Anthologie de la
littérature américaine

Cordialement

Yves Carlet

Collection
Premier
Cycle

Anthologie de la littérature américaine

DANIEL ROYOT
Professeur de littérature et civilisation américaines
à l'Université Lyon III - Jean-Moulin

JEAN BÉRANGER
Professeur de littérature et civilisation américaines
à l'Université Bordeaux III

YVES CARLET
Professeur de littérature et civilisation américaines
à l'Université Montpellier III - Paul-Valéry

KERMIT VANDERBILT
Professeur de littérature américaine
à l'Université San Diego, Etats-Unis

Presses Universitaires de France

puf

ISBN 2 13 043246 8

Dépôt légal — 1re édition : 1991, février

Sommaire

Avant-propos

Cette anthologie de la littérature américaine répond pour l'essentiel à une volonté pédagogique. Elle propose les grands jalons d'une évolution depuis la période coloniale jusqu'à nos jours. Elle s'inscrit en outre dans une double perspective. Aussi participe-t-elle d'abord du survey *qui dans la tradition anglo-saxonne vise à marquer les moments cruciaux et présenter les thèmes majeurs de l'histoire littéraire. Si nous avons dégagé des filiations et tenté de révéler les rapports parfois diffus entre tradition et innovation, nous nous sommes efforcés ensuite de préserver l'autonomie des textes, dont chacun devrait selon nous, refléter la richesse et l'originalité d'une création individuelle. C'est pourquoi nous avons conçu le choix des œuvres comme une mosaïque qui pourra être étudiée tant dans son ensemble que dans ses composantes.*

Les références historiques, sociales et culturelles que nous faisons figurer au fil des diverses introductions et notes d'élucidation ne sauraient naturellement hypothéquer le sens que le lecteur entendra donner aux textes. Respectant cette liberté de lecture, nous avons donc évité toute interprétation préalable de caractère contraignant. L'analyse critique est aujourd'hui servie par des concepts suffisamment élaborés pour qu'ils restituent, au travers d'explications méthodiques, la pleine valeur du récit, du discours et du réseau symbolique.

Pour chacune des phases majeures que nous présentons, nous avons offert une introduction générale. Les auteurs ont été ensuite regroupés selon des perspectives formelles ou thématiques qui font aussi l'objet d'une présentation. Nous avons enfin proposé une notice sur les écrivains pris séparément, en donnant à celle-ci une valeur biographique et thématique de nature à mieux désigner la place des passages comme des œuvres intégrales. Une bibliographie sélective suit l'introduction à l'auteur. Hormis la référence des œuvres complètes quand elles sont accessibles, nous nous sommes limités aux ouvrages critiques récents que les lecteurs pourront se procurer en librairie ou consulter dans des bibliothèques spécialisées. Dans la mesure des informations disponibles, nous avons inclus parmi les éléments bibliographiques, les travaux récents de la critique française dont nous savons que les Américains eux-mêmes apprécient toute la valeur. Les notes d'élucidation visent à clarifier certains aspects des textes qui pour des raisons diverses pourraient rester obscurs sans cet appareil pédagogique.

Un tableau chronologique permet de lier la fiction à son contexte historique, social et culturel. Des éléments de filmographie complètent cette anthologie et suggèrent de nouveaux champs d'exploration.

Nous avons donc opté pour cette stratégie pédagogique en recherchant rigueur et cohérence, en concevant cette anthologie pour un programme de lectures ou d'explications de textes au sein d'un enseignement progressif de la littérature américaine. Il demeure que nos lecteurs pourront remarquer d'inévitables absents. Nous avons certes suggéré maints prolongements dans nos introductions et cité nombre d'auteurs qui mériteraient à l'évidence de figurer ici. Toute anthologie présuppose des choix déchirants et nous assumons naturellement nos responsabilités en fonction de nos objectifs. Quand l'exigeaient à nos yeux la stature de l'auteur et l'exemplarité de son œuvre, nous avons délibérément consacré aux extraits un large espace, fût-ce en écartant, non sans regret, des ouvrages d'évidente valeur. La profusion des œuvres littéraires qui dans les dernières décennies ont renouvelé les thèmes et les formes de la fiction américaine nous a parfois contraints à laisser dans l'ombre quelques écrivains représentatifs. Nous avons néanmoins mis nos lecteurs sur des pistes qui leur permettront de faire d'autres découvertes.

Nous aurons réalisé nos ambitions si grâce à ce panorama nécessairement fragmentaire, nous avons su conduire nos lecteurs vers les incomparables richesses de la production littéraire des Etats-Unis.

Cette anthologie est le fruit d'une recherche collective dont chacun des coauteurs assume une part spécifique, Jean Béranger pour les XVIIe et XVIIIe siècles (I), Yves Carlet pour le XIXe (II), Kermit Vanderbilt avec mon concours pour les parties III, IV et V. J'ai enfin coordonné l'ensemble des travaux et assuré la direction de l'entreprise.

Ce travail collectif a bénéficié de l'aide et des conseils de nombreux collègues et amis, envers lesquels nous nous reconnaissons bien volontiers une dette. Que soient ici remerciés François Piquet pour son amical dévouement, Jean-Pierre Petit, Jean-François Gournay, Francis Bordat, Jean-Marie

Bonnet, Jean-Loup Bourget, François Laroque, Liliane Kerjan, Guy Dubois, Jean-Michel et Muriel Garnier, Robert Lerouge et Ozzie. André Lardinat et Françoise Vilain (Bibliothèques américaines de Paris et de Montpellier), Arthur Monke et Edward Geary, aux Etats-Unis, ont été comme à l'habitude d'une aide précieuse. Notre gratitude va enfin particulièrement à Maurice Gonnaud. La deuxième partie de cet ouvrage lui doit beaucoup.

Daniel ROYOT.

I – De l'Amérique coloniale à la Révolution

Il faut attendre le XIXe siècle, la déclaration d'indépendance littéraire de R. W. Emerson et le développement du transcendantalisme pour que les lettres américaines aient une spécificité bien admise. Il y a là l'achèvement d'une prise de conscience. Ceci laisse à la production des quelque deux cents premières années un rôle dans la gestation d'une identité.

La plupart des colons, des aventuriers, des engagés qui partent pour raisons économiques, pour faire fortune, pour la terre uniquement, ne s'intéressent pas à l'activité créatrice. Beaucoup ne lisent pas, pris qu'ils sont par le quotidien. Dans les familles une Bible, quelques livres de piété, un *Bay Psalm Book*, *The Day of Doom*, un *Abcd*, suffisent aux besoins spirituels et éducatifs. Toutes ne possèdent pas ces merveilleuses bibliothèques particulières qui font l'honneur des colonies, au sud comme au nord. Pourtant l'alphabétisation est considérable et le réseau d'écoles facilite l'accès d'un nombre important d'enfants et d'adolescents à des œuvres littéraires classiques. Par ailleurs beaucoup de coloniaux ou de voyageurs ne cultivent aucune différence. Certains ne font que passer. C'est le cas de Thomas Hariot qui resta moins d'un an à Roanoke, de John Smith qui ne séjourne véritablement que de 1607 à 1609. D'autres vont faire leur éducation dans la Mère Patrie et demeurent, comme William Byrd II, autant anglais que planteurs américains. Il y a ceux qui aimaient leur expérience et qui, victimes de circonstances, d'intolérance, se retournèrent, comme Thomas Morton, contre ceux qui bâtissaient le Nouveau Monde. Il y a ceux qui préfèrent être publiés à Londres plutôt qu'à Boston ou à Philadelphie. Les conditions favorables à l'éclosion d'une littérature originale sont difficiles à réunir.

La génération dite du transfert échoue dans son premier projet virginien d'une université mais implante Harvard College en 1636, créant un foyer intellectuel qui assure la transmission culturelle. Harvard — plus tard William and Mary en Virginie à la fin du siècle et Yale au début du XVIIIe siècle — reproduisent un modèle anglais avec ses modes de pensée, ses références religieuses très sélectionnées, et ses références littéraires. Les universités ne font que renforcer la culture diffusée dans les écoles et dans les églises. L'influence du puritanisme est déterminante. Rien d'autre ne vient l'équilibrer avant la fin du XVIIe siècle. De toute façon tout vient d'Europe puisque les Indiens, qui n'ont pas de littérature écrite au demeurant, sont au mieux promis à la conversion et à l'assimilation par les missionnaires et les écoles. De plus le puritanisme a banni le théâtre. Utiles au salut, les genres qui se développent sont le sermon, le journal intime et l'autobiographie. Les pamphlets, proches des sermons dans leur structure et leurs objectifs, et les récits historiques, proches du journal personnel ont beaucoup de succès : les uns et les autres peuvent servir une cause qui, de religieuse au départ, devient progressivement politique. Pasteurs ou laïcs, les coloniaux s'illustrèrent dans des genres considérés, il est vrai, comme mineurs. Les sermonnaires américains n'ont rien à envier à leurs homologues anglais. Leurs diaristes ont séduit. Leurs historiens ont été lus. Leurs pamphlétaires ont été efficaces. Enfin ils ont brillé, en moins grand nombre, en poésie. Les meilleurs écrivains ont été mesurés à la toise anglaise : tel journal a la qualité de celui de Pepys, tel poète est comparable aux grands « métaphysiques ». Mais l'Amérique coloniale n'a pas son Shakespeare, son Milton, ni son Defoe, ni son Swift, aucun écrivain qui ait à la fois cette stature et cette représentativité d'une culture. La spécificité de la littérature américaine tarde à apparaître. Pourtant elle pointe dans le préparationnisme simplifié des sermons de Thomas Hooker, dans la satire des modes européennes de N. Ward, dans l'expérience racontée de la captivité chez les Indiens, dans l'observation concrète de la nature par les Bartram, dans le bonheur bucolique du fermier James inventé par Crèvecœur qui donne à l'Amérique un embryon de roman. Et deux grands écrivains d'un Nouveau Monde émergent dès le XVIIIe siècle dans la vision mystique de Jonathan Edwards et dans le sens pratique et l'optimisme vainqueur de Benjamin Franklin.

1 – Chronique et histoire

De tous les genres pratiqués ce sont probablement les récits des chroniqueurs et des historiens qui ont immédiatement capté l'attention en Europe. L'exploration, la réflexion sur les découvertes et l'histoire des hommes en sont les thèmes principaux. Le premier est *A Brief and True Report of the New Found Land of Virginia* (1588) de Thomas Hariot (1560-1621), le savant cartographe et cosmographe qui passa onze mois sur l'île de Roanoke avec pour directive d'étudier les aborigènes et les ressources économiques. Il crée l'école de l'observation de la nature qu'illustrent John Smith pour la Nouvelle-Angleterre comme pour la Virginie continentale, William Byrd II, Robert Beverley (*c.* 1673-1722) avec le deuxième livre de *The History and Present State of Virginia* (1705), certaines lettres de Crèvecœur, l'œuvre de John et William Bartram. Sur l'observation de la nature et de la géographie, sur l'histoire naturelle, se greffe le récit des aventures humaines. Smith en commence la chronique. Mais c'est chez les écrivains de Nouvelle-Angleterre que l'histoire prend un sens. Le quotidien, le social, le politique sont éclairés par l'hypothèse d'un plan divin et d'une intervention de la Providence. D'où le caractère orienté de *The History of Plymouth Plantation* de W. Bradford, de *The History of New England 1630-1649* de John Winthrop, de *A Narrative of the Troubles with the Indians* (1677) de William Hubbard (1621-1704), de *Magnalia Christi Americana* et de *Wonders of the Invisible Word* de Cotton Mather. En dépit de ses prétentions au scrupule, cette histoire théocentrique doit être confrontée à d'autres textes polémiques comme celui de Thomas Morton pour Bradford et de Robert Calef pour Mather. La casuistique puritaine est mise à nu. Au XVIIIe siècle la chronique devient plus pédestre, plus politique, moins religieuse en tous cas. Fondée sur son observation personnelle *The History of the Five Indian Nations* (1727) de Cadwallader Colden (1688-1776) vise à réduire les prétentions françaises. Dans son *History of the Colony of Massachusetts Bay* (1764) Thomas Hutchinson (1711-1780), le gouverneur royal, veut donner une bonne image d'une colonie réputée politiquement rebelle.

JOHN SMITH, 1580-1631

Né à Willoughby dans une ferme du Lincolnshire, le futur capitaine Smith est d'abord apprenti chez un commerçant avant de s'engager comme soldat à seize ans. Après des aventures multiples en Europe il revient à Londres à temps pour s'intéresser aux projets de colonisation en Virginie. Débarquant à Jamestown en 1607 il explore le pays, négociant des vivres avec les Indiens dont il fut un instant prisonnier. Ses relations avec le chef Powathan et sa fille Pocahontas font partie de la légende des premiers jours. Ecarté jusqu'alors des responsabilités, il accède à la présidence de la plantation en 1608, mais, blessé, doit rentrer en Angleterre en 1609 où il se défend contre des adversaires. Mais cet aventurier et explorateur infatigable reprend la mer pour visiter la côte de Nouvelle-Angleterre en 1614. Candidat planteur, il ne parvient pas à s'entendre avec les gens de la Grande Migration de 1630 qui avaient pourtant mis à profit son troisième livre *A Description of New England* (1616). Le colon manqué devient écrivain, publiant en tout huit ouvrages. Il avait inauguré cette autre carrière avec *A True Relation of Such Occurences and Accidents of Noate as Hath Hapned in Virginia since the First Planting of that Collony* (1608).

BIBLIOGRAPHIE SÉLECTIVE. — Barbour (Philip L.), ed., *The Complete Works of Captain John Smith (1580-1631)*, 3 vol., Chapel Hill, The University of North Carolina Press, 1986 ; Leary (Lewis), Adventures of John Smith as Heroic Legend, *Essays on Early Virginia Literature Honoring Richard Beale Davis*, ed. Leo Lemay, New York, Burt Franklin, 1977.

A True Relation[1]

Arriving at Werawocomoco,[2] their Emperour proudly lying uppon a Bedstead a foote high upon tenne or twelve Mattes, richly hung with manie Chaynes of great Pearles about his necke, and covered with a great Covering of *Rahaughcums*:[3] At his heade sat a woman, at his feete another, on each side sitting uppon a Matte uppon the ground were raunged his chiefe men on each side the fire, tenne in a ranke, and behinde them as many yong women, each a great Chaine of white Beades over their shoulders, their heades painted in redde, and [he] with such a grave and Majesticall countenance, as drave me into admiration to see such state in a naked Salvage, [...][4] hee kindly welcomed me with good wordes, and great Platters of sundrie Victuals, assuring mee his friendship, and my libertie within foure dayes; hee much delighted in Opechancanoughs[5] relation of what I had described to him, and oft examined me upon the same. He asked mee the cause of our comming; I tolde him, being in fight with the Spaniards our enemie, beeing over powred, neare put to retreat, and by extreame weather put to this shore, where landing at Chesipiake, the people shot us, but at Kequoughtan they kindly used us; we by signes demaunded fresh water; they described us up the River was all fresh water; at Paspahegh, also they kindly used us; our Pinnasse being leake wee were inforced to stay to mend her, till Captaine Newport[6] my father came to conduct us away. He demaunded why we went further with our Boate; I tolde him, in that I would have occasion to talke of the backe Sea, that on the other side the

1. 1608. Voir introduction.
2. Début de l'épisode dans lequel Pocahontas est impliquée sans être encore mentionnée.
3. Ragondin.
4. C'est la première fois que Smith emploie ce mot au lieu d'Indien.
5. Redoutable successeur de Powathan de 1619 à 1645.
6. Responsable de l'expédition de 1606-1607.

maine, where was salt water, my father had a childe slaine, whiche wee supposed Monocan his enemie had done whose death we intended to revenge.

After good deliberation, hee began to describe mee the Countreys beyonde the Falles, with many of the rest, confirming what not onely Opechancanoyes, and an Indian which had beene prisoner to Powhatan had before tolde mee, but some called if five dayes, some sixe, some eight, where the sayde water dashed amongest many stones and rockes, each storme which caused oft tymes the heade of the River to bee brackish: Anchanachuck he described to bee the people that had slaine my brother, whose death hee would revenge. Hee described also upon the same Sea a mighty Nation called Pocoughtronack, a fierce Nation that did eate men, and warred with the people of Moyaoncer, and Pataromerke,[1] Nations upon the toppe of the heade of the Bay, under his territories, where the yeare before they had slain an hundred; he signified their crownes were shaven, long haire in the necke, tied on a knot, Swords like Pollaxes.[2]

Beyond them he described people with short Coates, and Sleeves to the Elbowes, that passed that way in Shippes like ours. Many Kingdomes hee described mee to the heade of the Bay, which seemed to bee a mightie River, issuing from mightie Mountaines betwixt the two Seas. The people cloathed at Ocanahonan he also confirmed, and the Southerly Countries also, as the rest, that reported us to be within a day and a halfe of Mangoge, two dayes of Chawwonock, 6. from Roanoke, to the south part of the backe sea: he described a countrie called Anone, where they have abundance of Brasse, and houses walled as ours. I requited his discourse, seing what pride hee had in his great and spacious Dominions, seeing that all hee knewe were under his Territories.

1. Potomac.
2. Tomahawks.

WILLIAM BRADFORD, 1590-1657

Né à Austerfield, fils d'un cultivateur prospère du Yorkshire, il est élevé par son grand-père et ses oncles à la mort de son père. Il apprend le métier de fermier. Mais à douze ans il entend les sermons du pasteur non conformiste Richard Clyfton. Bientôt il devient membre de la congrégation séparatiste de Scrooby, Nottinghamshire, et rencontre ses deux grands amis William Brewster (1567-1644) et John Robinson. En 1608 la petite communauté émigre aux Pays-Bas. Il exerce comme tisserand, achète une maison, se marie. Sa foi, sa conscience historique le conduisent à partir avec Brewster en Amérique à bord du *Mayflower*, laissant Robinson, leur pasteur malade, en Hollande. A la mort de John Carver (1576-1621), premier gouverneur, il est élu pour le remplacer dans des fonctions qu'il exercera presque sans interruption. Cet autodidacte trouve le temps de se cultiver, d'apprendre l'hébreu. Il écrit. Coauteur de *Mourt's Relation* (1622), poète occasionnel, il atteint la renommée posthume par un texte partiellement égaré, retrouvé chez l'évêque de Londres, et publié pour la première fois en 1856 sous le titre de *History of Plymouth Plantation*. Il y révèle son talent de narrateur, la qualité d'une prose simple et sobre que sous-tend l'émotion d'une expérience exceptionnelle.

BIBLIOGRAPHIE SÉLECTIVE. — Morison (Samuel E.), ed., *Of Plymouth Plantation 1620-1647 by William Bradford, Sometime Governor Thereof*, New York, Knopf, 1952 ; Westbrook (Perry D.), *William Bradford*, Boston, Twayne, 1978 ; Rosenmeier (Jesper), With my owne eyes : William Bradford's Of Plymouth Plantation, *in* Sacvan Bercovitch, *The American Puritan Imagination*, London, Cambridge University Press, 1968, 77-106.

Of Plymouth Plantation[1]

Septembre 6. These troubles being blown over, and now all being compact together in one ship, they put to sea again with a prosperous wind, which continued divers days together, which was some encouragement unto them; yet, according to the usual manner, many were afflicted with seasickness. And I may not omit here a special work of God's providence. There was a proud and very profane young man, one of the seamen, of a lusty, able body, which made him the more haughty; he would alway be contemning the poor people in their sickness and cursing them daily with grievous execrations; and did not let to tell them that he hoped to help to cast half of them overboard before they came to their journey's end, and to make merry with what they had; and if he were by any gently reproved, he would curse and swear most bitterly. But it pleased God before they came half seas over, to smite this young man with a grievous disease, of which he died in a desperate manner, and so was himself the first that was thrown overboard. Thus his curses light on his own head, and it was an astonishment to all his fellows for they noted it to be the just hand of God upon him.

After they had enjoyed fair winds and weather for a season, they were encountered many times with cross winds and met with many fierce storms with which the ship was shroudly[2] shaken, and her upper works made very leaky; and one of the main beams in the midships was bowed and cracked, which put them in some fear that the ship could not be able to perform the voyage. So some of the chief of the company, perceiving the mariners to fear the sufficiency of the ship as appeared by their mutterings, they entered into serious consultation with the master and other officers of the ship, to consider in time of the danger, and rather to return than to cast themselves into a desperate and inevitable peril. And truly there was great distraction and difference of opinion amongst the mariners themselves; fain would they do what could be done for their wages' sake (being now near half the seas over) and on the other hand they were loath to hazard their lives too desperately. But in examining of all opinions, the master and others affirmed

1. 1647. Titre modernisé du manuscrit publié en 1856 : *History of Plymouth Plantation.*
2. Sens premier : méchamment.

they knew the ship to be strong and firm under water; and for the buckling of the main beam, there was a great iron screw the passengers brought out of Holland, which would raise the beam into his place; the which being done, the carpenter and master affirmed that with a post put under it, set firm in the lower deck and otherways bound, he would make it sufficient. And as for the decks and upper works, they would caulk them as well as they could, and though with the working of the ship they would not long keep staunch, yet there would otherwise be no great danger, if they did not overpress her with sails. So they committed themselves to the will of God and resolved to proceed.

In sundry of these storms the winds were so fierce and the seas so high, as they could not bear a knot of sail, but were forced to hull[1] for divers days together. And in one of them, as they thus lay at hull in a mighty storm, a lusty[2] young man called John Howland, coming upon some occasion above the gratings was, with a seele[3] of the ship, thrown into sea; but it pleased God that he caught hold of the topsail halyards which hung overboard and ran out at length. Yet he held his hold (though he was sundry fathoms under water) till he was hauled up by the same rope to the brim of the water, and then with a boat hook and other means got into the ship again and his life saved. And though he was something ill with it, yet he lived many years after and became a profitable member both in church and commonwealth. In all this voyage there died but one of the passengers, which was William Butten, a youth, servant to Samuel Fuller, when they drew near the coast.

But to omit other things (that I may be brief) after long beating at sea they fell with that land which is called Cape Cod;[4] the which being made and certainly known to be it, they were not a little joyful. After some deliberation had amongst themselves and with the master of the ship, they tacked about and resolved to stand for the southward (the wind and weather being fair) to find some place about Hudson's River for their habitation.[5] But after they had sailed that course about half the day, they fell amongst dangerous shoals and roaring breakers, and they were so far

1. Se mettre en panne.
2. Gai.
3. Mouvement : roulis ou tangage.
4. Au point du jour du 19 novembre 1620.
5. Première mention de la destination des émigrants.

entangled therewith as they conceived themselves in great danger; and the wind shrinking upon them withal, they resolved to bear up again for the Cape and thought themselves happy to get out of those dangers before night overtook them, as by God's good providence they did. And the next day[1] they got into the Cape Harbor[2] where they rid in safety.

A word or two by the way of this cape. It was thus first named by Captain Gosnold and his company,[3] Anno 1602, and after by Captain Smith was called Cape James; but it retains the former name amongst seamen. Also, that point which first showed those dangerous shoals unto them they called Point Care, and Tucker's Terrour; but the French and Dutch to this day call it Malabar by reason of those perilous shoals and the losses they have suffered there.

Being thus arrived in a good harbor, and brought safe to land, they fell upon their knees and blessed the God of Heaven[4] who had brought them over the vast and furious ocean, and delivered them from all the perils and miseries thereof, again to set their feet on the firm and stable earth, their proper element. And no marvel if they were thus joyful, seeing wise Seneca was so affected with sailing a few miles on the coast of his own Italy, as he affirmed, that he had rather remain twenty years on his way by land than pass by sea to any place in a short time, so tedious and dreadful was the same unto him.[5]

COTTON MATHER, 1663-1728

Ce Bostonien a pour père Increase Mather (1639-1723), un personnage considérable : grand ministre du culte congrégationaliste, écrivain prolifique, homme politique habile, président de Harvard. Sa mère est la fille de John

1. La traversée avait duré soixante-cinq jours.
2. Provincetown aujourd'hui.
3 Ils avaient pris beaucoup de morue.
4. Daniel II. 19.
5. Sénèque, *Ad Lucilium Epistulae Morales*, LIII.

Cotton (1584-1652). Après des études à la Boston Latin School, il entre à l'université à douze ans. Excellent helléniste et latiniste, c'est un jeune homme plein de promesses. En 1685 il devient l'assistant de son père à la Second Church. Il lui succède en 1723. Il prend part aux événements de 1689, est élu *fellow* de Harvard, mais reste dans l'ombre d'un homme à qui il ne parvient pas à succéder comme président en 1701. Son intérêt pour les sciences lui assure son élection à la Royal Society en 1714. Le bégaiement dont il a souffert semble lui interdire une carrière de prédicateur : il y excelle. Il finit par dépasser son père avec ses 445 ouvrages, tous publiés. Si le volumineux *Diary* (1911) nous révèle l'homme, *Magnalia Christi Americana* (1702) est le grand œuvre d'histoire. *The Wonders of the Invisible World*, rédigé en 1692 pour défendre les juges de Salem, justifier la répression de la sorcellerie à laquelle il croit, et mettre en garde contre les excès, montre la complexité d'une personnalité dont la réputation demeure affectée par ses prises de position.

BIBLIOGRAPHIE SÉLECTIVE. — Mather (Cotton), *The Wonders of the Invisible World*, London, John Russell Smith, 1862 ; Middlekauf (Robert), *The Mathers, Three Generations of Puritan Intellectuals, 1596-1728*, New York, Oxford University Press, 1971 ; Silverman (Kenneth), *The Life and Times of Cotton Mather*, New York, Harper, 1984.

The Wonders of the Invisible World[1]

§ II. The *New-Englanders* are a People of God settled in those, which were once the *Devil's* Territories; and it may easily be supposed that the *Devil* was exceedingly disturbed, when he perceived such a People here accomplishing the Promise of old made unto our Blessed Jesus, *That He should have the Utmost parts of the Earth for his Possession.*[2] There was not a greater Uproar among the *Ephesians*, when the Gospel was first brought among them, than there was among, *The Powers of the Air* (after whom those

1. 1693. Récit composé à la demande des juges de Salem. Pour C. Mather Satan est l'instigateur de la sorcellerie, une forme de son combat contre Dieu. Les accusés étaient passibles de la peine de mort comme dans la Bible. Le pasteur avait des doutes sur les preuves.

2. Allusion à la tentation du Christ. Voir Mathieu 4 . 8-9 ou Luc 4 . 5-7.

Ephesians walked)[1] when first the *Silver Trumpets* of the Gospel here made the *Joyful Sound.* The Devil thus Irritated, immediately try'd all sorts of Methods to overturn this poor Plantation: and so much of the Church, as was *Fled into this Wilderness*, immediately found *The Serpent cast out of his Mouth a Flood for the carrying of it away.*[2] I believe that never were more *Satanical Devices* used for the Unsetling of any People under the Sun, than what have been Employ'd for the Extirpation of the *Vine* which God has here *Planted, Casting out the Heathen, and preparing a Room before it, and causing it to take deep Root, and fill the Land, so that it sent its Boughs unto the* Atlantic *Sea* Eastward, *and its Branches unto the* Connecticut *River* Westward, *and the Hills were covered with the shadow thereof.*[3] But, All those Attempts of Hell, have hitherto been Abortive, many an *Ebenezer*[4] has been Erected unto the Praise of God, by his Poor People here; and *Having obtained Help from God, we continue to this Day.* Wherefore the Devil is now making one Attempt more upon us; an Attempt more Difficult, more Surprizing, more snarl'd with unintelligible Circumstances than any that we have hitherto Encountred; an Attempt so *Critical*, that if we get well through, we shall soon enjoy *Halcyon* Days with all the *Vultures* of Hell *Trodden under our Feet.* He has wanted his *Incarnate Legions* to Persecute us, as the People of God have in the other Hemisphere been Persecuted: he has therefore drawn forth his more *Spiritual* ones to make an Attacque upon us. We have been advised by some Credible Christians yet alive, that a Malefactor, accused of *Witchcraft* as well as *Murder*, and Executed in this place more than Forty Years ago,[5] did then give Notice of, *An Horrible* PLOT *against the Country by* WITCHCRAFT, *and a Foundation of* WITCHCRAFT *then laid, which if it were not seasonably discovered, would probably Blow up, and pull down all the Churches in the Country.* And we have now with Horror seen the *Discovery* of such a *Witchcraft*! An Army of *Devils* is horribly broke in upon the place which is the *Center*, and after a sort, the *First-born* of our *English* Settlements[6]: and the Houses of the Good People there are fill'd with the doleful Shrieks of their Children and Servants,

1. Saint Paul fut mal reçu en Asie Mineure à Ephèse. Voir Ephésiens 2 . 2.
2. Apocalypse 13, 14-5.
3. Adaptée à la Nouvelle-Angleterre c'est une paraphrase des Psaumes 20, 8-11.
4. Monument commémoratif semblable à celui qu'érigea Samuel pour sa victoire sur les Philistins. Voir I Samuel 7-12.
5. Une vague de sorcellerie avait déferlé entre 1650 et 1659.
6. Salem fut fondée en 1629 avant le début de la Grande Migration en 1630.

Tormented by Invisible Hands, with Tortures altogether preternatural. After the Mischiefs there Endeavoured, and since in part Conquered, the terrible Plague, of *Evil Angels*, hath made its Progress into some other places, where other Persons have been in like manner Diabolically handled. These our poor Afflicted Neighbours, quickly after they become *Infected* and *Infested* with these *Dæmons*, arrive to a Capacity of Discerning those which they conceive the *Shapes* of their Troublers; and notwithstanding the Great and Just Suspicion, that the *Dæmons* might Impose the *Shapes* of Innocent Persons in their *Spectral Exhibitions* upon the Sufferers (which may perhaps prove no small part of the *Witch-Plot* in the issue) yet many of the Persons thus Represented, being Examined, several of them have been Convicted of a very Damnable *Witchcraft*: yea, more than One *Twenty* have *Confessed*, that they have Signed unto a *Book*, which the Devil show'd them, and Engaged in his Hellish Design of *Bewitching* and *Ruining* our Land. *We* know not, at least *I* know not, how fat the *Delusions* of Satan may be Interwoven into some Circumstances of the *Confessions*; but one would think, all the Rules of Understanding Humane Affairs are at an end, if after so many most Voluntary Harmonious *Confessions*, made by Intelligent Persons of all Ages, in sundry Towns, at several Times, we must not Believe the *main strokes* wherein those *Confessions* all agree: especially when we have a thousand preternatural Things every day before our eyes, wherein the *Confessors* do acknowledge their Concernment, and give Demonstration of their being so Concerned. If the Devils now can strike the minds of men with any *Poisons* of so fine a Composition and Operation, that Scores of Innocent People shall Unite, in *Confessions* of a Crime, which we see actually committed, it is a thing prodigious, beyond the Wonders of the former Ages, and it threatens no less than a sort of a Dissolution upon the World. Now, by these *Confessions* 'tis Agreed, *That* the Devil has made a dreadful Knot of *Witches* in the Country, and by the help of *Witches* has dreadfully increased that Knot: *That* these *Witches* have driven a Trade of Commissioning their *Confederate Spirits*, to do all sorts of Mischiefs to the Neighbours, whereupon there have ensued such Mischievous consequences upon the Bodies and Estates of the Neighbourhood, as could not otherwise be accounted for: yea, *That* at prodigious *Witch-Meetings*, the Wretches have proceeded so far, as to Concert and Consult the Methods of Rooting out the

Christian Religion from this Country, and setting up instead of it, perhaps a more gross *Diabolism*, than ever the World saw before. And yet it will be a thing little short of *Miracle*, if in so *spread* a Business as this, the Devil should not get in some of his Juggles[1], to confound the Discovery of all the rest.

WILLIAM BYRD II, 1674-1744

Fils d'un riche planteur qui commerce beaucoup avec les Indiens, William Byrd naît à « Belvedere », le domaine familial dans le périmètre actuel de Richmond, Virginie. A sept ans son père l'envoie en Hollande puis à Londres où il poursuit des études de droit à Middle Temple. Très introduit dans la bonne société, ce mondain, amateur de femmes et de théâtre, est élu à la Royal Society en 1696. Rappelé à la colonie pour diriger les affaires, il devient un notable. En 1728, l'administration locale le charge de présider la commission *ad hoc* pour établir la frontière contestée avec la Caroline du Nord. Ses observations servent de base à deux textes dont le second, *The History of the Dividing Line,* assure sa réputation littéraire. Il révèle sa passion de la nature et de ses paysages, le don de décrire avec cet œil vif et une pointe d'humour qui le caractérisent. Perfectionniste, il ne parvient pas à publier son livre auquel Thomas Jefferson s'intéresse mais qui ne sort des presses qu'en 1841. Ce planteur plein d'idées, cet homme d'esprit très à l'aise dans toutes les situations, auteur d'œuvres variées, cet homme concret, ce grand lecteur laisse à sa mort à sa femme et à ses nombreux enfants une splendide maison de style georgien, une bibliothèque de 3 600 volumes et 170 000 acres de terre.

BIBLIOGRAPHIE SÉLECTIVE. — Wright (Louis B.), ed., *The Prose Works of William Byrd of Westover : Narratives of a Colonial Virginian,* Cambridge, Mass., Belknap Press of Harvard University Press, 1966 ; Marambaud (Pierre), *William Byrd of Westover (1674-1744),* Charlottesville, Va., University Press of

1. Tour de passe-passe.

Virginia, 1971 ; Davis (Richard B.), William Byrd. Taste and Tolerance, 151-177, *in* Everett Emerson, *Major Writers of Early American Literature,* Madison, Wisc., The University of Wisconsin Press, 1972.

History of the Dividing Line[1]

22. Early in the morning we sent back two men to make farther search for the horse that was strayed away. We were unwilling the poor man should sustain such a damage as would eat out a large part of his pay or that the public should be at the expense of reimbursing him for it. These foresters hunted all over the neighboring woods and took as much pains as if the horse had been their own property, but all their diligence was to no purpose. The surveyors, in the meantime, being fearful of leaving these men too far behind, advanced the line no farther than 1 mile and 230 poles.[2]

As we rode along we found no less than three bears and a fat doe, that our Indian, who went out before us, had thrown in our course, and we were very glad to pick them up. About a mile from the camp we crossed Miry Creek, so called because several of the horses were mired in its branches. About 230 poles beyond that, the line intersected another river that seemed to be a branch of the Irvin, to which we gave the name of the Mayo in compliment to the other of our surveyors. It was about fifty yards wide where we forded it, being just below a ledge of rocks which reached across the river and made a natural cascade. Our horses could hardly keep their feet over these slippery rocks, which gave some of their riders no small palpitation. This river forks about a quarter of a mile below the ford and has some scattering canes growing near the mouth of it.

We pitched our tent on the western banks of the Mayo, for the pleasure of being lulled to sleep by the cascade. Here our hunters had leisure to go out and try their fortunes, and returned loaded with spoil. They brought in no less than six bears, exceedingly fat, so that the frying pan had no rest all night. We had now the opportunity of trying the speed of these lumpish animals by a fair course it had with the nimblest of our surveyors. A cub of a year old

1. Ecrit entre 1728-1738. Publié 1841.
2. Mesure : 16,5 pieds.

will run very fast, because, being upon his growth, he is never encumbered with too much fat; but the old ones are more sluggish and unwieldy, especially when mast[1] is plenty. Then their nimblest gait is only a heavy gallop, and their motion is still slower downhill, where they are obliged to sidle along very awkwardly to keep their lights from rising up into their throat. These beasts always endeavor to avoid a man, except they are wounded or happen to be engaged in the protection of their cubs. By the force of these instincts and that of self-preservation, they will now and then throw off all reverence for their Maker's image. For that reason, excess of hunger will provoke them to the same desperate attack for the support of their being. A memorable instance of the last case is said to have happened not long ago in New England, where a bear assaulted a man just by his own door, and rearing himself upon his haunches, offered to take him lovingly into his hug. But the man's wife, observing the danger her husband was in, had the courage to run behind the bear and thrust her two thumbs into his eyes. This made Bruin[2] quit the man and turn short upon the woman to take his revenge, but she had the presence of mind to spring back with more than female agility, and so both their lives were preserved.

23. At the distance of sixty-two poles from where we lay, we crossed the south branch of what we took for the Irvin, nor was it without difficulty we got over, though it happened to be without damage. Great part of the way after that was mountainous, so that we were no sooner got down one hill but we were obliged to climb up another. Only for the last mile of our stage we encountered a locust thicket, that was level but interlaced terribly with briers and grapevines. We forded a large creek no less than fives times, the banks of which were so steep that we were forced to cut them down with a hoe. We gave it the name of Crooked Creek because of its frequent meanders. The sides of it were planted with shrub canes extremely inviting to the horses, which were now quite jaded with clambering up so many precipices and tugging through so many dismal thickets; notwithstanding which we pushed the line this day four miles, sixty-nine poles.

The men were so unthrifty this morning as to bring but a small

1. Châtaignes.
2. Martin.

portion of their abundance along with them. This was the more unlucky because we could discover no sort of game the whole livelong day. Woodsmen are certainly good Christians in one respect at least, that they always leave the morrow to care for itself; though for that very reason they ought to pray more fervently for their daily bread than most of them remember to do.

The mountains were still concealed from our eyes by a cloud of smoke. As we went along we were alarmed at the sight of a great fire which showed itself to the northward. This made our small corps march in closer order than we used to do, lest perchance we might be waylaid by Indians. It made us look out sharp to see if we could discover any track or other token of these insidious foresters, but found none. In the meantime, we came often upon the track of bears, which can't without some skill be distinguished from that of human creatures made with naked feet. And, indeed, a young woodsman would be puzzled to find out the difference, which consists principally in a bear's paws being something smaller than a man's foot and in its leaving sometimes the mark of its claws in the impression made upon the ground.

The soil where the locust thicket grew was exceedingly rich, as it constantly is where that kind of tree is naturally and largely produced. But the desolation made there lately, either by fire or caterpillars, had been so general that we could not see a tree of any bigness standing within our prospect. And the reason why a fire makes such havoc in these lonely parts is this: the woods are not there burnt every year as they generally are amongst the inhabitants. But the dead leaves and trash of many years are heaped up together, which, being at length kindled by the Indians that happen to pass that way, furnish fuel for a conflagration that carries all before it.

There is a beautiful range of hills, as level as a terrace walk, that overlooks the valley through which Crooked Creek conveys its spiral stream. This terrace runs pretty near east and west about two miles south of the line and is almost parallel with it. The horses had been too much harassed to permit us to ride at all out of our way for the pleasure of any prospect or the gratification of any curiosity. This confined us to the narrow sphere of our business and is at the same time a just excuse for not animating our story with greater variety.

WILLIAM BARTRAM, 1739-1823

Né à Kinsessing, Pennsylvanie, ce fils de quaker se montre doué pour le dessin et la botanique. Son père John Bartram (1699-1777), le créateur des jardins botaniques, le met à dix-sept ans en apprentissage chez un marchand de Philadelphie. William ne réussit pas dans le commerce en Caroline du Nord, et échoue comme planteur de riz et d'indigo en Floride. Initié par une expédition avec son père, il attend sa chance. Aidé par le Dr Fothergill, qui le dirige, il entreprend de 1773 à 1777 un long voyage solitaire dont il rapporte les notes de son unique livre de *Travels* dont une version fut publiée en 1791 et l'autre en 1843. « Puc Puggy » — le chasseur de fleurs — comme l'appellent les Séminoles, a le sens du détail d'un peintre que révèlent ses dessins de plantes et d'animaux autant que sa prose. L'exactitude de ses observations a été confirmée par John James Audubon (1785-1851). Moins apprécié chez lui qu'en Europe, son exotisme a séduit Chateaubriand et Wordsworth. Carlyle en recommande la lecture à R. W. Emerson tant le texte lui paraît américain dans son sujet et dans son style. Coleridge y voit plus une série de poèmes qu'un récit. Emerveillé à jamais par le spectacle de la nature en laquelle il voit la bonté de Dieu, il passe les quarante-six dernières années de sa vie dans le jardin de son père, négligeant la chaire de botanique que l'Université de Pennsylvanie lui offre, et les séances de l'American Philosophical Society à laquelle il est élu.

BIBLIOGRAPHIE SÉLECTIVE. — Bartram (William), *Travels through North & South Carolina, East & West Florida*, Charlottesville, Va., University Press of Virginia, 1980 ; Earnest (Ernest), *John and William Bartram, Botanists and Explorers*, Philadelphia, Pa., University of Pennsylvania Press, 1940 ; Lee (Berta G.), William Bartram : Naturalist or « Poet » ?, *Early American Literature*, vol. VII, n° 2, 124-129.

Travels[1]

The evening was temperately cool and calm. The crocodiles began to roar and appear in uncommon numbers along the shores and in the river. I fixed my camp in an open plain near the utmost projection of the promontory, under the shelter of a large live oak which stood on the highest part of the ground but a few yards from my boat. From this open, high situation, I had a free prospect of the river, which was a matter of no trivial consideration to me, having good reason to dread the subtle attacks of the alligators who were crowding about my harbor. Having collected a good quantity of wood for the purpose of keeping up a light and smoke during the night, I began to think of preparing my supper when, upon examining my stores, I found but a scanty provision. I thereupon determined, as the most expeditious way of supplying my necessities, to take my bob and try for some trout. About one hundred yards above my harbor began a cove or bay of the river, out of which opened a large lagoon. The mouth or entrance from the river to it was narrow, but the waters soon after spread and formed a little lake, extending into the marshes. Its entrance and shores within I observed to be verged with floating lawns of pistia[2] and nymphea and other aquatic plants; these I knew were excellent haunts for trout.

The verges and islets of the lagoon were elegantly embellished with flowering plants and shrubs; the laughing coots[3] with wings half spread were tripping over the little coves and hiding themselves in the tufts of grass; young broods of the painted summer teal, skimming the still surface of the waters and following the watchful parent, unconscious of danger, were frequently surprised by the voracious trout; and he, in turn, as often by the subtle, greedy alligator. Behold him rushing forth from the flags and reeds. His enormous body swells. His plaited tail, brandished high, floats upon the lake. The waters like a cataract descend from his opening jaws. Clouds of smoke issue from his dilated nostrils. The earth trembles with his thunder. When immediately from the opposite coast of the lagoon emerges from the deep his rival

1. *Travels &*., 1791. Ce passage avait fasciné Coleridge.
2. Laitue d'eau.
3. Foulque.

champion. They suddenly dart upon each other. The boiling surface of the lake marks their rapid course, and a terrific conflict commences. They now sink to the bottom folded together in horrid wreaths. The water becomes thick and discolored. Again they rise; their jaws clap together, re-echoing through the deep surrounding forests. Again they sink, when the contest ends at the muddy bottom of the lake, and the vanquished makes a hazardous escape, hiding himself in the muddy, turbulent waters and sedge on a distant shore. The proud victor, exulting, returns to the place of action. The shores and forests resound his dreadful roar, together with the triumphing shouts of the plaited tribes around, witnesses of the horrid combat.

My apprehensions were highly alarmed after being a spectator of so dreadful a battle. It was obvious that every delay would but tend to increase my dangers and difficulties, as the sun was near setting, and the alligators gathered around my harbor from all quarters. From these considerations I concluded to be expeditious in my trip to the lagoon, in order to take some fish. Not thinking it prudent to take my fusee[1] with me, lest I might lose it overboard in case of a battle, which I had every reason to dread before my return, I therefore furnished myself with a club for my defense, went on board, and penetrated the first line of those which surrounded my harbor. They gave way; but being pursued by several very large ones, I kept strictly on the watch and paddled with all my might towards the entrance of the lagoon, hoping to be sheltered there from the multitude of my assailants. But, ere I had halfway reached the place, I was attacked on all sides, several endeavoring to overset the canoe.

My situation now became precarious to the last degree. Two very large ones attacked me closely at the same instant, rushing up with their heads and part of their bodies above the water, roaring terribly and belching floods of water over me. They struck their jaws together so close to my ears as almost to stun me, and I expected every moment to be dragged out of the boat and instantly devoured. But I applied my weapons so effectually about me, though at random, that I was so successful as to beat them off a little. When I found that they designed to renew the battle, I made for the shore as the only means left me for my preservation.

1. Fusil.

By keeping close to it I should have my enemies on one side of me only, whereas, I was before surrounded by them. Now there was a probability, if pushed to the last extremity, of saving myself by jumping out of the canoe on shore, as it is easy to outwalk them on land, although comparatively as swift as lightning in the water. I found this last expedient alone could fully answer my expectations, for as soon as I gained the shore, they drew off and kept aloof. This was a happy relief, as my confidence was, in some degree, recovered by it.

On recollecting myself, I discovered that I had almost reached the entrance of the lagoon, and determined to venture in, if possible, to take a few fish and then return to my harbor while daylight continued. I could now, with caution and resolution, make my way with safety along shore; and indeed there was no other way to regain my camp without leaving my boat and making my retreat through the marshes and reeds which, if I could even effect, would have been in a manner throwing myself away, for then there would have been no hopes of ever recovering my bark and returning in safety to any settlements of men. I accordingly proceeded and made good my entrance into the lagoon, though not without opposition from the alligators, who formed a line across the entrance, but did not pursue me into it, nor was I molested by any there, though there were some very large ones in a cove at the upper end. I soon caught more trout than I had present occasion for, and the air was too hot and sultry to admit of their being kept for many hours, even though salted or barbecued.

MICHEL-GUILLAUME-JEAN DE CRÈVECŒUR (1735-1813)

Né à Caen dans une famille de petite noblesse, instruit chez les Jésuites, il part à dix-neuf ans chez des parents en Angleterre, puis gagne le Canada en 1755. Il y sert comme arpenteur et cartographe. Un an après avoir obtenu un brevet de lieutenant dans l'armée royale, il est blessé à Québec, démissionne pour rester en Amérique. Pendant dix ans il voyage, commerce avec les Indiens, devient en 1765 citoyen de New York sous le nom de James Hector St John de Crèvecœur. Marié en 1769 il achète Pine Hill, 120 acres dans le comté d'Orange, vit en fermier. La guerre détruit ce bonheur. Suspecté par tous, il parvient à gagner Londres en 1780. Il y vend une partie de ses manuscrits qui connaissent un énorme succès dès leur parution en 1782 sous le titre de *Letters from an American Farmer*. Nommé consul de France en 1783, il conserve son poste à New York jusqu'en 1790 et quitte définitivement les Etats-Unis. Echappant à la Terreur en 1794, il va en Allemagne jusqu'en 1796, y retourne de 1806 à 1809. *Les lettres d'un cultivateur américain,* publiées à Paris en 1784 et 1787, sont des versions très différentes du texte anglais, destinées aux américanophiles français. Mais ce protégé de Mme d'Houdetot et du marquis de Turgot est aussi l'observateur attentif du Nouveau Monde qui n'est pas sans affinités avec Thoreau. Créateur de fiction il a également imaginé l'Amérique par narrateur interposé.

BIBLIOGRAPHIE SÉLECTIVE. — Stone Jr (Albert E.), ed., *Letters from an American Farmer and Sketches of Eighteenth Century America,* New York, Penguin American Library, 1981 ; Allen (Gay Wilson) et Asselineau (Roger), *St John de Crèvecœur, The Life of an American Farmer,* New York, Viking Penguin Inc., 1987 ; Rice (Howard C.), *Le cultivateur américain, étude sur l'œuvre de Saint John de Crèvecœur* (1932), Genève, Suisse, Slatkine Reprints, 1978 ; Béranger (Jean), The Desire for Communication : narrator and narratee in *Letters from an American Farmer, Early American Literature* (1977), 73-85 ; Chevignard (Bernard), Mémoire et création dans *Letters from an American Farmer, Actes du Colloque Mémoire et création dans le monde anglo-américain aux XVIIe et XVIIIe siècles,* Strasbourg, Université de Strasbourg II, 1984, 125-135.

Letters from an American Farmer[1]

In order to view the island in its longest direction from the town, I took a ride to the easternmost parts of it, remarkable only for the Pochick Rip,[2] where their best fish are caught. I passed by

1. 1782. Lettre VIII. Le narrateur, Farmer James, a visité l'île idéale de Nantucket.
2. Banc de sable

the Tetoukèmah lots, which are the fields of the community; the fences were made of cedar posts and rails, and looked perfectly straight and neat; the various crops they enclosed were flourishing; thence I descended into Barry's Valley, where the blue and the spear grass[1] looked more abundant than I had seen on any other part of the island; thence to Gib's Pond; and arrived at last at Siasconcet.[2] Several dwellings had been erected on this wild shore for the purpose of sheltering the fishermen in the season of fishing; I found them all empty, except that particular one to which I had been directed. It was like the others, built on the highest part of the shore, in the face of the great ocean; the soil appeared to be composed of no other stratum but sand, covered with a thinly scattered herbage. What rendered this house still more worthy of notice in my eyes was that it had been built on the ruins of one of the ancient huts erected by the first settlers for observing the appearance of the whales. Here lived a single family without a neighbour; I had never before seen a spot better calculated to cherish contemplative ideas, perfectly unconnected with the great world, and far removed from its perturbations.[3] The ever-raging ocean was all that presented itself to the view of this family; it irresistibly attracted my whole attention: my eyes were involuntarily directed to the horizontal line of that watery surface, which is ever in motion and ever threatening destruction to these shores. My ears were stunned with the roar of its waves rolling one over the other, as if impelled by a superior force to overwhelm the spot on which I stood. My nostrils involuntarily inhaled the saline vapours which arose from the dispersed particles of the foaming billows or from the weeds scattered on the shores. My mind suggested a thousand vague reflections, pleasing in the hour of their spontaneous birth, but now half forgotten, and all indistinct; and who is the landman that can behold without affright so singular an element, which by its impetuosity seems to be the destroyer of this poor planet, yet at particular times accumulates the scattered fragments and produces islands and continents fit for men to dwell on! Who can observe the regular vicissitudes of its waters without astonishment, now swelling themselves in order to

1. Chiendent.
2. Sorte d'île dans l'île.
3. James est en quête d'un lieu solitaire, véritable obsession, où il peut méditer sur l'ambivalence de la nature.

penetrate through every river and opening and thereby facilitate navigation, at other times retiring from the shores to permit man to collect that variety of shell-fish which is the support of the poor? Who can see the storms of wind, blowing sometimes with an impetuosity sufficiently strong even to move the earth, without feeling himself affected beyond the sphere of common ideas? Can this wind which but a few days ago refreshed our American fiedls and cooled us in the shade be the same element which now and then so powerfully convulses the waters of the sea, dismasts vessels, causes so many shipwrecks and such extensive desolations? How diminutive does a man appear to himself when filled with these thoughts, and standing as I did on the verge of the ocean! This family lived entirely by fishing, for the plough has not dared yet to disturb the parched surface of the neighbouring plain; and to what purpose could this operation be performed! Where is it that mankind will not find safety, peace, and abundance, with freedom and civil happiness? Nothing was wanting here to make this a most philosophical retreat but a few ancient trees[1] to shelter contemplation in its beloved solitude. There I saw a numerous family of children of various ages—the blessings of an early marriage; they were ruddy as the cherry, healthy as the fish they lived on, hardy as the pine knots; the eldest were already able to encounter the boisterous waves and shuddered not at their approach, early initiating themselves in the mysteries of that seafaring career, for which they were all intended; the younger, timid as yet, on the edge of a less agitated pool, were teaching themselves with nut-shells and pieces of wood, in imitation of boats, how to navigate in a future day the larger vessels of their father through a rougher and deeper ocean. I stayed two days there on purpose to become acquainted with the different branches of their economy and their manner of living in this singular retreat. The clams, the oysters of the shores, with the addition of Indian dumplings, constituted their daily and most substantial food. Larger fish were often caught on the neighbouring rip; these afforded them their greatest dainties; they had likewise plenty of smoked bacon. The noise of the wheels announced the industry of the mother and daughters;[2] one of them

1. L'absence d'arbres est attestée à Nantucket.
2. James chante les vertus des femmes américaines.

had been bred a weaver, and having a loom in the house, found means of clothing the whole family; they were perfectly at ease and seemed to want for nothing. I found very few books among these people, who have very little time for reading; the Bible and a few school tracts, both in the Nattic[1] and English languages, constituted their most numerous libraries. I saw indeed several copies of Hudibras and Josephus,[2] but no one knows who first imported them. It is something extraordinary to see this people, professedly so grave and strangers to every branch of literature, reading with pleasure the former work, which should seem to require some degree of taste and antecedent historical knowledge. They all read it much and can by memory repeat many passages, which yet I could not discover that they understood the beauties of. Is it not a little singular to see these books in the hands of fishermen, who are perfect strangers almost to any other? Josephus' history is indeed intelligible and much fitter for their modes of education and taste, as it describes the history of a people from whom we have received the prophecies which we believe and the religious laws which we follow.

1. John Eliot (1604-1690) avait traduit la Bible en natick, dialecte algonquin du Massachusetts (1663), rédigé un *Indian Primer* (1669).

2. *Hudibras :* satire contre les puritains de Samuel Butler (1612-1680), écrivain anglais : Joseph, le patriarche hébreu, Genèse 37, 39-50.

2 – *Sermons et libelles*

Au XVIIe siècle, surtout dans le Nord, les colons font une consommation immodérée de sermons. Tout, il est vrai, est prétexte à l'exercice de cet art de l'endoctrinement et de confort : les services religieux, les cérémonies officielles avec l'installation de nouveaux magistrats, les séances des assemblées coloniales, les commémorations annuelles. Sermons ordinaires, d'humiliation publique ou d'exécution de sentences, ils sont composés et dits par des pasteurs rompus à l'utilisation de la rhétorique, aux méthodes de préparation au salut enseignées aux puritains par l'Anglais Perkins. John Cotton en applique scrupuleusement le moule avec talent et simplicité. Thomas Hooker excelle dans l'art d' « ouvrir » le sens biblique sans recours aux figures anglicanes et en se servant de métaphores familières. Thomas Shepard fut sacré meilleur styliste de son temps avec *The Sincere Convert* (1640). Avec son fils Thomas (1635-1677) apparaît la « jérémiade » qui évoque le déclin supposé de la foi pour la revivifier. Cette modalité est reprise par Jonathan Edwards dans *Sinners in the Hands of an Angry God* (1741). Le sermon devient de plus en plus politique au XVIIIe siècle comme en témoigne *The Snare Broken* (1766), composé pour célébrer l'abandon du Stamp Act par Jonathan Mayhew (1720-1766). Les laïcs prêchent aussi : John Winthrop le démontre avec *Christian Charitie* (1630). Du sermon au libelle il n'y a qu'un pas comme on le voit avec Nathaniel Ward dans *The Simple Cobler of Aggawam*, et comme le rappelle la rhétorique de Thomas Paine dans *Common Sense.* De la longue controverse entre Roger Williams et John Cotton sur la tolérance aux textes de Dickinson, Jefferson, Otis dans la période révolutionnaire, les futurs Américains se montrent des écrivains compétents, efficaces et, souvent, talentueux.

THOMAS HOOKER, 1586-1647

Né à Marfield, Leicestershire, Thomas Hooker fait de bonnes études à Queen's College, Cambridge, puis à Emmanuel où il passe quatorze ans. Converti au sens puritain il choisit le ministère sacré. Il s'y taille une belle réputation qui lui attire les foudres de l'archevêque Laud. Il s'enfuit d'abord en Hollande qu'il quitte pour la Baie en 1633 en compagnie de John Cotton, son brillant collègue, un ancien de Cambridge. Quelques tensions entre ecclésiastiques et surtout des querelles de terres avec les gouverneurs le font partir après trois ans à New Town (Cambridge) avec une grande partie de sa congrégation. Il fonde la colonie du Connecticut où il meurt trente et un ans plus tard. Homme d'Etat et pasteur charismatique de Hartford, il collabore avec ses voisins aux synodes de 1637 — qui règle la crise antinomienne — et de 1643 qui écarte la voie presbytérienne. L'un de ses 22 livres, le *Survey of the Summe of Church-Discipline* (1648), est l'exposé définitif de la conception congrégationaliste du christianisme. Persuadé de la corruption totale de l'homme, il tente par ses sermons d'enseigner les étapes du salut — le préparationisme — et de persuader les pécheurs de se réformer. Sa qualité maîtresse est de savoir s'adapter à son public, d'expliquer clairement, avec des images familières, une foi intransigeante.

BIBLIOGRAPHIE SÉLECTIVE. — Bush Jr (Sargent), ed., *The Writings of Thomas Hooker : Spiritual Adventure in Two Worlds,* Madison, University of Wisconsin Press, 1980 ; Hooker (Thomas), *Redemption, three Sermons (1637-1656),* facs. reprint, introduction Everett H. Emerson, Delmar, NY, Scholars Fac. & Reprint, 1977 ; Shuffelton (Frank), *Thomas Hooker 1586-1647,* Princeton, Princeton University Press, 1977.

The Soules Ingrafting into Christ[1]

The first sort is all carnall' profane opposers of the Lord Jesus: The carnall Gospeller[2] is content that Christ should undertake for him, and bee his Protector, to defend him from the plague of sinne; but he is not content that Christ should rule in him. He doth as the Inne-keeper, that receives a guest into his house, to make an advantage of him: for as the Inne-keeper will come to his guest, & pretend great matters to him, not because he would have his guest to possesse him, but because he would be possesser of his money; so the carnall Gospeller would have Christ for his owne turne, hee would dispose of Christ and mercy for his owne purpose: and hence come all those speeches, God is mercifull, and, Hath the Lord Christ created men to damne them: Oh, but mercy is sweet, and pardon is good. This is thus much, you would have Christ to pardon sinne, that you might commit it with lesse seare and more freedome. If you did see no Saviour, but that[3] you must needs be damned for it, you would startle at it. But you would have Christ to stand by you that you might sinne the more freely. Oh be not deceived; doe you thinke that Christ will come to bee an underling[4] to your lusts, and a drudge to your base distempers, whose condemnation is just, saith the Apostle? No, you are deceived, you shall not have Christ a servant to carry your lusts and pleasures to heaven with you. The truth is, the Lord Jesus will never bring comfort nor consolation to thee that wilt not bee possessed of him; either have both or neither, chuse whether you will.

The second sort to be reproved, are a company of slye hypocrites, that would part stakes with Christ, and part houses with him; they could bee content that hee should have some roome in the house, but they will dispose of all themselves: as a man that lets some roomes in his house, upon this condition, that he may have them when hee lists. You will pray against sinne, provided that now and then Christ will give you leave to practise it; and you will cry out against it, provided that you may have a privie seale, and some secret licence for it; and you will prosesse bitterly against base courses, so you may have some backe doore and inward lust

1. 1637. Conclusion du sermon sur ceux qui se méprennent, sur le sens de la greffe du cœur en Christ.
2. Prédicateur mondain.
3. Et que.
4. Esclave.

still, The Lord Jesus doth not share with any man: can he have a part and the Divell a part: nay, hee will have either all or none. It was the trick of an adulterous heart: for when there was contention for the children, the harlot said, *Let it bee neither thine nor mine, but divide it:* Nay, saith the mother, *let her have all.*[1] She was the harlot that would have the childe divided. So it is an adulterous and dissembling heart that saith, Let Christ have a part, and the world a part; let lusts and pompe have a part, and Christ a part, this is dissimulation with God, and shall receive condemnation: there must be no sharing. If your hearts be guilty of this, I charge you in the name of the Lord Jesus consider it, the Lord never came into your soules: you must resigne all to him, and then hee will save all: hee will pardon all sinne, and give power against it. What a fearefull thing were it, if the Lord should deale with you as you deale with him. Suppose thou couldst be half damned; wouldst thou be content to have thy heart go to hell and thine eye to heaven, or thy body to hell and thy soule to heaven: therefore that thy body and soule may both be saved, resigne up all into the hands of thy Saviour, and let him dispose of all here in the kingdome of grace, and then he will take all to himselfe in glory for ever.

Use 1. If the Lord Jesus be the possessor of all the house, then let every one have his own, doe not withdraw from Christ that which is his. Whose image and superscription hath the soule: Christ Jesus hath the protection of it, therefore let him have all: let thine eye see his works, and wonder and admire at them; let thy minde know Jesus Christ, whom to know is eternall life; but doe not withdraw any thing from the true owner thereof, that hath purchased it full deare. 1 Cor. 5, 15: *Shall I take the members of Christ, and make them the members of an harlot? God forbid.* Thine eye, and thy tongue, and thy hand, and thy heart, they are all Christs members, hee hath bought all with his blood, and thou hast nothing to doe with that which Christ hath bought: therefore whensoever thy corruptions stirre, and Satan tempts and begges for the use of thy minde or heart, make answer and say, Shall I take that heart that is Christs, and thinke basely. God forbid: Shall I take the hand of Christ and worke wickednesse with it? The holy Apostle is marvellous peremptory in this case: as 1 Cor. 6, 19: *Glorifie God in your body and in your spirit, which are Gods,* and he hath bought you with a price:

1. I Rois, 3, 26.

your bodies and soules are the Lords, he undertakes for both, therefore glorifie God in both. If a man did come to your house, and take the meat and drinke that you have provided, and rob you of your mony, you would take it very hardly, and say, It is my owne. So you are not you owne. Therefore if the Divell or the world would prevaile with you, and enter into the use of your heart or minde, tell him they are not thy owne, they are the Lords: Jesus Christ hath come into thy heart and minde in mercy, and therefore say it is the Lords, let him doe what he will with it.

ROGER WILLIAMS (*c.* 1603-1683)

Londonien, fils de tailleur, il attire l'attention de Sir Edward Coke, le grand juriste, qui facilite son admission à Charterhouse, puis à Pembroke Hall, Cambridge. Devenu chapelain de Sir William Masham, il quitte sa place pour la colonie de la Baie. Arrivé en février 1631 il refuse de diriger une congrégation non séparatiste. Convaincu du caractère absolument privé de la foi, de la nécessité d'une séparation complète de l'Eglise et de l'Etat, de l'obligation pour les colons d'acheter leur terre aux Indiens, il se rend indésirable. Banni en 1635, fuyant la déportation en Angleterre, il va chez les Narragansetts et fonde Providence en 1636. Cultivant ses bonnes relations avec les Indiens il gère le Rhode Island selon ses principes. En 1643, il se rend à Londres pour obtenir une charte, rédige sa *Key into the Language of America* pendant le voyage, commence ses attaques contre John Cotton (1584-1652). Il écrit le premier d'une série de libelles, *A Bloody Tenent of Persecution* (1644). Il rentre à Providence où il est élu Président de la colonie, fonction qu'il garde jusqu'en 1657. Son combat contre l'éminence grise du pouvoir politique à Boston et sa défense de la liberté de conscience au nom d'un calvinisme exalté rendent célèbre le brillant pasteur. Mais le violent débat qui l'oppose aux quakers en 1672 porte une ombre à la réputation de tolérance qu'il avait acquise.

BIBLIOGRAPHIE SÉLECTIVE. — Caldwell (Samuel L.) *et al.*, eds, *The Complete Writings of Roger Williams*, 7 vol., New York, Russell & Russel, 1963 ; Gilpin (W. Clark), *The Millenariam Piety of Roger Williams*, Chicago, University of Chicago Press, 1979 ; Miller (Perry), *Roger Williams, His Contribution to the American Tradition*, New York, Atheneum, 1962.

The Bloody Tenent of Persecution[1]

TO EVERY COURTEOUS READER

While I plead the Cause of *Truth* and *Innocencie* against the bloody *Doctrine* of *Persecution* for cause of *conscience*, I judge it not unfit to give *alarme* to my selfe, and all men to prepare to be *persecuted* or hunted for cause of *conscience*.

Whether thou standest charged with 10 or but 2 *Talents*,[2] if thou huntest any for cause of *conscience*, how canst thou say thou followest the *Lambe* of *God* who so abhorr'd that practice?

If *Paul*, if *Jesus Christ* were present here at *London*, and the *question* were proposed what *Religion* would they approve of: The *Papists*, *Prelatists*,[3] *Presbyterians*, *Independents*, &c. would each say, Of mine, of mine.

But put the second question, if one of the severall sorts should by *major vote* attaine the *Sword* of steele: what weapons doth Christ Jesus authorize them to fight with in His cause? Doe not all men hate the *persecutor*, and every *conscience* true or false complaine of cruelty, tyranny? &c.

Two *mountaines* of crying *guilt* lye heavie upon the backes of All that name the name of *Christ* in the eyes of *Jewes*, *Turkes* and *Pagans*.

First, The blasphemies of their *Idolatrous inventions*, *superstitions*, and most *unchristian conversations*.

Secondly, The bloody irreligious and inhumane *oppressions* and *destructions* under the maske or vaile of the Name of *Christ*, &c.

O how like is the *jealous Jehovah*, the consuming fire to end these *slaughters* in a greater slaughter of the holy Witnesses? *Rev.* 11.

1. *The Bloody Tenent of Persecution for Cause of Conscience, discussed, in a Conference between Truth and Peace*, 1644.
2. Sens obsolète : disposition au mal.
3. Episcopaliens.

Six yeares preaching of so much Truth of *Christ* (as that time afforded in *K. Edwards*[1] dayes) kindles the flames of *Q. Maries*[2] bloody *persecutions*.

Who can now but expect that after so many scores of yeares *preaching* and *professing* of more *Truth*, and amongst so many great *contentions* amongst the very best of *Protestants*, a fierie furnace should be heat, and who sees not now the *fires* kindling?

I confesse I have little hopes till those flames are over, that this Discourse against the *doctrine of persecution* for cause of *conscience* should passe currant (I say not amongst the *Wolves* and *Lions*, but even amongst the *Sheep* of *Christ* themselves) yet *liberavi animam meam*,[3] I have not hid within my *breast* my *souls* belief: And although sleeping on the bed either of the pleasures or profits of sinne thou thinkest thy conscience bound to smite at him that dares to waken thee? Yet in the middest of all these *civill* and *spirituall Wars*[4] (I hope we shall agree in these particulars).

First, how ever the proud (upon the advantage of an higher earth or ground) or'elooke the poore and cry out *Schismatickes, Hereticks*, &c. shall *blasphemers* and *seducers* scape unpunished? &c. Yet there is a sorer punishment in the *Gospel* for despising of *Christ* then *Moses*, even when the despiser of *Moses* was put to death without mercie, *Heb*. 10. 28, 29. He that beleeveth not shall bee damned, *Marke* 16. 16.

Secondly, what ever Worship, Ministry, Ministration, the best and purest are practised without *faith* and true perswation that they are the true institutions of God, they are sin, sinfull worships, Ministries, &c. And however in Civill things we may be servants unto men, yet in Divine and Spirituall things the poorest *pesant* must disdaine the service of the highest *Prince*: Be ye not the servants of men, 1 Cor. 14. [vii: 23.]

Thirdly, without search and triall no man attaines this faith and right perswasion, 1 *Thes. 5.* Try all things.

In vaine have *English Parliaments* permitted *English Bibles* in the poorest *English* houses, and the simplest man or woman to search the Scriptures, if yet against their soules perswasion from the

1. Edouard VI (1547-1553).
2. Reine Marie (1553-1558).
3. J'ai libéré mon âme.
4. La guerre civile commencée en 1642.

Scripture, they should be forced (as if they lived in *Spaine* or *Rome* it selfe without the sight of a *Bible*) to beleeve as the Church beleeves.

Fourthly, having tried, we must hold fast, 1 *Thessal.* 5. upon the losse of a Crowne, *Revel.* 13. [iii: 11.] we must not let goe for all the flea bitings of the present afflictions, &c. having bought Truth deare, we must not sell it cheape, not the least graine of it for the whole World, no not for the saving of Soules, though our owne most precious; least of all for the bitter sweetning of a little vanishing pleasure.

For a little puffe of credit and reputation from the changeable breath of uncertaine sons of men.[:]

For the broken bagges of Riches on Eagles wings: For a dreame of these, any or all of these which on our death-bed vanish and leave tormenting stings behinde them: Oh how much better is it from the love of Truth, from the love of the Father of lights, from whence it comes, from the love of the Sonne of God, who is the way and the Truth, to say as he, *John* 18. 37. for this end was I borne, and for this end came I into the World that I might beare witnesse to the Truth.

NATHANIEL WARD (*c.* 1578-1652)

Descendant de bonne famille, fils de pasteur, il est né à Haverhill, Suffolk. Admis à Emmanuel College, Cambridge, en 1596, il poursuit, après son MA, des études de droit à Lincoln's Inn. Inscrit au barreau en 1615, il voyage en Europe. Ordonné en Allemagne en 1618 il devient chapelain de marchands anglais en Prusse. De retour en Angleterre il exerce son ministère jusqu'à ses démêlés avec l'archevêque Laud. Au décès de sa femme il émigre en 1633 avec ses enfants. Il est pasteur d'Ipswich pendant trois ans. Nommé membre de la commission *ad hoc* il est le principal auteur du *Body of Liberties of Massachusetts Bay* (1641). Il reçoit 600 acres de terre à Haverhill sur lesquelles il ne s'installe pas pour raisons de santé. Il lègue son bien à Harvard College. Replié à Boston il rédige *The Simple Cobler of Aggawan* (1647) qui paraît à Londres l'année de son retour définitif et qui lui vaut un franc succès. Invité à prêcher au Parlement, il écrit d'autres libelles et quelques vers. Mais sa réputation repose sur ce sermon burlesque, cet essai, ce pamphlet qui captive par la liberté du propos, une faconde, un sens de la parodie, un humour qui côtoie la satire violente, une boulimie verbale créatrice qui caractérise une œuvre au style original, débordant de références, à effets multiples par lequel Ward défend l'ordre puritain.

BIBLIOGRAPHIE SÉLECTIVE. — Zall (P. W.), ed., *The Simple Cobler of Aggawam in America by Nathaniel Ward,* Lincoln, Nebraska, 1969 ; Béranger (Jean), *Nathaniel Ward,* Bordeaux, Sobodi, 1969 ; Royot (Daniel), *L'humour américain. Des puritains aux yankees,* Lyon, Presses Universitaires de Lyon, 1980 ; Arndt (Robert D.), The Simple Cobler of Aggawam : Nathaniel Ward and the Rhetoric of Satire, *Early American Literature,* vol. V, n° 8, 3-16 ; Béranger (Jean), Voices of Humor in Nathaniel Ward, *Studies in American Humor,* vol. II, 2, 1975, 96-104 ; Scheick (William J.), The Widower Narrator in Nathaniel Ward's *The Simple Cobler of Aggawam in American, The New England Quarterly,* vol. XLVII, I, 1974.

The Simple Cobler of Aggawam in America[1]

Should I not keepe promise in speaking a little to Womens fashions, they would take it unkindly: I was loath to pester better matter with such stuffe; I rather thought it meet to let them stand by themselves, like the *Quæ Genus*[2] in the Grammer, being Deficients, or Redundants, not to be brought under any Rule: I shall therefore make bold for this once, to borrow a little of their loose tongued Liberty, and mispend a word or two upon their long-wasted, but short-skirted patience: a little use of my stirrup will doe no harme.

Ridentem dicere verum, quid prohibet?[3]

Gray Gravity it selfe can well beteam,
That Language be adapted to the Theme.
He that to Parrots speaks, must parrotise:
He that instructs a foole, may act th'unwise.

1. 1647. Quatrième édition.
2. Quel genre ?
3. Qu'est-ce qui m'empêche de dire la vérité en riant ? (Horace, *Satires,* I, i, 24-25.)

It is known more then enough, that I am neither Nigard, nor Cinick, to the due bravery of the true Gentry: if any man mislikes a bullymong drossock[1] more then I, let him take her for his labour: I honour the woman that can honour her selfe with her attire: a good Text alwayes deserves a fair Margent; I am not much offended, if I see a trimme, far trimmer than she that weares it: in a word, whatever Christianity or Civility will allow, I can afford with *London* measure: but when I heare a nugiperous[2] Gentledame inquire what dresse the Queen is in this week: what the nudiustertian[3] fashion of the Court; with egge to be in it in all haste, whatever it be; I look at her as the very gizzard of a trifle, the product of a quarter of a cypher, the epitome of Nothing, fitter to be kickt, if shee were of a kickable substance, than either honour'd or humour'd.

To speak moderately, I truly confesse it is beyond the ken of my understanding to conceive, how those women should have any true grace, or valuable vertue, that have so little wit, as to disfigure themselves with such exotick garbes, as not only dismantles their native lovely lustre, but transclouts[4] them into gant-bar-geese[5], ill-shapen-shotten-shell-fish[6], Egyptian Hyeroglyphicks, or at the best into French flurts[7] of the pastery, which a proper English woman should scorne with her heels: it is no marvell they weare drailes[8] on the hinder part of their heads, having nothing as it seems in the fore-part, but a few Squirrils brains to help them frisk from one ill-favour'd fashion to another.

These whimm' Crown'd shees, these fashion-fansyingwits,
Are empty thin brain'd shells, and fidling Kits.

The very troublers and impoverishers of mankind, I can hardly forbeare to commend to the world a saying of a Lady living sometime with the Queen of *Bohemia*, I know not where shee found it, but it is pitty it should be lost.

1. Une femme malpropre.
2. Marchande de colifichets.
3. D'il y a trois jours.
4. Déguise.
5. Oie sauvage.
6. Crustacés biscornus et sans frai.
7. Fleurtés (fleuretté + flirté).
8. Coiffure avec traîne.

The world is full of care, much like unto a bubble;
Women and care, and care and women, and women and
care and trouble.

The Verses are even enough for such odde pegma's[1] I can make my selfe sicke at any time, with comparing the dazling splender wherewith our Gentlewomen were imbellished in some former habits, with the gut-foundred goosdom,[2] wherewith they are now surcingled[3] and debauched. Wee have about five or six of them in our Colony: if I see any of them accidentally, I cannot cleanse my phansie of them for a moneth after. I have been a solitary widdower almost twelve yeares, purposed lately to make a step over to my Native Country for a yoke-fellow: but when I consider how women there have tripe-wifed themselves[4] with their cladments, I have no heart to the voyage, least their nauseous shapes and the Sea, should work too sorely upon my stomach. I speak sadly; me thinkes it should breake the hearts of English-men, to see so many goodly English-women imprisoned in French Cages, peering out of their hood-holes for some men of mercy to help them with a little wit, and no body relieves them.

JONATHAN EDWARDS (1703-1758)

Né à East Windsor, Connecticut, fils de pasteur, petit-fils de l'influent Solomon Stoddard (1643-1729), enfant à la vive sensibilité religieuse, il est élevé chez ses parents avant d'entrer à Yale College en 1716 où il poursuit des études de théologie après son BA. En 1722, il s'occupe d'une église presbytérienne de New York puis il revient à Yale de 1724 à 1726, date à laquelle il rejoint son grand-père à Northampton, Massachusetts. Ordonné en 1727, il est le maître de la congrégation au décès de celui dont le nom est attaché à l'assouplissement des conditions d'entrée dans

1. Inscription.
2. Stupide ventrèche.
3. Enceintes.
4. Habillées en tripières.

l'église congrégationaliste. Jonathan fait l'inverse, exigeant une déclaration publique de conversion avant d'admettre à communion. A partir de 1734 il s'engage dans l'œuvre du Grand Réveil, persuadé que l'émotion doit accompagner la conviction intellectuelle. Il prêche des sermons remarquables pour convaincre. Mais ce grand calviniste lasse par sa sévérité. En 1750 les fidèles votent massivement contre lui. Démis, il accepte de devenir missionnaire auprès des Indiens à Stockbridge sur la frontière. C'est là qu'il rédige quelques-uns de ses grands traités. Devenu président du College of New Jersey en 1758, il meurt trois mois plus tard de la petite vérole, laissant de nombreux manuscrits dont certains, récemment publiés, éclairent l'œuvre d'un philosophe et d'un théologien de grande stature qui ouvre la voie aux transcendantalistes.

BIBLIOGRAPHIE SÉLECTIVE. — Smith (John F.), ed., *The Works of Jonathan Edwards,* 7 vol. parus, New Haven, Conn., Yale University Press, 1957 ; Delattre (Roland A.), *Beauty and sensibility in the Thought of Jonathan Edwards,* New Haven, Conn., Yale University Press, 1968 ; Lowance Jr (Mason I.), *The Language of Canaan,* chap. 8, Cambridge, Mass., Harvard University Press, 1980 ; Béranger (Jean), Interprétation et utilisation de l'*Apocalypse* par Jonathan Edwards, 30-47, *Le facteur religieux en Amérique du Nord,* n° 2, CEC-CRAA, Bordeaux, MSHA, 46, Diffusion Presses Universitaires de Bordeaux, 1981.

Notes on the Apocalypse[1]

Ans. 2. The church of God may suffer extreme oppression, and be brought very low just before the final destruction of Antichrist; but not directly by the power of Antichrist, but some other way, yet in general by things of the same tendency, and all by Satan, the grand adversary of God's church and head of all her enemies.

So it was after the deliverance out of Egypt, before the children of Israel were possessed of Canaan. They suffered extremely for

1. Titre du manuscrit rédigé entre 1723 et 1755. Commentaire de l'Apocalypse II, 3 : mille deux cent soixante ans de règne du Malin nous séparent du retour du Christ. Etablissant des parallèles typologiques entre l'histoire biblique et l'histoire chrétienne contemporaine, Edwards s'interroge sur les signes de la destruction qu'il croit prochaine de l'Antéchrist.

40 years in the wilderness. So it was with David after his begun deliverance from Saul. Just before his being made king over Israel, he was reduced to the last extremity by the Amalekites [I Sam. 30, 1-31]; and then again, before the setting up his throne in Jerusalem over all Israel, he had much trouble from Ishbosheth and his adherents [II Sam. 2, 8-4:12]. So after the partial restoration of the Jews by the decree of Cyrus,[1] they suffered extremely from the Samaritans, and were well nigh overcome by their attempts and devices [Ezra 4], before the more complete restoration by Artaxerxes in Ezra's time [Ezra 7].

So since the Reformation, the church of God is now reduced very lower and to great extremity, through the prevalence of deism, atheism, heresy and profaneness.

Ans. 3. The same ends may be obtained. The church of God may be as much and in like manner prepared, for that great salvation she is to receive at the downfall of Antichrist, without her being brought to her lowest state, through the power and prevalence of her antichristian enemies. 'Tis manifest that immediately before that glorious event, the popish powers[2] will collect all their strength. They will, in the height of the exercise of their malice and envy against God's will, rage in a most terrible manner, as Antiochus' rage was the greatest just before his death.[3] They shall join hand in hand; the combination will be exceeding strong. Their schemes shall be laid very deep; their preparations shall be immense. The devil will assist them to his utmost. All the powers of hell shall be awakened and engaged. Satan will engage other parts of his kingdom of darkness in the world, to engage in the help of the Romish power. Strong leagues and alliances shall be entered into. The ends of the earth, as it were, shall be stirred. Emissaries shall be most busily and successfully employed, in order to the most formidable and vast preparations. They shall be like Pharaoh with all the strength of Egypt, and his mighty host of chariots and horsemen, all ready for the battle, and in their own imagination sure of success, vaunting in themselves, in their greatly exceeding the people of God in external pomp and power,

1. Cyrus, roi de Perse (553-529 av. J.-C.), permit aux juifs de regagner la Palestine et de rebâtir le Temple.

2. Les Etats catholiques sont les instruments de l'Antéchrist.

3. Antiochus IV, roi de Syrie (175-164 av. J.-C.), mit à sac Jérusalem, hellénisa la ville, souilla le Temple en 168. Il passe pour être devenu fou avant sa mort.

so that they shall seem as nothing to 'em. They, greatly irritated and enraged, shall come with whetted resolutions of the most merciless cruelties. The appearances will be such as strongly to impress the minds of God's people, with a sense of their enemies' power and their own comparative weakness, and the greatness of the sufferings intended them, and lively apprehensions of their danger, any otherwise than as their faith shall overcome all these threatening appearances, and fill 'em with holy fortitude. Probably some of God's people will suffer. The enemy shall begin to prevail and exercise their cruelties, raising the pride and vaunting of the enemy, and giving God's people a full idea of the extreme sufferings they are threatened with.

Now these things will be as good a preparation for the glorious deliverance and salvation, which God shall work for his people, and the triumph they shall have over them, as though their enemies should be suffered actually to prevail and conquer God's people, and reduce 'em to the most extreme distress, and to appearance hopeless and extreme, immediately before their complete deliverance. Such a state of things with respect to God's people and their enemies, will be as good a preparation for the giving the world an affecting sense of God's glory as above that of his enemies', and [a sense] of the vanity of the pride and loftiness of men, and the folly their envy, malice and self-confidence, and to give God's people a sense of God's great grace and mercy to them, and will as well prepare the way for the glory of their triumph, and for the increase of the ardor of their praises.

Such were the circumstance of the great salvation God wrought for Israel at the Red Sea, that perhaps the preparation for the manifestation of God's glory in that work, and the preparation of God's people for their deliverance, their victory over the enemies, and praises to their glorious deliverer, was as great as if Pharaoh had been suffered for a little season actually to prevail, and had taken Israel captive, and they had suddenly and in some wonderful way been rescued, and their enemies miraculously destroyed.

93. Chapter 16, 13-14. "And I saw three unclean spirits like frogs come out of the mouth of the dragon, and out of the mouth of the beast, and out of the mouth of the false prophet. For they are the spirits of devils, working miracles, which go forth unto the kings of the earth and of the whole world, to

gather them to the battle of that great day of God Almighty." One main thing here intended and represented, seems to me to be the great prevailing of the delusions of the devil in counterfeit illuminations, and false affections, and enthusiasm,[1] by which the devil, imitating the great and wonderful works of God's Holy Spirit, shall deceive vast multitudes everywhere, and of all ranks and degrees, as they shall be led away by these things, and shall deceive others by hereby greatly prejudicing them against the power of godliness. Though this enthusiastical spirit shall operate different ways among different kinds of people, as it is not spoken as one spirit, but three unclean spirits out of the mouths of three different creatures.

SAMUEL LANGDON (1723-1797)

Né à Boston, Samuel Langdon étudie à Harvard College dont il sort diplômé en 1740. Maître d'école temporaire et prédicateur occasionnel jusqu'en 1747, il est ordonné par la congrégation de la First Church de Portsmouth, New Hampshire. Son nom est associé à la création de Dartmouth College. En 1774 il accède aux fonctions de président de son université. Il démissionne en 1780 et reprend une place de pasteur à Hampton Falls, New Hampshire. Patriote, il défend sa terre dans ses sermons. Il adopte la cause des futurs insurgés comme en témoigne un texte prêché devant une assemblée illégale le 31 mai 1775, peu après Lexington. Dans ce discours de circonstance S. Langdon fait revivre l'émotion et la rhétorique de ses grands prédécesseurs dont il retrouve les thèmes. Grâce aux relations de plus en plus tendues avec la mère patrie, les Nouveaux-Anglais revigorent l'art du sermon. Il est moins question de l'apostasie à la mode il y a peu, et

1. Trop de confiance en l'intuition pouvait mener à l'illuminisme dont les Antinomiens avaient été un exemple à Boston en 1637. Trop de recours à l'émotion pouvait conduire à l'enthousiasme religieux qui guettait les adeptes du Grand Eveil. Edwards prit conscience du danger.

beaucoup plus de la nouvelle mission. Homme politique, S. Langdon fut délégué à la Convention. Il recommanda la ratification de la Constitution en 1788.

BIBLIOGRAPHIE SÉLECTIVE. — Plumstead (A. W.), ed., *The Wall and the Garden. Selected Massachusetts Election Sermons 1670-1775*, Minneapolis, Minnesota, University of Minnesota Press, 1968.

Government Corrupted by Vice and Recovered by Righteousness[1]

It is now ten months since this Colony has been deprived of the benefit of that government which was so long enjoyed by charter.[2] They have had no general assembly for matters of legislation and the public revenue. The courts of justice have been shut up and almost the whole executive power has ceased to act. Yet order among the people has been remarkably preserved; few crimes have been committed punishable by the judge; even former contentions betwixt one neighbor and another have ceased; nor have fraud and rapine taken advantage of the imbecility of the civil powers.

The necessary preparations for the defense of our liberties required not only the collected wisdom and strength of the Colony, but an immediate cheerful application of the wealth of individuals to the public service, in due proportion; or a taxation which depended on general consent. Where was the authority to vote, collect, or receive the large sums required, and make provision for the utmost extremities? A congress succeeded to the honors of a general assembly as soon as the latter was crush'd by the hand of power.[3] It gained all the confidence of the people. Wisdom and prudence secur'd all that the laws of the former constitution could have given. And we now observe with astonishment an army of many thousands of well-disciplined troops suddenly assembled

1. 1775. Titre du sermon qu'il avait été invité à prêcher devant l'illégal et tout récent Congrès de la colonie de la Baie du Massachusetts réuni à Watertown pour sa troisième séance le 31 mai, date fixée par la Charte pour l'élection des conseillers.

2. Le Massachusetts Government Act de 1774 supprimait l'élection prévue par la Charte de 1691 et son remplacement par la désignation de Conseillers du Roi que le souverain devait nommer.

3. En septembre 1774 le général Gage, gouverneur, avait convoqué la Cour générale, puis annulé. Les représentants passèrent outre et formèrent la Cour provinciale devant laquelle Langdon fit son sermon selon la tradition.

and abundantly furnished with all necessary supplies in defense of the liberties of America.

But is it proper or safe for the Colony to continue much longer in such imperfect order? Must it not appear rational and necessary to every man that understands the various movements requisite to good government that the many parts should be properly settled, and every branch of the legislative and executive authority restored to that order and vigor on which the life and health of the body politic depend? To the honorable gentlemen now met in this new congress as the fathers of the people, this weighty matter must be referred. Who knows but in the midst of all the distresses of the present war to defeat the attempts of arbitrary power, God may in mercy restore to us our judges as at the first, and our counselors as at the beginning.

On your wisdom, religion, and public spirit, honored gentlemen, we depend, to determine what may be done as to the important matter of reviving the form of government and settling all necessary affairs relating to it in the present critical state of things, that we may again have law and justice, and avoid the danger of anarchy and confusion. May God be with you, and by the influences of his Spirit direct all your counsels and resolutions for the glory of his name and the safety and happiness of this Colony. We have great reason to acknowledge with thankfulness the evident tokens of the divine Presence with the former congress, that they were led to foresee present exigencies and make such effectual provision for them. It is our earnest prayer to the Father of lights that he would irradiate your minds, make all your way plain, and grant you may be happy instruments of many and great blessings to the people by whom you are constituted, to New England, and all the united colonies.

Let us praise our God for the advantages already given us over the enemies of liberty; particularly, that they have been so dispirited by repeated experience of the efficacy of our arms; and that in the late action at Chelsea, when several hundreds of our soldiery, the greater part open to the fire of so many cannon, swivels, and muskets from a battery advantageously situated, from two armed cutters and many barges full of marines, and from ships of the line in the harbor, not one man on our side was killed and but two or three wounded; when, by the best intelligence, a great number were killed and wounded on the other side, and one of their cutters was taken and burnt, the other narrowly escaping with great damage.[1]

If God be for us, who can be against us?[2] The enemy has reproached us for calling on his name and professing our trust in him. They have made a mock of our solemn fasts and every appearance of serious Christianity in the land. On this account, by way of contempt, they call us "saints"; and that they themselves may keep at the greatest distance from this character, their mouths are full of horrid blasphemies, cursing, and bitterness, and vent all the rage of malice and barbarity. And may we not be confident that the most High who regards these things will vindicate his own honor, and plead our righteous cause against such enemies to his government as well as our liberties. O, may our camp be free from every accursed thing! May our land be purged from all its sins! May we be truly a holy people, and all our towns, cities of righteousness! Then the Lord will be our refuge and strength, a very present help in trouble;[3] and we shall have no reason to be afraid though thousands of enemies set themselves against us round about—tho' all nature should be thrown into tumults and convulsions. He can command the stars in their courses to fight his battles, and all the elements to wage war with his enemies. He can destroy them with innumerable plagues, or send faintness into their hearts so that the men of might shall not find their hands. In a variety of methods he can work salvation for us, as he did for his people in ancient days, and according to the many remarkable deliverances granted in former times to Great Britain and New England, when popish machinations threatened both countries with civil and ecclesiastical tyranny.[4]

May the Lord hear us in this day of trouble and the name of the God of Jacob defend us; send us help from his sanctuary; and strengthen us out of Zion. We will rejoice in his salvation, and in the name of our God we will set up our banners; let us look to him to fulfill all our petitions. FINIS.

1. Compte rendu légèrement inexact : les Anglais perdirent 2 hommes.
2. Romains 8, 31.
3. Psaumes 46, I.
4. Langdon fait allusion aux intrigues de Rome, aux échecs de Jacques II le catholique, à l'élimination de la menace française au Canada malgré le Quebec Act (1774) qui maintient l'Eglise catholique.

THOMAS PAINE (1737-1809)

Ce mal-aimé est né à Thetford, Norfolk, fils d'un pauvre corsetier quaker. Après avoir étudié les sciences à la *grammar school* locale, il apprend le métier de son père. Devenu employé des douanes, il est renvoyé pour avoir écrit un texte demandant une augmentation de salaire. Il émigre à Philadelphie en 1774 et prend la rédaction du *Pennsylvania Magazine*. C'est en composant *Common Sense* qu'il attire enfin l'attention : il cristallise les volontés empruntant au sermon sa rhétorique de persuasion. En juillet 1776 il s'engage. Nommé aide de camp du général Greene, il écrit *The American Crisis* qui galvanise les Américains après la retraite de Trenton. Le Congrès le nomme secrétaire aux Affaires étrangères. Il accompagne Henry Laurens en France pour négocier argent et équipements. Il sert en Pennsylvanie. Mais la vigueur de ses raisonnements, son franc-parler lui font des ennemis. Il se tourne vers l'Angleterre et la France où les événements révolutionnaires le passionnent. Il écrit deux grands textes : *Rights of Man* (1791-1792) et *The Age of Reason* (1794-1795). Un des premiers à demander la République après Varennes, élu à la Convention, il vote contre la mort du roi, échappe de peu à la guillotine. Discrédité en Amérique par sa profession de foi déiste et antichrétienne, sa lettre ouverte au traître Washington l'achève. Invité par Jefferson à rentrer, il vit dans l'oubli, la maladie et la pauvreté de 1802 à sa mort à New Rochelle.

BILIOGRAPHIE SÉLECTIVE. — Foner (Philips S.), *The Complete Writings of Thomas Paine,* 2 vol., New York, Citadel Press, 1945 ; Aldridge (Alfred O.), *Thomas Paine's American Ideology,* Newark, University of Delaware Press, 1984 ; Vincent (Bernard), *Thomas Paine ou la religion de la liberté,* Paris, Aubier, 1987 ; Le Moal (Paul), Un « best-seller » de la révolution : Le *Common Sense* de Thomas Paine, 310-319, *Etudes anglaises*, XXIX, n° 3, 1976.

Common Sense[1]

I challenge the warmest advocate for reconciliation to show a single advantage that this continent can reap by being connected with Great Britain. I repeat the challenge; not a single advantage is derived. Our corn will fetch its price in any market in Europe, and our imported goods must be paid for, buy them where we will.

But the injuries and disadvantages which we sustain by that connection, are without number; and our duty to mankind at large, as well as to ourselves, instructs us to renounce the alliance: because, any submission to, or dependence on, Great Britain, tends directly to involve this continent in European wars and quarrels, and set us at variance with nations who would otherwise seek our friendship, and against whom we have neither anger nor complaint. As Europe is our market for trade, we ought to form no partial connection with any part of it. It is the true interest of America to steer clear of European contentions, which she never can do, while, by her dependence on Britain, she is made the makeweight in the scale of British politics.

Europe is too thickly planted with kingdoms to be long at peace, and whenever a war breaks out between England and any foreign power, the trade of America goes to ruin, *because of her connection with Britain.* The next war may not turn out like the last,[2] and should it not, the advocates for reconciliation now will be wishing for separation then, because neutrality in that case would be a safer convoy than a man of war.[3] Every thing that is right or reasonable pleads for separation. The blood of the slain, the weeping voice of nature cries, 'TIS TIME TO PART. Even the distance at which the Almighty hath placed England and America is a strong and natural proof that the authority of the one over the other, was never the design of heaven. The time likewise at which the continent was discovered, adds weight to the argument, and the manner in which it was peopled, encreases the force of it. The Reformation was preceded by the discovery of America: As if the Almighty graciously meant to open a sanctuary to the persecuted

1. Publié anonymement le 10 janvier 1776.

2. La guerre de Sept ans — appelée French and Indian War en Amérique — s'était terminée avec le traité de Paris en 1763.

3. Navire de guerre.

in future years, when home should afford neither friendship nor safety.

The authority of Great Britain over this continent, is a form of government, which sooner or later must have an end. And a serious mind can draw no true pleasure by looking forward, under the painful and positive conviction that what he calls "the present constitution" is merely temporary. As parents, we can have no joy, knowing that this government is not sufficiently lasting to insure any thing which we may bequeath to posterity. And by a plain method of argument, as we are running the next generation into debt, we ought to do the work of it, otherwise we use them meanly and pitifully. In order to discover the line of our duty rightly, we should take our children in our hand, and fix our station a few years farther into life; that eminence will present a prospect which a few present fears and prejudices conceal from our sight.

Though I would carefully avoid giving unnecessary offence, yet I am inclined to believe, that all those who espouse the doctrine of reconciliation, may be included within the following descriptions.

Interested men, who are not to be trusted, weak men who *cannot* see, prejudiced men who will not see, and a certain set of moderate men who think better of the European world than it deserves; and this last class, by an ill-judged deliberation, will be the cause of more calamities to this continent than all the other three.

It is the good fortune of many to live distant from the scene of present sorrow; the evil is not sufficiently brought to their doors to make them feel the precariousness with which all American property is possessed. But let our imaginations transport us a few moments to Boston; that seat of wretchedness will teach us wisdom, and instruct us for ever to renounce a power in whom we can have no trust. The inhabitants of that unfortunate city who but a few months ago were in ease and affluence, have now no other alternative than to stay and starve, or turn out to beg.[1] Endangered by the fire of their friends if they continue within the city, and plundered by the soldiery if they leave it, in their present situation they are prisoners without the hope of redemption, and

1. Pour punir les Bostoniens d'avoir jeté 342 caisses de thé dans le port, le Parlement britannique avait voté quatre lois dont l'une fermait le port au trafic à partir du 1er juin 1774. Une autre loi autorisait le logement de la troupe chez l'habitant. Il est exact que près d'un an plus tard des milliers de personnes étaient dans le dénuement.

in a general attack for their relief they would be exposed to the fury of both armies.

Men of passive tempers look somewhat lightly over the offences of Great Britain, and, still hoping for the best, are apt to call out, *Come, come, we shall be friends again for all this*. But examine the passions and feelings of mankind: bring the doctrine of reconciliation to the touchstone of nature, and then tell me whether you can hereafter love, honor, and faithfully serve the power that hath carried fire and sword into your land? If you cannot do all these, then are you only deceiving yourselves, and by your delay bringing ruin upon posterity. Your future connection with Britain, whom you can neither love nor honor, will be forced and unnatural, and being formed only on the plan of present convenience, will in a little time fall into a relapse more wretched than the first. But if you say, you can still pass the violations over, then I ask, hath your house been burnt? Hath your property been destroyed before your face? Are your wife and children destitute of a bed to lie on, or bread to live on? Have you lost a parent or a child by their hands, and yourself the ruined and wretched survivor? If you have not, then are you not a judge of those who have. But if you have, and can still shake hands with the murderers, then are you unworthy the name of husband, father friend, or lover, and whatever may be your rank or title in life, you have the heart of a coward, and the spirit of a sycophant.

This is not inflaming or exaggerating matters, but trying them by those feelings and affections which nature justifies, and without which we should be incapable of discharging the social duties of life, or enjoying the felicities of it. I mean not to exhibit horror for the purpose of provoking revenge, but to awaken us from fatal and unmanly slumbers, that we may pursue determinately some fixed object. 'Tis not in the power of Britain or of Europe to conquer America, if she doth not conquer herself by delay and timidity. The present winter is worth an age if rightly employed, but if lost or neglected the whole continent will partake of the misfortune; and there is no punishment which that man doth not deserve, be he who, or what, or where he will, that may be the means of sacrificing a season so precious and useful.

'Tis repugnant to reason, to the universal order of things, to all examples from former ages, to suppose that this continent can long remain subject to any external power. The most sanguine in

Britain doth not think so. The utmost stretch of human wisdom cannot, at this time, compass a plan, short of separation, which can promise the continent even a year's security. Reconciliation is *now* a fallacious dream. Nature has deserted the connection, and art cannot supply her place. For, as Milton wisely expresses, "never can true reconcilement grow where wounds of deadly hate have pierced so deep".[1]

Every quiet method for peace hath been ineffectual. Our prayers have been rejected with disdain; and hath tended to convince us that nothing flatters vanity or confirms obstinacy in kings more than repeated petitioning—and nothing hath contributed more than that very measure to make the kings of Europe absolute. Witness Denmark and Sweden. Wherefore, since nothing but blows will do, for God's sake let us come to a final separation, and not leave the next generation to be cutting throats under the violated unmeaning names of parent and child.

1. *Paradis perdu*, IV, 98-99.

3 – Journaux intimes et autobiographies

Il y a là un mode littéraire dans lequel les futurs Américains furent portés à s'illustrer. L'habitude du journal, imposé par l'éducation religieuse, l'éloignement et l'isolement colonial, la lecture de la Bible ont quelque responsabilité dans la cultivation du moi. Bon nombre de ces cahiers intimes demeurèrent inconnus. Ceux qui nous sont parvenus ont en commun la relation d'un itinéraire spirituel et le décompte journalier des progrès et des échecs. Mais ils sont très différents comme le *Journal of Michael Wigglesworth 1633-1657*, hanté par la corruption de l'homme et le désespoir, et celui d'un Samuel Sewall (1674-1729) dans lequel l'humour vient soulager les inquiétudes et que certains ont comparé au *Journal* de S. Pepys. Les diaristes ne sont pas tous puritains : le quaker John Woolman, ou le baptiste Isaac Backus (1724-1806) en sont de bons exemples au XVIIIe siècle. Proche du journal, l'autobiographie s'en distingue par sa dimension rétrospective. Il en est de deux types : à usage personnel ou destiné à un lecteur privilégié. John Winthrop relève de la première catégorie avec *Experientia* tandis qu'Anne Bradstreet écrit pour ses enfants. Thomas Shepard a dédicacé à son fils un texte dont la qualité littéraire a été reconnue. Cotton Mather, qui rédige un abondant *Journal* d'introverti, se met en scène pour son fils Increase dans *Paterna* (1700). Benjamin Franklin a besoin de son fils pour construire un portrait de lui-même et offrir un manuel de vie en société. Sa démarche est totalement opposée à celle d'un

Jonathan Edwards qui n'avait jamais songé à se positionner que devant Dieu. L'objectif est toujours le même, mais Franklin recherche l'approbation des hommes. L'autobiographie du grand polygraphe donne ses lettres de noblesse au genre en Amérique. Proches, les récits de captivité chez les Indiens ont fleuri comme une variante bien spécifique de l'autobiographie religieuse jusqu'à John Gyles (1678-1755) qui marque le point de départ de la sécularisation.

JOHN WINTHROP (1588-1649)

Fils du maître du manoir de Groton, Suffolk, John Winthrop est élevé sur place. En 1603 — il a quatorze ans — il entre à Trinity College, Cambridge. Pendant ce séjour il tombe gravement malade et fait l'expérience d'une profonde conversion religieuse. Il est désormais associé aux puritains. En 1605 il se marie, vit chichement. En 1613 il étudie le droit à Gray's Inn, devient juge de paix. Il perd sa femme, se remarie aussitôt. Sa seconde épouse meurt en 1617. Sa troisième union en 1618 dure trente ans. Juge à la Court of Wards and Liveries en 1627, il songe à émigrer, prépare soigneusement son départ, est nommé gouverneur de la Compagnie de la Baie avant le voyage. Il prêche un célèbre sermon *Of Christian Charitie, A Modell Hereof* à bord de l'*Arbella*. Gouverneur pendant dix ans, gouverneur-adjoint durant neuf ans, il dirige la colonie avec perspicacité et une autorité qui lui est parfois reprochée. Accusé en 1644, acquitté en 1645, il expose à la Cour le sens de la liberté pour un calviniste. Le *Journal* qu'il tient de 1630 à 1648, publié sous le titre de *History of New England*, est un mélange de mémoires et d'histoire, sources qui révèlent l'homme. *Experientia*, commencée en 1607, est son autobiographie religieuse. Elle nous montre la profondeur de sa foi.

BIBLIOGRAPHIE SÉLECTIVE. — Forbes (Allyn B.), ed., *Winthrop Papers*, 5 vol., Boston, Massachusetts Historical Society, 1925-1947 ; Morgan (Edmund S.), *The Puritan Dilemma, The*

Story of John Winthrop, Boston, Little, Brown, 1962 ; Shea (Daniel B.), *Spiritual Autobiography in Early America*, Princeton, Princeton University Press, 1968.

Experientia[1]

I finde by often experience that the most usuall thinge that breakes off my comfort in God, and delight in heavenly things, is the entertaininge the love of earthly things; for having so often given myselfe unto the Lord, by particular solemne Covenants,[2] as upon my recoverye out of my quartan,[3] the deathe of my former wife,[4] deliverance from speciall sicknesses, etc., and now againe upon the renuinge of my repentance in this last affliction by the deathe of my other wife,[5] the Lord will not endure it that I should steale my affection from him, to sett it againe upon the world; so as I perceive that lett me doe what duties I will, yet if my heart be roaminge after pleasure, glorie, profitt, etc.: he abhorres bothe me and my service; so as I see that if he may not have my heart, he will have nothinge: Heerupon it hathe fallen out often that I have bestowed a great deale of tyme in prayer, and other duties, and have founde no other answeare but a wounded and discontented mind, and all because I have brought an heart haltinge betweene God and the worlde, desirous of his favour, and yet not resolved upon the deniall of this worlde and myselfe; not weighinge that sentence of Christ "He that wilbe my disciple, must denie himselfe," etc.: Againe on the other side sometymes upon a short meditation, or prayer, a secreat grone, or desire sent up into heaven, etc., I have founde unspeakable peace and comforte, for then my heart would repose itselfe in God, and yield to him sayinge with Paul, Lord, what wilt thou have me to doe? Whereupon I conclude that I cannot serve 2 masters; if I love the world, the love of the father can have no abidinge in me. This benumbs the hand of faith, casts a mist before the eyes of it, cooles the zeale of prayer,

1. Titre, publié en 1790. Segment daté 1616.
2. Pactes conclus avec le Seigneur selon l'usage puritain.
3. Fièvre quarte.
4. Mary Forth, dont il eut six enfants.
5. Thomazine Clopton, épousée en 1616, lui donna une fille.

quenchethe the spirit, and all spirituall affections, and layes the heart open to the force of all temptations.

. . . .

God by his great mercie brought me to a sight of my sinnes, and so to repentance, never (I hope) to be repented of, true Repentance, sweet thoughe sharpe repentance; O most happie, and wholesome Repentance, more welcome to me then all earthly pleasures,—for want of it (it havinge been longe absent) my poore soule was allmost famished; when by it God opened before mine eyes the state of my soule, O what a poluted conscience found I; what impure affections, what unruly desires, what blindnesse of minde, what fearfull hardnesse of heart, which althoughe it were shaken and stirred to consideration and slight relentings, sometymes ofte in a day by occasion of readinge, or prayer, etc., yet it soone shooke off all suche motions, and grewe more stiff necked against God, untill it was allmost at that passe that it could not repente: But when it pleased God to have mercye upon me, and to sett my wickednesse upon me, I thought then suerly he would be doone with me, for my former boldnesse in sinninge and daliance with the breache of his Commandements: but I founde him more gracious then I durst conceive, or make use of for the present; my former rebellion, ingratitude, self love, slouthe, carnallitie, tyme servinge, etc., came so freshe before me, and shewed so foul and odious unto me: Oh that not onely my eyes, but that my very heart could melt in teares, that I might mourne night and daye for my sinnes against my good Father. O when shall I be ridde of the burthen of this sinful fleshe! Would any that had knowne the sweet mercies that I had received from him, ever have beleeved that I should have turned from him, to goe roaminge after worldly pleasures? Could I so soone forgett the pleasures, etc., which his presence was wont to afforde me, as I had learned out of Psal: 16. and 36. and prov: 3.

Amongst other sinnes which I founde in my selfe, I sawe my great unbeleefe was one of the cheifest, for I had not nourished my faithe in Christ and in his worde, but had given waye to doubtinge and distrust so farre, as I had neere lost the use of Gods worde, which althoughe I continued to read dailye, yet my faithe was so weakned through difficulties and delayes, as I had lefte off to live by faithe in the worde: and so for want of faithe my prayers failed, my meditations, readinge, and all grewe teadious and unprofitable, I had no heart to any Christian dutye, I thoughte all was in vaine. Heerupon I prayed earnestly and mourningly to have my faithe strengthened, and God soone heard me and by occasion in my familye exercises, I fealt my faithe beginne to revive as a man out of a dreame. I acknowledged the infallible truthe and certainty of Goods most pure and perfecte worde; my heart leaped within me when I considered it, I embraced it, I cast my selfe in to it: as fast as temptations came either to feare, doubt, of difficultie or danger etc., the very first thought of Gods words, Gods trueth, did easyly dispell them; and whereas before all my care was to gather peace to my heart from the smalnesse of my infirmities etc., nowe my comforte was in bringinge them (smale or great) unto the bloud of Christ, and by applyinge the promise I founde howe the crimson sinnes might be made white as well as the palest-coloured. *Gods trueth* caried all before it: I founde my heart, upon this meditation, willinge to sett upon any dutye, whilest I behelde my warrant in Gods book: and whereas sometymes many things did discourage me from dutye, as the iudgment of the greatest parte, the unlikelynesse of successe, the evill acceptation of others, the feare of losse, disgrace, health, etc., now I remembred what Christ sayed "Woe to the world because of offences, and blessed are they that shall not be offended in me:" I perceived that these and suche like rubbes to our faithe were the offences that Christ dothe partlye meane there, and I see that they that will take offence from the opinion of others, their owne corrupt reason, common experience, etc., shall never enioye the comforte of livinge by faithe, for the Childe of God must breake throughe all these and saye with Paul, Rom: [3. 4.] Let God be true and every man a liar. O Lord I have sinned in that I have not beleeved thy worde that I might sanctifie thy name before thy people, but by thy grace I shall not dare heerafter once to doubt of thy holy and eternall truethe: Let it be sufficient encouragement and warrant to me in any thinge, that it is thy Commandment, thy promise etc.

THOMAS SHEPARD (1605-1649)

Né à Towcester, Northamptonshire, il est le fils d'un apprenti chez un épicier et de la fille de celui-ci. Son enfance est troublée par le décès de sa mère alors qu'il a trois ans. Il est ballotté entre les parents qui, successivement, le prennent en charge. Il en veut à son père de s'être remarié. Il le perd définitivement quand il a dix ans. Admis à Emmanuel College à quinze ans, il obtient son BA en 1623 et son MA en 1627. La même année il est ordonné ministre du culte. Auparavant il avait vécu à Cambridge sa conversion. Trois ans plus tard l'archevêque Laud le réduit au silence. Il devient tuteur et chapelain de la famille Darley. Mais il veut émigrer. Dès son arrivée il est élu pasteur de New Town, se distingue comme l'un des grands prédicateurs de Nouvelle-Angleterre auquel Jonathan Edwards empruntera, dit-on, de nombreuses citations. Le « Pastor Evangelicus » comme l'appelle Cotton Mather, est l'un des maîtres d'œuvre du congrégationalisme, présent dans toutes les crises, et principal responsable du choix de Cambridge comme lieu d'implantation de Harvard College. Son journal paraît en 1647 sous le titre de *Private Diary* dans un ensemble de textes. L'*Autobiography*, récit plein d'émotion rétrospective, demeure en manuscrit jusqu'à sa publication — expurgée — en 1832.

BIBLIOGRAPHIE SÉLECTIVE. — McGiffert (Michael), ed., *God's Plot. The Paradoxes of Puritan Piety, Being the Autobiography and Journal of Thomas Shepard*, Amherst, University of Massachusetts Press, 1972 ; Shea (Daniel B.), *Spiritual Autobiography in Early America*, Princeton, Princeton University Press, 1968 ; Cappello (Mary), The Authority of Self-Definition in Thomas Shepard's *Autobiography* and *Journal*, *Early American Literature*, 24, n° 1 (1989), 35-51.

Autobiography[1]

Although my sins might hinder him from doing this, yet I told the Lord his mercy should be the more wonderful if in healing my child of his sickness he would withal heal me of my sins. And thus after a sad heavy night the Lord shined upon me in the morning, for I found him suddenly and strangely amended of his sore mouth which I did expect would have been his death. Oh, the tenderness of our God! Remember, therefore, my son, this mercy of the Lord to thee. Thus the child with the mother having recovered their strength, we set a second time to sea,[2] and when we went the child was so feeble that diverse of our friends did conclude the child could [not] live until it came to New England in a close ship, but the care of God was so great that it was made much better by the sea and more lively and strong. And in this voyage it and all of us were in danger to be drowned by a most terrible leak which the Lord stopped for us. Another danger in the ship that the Lord delivered it from was this: the ship in a storm tumbling suddenly on the one side, my wife having the child in her arms was almost pitched with her head and child in her arms against a post in the ship, and being ready to fall she felt herself plucked back by she knew not what, whereby she and the child were again preserved, and I cannot ascribe this to any other but the angels of God who are ministering spirits for the heirs of life. And thus after a[n] eleven weeks' sail from old England we came to New England shore where the mother fell sick of a consumption and thou, my child, wert put to [one word illegible] nurse to one goodwife Hopkins who was very tender of thee. And after we had been here diverse weeks, on the seventh of February or thereabout God gave thee the ordinance of baptism whereby God is become thy God and is beforehand with thee that whenever thou shalt return to God, he will undoubtedly receive thee—and this is a most high and happy privilege, and therefore bless God for it. And now after that this had been done thy dear mother died in the Lord,[3]

1. Probablement achevée en1646 (cf. McGiffert, p.33, 70-73).

2. Le départ tenté le 16 octobre 1634 échoue, la tempête rejetant le navire sur la côte. Quinze jours plus tard, le premier fils Thomas meurt à Yarmouth. Le second fils, appelé Thomas en souvenir de l'enfant perdu, naît en avril 1635, l'année de la traversée réussie.

3. Margaret Tauteville, la première de ses trois épouses, rencontrée alors qu'il était chapelain de Sir Richard Darley.

departing out of this world to another, who did lose her life by being careful to preserve thine, for in the ship thou wert so feeble and froward both in the day and night that hereby she lost her strength and at last her life. She hath made also many a prayer and shed many a tear in secret for thee, and this hath been oft her request: that if the Lord did not intend to glorify himself by thee, that he would cut thee off by death rather than to live to dishonor him by sin. And therefore know it: if thou shalt turn rebel against God and forsake God and care not for the knowledge of him nor to believe in his Son, the Lord will make all these mercies *woes* and all thy mother's prayers, tears, and death to be a swift witness against thee at the great day.

Thus the Lord taking away thy dear mother's life, the Lord takes care for thee and preserved thee in health until the spring, May 1, 1636: and now the hand of the Lord was stretched out against my child so that he had for diverse weeks a sore mouth both within and without, cheeks and lips full of blisters so as that he could eat no meat, only suck the breast, by which only he lived a long time, which I did think would have been its death again. But the Lord, being sought unto, recovered him again. And then the humor fell into his eyes which grew so sore that partly by the humor and partly by the ill handling and applying medicines to them his eyes grew stark blind with pearls upon both eyes and a white film, insomuch as it was a most dreadful sight unto all the beholders of him and very pitiful, which was such a misery that methought now I had rather that the Lord would take away my child by death than let it live a blind and a miserable life. But the Lord saw my sorrows, my tears, my poor prayers which were in bitterness for him. And after that I had concluded I must have a blind child to be a constant sorrow to me till my death and was made to be contented to bear the indignation of the Lord because I had sinned, resolving now to fear nor care nor grieve no more, but to be thankful nay, to love the Lord's will—presently, I say, upon this by a poor weak means, viz., the oil of white pasec, the Lord restored my child to his sight suddenly and strangely—I may almost say miraculously—again, which was no small joy to me and no little encouragement to do the Lord's work that took so much care for me and mine. Now consider, my son, of this great care of God for thee, and remember to lift up thy eyes to heaven to God in everlasting praises of him and dependence upon him, and take heed thou dost not make thy eyes windows of lust, but give thy eyes, nay, thy heart and whole soul and body, to him that hath been so careful of thee when thou couldst not care for thyself.

MARY ROWLANDSON (*c.* 1635-*c.* 1679)

Née sans doute à South Patherton, Somerset, elle émigre avec sa famille en 1639 pour rejoindre son père à Salem, Massachusetts. Son père, John White est devenu un riche propriétaire terrien quand elle épouse, en 1656, Joseph Rowlandson, premier pasteur de Lancaster. Un de ses quatre enfants meurt en bas âge avant que, le 20 février 1676, elle soit faite prisonnière dans l'attaque du bourg. La grande guerre du roi Philippe — Metacomet, chef des Wampanoaghs — avait éclaté en juin 1675 et embrasé toute la Nouvelle-Angleterre. Pendant ses pérégrinations elle perd sa petite fille qui meurt dans ses bras. Elle est séparée de ses deux autres enfants. Vivant à l'indienne chez Westamee, chef squaw des Pocassets et son mari Quanopen, chef narragansett, elle est soutenue dans les épreuves par sa foi et sa mémoire de la Bible : ses tribulations sont semblables à celles des Hébreux ; l'aventure, salutaire, illustre la Providence. Libérée le 2 mai 1676 à Princeton, Massachusetts, elle retrouve bientôt ses deux enfants. Son mari devient pasteur de Wethersfield, Connecticut, où elle a sans doute écrit son récit. En 1679 elle reçoit £30 de pension annuelle au décès de son époux. Sa trace se perd. Reste son œuvre, la plus célèbre du genre, publiée trois fois en 1682. Très personnel, très puritain, très humain, très vrai, c'est un classique.

BIBLIOGRAPHIE SÉLECTIVE. — Vaughan (Alden T.) et Clark (Edward W.), eds, *Puritans among the Indians, Accounts of Captivity and Redemption 1676-1724*, Cambridge, Harvard University Press, 1986 ; Slotkin (Richard), *Regeneration through Violence. The Mythology of the American Frontier, 1600-1860*, Middleton, Conn., Wesleyan University Press, 1973 ; Van Der Beets (Richard), *The Indian Captivity Narrative. An American Genre*, Washington, DC, University Press of America, 1984.

A Narrative of the Captivity and Restoration of Mrs Mary Rowlandson[1]

5. Another thing that I would observe is, the strange providence of God, in turning things about when the Indians was at the highest, and the English at the lowest. I was with the Enemy eleven weeks and five dayes, and not one Week passed without the fury of the Enemy, and some desolation by fire and sword upon one place or other. They mourned (with their black faces) for their own losses, yet triumphed and rejoyced in their inhumane, and many times devilish cruelty to the English. They would boast much of their Victories,[2] saying, that in two hours time they had destroyed such a Captain, and his Company at such a place; and such a Captain and his Company in such a place; and such a Captain and his Company in such a place: and boast how many Towns they had destroyed, and then scoffe, and say. They had done them a good turn, to send them to Heaven so soon. Again, they would say, This Summer that they would knock all the Rogues[3] in the head, or drive them into the Sea, or make them flie the Countrey: thinking surely, Agag-like, *The bitterness of Death is past.*[4] Now the Heathen begins to think all is their own, and the poor Christians hopes to fail (as to man) and now their eyes are more to God, and their hearts sigh heaven-ward: and to say in good earnest, *Help Lord, or we perish:* When the Lord had brought his people to this, that they saw no help in any thing but himself: then he takes the quarrel into his own hand: and though they had made a pit,[5] in their own imaginations, as deep as hell for the Christians that Summer, yet the Lord hurll'd them selves into it. And the Lord had not so many wayes before to preserve them, but now he hath as many to destroy them.

But to return again to my going home, where we may see a remarkable change of Providence: At first they were all against it, except my Husband would come for me; but afterwards they assented to it, and seemed much to rejoyce in it; some askt me to

1. *The Sovereignty and Goodness of God, together with the faithfulness of his Promises Displayed ; being a Narrative*, 1682. L'extrait est pris dans la vingtième section, la conclusion.

2. Coutume courante à l'époque chez les Indiens.

3. L'objectif des Wampanoaghs et de leurs alliés était bien de tuer ou de jeter à la mer tous les envahisseurs blancs, tous ces fourbes.

4. Agag, roi des Amalécites, battu par Saül, se croit épargné. Il est tué par Samuel (I Samuel 15, 32).

5. Gouffre. L'écho biblique est immédiat.

send them some Bread, others some Tobacco, others shaking me by the hand, offering me a Hood and Scarfe to ride in; not one moving hand or tongue against it. Thus hath the Lord answered my poor desire, and the many earnest requests of others put up unto God for me. In my travels an Indian came to me, and told me, if I were willing, he and his Squaw would run away, and go home along with me: I told him No: I was not willing to run away, but desired to wait Gods time, that I might go home quietly, and without fear. And now God hath granted me my desire. O the wonderfull power of God that I have seen, and the experience that I have had: I have been in the midst of thoses roaring Lyons, and Salvage Bears, that feared neither God, nor Man, nor the Devil; by night and day, alone and in company: sleeping all sorts together, and yet not one of them ever offered me the least abuse of unchastity to me, in world or action.[1] Though some are ready to say, I speak it for my own credit; But I speak it in the presence of God, and to his Glory. Gods Power is as great now, and as sufficient to save, as when he preserved Daniel in the Lions Den; or the three Children in the fiery Furnace.[2] I may well say as his Psal. 107. 12, *Oh give thanks unto the Lord for he is good, for his mercy endureth for ever.* Let the Redeemed of the Lord say so, whom he hath redeemed from the hand of the Enemy, especially that I should come away in the midst of so many hundreds of Enemies quietly and peacably, and not a Dog moving his tongue. So I took my leave of them, and in coming along my heart melted into tears, more then all the while I was with them, and I was almost swallowed up with the thoughts that ever I should go home again. About the Sun going down, Mr. Hoar,[3] and my self, and the two Indians came to Lancaster, and a solemn sight it was to me. There had I lived many comfortable years amongst my Relations and Neighbours, and now not one Christian to be seen, nor one house left standing. We went on to a Farm house that was yet standing, where we lay all night: and a comfortable lodging we had, though nothing but straw to ly on. The Lord preserved us in safety that night, and

1. Les Indiens de l'Est ne violaient pas les captives blanches. La continence faisait partie du rituel de purification des guerriers. Enfreindre la règle les eût affaiblis.

2. Jeté dans la fosse aux lions le prophète Daniel en ressortit indemne (Daniel 6, 1-29). Shadrach, Meshach, et Abednego refusèrent d'adorer de faux dieux. Jetés dans une fournaise, ils furent sauvés par un ange (Daniel 3, 13-20).

3. John Hoar, de Concord, Massachusetts, l'émissaire du pasteur Rowlandson, qui avait négocié la rançon avec le Conseil des Indiens Sagamores.

raised us up again in the morning, and carried us along, that before noon, we came to Concord. Now was I full of joy, and yet not without sorrow: joy to see such a lovely sight, so many Christians together, and some of them my Neighbours: There I met with my Brother, and my Brother in Law, who asked me, if I knew where his Wife was? Poor heart! he had helped to bury her, and knew it not; she being shot down by the house was partly burnt: so that those who were at Boston at the desolation of the Town, and came back afterward, and buried the dead, did not know her. Yet I was not without sorrow, to think how many were looking and longing, and my own Children amongst the rest, to enjoy that deliverance that I had now received, and I did not know whither ever I should see them again. Being recruited with food and raiment we went to Boston that day, where I met with my dear Husband, but the thoughts of our dear Children, one being dead, and the other we could not tell where, abated our comfort each to other. I was not before so much hem'd in with the merciless and cruel Heathen, but now as much with pittiful, tender-hearted and compassionate Christians.

JOHN WOOLMAN (1720-1772)

Né à Rancocas, New Jersey, dans une famille de colons quakers, à quelques milles à l'est de Philadelphie, il est élevé à la ferme et reçoit une instruction élémentaire à l'école des Amis de Mount Holly, la bourgade voisine. L'éducation familiale, la fréquentation des réunions des adeptes favorisent le développement d'une forte vie spirituelle. Après avoir connu une phase d'éloignement mondain vers sa seizième année, il revient vite à la religion. A vingt et un ans il quitte la ferme pour devenir boutiquier et tailleur à Mount Holly. D'abord employé, puis patron, il réduit son activité commerçante parce qu'il se croit appelé par Dieu. En 1749 il épouse Sarah Ellis, une amie d'enfance dont il aura deux enfants. Dès 1743 il entreprend son action missionnaire. Il voyage beaucoup du New Hampshire à la Caroline du Nord. Dès 1754 il écrit *Some Considerations on the Keeping of Negroes*, et une suite en 1762. En 1763 il se rend chez les Indiens de l'ouest de la Pennsylvanie dont il défend les droits. En 1772 il va porter la bonne parole en Angleterre et meurt à York de la petite vérole. Autodidacte, il avait appris un peu de droit, servait d'écrivain public, rédigeait des testaments. Cet homme bon se méfie de l'argent, du succès, recherche la simplicité que lui enseigne sa foi. Sans cesse réédité depuis 1774, son *Journal* contribue à une notoriété qu'il avait évitée.

BIBLIOGRAPHIE SÉLECTIVE. — Moulton (Phillips S.), ed., *Journal and Major Essays of John Woolman*, Philadelphia, Philadelphia Yearly Meeting, 1971 ; Rosenblatt (Paul), *John Woolman*, New York, Twayne, 1969 ; Shea (Daniel B.), *Spiritual Autobiography in Early America*, Princeton, Princeton University Press, 1968, 45-84 ; Cassagne (Ella), L'anti-esclavagisme de John Woolman, *Etudes anglaises*, XXI, 2, 1968, 142-151.

The Journal[1]

In the management of my outward affairs, I may say with thankfulness, I found truth to be my support; and I was respected in my master's family, who came to live in Mount Holly[2] within two years after my going there.

In a few months after I came here, my master bought[3] several Scotchmen servants, from on board a vessel, and brought them to Mount Holly to sell, one of whom was taken sick and died. In the latter part of his sickness, being delirious, he used to curse and swear most sorrowfully; and the next night after his burial I was left to sleep alone in the chamber where he died. I perceived in me a timorousness; I knew, however, I had not injured the man, but assisted in taking care of him according to my capacity. I was not free to ask any one on that occasion to sleep with me. Nature was feeble; but every trial was a fresh incitement to give myself up wholly to the service of God, for I found no helper like him in times of trouble.

1. 1774.
2. Bourg qui abrite une forte communauté de quakers anglais.
3. Le propriétaire du magasin achète le contrat des engagés écossais.

About the twenty-third year of my age, I had many fresh and heavenly openings,[1] in respect to the care and providence of the Almighty over his creatures in general, and over man as the most noble amongst those which are visible. And being clearly convinced in my judgment that to place my whole trust in God was best for me, I felt renewed engagements that in all things I might act on an inward principle of virtue, and pursue worldly business no further than as truth opened my way.

About the time called Christmas I observed many people, both in town and from the country, resorting to public-houses, and spending their time in drinking and vain sports, tending to corrupt one another; on which account I was much troubled. At one house in particular there was much disorder; and I believed it was a duty incumbent on me to speak to the master of that house. I considered I was young, and that several elderly friends in town had opportunity to see these things; but though I would gladly have been excused, yet I could not feel my mind clear.

The exercise was heavy; and as I was reading what the Almighty said to Ezekiel,[2] respecting his duty as a watchman, the matter was set home more clearly. With prayers and tears I besought the Lord for his assistance, and He, in loving-kindness, gave me a resigned heart. At a suitable opportunity I went to the public-house; and seeing the man amongst much company, I called him aside, and in the fear and dread of the Almighty expressed to him what rested on my mind. He took it kindly, and afterwards showed more regard to me than before. In a few years afterwards he died, middle-aged; and I often thought that had I neglected my duty in that case it would have given me great trouble; and I was humbly thankful to my gracious Father, who had supported me herein.

My employer, having a negro woman,[3] sold her, and desired me to write a bill of sale, the man being waiting who bought her. The thing was sudden; and though I felt uneasy at the thoughts of writing an instrument of slavery for one of my fellow-creatures, yet I remembered that I was hired by the year, that it was my master who directed me to do it, and that it was an elderly man, a member

1. Messages directs (terminologie quaker).
2. Ezéchiel le prophète, 3, 17.
3. Le New Jersey comptait de nombreux esclaves noirs à l'époque.

of our Society,[1] who bought her; so through weakness I gave way, and wrote it; but at the executing of it I was so afflicted in my mind, that I said before my master and the Friend[2] that I believed slave-keeping to be a practice inconsistent with the Christian religion. This, in some degree, abated my uneasiness; yet as often as I reflected seriously upon it I thought I should have been clearer if I had desired to be excused from it, as a thing against my conscience; for such it was. Some time after this a young man of our Society spoke to me to write a conveyance of a slave to him, he having lately taken a negro into his house. I told him I was not easy to write it; for, though many of our meeting and in other places kept slaves, I still believed the practice was not right, and desired to be excused from the writing. I spoke to him in good-will; and he told me that keeping slaves was not altogether agreeable to his mind; but that the slave being a gift made to his wife he had accepted her.

BENJAMIN FRANKLIN (1706-1790)

Né à Boston, fils de Josiah Franklin, un humble chandelier très dévot qui avait immigré en 1682, il reçoit une maigre instruction formelle. Son père, qui a dix-sept enfants avec ses deux épouses, n'a pas les moyens d'en faire un pasteur. D'ailleurs Benjamin est inégalement doué. Il le met en apprentissage. Sans vocation précise, l'adolescent devient imprimeur, sa chance. Il se querelle vite avec son frère James, l'imprimeur patenté, et à dix-sept ans va à Philadelphie, et, bientôt victime du gouverneur Keith, à Londres. Mais il a l'instinct de la réussite. Parti en 1724, de retour deux ans plus tard, il est propriétaire de son imprimerie en 1730, année de son mariage avec Deborah Read. Sa carrière, irrésistible, commence alors : imprimeur, négociateur, diplomate, homme politique, il

1. La Société des Amis, l'Eglise des quakers.
2. Beaucoup d'Amis étaient encore propriétaires d'esclaves. En 1758 l'Assemblée annuelle décida à Philadelphie de désavouer ceux qui garderaient ou importeraient des Noirs.

est présent partout jusqu'à la convention constitutionnelle de 1783. C'est aussi un savant et un inventeur d'objets pratiques. Ecrivain, il est auteur d'essais à la manière d'Addison, de satires, de textes politiques et scientifiques, mais, difficilement saisissable, cet homme qui a incarné longtemps une image type de l'Américain, se révèle plus dans sa correspondance et dans la première partie de l'*Autobiographie*, l'œuvre la plus connue bien qu'inachevée, qu'il compose à plusieurs reprises : en 1771 à Twyford, en 1784 à Passy, chez lui en 1788.

BIBLIOGRAPHIE SÉLECTIVE. — Labaree (Leonard W.) *et al.*, *The Papers of Benjamin Franklin*, 27 vol. parus, New Haven, Conn., Yale University Press, 1959- ; Clark (Ronald W.), *Benjamin Franklin, A Biography*, New York, Random House, 1983 ; Royot (Daniel), *L'humour américain*, Lyon, Presses Universitaires de Lyon, 1980, 74-97 ; Bercovitch (Sacvan), The Ritual of American Autobiography : Edwards, Franklin, Thoreau, *Revue française d'Etudes américaines*, n° 14, mai 1982, 139-149 ; Lynen (John F.), Benjamin Franklin and the choice of a single point of view, *in* Sacvan Bercovitch, ed., *The American Puritan Imagination*, London, Cambridge University Press, 1974, 173-195.

The Autobiography[1]

There was another bookish lad in the town, John Collins by name, with whom I was intimately acquainted. We sometimes disputed, and very fond we were of argument, and very desirous of confuting one another—which disputatious[2] turn, by the way, is apt to become a very bad habit, making people often extremely disagreeable in company, by the contradiction that is necessary to bring it into practice; and thence besides souring and spoiling the conversation, it is productive of disgusts and perhaps enmities where you may have occasion for friendship. I had caught it by reading my father's books of dispute on religion. Persons of good sense, I have since observed, seldom fall into it, except lawyers, university men, and men of all sorts who have been bred at

1. 1790. La première partie traite des origines et de la formation.
2. Raisonneur. La *disputatio*, principe et élément de la rhétorique du discours, était enseignée dans les universités médiévales et coloniales.

Edinburgh.[1] A question was once somehow or other started between Collins and me on the propriety of educating the female sex in learning and their abilities for study. He was of opinion that it was improper and that they were naturally unequal to it. I took the contrary side, perhaps a little for dispute sake. He was naturally more eloquent, having a greater plenty of words, and sometimes, as I thought, I was vanquished more by his fluency than by the strength of his reasons. As we parted without settling the point and were not to see one another again for some time, I sat down to put my arguments in writing, which I copied fair and sent to him. He answered and I replied. Three or four letters on a side had passed, when my father happened to find my papers and read them. Without entering into the subject in dispute, he took occasion to talk with me about my manner of writing, observed that though I had the advantage of my antagonist in correct spelling and pointing[2] (which I owed to the printing house) I fell far short in elegance of expression, in method, and in perspicuity[3]—of which he convinced me by several instances. I saw the justice of his remarks and thence grew more attentive to my manner of writing, and determined to endeavour to improve my style.

About this time I met with an odd volume of the *Spectator*.[4] It was the third. I had never before seen any of them. I bought it, read it over and over, and was much delighted with it. I thought the writing excellent and wished if possible to imitate it. With that view, I took some of the papers, and making short hints of the sentiment in each sentence, laid them by a few days, and then without looking at the book, tried to complete the papers again by expressing each hinted sentiment at length and as fully as it had been expressed before, in any suitable words that should occur to me. Then I compared my *Spectator* with the original, discovered some of my faults, and corrected them. But I found I wanted a stock of words or a readiness in recollecting and using them, which I thought I should have acquired before that time if I had gone on making verses; since the continual search for words of the same

1. Les presbytériens écossais avaient une réputation de chicane.
2. Ponctuation. A l'époque l'orthographe n'était pas standardisée.
3. Clarté dans le développement des idées.
4. Périodique anglais (1711-1712 et 1714) consacré aux essais littéraires et moraux de J. Addison (1672-1719) et R. Steele (1672-1729), hommes de lettres célèbres et modèles de style.

import but of different length to suit the measure,[1] or of different sound for the rhyme would have laid me under a constant necessity of searching for variety, and also have tended to fix that variety in my mind, and make me master of it. Therefore I took some of the tales in the *Spectator* and turned them into verse, and after a time, when I had pretty well forgotten the prose, turned them back again.

I also sometimes jumbled my collections of hints into confusion, and after some weeks endeavoured to reduce them into the best order before I began to form the full sentences and complete the paper. This was to teach me method in the arrangement of the thoughts. By comparing my work afterwards with the original, I discovered many faults and corrected them; but I sometimes had the pleasure of fancying that in certain particulars of small import I had been lucky enough to improve the method or the language, and this encouraged me to think that I might possibly in time come to be a tolerable English writer, of which I was extremely ambitious.

The time I allotted for these exercises and for reading, was at night after work, or before it began in the morning, or on Sundays, when I contrived to be in the printing house alone, avoiding as much as I could the common attendance on public worship which my father used to exact of me when I was under his care[2] and which, indeed, I still thought a duty, though I could not, as it seemed to me, afford the time to practise it.

When about sixteen years of age I happened to meet with a book written by one Tryon,[3] recommending a vegetable diet. I determined to go into it. My brother,[4] being yet unmarried, did not keep house but boarded himself and his apprentices in another family. My refusing to eat flesh occasioned an inconveniency, and I was frequently chid for my singularity. I made myself acquainted with Tryon's manner of preparing some of his dishes, such as boiling potatoes or rice, making hasty pudding,[5] and a few others;

1. Mètre.

2. Issu d'une famille partiellement non conformiste, et fier de sa confession, Josiah Franklin avait quitté Ecton, Northamptonshire, lorsque les conventicules étaient interdits. Il avait parlé d'offrir son dixième fils à l'Eglise — sa « — dîme » et aurait aimé qu'il devînt pasteur congrégationaliste.

3. Thomas Tryon, *Way to Health and Happiness*, 1682.

4. James l'imprimeur (1697-1735), fondateur du *New England Courant* (1721-1726).

5. Bouillie d'avoine ou de maïs.

and then proposed to my brother that if he would give me weekly half the money he paid for my board, I would board myself. He instantly agreed to it, and I presently found that I could save half what he paid me. This was an additional fund for buying of books. But I had another advantage in it. My brother and the rest going from the printing house to their meals, I remained there alone, and dispatching presently my light repast (which often was no more than a biscuit or a slice of bread, a handful of raisins or a tart from the pastry cook's, and a glass of water) had the rest of the time till their return for study, in which I made the greater progress from that greater clearness of head and quicker apprehension which generally attend temperance in eating and drinking. Now it was that being on some occasion made ashamed of my ignorance in figures, which I had twice failed in learning when at school,[1] I took Cocker's book of arithmetic,[2] and went through the whole by myself with the greatest ease. I also read Seller's and Sturmy's[3] book on navigation and became acquainted with the little geometry it contains, but I never proceeded far in that science. I read about this time Locke *On Human Understanding*,[4] and *The Art of Thinking* by Messrs. du Port Royal.[5]

1. A la « grammar school » à huit ans, puis à l'école primaire plus tard.
2. Edward Cocker, *Arithmetic* (1677). Eut un énorme succès.
3. Franklin était passionné par le sujet de John Seller, *An Epitome of the Art of Navigation* (1681) et de Samuel Sturmy, *The Mariner's Magazine* (1699).
4. Le philosophe John Locke avait publié *An Essay Concerning Human Understanding* (1690).
5. *Logic, or the Art of Thinking* (1687), version anglaise du livre d'Antoine Arnauld et Pierre Nicole, paru en latin en 1662.

4 – La poésie

Elle souffre d'avoir été trop longtemps ignorée ou méprisée. L'Amérique coloniale n'a donné naissance ni à un Milton ni à un Pope à l'époque où l'Angleterre atteignait des sommets. Il faut attendre 1960 pour découvrir dans sa plénitude le meilleur des poètes qui supporte la comparaison avec Herbert, Francis Quarles ou John Donne. Ce n'est pas avant 1968 que paraît, aux Etats-Unis, l'anthologie de H. T. Meserole : enfin 500 pages consacrées à la poésie du XVIIe siècle. A cette situation il y a une première raison : beaucoup d'œuvres demeurent en manuscrit par négligence, volonté expresse, ou ignorance. Le travail d'édition n'est d'ailleurs pas achevé. D'autre part cette poésie des deux premiers siècles a paru trop exclusivement religieuse quand elle n'était pas dictée par l'occasion. L'exhumation des poèmes de Taylor à partir de 1937 ne change rien à l'image reçue. Le premier livre imprimé à la colonie est *The Bay Psalm Book* (1639), traduction anonyme en vers destinée à être chantée dans les congrégations. L'immense succès du *Day of Doom* de Michael. Wigglesworth fait le reste. Mais cette vue cavalière omet la voix bien singulière d'une femme, Anne Bradstreet, à qui John Berryman rend hommage en notre siècle. Elle oublie Benjamin Tompson qui satirise Puritains et Indiens. Elle passe sous silence de charmants vers de circonstance. Elle ne tient pas compte de la poésie écrite au Sud et au XVIIIe siècle. De son voyage au Maryland Ebenezer Cook rapporte la matière de sa satire *The Sot-Weed Factor* (1708). Richard Lewis est le meilleur poète de la nature américaine avant Philip Freneau. Son *Journey from Patapsco to Annapolis* paraît en 1731. Il faut citer Francis Hopkinson, auteur de

The Battle of the Kegs (1778), ballade satirique, et Phyllis Wheatley, la première poétesse noire. Tout n'a cependant pas été méconnu. Certains furent assez heureux pour être publiés en Angleterre : Ebenezer Cook, bien sûr, et Anne Bradstreet ou Benjamin Tompson.

MICHAEL WIGGLESWORTH (1631-1705)

Né en Angleterre, probablement au Yorkshire, il quitte le pays en 1638 avec ses parents. Son père, homme d'affaires prospère, s'installe comme colon à New Haven, Connecticut. C'est là qu'Ezechiel Cheever, le grand maître, lui apprend le latin et le prépare pour entrer à l'université. Mais son père, blessé et malade, doit abandonner son nouveau métier d'agriculteur. Le fils est retiré de l'école pour travailler la terre. Cinq ans plus tard, il reprend ses études et est enfin admis à Harvard à dix-sept ans. Titulaire de son BA et de son AM, il reste comme tuteur aux appointements de £2 par an. Puis il devient pasteur de Malden en 1656 tout en exerçant la médecine apprise au Collège. De 1657 à 1686 une longue maladie l'empêche pratiquement d'accomplir ses fonctions pastorales. Sa foi exigeante, fondée sur l'expérience de la conversion puritaine, lui dicte son *Autobiography*, des poèmes, dont *The Day of Doom* (1662) qui eut un immense retentissement avec 1 800 exemplaires vendus en un an. Au classement des lectures il suit la Bible et le Catéchisme abrégé. Enfants et adultes l'apprennent par cœur. Cette mémorisation est facilitée par l'utilisation du mètre des hymnes, de ces vers hexasyllabiques et octosyllabiques répartis en 224 strophes de huit.

BIBLIOGRAPHIE SÉLECTIVE. — Meserole (Harrison T.), ed., *Seventeenth-Century American Poetry*, Garden City, NY, Doubleday, 1968, 37-118 ; Morgan (Edmund S.), ed., *The Diary of Michael Wigglesworth, 1653-1657*, New York, Harper, 1965 ; Crowder (Richard), *No Featherbed to Heaven : A Biography of Michael Wigglesworth*, East Lansing, Mich., Michigan State University Press, 1962.

The Day of Doom[1]

180

Psa. 58, 3
Ro. 6, 23
Gal. 3, 10
Rom. 8, 29, 30
and 11, 7
Rev. 21, 27
Luk. 12, 48

You sinners are, and such a share
as sinners may expect,
Such you shall have; for I do save
none but mine own Elect.[2]
Yet to compare your sin with their,
who liv'd a longer time,
I do confess yours is much less,
though every sin's a crime

181

Mat. 11, 22
The wicked all convinced and put to silence.
Ro. 3, 19
Mat. 22, 12

A crime it is, therefore in bliss
you may not hope to dwell;
But unto you I shall allow
the easiest room in Hell.
The glorious King thus answering,
they cease, and plead no longer:
Their Consciences must needs confess
his Reasons are the stronger.

182

Behold the formidable estate of all the ungodly, as they stand hopeless and helpless before an impartial Judge, expecting their final sentence.
Rev. 6, 16, 17

Thus all mens Pleas the Judge with ease
doth answer and confute,
Until that all, both great and small,
are silenced and mute.
Vain hopes are cropt, all mouths are stopt,
sinners have nought to say,
But that 'tis just, and equal most
they should be damn'd for ay.[3]

1. 1662. Destiné à tous publics le poème a 224 strophes.
2. Ceux dont Dieu a décidé le salut de toute éternité.
3. Toujours.

183

Now what remains, but that to pains
 and everlasting smart,[1]
Christ should condemn the Sons of men,
 which is their just desert;[2]
Oh, rueful plights of sinful wights![3]
 Oh wretches all forlorn!
'T had happy been they ne're had seen
 the Sun, or not been born.

184

Yea, now it would be good they could
 themselves annihilate,
And cease to be, themselves to free
 from such a fearful state.
Oh happy Dogs, and Swine, and Frogs:
 yea Serpents generation,
Who do not fear this doom to hear,
 and sentence of Damnation!

185

Psa. 139, 2, 3, 4
Eccl. 12, 14

This is their state so desperate:
 their sins are fully known;
Their vanities and villanies
 before the world are shown.
As they are gross and impious,
 so are their numbers more
Than motes i' th' Air, or then their hair,
 or sands upon the shore.

186

Divine Justice offended is
 and Satisfaction claimeth:

1. Douleur cuisante.
2. Ce qu'ils méritent.
3. Ames.

God's wrathful ire kindled like fire,
against them fiercely flameth.
Their Judge severe doth quite cashier[1]
Mat. 25, 45 and all their Pleas off take,
That never a man, or dare, or can
a further Answer make.

ANNE BRADSTREET, *c.* 1612-1672

Née dans le Northamptonshire, Anne Dudley appartient à une bonne famille. Son père Thomas est l'intendant du comte de Lincoln, ce qui lui ouvre une riche bibliothèque de classiques et de contemporains. Elle reçoit une éducation très supérieure à celle d'une jeune fille de son temps. A sept ans elle apprend les langues, la musique, la danse avec huit tuteurs. Elle rencontre un jeune diplômé de Cambridge, Simon Bradstreet, qu'elle épouse en 1628. Simon s'occupe de la Compagnie de la Baie en gestation. Elle le suit à bord de l'*Arbella* en 1630 bien qu'elle souffre de quitter un monde brillant pour le désert puritain. Le couple finit par se fixer à North Andover en 1645. Elle y reste jusqu'à sa mort, frêle et active, élevant ses nombreux enfants et écrivant tandis que son mari est très pris par le secrétariat de la Compagnie. En 1650 son beau-frère, John Woodbridge, pasteur d'Andover, publie à Londres, peut-être à son insu, *The Tenth Muse*, un volume de ses premiers vers qui connaissent un vif succès. Mais c'est par sa poésie posthume que nous nous souvenons de la « Mère de la poésie américaine ». La chair, l'amour terrestre y sont présents avec une pointe d'érotisme discret. Et si Anne Bradstreet est aussi contemplative et aspire à la vie éternelle c'est parce qu'elle est éblouie par le monde d'ici-bas.

1. Chasse.

BIBLIOGRAPHIE SÉLECTIVE. — McElrath, Jr. (Joseph) et Robb (Allan P.), eds, *The Complete Works of Anne Bradstreet*, Boston, Twayne, 1981 ; Stanford (Anne), *Anne Bradstreet, the Wordly Puritan*, New York, Burt Franklin, 1974 ; Richardson (Robert D.), The Puritan Poetry of Anne Bradstreet, *Texas Studies in Literature and Language*, IX (1967), 317-331.

Contemplations[1]

Some time now past in the autumnal tide,
When Phoebus[2] wanted but one hour to bed,
The trees all richly clad, yet void of pride,
Where gilded o'er by his rich golden head.
Their leaves and fruits seemed painted, but was true,
Of green, of red, of yellow, mixed hue;
Rapt were my senses at this delectable view.

2

I wist not what to wish, yet sure thought I,
If so much excellence abide below,
How excellent is He that dwells on high,
Whose power and beauty by his works we know?
Sure he is goodness, wisdom, glory, light,
That hath this under world so richly dight;[3]
More heaven than earth was here, no winter and no night.

3

Then on a stately oak I cast mine eye,
Whose ruffling top the clouds seemed to aspire;
How long since thou wast in thine infancy?
Thy strength, and stature, more thy years admire,
Hath hundred winters past since thou wast born?
Or thousand since thou brakest thy shell of horn?
If so, all these as nought, eternity doth scorn.

1. Publié en 1678, ce poème a 33 strophes.
2. Apollon, le dieu soleil.
3. Paré.

4

Then higher on the glistering Sun I gazed,
Whose beams was shaded by the leavie tree;
The more I looked, the more I grew amazed,
And softly said, "What glory's like to thee?"
Soul of this world, this universe's eye,
No wonder some made thee a deity;
Had I not better known, alas, the same had I.

5

Thou as a bridegroom from thy chamber rushes,
And as a strong man, joys to run a race;[1]
The morn doth usher thee with smiles and blushes;
The Earth reflects her glances in thy face.
Birds, insects, animals with vegative,
Thy heat from death and dullness doth revive,
And in the darksome womb of fruitful nature dive.

6

Thy swift annual and diurnal course,
Thy daily straight and yearly oblique path,
Thy pleasing fervor and thy scorching force,
All mortals here the feeling knowledge hath.
Thy presence makes it day, thy absence night,
Quaternal seasons caused by thy might:
Hail creature, full of sweetness, beauty, and delight.

A letter to her husband,[2]
absent upon public employment

My head, my heart, mine eyes, my life, nay, more,
My joy, my magazine[3] of earthly store,
If two be one, as surely thou and I,

1. Paraphrase de Psaumes 19, 4-5.
2. Publié en 1678. Simon Bradstreet, magistrat de la colonie, était fréquemment absent.
3. Entrepôt.

How stayest thou there, whilst I at Ipswich[1] lie?
So many steps, head from the heart to sever,
If but a neck, soon should we be together.
I, like the Earth this season, mourn in black,
My Sun is gone so far in's zodiac,
Whom whilst I'joyed, nor storms, nor frost I felt,
His warmth such frigid colds did cause to melt.
My chilled limbs now numbed lie forlorn;
Return, return, sweet Sol, from Capricorn;[2]
In this dead time, alas, what can I more
Than view those fruits which through thy heat I bore?
Which sweet contentment yield me for a space,
True living pictures of their father's face.
O strange effect! now thou art southward gone,
I weary grow the tedious day so long;
But when thou northward to me shalt return,
I wish my Sun may never set, but burn
Within the Cancer[3] of my glowing breast,
The welcome house of him my dearest guest.
Where ever, ever stay, and go not thence,
Till nature's sad decree shall call thee hence;
Flesh of thy flesh,[4] bone of thy bone,
I there, thou there, yet both but one.

In memory of my dear grandchild Elizabeth[5] Bradstreet, who deceased August, 1665, being a year and half old

Farewell dear babe, my heart's too much content,
Farewell sweet babe, the pleasure of mine eye,
Farewell fair flower that for a space was lent,
Then ta'en away unto eternity.

1. La référence à Ipswich — Aggawam — permet de donner une fourchette de date du poème : 1636-1643.
2. Sol(eil). Le capricorne représente l'hiver.
3. Quatrième signe du zodiaque : l'été.
4. Genèse 2, 23-4.
5. Fille de son fils Samuel.

Blest babe, why should I once bewail thy fate,
Or sigh thy days so soon were terminate,
Sith thou art settled in an everlasting state.

2

By nature trees do rot when they are grown,
And plums and apples thoroughly ripe do fall,
And corn and grass are in their season mown,
And time brings down what is both strong and tall.
But plants new set to be eradicate,
And buds new blown to have so short a date,
Is by His hand alone that guides nature and fate.

BENJAMIN TOMPSON (1642-1714)

Fils de William Tompson, diplômé de Brasenose College, Oxford, qui émigre en 1636 avec sa femme et ses trois enfants pour se rendre dans le Maine, il naît à Braintree — aujourd'hui Quincy — Massachusetts, en 1642, trois ans après que son père eut accepté d'en être le pasteur. Mais trois mois après sa naissance ce père s'en va en Virginie ; sa mère meurt. A son retour du Sud William ne semble pas avoir cherché à reprendre son fils qui est élevé par les Blanchard. Il étudie à Harvard qu'il quitte en 1662. Peu attiré par le service de Dieu, il enseigne et exerce la médecine. Il écrit de la poésie. Maître d'école à Braintree en 1667 et 1668, il l'est à nouveau et pour vingt ans en 1678. Il meurt pauvre en 1714, laissant une veuve et huit enfants. Connu pour divers poèmes, il compose son œuvre principale avec *New England's Crisis*, publié en 1676. Ce texte héroï-comique est une jérémiade en vers dans laquelle il n'épargne ni les Indiens ni — ce qui est moins fréquent — ses compatriotes.

BIBLIOGRAPHIE SÉLECTIVE. — White (Peter), ed., *Benjamin Tompson, Colonial Bard, A Critical edition*, University Park, Pa., Pennsylvania State University Press, 1980; Fussell (Edwin S.), Benjamin Tompson, Public Poet, *New England Quarterly*, 26 (1953), 494-511.

New Englands Crisis,[1] The Prologue.

The times wherein old *Pompion*[2] was a Saint,
When men far'd hardly yet without complaint
On vilest *Cates*,[3] the dainty *Indian Maize*
Was eat with *Clamp-shells* out of wooden Trayes
Under thatcht *Hutts* without the cry of *Rent*,
And the best *Sawce* to every Dish, *Content*.
When Flesh was food, and hairy skins made coats,
And men as wel as birds had chirping Notes.
When Cimnels[4] were accounted noble bloud
Among the tribes of common herbage food.
Of *Ceres* bounty form'd was many a knack
Enough to fill *poor Robins Almanack*.
These golden times (too fortunate to hold)
Were quickly sin'd away for love of gold.
Twas then among the bushes, not the street
If one in place did an inferiour meet,
Good morrow Brother, is there ought you want?
Take freely of me, what I have you ha'nt.
Plain *Tom* and *Dick* would pass as currant now,
As ever since *Your Servant Sir* and bow.
Deep-skirted doublets,[5] *puritanick* capes
Which now would render men like upright Apes,
Was comlier wear our wiser Fathers thought
Than the cast[6] fashions from all *Europe* brought.
Twas in those dayes an honest *Grace* would hold
Till an hot puddin grew at heart a cold.

1. 1676.
2. Pompion: melon/lourdaud.
3. Nourritures.
4. Biscuits.
5. Pourpoints.
6. Empesées.

And men had better stomachs to religion
Than I to capon, turkey-cock or pigeon.
When honest Sisters met to pray not prate
About their own and not their neighbours state.
During *Plain Dealings*[1] Reign, that worthy Stud
Of th' ancient planters race before the flood
These times were good, Merchants car'd not a rush
For other fare than *Jonakin*[2] *and Mush*.
Although men far'd and lodged very hard
Yet Innocence was better than a Guard.
Twas long before spiders and wormes had drawn
Their dungy webs or hid with cheating Lawne
New-Englands beautyes, which stil seem'd to me
Illustrious in their own simplicity.
Twas ere the neighbouring *Virgin-land* had broke
The Hogsheads of her worse than hellish smoak.[3]
Twas ere the Islands sent their Presents in,
Which but to use was counted next to sin.
Twas ere a *Barge* had made so rich a fraight
As *Chocholatte*, dust-gold and bitts of eight.[4]
Ere wines from *France* and *Moscovadoe*[5] too
Without the which the drink will scarsly doe,
From western Isles, ere fruits and dilicacies,
Did rot maids teeth and spoil their hansome faces.
Or ere these times did chance the noise of war
Was from our towns and hearts removed far.
No Bugbear Comets in the chrystal air
To drive our christian Planters to despair.
No sooner pagan malice peeped forth
But Valour snib'd[6] it; then were men of worth
Who by their prayers slew thousands Angel like,
Their weapons are unseen with which they strike.
Then had the Churches rest, as yet the coales
Were covered up in most contentious souls.

1. Libelle de Thomas Lechford publié à Londres (1642). Assez critique des puritains.
2. Johnny-cake : sorte de pain plat, de grosse crêpe.
3. Muids de tabac de Virginie.
4. Huitièmes de peso espagnol.
5. Sucre non raffiné.
6. Repoussait.

Freeness in Judgment, union in affection,
Dear love, sound truth they were our grand protection.
These were the twins which in our Councells sate,
These gave prognosticks of our future fate,
If these be longer liv'd our hopes increase,
These warrs will usher in a longer peace:
But if *New-Englands* love die in its youth
The grave will open next for blessed Truth.
This *Theame* is out of date, the peacefull hours
When Castles needed not but pleasant bowers.
Not ink, but bloud and tears now serve the turn
To draw the figure of *New-Englands* Urne.[1]
New Englands hour of passion is at hand,
No power except Divine can it withstand;
Scarce hath her glass[2] of fifty years run out,
But her old prosperous Steeds turn heads about,
Tracking themselves back to their poor beginnings,
To fear and fare upon their fruits of sinnings:
So that the mirrour of the Christian world
Lyes burnt to heaps in part, her Streamers[3] furl'd
Grief reigns, joyes flee and dismal fears surprize,
Not dastard spirits only but the wise.
Thus have the fairest hopes deceiv'd the eye
Of the big swoln Expectant standing by.
Thus the proud Ship after a little turn
Sinks into *Neptunes* arms to find its Urn.
Thus hath the heir to many thousands born
Been in an instant from the mother torn.
Ev'n thus thine infant cheeks begin to pale,
And thy supporters through great losses fail.
This is the *Prologue* to thy future woe,
The *Epilogue* no mortal yet can know.

1. Urne/urne funéraire.
2. Sablier.
3. Etendards.

EDWARD TAYLOR (*c.* 1642-1729)

Né vraisemblablement à Sketchley, Leicestershire, élevé à la ferme, il reçoit une éducation non conformiste. Refusant l'Acte de Conformité en 1662, il ne peut continuer d'enseigner ou de suivre, librement, le culte de son choix. Il se décide à émigrer et, en 1668, débarque à Boston. Après une entrevue avec le président Charles Chauncy, il entre à Harvard. Diplômé en 1671, il envisage de rester, mais accepte l'invitation de devenir pasteur à Westfield, sur la frontière. En 1674 il se marie et aura huit enfants. Demeurant sur place il échappe aux violences de la guerre du roi Philippe, et parvient enfin à organiser son église. Ordonné en 1679 il partage ses activités entre le ministère des âmes et celui du corps, car il est devenu médecin. A la mort de son épouse, il se remarie et a six nouveaux enfants. Ce calviniste sévère a son jardin secret : la poésie. Rimailleur en Angleterre et à Harvard, il écrit de nombreux poèmes de circonstance. Il atteint la renommée posthume par sa poésie religieuse, moins par *God's Determination* que par ses quelque deux cents *Preparatory Meditations*, sorte de journal intime et spirituel entre 1682 et 1725. Ce sont pour la plupart des commentaires de versets bibliques qu'il choisissait pour ses sermons de communion aux convertis. L'inspiration poétique est celle des « métaphysiques » anglais de la grande époque.

BIBLIOGRAPHIE SÉLECTIVE. — Stanford (Donald E.), ed., *The Poems of Edward Taylor*, New Haven, Yale University Press, 1960 ; Gatta (John), *Gracious Laughter : The Meditative Wit of Edward Taylor*, Columbia, Missouri, University of Missouri Press, 1989 ; Grabo (Norman S.), *Edward Taylor*, New York, Twayne, 1961.

Huswifery[1]

Make me, O Lord, thy Spin[n]ing Wheele[2] compleate;
Thy Holy Worde my Distaff make for mee.
Make mine Affections thy Swift Flyers neate,
And make my Soule thy holy Spoole to bee.
My Conversation make to be thy Reele,
And reele the yarn[3] thereon spun of thy Wheele.

Make me thy Loome[4] then, knit therein this Twine:
And make thy Holy Spirit, Lord, winde quills:[5]
Then weave the Web thyselfe. The yarn is fine,
Thine Ordinances make my Fulling Mills.[6]
Then dy the same in Heavenly Colours Choice,
All pinkt[7] with Varnish't Flowers of Paradise.

Then cloath therewith mine Understanding, Will,
Affections, Judgment, Conscience, Memory;
My Words and Actions, that their shine may fill
My wayes with glory and thee glorify.
Then mine apparell shall display before yee
That I am Cloathd in Holy robes for glory.

16. Meditation. Lu. 7, 16. A greate prophet is risen up[8]

Leafe Gold, Lord of thy Golden Wedge o'relaid[9]
My Soul at first, thy Grace in e'ry part
Whose peart,[10] fierce Eye thou such a Sight hadst made
Whose brightsom beams could break into thy heart
Till thy Curst Foe had with my Fist mine Eye
Dasht out, and did my Soule Unglorify.

1. Publié en 1939. C'est le poème sur l'économie domestique, image de l'économie divine.
2. Image créatrice du rouet.
3. Fil.
4. Métier.
5. Semblable à une bobine.
6. Moulin à foulon où le tissu (de l'âme) est nettoyé par les ordonnances de Dieu — allusion théologique.
7. Orné.
8. Première série de *Méditations*. Daté 6 mars 1686. Publié en 1939.
9. Overlaid : Jésus, orfèvre, utilise des triangles de feuilles d'or.
10. Vifs.

I cannot see, nor Will thy Will aright.
Nor see to waile[1] my Woe, my loss and hew
Nor all the Shine in all the Sun can light
My Candle, nor its Heate my Heart renew.
See, waile, and Will thy Will, I must, or must
From Heavens sweet Shine to Hells hot flame be thrust.

Grace then Conceald in God himselfe, did rowle[2]
Even Snow Ball like into a Sunball Shine
And nestles all its beams buncht in thy Soule
My Lord, that sparkle in Prophetick Lines.
Oh! Wonder more than Wonderfull! this Will
Lighten the Eye which Sight Divine did spill.

What art thou, Lord, this Ball of Glory bright?
A Bundle of Celestiall Beams up bound
In Graces band fixt in Heavens topmost height
Pouring thy golden Beams thence, Circling round
Which shew thy Glory, and thy glories Way
And ery Where will make Celestiall Day.

Lord let thy Golden Beams pierce through mine Eye
And leave therein an Heavenly Light to glaze
My Soule with glorious Grace all o're, whereby
I may have Sight, and Grace in mee may blaze.
Lord ting[3] my Candle at thy Burning Rayes,
To give a gracious Glory to thy Prayse.

Thou Lightning Eye, let some bright Beames of thine
Stick in my soul, to light and liven it:
Light, Life, and Glory, things that are Divine;
I shall be grac'd withall for glory fit.
My Heart then stufft with Grace, Light, Life, and Glee
I'le sacrifice in Flames of Love to thee.

1. Fleurer.
2. Roll.
3. Colore légèrement.

56. Meditation. Joh. 15,24. Had I not done amongst them the works, that none other man hath done, etc.[1]

Should I with silver tooles delve through the Hill
 Of Cordilera[2] for rich thoughts, that I
My Lord, might weave with an angelick skill
 A Damask Web of Velvet Verse thereby
 To deck thy Works up, all my Web would run
 To rags, and jags: so snicksnarld to the thrum.[3]

Thine are so rich: Within, Without. Refin'd.
 No workes like thine. No Fruits so sweete that grow
On th'trees of righteousness, of Angell kinde
 And Saints, whose limbs reev'd[4] with them bow down low.
 Should I search ore the Nutmeg Gardens shine
 Its fruits in flourish are but skegs[5] to thine.

The Clove, when in its White-green'd blossoms shoots,
 Some Call the pleasentst sent the World doth show.
None Eye e're saw, nor nose e're smelt such Fruits
 My Lord, as thine, Thou Tree of Life in'ts blow.
 Thou Rose of Sharon,[6] Vallies Lilly true
 Thy Fruits most sweet and Glorious ever grew.

Thou art a Tree of Perfect nature trim
 Whose golden lining is of perfect Grace
Perfum'de with Deity unto the brim,
 Whose fruits, of the perfection, grow, of Grace.
 Thy Buds, thy Blossoms, and thy fruits adorne
 Thyselfe, and Works, more shining than the morn.

. . . .

Nature doth better work than Art: yet thine
 Out vie both works of nature and of Art.

1. Deuxième série de *Méditations*, strophes 5-8 omises. Daté 1703. Publié en 1939.
2. La Cordillère des Andes et les chaînes du Mexique.
3. Fil emmêlé qui reste sur le métier.
4. Couverts.
5. Prune sauvage.
6. Fleur de la Bible, tulipe ou narcisse probablement.

Natures Perfection and the perfect shine
    Of Grace attend thy deed in ev'ry part.
    A Thought, a Word, and Worke of thine, will kill
    Sin, Satan, and the Curse: and Law fulfill.

Thou art the Tree of Life in Paradise,
    Whose lively branches are with Clusters hung
Of Lovely fruits, and Flowers more sweet than spice
    Bende down to us: and doe out shine the sun,
    Delightfull unto God, doe man rejoyce
    The pleasentst fruits in all Gods Paradise.

Lord feed mine eyes then with thy Doings rare,
    And fat my heart with these ripe fruites thou bearst.
Adorn my Life well with thy works, make faire
    My Person with apparrell thou prepar'st.
    My Boughs shall loaded bee with fruits that spring
    Up from thy Works, while to thy praise I sing.

II – Les années de maturation

De 1790 à 1865, les Etats-Unis jettent les bases de leur puissance future. Celles-ci sont tout d'abord politiques : les « Pères fondateurs » (c'est ainsi que l'on appelle les auteurs de la Constitution) ont mis en place des institutions dont la cohérence et la viabilité s'imposent aux plus sceptiques. Dès le début du XIXe siècle, il est clair que l'émancipation politique de la jeune nation est irréversible. L'expansion territoriale et démographique est encore plus frappante : de 1789 à 1865, le territoire des Etats-Unis passe de 2 millions et demi à 8 millions de kilomètres carrés : en 1790, il y a 4 millions d'Américains ; en 1860, 31 millions et demi. Enfin, la transformation des structures économiques est considérable, qu'il s'agisse des voies de communication (canaux et voies navigables, puis chemins de fer), de l'agriculture (essor de la culture du coton dans le Sud, développement rapide du Middle West) ou de l'industrie (sidérurgique, textile, etc.).

Au lendemain de l'Indépendance, nombre de voix se font entendre pour annoncer l'émancipation culturelle de la nouvelle nation ; mais il faudra vite déchanter : celle-ci ne se fera que lentement, douloureusement, et l'écart se creusera au fil des ans entre le dynamisme politique et économique des Etats-Unis et leur incapacité à se libérer, dans le domaine littéraire ou artistique, des modèles britanniques. En 1837, Ralph Waldo Emerson déplore encore, dans un discours qui fera date, « The American Scholar », l'esprit d'imitation qui maintient ses compatriotes dans une dépendance quasi coloniale : « We have listened too long to the courtly muses of Europe. » On ne s'étonnera donc pas que les gloires incontestées de cette période — les Freneau, les Bryant, les Longfellow — aient peu à peu perdu leur prestige, tandis que des créateurs solitaires et méconnus de leur vivant étaient réhabilités bien après leur mort. Il a fallu attendre les années 1920 pour que *Moby Dick* de Herman Melville soit redécouvert.

Même si l'on se limite aux quelques écrivains qui seront présentés dans ce chapitre, on constate qu'ils sont tous natifs des Etats de la côte Est : Irving, Cooper, Melville et Whitman naissent dans l'Etat de New York, Hawthorne, Emerson et Thoreau au Massachusetts, Poe en Virginie. Aucun d'eux ne passe dans l'Ouest plus de quelques semaines. En revanche, la plupart d'entre eux séjournent en Europe, parfois longuement (cinq ans pour Poe, sept ans pour Hawthorne, près de vingt ans pour Irving), même si l'on trouve également quelques irréductibles comme Thoreau et Whitman, qui ne quitteront jamais le continent américain.

Le monde de l'édition est tout aussi limité géographiquement, et tout aussi tourné vers l'Angleterre : il se limite en fait à trois métropoles, New York, Philadelphie et Boston, qui reçoivent les ouvrages britanniques dès leur publication et les impriment à leur tour. Ces éditions « piratées » sont bien sûr dénoncées par ceux qui en sont les victimes, mais il faudra attendre 1891 pour que le Congrès les interdise. Comment un jeune écrivain américain pourrait-il s'imposer face à un tel déferlement ? Journalistes et chroniqueurs ont beau appeler de leurs vœux l'arrivée d'une littérature nationale, autonome, qui véhiculerait des valeurs démocratiques au lieu de reproduire servilement celles de l'aristocratie anglaise : le public, lui, dévore Walter Scott et Charles Dickens (qui fera une tournée triomphale en 1841).

On pourrait dire que l'écrivain américain, pendant ces années de maturation, souffre d'un double ostracisme : celui de la critique britannique, qui traite les productions littéraires de la jeune république avec une condescendance parfois insultante (ainsi, la *Quarterly review* demande en 1820 : « Who reads an American book ? ») ; et celle d'un public indifférent aux tentatives d'expression originales, peu soucieux de promouvoir la production autochtone, comblé par la lecture d'*Ivanhoe* ou d'*Oliver Twist*.

A ces obstacles extérieurs s'ajoutent les contraintes contradictoires qui s'exercent sur les écrivains : d'une part, ils héritent d'une culture post-révolutionnaire qui proclame le rejet de modes de vie et de pensée inhérents aux traditions européennes ; d'autre part, ils cherchent vainement dans leur propre culture les modèles qu'ils pourraient leur substituer. Henry James décrira ce dilemme dans son étude sur Hawthorne, et s'amusera à faire la liste de tous les éléments qui, dans les grandes nations européennes, contribuent à créer une « haute civilisation », et qui font défaut dans la jeune nation. Hawthorne lui-même, dans sa préface à *The Marble Faun*, justifie le choix de l'Italie comme cadre de son dernier roman en invoquant la pauvreté des sujets proposés par la société américaine.

Dans cette préface, Hawthorne n'évoque pas seulement la jeunesse relative de cette société : il souligne également les effets négatifs sur la création littéraire d'un fait socialement bénéfique : la prospérité ambiante, qui fait régner au moins dans les classes moyennes une lumière uniforme peu propice aux ombres et aux nuances de la fiction, et une atmosphère prosaïque propre à décourager le poète. Pourtant, d'autres souligneront l'infinie richesse du matériau qu'offre la réalité américaine. Emerson écrit en 1844 qu'il cherche vainement le poète capable de chanter cette réalité multiple, mais que celui-ci ne saurait tarder à apparaître : « Our log-rolling, our stumps and our politics, our fisheries, our Negroes and Indians, our boats and our repudiations, the wrath of rogues and the pusillanimity of honest men, the northern trade, the southern planting, the western clearing, Oregon and Texas, are yet unsung. Yet America is a poem in our eyes ; its ample geography dazzles the imagination, and it will not wait long for meters » (« The Poet »). Cette prophétie ne tardera pas à se réaliser, puisque, onze ans plus tard, Whitman publiera la première édition de ses *Leaves of Grass* ; mais il est significatif qu'il faille attendre 1855 pour qu'un poète américain ose chanter l'Amérique.

En fait, le vrai problème est moins le manque de « sujets » que l'indifférence ou l'hostilité du public, largement intériorisée par l'écrivain, et qu'il doit exorciser pour écrire. Dans l'Amérique de 1840 ou de 1850, l'écrivain qui n'a pas de par sa naissance et son éducation une place de choix dans la société patricienne des grandes métropoles est condamné à rester un marginal, et à passer pour un parasite dans un monde entièrement tourné vers des tâches immédiates. Il en souffre et s'en ouvre parfois obliquement au lecteur, sur le mode confidentiel, comme Hawthorne dans l'introduction à *The Scarlet Letter*, ou sur le mode polémique et provocateur, comme Thoreau dans le premier chapitre de *Walden* ; ou encore il contourne l'obstacle en se construisant un personnage, comme Whitman. Dans tous les cas, la marge de manœuvre est étroite, puisqu'il s'agit de proposer fiction ou poésie à une Amérique apparemment vouée au principe de réalité ; d'où peut-être la prolifération des œuvres hybrides, qui se situent à mi-chemin entre l'imaginaire et le réel — ou le présumé tel : la conférence, l'essai, le récit de voyage, le témoignage. Il arrive même qu'une œuvre de fiction soit présentée comme un document authentique : dans l'introduction à *The Scarlet Letter*, Hawthorne prétend — avec, il est vrai, une forte dose de dérision et d'humour — avoir découvert dans les combles de la douane de Salem un manuscrit dont le texte n'est autre que celui du roman.

Enfin, et surtout, le décalage est manifeste dans les cercles cultivés de l'Amérique post-révolutionnaire entre l'appel quasi général à une thématique nationale, voire patriotique, et la soumission aux formes et aux modèles esthétiques européens. On attend de l'écrivain qu'il coule dans des moules pré-existants un matériau emprunté à l'histoire nationale (plutôt qu'aux réalités contemporaines ; Emerson est, à cet égard, une exception). D'où diverses tentatives qui évoquent le décalque plus que la création, et qui ont disparu dans les oubliettes de l'histoire littéraire. Même chez d'authentiques créateurs, comme Irving et Cooper, l'œuvre ne peut se développer indépendamment des normes imposées par une tradition littéraire et des codes liés aux genres que cette tradition a fait connaître — l'essai dans la manière de Steele et Addison, chez Irving ; le roman historique de Scott, chez Cooper. Ils occupent donc une place intermédiaire entre l'écriture mimétique dont il a été question plus haut et l'explosion littéraire à laquelle la critique donne le nom de « Renaissance américaine » : Irving et Cooper ne se contentent pas de reproduire des modèles ; ils parviennent à les « naturaliser », jouant ainsi le rôle de médiateurs.

Il convient d'ailleurs de ne pas oublier la chronologie : Irving gagne la faveur du public britannique et américain entre 1807 et 1820 ; Cooper fait de même de 1821 à 1823. Si nous passons à la carrière de Poe et Hawthorne, nous constatons que le premier ne sort — très partiellement — de l'obscurité qu'entre 1840 et 1844, et que le second connaît un succès d'estime à partir de 1837. L'écart avec Irving et Cooper n'est pas seulement chronologique : il ne s'agit plus seulement de recourir à des recettes éprouvées en les adaptant à un matériau neuf, mais de construire une œuvre ancrée dans le passé de la Nouvelle-Angleterre ou du Sud, d'apporter à la construction du conte ou du roman une exigence sans faille. Une telle entreprise, dans l'Amérique de 1840, ne peut conduire à la notoriété : Poe et Hawthorne écriront dans la solitude ; le premier mourra prématurément, tragiquement ; le second, malgré le relatif succès de *The Scarlet Letter*, en 1850, s'enfoncera peu à peu dans la stérilité.

Le parcours d'Emerson et de Thoreau est fort différent : tous deux adhèrent à un mouvement mi-religieux, mi-littéraire qui prétend régénérer l'individu, le transcendantalisme. Leur œuvre se crée donc en marge des genres littéraires reconnus : les « essais » d'Emerson ont peu de points communs avec ceux d'Irving, et s'inscrivent dans une tradition qui remonte aux origines de la Nouvelle-Angleterre : celle du sermon puritain, dont il nous offre une version sécularisée, propre à répondre aux exigences de son temps. Quant à *Walden* de Thoreau (1854), c'est un livre inclassable, où l'on a vu une autobiographie, un traité d'histoire naturelle, un évangile, ou un poème. On pourrait presque dire qu'Emerson et Thoreau ouvrent des voies nouvelles à la littérature américaine parce que leur entreprise n'est pas, à proprement parler, littéraire : leur messianisme les met à l'abri des contraintes qui ont un effet stérilisant sur tant de leurs contemporains.

Melville et Whitman opèrent en quelque sorte la synthèse des deux démarches précédentes : tout en se situant, comme Poe et Hawthorne, à l'intérieur d'un cadre littéraire défini (l'un écrit des romans, l'autre des poèmes), ils font éclater ce cadre et s'engagent dans une véritable aventure, modèle inépuisable pour les écrivains qui leur succéderont.

1 – Les médiateurs

Les trente années qui suivent l'élection de Washington en 1789 se caractérisent par une grande espérance, suivie d'une grande déception. Au lendemain de l'Indépendance, et à nouveau après la seconde guerre contre l'Angleterre (1812-1815), les périodiques américains proclament l'émancipation culturelle de la jeune nation, allant parfois jusqu'à annoncer l'apparition imminente d'un Homère ou d'un Milton américain. Certains, comme Noah Webster, auteur du premier dictionnaire américain, souhaitent l'émergence d'une langue proche, mais distincte de l'anglais britannique. Ces accès de nationalisme ne sauraient faire oublier que la plupart des journaux littéraires sont aux mains de Fédéralistes aussi anglophiles que conservateurs, toujours prêts à opposer le provincialisme et la grossièreté de la culture environnante au raffinement et à la richesse de l'ex-mère patrie. De plus, ces critiques se réclament de normes classiques pour rejeter les audaces de Wordsworth, Southey et Coleridge. Le romantisme ne pénétrera que difficilement aux Etats-Unis.[1]

Les productions littéraires des premières années ne sont guère que des copies de modèles empruntés au théâtre anglais (ex. *The Contrast*, pièce de Royall Tyler, 1787) au récit picaresque (*Modern Chivalry* de Hugh Henry Brackenridge, publié de 1792 à 1815) ou au roman gothique (*Wieland* de Charles Brockden Brown, 1798).

1. Voir Jean-Marie Bonnet, *La critique littéraire aux Etats-Unis, 1783-1837*, Lyon, PUL, 1982.

De même, le groupe de poètes connus sous le nom de « *Connecticut Wits* » manie avec un bonheur inégal les codes de la satire (John Trumbull) ou de la poésie épique (Timothy Dwight). Cette dernière connaît, assez logiquement, un essor particulier après l'Indépendance : Joel Barlow chante le destin national dans *The Columbiad* (1807), hymne en neuf livres à la nation américaine, de facture lourdement conventionnelle.

Force est donc de constater que l'explosion littéraire annoncée ne se produit pas : non seulement la jeune nation n'innove pas, mais elle reste attachée à des modèles néo-classiques qui n'ont plus cours en Angleterre. Ainsi Philip Freneau (1752-1832), poète-lauréat de la Révolution américaine, chante l'indianité ou la flore et la faune du Nouveau Monde sans se libérer d'une diction poétique héritée du XVIIIe siècle. William C. Bryant (1794-1878), salué de son vivant comme le grand poète de la Nouvelle-Angleterre, évoque la forêt inviolée ou l'immensité de la Prairie en des accents trop sages dont la régularité même paraît aujourd'hui totalement inadaptée à la nature de ses sujets.

C'est en fait dans le domaine de la fiction que l'Amérique trouvera ses premiers écrivains authentiques.

WASHINGTON IRVING, 1783-1859

Washington Irving occupe une place particulière dans les lettres américaines : premier écrivain de la jeune République à gagner le public britannique (Scott, Dickens, Thackeray ne tariront pas d'éloges sur le *Sketch-Book*), il est également salué dans son propre pays, qu'il quitte pourtant pendant près de vingt ans, comme un essayiste et un conteur de talent. En fait, Irving joue le rôle de médiateur entre les deux continents.

Né à New York d'une famille aisée — son père était un marchand prospère —, il publie en 1807 avec son frère et son beau-frère une satire de la démocratie américaine, *Salmagundi*, qui se présente comme les réflexions d'un certain Launcelot Langstaff, conservateur éclairé sorti tout droit du *Spectator*, l'organe d'Addison et Steele. Son œuvre suivante, *A History of New York*, est également publiée comme émanant d'un personnage créé de toutes pièces par Irving, et dont le nom, Knickerbocker, servira de signe de ralliement à un groupe d'hommes de lettres new-yorkais pendant les années 1820. Irving y retrace avec une verve et une irrévérence surprenantes le parcours de ses ancêtres hollandais depuis la fondation de New Amsterdam (la future New York). Le livre rappelle le XVIIIe siècle anglais par la manière dont il reprend les codes héroï-comiques, mais annonce par son goût de l'extravagance et de l'hyperbole les humoristes américains de la génération suivante.

Après avoir délaissé pendant une décennie la littérature pour le commerce, et quitté en 1815 les Etats-Unis pour l'Angleterre, Irving reviendra aux lettres après la faillite de l'entreprise familiale. *The Sketch-Book*, publié en 1819-1820, est immédiatement salué comme une œuvre majeure par la critique britannique ; on y trouve côte à côte des essais et des croquis ou de courts récits consacrés aussi bien à Londres ou à la campagne anglaise qu'à l'Amérique coloniale et aux guerres indiennes. Les deux contes qui feront la fortune d'Irving, « Rip Van Winkle » et « The Legend of Sleepy Hollow », se situent dans la vallée de l'Hudson, mais le cadre d'un autre conte, « The Spectre Bridegroom », est l'Allemagne féodale. C'est sans doute cette rencontre incongrue des deux continents qui explique le succès du livre.

Diplomate en Espagne et en Angleterre de 1826 à 1832, Irving devient également une sorte de plénipotentiaire littéraire, en faisant connaître au public américain le folklore allemand (*Tales of a Traveller*, 1824) ou espagnol (*The Alhambra*, 1832), et en donnant parallèlement une sorte de caution de respectabilité à la jeune littérature américaine en Europe.

BIBLIOGRAPHIE SÉLECTIVE. — *The Complete Works of Washington Irving* (en cours de publication), eds Henry Pochmann, Herbert Keinfield, Boston, Twayne, 1977- ; *History, Tales and Sketches*, New York, Library of America, 1983 (3 autres vol. en préparation) ; Bowden (Mary), *Washington Irving*, Boston, Twayne, 1981 ; Hedges (William), *Washington Irving, an American Study, 1802-1832*, Baltimore, John Hopkins, 1965 ; Leary (Lewis), *Washington Irving*, Minneapolis, University of Minnesota

Pamphlets, 1963 ; Roth (Martin), *Comedy and America : The Lost World of Washington Irving*, Port Washington, Kennikat Press, 1976 ; Wagenknecht (Edward), *Washington Irving : Moderation Displayed*, New York, Oxford UP, 1962.

Rip Van Winkle[1]

Dans un paisible village niché au cœur des montagnes Catskill, dans ce qui est devenu l'Etat de New York, Rip Van Winkle trouve dans la chasse le moyen d'échapper au travail de la ferme, qu'il a en horreur, et aux récriminations de son acariâtre épouse. Un jour qu'il est parti dans la montagne avec son chien Wolf, il rencontre d'étranges personnages qui lui offrent un breuvage inconnu. Il sombre dans un profond sommeil.

[...] On awaking he found himself on the green knoll from whence he had first seen the old man of the glen. He rubbed his eyes—it was a bright, sunny morning. The birds were hopping and twittering among the bushes, and the eagle was wheeling aloft and breasting the pure mountain breeze. "Surely," thought Rip, "I have not slept here all night." He recalled the occurrences before he fell asleep. The strange man with a keg of liquor—the mountain ravine—the wild retreat among the rocks—the woe begone party at ninepins[2]—the flagon—"ah! that flagon! that wicked flagon!" thought Rip—"what excuse shall I make to Dame Van Winkle?"

He looked round for his gun, but in place of the clean well oiled fowling piece he found an old firelock lying by him, the barrel encrusted with rust; the lock falling off and the stock worm eaten. He now suspected that the grave roysters[3] of the mountain had put a trick upon him, and having dosed him with liquor, had robbed him of his gun. Wolf too had disappeared, but he might have strayed away after a squirrel or partridge. He whistled after him

1. Publié dans le *Sketch-Book* (1819-1820), ce conte est en fait inspiré d'une légende allemande ; mais Irving l'a « naturalisé », en l'ancrant dans un cadre géographique et culturel proprement américain — celui de la colonie hollandaise dont étaient issus ses ancêtres — et en le situant historiquement : la perplexité de Rip face à l'Amérique post-révolutionnaire permet à l'auteur d'évoquer à mots couverts les traumatismes liés à l'Indépendance.

2. Les étranges personnages étaient occupés à jouer aux quilles.

3. = *roisterers* [du franç. « rustre »] : festoyeurs.

and shouted his name—but all in vain; the echoes repeated his whistle and shout, but no dog was to be seen.

He determined to revisit the scene of the last evening's gambol, and if he met with any of the party, to demand his dog and gun. As he arose to walk he found himself stiff in the joints and wanting in his usual activity. "These mountain beds do not agree with me," thought Rip, "and if this frolick should lay me up with a fit of the rheumatism, I shall have a blessed time with Dame Van Winkle." With some difficulty he got down into the glen; he found the gully up which he and his companion had ascended the preceding evening, but to his astonishment a mountain stream was now foaming down it; leaping from rock to rock, and filling the glen with babbling murmurs. He, however, made shift to scramble up its sides working his toilsome way through thickets of birch, sassafras and witch hazel, and sometimes tripped up or entangled by the wild grape vines that twisted their coils and tendrils from tree to tree, and spread a kind of net work in his path.

At length he reached to where the ravine had opened through the cliffs, to the amphitheatre—but no traces of such opening remained. The rocks presented a high impenetrable wall over which the torrent came tumbling in a sheet of feathery foam, and fell into a broad deep basin black from the shadows of the surrounding forest. Here then poor Rip was brought to a stand. He again called and whistled after his dog—he was only answered by the cawing of a flock of idle crows, sporting high in air about a dry tree that overhung a sunny precipice; and who, secure in their elevation seemed to look down and scoff at the poor man's perplexities.

What was to be done? The morning was passing away and Rip felt famished for want of his breakfast. He grieved to give up his dog and gun; he dreaded to meet his wife; but it would not do to starve among the mountains. He shook his head, shouldered the rusty fire lock and with a heart full of trouble and anxiety, turned his steps homeward.

As he approached the village he met a number of people, but none whom he knew, which somewhat surprised him, for he had thought himself acquainted with every one in the country round. Their dress too was of a different fashion from that to which he was accustomed. They all stared at him with equal marks of surprise, and whenever they cast their eyes upon him, invariably stroked their chins. The constant recurrence of this gesture induced Rip involuntarily to do the same, when to his astonishment he found his beard had grown a foot long!

He had now entered the skirts of the village. A troop of strange children ran at his heels, hooting after him and pointing at his grey beard. The dogs too, not one of which he recognized for an old acquaintance, barked at him as he passed. The very village was altered—it was larger and more populous. There were rows of houses which he had never seen before, and those which had been his familiar haunts had disappeared. Strange names were over the doors—strange faces at the windows—every thing was strange. His mind now misgave him; he began to doubt whether both he and the world around him were not bewitched. Surely this was his native village which he had left but the day before. There stood the Kaatskill mountains—there ran the silver Hudson at a distance—there was every hill and dale precisely as it had always been—Rip was sorely perplexed—"That flagon last night," thought he, "has addled my poor head sadly!"

It was with some difficulty that he found the way to his own house, which he approached with silent awe, expecting every moment to hear the shrill voice of Dame Van Winkle. He found the house gone to decay—the roof fallen in, the windows shattered and the doors off the hinges. A half starved dog that looked like Wolf was skulking about it. Rip called him by name but the cur snarled, shewed his teeth and passed on. This was an unkind cut indeed—"My very dog," sighed poor Rip, "has forgotten me!"

He entered the house, which, to tell the truth, Dame Van Winkle had always kept in neat order. It was empty, forlorn and apparently abandoned. This desolateness overcame all his connubial fears—he called loudly for his wife and children—the lonely chambers rung for a moment with his voice, and then all again was silence.

He now hurried forth and hastened to his old resort, the village inn—but it too was gone. A large, ricketty wooden building stood in its place, with great gaping windows, some of them broken, and mended with old hats and petticoats, and over the door was printed "The Union Hotel, by Jonathan Doolittle". Instead of the great tree, that used to shelter the quiet little Dutch inn of yore, there now was reared a tall naked pole with something on top that looked like a red night cap,[1] and from it was fluttering a flag on which was a singular assemblage of stars and stripes—all this was strange and incomprehensible. He recognized on the sign, however, the ruby face of King George[2] under which he had smoked so many a peaceful pipe, but even this was singularly metamorphosed. The red coat was changed for one of blue and buff; a sword was held in the hand instead of a sceptre; the head was decorated with a cocked hat, and underneath was printed in large characters GENERAL WASHINGTON.

There was as usual a crowd of folk about the door; but none that Rip recollected. The very character of the people seemed changed. There was a busy, bustling disputatious tone about it, instead of the accustomed phlegm and drowsy tranquility. He looked in vain for the sage Nicholaus Vedder with his broad face, double chin and fair long pipe, uttering clouds of tobacco smoke instead of idle speeches. Or Van Bummel the schoolmaster doling forth the contents of an ancient newspaper. In place of these a lean bilious looking fellow with his pockets full of hand bills, was haranguing vehemently about rights of citizens—elections—members of Congress—liberty—Bunker's hill[3]—heroes of seventy six—and other words which were a perfect babylonish jargon to the bewildered Van Winkle.

The appearance of Rip with his long grizzled beard, his rusty fowling piece, his uncouth dress and an army of women and children at his heels soon attracted the attention of the tavern politicians. They crowded around him eying him from head to foot, with great curiosity. The orator bustled up to him, and drawing him partly aside, enquired "on which side he voted?"—Rip stared in vacant stupidity. Another short but busy little fellow pulled him by the arm and rising on tiptoe, enquired in his ear "whether he was Federal or Democrat?"[4]—Rip was equally at a loss to comprehend the question—when a knowing, self important old gentleman, in a sharp cocked hat, made his way through the crowd, putting them to the right and left with his

1. Le bonnet phrygien.

2. George III, roi d'Angleterre à l'époque de la guerre d'Indépendance.

3. Lieu d'une bataille célèbre qui se déroula près de Boston en 1775. L'évocation du fanatisme républicain rappelle *Salmagundi*.

4. Après l'Indépendance, les Fédéralistes de Washington et Hamilton s'opposent aux Démocrates (ou Républicains-Démocrates) de Jefferson.

elbows as he passed, and planting himself before Van Winkle, with one arm akimbo, the other resting on his cane, his keen eyes and sharp hat penetrating as it were into his very soul, demanded in an austere tone—"what brought him to the election with a gun on his shoulder and a mob at his heels, and whether he meant to breed a riot in the village?"—"Alas gentlemen," cried Rip, somewhat dismayed, "I am a poor quiet man, a native of the place, and a loyal subject of the King—God bless him!"

Here a general shout burst from the bystanders—"A tory! a tory![1] a spy! a Refugee! hustle him! away with him!"—It was with great difficulty that the self important man in the cocked hat restored order; and having assumed a ten fold austerity of brow demanded again of the unknown culprit, what he came there for and whom he was seeking. The poor man humbly assured him that he meant no harm; but merely came there in search of some of his neighbours, who used to keep about the tavern.

"—Well—who are they?—name them."

Rip bethought himself a moment and enquired, "Where's Nicholaus Vedder?"

There was a silence for a little while, when an olf man replied, in a thin, piping voice, "Nicholaus Vedder? why he is dead and gone these eighteen years! There was a wooden tombstone in the church yard that used to tell all about him, but that's rotted and gone too."

"Where's Brom Dutcher?"

"Oh he went off to the army in the beginning of the war; some say he was killed at the storming of Stoney Point—others say he was drowned in a squall at the foot of Antony's Nose[2]—I don't know—he never came back again."

"Where's Van Bummel the schoolmaster?"

"He went off to the wars too—was a great militia general, and is now in Congress."

Rip's heart died away at hearing of these sad changes in his home and friends, and finding himself thus alone in the world—every answer puzzled him too by treating of such enormous lapses of time and of matters which he could not understand—war—Congress, Stoney Point—he had no courage

1. On appelait *Tories* les loyalistes, ennemis de la Révolution.
2. Stoney Point, Antony's Nose : lieux de batailles révolutionnaires sur les rives du fleuve Hudson.

to ask after any more friends, but cried out in despair, "Does nobody here know Rip Van Winkle?"

"Oh. Rip Van Winkle?" exclaimed two or three—"oh to be sure!—that's Rip Van Winkle—yonder—leaning against the tree."

Rip looked and beheld a precise counterpart of himself, as he went up the mountain: apparently as lazy and certainly as ragged! The poor fellow was now completely confounded. He doubted his own identity, and whether he was himself or another man. In the midst of his bewilderment the man in the cocked hat demanded who he was,—what was his name?

"God knows," exclaimed he, at his wit's end, "I'm not myself.—I'm somebody else—that's me yonder—no—that's somebody else got into my shoes—I was myself last night; but I fell asleep on the mountain—and they've changed my gun—and every thing's changed—and I'm changed—and I can't tell what's my name, or who I am!"

The bystanders began now to look at each other, nod, wink significantly and tap their fingers against their foreheads. There was a whisper also about securing the gun, and keeping the old fellow from doing mischief—at the very suggestion of which, the self important man in the cocked hat retired with some precipitation. At this critical moment a fresh likely looking woman pressed through the throng to get a peep at the greybearded man. She had a chubby child in her arms, which frightened at his looks began to cry. "Hush Rip," cried she, "hush you little fool, the old man won't hurt you." The name of the child, the air of the mother, the tone of her voice all awakened a train of recollections in his mind. "What is your name my good woman?" asked he.

"Judith Gardenier."

"And your father's name?"

"Ah, poor man, Rip Van Winkle was his name, but it's twenty years since he went away from home with his gun and never has been heard of since—his dog came home without him—but whether he shot himself, or was carried away by the Indians no body can tell. I was then but a little girl."

Rip had but one question more to ask, but he put it with a faltering voice—

"Where's your mother?"—

Oh she too had died but a short time since—she broke a blood vessel in a fit of passion at a New England pedlar.—

There was a drop of comfort at least in this intelligence. The honest man could contain himself no longer—he caught his daughter and her child in his arms.—"I am your father!" cried he—"Young Rip Van Winkle once—old Rip Van Winkle now!—does nobody know poor Rip Van Winkle!"

All stood amazed, until an old woman tottering out from among the crowd put her hand to her brow and peering under it in his face for a moment exclaimed—"Sure enough!— it is Rip Van Winkle—it is himself—welcome home again old neighbour—why, where have you been these twenty long years?"

Rip's story was soon told, for the whole twenty years had been to him but as one night. The neighbours stared when they heard it; some were seen to wink at each other and put their tongues in their cheeks, and the self important man in the cocked hat, who when the alarm was over had returned to the field, screwed down the corners of his mouth and shook his head—upon which there was a general shaking of the head throughout the assemblage.

It was determined, however, to take the opinion of old Peter Vanderdonk, who was seen slowly advancing up the road. He was a descendant of the historian of that name, who wrote one of the earliest accounts of the province. Peter was the most ancient inhabitant of the village and well versed in all the wonderful events and traditions of the neighbourhood. He recollected Rip at once, and corroborated his story in the most satisfactory manner. He assured the company that it was a fact handed down from his ancestor the historian,[1] that the Kaatskill mountains had always been haunted by strange beings. That it was affirmed that the great Hendrick Hudson,[2] the first discoverer of the river and country, kept a kind of vigil there every twenty years, with his crew of the Half Moon—being permitted in this way to revisit the scenes of his enterprize and keep a guardian eye upon the river and the great city called by his name. That his father had once seen them in their old Dutch dresses playing at nine pins in a hollow of the

1. Adriaen Van der Donck, historien hollandais qui avait écrit une histoire des colonies hollandaises en Amérique.

2. Henry Hudson (le prénom est ici « hollandisé ») découvrit le fleuve qui devait porter son nom en 1609.

mountain; and that he himself had heard one summer afternoon the sound of their balls, like distant peals of thunder.

To make a long story short—the company broke up, and returned to the more important concerns of the election. Rip's daughter took him home to live with her; she had a snug well furnished house, and a stout cheery farmer for a husband whom Rip recollected for one of the urchins that used to climb upon his back. As to Rip's son and heir, who was the ditto of himself seen leaning against the tree; he was employed to work on the farm; but evinced an hereditary disposition to attend to any thing else but his business.

Rip now resumed his old walks and habits; he soon found many of his former cronies, though all rather the worse for the wear and tear of time; and preferred making friends among the rising generation, with whom he soon grew into great favour. Having nothing to do at home, and being arrived at that happy age when a man can be idle, with impunity, he took his place once more on the bench at the inn door and was reverenced as one of the patriarchs of the village and a chronicle of the old times "before the war." It was some time before he could get into the regular track of gossip, or could be made to comprehend the strange events that had taken place during his torpor. How that there had been a revolutionary war—that the country had thrown off the yoke of Old England and that instead of being a subject of his majesty George the Third, he was now a free citizen of the United States. Rip in fact was no politician; the changes of states and empires made but little impression on him; but there was one species of despotism under which he had long groaned and that was petticoat government. Happily that was at an end—he had got his neck out of the yoke of matrimony, and could go in and out whenever he pleased without dreading the tyranny of Dame Van Winkle. Whenever her name was mentioned, however, he shook his head, shrugged his shoulders and cast up his eyes; which might pass either for an expression of resignation to his fate or joy at his deliverance.

He used to tell his story to every stranger that arrived at Mr. Doolittle's Hotel. He was observed at first to vary on some points, every time he told it, which was doubtless owing to his having so recently awaked. It at last settled down precisely to the tale I have related and not a man woman or child in the neighbourhood but knew it by heart. Some always pretended to doubt the reality of it, and insisted that Rip had been out of his head, and that this was one point on which he always remained flighty. The old Dutch inhabitants, however, almost universally gave it full credit—Even to this day they never hear a thunder storm of a summer afternoon about the Kaatskill, but they say Hendrick Hudson and his crew are at their game of nine pins; and it is a common wish of all henpecked husbands in the neighbourhood, when life hangs heavy on their hands, that they might have a quieting draught out of Rip Van Winkle's flagon.

NOTE[1]

The foregoing tale one would suspect had been suggested to Mr. Knickerbocker by a little German superstition about the emperor Frederick *der Rothbart* and the Kypphauser Mountain; the subjoined note, however, which he had appended to the tale, shews that it is an absolute fact, narrated with his usual fidelity.—

"The story of Rip Van Winkle may seem incredible to many, but nevertheless I give it my full belief, for I know the vicinity of our old Dutch settlements to have been very subject to marvellous events and appearances. Indeed I have heard many stranger stories than this, in the villages along the Hudson; all of which were too well authenticated to admit of a doubt. I have even talked with Rip Van Winkle myself, who when last I saw him was a very venerable old man and so perfectly rational and consistent on every other point, that I think no conscientious person could refuse to take this into the bargain—nay I have seen a certificate on the subject taken before a country justice and signed with a cross in the justice's own hand writing. The story therefore is beyond the possibility of doubt.

D.K."

1. Cette note représente une sorte de post-scriptum comique, dont l'humour est lié à la tentative du narrateur pour authentifier un récit invraisemblable. Cette technique sera reprise par les humoristes du Sud-Ouest (voir chap. 2) : « Rip Van Winkle » peut être lu comme une version patricienne — et précoce — de la *tall tale*, à cette différence près que Rip ne raconte pas ses propres aventures. Selon une perspective toute différente, on peut voir dans cette conclusion une technique destinée à masquer la dimension mythique du conte, qui contient un double mythe d'origines : origines de la colonie hollandaise (Henry Hudson) et origines de la nation américaine.

JAMES FENIMORE COOPER, 1789-1851

A la différence d'Irving, Cooper conquiert le public américain — et européen — en ouvrant la voie à une mythologie du Nouveau Monde ; mais on aurait tort de l'identifier à son héros, le très démocratique Bas-de-Cuir (Leatherstocking). C'est en fait, par naissance et par mariage, un patricien. Après une enfance passée dans la propriété familiale, dans la partie la plus sauvage de l'Etat de New York, il est exclu de l'Université de Yale pour indiscipline, et s'engage dans la marine, ce qui lui permet d'écrire le premier roman maritime américain, *The Pilot* (1824). Auparavant, il a déjà connu le succès avec un roman historique dans le style de Walter Scott, dont l'action se déroule pendant la Révolution américaine, *The Spy* (1821).

Mais le nom de Cooper est associé pour d'innombrables lecteurs des deux continents aux cinq romans dont le héros est Natty Bumppo, *alias* Œil de Faucon, *alias* Bas-de-Cuir. Celui-ci apparaît, curieusement, sous les traits d'un vieux chasseur usé et aigri dans *The Pioneers* (1823), avant de rajeunir, trois ans plus tard, dans *The Last of the Mohicans*. Dans ce second récit, il noue une amitié improbable avec le vieux chef indien Chingachcook (« prononcez Chicago », dira Mark Twain, qui brocardera Cooper dans un essai féroce, « The Literary Offences of Fenimore Cooper »). Le roman suivant, *The Prairie* (1827), présente Natty Bumppo comme un noble vieillard et se conclut par sa disparition, mais il renaît dans *The Pathfinder* (1840) et *The Deerslayer* (1841), tous deux consacrés à ses années d'apprentissage. L'étrange chronologie des « Leatherstocking novels » fera dire à D. H. Lawrence, dans ses *Studies of Classic American Literature* : « They go backwards, from old age to golden youth. That is the true myth of America. She starts old, wrinkled and writhing in an old skin. And there is a gradual sloughing of the old skin, towards a new youth. »

Il faut résister à la tentation de simplifier le personnage de Natty Bumppo : s'il *devient* dans les deux derniers romans du cycle une sorte de prototype du *cowboy*, héros solitaire incarnant l'ordre dans un monde menacé par la violence primitive, il apparaît tout d'abord comme un vieil homme désabusé, assistant impuissant au viol de la terre américaine. Cooper est généralement présenté comme le créateur du premier protagoniste issu de la démocratie ; mais il consacrera ses dernières œuvres (par exemple les essais publiés en 1838 sous le titre *The American Democrat*) à une critique amère de cette même démocratie. En fin de compte, le titre de « Scott américain », que devait lui confier — à son corps défendant — la critique anglaise, n'est pas aussi incongru qu'il paraît : si l'œuvre de Scott exalte un univers aristocratique condamné par l'histoire, celle de Cooper évoque une « aristocratie naturelle », dont Natty Bumppo est l'incarnation, et qui est également condamnée par la progression de la « civilisation ».

BIBLIOGRAPHIE SÉLECTIVE. — *The Writings of James Fenimore Cooper*, ed. James Franklin Beard (en cours de publication), State of New York UP, 1968 ; *The Leatherstocking Tales*, ed. Blake Nevins (3 autres vol. en préparation), New York, Library of America ; Dekker (George) et McWilliams (John), *Fenimore Cooper : The Critical Heritage*, London, Methuen, 1973 ; Fields (Wayne), ed., *James Fenimore Cooper : a Collection of Critical Essays*, Englewood Cliffs, NJ, Prentice-Hall, 1979 ; McWilliams (John), *Political Justice in a Republic : James Fenimore Cooper's America*, Berkeley, U. of California Press, 1972 ; Slotkin (Richard), *Regeneration through Violence : the Mythology of the American Frontier, 1600-1860*, Middleton, Conn., Wesleyan UP, 1973 ; Test (George), ed., *James Fenimore Cooper : His Country and His Heart*, Oneonta, NY, SUNY College, 1987.

The Prairie[1]

FIN DU CHAPITRE 1

L'action de The Prairie *se situe en 1804, un an après l'achat de la Louisiane — c'est-à-dire d'un immense territoire à l'ouest du Mississippi — par Jefferson. Le roman s'ouvre avec l'arrivée dans ces solitudes désolées d'Ishmael Bush, pionnier fruste et brutal, de sa*

1. Publié en 1827. Cooper s'est inspiré du rapport sur l'expédition de Stephen Long dans l'Ouest en 1820.

femme Esther, de ses sept fils, de sa fille Esther, et de son beau-frère Abiram White. Ils rencontrent un vieillard de plus de quatre-vingts ans qui n'est autre que Natty Bumppo.

[...] From the moment when it had thus unaccountably appeared, as it were, between the heavens and the earth, the stranger's figure had neither moved nor given the smallest evidence of hostility. Had he harbored any such evil intention, the individual who now came plainly into view seemed but little qualified to execute them.

A frame that had endured the hardships of more than eighty seasons was not qualified to awaken apprehension in the breast of one as powerful as the emigrant. Notwithstanding his years and his look of emaciation, if not of suffering, there was that about this solitary being, however, which said that time, and not disease, had laid his hand heavily on him. His form had withered, but it was not wasted. The sinews and muscles, which had once denoted great strength, though shrunken, were still visible; and his whole figure had attained an appearance of induration, which, if it were not for the well-known frailty of humanity, would have seemed to bid defiance to the further approaches of decay. His dress was chiefly of skins, worn with the hair to the weather; a pouch and horn were suspended from his shoulders; and he leaned on a rifle of uncommon length, but which, like its owner, exhibited the wear of long and hard service.

As the party drew nigher to this solitary being and came within a distance to be heard, a low growl issued from the grass at his feet, and then a tall, gaunt, toothless hound arose lazily from his lair, and shaking himself, made some show of resisting the nearer approach of the travelers.[1]

"Down, Hector, down," said his master in a voice that was a little tremulous and hollow with age. "What have ye to do, pup, with men who journey on their lawful callings?"

"Stranger, if you are much acquainted in this country," said the leader of the emigrants, "can you tell a traveler where he may find necessaries for the night?"

1. Le mystère qui entoure d'emblée le personnage — on ignore tout de lui, et il est présenté, littéralement, comme une apparition — lui donne bien évidemment un tout autre statut que celui dont pouvait jouir le pauvre Rip ; mais ce vieux chasseur, armé d'un fusil comme on n'en fait plus, semble lui aussi surgir du passé.

"Is the land filled on the other side of the big river?" demanded the old man solemnly and without appearing to hearken to the other's question; "or why do I see a sight I had never thought to behold again?"

"Why, there is country left, it is true, for such as have money and are not particular in the choice," returned the emigrant; "but to my taste, it is getting crowdy. What may a man call the distance from this place to the nighest point on the main river?"

"A hunted deer could not cool his sides in the Mississippi without traveling a weary five hundred miles."

"And what may you name the district hereaway?"

"By what name," returned the old man, pointing significantly upwards, "would you call the spot where you see yonder cloud?"

The emigrant looked at the other like one who did not comprehend his meaning and who half suspected he was trifled with; but he contented himself by saying. "You are but a new inhabitant, like myself, I reckon, stranger, or otherwise you would not be backward in helping a traveler to some advice; words cost but little, and sometimes lead to friendships."

"Advice is not a gift, but a debt that the old owe to the young. What would you wish to know?"

"Where I may camp for the night. I'm no great difficulty maker as to bed and board; but all old journeyers like myself know the virtue of sweet water and a good browse for the cattle."

"Come, then, with me, and you shall be master of both; and little more is it that I can offer on this hungry prairie."

As the old man was speaking, he raised his heavy rifle to his shoulder with a facility a little remarkable for his years and appearance, and without further words led the way over the acclivity to the adjacent bottom.

CHAPITRE 7

Le campement d'Ishmael Bush ne tarde pas à être attaqué par les Sioux. Privés de leurs chevaux, les voyageurs se retrouvent dans une situation peu enviable.

[...] Ishmael and his sons, together with the forbidding-looking brother of his wife, were all speedily afoot; and then, as the sun began to shed his light on the place, they became gradually apprised of the extent of their loss.

Ishmael looked round upon the motionless and heavily loaded vehicles with his teeth firmly compressed, cast a glance at the amazed and helpless group of children, which clustered around their sullen but desponding mother, and walked out upon the open land as if he found the air of the encampment too confined. He was followed by several of the men, who were attentive observers, watching the dark expression of his eye as the index of their own future movements. The whole proceeded in profound and moody silence to the summit of the nearest swell, whence they could command an almost boundless view of the naked plains. Here nothing was visible but a solitary buffalo, that gleaned a meager subsistence from the decaying herbage at no great distance, and the ass of the physician, who profited by his freedom to enjoy a meal richer than common.[1]

"Yonder is one of the creatures left by the villains to mock us," said Ishmael, glancing his eye towards the latter, "and that the meanest of the stock. This is a hard country to make a crop in, boys; and yet food must be found to fill many hungry mouths!"

"The rifle is better than the hoe in such a place as this," returned the eldest of his sons, kicking the hard and thirsty soil on which he stood with an air of contempt. "It is good for such as they who make their dinner better on beggars' beans than hominy.[2] A crow would shed tears if obliged by its errand to fly across the district."

"What say you, trapper?" returned the father, showing the slight impression his powerful heel had made on the compact earth and laughing with frightful ferocity. "Is this the quality of land a man would choose who never troubles the county clerk with title deeds?"

"There is richer soil in the bottoms," returned the old man calmly, "and you have passed millions of acres to get to this dreary spot, where he who loves to till the 'arth might have received bushels[3] in return for pints, and that too at the cost of no very

1. Le Dr Obed Battius vient de faire irruption dans le campement. Cet ancêtre du Pr Tournesol permet à Cooper d'introduire un élement de comédie dans l'univers très sombre des premiers chapitres.

2. Mas concassé et bouilli.

3. Des boisseaux (environ un décalitre).

grievous labor. If you have come in search of land, you have journeyed hundreds of miles too far, or as many leagues too little."

"There is then a better choice towards the other ocean?" demanded the squatter, pointing in the direction of the Pacific.

"There is, and I have seen it all," was the answer of the other, who dropped his rifle to the earth and stood leaning on its barrel like one who recalled the scenes he had witnessed with melancholy pleasure. "I have seen the waters of the two seas! On one of them was I born and raised to be a lad like yonder tumbling boy. America has grown, my men, since the days of my youth to be a country larger than I once had thought the world itself to be. Near seventy years I dwelt in York, province and state together; you've been in York, 'tis like?"[1]

"Not I—not I; I never visited the towns, but often have heard the place you speak of named. 'Tis a wide clearing there, I reckon."

"Too wide! Too wide! They scourge the very 'arth with their axes. Such hills and hunting grounds as I have seen stripped of the gifts of the Lord, without remorse or shame! I tarried till the mouths of my hounds were deafened by the blows of the chopper, and then I came west in search of quiet. It was a grievous journey that I made, a grievous toil to pass through falling timber and to breathe the thick air of smoky clearings week after week as I did! 'Tis a far country too, that state of York, from this!"

"It lies ag'in in the outer edge of old Kentuck, I reckon, though what the distance may be I never knew."

"A gull would have to fan a thousand miles of air to find the eastern sea. And yet it is no mighty reach to hunt across when shade and game are plenty! The time has been when I followed the deer in the mountains of the Delaware and Hudson and took the beaver on the streams of the upper lakes in the same season; but my eye was quick and certain at that day, and my limbs were like the legs of a moose! The dam[2] of Hector"—dropping his look kindly to the aged hound that crouched at his feet—"was then a pup, and apt to open on the game the moment she struck the scent. She gave me a deal of trouble, that slut, she did!"

1. L'Etat de New York, dont Cooper évoquait la transformation dans *The Pioneers*. Natty Bumppo y apparaissait déjà comme l'incarnation d'un ordre disparu.

2. La mère (d'un animal).

"Your hound is old, stranger, and a rap on the head would prove a mercy to the beast."

"The dog is like his master," returned the trapper without appearing to heed the brutal advice the other gave, "and will number his days when his work amongst the game is over, and not before. To my eye things seem ordered to meet each other in this creation. 'Tis not the swiftest-running deer that always throws off the hounds, nor the biggest arm that holds the truest rifle. Look around you, men; what will the Yankee choppers say when they have cut their path from the eastern to the western waters and find that a hand, which can lay the 'arth bare at a blow, has been here and swept the country in very mockery of their wickedness. They will turn on their tracks like a fox that doubles, and then the rank smell of their own footsteps will show them the madness of their waste. Howsomever, these are thoughts that are more likely to rise in him who has seen the folly of eighty seasons than to teach wisdom to men still bent on the pleasures of their kind! You have need yet of a stirring time if you think to escape the craft and hatred of the burntwood Indians. They claim to be the lawful owners of this country and seldom leave a white more than the skin he boasts of when once they get the power, as they always have the will, to do him harm."

"Old man," said Ishmael sternly, "to which people do you belong? You have the color and speech of a Christian, while it seems that your heart is with the redskins."[1]

"To me there is little difference in nations. The people I loved most are scattered as the sands of the dry riverbeds fly before the fall hurricanes, and life is too short to make use and custom with strangers, as one can do with such as he has dwelt amongst for years. Still am I a man without the cross of Indian blood; and what is due from a warrior to his nation is owing by me to the people of the States, though little need have they, with their militia and their armed boats, of help from a single arm of fourscore."

"Since you own your kin, I may ask a simple question. Where are the Siouxes who have stolen my cattle?"

"Where is the herd of buffaloes which was chased by the

1. On ne saurait mieux résumer la nature hybride — et mythique — de Natty Bumppo, figure solitaire qui n'appartient ni à la tribu indienne ni à la société des Blancs, mais qui participe de l'une et de l'autre.

panther across this plain no later than the morning of yesterday! It is as hard—"

"Friend," said Dr. Battius, who had hitherto been an attentive listener, but who now felt a sudden impulse to mingle in the discourse, "I am grieved when I find a venator, or hunter, of your experience and observation following the current of vulgar error. The animal you describe is in truth a species of the *Bos ferus* (or *Bos sylvestris*, as he has been happily called by the poets), but though of close affinity, it is altogether distinct from the common bubulus. Bison is the better word, and I would suggest the necessity of adopting it in future when you shall have occasion to allude to the species."

"Bison or buffalo, it makes but little matter. The creatur' is the same, call it by what name you will, and—"

"Pardon me, venerable venator; as classification is the very soul of the natural sciences, the animal or vegetable must of necessity be characterized by the peculiarities of its species, which is always indicated by the name—"

"Friend," said the trapper a little positively, "would the tail of a beaver make the worse dinner for calling it a mink; or could you eat of the wolf with relish because some bookish man had given it the name of venison?"

As these questions were put with no little earnestness and some spirit, there was every probability that a hot discussion would have succeeded between two men, of whom one was so purely practical and the other so much given to theory, had not Ishmael seen fit to terminate the dispute by bringing into view a subject that was much more important to his own immediate interests.

"Beavers' tails and minks' flesh may do to talk about before a maple fire and a quiet hearth," interrupted the squatter without the smallest deference to the interested feelings of the disputants, "but something more than foreign words, or words of any sort, is now needed. Tell me, trapper, where are your Siouxes skulking?"

"It would be as easy to tell you the colors of the hawk that is floating beneath yonder white cloud! When a redskin strikes his blow, he is not apt to wait until he is paid for the evil deed in lead."

"Will the beggarly savages believe they have enough when they find themselves masters of all the stock?"

"Natur' is much the same, let it be covered by what skin it may. Do you ever find your longings after riches less when you have made a good crop than before you were master of a kernel of corn? If you do, you differ from what the experience of a long life tells me is the common cravings of man."

"Speak plainly, old stranger," said the squatter, striking the butt of his rifle heavily on the earth, his dull capacity finding no pleasure in a discourse that was conducted in so obscure allusions; "I have asked a simple question, and one I know well that you can answer."

"You are right, you are right. I can answer, for I have too often seen the disposition of my kind to mistake it when evil is stirring. When the Siouxes have gathered in the beasts and have made sure that you are not upon their heels, they will be back nibbling like hungry wolves to take the bait they have left; or it may be, they'll show the temper of the great bears that are found at the falls of the Long tiver[1] and strike at once with the paw, without stopping to nose their prey."

"You have then seen the animals you mention!" exclaimed Dr. Battius, who had now been thrown out of the conversation quite as long as his impatience could well brook, and who approached the subject with his tablets ready opened as a book of reference. "Can you tell me if what you encountered was of the species *Ursus horribilis*—with the ears rounded—front arquated—eyes destitute of the remarkable supplemental lid—with six incisors, one false, and four perfect molars—"

"Trapper, go on, for we are engaged in reasonable discourse," interrupted Ishmael; "you believe we shall see more of the robbers."

"Nay—nay—I do not call them robbers, for it is the usage of their people, and what may be called the prairie law."

"I have come five hundred miles to find a place where no man can ding the words of the law in my ears," said Ishmael fiercely[2] "and I am not in a humor to stand quietly at a bar while a redskin sits in judgment. I tell you, trapper, if another Sioux is seen prowling around my camp, wherever it may be, he shall feel the contents of old Kentuck"—slapping his rifle in a manner that

1. Nom donné par les Indiens au Mississippi.

2. Ishmael Bush a eu des démêlés avec la justice ; c'est en partie pour lui échapper qu'il s'aventure dans cette contrée inhospitalière. C'est, comme l'écrit D. H. Lawrence dans une belle formule, « the pioneering brute invasion of the West, crime-tinged ».

could not be easily misconstrued—"though he wore the medal of Washington* himself. I call the man a robber who takes that which is not his own."

"The Teton, and the Pawnee, and the Konza, and men of a dozen other tribes claim to own these naked fields."

"Natur' gives them the lie in their teeth. The air, the water, and the ground are free gifts to man, and no one has the power to portion them out in parcels. Man must drink, and breathe, and walk, and therefore each has a right to his share of 'arth. Why do not the surveyors of the States set their compasses and run their lines over our heads as well as beneath our feet? Why do they not cover their shining sheepskins with big words, giving to the landholder, or perhaps he should be called airholder, so many rods of heaven, with the use of such a star for a boundary mark, and such a cloud to turn a mill?"

As the squatter uttered his wild conceit, he laughed from the very bottom of his chest, in scorn. The deriding but frightful merriment passed from the mouth of one of his ponderous sons to that of the other until it had made the circuit of the whole family.

"Come, trapper," continued Ishmael in a tone of better humour, like a man who feels that he has triumphed, "neither of us, I reckon, has ever had much to do with title deeds, or county clerks, or blazed trees; therefore we will not waste words on fooleries. You are a man that has tarried long in this clearing; and now I ask your opinion face to face, without fear or favor, if you had the lead in my business, what would you do?"

The old man hesitated and seemed to give the required advice with deep reluctance. As every eye, however, was fastened on him, and whichever way he turned his face he encountered a look riveted on the lineaments of his own working countenance, he answered in a low, melancholy tone, "I have seen too much mortal blood poured out in empty quarrels to wish ever to hear an angry rifle again. Ten weary years have I sojourned alone on these naked plains waiting for my hour, and not a blow have I struck ag'in an enemy more humanized than the grizzly bear."

"*Ursus horribilis*," muttered the doctor.

* The American government creates chiefs among the western tribes, and decorates them with silver medals bearing the impression of the different presidents. That of Washington is the most prized (note de Cooper).

The speaker paused at the sound of the other's voice, but perceiving it was no more than a sort of mental ejaculation, he continued in the same strain, "More humanized than the grizzly bear or the panther of the Rocky Mountains, unless the beaver, which is a wise and knowing animal, may be so reckoned. What would I advise? Even the female buffalo will fight for her young!"

"It never then shall be said that Ishmael Bush has less kindness for his children than the bear for her cubs!"

CHAPITRE 32

L'intrigue tortueuse du roman ne peut être résumée ici. Le chapitre 32 est consacré à l'exécution d'Abiram White, coupable d'avoir tué le fils d'Ishmael Bush. La brutalité de l'univers évoqué au début du roman trouve ici son apogée. Le criminel a été placé, la corde au cou et les bras liés, au bord d'une étroite saillie rocheuse qui domine le gouffre. Ishmael rejoint sa femme et ses fils.

[...] No questions nor explanations passed between the husband and his wife. It was only as the latter was about to withdraw among her children for the night that the former saw her taking a furtive look at the pan of his rifle. Ishmael bade his sons seek their rest, announcing his intention to look to the safety of the camp in person. When all was still, he walked out upon the prairie with a sort of sensation that he found his breathing among the tents too straitened. The night was well adapted to heighten the feelings which had been created by the events of the day.

The wind had risen with the moon, and it was occasionally sweeping over the plain in a manner that made it not difficult for the sentinel to imagine strange and unearthly sounds were mingling in the blast. Yielding to the extraordinary impulses of which he was the subject, he cast a glance around to see that all were slumbering in security, and then he strayed towards the swell of land already mentioned. Here the squatter found himself at a point that commanded a view to the east and to the west. Light fleecy clouds were driving before the moon, which was cold and watery, though there were moments when its placid rays were shed from clear-blue fields, seeming to soften objects to its own mild loveliness.

For the first time, in a life of so much wild adventure, Ishmael felt a keen sense of solitude. The naked prairies began to assume the forms of illimitable and dreary wastes, and the rushing of the wind sounded like the whisperings of the dead. It was not long before he thought a shriek was borne past him on a blast. It did not sound like a call from earth, but it swept frightfully through the upper air, mingled with the hoarse accompaniment of the wind. The teeth of the squatter were compressed, and his huge hand grasped the rifle as if it would crush the metal. Then came a lull, a fresher blast, and a cry of horror that seemed to have been uttered at the very portals of his ears. A sort of echo burst involuntarily from his own lips, as men shout under unnatural excitement, and throwing his rifle across his shoulder, he proceeded towards the rock with the strides of a giant.

It was not often that the blood of Ishmael moved at the rate with which the fluid circulates in the veins of ordinary men, but now he felt it ready to gush from every pore in his body. The animal was aroused in his most latent energies. Ever as he advanced he heard those shrieks, which sometimes seemed ringing among the clouds and sometimes passed so nigh as to appear to brush the earth. At length there came a cry in which there could be no delusion or to which the imagination could lend no horror. It appeared to fill each cranny of the air, as the visible horizon is often charged to fullness by one dazzling flash of the electric fluid. The name of God was distinctly audible, but it was awfully and blasphemously blended with sounds that may not be repeated. The squatter stopped, and for a moment he covered his ears with his hands. When he withdrew the latter, a low and husky voice at his elbow asked in smothered tones, "Ishmael, my man, heard ye nothing?"

"Hist!" returned the husband, laying a powerful arm on Esther without manifesting the smallest surprise at the unlooked-for presence of his wife. "Hist, woman! If you have the fear of heaven, be still!"

A profound silence succeeded. Though the wind rose and fell as before, its rushing was no longer mingled with those fearful cries. The sounds were imposing and solemn, but it was the solemnity and majesty of nature.

"Let us go on," said Esther; "all is hushed."

"Woman, what has brought you here?" demanded her husband, whose blood had returned into its former channels and whose thoughts had already lost a portion of their excitement.

"Ishmael, he murdered our firstborn, but it is not meet that the son of my mother should lie upon the ground like the carrion of a dog."

"Follow!" returned the squatter, again grasping his rifle and striding towards the rock. The distance was still considerable, and their approach as they drew nigh the place of execution was moderated by awe. Many minutes had passed before they reached a spot where they might distinguish the outlines of the dusky objects.

"Where have you put the body?" whispered Esther. "See, here are pick and spade, that a brother of mine may sleep in the bosom of the earth!"

The moon broke from behind a mass of clouds, and the eye of the woman was enabled to follow the finger of Ishmael. It pointed to a human form swinging in the wind beneath the ragged and shining arm of the willow. Esther bent her head and veiled her eyes from the sight. But Ishmael drew nigher and long contemplated his work in awe, though not in compunction. The leaves of the sacred book were scattered on the ground, and even a fragment of the shelf had been displaced by the kidnapper in his agony. But all was now in the stillness of death. The grim and convulsed countenance of the victim was at times brought full into the light of the moon, and again as the wind lulled the fatal rope drew a dark line across its bright disk. The squatter raised his rifle with extreme care and fired. The cord was cut, and the body came lumbering to the earth, a heavy and insensible mass.

FIN DU CHAPITRE 34

La violence de la scène précédente contraste avec la sérénité de la conclusion, consacrée à la mort paisible et digne de Natty Bumppo, au sein d'une tribu indienne amie.

[...] The trapper had remained nearly motionless for an hour. His eyes alone had occasionally opened and shut. When opened, his gaze seemed fastened on the clouds which hung around the western horizon, reflecting the bright colors and giving form and loveliness to the glorious tints of an American sunset. The hour, the calm beauty of the season, the occasion—all conspired to fill the spectators with solemn awe. Suddenly, while musing on the remarkable position in which he was placed, Middleton[1] felt the hand which he held grasp his own with incredible power, and the old man, supported on either side by his friends, rose upright to his feet. For a moment he looked about him as if to invite all in presence to listen (the lingering remnant of human frailty), and then, with a fine military elevation of the head and with a voice that might be heard in every part of that numerous assembly, he pronounced the word "Here!"

A movement so entirely unexpected, and the air of grandeur and humility which were so remarkably united in the mien of the trapper, together with the clear and uncommon force of his utterance, produced a short period of confusion in the faculties of all present. When Middleton and Hard Heart,[2] each of whom had involuntarily extended a hand to support the form of the old man, turned to him again, they found that the subject of their interest was removed forever beyond the necessity of their care. They mournfully placed the body in its seat, and Le Balafré arose to announce the termination of the scene to the tribe. The voice of the old Indian seemed a sort of echo from that invisible world to which the meek spirit of the trapper had just departed.

"A valiant, a just, and a wise warrior has gone on the path which will lead him to the blessed grounds of his people!" he said. "When the voice of the Wahcondah called him, he was ready to answer. Go, my children; remember the just chief of the palefaces, and clear your own tracks from briers!"

The grave was made beneath the shade of some noble oaks. It has been carefully watched to the present hour by the Pawnees of the Loup and is often shown to the traveler and the trader as a spot where a just white man sleeps. In due time the stone was placed at its head, with the simple inscription which the trapper had himself requested. The only liberty taken by Middleton was to add: "May no wanton hand ever disturb his remains!"

1. Jeune capitaine de cavalerie qui assiste aux derniers instants de Natty Bumppo.
2. Brave Indien qui est l'ami de Natty.

2 – Deux génies contraints

L'œuvre de Poe et celle de Hawthorne invitent à la comparaison, à la fois par ce qui les sépare et par ce qui les rapproche : très dissemblables par leurs origines (l'un était natif de Virginie, l'autre du Massachusetts) et par leurs parcours respectifs (météorique et tragique chez Poe, beaucoup moins flamboyant chez Hawthorne), les deux écrivains se rejoignent dans leur rapport ambigu à leur culture — « aristocratie » sudiste chez l'un, tradition puritaine chez l'autre —, dans leur solitude morbide, dans leur rejet de la poésie spontanée et leur conscience aiguë des contraintes formelles qui s'imposent à l'artiste, dans leur prédilection pour le conte et la nouvelle.

On ne peut comprendre la carrière littéraire de Poe et de Hawthorne sans avoir quelque idée du petit monde en marge duquel elle s'est développée. Dans le Sud comme en Nouvelle-Angleterre, les cercles littéraires sont dominés par une société patricienne (planteurs de Virginie, armateurs bostoniens) dont les modèles sont britanniques : tout d'abord Addison, Goldsmith, Sterne, puis le romantisme, particulièrement Walter Scott, qui est l'objet d'un véritable culte dans le « vieux Sud ». Un romancier comme John P. Kennedy tente dans *Swallow Barn* (1832) d'exalter le passé virginien comme Scott a exalté le passé écossais, tandis que William G. Simms évoque dans ses « *border romances* » le monde plus animé de la « frontière » du Sud-Ouest. Ainsi s'élabore le mythe du Sud nourri de fierté régionale, de conservatisme social et de pittoresque, qui fleurira après la guerre de Sécession.

Parallèlement, on voit apparaître en Nouvelle-Angleterre une tradition qui, elle aussi, se développera après 1865 : la « tradition distinguée » *(« genteel tradition »)*, faite de décorum, d'élitisme social, d'attachement au passé de la Nouvelle-Angleterre et de moralisme rigoureux. Henry Longfellow (1807-1882), professeur à Harvard, acquiert avec des récits pittoresques en forme de ballades (*Evangeline*, 1847 ; *Hiawatha*, 1855) une réputation qui n'a pas résisté à l'épreuve du temps. De même, les romans et les essais d'Oliver Wendell Holmes (1809-1894), médecin, enseignant et lettré bostonien sont bien oubliés aujourd'hui, ainsi qu'une grande partie de l'œuvre d'un autre patricien, James Russell Lowell. Il faut cependant faire une exception, dans la production de ce dernier, pour *A Fable for Critics*, satire alerte des milieux littéraires, et *The Biglow Papers* (1846), série de lettres écrites dans le patois de la Nouvelle-Angleterre. L'historien Francis Parkman écrit, de son côté, un récit de voyage qui restera un classique, *The Oregon Trail* (1849).

EDGAR ALLAN POE, 1809-1849

La critique américaine a souvent réagi avec quelque perplexité à l'enthousiasme du public français pour « Edgarpo » : la réputation de Poe dans notre pays — due, en partie du moins, au zèle de Baudelaire et Mallarmé, qui ont été les premiers à le traduire — contraste en effet avec l'obscurité dans laquelle il est longtemps resté aux Etats-Unis.

Sa carrière est brève et tragique. Fils d'acteurs itinérants, orphelin à l'âge de deux ans, il est recueilli par un couple de riches commerçants de Virginie, qui l'inscrivent dans d'excellentes institutions anglaises. Son comportement pendant ses études à l'Université de Virginie (il joue et s'endette) amène son tuteur à lui couper les vivres. Nous sommes en 1826, et Poe a dix-sept ans. Tout en composant ses premiers poèmes, publiés à compte d'auteur en 1827, le jeune homme cherche un moyen de subsistance. Après un bref séjour dans l'armée, il est renvoyé de West Point en 1831 et passe quelques années dans le plus grand dénuement à Baltimore, chez sa tante, dont il épouse en 1836 la fille Virginia, âgée de quatorze ans. Celle-ci mourra de tuberculose en 1847.

L'insuccès des trois volumes de poèmes publiés de 1827 à 1831 amène Poe à écrire pour diverses revues ; hormis ses premiers contes, il rédige ainsi des articles littéraires qui révèlent — outre une verve parfois féroce — un jugement très sûr, fondé sur une conception exigeante de son art. En 1846, il présente dans un essai théorique, « The Philosophy of Composition », sa théorie de la beauté et son refus de l'inspiration chère aux romantiques, insistant en revanche sur la recherche patiente et systématique de l'effet.

Parallèlement à ces essais critiques, Poe publie un nouveau volume de poèmes (*« The Raven » and Other Poems*, 1845), *The Narrative of Arthur Gordon Pym* (1838), récit fantastique dont le début, très réaliste, trompera nombre de lecteurs, et deux volumes de contes (*Tales of the Grotesque and Arabesque*, 1840) suivis d'un troisième volume en 1845 (*Tales*). La plupart de ces contes ont déjà été publiés dans divers périodiques. La dernière œuvre publiée du vivant de Poe, *Eureka, A Prose Poem* (1848), est une sorte de testament philosophique.

Il a fallu toute la patience des biographes et des critiques pour faire un sort aux mythes répandus à propos de Poe à la fois par ses ennemis, comme Rufus Griswold, chargé bien naïvement par l'auteur d'éditer ses ouvrages (Griswold alla jusqu'à réécrire certaines lettres, fit croire à l'opiomanie de Poe, le présenta comme un monstre prêt aux pires infamies) et par ses disciples ou thuriféraires comme Charles Baudelaire, largement responsable du mythe du poète maudit. Mais Poe lui-même, par sa mythomanie, avait en quelque sorte montré le chemin, et il a fallu près d'un siècle pour que la critique suive à son propos le conseil de D. H. Lawrence : « Never trust the artist. Trust the tale. The proper function of a critic is to save the tale from the artist who created it » (*Studies in Classic American Literature,* chap. 1).

BIBLIOGRAPHIE SÉLECTIVE. — The Collected Works of Edgar Allan Poe, ed. T. O. Mabbott *et al.* (3 vol. parus), Cambridge, Mass., Harvard UP, 1969 ; *Poetry and Tales, Essays and Reviews,* New York, Library of America, 1984 ; *Contes, Essais, Poèmes* (traductions), éd. Claude Richard, Paris, Laffont, 1989 ; Cabau (Jacques), *Edgar Poe par lui-même,* Paris, Seuil, 1960 ; Dayan (Joan), *Fables of Mind : an Inquiry into Poe's Fiction,* New York, Oxford UP, 1987 ; Halliburton (David), *Edgar Allan Poe, a Phenomenological View,* Princeton UP, 1973 ; Hoffman (Daniel), Poe Poe Poe Poe Poe Poe Poe, Garden City, NY, Doubleday, 1972 ; Pinto (Evelyne), *Edgar Poe ou l'art d'inventer,* Paris, Klincksieck, 1983 ; Richard (Claude), *Configuration critique d'Edgar Poe,* Paris, Minard, 1969 ; *Edgar Poe, journaliste et critique,* Paris, Klincksieck, 1978. Voir également les n°s 1 et 12 de la revue *Delta* (Montpellier).

Poems

TO ONE IN PARADISE[1]

Ah, dream too bright to last!
   Ah, starry Hope! that didst arise
But to be overcast!
   A voice from out the Future cries,
"On! on!"—but o'er the Past
   (Dim gulf!) my spirit hovering lies
Mute, motionless, aghast!

For, alas! alas! with me
   The light of Life is o'er!
No more—no more—no more—
   (Such language holds the solemn sea
To the sands upon the shore)
   Shall bloom the thunder-blasted tree,
Or the stricken eagle soar!

1. Ce poème inspiré de Byron fut publié en janvier 1834 dans le *Godey's Lady's Book,* et inclus dans le recueil *The Raven and Other Poems*, 1845.

And all my days are trances,
  And all my nightly dreams
Are where thy grey eyes glances,
  And where thy footstep gleams—
In what ethereal dances,
  By what eternal streams.

Thou wast that all to me, love,
  For which my soul did pine—
A green isle in the sea, love,[1]
  A fountain and a shrine,
All wreathed with fairy fruits and flowers,
  And all the flowers were mine.

ANNABEL LEE[2]

It was many and many a year ago,
    In a kingdom by the sea,
That a maiden there lived whom you may know
    By the name of Annabel Lee;—
And this maiden she lived with no other thought
    Than to love and be loved by me.

She was a child and *I* was a child,
    In this kingdom by the sea,[3]
But we loved with a love that was more than love—
    I and my Annabel Lee—
With a love that the wingéd seraphs of Heaven
    Coveted her and me.

1. Baudelaire, premier traducteur de Poe, chantera « le vert paradis des amours enfantines ». L'image de l'île verte est déjà chez Byron et Shelley un symbole d'amour juvénile : bel exemple d'intertextualité, de la manière dont certaines métaphores ont pu « drageonner » d'une littérature nationale à une autre.

2. Publié dans la *Daily Tribune* le 9 octobre 1849, soit deux jours après la mort de Poe, « Annabel Lee » est un peu son testament poétique : il est entièrement conforme à sa conception de la poésie comme ensemble d'échos (allitérations et rimes) dont l'agencement traduit l'harmonie du monde.

3. On retrouve ici le thème des amours enfantines, associé à la mort et au regret.

And this was the reason that, long ago,
In this kingdom by the sea,
A wind blew out of a cloud by night
Chilling my Annabel Lee;
So that her highborn kinsmen came
And bore her away from me,
To shut her up in a sepulchre
In this kingdom by the sea.

The angels, not half so happy in Heaven,
Went envying her and me:—
Yes! that was the reason (as all men know,
In this kingdom by the sea)
That the wind came out of a cloud, chilling
And killing my Annabel Lee.

But our love it was stronger by far than the love
Of those who were older than we—
Of many far wiser than we—
And neither the angels in Heaven above
Nor the demons down under the sea,
Can ever dissever my soul from the soul
Of the beautiful Annabel Lee:—

For the moon never beams without bringing me dreams
Of the beautiful Annabel Lee;
And the stars never rise but I see the bright eyes
Of the beautiful Annabel Lee;
And so, all the night-tide, I lie down by the side
Of my darling, my darling, my life and my bride,
In her sepulchre there by the sea—
In her tomb by the side of the sea.

Contes

THE BLACK CAT[1]

For the most wild yet most homely narrative which I am about to pen, I neither expect nor solicit belief. Mad indeed would I be to expect it, in a case where my very senses reject their own evidence. Yet, mad am I not—and very surely do I not dream. But to-morrow I die, and to-day I would unburthen my soul. My immediate purpose is to place before the world, plainly, succinctly, and without comment, a series of mere household events. In their consequences, these events have terrified—have tortured—have destroyed me. Yet I will not attempt to expound them. To me, they have presented little but horror—to many they will seem less terrible than *baroques*. Hereafter, perhaps, some intellect may be found which will reduce my phantasm to the commonplace—some intellect more calm, more logical, and far less excitable than my own, which will perceive, in the circumstances I detail with awe, nothing more than an ordinary succession of very natural causes and effects.[2]

From my infancy I was noted for the docility and humanity of my disposition. My tenderness of heart was even so conspicuous as to make me the jest of my companions. I was especially fond of animals, and was indulged by my parents with a great variety of pets. With these I spent most of my time, and never was so happy as when feeding and caressing them. This peculiarity of character grew with my growth, and, in my manhood, I derived from it one of my principal sources of pleasure. To those who have cherished an affection for a faithful and sagacious dog, I need hardly be at the trouble of explaining the nature or the intensity of the gratification thus derivable. There is something in the unselfish and self-sacrificing love of a brute, which goes directly to the heart of

1. Paru dans le *United States Saturday Post,* journal de Philadelphie, le 19 août 1843, et inclus dans *Tales,* 1845.

2. On distingue généralement entre les contes fantastiques et les récits dits de « ratiocination » (qui prennent souvent la forme d'une enquête policière, comme « The Murders in the Rue Morgue », « The Mystery of Marie Roget » ou « The Purloined Letter »). Cette invitation à une lecture rationnelle, au seuil d'un conte fantastique, montre que les choses sont plus complexes : le rationnel et l'irrationnel peuvent se disputer le lecteur, et cette concurrence peut créer une tension propice à l'intérêt dramatique.

him who has had frequent occasion to test the paltry friendship and gossamer fidelity[1] of mere *Man*.

I married early, and was happy to find in my wife a disposition not uncongenial with my own. Observing my partiality for domestic pets, she lost no opportunity of procuring those of the most agreeable kind. We had birds, gold-fish, a fine dog, rabbits, a small monkey, and a *cat*.

This latter was a remarkably large and beautiful animal, entirely black, and sagacious to an astonishing degree. In speaking of his intelligence, my wife, who at heart was not a little tinctured with superstition, made frequent allusions to the ancient popular notion, which regarded all black cats as witches in disguise. Not that she was ever *serious* upon this point—and I mention the matter at all for no better reason than that it happens, just now, to be remembered.

Pluto—this was the cat's name[2]—was my favorite pet and playmate. I alone fed him, and he attended me wherever I went about the house. It was even with difficulty that I could prevent him from following me throught the streets.

Our friendship lasted, in this manner, for several years, during which my general temperament and character—through the instrumentality of the Fiend Intemperance[3]—had (I blush to confess it) experienced a radical alteration for the worse. I grew, day by day, more moody, more irritable, more regardless of the feelings of others. I suffered myself to use intemperate language to my wife. At length, I even offered her personal violence. My pets, of course, were made to feel the change in my disposition. I not only neglected, but ill-used them. For Pluto, however, I still retained sufficient regard to restrain me from maltreating him, as I made no scruple of maltreating the rabbits, the monkey, or even the dog, when, by accident, or through affection, they came in my way. But my disease grew upon me—for what disease is like Alcohol!—and at length even Pluto, who was now becoming old, and consequently somewhat peevish—even Pluto began to experience the effects of my ill temper.

1. Cette image suggère soit une toile d'araignée (= fils de la vierge), soit une gaze très fragile.

2. Le nom du chat, Pluton, suggère bien entendu l'émergence d'une figure infernale ; mais ne lui a-t-il pas été donné par son maître, et ne traduit-il pas la *vision* que celui-ci a de lui ?

3. Mot désignant, au XIXe siècle, une consommation excessive d'alcool. Le fait que Poe ait été, lui aussi, alcoolique ne nous autorise pas à assimiler le narrateur à l'auteur.

One night, returning home, much intoxicated, from one of my haunts about town, I fancied that the cat avoided my presence. I seized him; when, in his fright at my violence, he inflicted a slight wound upon my hand with his teeth. The fury of a demon instantly possessed me. I knew myself no longer. My original soul seemed, at once, to take its flight from my body; and a more than fiendish malevolence, gin-nurtured, thrilled every fibre of my frame. I took from my waistcoat-pocket a penknife, opened it, grasped the poor beast by the throat, and deliberately cut one of its eyes from the socket! I blush, I burn, I shudder, while I pen the damnable atrocity.

When reason returned with the morning—when I had slept off the fumes of the night's debauch—I experienced a sentiment half of horror, half of remorse, for the crime of which I had been guilty; but it was, at best, a feeble and equivocal feeling, and the soul remained untouched. I again plunged into excess, and soon drowned in wine all memory of the deed.

In the meantime the cat slowly recovered. The socket of the lost eye presented, it is true, a frightful appearance, but he no longer appeared to suffer any pain. He went about the house as usual, but, as might be expected, fled in extreme terror at my approach. I had so much of my old heart left, as to be at first grieved by this evident dislike on the part of a creature which had once so loved me. But this feeling soon gave place to irritation. And then came, as if to my final and irrevocable overthrow, the spirit of PERVERSENESS.[1] Of this spirit philosophy takes no account. Yet I am not more sure that my soul lives, than I am that perverseness is one of the primitive impulses of the human heart—one of the indivisible primary faculties, or sentiments, which give direction to the character of Man. Who has not, a hundred times, found himself committing a vile or a silly action, for no other reason than because he knows he should *not?* Have we not a perpetual inclination, in the teeth of our best judgment, to violate that which is *Law*, merely because we understand it to be such? This spirit of perverseness, I say, came to my final overthrow. It was this unfathomable longing of the soul to *vex itself*—to offer violence to its own nature—to do wrong for the wrong's sake only—that

1. Mot complexe, qui suggère la méchanceté, l'entêtement et le caprice. Voir le conte intitulé « The Imp of the Perverse ».

urged me to continue and finally to consummate the injury I had inflicted upon the unoffending brute. One morning, in cool blood, I slipped a noose about its neck and hung it to the limb of a tree—hung it with the tears streaming from my eyes, and with the bitterest remorse at my heart—hung it *because* I knew that it had loved me, and *because* I felt it had given me no reason of offence;—hung it *because* I knew that in so doing I was committing a sin—a deadly sin that would so jeopardize my immortal soul as to place it—if such a thing were possible—even beyond the reach of the infinite mercy of the Most Merciful and Most Terrible God.

On the night of the day on which this cruel deed was done, I was aroused from sleep by the cry of fire. The curtains of my bed were in flames. The whole house was blazing. It was with great difficulty that my wife, a servant, and myself, made our escape from the conflagration. The destruction was complete. My entire worldly wealth was swallowed up, and I resigned myself thenceforward to despair.

I am above the weakness of seeking to establish a sequence of cause and effect, between the disaster and the atrocity. But I am detailing a chain of facts—and wish not to leave even a possible link imperfect. On the day succeeding the fire, I visited the ruins. The walls, with one exception, had fallen in. This exception was found in a compartment wall, not very thick, which stood about the middle of the house, and against which has rested the head of my bed. The plastering had here, in great measure, resisted the action of the fire—a fact which I attributed to its having been recently spread. About this wall a dense crowd were collected, and many persons seemed to be examining a particular portion of it with very minute and eager attention. The words "strangel!" "singular!" and other similar expressions, excited my curiosity. I approached and saw, as if graven in *bas-relief* upon the white surface, the figure of a gigantic *cat*. The impression was given with an accuracy truly marvellous. There was a rope about the animal's neck.

When I first beheld this apparition—for I could scarcely regard it as less—my wonder and my terror were extreme. But at length reflection came to my aid. The cat, I remembered, had been hung in a garden adjacent to the house. Upon the alarm of fire, this garden had been immediately filled by the crowd—by some one of whom the animal must have been cut from the tree and thrown, through an open window, into my chamber. This had probably been done with the view of arousing me from sleep. The falling of other walls had compressed the victim of my cruelty into the substance of the freshly-spread plaster; the lime of which, with the flames, and the *ammonia* from the carcass, had then accomplished the portraiture as I saw it.

Although I thus readily accounted to my reason, if not altogether to my conscience, for the startling fact just detailed, it did not the less fail to make a deep impression upon my fancy. For months I could not rid myself of the phantasm[1] of the cat; and, during this period, there came back into my spirit a half-sentiment that seemed, but was not, remorse. I went so far as to regret the loss of the animal, and to look about me, among the vile haunts which I now habitually frequented, for another pet of the same species, and of somewhat similar appearance, with which to supply its place.

One night as I sat, half stupefied, in a den of more than infamy, my attention was suddenly drawn to some black object, reposing upon the head of one of the immense hogsheads of Gin, or of Rum, which constituted the chief furniture of the apartment. I had been looking steadily at the top of this hogshead for some minutes, and what now caused me surprise was the fact that I had not sooner perceived the object thereupon. I approached it, and touched it with my hand. It was a black cat—a very large one—fully as large as Pluto, and closely resembling him in every respect but one. Pluto had not a white hair upon any portion of his body; but this cat had a large, although indefinite splotch of white, covering nearly the whole region of the breast.

Upon my touching him, he immediately arose, purred loudly, rubbed against my hand, and appeared delighted with my notice. This, then, was the very creature of which I was in search. I at once offered to purchase it of the landlord; but this person made no claim to it—knew nothing of it—had never seen it before.

I continued my caresses, and when I prepared to go home, the animal evinced a disposition to accompany me. I permitted it to do so; occasionally stooping and patting it as I proceeded. When it

1. Baudelaire traduit par « fantôme », mais le terme « *phantasm* » suggère, comme le français « fantasme », une hallucination — en dépit du paragraphe qui précède, consacré à une « succession ordinaire de causes et d'effets ».

reached the house it domesticated itself at once, and became immediately a great favorite with my wife.

For my own part, I soon found dislike to it arising within me. This was just the reverse of what I had anticipated; but—I know not how or why it was—its evident fondness for myself rather disgusted and annoyed. By slow degrees these feelings of disgust and annoyance rose into the bitterness of hatred. I avoided the creature; a certain sense of shame, and the remembrance of my former deed of cruelty, prevented me from physically abusing it. I did not, for some weeks, strike, or otherwise violently ill use it; but gradually—very gradually—I came to look upon it with unutterable loathing, and to flee silently from its odious presence, as from the breath of a pestilence.

What added, no doubt, to my hatred of the beast, was the discovery, on the morning after I brought it home, that, like Pluto, it also had been deprived of one of its eyes. This circumstance, however, only endeared it to my wife, who, as I have already said, possessed, in a high degree, that humanity of feeling which had once been my distinguishing trait, and the source of many of my simplest and purest pleasures.

With my aversion to this cat, however, its partiality for myself seemed to increase. It followed my footsteps with a pertinacity which it would be difficult to make the reader comprehend. Wherever I sat, it would crouch beneath my chair, or spring upon my knees, covering me with its loathsomes caresses. If I arose to walk it would get between my feet and thus nearly throw me down, or, fastening its long and sharp claws in my dress, clamber, in this manner, to my breast. At such times, although I longed to destroy it with a blow, I was yet withheld from so doing, partly by a memory of my former crime, but chiefly—let me confess it at once—by absolute *dread* of the beast.

This dread was not exactly a dread of physical evil—and yet I should be at a loss how otherwise to define it. I am almost ashamed to own—yes, even, in this felon's cell, I am almost ashamed to own—that the terror and horror with which the animal inspired me, had been heightened by one of the merest chimeras it would be possible to conceive. My wife had called my attention, more than once, to the character of the mark of white hair, of which I have spoken, and which constituted the sole visible difference between the strange beast and the one I had destroyed. The reader will remember that this mark, although large, had been originally very indefinite; but, by slow degrees—degrees nearly imperceptible, and which for a long time my reason struggled to reject as fanciful—it had, at length, assumed a rigorous distinctness of outline. It was now the representation of an object that I shudder to name—and for this, above all, I loathed, and dreaded, and would have rid myself of the monster *had I dared*—it was now, I say, the image of a hideous—of a ghastly thing—of the GALLOWS!—oh, mournful and terrible engine of Horror and of Crime—of Agony and of Death!

And now I was indeed wretched beyond the wretchedness of mere Humanity. And *a brute beast*—whose fellow I had contemptuously destroyed—*a brute beast* to work out for *me*—for me, a man fashioned in the image of the High God[1]—so much of insufferable wo! Alas! neither by day nor by night knew I the blessing of Rest any more! During the former the creature left me no moment alone, and in the latter I started hourly from dreams of unutterable fear to find the hot breath of *the thing* upon my face, and its vast weight—an incarnate Night-Mare[2] that I had no power to shake off—incumbent eternally upon my *heart!*

Beneath the pressure of torments such as these feeble remnant of the good within me succumbed. Evil thoughts became my sole intimates—the darkest and most evil of thoughts. The moodiness of my usual temper increased to hatred of all things and of all mankind; while from the sudden, frequent, and ungovernable outbursts of a fury to which I now blindly abandoned myself, my uncomplaining wife, alas! was the most usual and the most patient of sufferers.

One day she accompanied me, upon some household errand, into the cellar of the old building which our poverty compelled us to inhabit. The cat followed me down the steep stairs, and, nearly throwing me headlong, exasperated me to madness. Uplifting an axe, and forgetting in my wrath the childish dread which had hitherto stayed my hand, I aimed a blow at the animal, which, of course, would have proved instantly fatal had it descended as I wished. But this blow was arrested by the hand of my wife. Goaded by the interference into a rage more than demoniacal, I withdrew

1. Citation de la Genèse, I, 27.

2. La graphie du mot lui restitue son sens étymologique — l'incube de la nuit. Voir le célèbre tableau de Füssli, *Le Cauchemar* (1781).

my arm from her grasp and buried the axe in her brain. She fell dead upon the spot without a groan.

This hideous murder accomplished, I set myself forthwith, and with entire deliberation, to the task of concealing the body. I knew that I could not remove it from the house, either by day or night, without the risk of being observed by the neighbors. Many projects entered my mind. At one period I thought of cutting the corpse into minute fragments, and destroying them by fire. At another, I resolved to dig a grave for it in the floor of the cellar. Again, I deliberated about casting it in the well in the yard—about packing it in a box, as if merchandise, with the usual arrangements, and so getting a porter to take it from the house. Finally I hit upon what I considered a far better expedient than either of these. I determined to wall it up in the cellar—as the monks of the Middle Ages are recorded to have walled up their victims.

For a purpose such as this the cellar was well adapted. Its walls were loosely constructed, and had lately been plastered throughout with a rough plaster, which the dampness of the atmosphere had prevented from hardening. Moreover, in one of the walls was a projection, caused by a false chimney, or fire-place, that had been filled up and made to resemble the rest of the cellar. I made no doubt that I could readily displace the bricks at this point, insert the corpse, and wall the whole up as before, so that no eye could detect any thing suspicious.

And in this calculation I was not deceived. By means of a crow-bar I easily dislodged the bricks, and, having carefully deposited the body against the inner wall, I propped it in that position, while with little trouble I relaid the whole structure as it originally stood. Having procured mortar, sand, and hair, with every possible precaution, I prepared a plaster which could not be distinguished from the old, and with this I very carefully went over the new brick-work. When I had finished, I felt satisfied that all was right. The wall did not present the slightest appearance of having been disturbed. The rubbish on the floor was picked up with the minutest care. I looked around triumphantly, and said to myself—"Here at least, then, my labor has not been in vain."

My next step was to look for the beast which had been the cause of so much wickedness; for I had, at length, firmly resolved to put it to death. Had I been able to meet with it at the moment, there could have been no doubt of its fate; but it appeared that the crafty animal had been alarmed at the violence of my previous anger, and forebore to present itself in my present mood. It is impossible to describe or to imagine the deep, the blissful sense of relief which the absence of the detested creature occasioned in my bosom. It did not make its appearance during the night—and thus for one night, at least, since its introduction into the house, I soundly and tranquilly slept; aye, *slept* even with the burden of murder upon my soul.

The second and the third day passed, and still my tormentor came not. Once again I breathed as a free man. The monster, in terror, had fled the premises for ever! I should behold it no more! My happiness was supreme! The guilt of my dark deed disturbed me but little. Some few inquiries had been made, but these had been readily answered. Even a search had been instituted—but of course nothing was to be discovered. I looked upon my future felicity as secured.

Upon the fourth day of the assassination, a party of the police came, very unexpectedly, into the house, and proceeded again to make rigorous investigation of the premises. Secure, however, in the inscrutability of my place of concealment, I felt no embarrassment whatever. The officers bade me accompany them in their search. They left no nook or corner unexplored. At length, for the third of fourth time, they descended into the cellar. I quivered not in a muscle. My heart beat calmly as that of one who slumbers in innocence. I walked the cellar from end to end. I folded my arms upon my bosom, and roamed easily to and fro. The police were thoroughly satisfied and prepared to depart. The glee at my heart was too strong to be restrained. I burned to say if but one word, by way of triumph, and to render doubly sure their assurance of my guiltlessness.

"Gentlemen," I said at last, as the party ascended the steps, "I delight to have allayed your suspicions. I wish you all health and a little more courtesy. By the bye, gentlemen, this—this is a very well-constructed house," (in the rabid desire to say something easily, I scarcely knew what I uttered at all),—"I may say an *excellently* well-constructed house. These walls—are you going, gentlemen?—these walls are solidly put together"; and here, through the mere frenzy of bravado, I rapped heavily with a cane which I held in my hand, upon that very portion of the brickwork behind which stood the corpse of the wife of my bosom.

But may God shield and deliver me from the fangs of the Arch-Fiend![1] No sooner had the reverberation of my blows sunk into silence, than I was answered by a voice from within the tomb!—by a cry, at first muffled and broken, like the sobbing of a child, and then quickly swelling into one long, loud and continuous scream, utterly anomalous and inhuman—a howl—a wailing shriek, half of horror and half of triumph, such as might have arisen only out of hell, conjointly from the throats of the damned in their agony and of the demons that exult in the damnation.

Of my own thoughts it is folly to speak. Swooning, I staggered to the opposite wall. For one instant the party on the stairs remained motionless through extremity of terror and awe. In the next a dozen stout arms were toiling at the wall. It fell bodily. The corpse, already greatly decayed and clotted with gore, stood erect before the eyes of the spectators. Upon its head, with red extended mouth and solitary eye of fire, sat the hideous beast whose craft had seduced me into murder,[2] and whose informing voice had consigned me to the hangman. I had walled the monster up within the tomb.

The Narrative of Arthur Gordon Pym of Nantucket[3]

CHAPITRE X

Le narrateur et ses deux amis, Augustus et Peters, sont venus à bout des mutins qui avaient pris possession du brick le Grampus *et les ont tous exterminés, à l'exception d'un seul, Parker ; mais le bateau, fort endommagé par une terrible tempête, prend l'eau, et les trois hommes sont en proie à la faim et à la soif.*

Shortly afterward an incident occurred which I am induced to look upon as more intensely productive of emotion, as far more

1. Le mot « *fangs* » (griffes) rappelle la morsure du chat au début du conte.

2. « *Craft* » suggère « *witchcraft* », et « *seduce* » invite à voir dans le chat une figure diabolique; mais cette phrase peut légitimer une lecture fantastique, ou invalider cette lecture, selon qu'on croit le narrateur possédé, ou simplement dément.

3. Ce récit fut publié par *Harper* en 1838. Les trois premiers chapitres avaient paru en feuilleton dans le *Southern Literary Messenger* l'année précédente. Harper parvint à faire croire à certains critiques qu'il s'agissait d'un témoignage authentique.

replete with the extremes first of delight and then of horror, than even any of the thousand chances which afterward befell me in nine long years, crowded with events of the most startling and, in many cases, of the most unconceived and unconceivable character. We were lying on the deck near the companion-way,[1] and debating the possibility of yet making our way into the storeroom, when, looking toward Augustus, who lay fronting myself, I perceived that he had become all at once deadly pale, and that his lips were quivering in the most singular and unaccountable manner. Greatly alarmed, I spoke to him, but he made me no reply, and I was beginning to think that he was suddenly taken ill, when I took notice of his eyes, which were glaring apparently at some object behind me. I turned my head, and shall never forget the ecstatic joy which thrilled through every particle of my frame, when I perceived a large brig bearing down upon us, and not more than a couple of miles off. I sprung to my feet as if a musket bullet had suddenly struck me to the heart; and, stretching out my arms in the direction of the vessel, stood in this manner, motionless, and unable to articulate a syllable. Peters and Parker were equally affected, although in different ways. The former danced about the deck like a madman, uttering the most extravagant rhodomontades, intermingled with howls and imprecations, while the latter burst into tears, and continued for many minutes weeping like a child.

The vessel in sight was a large hermaphrodite brig,[2] of a Dutch build, and painted black, with a tawdry gilt figure-head. She had evidently seen a good deal of rough weather, and, we supposed, had suffered much in the gale which had proved so disastrous to ourselves; for her foretopmast[3] was gone, and some of her starboard bulwarks.[4] When we first saw her, she was, as I have already said, about two miles off and to windward, bearing down upon us. The breeze was very gentle, and what astonished us chiefly was, that she had no other sails set than her foremast and mainsail, with a flying jib[5]—of course she came down but slowly, and our impatience amounted nearly to phrensy. The awkward

1. Echelle reliant les cabines au pont.
2. Brick-goëlette.
3. Mât de misaine.
4. Mur de tribord.
5. Foc, voile triangulaire à l'avant du navire.

manner in which she steered, too, was remarked by all of us, even excited as we were. She yawed about[1] so considerably, that once or twice we thought it impossible she could see us, or imagined that, having seen us, and discovered no person on board, she was about to tack[2] and make off in another direction. Upon each of these occasions we screamed and shouted at the top of our voices, when the stranger would appear to change for a moment her intention, and again hold on toward us—this singular conduct being repeated two or three times, so that at last we could think of no other manner of accounting for it than by supposing the helmsman to be in liquor.

No person was seen upon her decks until she arrived within about a quarter of a mile of us. We then saw three seamen, whom by their dress we took to be Hollanders. Two of these were lying on some old sails near the forecastle,[3] and the third, who appeared to be looking at us with great curiosity, was leaning over the starboard bow near the bowsprit.[4] This last was a stout and tall man, with a very dark skin. He seemed by his manner to be encouraging us to have patience, nodding to us in a cheerful although rather odd way, and smiling constantly, so as to display a set of the most brilliantly white teeth. As his vessel drew nearer, we saw a red flannel cap which he had on fall from his head into the water; but of this he took little or no notice, continuing his odd smiles and gesticulations. I relate these things and circumstances minutely, and I relate them, it must be understood, precisely as they *appeared* to us.[5]

The brig came on slowly, and now more steadily than before, and—I cannot speak calmly of this event—our hearts leaped up wildly within us, and we poured out our whole souls in shouts and thanksgiving to God for the complete, unexpected, and glorious deliverance that was so palpably at hand. Of a sudden, and all at once, there came wafted over the ocean from the strange vessel (which was now close upon us) a smell, a stench, such as the whole world has no name for—no conception of—hellish—utterly

1. Faire des embardées.
2. Virer de bord.
3. Gaillard d'avant, partie antérieure du pont.
4. Beaupré, mât oblique placé à l'avant du navire.
5. Cette intervention du narrateur, ajoutée aux multiples précisions topographiques, crée un effet de réel qui contribue à authentifier le récit et à réduire les éventuelles réticences du lecteur. Le choc du paragraphe suivant n'en sera que plus violent.

suffocating—insufferable, inconceivable. I gasped for breath, and turning to my companions, perceived that they were paler than marble. But we had now no time left for question or surmise—the brig was within fifty feet of us, and it seemed to be her intention to run under our counter, that we might board her without putting out a boat. We rushed aft, when, suddenly, a wide yaw threw her off full five or six points from the course she had been running, and, as she passed under our stern at the distance of about twenty feet, we had a full view of her decks. Shall I ever forget the triple horror of that spectacle? Twenty-five or thirty human bodies, among whom were several females, lay scattered about between the counter and the galley[1] in the last and most loathsome state of putrefaction. We plainly saw that not a soul lived in that fated vessel! Yet we could not help shouting to the dead for help! Yes, long and loudly did we beg, in the agony of the moment, that those silent and disgusting images would stay for us, would not abandon us to become like them, would receive us among their goodly company! We were raving with horror and despair—thoroughly mad through the anguish of our grievous disappointment.

As our first loud yell of terror broke forth, it was replied to by something, from near the bowsprit of the stranger, so closely resembling the scream of a human voice that the nicest ear might have been startled and deceived. At this instant another sudden yaw brought the region of the forecastle for a moment into view, and we beheld at once the origin of the sound. We saw the tall stout figure still leaning on the bulwark, and still nodding his head to and fro, but his face was now turned from us so that we could not behold it. His arms were extended over the rail,[2] and the palms of his hands fell outward. His knees were lodged upon a stout rope, tightly stretched, and reaching from the heel of the bowsprit to a cathead.[3] On his back, from which a portion of the shirt had been torn, leaving it bare, there sat a huge sea-gull, busily gorging itself with the horrible flesh, its bill and talons deep buried, and its white plumage spattered all over with blood. As the brig moved farther round so as to bring us close in view, the bird, with much apparent difficulty, drew out its crimsoned head, and, after eyeing us for a

1. Entre l'arrière et la cuisine.
2. La lisse, assemblage de barres de bois horizontales servant de garde-fou.
3. Un bossoir, grosse pièce saillante placée à l'avant et servant à la manœuvre d'une ancre.

moment as if stupefied, arose lazily from the body upon which it had been feasting, and, flying directly above our deck, hovered there a while with a portion of clotted and liverlike substance in its beak. The horrid morsel dropped at length with a sullen splash immediately at the feet of Parker. May God forgive me, but now, for the first time, there flashed through my mind a thought, a thought which I will not mention, and I felt myself making a step toward the ensanguined spot. I looked upward, and the eyes of Augustus met my own with a degree of intense and eager meaning which immediately brought me to my senses. I sprang forward quickly, and, with a deep shudder, threw the frightful thing into the sea.

The body from which it had been taken, resting as it did upon the rope, had been easily swayed to and fro by the exertions of the carnivorous bird, and it was this motion which had at first impressed us with the belief of its being alive. As the gull relieved it of its weight, it swung round and fell partially over, so that the face was fully discovered. Never, surely, was any object so terribly full of awe! The eyes were gone, and the whole flesh around the mouth, leaving the teeth utterly naked. This, then, was the smile which had cheered us on to hope! this the—but I forbear. The brig, as I have already told, passed under our stern, and made its way slowly but steadily to leeward. With her and with her terrible crew went all our gay visions of deliverance and joy. Deliberately as she went by, we might possibly have found means of boarding her, had not our sudden disappointment, and the appalling nature of the discovery which accompanied it, laid entirely prostrate every active faculty of mind and body. We had seen and felt, but we could neither think nor act, until, alas! too late. How much our intellects had been weakened by this incident may be estimated by the fact, that when the vessel had proceeded so far that we could perceive no more than the half of her hull, the proposition was seriously entertained of attempting to overtake her by swimming!

I have, since this period, vainly endeavoured to obtain some clew to the hideous uncertainty which enveloped the fate of the stranger.[1] Her build and general appearance, as I have before

1. On note que cette vision d'horreur reste mystérieuse ; mais les tentatives du narrateur pour lui trouver une explication rationnelle l'arrachent au fantastique pour l'intégrer à une expérience vécue. L'art de Poe, ici comme dans « The Black Cat », consiste à repousser les limites du vraisemblable.

stated, led us to the belief that she was a Dutch trader, and the dresses of the crew also sustained this opinion. We might have easily seen the name upon her stern, and, indeed, taken other observations, which would have guided us in making out her character; but the intense excitement of the moment blinded us to every thing of that nature. From the saffron-like hue of such of the corpses as were not entirely decayed, we concluded that the whole of her company had perished by the yellow fever, or some other virulent disease of the same fearful kind. If such were the case (and I know not what else to imagine), death, to judge from the positions of the bodies, must have come upon them in a manner awfully sudden and overwhelming, in a way totally distinct from that which generally characterizes even the most deadly pestilences with which mankind are acquainted. It is possible, indeed, that poison, accidentally introduced into some of their sea-stores, may have brought about the disaster; or that the eating of some unknown venomous species of fish, or other marine animal, or oceanic bird, might have induced it,—but it is utterly useless to form conjectures where all is involved, and will, no doubt, remain for ever involved, in the most appalling and unfathomable mystery.

NATHANIEL HAWTHORNE, 1804-1864

L'œuvre de Nathaniel Hawthorne est aussi inséparable de la Nouvelle-Angleterre que celle de Faulkner du Sud ; mais sa relation à sa terre natale est loin d'être simple. Lui-même rappelle dans la longue introduction à *The Scarlet Letter* intitulée « The Custom-House » qu'il se sent comme enchaîné à la ville de Salem, et qu'il écrit en partie pour exorciser les souvenirs liés au passé familial (le fondateur de la lignée a été juge, et son fils a fait condamner les sorcières en 1692).

Le père du jeune Nathaniel, capitaine au long cours, meurt brutalement en 1808, et sa veuve doit pour élever ses trois enfants accepter l'aide de sa famille ; le jeune homme pourra cependant faire des études à Bowdoin College, dans le Maine, après quoi il renoncera à s'engager dans une profession et passera douze ans de retraite studieuse dans la maison maternelle : il lit, écrit, et publie ses premières œuvres — un roman encore maladroit, *Fanshawe* (1828) et des contes qui paraissent dans divers périodiques avant d'être réunis en 1837 dans un volume, sous le titre de *Twice-Told Tales*. On y trouve déjà des chefs-d'œuvre comme « The Minister's Black Veil », « The May-pole of Merry Mount », « The Gentle Boy », et « Wakefield ».

La publication de ce recueil marque la fin de la retraite : Hawthorne occupe deux ans un poste à la douane de Boston, participe brièvement à la communauté utopique de Brook Farm (il tirera de cette expérience un roman, *The Blithedale Romance*, publié en 1852), se marie et s'installe avec sa jeune épouse à Concord, à proximité d'Emerson et de Thoreau, dans un ancien presbytère ; d'où le titre du second recueil de contes qu'il publie en 1846, *Mosses from an Old Manse* (« Young Goodman Brown », « Rappaccini's Daughter », « Roger Malvin's Burial »). Un dernier recueil de contes suivra en 1852, *The Snow Image, and Other Twice-Told Tales* (« Ethan Brand », « My Kinsman, Major Molineux »).

Après avoir écrit *The Scarlet Letter,* en 1850, Hawthorne s'installe dans les Berkshires, à la frontière du Massachusetts et de l'Etat de New York. Il y rencontre Herman Melville, et y écrit *The House of the Seven Gables*. Consul à Liverpool de 1853 à 1857, il séjourne deux ans à Rome et Florence et écrit *The Marble Faun* (1860). Les quatre œuvres qu'il tentera d'écrire après son retour aux Etats-Unis resteront inachevées.

Hawthorne a défini dans les préfaces de ses romans ce qui distingue son œuvre du récit réaliste : au lieu de donner à un univers fictif l'apparence de la réalité, il se situe au contraire dans un « territoire neutre, quelque part entre le monde réel et le monde féerique, où le réel et l'imaginaire peuvent se rencontrer » ; et il donne à ce nouveau type de fiction le nom de « *romance* ».

BIBLIOGRAPHIE SÉLECTIVE. — *Works,* Centenary Edition, eds. W. Charvat, R. H. Pearce (16 vol.), Columbus, Ohio State UP, 1962-1985; *Tales & Sketches,* ed. R. H. Pearce, New York, Library of America, 1982 ; *Novels,* ed. Millicent Bell, même édition, 1983 (3 autres vol. en préparation) ; Colacurcio

(Michael), *New Essays on The Scarlet Letter,* Cambridge, Cambridge UP, 1985 ; Crews (Frederick), *The Sins of the Fathers : Hawthorne's Psychological Themes,* New York, Oxford UP, 1966 ; Kaul (A. N.), ed., *Hawthorne : a Collection of Critical Essays,* Englewood Cliffs, NJ, Prentice-Hall, 1966 ; Normand (Jean), *Nathaniel Hawthorne : esquisse d'une analyse de la création artistique,* Paris, PUF, 1964 ; Stubbs (John), *The Pursuit of Form : a Study of Hawthorne and the Romance,* U. of Illinois Press, 1970.

The Scarlet Letter

CHAPITRE 3 : THE RECOGNITION

Ce roman fut publié en 1850. Dans ce chapitre, précédée du bedeau, une jeune femme portant sur sa poitrine une lettre A brodée au fil rouge, et tenant dans ses bras un nouveau-né, se rend de la prison au pilori, où elle doit comparaître devant ses juges. Nous sommes à Boston, quinze à vingt ans après la fondation de la colonie puritaine. Depuis le pilori, Hester Prynne reconnaît dans la foule son mari, Roger Chillingworth, qu'elle croyait mort (on apprendra plus tard qu'il a vécu chez les Indiens, avant de rejoindre Boston... et d'arriver le jour du procès). Le vénérable pasteur John Wilson l'adjure de livrer le nom de son amant — car elle est accusée d'adultère —, et devant son refus, s'adresse à son jeune confrère, Arthur Dimmesdale.

[...] "Speak to the woman, my brother," said Mr. Wilson. "It is of moment to her soul, and therefore, as the worshipful Governor says, momentous to thine own, in whose charge hers is. Exhort her to confess the truth!"

The Reverend Mr. Dimmesdale bent his head, in silent prayer, as it seemed, and then came forward.

"Hester Prynne," said he, leaning over the balcony, and looking down steadfastly into her eyes, "thou hearest what this good man says, and seest the accountability under which I labor.[1] If thou feelest it to be for thy soul's peace, and that thy earthy punishment will thereby be made more effectual to salvation,[2] I charge thee to speak out the name of thy fellow-sinner and fellow-sufferer! Be not silent from any mistaken pity and

1. Quelle lourde responsabilité je me vois confier. Dimmesdale tutoie Hester *(thou)*.
2. (Si tu sens) qu'il rendra ton châtiment sur terre plus efficace pour te gagner le salut.

tenderness for him; for, believe me, Hester, though he were to step down from a high place, and stand there beside thee, on thy pedestal of shame, yet better were it so,[1] than to hide a guilty heart through life. What can thy silence do for him, except it tempt him[2]—yea, compel him, as it were—to add hypocrisy to sin? Heaven hath granted thee an open ignominy, that thereby thou mayest[3] work out an open triumph over the evil within thee, and the sorrow without. Take heed how thou deniest to him[4]—who, perchance, hath not the courage to grasp it for himself—the bitter, but wholesome, cup that is now presented to thy lips!"

The young pastor's voice was tremulously sweet, rich, deep, and broken. The feeling that it so evidently manifested, rather than the direct purport of the words, caused it to vibrate within all hearts, and brought the listeners into one accord of sympathy. Even the poor baby, at Hester's bosom, was affected by the same influence; for it directed its hitherto vacant gaze towards Mr. Dimmesdale, and held up its little arms, with a half pleased, half plaintive murmur. So powerful seemed the minister's appeal, that the people could not believe but that Hester Prynne would speak out the guilty name; or else that the guilty one himself,[5] in whatever high or lowly place he stood, would be drawn forth by an inward and inevitable necessity, and compelled to ascend the scaffold.

Hester shook her head.

"Woman, transgress not beyond the limits of Heaven's mercy!" cried the Reverend Mr. Wilson, more harshly than before. "That little babe hath been gifted with a voice, to second and confirm the counsel which thou hast heard. Speak out the name! That, and thy repentance, may avail to take the scarlet letter off thy breast."

"Never!" replied Hester Prynne, looking, not at Mr. Wilson, but into the deep and troubled eyes of the younger clergyman. "It is too deeply branded. Ye cannot take it off. And would that I might endure his agony, as well as mine!"

1. = *it would be better so...*
2. = *except tempt him...*
3. Afin que tu puisses par ce moyen...
4. Prends garde de ne pas lui refuser...
5. Ne pouvaient imaginer qu'Hester puisse refuser... ; à moins que le coupable lui-même... L'intervention du narrateur, interprète de la communauté puritaine, conduit à un double leurre : en présentant comme une évidence une interprétation erronée de l'échange qui s'est établi entre Hester et Dimmesdale, elle trompe le lecteur à la fois sur la situation et sur la capacité de la communauté puritaine à l'analyser.

"Speak, woman!" said another voice, coldly and sternly, proceeding from the crowd about the scaffold. "Speak; and give your child a father!"

"I will not speak!" answered Hester, turning pale as death, but responding to this voice, which she too surely recognized. "And my child must seek a heavenly Father; she shall never know an earthly one!"

"She will not speak!" murmured Mr. Dimmesdade, who, leaning over the balcony, with his hand upon his heart, had awaited the result of his appeal. He now drew back, with a long respiration. "Wondrous strength and generosity of a woman's heart! She will not speak!"

Discerning the impracticable state of the poor culprit's mind, the elder clergyman, who had carefully prepared himself for the occasion, addressed to the multitude a discourse on sin, in all its branches, but with continual reference to the ignominious letter. So forcibly did he dwell upon this symbol, for the hour or more during which his periods were rolling over the people's heads, that it assumed new terrors in their imagination, and seemed to derive its scarlet hue from the flames of the infernal pit. Hester Prynne, meanwhile, kept her place upon the pedestal of shame, with glazed eyes, and an air of weary indifference. She had borne, that morning, all that nature could endure; and as her temperament was not of the order that escapes from too intense suffering by a swoon, her spirit could only shelter itself beneath a stony crust of insensibility, while the faculties of animal life remained entire. In this state, the voice of the preacher thundered remorselessly, but unavailingly, upon her ears. The infant, during the latter portion of her ordeal, pierced the air with its wailings and screams; she strove to hush it, mechanically, but seemed scarcely to sympathize with its trouble. With the same hard demeanour, she was led back to prison, and vanished from the public gaze within its iron-clamped portal. It was whispered, by those who peered after her, that the scarlet letter threw a lurid gleam along the dark passage-way of the interior.[1]

1. En focalisant la lecture, dans ce dernier paragraphe, sur les sentiments de Hester, Hawthorne utilise à nouveau le privilège du romancier auquel il a renoncé dans cette scène très dramatique : la position des juges surplombant le pilori, de Hester au centre de la place, de la communauté elle-même fait songer à une représentation. Les chapitres 12 et 23, tout aussi dramatiques, nous ramèneront à ce cœur de la colonie puritaine.

CHAPITRE 8 : THE ELF-CHILD AND THE MINISTER

Le Dr Roger Chillingworth rend visite à Hester dans sa cellule, officiellement pour la soigner, en fait pour lui arracher le nom de son amant : il n'y parvient pas mieux que Wilson et Dimmesdale. Bientôt, Hester quitte la prison pour vivre avec sa fille dans une petite chaumière située à la limite du village, entre la forêt et l'océan, et tente du mieux qu'elle peut d'élever sa fille, rebelle à toutes les règles. Ayant appris que l'on songe en haut lieu à lui retirer la garde de Pearl, âgée de trois ans, elle décide d'aller plaider sa cause chez le gouverneur Bellingham.

[...] Governor Bellingham stepped through the window into the hall, followed by his three guests.

"Hester Prynne," said he, fixing his naturally stern regard on the wearer of the scarlet letter, "there hath been much question concerning thee, of late. The point hath been weightily discussed, whether we, that are of authority and influence, do well discharge our consciences by trusting an immortal soul, such as there is in yonder child, to the guidance of one who hath stumbled and fallen, amid the pitfalls of this world.[1] Speak thou, the child's own mother! Were it not, thinkest thou, for thy little one's temporal and eternal welfare, that[2] she be taken out of thy charge, and clad soberly, and disciplined strictly, and instructed in the truths of heaven and earth? What canst thou do for the child, in this kind?"

"I can teach my little Pearl what I have learned from this!" answered Hester Prynne, laying her finger on the red token.

"Woman, it is thy badge of shame!" replied the stern magistrate. "It is because of the stain which that letter indicates, that we would transfer thy child to other hands."

"Nevertheless," said the mother calmly, though growing more pale, "this badge hath taught me,—it daily teaches me,—it is teaching me at this moment,—lessons whereof my child may be the wiser and better, albeit they can profit nothing to myself."[3]

"We will judge warily," said Bellingham, "and look well what we are about to do. Good Master Wilson, I pray you, examine this Pearl,—since that is her name,—and see whether she hath had such Christian nurture as befits a child of her age."

1. En d'autres termes, peut-on confier à une pécheresse l'instruction de son enfant ?
2. Ne penses-tu pas qu'il serait préférable, pour le bien-être de ton enfant comme pour son salut...
3. *Whereof :* from which ; *albeit :* though.

The old minister seated himself in an arm-chair, and made an effort to draw Pearl betwixt his knees. But the child, unaccustomed to the touch of familiarity of any but her mother, escaped through the open window and stood on the upper step, looking like a wild, tropical bird, of rich plumage, ready to take flight into the upper air. Mr. Wilson, not a little astonished at this outbreak,—for he was a grandfatherly sort of personage, and usually a vast favorite with children,—essayed, however, to proceed with the examination.

"Pearl," said he, with great solemnity, "thou must take heed to instruction, that so, in due season, thou mayest wear in thy bosom the pearl of great price.[1] Canst thou tell me, my child, who made thee?"

Now Pearl knew well enough who made her; for Hester Prynne, the daughter of a pious home, very soon after her talk with the child about her Heavenly Father, had begun to inform her of those truths which the human spirit, at whatever stage of immaturity, imbibes with such eager interest. Pearl, therefore, so large were the attainments of her three years' lifetime, could have borne a fair examination in the New England Primer, or the first column of the Westminster Catechism,[2] although unacquainted with the outward form of either of those celebrated works. But that perversity,[3] which all children have more or less of, and of which little Pearl had a tenfold portion, now, at the most inopportune moment, took thorough possession of her, and closed her lips, or impelled her to speak words amiss. After putting her finger in her mouth, with many ungracious refusals to answer good Mr. Wilson's question, the child finally announced that she had not been made at all, but had been plucked by her mother off the bush of wild roses, that grew by the prison-door.

This fantasy was probably suggested by the near proximity of the Governor's red roses, as Pearl stook outside of the window; together with her recollection of the prison rose-bush, which she had passed in coming hither.

Old Roger Chillingworth, with a smile on his face, whispered

1. Cf. Mathieu, 13, 45-46 : « Again, the kingdom of heaven is like unto a merchant man, seeking goodly pearls : Who, when he found one pearl of great price, went and sold all that he had, and bought it. »

2. Ouvrages utilisés par les puritains pour l'instruction religieuse. Cf. ci-dessous, *Walden*, « Economy », n. 2, p.181.

3. Cf. ci-dessus, « The Black Cat », n. 6, p.133.

something in the young clergyman's ear. Hester Prynne looked at the man of skill, and even then, with her fate hanging in the balance, was startled to perceive what a change had come over his features,—how much uglier they were,—how his dark complexion seemed to have grown duskier, and his figure more misshappen,—since the days when she had familiarly known him. She met his eyes for an instant, but was immediately constrained to give all her attention to the scene now going forward.

"This is awful!" cried the Governor, slowly recovering from the astonishment into which Pearl's response had thrown him. "Here is a child of three years old, and she cannot tell who made her! Without question, she is equally in the dark as to her soul, its present depravity, and future destiny! Methinks, gentlemen, we need inquire no further."

Hester caught hold of Pearl, and drew her forcibly into her arms, confronting the old Puritan magistrate with almost a fierce expression. Alone in the world, cast off by it, and with this sole treasure to keep her heart alive, she felt that she possessed indefeasible rights[1] against the world, and was ready to defend them to the death.

"God gave me the child!" cried she. "He gave her, in requital of all things else, which ye had taken from me. She is my happiness!—she is my torture, none the less! Pearl keeps me here in life! Pearl punishes me too! See ye not, she is the scarlet letter, only capable of being loved, and so endowed with a million-fold the power of retribution[2] for my sin? Ye shall not take her! I will die first!"

"My poor woman," said the not unkind old minister, "the child shall be well cared for!—far better than thou canst do it."

"God gave her into my keeping," repeated Hester Prynne, raising her voice almost to a shriek. "I will not give her up!"—And here, by a sudden impulse, she turned to the young clergyman, Mr. Dimmesdale, at whom, up to this moment, she had seemed hardly so much as once to direct her eyes.—"Speak thou for me!" cried she. "Thou wast my pastor, and hadst charge of my soul, and

1. Les termes utilisés ici rappellent — ou annoncent ! — ceux de la Déclaration d'Indépendance : « We hold these truths to be self-evident, that all men are created equal, that they are endowed by their Creator with certain inalienable Rights, that among these are Life, Liberty and the Pursuit of Happiness. » Hester ne dit-elle pas, un peu plus loin : « She is my happiness » ?

2. Terme religieux désignant le châtiment divin.

knowest me better than these men can. I will not lose the child! Speak for me! Thou knowest,—for thou hast sympathies which these men lack!—thou knowest what is in my heart, and what are a mother's rights, and how much the stronger they are, when that mother has but her child and the scarlet letter! Look thou to it! I will not lose the child! Look to it!"

CHAPITRE 10 : THE LEECH AND HIS PATIENT

Le bon Dr Chillingworth vit maintenant aux côtés du jeune pasteur, affligé d'un mal étrange. Un jour qu'ils conversent du péché et de la dissimulation, ils entendent une voix d'enfant.

[...] Before Roger Chillingworth could answer, they heard the clear, wild laughter of a young child's voice, proceeding from the adjacent burial-ground. Looking instinctively from the open window,—for it was summer-time,—the minister beheld Hester Prynne and little Pearl passing along the footpath that traversed the inclosure. Pearl looked as beautiful as the day, but was in one of those moods of perverse merriment which, whenever they occurred, seemed to remove her entirely out of the sphere of sympathy or human contact. She now skipped irreverently from one grave to another; until, coming to the broad, flat, armorial tombstone of a departed worthy,—perhaps of Isaac Johnson himself,[1]—she began to dance upon it. In reply to her mother's command and entreaty that she would behave more decorously, little Pearl paused to gather the prickly burrs from a tall burdock,[2] which grew beside the tomb. Taking a handful of these, she arranged them along the lines of the scarlet letter that decorated the maternal bosom, to which the burrs, as their nature was, tenaciously adhered. Hester did not pluck them off.

Roger Chillingworth had by this time approached the window, and smiled grimly down.

"There is no law, nor reverence for authority, no regard for human ordinances or opinions, right or wrong, mixed up with that child's composition," remarked he, as much to himself as to his companion. "I saw her, the other day, bespatter the Governor

1. L'un des fondateurs de la colonie puritaine, mort peu après le débarquement en 1630.
2. Bardane, plante dont les fruits piquants s'accrochent aux cheveux et aux vêtements.

himself with water, at the cattle-trough in Spring Lane. What, in Heaven's name, is she? Is the imp altogether evil? Hath she affections? Hath she any discoverable principle of being?"

"None,—save the freedom of a broken law,"—answered Mr. Dimmesdale, in a quiet way, as if he had been discussing the point within himself. "Whether capable of good, I know not."

The child probably overheard their voices; for, looking up to the window, with a bright, but naughty smile of mirth and intelligence, she threw one of the prickly burrs at the Reverend Mr. Dimmesdale. The sensitive clergyman shrunk, with nervous dread, from the light missile. Detecting his emotion, Pearl clapped her little hands in the most extravagant ecstasy. Hester Prynne, likewise, had involuntarily looked up; and all these four persons, old and young, regarded one another in silence, till the child laughed aloud, and shouted,—"Come away, mother! Come away, or yonder old Black Man will catch you! He hath got hold of the minister already. Come away, mother, or he will catch you! But he cannot catch little Pearl!"

So she drew her mother away, skipping, dancing, and frisking fantastically among the hillocks of the dead people, like a creature that had nothing in common with a bygone and buried generation, nor owned herself akin to it. It was as if she had been made afresh, out of new elements, and must perforce be permitted to live her own life, and be a law unto herself, without her eccentricities being reckoned to her for a crime.[1]

"There goes a woman", resumed Roger Chillingworth, after a pause, "who, be her demerits what they may, hath none of that mystery of hidden sinfulness which you deem so grievous to be borne. Is Hester Prynne the less miserable, think you, for that scarlet letter on her breast?"

"I do verily believe it," answered the clergyman, "Nevertheless, I cannot answer for her. There was a look of pain in her face, which I would gladly have been spared the sight of. But still, methinks, it must needs be better for the sufferer to be free to show his pain, as this poor woman Hester is, than to cover it all up in his heart."

1. La liberté de Pearl dansant sur les tombes, se réclamant d'une loi intérieure et refusant les interdits de la société est très proche de celle qu'évoque Emerson dans « Self-Reliance » (cf. ci-dessous, p. 175-177).

CHAPITRE 12 : THE MINISTER'S VIGIL

Chillingworth ne tarde pas à percer le secret de Dimmesdale. Sans lui révéler sa véritable identité, il fait subir au jeune pasteur de subtiles tortures qui s'ajoutent au remords de ce dernier, incapable de confesser sa faute et jouissant dans la communauté d'un respect immérité.

Walking in the shadow of a dream, as it were, and perhaps actually under the influence of a species of somnambulism, Mr. Dimmesdale reached the spot, where, now so long since, Hester Prynne had lived through her first hour of public ignominy. The same platform or scaffold, black and weather-stained with the storm or sunshine of seven long years, and foot-worn, too, with the tread of many culprits who had since ascended it, remained standing beneath the balcony of the meeting-house. The minister went up the steps.

It was an obscure night of early May. An unvaried pall of cloud[1] muffled the whole expanse of sky from zenith to horizon. If the same multitude which had stood as eyewitnesses while Hester Prynne sustained her punishment could now have been summoned forth, they would have discerned no face above the platform, nor hardly the outline of a human shape, in the dark gray of the midnight. But the town was all asleep. There was no peril of discovery. The minister might stand there, if it so pleased him, until morning should redden in the east, without other risk than that the dank and chill night-air would creep into his frame, and stiffen his joints with rheumatism, and clog his throat with catarrh and cough; thereby defrauding the expectant audience of to-morrow's prayer and sermon. No eye could see him, save that everwakeful one which had seen him in his closet, wielding the bloody scourge.[2] Why, then, had he come hither? Was it but the mockery of penitence? A mockery, indeed, but in which his soul trifled with itself! A mockery at which angels blushed and wept, while fiends rejoiced, with jeering laughter! He had been driven hither by the impulse of that Remorse which dogged him

1. Les nuages forment comme un drap mortuaire, et ajoutent à l'atmosphère oppressante de cette nuit sans lune — atmosphère propice au drame intime et dérisoire qui va se jouer sur le pilori, lieu du châtiment public.

2. Consumé par le remords, Dimmesdale s'est à plusieurs reprises donné le fouet dans la solitude de sa chambre.

everywhere, and whose own sister and closely linked companion was that Cowardice[1] which invariably drew him back, with her tremulous gripe, just when the other impulse had hurried him to the verge of a disclosure. Poor, miserable man! what right had infirmity like his to burden itself with crime? Crime is for the iron-nerved, who have their choice either to endure it, or, if it press too hard, to exert their fierce and savage strength for a good purpose, and fling it off at once! This feeble and most sensitive of spirits could do neither, yet continually did one thing or another, which intertwined, in the same inextricable knot, the agony of heaven-defying guilt and vain repentance.

And thus, while standing on the scaffold, in this vain show of expiation, Mr. Dimmesdale was overcome with a great horror of mind, as if the universe were gazing at a scarlet token on his naked breast, right over his heart. On that spot, in very truth, there was, and there had long been, the gnawing and poisonous tooth of bodily pain. Without any effort of his will, or power to restrain himself, he shrieked aloud; an outcry that went pealing through the night, and was beaten back from one house to another, and reverberated from the hills in the background; as if a company of devils, detecting so much misery and terror in it, had made a plaything of the sound, and were bandying it to and fro.

"It is done!" muttered the minister, covering his face with his hands. "The whole town will awake, and hurry forth, and find me here!"

But it was not so. The shriek had perhaps sounded with a far greater power, to his own startled ears, than it actually possessed. The town did not awake; or, if it did, the drowsy slumberers mistook the cry either for something frightful in a dream, or for the noise of witches; whose voices, at that period, were often heard to pass over the settlements or lonely cottages, as they rode with Satan through the air. The clergyman, therefore, hearing no symptoms of disturbance, uncovered his eyes and looked about him. At one of the chamber-windows of Governor Bellingham's mansion, which stood at some distance, on the line of another street, he beheld the appearance of the old magistrate himself, with a lamp in his hand, a white night-cap on his head, and a long

1. *Remorse, Cowardice :* on note le recours à l'allégorie, figure fréquemment utilisée par les prédicateurs puritains.

white gown enveloping his figure. He looked like a ghost, evoked unseasonably from the grave. The cry had evidently startled him. At another window of the same house, moreover, appeared old Mistress Hibbins, the Governor's sister, also with a lamp, which, even thus far off, revealed the expression of her sour and discontented face. She thrust forth her head from the lattice, and looked anxiously upward. Beyond the shadow of a doubt, this venerable witch-lady had heard Mr. Dimmesdale's outcry, and interpreted it, with its multitudinous echoes and reverberations, as the clamor of the fiends and night-hags,[1] with whom she was well known to make excursions into the forest.

CHAPITRE 17 : THE PASTOR AND HIS PARISHIONER

Hester décide de révéler à Dimmesdale l'identité de Chillingworth. Elle se rend donc dans la forêt avec Pearl pour attendre le pasteur, qui revient d'une mission chez les Indiens. Dimmesdale lui avoue la solitude et l'horreur de son existence.

[...] Such was the ruin to which she had brought the man, once,—nay, why should we not speak it?—still so passionately loved! Hester felt that the sacrifice of the clergyman's good name, and death itself, as she had already told Roger Chillingworth, would have been infinitely preferable to the alternative which she had taken upon herself to choose.[2] And now, rather than have had this grievous wrong to confess, she would gladly have lain down on the forest-leaves, and died there, at Arthur Dimmesdale's feet.

"O Arthur," cried she, "forgive me! In all things else, I have striven to be true! Truth was the one virtue which I might have held fast, and did hold fast through all extremity; save when thy good,—thy life,—thy fame,—were put in question! Then I consented to a deception. But a lie is never good, even though death threaten on the other side! Dost thou not see what I would say? That old man!—the physician!—he whom they call Roger Chillingworth!—he was my husband!"

The minister looked at ther, for an instant, with all that violence of passion, which—intermixed, in more shapes than one,

1. = *witches*. La sœur du gouverneur Bellingham, curieusement, est une sorcière.

2. C'est-à-dire la décision (prise il y a sept ans) de cacher à Dimmesdale que Chillingworth est son mari.

with his higher, purer, softer qualities—was, in fact, the portion of him which the Devil claimed, and through which he sought to win the rest. Never was there a blacker or a fiercer frown, than Hester now encountered. For the brief space that it lasted, it was a dark transfiguration. But his character had been so much enfeebled by suffering, that even its lower energies were incapable of more than a temporary struggle. He sank down on the ground, and buried his face in his hands.

"I might have known it!" murmured he. "I did know it![1] Was not the secret told me in the natural recoil of my heart, at the first sight of him, and as often as I have seen him since? Why did I not understand? O Hester Prynne, thou little, little knowest all the horror of this thing! And the shame!—the indelicacy!—the horrible ugliness of this exposure of a sick and guilty heart to the very eye that would gloat over it! Woman, woman, thou art accountable for this! I cannot forgive thee!"

"Thou shalt forgive me!" cried Hester, flinging herself on the fallen leaves beside him. "Let God punish! Thou shalt forgive!"

With sudden and desperate tenderness, she threw her arms around him, and pressed his head against her bosom; little caring though his cheek rested on the scarlet letter. He would have released himself, but strove in vain to do so. Hester would not set him free, lest he should look her sternly in the face. All the world had frowned on her,—for seven long years had it frowned upon this lonely woman,—and still she bore it all, nor ever once turned away her firm, sad eyes. Heaven, likewise, had frowned upon her, and she had not died. But the frown of this pale, weak, sinful, and sorrow-stricken man was what Hester could not bear, and live!

"Wilt thou yet forgive me?" she repeated, over and over again. "Wilt thou not frown? Wilt thou forgive?"

"I do forgive you, Hester," replied the minister, at length, with a deep utterance out of an abyss of sadness, but no anger. "I freely forgive you now. May God forgive us both! We are not, Hester, the worst sinners in the world. There is one worse than even the polluted priest! That old man's revenge has been blacker than my

1. Cet étrange aveu, conforme à l'analyse de l'acte manqué par Freud, montre que Dimmesdale ne *voulait* pas le savoir — ce qui retire toute justification à la condamnation qui va suivre (« Woman, thou art accountable for this ! »).

sin. He has violated, in cold blood, the sanctity of a human heart. Thou and I, Hester, never did so!"

"Never, never!" whispered she. "What we did had a consecration of its own. We felt it so! We said so to each other! Hast thou forgotten it?"

"Hush, Hester!" said Arthur Dimmesdale, rising from the ground. "No; I have not forgotten!"

They sat down again, side by side, and hand clasped in hand, on the mossy trunk of the fallen tree. Life had never brought them a gloomier hour; it was the point whither their pathway had so long been tending, and darkening ever, as it stole along;—and yet it inclosed a charm that made them linger upon it, and claim another, and another, and, after all, another moment. The forest was obscure around them, and creaked with a blast that was passing through it. The boughs were tossing heavily above their heads; while one solemn old tree groaned dolefully to another, as if telling the sad story of the pair that sat beneath, or constrained to forebode evil to come.

And yet they lingered. How dreary looked the forest-track that led backward to the settlement, where Hester Prynne must take up again the burden of her ignominy, and the minister the hollow mockery of his good name! So they lingered an instant longer. No golden light had ever been so precious as the gloom of this dark forest. Here, seen only by his eyes, the scarlet letter need not burn into the bosom of the fallen woman! Here, seen only by her eyes, Arthur Dimmesdale, false to God and man, might be, for one moment, true!

He started at a thought that suddenly occurred to him.

"Hester," cried he, "here is a new horror! Roger Chillingworth knows your purpose to reveal his true character. Will he continue, then, to keep our secret? What will now be the course of his revenge?"

"There is a strange secrecy in his nature," replied Hester, thoughtfully; "and it has grown upon him by the hidden practices of his revenge. I deem it not likely that he will betray the secret. He will doubtless seek other means of satiating his dark passion."

"And I!—how am I to live longer, breathing the same air with this deadly enemy?" exclaimed Arthur Dimmesdale, shrinking within himself, and pressing his hand nervously against his heart,—a gesture that had grown involuntary with him. "Think for me, Hester! Thou art strong. Resolve for me!"[1]

"Thou must dwell no longer with this man," said Hester, slowly and firmly. "Thy heart must be no longer under his evil eye!"

"It were far worse than death!" replied the minister. "But how to avoid it? What choice remains to me? Shall I lie down again on these withered leaves, where I cast myself when thou didst tell me what he was? Must I sink down there, and die at once?"

"Alas, what a ruin has befallen thee!" said Hester, with the tears gushing into her eyes. "Wilt thou die for very weakness? There is no other cause!"

"The judgment of God is on me," answered the conscience-stricken priest. "It is too mighty for me to struggle with!"

"Heaven would show mercy," rejoined Hester, "hadst thou but the strength to take advantage of it."

"Be thou strong for me!" answered he. "Advise me what to do."

"Is the world then so narrow?" exclaimed Hester Prynne, fixing her deep eyes on the minister's, and instinctively exercising a magnetic power over a spirit so shattered and subdued, that it could hardly hold itself erect. "Doth the universe lie within the compass of yonder town, which only a little time ago was but a leaf-strewn desert, as lonely as this around us? Whither leads yonder forest-track? Backward to the settlement, thou sayest! Yes; but onward, too! Deeper it goes, and deeper, into the wilderness, less plainly to be seen at every step; until, some few miles hence, the yellow leaves will show no vestige of the white man's tread. There thou art free! So brief a journey would bring thee from a world where thou hast been most wretched, to one where thou mayest still be happy! Is there not shade enough in all this boundless forest to hide thy heart from the gaze of Roger Chillingworth?"

"Yes, Hester; but only under the fallen leaves!" replied the minister, with a sad smile.

"Then there is the broad pathway of the sea!" continued

1. On note la manière dont les rôles traditionnels sont ici inversés — nouveau paradoxe d'un roman qui brouille les frontières habituelles entre la vertu et le péché, la loi et la transgression, le pardon et la faute (la vraie faute de Hester — celle qui est liée à son mensonge — n'a-t-elle pas été inspirée par le désir de souffrir à la place de Dimmesdale ?).

Hester. "It brought thee hither. If thou so choose, it will bear thee back again. In our native land, whether in some remote rural village or in vast London,—or, surely, in Germany, in France, in pleasant Italy,—thou wouldst be beyond his power and knowledge! And what hast thou to do with all these iron men, and their opinions? They have kept thy better part in bondage too long already!"[1]

"It cannot be!" answered the minister, listening as if he were called upon to realize a dream. "I am powerless to go. Wretched and sinful as I am, I have had no other thought than to drag on my earthly existence in the sphere where Providence hath placed me. Lost as my own soul is, I would still do what I may for other human souls! I dare not quit my post, though an unfaithful sentinel, whose sure reward is death and dishonor, when his dreary watch shall come to an end!"

"Thou art crushed under this seven years' weight of misery," replied Hester, fervently resolved to buoy him up with her own energy. "But thou shalt leave it all behind thee! It shall not cumber thy steps, as thou treadest along the forest-path; neither shalt thou freight the ship with it, if thou prefer to cross the sea. Leave this wreck and ruin here where it hath happened! Meddle no more with it! Begin all anew! Hast thou exhausted possibility in the failure of this one trial? Not so! The future is yet full of trial and success. There is happiness to be enjoyed! There is good to be done! Exchange this false life of thine for a true one. Be, if thy spirit summon thee to such a mission, the teacher and apostle of the red men. Or,—as is more thy nature,—be a scholar and a sage among the wisest and the most renowned of the cultivated world. Preach! Write! Act! Do any thing, save to lie down and die! Give up this name of Arthur Dimmesdale, and make thyself another, and a high one, such as thou canst wear without fear or shame. Why shouldst thou tarry so much as one other day in the torments that have so gnawed into thy life!—that have made thee feeble to will and to do!—that will leave thee powerless even to repent! Up, and away!"

1. A l'espace puritain, constrictif et centripète (la colonie doit se défendre à la fois contre la décadence européenne et contre la corruption de la forêt, lieu du Malin) se substitue un nouvel espace, centrifuge et expansif. On remarque que pour Hester, la libération peut venir soit de l'Ouest, soit d'un retour à l'Europe : elle annonce ainsi la démarche de Twain comme celle de James et des « expatriés ».

"O Hester!" cried Arthur Dimmesdale, in whose eyes a fitful light, kindled by her enthusiasm, flashed up and died away, "thou tellest of running a race to a man whose knees are tottering beneath him! I must die here. There is not the strength or courage left me to venture into the wide, strange, difficult world, alone!"

It was the last expression of the despondency of a broken spirit. He lacked energy to grasp the better fortune that seemed within his reach.

He repeated the word.

"Alone, Hester!"

"Thou shalt not go alone!" answered she, in a deep whisper.

Then, all was spoken!

CHAPITRE 23 : THE REVELATION OF THE SCARLET LETTER

Hester parvient à rencontrer le capitaine d'un bateau en partance pour l'Europe ; mais Chillingworth apprend son projet, et le lui révèle au moment où commence la « fête puritaine » — l'élection du nouveau gouverneur de la colonie. Après un office religieux, au cours duquel Dimmesdale prononce un sermon mémorable, le cortège des dignitaires se dirige vers la place du marché.

[...] As the ranks of military men and civil fathers moved onward, all eyes were turned towards the point where the minister was seen to approach among them. The shout died into a murmur, as one portion of the crowd after another obtained a glimpse of him. How feeble and pale he looked amid all his triumph! The energy—or say, rather, the inspiration which had held him up, until he should have delivered the sacred message that brought its own strength along with it from heaven—was withdrawn, now that it had so faithfully performed its office. The glow, which they had just before beheld burning on his cheek, was extinguished, like a flame that sinks down hopelessly among the late-decaying embers. It seemed hardly the face of a man alive, with such a deathlike hue; it was hardly a man with life in him, that tottered on his path so nervelessly, yet tottered, and did not fall!

One of his clerical brethren,—it was the venerable John Wilson,—observing the state in which Mr. Dimmesdale was left by the retiring wave of intellect and sensibility, stepped forward hastily to offer his support. The minister tremulously, but decidedly, repelled the old man's arm. He still walked onward, if that movement could be so described, which rather resembled the wavering effort of an infant, with its mother's arms in view, outstretched to tempt him forward.[1] And now, almost imperceptible as were the latter steps of his progress, he had come opposite the well-remembered and weather-darkened scaffold, where, long since, with all that dreary lapse of time between, Hester Prynne had encountered the world's ignominious stare. There stood Hester, holding little Pearl by the hand! And there was the scarlet letter on her breast! The minister here made a pause; although the music still played the stately and rejoicing march to which the procession moved. It summoned him onward,—onward to the festival!—but here he made a pause.

Bellingham, for the last few moments, had kept an anxious eye upon him. He now left his own place in the procession, and advanced to give assistance; judging from Mr. Dimmesdale's aspect that he must otherwise inevitably fall. But there was something in the latter's expression that warned back the magistrate, although a man not readily obeying the vague intimations that pass from one spirit to another. The crowd, meanwhile, looked on with awe and wonder. This earthly faintness was, in their view, only another phase of the minister's celestial strength; nor would it have seemed a miracle too high to be wrought for one so holy, had he ascended before their eyes, waxing dimmer and brighter, and fading at last into the light of heaven!

He turned towards the scaffold, and stretched forth his arms.

"Hester," said he, "come hither! Come, my little Pearl!"

It was a ghastly look with which he regarded them; but there was something at once tender and strangely triumphant in it. The child, with the bird-like motion which was one of her characteristics, flew to him, and clasped her arms about his knees. Hester Prynne—slowly, as if impelled by inevitable fate, and against her strongest will—likewise drew near, but paused before she reached him. At this instant old Roger Chillingworth thrust himself through the crowd,—or, perhaps, so dark, disturbed, and evil was his look, he rose up out of some nether region,[2]—to snatch

1. Cette image ironique suggère que l'apparente métamorphose de Dimmesdale (n'apprend-il pas à marcher seul ?) se réduit en fin de compte à un changement de tutelle.

2. = Below the earth's surface.

back his victim from what he sought to do! Be that as it might, the old man rushed forward and caught the minister by the arm.

"Madman, hold! What is your purpose?" whispered he. "Wave back that woman! Cast off this child! All shall be well! Do not blacken your fame, and perish in dishonor! I can yet save you! Would you bring infamy on your sacred profession?"

"Ha, tempter! Methinks thou art too late!" answered the minister, encountering his eye, fearfully, but firmly. "Thy power is not what it was! With God's help, I shall escape thee now!"

He again extended his hand to the woman of the scarlet letter.

"Hester Prynne," cried he, with a piercing earnestness, "in the name of Him, so terrible and so merciful, who gives me grace, at this last moment, to do what—for my own heavy sin and miserable agony—I withheld myself from doing seven years ago, come hither now, and twine thy strength about me! Thy strength, Hester; but let it be guided by the will which God hath granted me! This wretched and wronged old man is opposing it with all his might!—with all his own might and the fiend's! Come, Hester, come! Support me up yonder scaffold!"

The crowd was in a tumult. The men of rank and dignity, who stood more immediately around the clergyman, were so taken by surprise, and so perplexed as to the purport of what they saw,—unable to receive the explanation which most readily presented itself, or to imagine any other,—that they remained silent and inactive spectators of the judgment which Providence seemed about to work.[1] They beheld the minister, leaning on Hester's shoulder and supported by her arm around him, approach the scaffold, and ascend its steps; while still the little hand of the sin-born child was clasped in his. Old Roger Chillingworth followed, as one intimately connected with the drama of guilt and sorrow in which they had all been actors, and well entitled, therefore, to be present at its closing scene.[2]

"Hadst thou sought the whole earth over," said he, looking darkly at the clergyman, "there was no one place so secret,—no

1. L'évidente démission des dignitaires est particulièrement significative en ce jour d'élection. La crise personnelle de Dimmesdale devient ainsi le révélateur d'une crise plus profonde, collective et politique.

2. On note la présence ici de termes empruntés au théâtre : les trois « scènes » qui se déroulent sur la place du marché (chap. 3, 12, 23) forment ainsi une sorte de « pièce dans le roman ».

high place nor lowly place,[1] where thou couldst have escaped me,—save on this very scaffold!"

"Thanks be to Him who hath led me hither!" answered the minister.

Yet he trembled, and turned to Hester with an expression of doubt and anxiety in his eyes, not the less evidently betrayed, that there was a feeble smile upon his lips.

"Is not this better," murmured he, "than what we dreamed of in the forest?"

"I know not! I know not!" she hurriedly replied. "Better? Yea; so we may both die, and little Pearl die with us!"

"For thee and Pearl, be it as God shall order," said the minister; "and God is merciful![2] Let me now do the will which he hath made plain before my sight. For, Hester, I am a dying man. So let me make haste to take my shame upon me."

Partly supported by Hester Prynne, and holding one hand of little Pearl's, the Reverend Mr. Dimmesdale turned to the dignified and venerable rulers; to the holy ministers, who were his brethren; to the people, whose great heart was thoroughly appalled, yet overflowing with tearful sympathy, as knowing that some deep life-matter—which, if full of sin, was full of anguish and repentance likewise—was now to be laid open to them.[3] The sun, but little past its meridian, shone down upon the clergyman, and gave a distinctness to his figure, as he stood out from all the earth to put in his plea of guilty at the bar of Eternal Justice.[4]

1. Cf. chap. 3 : « though he were to step down from a high place ».

2. Hester et Pearl survivront en effet à Dimmesdale ; la première reviendra vivre dans sa chaumière, enfin respectée, et sera enterrée aux côtés de Dimmesdale — bien que dans une tombe séparée ; la seconde épousera un noble anglais ; c'est du moins ce que semblent indiquer les divers indices du chapitre 24.

3. La sympathie du peuple contraste avec la démission des dignitaires : on est tenté de parler ici « d'intelligence du cœur » ; mais le chapitre 24 corrigera cette impression, puisqu'une partie de l'assistance refusera d'admettre l'évidence, et verra dans le geste du pasteur une nouvelle preuve de sa sainteté.

4. Le soleil était à son zénith au chapitre 3 ; le chapitre 12 se déroulait au cœur de la nuit ; les trois chapitres sont liés par un véritable réseau de symétries et d'oppositions.

3 – Témoins et prophètes

Les deux écrivains que nous abordons maintenant ne sont pas mieux acceptés par l'intelligentsia de leur temps que Poe ou Hawthorne ; mais s'ils écrivent en marge des cercles littéraires, ils n'en ont pas moins la certitude d'incarner ce que l'un d'eux, Ralph Waldo Emerson, appelle « le Parti de l'Espérance » — c'est-à-dire les forces vives de la nation, étouffées par le poids des traditions et des habitudes, des institutions et des rituels. Ils partagent cet optimisme paradoxal avec une pléiade d'autres prophètes, fils comme eux de la Nouvelle-Angleterre, auxquels on donnera bientôt par dérision le nom de transcendantalistes.

Les origines du mouvement sont plus religieuses que littéraires : la plupart de ses fondateurs sont des unitariens, calvinistes libéraux qui veulent débarrasser la religion protestante de ses dogmes les plus austères, comme la prédestination ou la corruption absolue de l'homme non touché par la Grâce. La Mecque de l'unitarisme est Harvard, d'où sont issus la plupart des futurs transcendantalistes. Sous l'influence du romantisme allemand, filtré par Coleridge et Carlyle, un certain nombre de jeunes unitariens dénoncent la prudence excessive de leurs aînés, et proclament un nouvel Evangile, fondé sur la divinité de l'homme, l'identité profonde de toutes les religions, et le caractère sacré de la nature. Le terme de transcendantalisme est en fait impropre pour désigner une philosophie qui postule l'immanence du divin dans le monde, et l'aptitude de l'homme à se régénérer sans le secours des religions constituées.

C'est au cours des années 1830 que le nouveau mouvement se cristallise. Le petit livre publié par Emerson en 1836, *Nature,* joue un rôle de catalyseur. Bientôt, les novateurs organisent des « conversations », et créent leur propre journal, le *Dial,* qui paraîtra de 1840 à 1844. A partir de cette aspiration commune vont se développer des entreprises très diverses, et souvent éphémères, visant à transformer l'individu ou la société ; ainsi, A. B. Alcott cherche à renouveler la pédagogie à partir de l'Evangile, tandis que Theodore Parker attire des foules immenses en tonnant en chaire contre la corruption ou l'esclavage. Quant à George Ripley, il crée la communauté utopique de Brook Farm (1841-1847), à laquelle Hawthorne participera quelques mois.

Quel est l'intérêt littéraire du transcendantalisme ? il est multiple, mais n'apparaîtra que bien après sa disparition. Tout d'abord, il exprime l'impatience d'une génération lasse de se conformer aux normes d'un autre temps. En traduisant Goethe, en présentant le romantisme allemand et anglais à ses compatriotes, Margaret Fuller permet à des créateurs authentiques d'échapper à ce carcan de règles qu'ont tenté d'imposer les périodiques littéraires. En proclamant le droit imprescriptible du citoyen américain à chanter la nature, Emerson et Thoreau libèrent des énergies créatrices qui permettront à Melville et à Whitman d'écrire en marge des codes, des normes et des modes dont un Bryant et un Longfellow ne se dégageront jamais. Mais, contrairement à ce qu'ont voulu faire croire ses détracteurs, le transcendantalisme ne s'est pas limité à substituer une esthétique romantique à une esthétique néo-classique : en affirmant l'identité profonde de l'inspiration religieuse et de l'imagination, il a donné droit de cité à l'écrivain, et ouvert la voie à une tradition spécifiquement américaine, même si elle a été annoncée par Carlyle — il faut rappeler que *Sartor Resartus* a été la bible d'Emerson, de Thoreau, de Melville et de Whitman : celle du poète-prophète dont la vision intime prétend faire obstacle aux trahisons de l'histoire, rendre l'Amérique à sa grandeur première, et faire du témoignage un nouveau genre littéraire.

RALPH WALDO EMERSON, 1803-1882

Peu connu en France, Emerson est souvent considéré aux Etats-Unis comme le Père fondateur de la littérature américaine. De Whitman à Robert Frost, on ne compte plus ceux qui ont exprimé leur dette à son égard. Pourtant, le début de sa carrière n'annonce guère un tel destin : héritier d'une longue lignée de pasteurs protestants, il se prépare à son tour au ministère, mais y renonce en 1832, après une grave crise de vocation, et s'installe non loin de Boston, dans la paisible bourgade de Concord.

Sa première œuvre publiée, *Nature* (1836), est immédiatement saluée par les transcendantalistes comme le manifeste de leur mouvement, mais n'est guère lue en dehors du groupe. En revanche, le discours qu'il prononce en 1837, « The American Scholar », est salué par nombre d'intellectuels comme la « déclaration d'indépendance culturelle » de la jeune République, selon le mot de l'un d'eux. De 1836 à 1844, l'activité d'Emerson est multiple : il donne plusieurs tournées de conférences, dirige la publication du *Dial*, et publie en 1841 et 1844 deux séries d'*Essais* qui sont généralement considérés comme son œuvre la plus remarquable. La première série est dans la droite ligne des textes antérieurs : elle affirme la nécessité d'échapper à l'étau des institutions (« Self-Reliance »), l'aptitude de chaque individu à retrouver le génie des grands créateurs ou la force des héros (« History »), la présence en l'homme d'une « sur-âme », preuve de sa divinité et promesse de perfection future (« The Over-soul ») ; la plasticité de la nature, qui permet à tout novateur de faire reculer les limites du possible (« Circles »). La seconde célèbre le poète comme le prêtre des Temps modernes, capable de déchiffrer pour nous le livre de la nature, et annonce l'imminence d'une poésie américaine (« The Poet »), mais exprime également l'irruption du doute et le passage progressif à une philosophie relativiste (« Experience », « Nominalist and Realist »).

Representative Men (1850) est le fruit de ce nouvel équilibre entre la foi et le scepticisme : c'est une galerie de portraits (Platon, Montaigne, Shakespeare, Napoléon, Goethe) qui fait apparaître les déséquilibres indissociables du génie ou de la force. De même, *English Traits* souligne à la fois la grandeur de la culture britannique et ses limites, liées à des structures sociales inadaptées au XIXe siècle. Ce livre est une nouvelle déclaration d'Indépendance déguisée en hommage.

The Conduct of Life (1860) révèle une fascination nouvelle pour le destin (« Fate ») en même temps qu'une tendance à exalter la puissance et la richesse (« Power », « Wealth »). En fait, il marque le début d'un déclin qui va s'accentuer après la guerre de Sécession, au moment même où, ironiquement, Emerson est enfin reconnu comme un grand écrivain.

BIBLIOGRAPHIE SÉLECTIVE. — *The Collected Works of R. W. Emerson* (en cours de publication), Alfred Ferguson *et al.*, eds, Cambridge, Mass., Harvard UP, 1971 ; *Essays and Lectures, Poetry and Later Writings* (2 vol.), New York, Library of America, 1985 (3 autres vol. en prép.) ; Gonnaud (Maurice), *Individu et société dans l'œuvre de Ralph Waldo Emerson,* Paris, Didier, 1964 ; Paul (Sherman), *Emerson's Angle of Vision : Man and Nature in American Experience,* Cambridge, Mass., Harvard UP, 1952 ; Robinson (David), *Apostle of Culture : Emerson as Preacher and Lecturer,* Philadelphia, U. of Pennsylvania P., 1982 ; Whicher (Stephen), *Freedom and Fate : an Inner Life of Ralph Waldo Emerson,* Philadelphia, U. of Pennsylvania P., 1953, 1970 ; Carlet (Yves), Révolution, révélation, résolution : Boston et l'image révolutionnaire, *Revue française d'études américaines,* 40, avril 1989, p. 187-200.

Nature[1]

Our age is retrospective. It builds the sepulchres of the fathers. It writes biographies, histories, and criticism. The foregoing generations beheld God and nature face to face; we, through their eyes. Why should not we also enjoy an original relation to the universe? Why should not we have a poetry and philosophy of

1. Cet extrait comprend le début de l'introduction et un passage célèbre du premier chapitre.

insight and not of tradition, and a religion by revelation to us,[1] and not the history of theirs? Embosomed for a season in nature, whose floods of life stream around and through us, and invite us by the powers they supply, to action proportioned to nature, why should we grope among the dry bones of the past, or put the living generation into masquerade out of its faded wardrobe? The sun shines to-day also. There is more wool and flax in the fields. There are new lands, new men, new thoughts. Let us demand our own works and laws and worship.

Undoubtedly we have no questions to ask which are unanswerable. We must trust the perfection of the creation so far, as to believe that whatever curiosity the order of things has awakened in our minds, the order of things can satisfy. Every man's condition is a solution in hieroglyphic[2] to those inquiries he would put. He acts it as life, before he apprehends it as truth. In like manner, nature is already, in its forms and tendencies, describing its own design. Let us interrogate the great apparition, that shines so peacefully around us. Let us inquire, to what end is nature?

. . . .

To speak truly, few adult persons can see nature. Most persons do not see the sun. At least they have a very superficial seeing. The sun illuminates only the eye of the man, but shines into the eye and the heart of the child. The lover of nature is he whose inward and outward senses are still truly adjusted to each other; who has retained the spirit of infancy even into the era of manhood. His intercourse with heaven and earth, becomes part of his daily food. In the presence of nature, a wild delight runs through the man, in spite of real sorrows. Nature says,—he is my creature, and maugre[3] all his impertinent griefs, he shall be glad with me. Not the sun or the summer alone, but every hour and season yields its tribute of

1. Le terme de « révélation » montre qu'Emerson se situe dans la droite ligne de la tradition protestante: pour Luther comme pour Calvin, l'homme a besoin d'être visité par la Grâce pour connaître la foi. Le transcendantalisme transfère ce pouvoir régénérateur de la Grâce à la Nature.

2. Champollion (1790-1832) venait de déchiffrer les hiéroglyphes égyptiens. Cette image résume pour les transcendantalistes — et pour Poe — la présence dans la nature de signes mystérieux, mais susceptibles d'être décryptés. Ainsi, la Nature devient le Livre de Dieu, et la lecture des signes naturels devient une nouvelle exégèse (l'exégèse biblique était l'interprétation des Ecritures).

3. Malgré (terme archaïque). On note ici la nostalgie de l'enfance, déjà présente chez Poe. La différence est que, chez Emerson, la Nature peut rendre à l'adulte sa jeunesse perdue. On songe une fois de plus au « mythe américain » selon D. H. Lawrence (cf. ci-dessus, Cooper).

delight; for every hour and change corresponds to and authorizes a different state of the mind, from breathless noon to grimmest midnight. Nature is a setting that fits equally well a comic or a mourning piece. In good health, the air is a cordial of incredible virtue. Crossing a bare common, in snow puddles, at twilight, under a clouded sky, without having in my thoughts any occurrence of special good fortune, I have enjoyed a perfect exhilaration. Almost I fear to think how glad I am. In the woods too, a man casts off his years, as the snake his slough, and at what period soever of life, is always a child. In the woods, is perpetual youth. Within these plantations of God,[1] a decorum and sanctity reign, a perennial festival is dressed, and the guest sees not how he should tire of them in a thousand years. In the woods, we return to reason and faith. There I feel that nothing can befal me in life,—no disgrace, no calamity (leaving me my eyes), which nature cannot repair. Standing on the bare ground,—my head bathed by the blithe air, and uplifted into infinite space,—all mean egotism vanishes. I become a transparent eye-ball. I am nothing. I see all. The currents of the Universal Being circulate through me; I am part or particle of God. The name of the nearest friend sounds then foreign and accidental. To be brothers, to be acquaintances,—master or servant, is then a trifle and a disturbance. I am the lover of uncontained and immortal beauty. In the wilderness, I find something more dear and connate[2] than in streets of villages. In the tranquil landscape, and especially in the distant line of the horizon, man beholds somewhat as beautiful as his own nature.

The greatest delight which the fields and woods minister, is the suggestion of an occult relation between man and the vegetable. I am not alone and unacknowledged. They nod to me and I to them. The waving of the boughs in the storm, is new to me and old. It takes me by surprise, and yet is not unknown. Its effect is like that of a higher thought or a better emotion coming over me, when I deemed I was thinking justly or doing right.

1. Le terme de « plantation » était celui que les Puritains appliquaient à leur colonie.
2. = *cognate :* parent, proche.

Journals (1837-1838)[1]

OCTOBER 23, 1837

Culture in the high sense does not consist in polishing or varnishing but in so presenting the attractions of Nature that the slumbering attributes of man may burst their iron sleep & rush full grown into day. Culture is not the trimming & turfing of gardens, but the showing the true harmony of the unshorn landscape with horrid thickets & bald mountains & the balance of the land & sea.

NOVEMBER 7?, 1837

"Miracles have ceased." Have they indeed? When? They had not ceased this afternoon when I walked into the wood & got into bright miraculous sunshine in shelter from the roaring wind. Who sees a pine cone or the turpentine exuding from the tree, or a leaf the unit of vegetation fall from its bough as if it said "The Year is finished," or hears in the quiet piny glen the titmouse, chirping his cheerful note, or walks along the lofty promontory-like ridges which like natural causeways traverse the morass, or gazes upward at the rushing clouds or downward at a moss or a stone & says to himself "Miracles have ceased"?

Tell me good friend when this hillock on which your foot stands, swelled from the level of the sphere by volcanic force. Pick up that pebble at your feet, look at its gray sides, its sharp crystal, & tell me what fiery inundation of the world melted the minerals like wax & as if the globe were one glowing crucible gave this stone its shape. There is the truth-speaking pebble itself to affirm to endless ages the thing was so. Tell me where is the manufactory of this air so thin, so blue, so restless which eddies around you, in which your lifes floats, of which your lungs are but an organ, and which you coin into musical words. I am agitated with curiosity to know the secret of Nature. Why cannot Geology, why cannot Botany speak & tell me what has been, what is, as I run along the forest promontory & ask when it rose like a blister on heated steel? Then I looked up & saw the Sun shining in the vast Sky & heard

1. Comme Thoreau, Emerson a tenu son journal jusqu'à sa mort. On y trouve à la fois les brouillons de ses *Essais* et des confessions personnelles qu'on ne retrouve pas dans les œuvres publiées de son vivant.

the wind bellow above & the water glistened in the vale. These were the forces that wrought then & work now. Yes there they grandly speak to all plainly in proportion as we are quick to apprehend.[1]

MAY 11, 1838

Last night the moon rose behind four distinct pine tree tops in the distant woods & the night at ten was so bright that I walked abroad. But the sublime light of night is unsatisfying, provoking, it astonishes but explains not. Its charm floats, dances, disappears, comes & goes, but palls in five minutes after you have left the house. Come out of your warm angular house resounding with few voices into the chill grand instantaneous night, with such a Presence as a full moon in the clouds, & you are struck with poetic wonder. In the instant you leave far behind all human relations, wife, mother, & child, & live only with the savages—water, air, light, carbon, lime, & granite. I think of Kuhleborn.[2] I become a moist cold element. "Nature grows over me." Frogs pipe; waters far off tinkle; dry leaves hiss; grass bends & rustles; I have died out of the human world & come to feel a strange cold, aqueous, terraqueous, aerial, ethereal sympathy & existence. I sow the sun & moon for seeds.

JUNE 22, 1838

Conjure with the great name. Who forbade you to create? Fear. & who made fear? Sin; Inaction; Ignorance. Was is this astounding greatness of other men that they should be as God to you? Why, it is two things: First, your littleness which makes them seem so large; & second, your identity with them which makes them delightful to you as the colossal portrait of yourself. If society sleeps & snores, if there is no art, no poetry, no genius, no virtue, do not say that such things cannot be, but remember in your own sorrowful life the Sin that is also in theirs, namely the surrender of hope, the voluntary abdication that somewhere was, covered up

1. Ici encore, on retrouve un grand thème romantique — l'abandon aux forces de la nature primitive —, mais qui prend une résonance particulière dans l'Amérique de 1837, encore largement livrée à la *wilderness*.

2. Esprit du torrent et de la tempête dans *Ondine*, conte alors célèbre de l'écrivain allemand Fouqué.

now in the bushes & wilderness of so many years when you said,—"As others do, so will I; I renounce, I am sorry for it, my early visions. I must eat the good of the land, & let learning & romantic expectations go until a more convenient season." Then died the man in you; then perished the buds of Art & poetry & genius. Had you stood firm, had many stood firm, Oh God! had all,—we should no longer speak of society with cold disapproval, warning you against it, but we should see in it the half gods whose traces are not yet quite obliterated careering in contest or in love in the still grand remains of Greek art.

Self Reliance[1]

[...] Trust thyself: every heart vibrates to that iron string. Accept the place the divine Providence has found for you; the society of your contemporaries, the connexion of events. Great men have always done so and confided themselves childlike to the genius of their age, betraying their perception that the absolutely trustworthy was seated at their heart, working through their hands, predominating in all their being. And we are now men, and must accept in the highest mind the same transcendent destiny; and not minors and invalids in a protected corner, not cowards fleeing before a revolution, but guides, redeemers, and benefactors, obeying the Almighty effort, and advancing on Chaos and the Dark.

What pretty oracles nature yields us on this text in the face and behavior of children, babes and even brutes. That divided and rebel mind, that distrust of a sentiment because our arithmetic has computed the strength and means opposed to our purpose, these have not. Their mind being whole, their eye is as yet unconquered, and when we look in their faces, we are disconcerted. Infancy conforms to nobody: all conform to it, so that one babe commonly makes four or five out of the adults who prattle and play to it. So God has armed youth and puberty and manhood no less with its own piquancy and charm, and made it enviable and gracious and its claims not to be put by, if it will stand by itself. Do not think the

1. Sans doute le plus célèbre des essais de la première série (1841). Le titre de cet essai en résume le message, qui est dans la droite ligne du texte précédent.

youth has no force because he cannot speak to you and me. Hark! in the next room his voice is sufficiently clear and emphatic. It seems he knows how to speak to his contemporaries. Bashful or bold, then, he will know how to make us seniors very unnecessary.

The nonchalance of boys who are sure of a dinner, and would disdain as much as a lord to do or say aught to conciliate one, is the healthy attitude of human nature. A boy is in the parlour what the pit is in the playhouse; independent, irresponsible, looking out from his corner on such people and facts as pass by, he tries and sentences them on their merits, in the swift summary way of boys, as good, bad, interesting, silly, eloquent, troublesome. He cumbers himself never about consequences, about interest: he gives an independent, genuine verdict. Thou must court him: he does not court you. But the man is, as it were, clapped into jail by his consciousness. As soon as he has once acted or spoken with eclat, he is a committed person, watched by the sympathy or the hatred of hundreds whose affections must now enter into his account. There is no Lethe for this. Ah, that he could pass again into his neutrality! Who can thus avoid all pledges, and having observed, observe again from the same unaffected, unbiassed, unbribable, unaffrighted innocence, must always be formidable. He would utter opinions on all passing affairs, which being seen to be not private but necessary, would sink like darts into the ear of men, and put them in fear.

These are the voices which we hear in solitude, but they grow faint and inaudible as we enter into the world. Society everywhere is in conspiracy against the manhood of every one of its members. Society is a joint-stock company in which the members agree for the better securing of his bread to each shareholder, to surrender the liberty and culture of the eater. The virtue in most request is conformity. Self-reliance is its aversion. It loves not realities and creators, but names and customs.

Whoso would be a man must be a nonconformist.[1] He who would gather immortal palms must not be hindered by the name of goodness, but must explore if it be goodness. Nothing is at last sacred but the integrity of your own mind. Absolve you to yourself,

1. Terme religieux désignant, au sens étroit du terme, le membre d'une secte n'acceptant pas l'autorité de l'Eglise d'Angleterre (synonyme de *dissenter*). Emerson l'emploie dans un sens beaucoup plus large, proche du mot français « *anti*-conformiste ».

and you shall have the suffrage of the world. I remember an answer which when quite young I was prompted to make to a valued adviser who was wont to importune me with the dear old doctrines of the church. On my saying, What have I to do with the sacredness of traditions, if I live wholly from within? my friend suggested—"But these impulses may be from below, not from above." I replied, "They do not seem to me to be such; but if I am the Devil's child, I will live then from the Devil."[1] No law can be sacred to me but that of my nature. Good and bad are but names very readily transferable to that or this; the only right is what is after my constitution, the only wrong what is against it. A man is to carry himself in the presence of all opposition as if every thing were titular and ephemeral but he. I am ashamed to think how easily we capitulate to badges and names, to large societies and dead institutions. Every decent and well-spoken individual affects and sways me more than is right. I ought to go upright and vital, and speak the rude truth in all ways.

Journals (1847)

JUNE?, 1847

[...] Alas for America as I must so often say, the ungirt, the diffuse, the profuse, procumbent,[2] one wide ground juniper, out of which no cedar, no oak will rear up a mast to the clouds! it all runs to leaves, to suckers, to tendrils, to miscellany. The air is loaded with poppy, with imbecility, with dispersion, & sloth.

Eager, solicitous, hungry, rabid, busy-bodied America attempting many things, vain, ambitious to feel thy own existence, & convince others of thy talent, by attempting & hastily accomplishing much; yes, catch thy breath & correct thyself and

1. Il est intéressant de songer à ce texte en lisant *Huckleberry Finn* de Mark Twain : la force de Huck vient du regard naïf, mais lucide qu'il jette sur le monde des adultes, et qui lui permet de percer à jour les mensonges de la société. Le chapitre 31 décrit un processus semblable à celui qu'évoque Emerson ici : après avoir failli renoncer, Huck choisit « d'aller en Enfer ».

2. (D'une plante) : rampante. Cette image permet à Emerson d'exprimer un sentiment, une intuition plus qu'une certitude. Cette manière de penser par métaphores fait déjà songer à Thoreau et à Melville.

failing here, prosper out there; speed & fever are never greatness; but reliance & serenity & waiting & perseverance, heed of the work & negligence of the effect.

Great country, diminutive minds.

English Traits[1]

[...] It requires, men say, a good constitution to travel in Spain. I say as much of England, for other cause, simply on account of the vigor and brawn of the people. Nothing but the most serious business could give one any counterweight to these Baresarks, though they were only to order eggs and muffins for their beakfast. The Englishman speaks with all his body. His elocution is stomachic,—as the American's is labial. The Englishman is very petulant and precise about his accommodation at inns and on the roads; a quiddle about his toast and his chop and every species of convenience, and loud and pungent in his expressions of impatience at any neglect. His vivacity betrays itself at all points, in his manners, in his respiration, and the inarticulate noises he makes in clearing the throat;—all significant of burly strength. He has stamina; he can take the initiative in emergencies. He has that *aplomb* which results from a good adjustment of the moral and physical nature and the obedience of all the powers to the will; as if the axes of his eyes were united to his backbone, and only moved with the trunk.

This vigor appears in the incuriosity and stony neglect, each of every other. Each man walks, eats, drinks, shaves, dresses, gesticulates, and, in every manner acts and suffers without reference to the bystanders, in his own fashion, only careful not to interfere with them or annoy them; not that he is trained to neglect the eyes of his neighbors,—he is really occupied with his own affair and does not think of them. Every man in this polished country consults only his convenience, as much as a solitary pioneer in Wisconsin. I know not where any personal eccentricity is so freely allowed, and no man gives himself any concern with it. An

1. Après un séjour en Angleterre (octobre 1847 - juillet 1848), Emerson tire de ses notes une série de conférences qu'il réunira sous un même titre, *English Traits*, en 1856. Voici un portrait du comportement anglais qu'il est tentant d'opposer à la critique de l'Amérique dans le texte précédent : le personnage décrit ici est aux antipodes de la « dispersion » américaine.

Englishman walks in a pouring rain, swinging his closed umbrella like a walking-stick; wears a wig, or a shawl, or a saddle, or stands on his head, and no remark is made. And as he has been doing this for several generations, it is now in the blood.

In short, every one of these islanders is an island himself, safe, tranquil, incommunicable. In a company of strangers you would think him deaf; his eyes never wander from his table and newspaper. He is never betrayed into any curiosity or unbecoming emotion. They have all been trained in one severe school of manners, and never put off the harness. He does not give his hand. He does not let you meet his eye. It is almost an affront to look a man in the face without being introduced. In mixed or in select companies they do not introduce persons; so that a presentation is a circumstance as valid as a contract. Introductions are sacraments. He withholds his name. At the hotel, he is hardly willing to whisper it to the clerk at the book-office. If he give you his private address on a card, it is like an avowal of friendship; and his bearing, on being introduced, is cold, even though he is seeking your acquaintance and is studying how he shall serve you.

HENRY DAVID THOREAU, 1817-1862

Contrairement à Emerson, Thoreau n'a trouvé que récemment sa place dans les anthologies américaines : il a longtemps été considéré comme un naturaliste ou un original plus que comme un écrivain ; mais sa réputation n'a cessé de grandir au cours du dernier demi-siècle.

Né à Concord au moment où cette petite ville n'est encore pas devenue le lieu de ralliement des poètes et des trancendantalistes, fils d'un modeste fabricant de crayons, le jeune Thoreau fait pourtant des études à Harvard. De retour à Concord, il se partage entre l'enseignement et des excursions au cours desquelles il étudie la flore et la faune de sa région. Cette seconde vocation — contrairement à la première — l'occupera jusqu'à sa mort. Ami et disciple d'Emerson, il commence un journal, écrit des poèmes et des essais dont certains seront publiés dans le *Dial*.

Le 4 juillet 1845 — date symbolique —, Thoreau s'installe à proximité de Concord, au bord du petit lac de Walden ; il y occupe pendant deux ans une hutte qu'il a construite lui-même, et y écrit son premier livre, *A Week on the Concord and Merrimack Rivers,* récit d'un voyage en barque fait quelques années plus tôt avec son frère, mort tragiquement depuis (1849). Il y rédige également la première version d'un livre qui sera constamment remanié jusqu'à sa publication en 1854, *Walden.* Ce chef-d'œuvre inclassable s'ouvre comme le compte rendu d'une expérience, interrompu çà et là de réflexions féroces sur la société contemporaine ; mais sans perdre cette dimension autobiographique et didactique, il devient peu à peu récit d'une quête spirituelle, mythe d'origines, poème en prose nourri d'innombrables lectures et porté par une langue prodigieusement dense et mobile.

De 1854 à sa mort en 1862, Thoreau écrit plusieurs récits de voyages publiés après sa mort : *The Maine Woods* (1864), *Cape Cod* (1865). Il rédige également les 7 000 pages de son journal, véritable trésor fait de descriptions, de courts récits, de réflexions et de (rares) confessions. L'élément central de cette œuvre hétéroclite est le culte à la fois exalté et méticuleux de la nature, dont il observe les phénomènes avec une infinie patience, et dont certains textes chantent le pouvoir régénérateur (« Walking », 1862).

On ne saurait rendre justice à l'œuvre de Thoreau sans évoquer les essais et pamphlets ; certains d'entre eux ont eu un impact surprenant aux Etats-Unis et ailleurs : ainsi, « Resistance to Civil Government » (1849 ; souvent intitulé improprement « Civil Disobedience ») est un appel à la désobéissance civile qui influencera Gandhi et Martin Luther King. Avant de mourir en 1862 de tuberculose, Thoreau consacre à l'action violente de John Brown plusieurs textes qui sont de véritables appels aux armes (par exemple « A Plea for Captain John Brown », 1859).

BIBLIOGRAPHIE SPÉCIFIQUE. — *The Writings of Henry D. Thoreau* (en cours de publication), Princeton UP, 1971- ; *Henry David Thoreau, Collected Works* (2 vol.), New York, Library of America, 1985 ;

Cavell (Stanley), *The Senses of Walden,* San Francisco, North Point P., 1981 ; Edel (Leon), *Henry D. Thoreau,* Minneapolis, U. of Minnesota Pamphlet, 1970 ; Lebeaux (Richard), *Young Man Thoreau,* U. of Massachusetts P., 1977 ; *Thoreau's Seasons,* même éd., 1984 ; Paul (Sherman), *The Shores of America : Thoreau's Inward Exploration,* U. of Illinois P., 1958. Voir également Granger (Michel), « Walden, ou l'autographie de H. D. Thoreau », *Revue française d'Etudes américaines,* 14 (mai 1982) ; Tissot (Roland), « Les douze échos d'économie dans *Walden* », *Etudes anglaises,* 24, 1981.

Walden

CHAPITRE 1 : ECONOMY[1]

[...] The mass of men lead lives of quiet desperation. What is called resignation is confirmed desperation. From the desperate city you go into the desperate country, and have to console yourself with the bravery of minks and muskrats. A stereotyped but unconscious despair is concealed even under what are called the games and amusements of mankind. There is no play in them, for this comes after work. But it is a characteristic of wisdom not to do desperate things.

When we consider what, to use the words of the catechism, is the chief end of man,[2] and what are the true necessaries and means of life, it appears as if men had deliberately chosen the common mode of living because they preferred it to any other. Yet they honestly think there is no choice left. But alert and healthy natures remember that the sun rose clear. It is never too late to give up our prejudices. No way of thinking or doing, however ancient, can be trusted without proof. What every body echoes or in silence passes by as true to-day may turn out to be falsehood to-morrow, mere smoke of opinion, which some had trusted for a cloud that would sprinkle fertilizing rain on their fields. What old people say you cannot do you try and find that you can. Old deeds for old people,

1. Le premier chapitre du livre n'est pas seulement une introduction : c'est aussi une manière de pamphlet, où l'ermite de Walden se fonde sur son expérience dans la nature pour attaquer le matérialisme et la routine de ses contemporains. On retrouve dans cet extrait l'opposition emersonienne de la vieillesse et de la jeunesse.

2. « What is the chief end of man ? Man's chief end is to glorify God and to enjoy him forever » (The Shorter Catechism, in *The New England Primer*). Cf. ci-dessus, *The Scarlet Letter*, n. 13.

and new deeds for new.[1] Old people did not know enough once, perchance, to fetch fresh fuel to keep the fire a-going ; new people put a little dry wood under a pot, and are whirled round the globe with the speed of birds, in a way to kill old people, as the phrase is.[2] Age is no better, hardly so well, qualified for an instructor as youth, for it has not profited so much as it has lost. One may almost doubt if the wisest man has learned any thing of absolute value by living. Practically, the old have no very important advice to give the young, their own experience has been so partial, and their lives have been such miserable failures, for private reasons, as they must believe; and it may be that they have some faith left which belies that experience, and they are only less young than they were. I have lived some thirty years on this planet, and I have yet to hear the first syllabe of valuable or even earnest advice from my seniors. They have told me nothing, and probably cannot tell me any thing, to the purpose. Here is life, an experiment to a great extent untried by me ; but it does not avail me that they have tried it. If I have any experience which I think valuable, I am sure to reflect that this my Mentors said nothing about.

CHAPITRE 5 : SOLITUDE

This is a delicious evening, when the whole body is one sense, and imbibes delight through every pore. I go and come with a strange liberty in Nature, a part of herself. As I walk along the stony shore of the pond in my shirt sleeves, though it is cool as well as cloudy and windy, and I see nothing special to attract me, all the elements are unusually congenial to me. The bullfrogs trump to usher in the night, and the note of the whippoorwill is borne on the rippling wind from over the water. Sympathy with the fluttering alder and poplar leaves almost takes away my breath; yet, like the lake, my serenity is rippled but not ruffled. These small waves raised by the evening wind are as remote from storm as the smooth reflecting surface. Though it is now dark, the wind still blows and roars in the wood, the waves still dash, and some

1. Voir l'extrait de *Nature*. Emerson et Thoreau répliquent au nom du « Parti de l'Avenir » aux récriminations et aux avertissements de leurs aînés — qui trouvent un écho dans le chapitre 7 de *The Prairie* ou dans « Rip Van Winkle ».

2. Allusion au chemin de fer, qui se développe très rapidement au cours des années 1840 et 1850. Voir ci-dessous, chap. 9.

creatures lull the rest with their notes. The repose is never complete. The wildest animals do not repose, but seek their prey now; the fox, and skunk, and rabbit, now roam the fields and woods without fear. They are Nature's watchmen,—links which connect the days of animated life.

When I return to my house I find that visitors have been there and left their cards, either a bunch of flowers, or a wreath of evergreen, or a name in pencil on a yellow walnut leaf or a chip. They who come rarely to the woods take some little piece of the forest into their hands to play with by the way, which they leave, either intentionally or accidentally. One has peeled a willow wand, woven it into a ring, and dropped it on my table. I could always tell if visitors had called in my absence, either by the bended twigs or grass, or the print of their shoes, and generally of what sex or age or quality they were by some slight trace left, as a flower dropped, or a bunch of grass plucked and thrown away, even as far off as the railroad, half a mile distant, or by the lingering odor of a cigar or pipe. Nay, I was frequently notified of the passage of a traveller along the highway sixty rods off by the scent of his pipe.

There is commonly sufficient space about us. Our horizon is never quite at our elbows. The thick wood is not just at our door, nor the pond, but somewhat is always clearing, familiar and worn by us, appropriated and fenced in some way, and reclaimed from Nature. For what reason have I this vast range and circuit, some square miles of unfrequented forest, for my privacy, abandoned to me by men? My nearest neighbor is a mile distant, and no house is visible from any place but the hill-tops within half a mile of my own. I have my horizon bounded by woods all to myself; a distant view of the railroad where it touches the pond on the one hand, and of the fence which skirts the woodland road on the other. But for the most part it is as solitary where I live as on the prairies. It is as much Asia or Africa as New England. I have, as it were, my own sun and moon and stars, and a little world all to myself. At night there was never a traveller passed my house, or knocked at my door, more than if I were the first or last man; unless it were in the spring, when at long intervals some came from the village to fish for pouts,—they plainly fished much more in the Walden Pond of their own natures, and baited their hooks with darkness,—but they soon retreated, usually with light baskets, and left "the world to darkness and to me,"[1] and the black kernel of the night was never profaned by any human neighborhood. I believe that men are generally still a little afraid of the dark, though the witches are all hung, and Christianity and candles have been introduced.

Yet I experienced sometimes that the most sweet and tender, the most innocent and encouraging society may be found in any natural object, even for the poor misanthrope and most melancholy man. There can be no very black melancholy[2] to him who lives in the midst of Nature and has his senses still. There was never yet such a storm but it was Æolian music[3] to a healthy and innocent ear. Nothing can rightly compel a simple and brave man to a vulgar sadness. While I enjoy the friendship of the seasons I trust that nothing can make life a burden to me. The gentle rain which waters my beans[4] and keeps me in the house to-day is not drear and melancholy, but good for me too. Though it prevents my hoeing them, it is of far more worth than my hoeing. If it should continue so long as to cause the seeds to rot in the ground and destroy the potatoes in the low lands, it would still be good for the grass on the uplands, and, being good for the grass, it would be good for me. Sometimes, when I compare myself with other men, it seems as if I were more favored by the gods than they, beyond any deserts that I am conscious of; as if I had a warrant and surety at their hands which my fellows have not, and were especially guided and guarded. I do not flatter myself, but if it be possible they flatter me. I have never felt lonesome, or in the least oppressed by a sense of solitude, but once, and that was a few weeks after I came to the woods, when, for an hour, I doubted if the near neighborhood of man was not essential to a serene and healthy life. To be alone was something unpleasant. But I was at the same time conscious of a slight insanity in my mood, and seemed to foresee my recovery. In the midst of a gentle rain while these thoughts prevailed, I was suddenly sensible of such sweet and beneficent society in Nature, in the very pattering of the drops, and in every sound and sight around my house, an infinite and unaccountable

1. Thomas Gray, « Elegy in a Country Churchyard » (1751). Walden est émaillé de citations qui montrent combien cette solitude était peuplée d'échos littéraires (cf. chap. 3, « Reading »). Mais cette présence humaine médiatisée par le livre ne fait nullement écran à l'échange avec la Nature.

2. Selon la théorie des humeurs, la mélancolie était causée par la bile noire.

3. La harpe éolienne (d'Eole, dieu du vent) est un instrument dont le vent fait vibrer les cordes. Thoreau en avait placé une sur le rebord de sa fenêtre.

4. Thoreau avait planté un champ de haricots non loin de sa hutte. Cf. chap. 7, « The Bean-Field ».

friendliness all at once like an atmosphere sustaining me, as made the fancied advantages of human neighborhood insignificant, and I have never thought of them since. Every little pine needle expanded and swelled with sympathy and befriended me. I was so distinctly made aware of the presence of something kindred to me, even in scenes which we are accustomed to call wild and dreary, and also that the nearest of blood to me and humanest was not a person nor a villager, that I thought no place could ever be strange to me again.—

> "Mourning untimely consumes the sad;
> Few are their days in the land of the living,
> Beautiful daughter of Toscar."[1]

Some of my pleasantest hours were during the long rain storms in the spring or fall, which confined me to the house for the afternoon as well as the forenoon, soothed by their ceaseless roar and pelting; when an early twilight ushered in a long evening in which many thoughts had time to take root and unfold themselves. In those driving north-east rains which tried the village houses so, when the maids stood ready with mop and pail in front entries to keep the deluge out, I sat behind my door in my little house, which was all entry, and thoroughly enjoyed its protection. In one heavy thunder shower the lightning struck a large pitch-pine across the pond, making a very conspicuous and perfectly regular spiral groove from top to bottom, an inch or more deep, and four of five inches wide, as you would groove a walking-stick. I passed it again the other day, and was struck with awe on looking up and beholding that mark, now more distinct than ever, where a terrific and resistless bolt came down out of the harmless sky eight years ago. Men frequently say to me, "I should think you would feel lonesome down there, and want to be nearer to folks, rainy and snowy days and nights especially." I am tempted to reply to such,—This whole earth which we inhabit is but a point in space. How far apart, think you, dwell the two most distant inhabitants of yonder star, the breadth of whose disk cannot be appreciated by our instruments? Why should I feel lonely? is not our planet in the Milky Way? This which you put seems to me not be the most important question. What sort of space is that which separates a

1. Traduction d'*Ossian* par Patrick Mac Gregor (Londres, 1841) ; l'une des lectures favorites de Thoreau.

man from his fellows and makes him solitary? I have found that no exertion of the legs can bring two minds much nearer to one another. What do we want most to dwell near to? Not to many men surely, the depot, the post-office, the bar-room, the meeting-house, the school-house, the grocery, Beacon Hill, or the Five Points,[1] where men most congregate, but to the perennial source of our life, whence in all our experience we have found that to issue; as the willow stands near the water and sends out its roots in that direction. This will vary with different natures, but this is the place where a wise man will dig his cellar. . . . I one evening overtook one of my townsmen, who has accumulated what is called "a handsome property",—though I never got a *fair* view of it,—on the Walden road, driving a pair of cattle to market, who inquired of me how I could bring my mind to give up so many of the comforts of life. I answered that I was very sure I liked it passably well; I was not joking.[2] And so I went home to my bed, and left him to pick his way through the darkness and the mud to Brighton,—or Bright-town,[3]—which place he would reach some time in the morning.

CHAPITRE 9 : THE PONDS

[...] When I first paddled a boat on Walden, it was completely surrounded by thick and lofty pine and oak woods, and in some of its coves grape vines had run over the trees next the water and formed bowers under which a boat could pass. The hills which form its shores are so steep, and the woods on them were then so high, that, as you looked down from the west end, it had the appearance of an amphitheatre for some kind of sylvan spectacle. I have spent many an hour, when I was younger, floating over its surface as the zephyr willed, having paddled my boat to the middle, and lying on my back across the seats, in a summer forenoon, dreaming awake, until I was aroused by the boat touching the sand, and I arose to

1. Beacon Hill, Five Points : quartiers de Boston et de New York.

2. Cette conversation imaginaire permet de distinguer entre Walden, lieu de la solitude et de la sérénité (c'est l'essentiel du message de ce texte, son *énoncé*), et *Walden*, œuvre littéraire où le monologue glisse vite vers le dialogue, où l'interlocuteur apparaît à travers la véhémence du ton, bref, où la société est constamment présente, en creux, dans *l'énonciation*.

3. Banlieue de Boston où se trouvaient de nombreux abattoirs.

see what shore my fates had impelled me to; days when idleness was the most attractive and productive industry.[1] Many a forenoon have I stolen away, preferring to spend thus the most valued part of the day; for I was rich, if not in money, in sunny hours and summer days, and spent them lavishly; nor do I regret that I did not waste more of them in the workshop or the teacher's desk.[2] But since I left those shores the woodchoppers have still further laid them waste, and now for many a year there will be no more rambling through the aisles of the wood, with occasional vistas through which you see the water. My Muse may be excused if she is silent henceforth. How can you expect the birds to sing when their groves are cut down?[3]

Now the trunks of trees on the bottom, and the old log canoe, and the dark surrounding woods, are gone, and the villagers, who scarcely know where it lies, instead of going to the pond to bathe or drink, are thinking to bring its water, which should be as sacred as the Ganges at least, to the village in a pipe, to wash their dishes with!—to earn their Walden by the turning of a cock or drawing of a plug![4] That devilish Iron Horse, whose ear-rending neigh is heard throughout the town, has muddied the Boiling Spring with his foot, and he it is that has browsed off all the woods on Walden shore; that Trojan horse, with a thousand men in his belly, introduced by mercenary Greeks! Where is the country's champion, the Moore of Moore Hall,[5] to meet him at the Deep

1. Thoreau donne à ce mot le sens que lui donnaient les Puritains : assiduité, zèle, goût du travail.

2. Thoreau avait été employé comme instituteur, et avait travaillé dans la fabrique de crayons de son père. On note la cohérence des métaphores, toutes empruntées au langage de l'argent *(stolen ; spend ; rich ; money ; lavishly ; waste)*. L'ermite de Walden choisit en somme de combattre la société sur son propre terrain. L'opposition qui se dessine ici va déboucher sur un triple développement : élégiaque, épique, et enfin lyrique.

3. Cette phrase rappelle la chanson populaire française : *Nous n'irons plus au bois, les lauriers sont coupés*. La structure du passage est paradoxale : cet aveu d'impuissance, loin de conduire au silence, va hâter le passage du mode élégiaque au mode épique.

4. Il avait été envisagé d'amener l'eau de Walden au village de Concord — sacrilège suprême pour Thoreau. On voit que les hymnes à la jeunesse et à l'esprit d'entreprise du premier chapitre sont trompeurs. *Walden*, comme *The Prairie*, est (entre autres choses) un tribut à une nature primitive en voie d'extinction.

5. Cette épopée spontanée se nourrit de mythologie grecque (le Cheval de Troie) et anglaise : « But More of More-Hall, with nothing at all / He slew the dragon of Wantley » (The Dragon of Wantley, *in* Percy, *Reliques of Ancient English Poetry*, 1765). Nous avons ici l'amorce d'une mythologie américaine, qui ferait du poète-prophète-ermite purifié par la Nature le héros vainqueur du nouveau dragon, ou du Cheval de Troie qui a envahi Walden : le chemin de fer.

Cut[1] and thrust an avenging lance between the ribs of the bloated pest?

Nevertheless, of all the characters I have known, perhaps Walden wears best, and best preserves its purity. Many men have been likened to it, but few deserve that honor. Though the woodchoppers have laid bare first this shore and then that, and the Irish have built their sties by it, and the railroad has infringed on its border, and the ice-men have skimmed it once,[2] it is itself unchanged, the same water which my youthful eyes fell on; all the change is in me. It has not acquired one permanent wrinkle after all its ripples. It is perennially young, and I may stand and see a swallow dip apparently to pick an insect from its surface as of yore. It struck me again tonight, as if I had not seen it almost daily for more than twenty years,—Why, here is Walden, the same woodland lake that I discovered so many years ago; where a forest was cut down last winter another is springing up by its shore as lustily as ever; the same thought is welling up to its surface that was then; it is the same liquid joy and happiness to itself and its Maker, ay, and it *may* be to me. It is the work of a brave man surely, in whom there was no guile![3] He rounded this water with his hand, deepened and clarified it in his thought, and in his will bequeathed it to Concord. I see by its face that it is visited by the same reflection; and I can almost ay, Walden, is it you?

It is no dream of mine,
To ornament a line;
I cannot come nearer to God and Heaven
Than I live to Walden even.
I am its stony shore,
And the breeze that passes o'er;
In the hollow of my hand
Are its water and its sand,
And its deepest resort
Lies high in my thought.[4]

1. Non loin du lac, on avait dû niveler le sol pour permettre le passage du chemin de fer.

2. Le chemin de fer avait été construit surtout par des ouvriers irlandais ; l'industrie de la glace était florissante à l'époque : on avait donc découpé des blocs de glace à la surface du lac pour les acheminer vers les métropoles.

3. « Behold, an Israelite indeed, in whom there is no guile » (Evangile selon saint Jean, 1, 1).

4. Ce poème est de Thoreau.

The cars never pause to look at it; yet I fancy that the engineers and firemen and brakemen, and those passengers who have a season ticket and see it often, are better men for the sight. The engineer does not forget at night, or his nature does not, that he has beheld this vision of serenity and purity once at least during the day. Though seen but once, it helps to wash out State-street[1] and the engine soot. One proposes that it be called « God's Drop ».[2]

1. Le quartier financier de Boston : victoire donc de la pureté lacustre et de la fontaine de Jouvence sur la corruption de l'argent et les modes éphémères qu'elle engendre.
2. Ralph Waldo Emerson.

4 – Les aventuriers

Pourquoi associer Melville, romancier, et Whitman, poète ? Tout d'abord pour des raisons de simple chronologie : nés la même année (1819), ils sont morts à un an de distance. Plus profondément, parce que tous deux ont tiré parti de l'exemple de leurs prédécesseurs — Hawthorne pour Melville, Emerson pour Whitman — tout en s'aventurant beaucoup plus loin des sentiers tracés par les traditions littéraires de leur temps : on est tenté d'utiliser pour définir leurs œuvres respectives une image maritime qu'ils auraient sans doute acceptée, et de dire qu'ils ont brisé les amarres, pour s'engager dans une aventure littéraire qui a fait d'eux des découvreurs, ouvrant aux écrivains de notre temps de nouveaux modes d'expression.

Placer Melville et Whitman côte à côte ne signifie pas réduire l'écart qui les sépare. Le premier connaît un succès précoce et passager avec des récits de voyage sans prétention, pour rencontrer avec *Moby Dick* l'incompréhension de la critique et du public, et sombrer dans l'obscurité (son œuvre ne sera redécouverte que dans les années 1920). Le second connaît dès la publication de *Leaves of Grass*, en 1855, un succès de scandale, et vit entouré d'un groupe de disciples, tout en étant mis hors la loi par la critique respectable de son temps. Le pessimisme de plus en plus sombre de Melville contraste avec l'optimisme parfois factice de Whitman. Mais malgré ces évidentes différences, les deux écrivains se rejoignent dans la facture conventionnelle de leurs premiers écrits, la manière dont ils découvrent peu à peu leur propre voie, et dont sans chercher à dépeindre l'Amérique ils parviennent à en livrer la démesure et la vitalité.

Il suffit pour avoir quelque idée de leur vision de la comparer à celle de leurs contemporains. De juin 1851 à avril 1852, Harriet Beecher Stowe publie en feuilleton un roman qui va bouleverser l'Amérique et connaître un succès immédiat : *Uncle Tom's Cabin*, récit édifiant, moralisateur et bavard, difficilement lisible pour le lecteur du XXe siècle. Qui, alors, aurait osé affirmer que le naufrage du *Pequod* aurait un siècle plus tard infiniment plus de prégance que la mort de l'oncle Tom ? A la même époque, le poète John G. Whittier (1807-1892) chante dans des vers tout aussi marqués par le propos moralisant les souffrances des esclaves, les humbles effusions des âmes simples et la cruauté de l'oppresseur. Quel lecteur contemporain aurait prédit que la postérité préférerait à ces poèmes généreux et nobles l'égotisme forcené de Whitman ?

UN HUMORISTE DU TERROIR

C'est peut-être chez les humoristes qu'il faut chercher une tradition proprement américaine, dont la fraîcheur et la hardiesse annoncent certaines pages de *Moby Dick* ou de *Leaves of Grass* : on voit apparaître de 1830 à 1860 une forme d'écriture qui se nourrit de culture populaire, même si celle-ci est revue et corrigée par des hommes cultivés, journalistes ou avocats. Ainsi, Seba Smith, journaliste du Maine, invente en 1830 Jack Downing, sorte de philosophe campagnard qui, pendant vingt-neuf ans, va dans ses « lettres » passer institutions et célébrités au crible de son solide bon sens. James Russell Lowell (cf. chap. 2) écrit *The Biglow Papers* en patois de Nouvelle-Angleterre. Mais c'est surtout dans le Sud-Ouest que va se créer un véritable genre littéraire, fondé sur les rodomontades de personnages truculents et sur une écriture hyperbolique, aux antipodes de l'*understatement* britannique : il s'agit de la *tall tale*, parfois anonyme, parfois transmise par des narrateurs qui seront mi-témoins, mi-conteurs. Augustus Longstreet publie en 1835 une série de portraits et d'esquisses intitulée *Georgia Scenes, Characters and Incidents* ; Thomas Thorpe écrit en 1841 un conte bientôt célèbre, « The Big Bear of Arkansas » ; Johnson Hooper conte les aventures d'un marginal qui fait déjà songer aux personnages de Mark Twain, Simon Suggs ; et George Washington Harris crée un anti-héros couard et misanthrope, mais cocasse, Sut Lovingwood.

BIBLIOGRAPHIE SÉLECTIVE. — Blair (Walter), *Native American Humor* (1937), San Francisco, Chandler, 1960 ; Blair (Walter) et Hamlin (Hill), *America's Humor*, New York, Oxford UP, 1978 ; Gale (Stephen), *Encyclopedia of American Humorists*, New York, Garland, 1988 ; Rourke (Constance), *American Humor : A Study of the National Character*, New York, Harcourt Brace, 1931 ; Thorp (Willard), *American Humorists*, Minneapolis, University of Minnesota Pamphlets, 1964 ; Royot (Daniel), *L'humour américain, des puritains aux yankees*, Lyon, PUL, 1980.

Theatrical Performance[1]

I was ridin along the Mississippi in my wagon, when I came acrost a feller floating down stream, settin in the starn[2] of his boat fast asleep. Well, I hadn't had a fight for ten days; felt as tho' I should have to kiver[3] myself up in a salt barrel, to keep so wolfy[4] about the shoulders. So says I, hallo stranger, if you don't mind your boat will run off and leave you. So he looked up at me slantindicular,[5] and I looked down on him slantindicular. He took out a chor[6] of tobacco, and says he, I don't vallee[7] you tantamount to that; and the varmant[8] clapped his wings and crowed. I ris up,[9] shuch[10] my mane, croocked my neck, and nickered[11] like a horse.

1. Ce texte, anonyme, fut publié par Lunenberg Abernathy dans *Laughable Anecdotes* (1832). Les journaux et almanachs du Sud présentaient fréquemment à leurs lecteurs ces tartarinades américaines.
2. = *a fellow... sitting in the stern.*
3. = *cover.*
4. Image traduisant l'agressivité.
5. Mot hybride : *slanting* + *perpendicular.*
6. = *chew.*
7. = *value.*
8. = *varmint*, vaurien (de *vermin*).
9. = *rose.*
10. = *shook.*
11. = *nighed.*

He run his boat plump head foremost ashore. I stopped my wagon, and set my triggers. Mister, says he, I can whip my weight in wild cats, and ride straight thro' a crab apple orchard on a flash of lightning—clear meat axe[1] disposition—the best man, if I an't, I wish I may be tetotaciously exfluncated.[2] So we come together; he was a pretty severe colt, but no part of a priming[3] for me. I put it to him mighty droll—in ten minutes he yelled enough, and swore I was a ripstaver![4] Says I, an't I the yallow flower of the forest ? And I'm all brimstone but[5] the head, and that's aquafortis! Says he, stranger, you're a beauty, and if I only know'd your name, I'd vote for you next election Says I, my name is Nimrod Wildfire—half horse, half alligator,[6] and a touch of the airthquake—that's got the prettiest sister, fattest horse, and ugliest dog in the district, and can out run, out jump, throw down, drag out and whip any man in all Kentuck![7]

HERMAN MELVILLE, 1819-1891

Comme Hawthorne, Melville appartient à une famille respectable (ses ancêtres se sont distingués pendant la Révolution) ; comme lui, il connaîtra très tôt l'expérience du deuil et de la souffrance. Son père, négociant aisé, fait faillite en 1830, sombre dans la démence et meurt en 1832, laissant huit orphelins. Herman a treize ans. Il sera employé de banque, fermier chez un de ses oncles, comptable dans un magasin de fourrures, puis instituteur. Mais il cède bientôt à l'appel de la mer, qu'il a si bien évoqué au premier chapitre de *Moby Dick* : mousse pendant quelques mois en 1837, puis matelot sur un baleinier en 1841, il déserte dans les îles Marquises,

1. Hachoir à viande.
2. Si je ne suis pas le meilleur, je veux bien être réduit en poudre.
3. Il ne faisait pas le poids.
4. Un champion.
5. = *about.*
6. Le nom et son attribut étaient souvent utilisés pour désigner l'homme de la frontière, également appelé « *ring-tailed roarer* ». Au théâtre, Nimrod Wildfire apparaît dans *The Lion of the West* (1830) de J. K. Paulding.
7. = Kentucky.

s'engage sur un second baleinier où éclate une mutinerie, puis sur un navire de guerre où il découvre la rude discipline militaire.

Le récit romancé de ces diverses aventures fera la matière de ses premières œuvres : *Typee, A Peep at Polynesian Life* (1846), et *Omoo, A Narrative of Adventures in the South Seas* (1847) rencontrent un succès immédiat. L'auteur se lasse pourtant d'être salué comme « l'homme qui a vécu parmi les cannibales ». Il a d'autres ambitions, lit Shakespeare, Spencer, Swift, Rabelais et Dante, et tire de ces lectures une allégorie quelque peu incohérente, *Mardi* (1849). L'échec du livre le contraint à revenir à sa veine première : *Redburn* (1849) et *White Jacket* (1850) sont deux romans inspirés respectivement de son expérience dans la marine marchande et dans la marine de guerre.

C'est à ce moment que Melville rencontre Hawthorne, dont il a lu avec enthousiasme les contes. C'est pour le jeune écrivain une révélation. Il décide de reprendre le nouveau récit qu'il vient de consacrer à l'aventure d'un baleinier. Ce récit, remanié, amplifié, deviendra *Moby Dick*, véritable « symphonie » littéraire (pour reprendre le titre du chap. 132) où se mêlent la dérision, l'extravagance, le pathétique, la rêverie, où le lecteur voit le roman d'aventures se métamorphoser en drame shakespearien, en conte philosophique, en poème en prose.

L'Amérique de 1851 n'est pas prête à accueillir une œuvre aussi singulière. Malgré quelques comptes rendus favorables, le livre est un échec, de même que *Pierre, or the Ambiguities*, publié l'année suivante. Les conférences données par Melville ne remportent pas plus de succès, et c'est un homme amer, déçu qui accepte un emploi d'inspecteur des douanes à New York. Il l'occupera près de vingt ans. L'écrivain ne renonce pas pour autant : il publie un roman historique, *Israel Potter* (1855), puis en 1856 un remarquable recueil de contes intitulé *Piazza Tales* (« Bartleby » et « Benito Cereno » en font partie), et en 1857 un récit étrange et ambigu — satire ? roman picaresque ? allégorie ? — dont le personnage principal est un charlatan, et dont l'action se déroule à bord d'un bateau, sur le Mississipi, *The Confidence-Man, His Masquerade.* Ces œuvres passeront inaperçues, de même que les quatre volumes de poésie publiés entre 1866 et 1891. Quelques mois avant sa mort, Melville écrit son testament littéraire, qui restera inédit jusqu'en 1924 : *Billy Budd*, court roman — ou longue nouvelle — maritime dont le jeune héros est un matelot, pendu après avoir frappé — et tué involontairement — un officier.

BIBLIOGRAPHIE SÉLECTIVE. — *The Writings of Herman Melville*, eds Harrison Hayford, Hershel Parker (15 vol.), en cours de publication, Evanston, Ill., 1968- ; *Typee, Omoo, Mardi ; Redburn, White-Jacket, Moby Dick ; Pierre, Israel Potter, The Confidence-Man, Tales & Billy Budd* (4e vol. en prép.), New York, Library of America, 1982-1983 ; Brodhead (Richard), *Hawthorne, Melville, and the Novel*, Chicago UP, 1973, 1982 ; Brodhead (Richard), ed., *New Essays on Moby Dick*, Cambridge UP, 1986 ; Durand (Régis), *Melville, signes et métaphores*, Lausanne, L'Age d'Homme, 1980 ; Jaworski (Philippe), *Melville, le désert et l'empire*, Paris, Presses de l'Ecole Normale supérieure, 1986 ; Mayoux (Jean-Jacques), *Melville par lui-même*, Paris, Seuil, 1958 ; Hayford (Harrison) et Hersel Parker, eds, *Moby Dick as Doubloon*, New York, Norton, 1970 ; Vincent (Howard), *Studies in Moby Dick*, Columbus, Ohio, Charles Merrill, 1969.

Moby Dick

CHAPITRE I : LOOMINGS

Call me Ishmael.[1] Some years ago—never mind how long precisely—having little or no money in my purse, and nothing particular to interest me on shore, I thought I would sail about a little and see the watery part of the world. It is a way I have of driving off the spleen, and regulating the circulation. Whenever I find myself growing grim about the mouth; whenever it is a damp, drizzly November in my soul; whenever I find myself involuntarily pausing before coffin warehouses, and bringing up the rear of every funeral I meet; and especially whenever my hypos[2] get such

1. Ishmael (en français Ismael) est mentionné dans l'Ancien Testament (Genèse 16, 11 et 12). Fils d'Abraham et de l'esclave Hagar, il est condamné dès sa naissance à l'errance et à la solitude : « And he will be a wild man ; his hand will be against every man, and every man's hand against him. » On se rappelle que le pionnier de *The Prairie* s'appelait Ishmael Bush.

2. Hypocondrie, état dépressif.

an upper hand of me, that it requires a strong moral principle to prevent me from deliberately stepping into the street, and methodically knocking people's hats off—then, I account it high time to get to sea as soon as I can. This is my substitute for pistol and ball. With a philosophical flourish Cato throws himself upon his sword; I quietly take to the ship. There is nothing surprising in this. If they but knew it, almost all men in their degree, some time or other, cherish very nearly the same feelings towards the ocean with me.

There now is your insular city of the Manhattoes,[1] belted round by wharves as Indian isles by coral reefs—commerce surrounds it with her surf. Right and left, the streets take you waterward. Its extreme down-town is the Battery, where that noble mole is washed by waves, and cooled by breezes, which a few hours previous were out of sight of land. Look at the crowds of water-gazers there.

Circumambulate the City of a dreamy Sabbath afternoon. Go from Corlears Hook to Coenties Slip, and from thence, by Whitehall, northward.[2] What do you see?—Posted like silent sentinels all around the town, stand thousands upon thousands of mortal men fixed in ocean reveries. Some leaning against the spiles; some seated upon the pier-heads; some looking over the bulwarks of ships from China; some high aloft in the rigging, as if striving to get a still better seaward peep. But these are all landsmen; of week days pent up in lath and plaster—tied to counters, nailed to benches, clinched to desks.[3] How then is this? Are the green fields gone? What do they here?

But look! here come more crowds, pacing straight for the water, and seemingly bound for a dive. Strange! Nothing will content them but the extremest limit of the land; loitering under the shady lee of yonder warehouses will not suffice. No. They must get just as nigh the water as they possibly can without falling in. And there they stand—miles of them—leagues. Inlanders all, they come from lanes and alleys, streets and avenues—north, east, south, and west. Yet here

1. C'est le nom qu'avait donné Irving aux habitants de New York dans sa *Knickerbocker History of New York*.

2. Cet itinéraire contourne la pointe de Manhattan par la rive de l'East River, puis de l'Hudson.

3. Dans « Bartleby », l'une des *Piazza Tales*, Melville décrit la morne existence d'un petit employé « rivé à son bureau ».

they all unite. Tell me, does the magnetic virtue in the needles of the compasses of all those ships attract them thither?

Once more. Say, you are in the country; in some high land of lakes. Take almost any path you please, and ten to one it carries you down in a dale, and leaves you there by a pool in the stream. There is magic in it. Let the most absent-minded of men be plunged in his deepest reveries—stand that man on his legs, set his feet a-going, and he will infallibly lead you to water, if water there be in all that region. Should you ever be athirst in the great American desert, try this experiment, if your caravan happen to be supplied with a metaphysical professor. Yes, as every one knows, meditation and water are wedded for ever.

But here is an artist. He desires to paint you the dreamiest, shadiest, quietest, most enchanting bit of romantic landscape in all the valley of the Saco.[1] What is the chief element he employs? There stand his trees, each with a hollow trunk, as if a hermit and a crucifix were within; and here sleeps his meadow, and there sleep his cattle; and up from yonder cottage goes a sleepy smoke. Deep into distant woodlands winds a mazy way, reaching to overlapping spurs of mountains bathed in their hill-side blue. But though the picture lies thus tranced, and though this pine-tree shakes down its sighs like leaves upon this shepherd's head, yet all were vain, unless the shepherd's eye were fixed upon the magic stream before him. Go visit the Prairies in June, when for scores on scores of miles you wade knee-deep among Tiger-lilies—what is the one charm wanting?—Water—there is not a drop of water there! Were Niagara but a cataract of sand, would you travel your thousand miles to see it? Why did the poor poet of Tennessee, upon suddenly receiving two handfuls of silver, deliberate whether to buy him a coat, which he sadly needed, or invest his money in a pedestrian trip to Rockaway Beach?[2] Why is almost every robust healthy boy with a robust healthy soul in him, at some time or other crazy to go to sea? Why upon your first voyage as a passenger, did you yourself feel such a mystical vibration, when first told that you and your ship were now out of sight of land? Why did the old Persians hold the sea holy? Why did the Greeks give it

1. Fleuve qui traverse le New Hampshire et le Maine.

2. Extrémité sud-ouest de Long Island. Allusion probable à Bayard Taylor, contemporain de Melville.

a separate deity,[1] and make him the own brother of Jove? Surely all this is not without meaning. And still deeper the meaning of that story of Narcissus, who because he could not grasp the tormenting, mild image he saw in the fountain, plunged into it and was drowned. But that same image, we ourselves see in all rivers and oceans. It is the image of the ungraspable phantom of life; and this is the key to it all.

CHAPITRE 28 : AHAB[2]

Ishmael se rend en compagnie de son nouvel ami Queequeg, natif des îles du Sud, à Nantucket où tous deux s'embarquent à bord du Pequod, *un baleinier. Le capitaine est tout d'abord étrangement invisible ; mais un jour, il apparaît sur le pont.*

[...] There seemed no sign of common bodily illness about him, nor of the recovery from any. He looked like a man cut away from the stake, when the fire has overrunningly wasted all the limbs without consuming them, or taking away one particle from their compacted aged robustness. His whole high, broad form, seemed made of solid bronze, and shaped in an unalterable mould, like Cellini's cast Perseus.[10] Threading its way out from among his grey hairs, and continuing right down one side of his tawny scorched face and neck, till it disappeared in his clothing, you saw a slender rod-like mark, lividly whitish. It resembled that perpendicular seam sometimes made in the straight, lofty trunk of a great tree, when the upper lightning tearingly darts down it, and without wrenching a single twig, peels and grooves out the bark from top to bottom, ere running off into the soil, leaving the tree still greenly alive, but branded. Whether that mark was born with him, or whether it was the scar left by some desperate wound, no one could certainly say. By some tacit consent, throughout the voyage little

1. Poséidon. Le nombre et la variété des références mythologiques dans ce premier chapitre montrent que chez Melville, comme chez Thoreau, le très fort ancrage géographique (Manhattan, Walden) est compatible avec une extrême réceptivité à des cultures multiples (la Bible, la mythologie et l'histoire classiques, etc.). De même, la surprenante familiarité du ton — qui rapproche Melville des humoristes — n'empêche nullement un recours inépuisable à la littérature américaine (cf. ici Irving), mais aussi classique, européenne, etc.

2. Le roi Achab (en anglais Ahab) est mentionné dans la Bible au chapitre des Rois. Indifférent aux prophéties d'Elie (Elijah en anglais ; un soi-disant prophète portant ce nom apparaîtra au chap. 19 de *Moby Dick*), il provoque la colère de Dieu. Il est tué au combat, et conformément à la prophétie, les chiens boivent son sang.

3. Le *Persée* de Benvenuto Cellini se trouve à Florence.

or no allusion was made to it, especially by the mates. But once Tashtego's senior, an old Gay-Head Indian[1] among the crew, superstitiously asserted that not till he was full forty years old did Ahab become that way branded, and then it came upon him, not in the fury of any mortal fray, but in an elemental strife at sea. Yet, this wild hint seemed inferentially negatived, by what a grey Manxman[2] insinuated, an old sepulchral man, who, having never before sailed out of Nantucket, had never ere this laid eye upon wild Ahab. Nevertheless, the old sea-traditions, the immemorial credulities, popularly invested this old Manxman with preternatural powers of discernment. So that no white sailor seriously contradicted him when he said that if ever Captain Ahab should be tranquilly laid out—which might hardly come to pass, so he muttered—then, whoever should do that last office for the dead, would find a birth-mark on him from crown to sole.

So powerfully did the whole grim aspect of Ahab affect me, and the livid brand which streaked it, that for the first few moments I hardly noted that not a little of this overbearing grimness was owing to the barbaric white leg upon which he partly stood. It had previously come to me that this ivory leg had at sea been fashioned from the polished bone of the sperm whale's jaw. "Aye, he was dismasted off Japan," saif the old Gay-Head Indian once; "but like his dismasted craft, he shipped another mast without coming home for it. He has a quiver of 'em."

I was struck with the singular posture he maintained. Upon each side of the Pequod's quarter deck, and pretty close to the mizen shrouds,[3] there was an auger hole, bored about half an inch or so, into the plank. His bone leg steadied in that hole; one arm elevated, and holding by a shroud; Captain Ahab stood erect, looking straight out beyond the ship's ever-pitching prow. There was an infinity of firmest fortitude, a determinate, unsurrenderable wilfulness, in the fixed and fearless, forward dedication of that glance. Not a word he spoke; nor did his officers say aught to him; though by all their minutest gestures and

1. Gayhead est un promontoire de l'île de Martha's Vineyard, non loin de Nantucket. Tashtego : l'un des trois harponneurs, Indien lui aussi. Le nom du baleinier rappelle, à une lettre près, celui d'une tribu indienne qui combattit contre les Puritains du Massachusetts, les Pequot.

2. Originaire de l'île de Man, dans la mer d'Irlande.

3. *Quarter-deck :* gaillard d'arrière ; *mizzen-shrouds :* haubans de misaine. Ahab s'adresse à l'équipage du *Pequod*, qu'il a réuni sur le gaillard d'arrière.

expressions, they plainly showed the uneasy, if not painful, consciousness of being under a troubled master-eye. And not only that, but moody stricken Ahab stood before them with a crucifixion in his face; in all the nameless regal overbearing dignity of some mighty woe.

CHAPITRE 36 : THE QUARTER-DECK

Ahab s'adresse à l'équipage du Pequod, *qu'il a réuni sur le gaillard d'arrière.*

[...] "All ye mast-headers have before now heard me give orders about a white whale. Look ye! d'ye see this Spanish ounce of gold?"—holding up a broad bright coin to the sun—"it is a sixteen dollar piece, men,—a doubloon. D'ye see it? Mr. Starbuck, hand me yon top-maul."[1]

While the mate was getting the hammer, Ahab, without speaking, was slowly rubbing the gold piece against the skirts of his jacket, as if to heighten its lustre, and without using any words was meanwhile lowly humming to himself, producing a sound so strangely muffled and inarticulate that it seemed the mechanical humming of the wheels of his vitality in him.

Receiving the top-maul from Starbuck, he advanced towards the main-mast with the hammer uplifted in one hand, exhibiting the gold with the other, and with a high raised voice exclaiming: "Whosoever of ye raises me a white-headed whale with a wrinkled brow and a crooked jaw; whosoever of ye raises me that white-headed whale, with three holes punctured in his starboard fluke[2]—look ye, whosoever of ye raises me that same white whale, he shall have this gold ounce, my boys!"

"Huzza! huzza!" cried the seamen, as with swinging tarpaulins they hailed the act of nailing the gold to the mast.

"It's a white whale, I say," resumed Ahab, as he threw down the top-maul; "a white whale. Skin your eyes for him, men; look sharp for white water; if ye see but a bubble, sing out."

All this while Tashtego, Daggoo, and Queequeg[3] had looked

1. Gros marteau, masse.
2. Nageoire de la queue.
3. Tashtego, l'Indien, Daggoo, un Noir africain, et Queequeg, Polynésien, sont les trois harponneurs. Le choix de ces trois ethnies par Melville n'est bien sûr pas un hasard : il s'agit de trois groupes qui ont été victimes de la colonisation européenne.

on with even more intense interest and surprise than the rest, and at the mention of the wrinkled brow and crooked jaw they had started as if each was separately touched by some specific recollection.

"Captain Ahab," saif Tashtego, "that white whale must be the same that some call Moby Dick."

"Moby Dick?" shouted Ahab, "Do ye know the white whale then, Tash?"

"Does he fan-tail a little curious, sir, before he goes down?" said the Gay-Header deliberately.

"And has he a curious spout, too," said Daggoo, "very bushy, even for a parmacetty,[1] and mighty quick, Captain Ahab?"

"And he have one, two, tree—oh! good many iron in him hide, too, Captain," cried Queequeg disjointedly, "all twiske-tee betwisk, like him—him—" faltering hard for a word, and screwing his hand round and round as though uncorking a bottle—"like him—him—"

"Corkscrew!" cried Ahab, "aye, Queequeg, the harpoons lie all twisted and wrenched in him; aye, Daggoo, his spout is a big one, like a whole shock of wheat, and white as a pile of our Nantucket wool after the great annual sheep-shearing; aye, Tashtego, and he fan-tails like a split jib in a squall.[2] Death and devils! men, it is Moby Dick ye have seen—Moby Dick—Moby Dick!"

"Captain Ahab," said Starbuck, who, with Stubb and Flask,[3] had thus far been eyeing his superior with increasing surprise, but at last seemed struck with a thought which somewhat explained all the wonder. "Captain Ahab, I have heard of Moby Dick—but it was not Moby Dick that took off thy leg?"

"Who told thee that?" cried Ahab; then pausing, "Aye, Starbuck; aye, my hearties all round; it was Moby Dick that dismasted me; Moby Dick that brought me to this dead stump I stand on now. Aye, aye," he shouted with a terrific, loud, animal sob, like that of a heart-stricken moose; "Aye, aye! it was that accursed white whale that razeed me; made a poor pegging

1. *Spout :* souffle, ou jet émis par la baleine ; *parmacetty : spermaceti*, cachalot recherché pour le *spermaceti* (blanc de baleine : cf. ci-dessous, chap. 94).

2. Comme un foc déchiré dans la tempête.

3. Les trois seconds d'Ahab.

lubber[1] of me for ever and a day!" Then tossing both arms, with measureless imprecations he shouted out: "Aye, aye! and I'll chase him round Good Hope, and round the Horn, and round the Norway Maelstrom, and round perdition's flames before I give him up. And this is what ye have shipped for, men! to chase that white whale on both sides of land, and over all siodes of earth, till he spouts black blood and rolls fin out. What say ye, men, will ye splice hands on it, now? I think ye do look brave."

"Aye, aye!" shouted the harpooneers and seamen, running closer to the excited old man: "A sharp eye for the White Whale; a sharp lance for Moby Dick!"

"God bless ye," he seemed to half sob and half shout. "God bless ye, men. Steward! go draw the great measure of grog. But what's this long face about, Mr. Starbuck; wilt thou not chase the white whale? art not game for Moby Dick?"

"I am game for his crooked jaw, and for the jaws of Death too, Captain Ahab, if it fairly comes in the way of the business we follow; but I came here to hunt whales, not my commander's vengeance.[2] How many barrels will thy vengeance yield thee even if thou gettest it, Captain Ahab? it will not fetch thee much in our Nantucket market."

"Nantucket market! Hoot! But come closer, Starbuck; thou requirest a little lower layer. If money's to be the measurer, man, and the accountants have computed their great counting-house the globe, by girdling it with guineas, one to every three parts of an inch; then, let me tell thee, that my vengeance will fetch a great premium *here*!"

"He smites his chest," whispered Stubb, "what's that for? methinks it rings most vast, but hollow."

"Vengeance on a dumb brute!" cried Starbuck, "that simply smote thee from blindest instinct! Madness! To be enraged with a dumb thing, Captain Ahab, seems blasphemous."

"Hark ye yet again,—the little lower layer.[3] All visible objects, man, are but as pasteboard masks. But in each event—in the living act, the undoubted deed—there, some

1. Lourdaud, empoté. Lors d'une chasse antérieure, Moby Dick a arraché une jambe à Ahab.

2. Starbuck tente vainement de s'opposer à l'entreprise d'Ahab, au nom de Dieu, mais aussi du profit (*star* + *buck*).

3. *Hark* = *hear*. Ahab invite Starbuck à percer la surface des choses pour le comprendre (« *the little lower layer* »). Mais ce plaidoyer se mue en aveu involontaire : en se comparant à un prisonnier tentant d'abattre le mur de sa prison, il désigne sa propre servitude.

unknown but still reasoning thing puts forth the mouldings of its features from behind the unreasoning mask. If man will strike, strike through the mask! How can the prisoner reach outside except by thrusting through the wall? To me, the white whale is that wall, shoved near to me. Sometimes I think there's naught beyond. But 'tis enough. He tasks me; he heaps me; I see in him outrageous strength, with an inscrutable malice sinewing it. That inscrutable thing is chiefly what I hate; and be the white whale agent, or be the white whale principal,[1] I will wreak that hate upon him. Talk not to me of blasphemy, man; I'd strike the sun if it insulted me."

CHAPITRE 94 : A SQUEEZE OF THE HAND

L'équipage du Pequod *a tué une baleine et l'a dépecée. Le passage qui suit décrit le travail des marins occupés à malaxer le blanc de baleine, partie concrète d'une huile qui se trouve dans les sinus crâniens. Cette opération devient peu à peu le symbole d'un échange fraternel et généreux qui fait équilibre à la quête solitaire d'Ahab. L'exaltation de l'amitié masculine dans ce texte fait songer à l'amour des « camarades » célébré dans certains poèmes de Whitman.*

[...] It had cooled and crystallized to such a degree, that when, with several others, I sat down before a large Constantine's[2] bath of it, I found it strangely concreted into lumps, here and there rolling about in the liquid part. It was our business to squeeze these lumps back into fluid. A sweet and unctuous duty! No wonder that in old times this sperm was such a favorite cosmetic. Such a clearer! such a sweetener! such a softener! such a delicious mollifier! After having my hands in it for only a few minutes, my fingers felt like eels, and began, as it were, to serpentine and spiralize.

As I sat there at my ease, cross-legged on the deck; after the bitter exertion at the windlass;[3] under a blue tranquil sky; the ship under indolent sail, and gliding so serenely along; as I bathed my hands among those soft, gentle globules of infiltrated tissues,

1. Que la baleine soit l'origine du crime, ou qu'elle n'en soit que l'instrument.
2. Constantin Ier, premier empereur chrétien.
3. Guindeau, treuil horizontal servant à lever l'ancre.

woven almost within the hour; as they richly broke to my fingers, and discharged all their opulence, like fully ripe grapes their wine; as I snuffed up that uncontaminated aroma,—literally and truly, like the smell of spring violets; I declare to you, that for the time I lived as in a musky meadow; I forgot all about our horrible oath;[1] in that inexpressible sperm, I washed my hands and my heart of it; I almost began to credit the old Paracelsan[2] superstition that sperm is of rare virtue in allaying the heat of anger: while bathing in that bath, I felt divinely free from all ill-will, or petulance, or malice, of any sort whatsoever.

Squeeze! squeeze! squeeze! all the morning long; I squeezed that sperm till I myself almost melted into it; I squeezed that sperm till a strange sort of insanity came over me; and I found myself unwittingly squeezing my co-laborers' hands in it, mistaking their hands for the gentle globules. Such an abounding, affectionate, friendly, loving feeling did this avocation beget; that at last I was continually squeezing their hands, and looking up into their eyes sentimentally; as much as to say,—Oh! my dear fellow beings, why should we longer cherish any social acerbities, or know the slightest ill-humor or envy! Come; let us squeeze hands all round; nay, let us all squeeze ourselves into each other; let ut squeeze ourselves universally into the very milk and sperm of kindness.

Would that I could keep squeezing that sperm for ever! For now, since by many prolonged, repeated experiences, I have perceived that in all cases man must eventually lower, or at least shift, his conceit of attainable felicity; not placing it anywhere in the intellect or the fancy; but in the wife, the heart, the bed, the table, the saddle, the fire-side, the country; now that I have perceived all this, I am ready to squeeze case eternally. In visions of the night, I saw long rows of angels in paradise, each with his hands in a jar of spermaceti.

1. Ahab a fait prêter serment à l'équipage au complet.
2. Paracelse, alchimiste et médecin suisse (1493-1541), père de la médecine hermétique.

CHAPITRE 135 : THE CHASE, THIRD DAY

L'affrontement entre le Pequod *et Moby Dick dure depuis trois jours. La baleine blanche a déjà coulé deux chaloupes, et vient de mettre hors d'état deux des trois barques qui ont été mises à la mer en ce troisième jour de chasse.*

[...] From the ship's bows, nearly all the seamen now hung inactive; hammers, bits of plank, lances, and harpoons, mechanically retained in their hands, just as they had darted from their various employments; all their enchanted eyes intent upon the whale, which from side to side strangely vibrating his predestinating head, sent a broad band of overspreading semicircular foam before him as he rushed. Retribution,[1] swift vengeance, eternal malice were in his whole aspect, and spite of all that mortal man could do, the solid white buttress of his forehead smote the ship's starboard bow, till men and timbers reeled. Some fell flat upon their faces. Like dislodged trucks, the heads of the harpooneers aloft shook on their bull-like necks. Through the breach, they heard the waters pour, as mountain torrents down a flume.

"The ship! The hearse!—the second hearse!" cried Ahab from the boat; "its wood could only be American!"[2]

Diving beneath the settling ship, the whale ran quivering along its keel; but turning under water, swiftly shot to the surface again, far off the other bow, but within a few yards of Ahab's boat, where, for a time, he lay quiescent.

"I turn my body from the sun. What ho, Tashtego! let me hear thy hammer. Oh! ye three unsurrendered spires of mine; thou uncracked keel; and only god-bullied hull; thou firm deck, and haughty helm; and Pole-pointed prow,—death-glorious ship! must ye then perish, and without me? Am I cut off from the last fond pride of meanest shipwrecked captains? Oh, lonely death on lonely life! Oh, now I feel my topmost greatness lies in my topmost grief. Ho, ho! from all your furthest bounds, pour ye now in, ye

1. Châtiment divin.

2. Ahab répète ici la prédiction de Fedallah, personnage ténébreux et inquiétant qui a apaisé les craintes du capitaine au chap. 117, en lui affirmant qu'il ne pouvait mourir avant d'avoir vu deux corbillards sur la mer : « The first not made by mortal hand; and the visible wood of the last must be grown in America. » Comme Macbeth trompé par les sorcières (« none of woman born / Shall harm Macbeth », IV, 1, 80), le tyran du *Pequod* découvre trop tard que l'impossible est en train de se réaliser.

bold billows of my whole foregone life, and top this one piled comber[1] of my death! Towards thee I roll, thou all-destroying but unconquering whale; to the last I grapple with thee; from hell's heart I stab at thee; for hate's sake I spit my last breath at thee. Sink all coffins and all hearses to one common pool! and since neither can be mine, let me then tow to pieces, while still chasing thee, though tied to thee, thou damned whale! *Thus*, I give up the spear!"

The harpoon was darted; the stricken whale flew forward; with igniting velocity the line[2] ran through the groove;—ran foul. Ahab stooped to clear it; he did clear it; but the flying turn caught him round the neck, and voicelessly as Turkish mutes bowstring their victim, he was shot out of the boat, ere the crew knew he was gone. Next instant, the heavy eye-splice in the rope's final end flew out of the stark-empty tub,[3] knocked down an oarsman, and smiting the sea, disappeared in its depths.

For an instant, the tranced boat's crew stood still; then turned. "The ship? Great God, where is the ship?" Soon they through dim, bewildering mediums saw her sidelong fading phantom, as in the gaseous Fata Morgana,[4] only the uppermost masts out of water; while fixed by infatuation, or fidelity, or fate, to their once lofty perches, the pagan harpooneers still maintained their sinking lookouts on the sea. And now, concentric circles seized the lone boat itself, and all its crew, and each floating oar, and every lance-pole, and spinning, animate and inanimate, all round and round in one vortex, carried the smallest chip of the *Pequod* out of sight.

But as the last whelmings[5] intermixingly poured themselves over the sunken head of the Indian at the mainmast, leaving a few inches of the erect spar yet visible, together with long streaming yards of the flag, which calmly undulated, with ironical coincidings, over the destroying billows they almost touched;—at that instant, a red arm and a hammer hovered backwardly uplifted in the open air, in the act of nailing the flag faster and yet

1. *Billow, comber* = vague.
2. La ligne, c'est-à-dire la corde attachée au harpon.
3. L'épissure qui termine la ligne gicle hors de la baille, récipient rond où celle-ci était enroulée.
4. Un mirage que l'on voit au large de la Calabre et du détroit de Messine. La légende l'attribue à Morgan Le Fay, sœur du roi Arthur dans le *Morte d'Arthur* de Malory (1485).
5. *To whelm = to overwhelm :* les remous, les tourbillons qui engloutissent le bateau.

faster to the subsiding spar.[1] A sky-hawk that tauntingly had followed the main-truck downwards from its natural home among the stars, pecking at the flag, and incommoding Tashtego there; this bird now chanced to intercept its broad fluttering wing between the hammer and the wood; and simultaneously feeling that etherial thrill, the submerged savage beneath, in his death-grasp, kept his hammer frozen there; and so the bird of heaven, with archangelic shrieks, and his imperial beak thrust upwards, and his whole captive form folded in the flag of Ahab, went down with his ship, which, like Satan, would not sink to hell till she had dragged a living part of heaven along with her, and helmeted herself with it.[2]

Now small fowls flew screaming over the yet yawning gulf; a sullen white surf beat against its steep sides; then all collapsed, and the great shroud of the sea rolled on as it rolled five thousand years ago.[3][7]

WALT WHITMAN, 1819-1892

Comme Melville, Whitman naît dans l'Etat de New York ; mais ses origines sont toutes différentes : fils de charpentier, il travaille très jeune comme apprenti chez un imprimeur, puis devient instituteur. Il se partage alors pendant plus de dix ans entre l'enseignement, le journalisme (il va créer plusieurs journaux, souvent éphémères) et le militantisme en faveur du Parti Démocrate, puis du tout nouveau *Free Soil Party*.

Les premières productions du jeune Whitman sont loin d'annoncer son œuvre future : il s'agit d'un roman didactique contre l'alcoolisme et d'articles politiques qui ne se distinguent en rien de ceux de ses confrères, avec leur patriotisme agressif et leur rhétorique pesante.

1. Seconde allusion à *Morte d'Arthur*, où l'on voit un bras nu sortir des eaux du lac en brandissant Excalibur.

2. Allusion au célèbre monologue de Satan dans *Paradise Lost* de Milton.

3. L'époque du Déluge, selon la chronologie biblique.

La métamorphose du journaliste en poète a fait couler beaucoup d'encre : est-elle due à la déception du militant ou du journaliste ? à une découverte de l'homosexualité, évoquée à mots couverts dans certains poèmes ? à diverses lectures, particulièrement des essais d'Emerson (lui-même dira : « I was simmering... Emerson brought me to a boil ») ? Quoi qu'il en soit, les années 1850 voient apparaître un nouveau Whitman, qui renonce au journalisme et à la vie politique, revient au métier de charpentier et souligne avec quelque ostentation ses origines prolétaires, tout en fréquentant assidûment l'opéra.

A partir de la première édition de *Leaves of Grass*, mince plaquette d'à peine 100 pages, l'évolution du poète se confond avec celle de ce livre qui va s'étoffer, d'édition en édition, sans perdre son titre initial. Il deviendra le plus bel exemple de ce que Sacvan Bercovitch a appelé « auto-American-biography » : une œuvre où l'écrivain américain raconte l'Amérique en se racontant. Le thème récurrent de *Leaves of Grass* est en effet la fusion de cette *persona* que chante « Song of Myself » et de la nation américaine, dans toute sa multiplicité.

BIBLIOGRAPHIE SÉLECTIVE. — *The Collected Writings of Walt Whitman* (22 vol., en cours de public.), eds Gay Wilson Allen, Sculley Bradley, New York UP, 1961- ; *Leaves of Grass*, Sculley Bradley, Harold Blodgett, eds, New York, Norton, 1973 ; Allen (Gay Wilson), *The Solitary Singer : a Critical Biography of Walt Whitman*, Chicago, U. of Chicago P., 1985 ; *The New Walt Whitman Handbook*, New York UP, 1986 ; Asselineau (Roger), *L'évolution de Walt Whitman après la première édition des « Feuilles d'herbe »*, Paris, Didier, 1954 ; Aspiz (Harold), *Walt Whitman and the Body Beautiful*, Urbana, U. of Illinois P., 1980 ; Black (Stephen), *Whitman's Journey into Chaos : A Psychoanalytical Study of the Poetic Process*, Princeton UP, 1975. Voir également le n° 16 de la revue *Delta* (mai 1983) ; Asselineau (Roger), *Leaves of Grass* (bilingue), Paris, Aubier, 1989 ; Darras (Jacques), *Feuilles d'herbe*, Paris, Grasset, 1989.

Song of Myself[1]

8

The little one sleeps in its cradle,
I lift the gauze and look a long time, and silently brush away flies with my hand.

The youngster and the red-faced girl turn aside up the bushy hill,
I peeringly view them from the top.

The suicide sprawls on the bloody floor of the bedroom,
I witness the corpse with its dabbled hair, I note where the pistol has fallen.

The blab of the pave, tires of carts, sluff[2] of boot-soles, talk of the promenaders,
The heavy omnibus, the driver with his interrogating thumb, the clank of the shod horses on the granite floor,
The snow-sleighs, clinking, shouted jokes, pelts of snow-balls,
The hurrahs for popular favorites, the fury of rous'd mobs,
The flap of the curtain'd litter, a sick man inside borne to the hospital,
The meeting of enemies, the sudden oath, the blows and fall,
The excited crowd, the policeman with his star quickly working his passage to the centre of the crowd,
The impassive stones that receive and return so many echoes,
What groans of over-fed or half-starv'd who fall sunstruck or in fits,

1. Sans doute le poème le plus célèbre de Whitman. Publié sans titre dans l'édition de 1855, il en occupait plus de la moitié. Intitulé « Poem of Walt Whitman, an American » en 1856, puis « Walt Whitman » en 1860, il devint « Song of Myself » en 1881. Le poème commence par une affirmation du « moi » (« I celebrate myself, and sing myself ») accompagnée d'un appel au lecteur (« And what I shall assume you shall assume »). La strophe 8 confère à cette auto-célébration une dimension nouvelle : la première personne du poème se voit offrir un pouvoir visionnaire qui lui donne une ubiquité créatrice, et permet à Whitman de mêler expérience personnelle et souvenirs littéraires ou artistiques. Le mariage du trappeur et de l'Indienne évoqué à la strophe 10 est inspiré d'un tableau du peintre Alfred Jacob Miller (1810-1874), *The Trapper's Bride*. Le texte est celui de la dernière édition (1892).

2. *Tires :* (bruit des) cercles de roues ; *sluff :* glissement.

What exclamations of women taken suddenly who hurry home
and give birth to babes,
What living and buried speech is always vibrating here, what
howls restrain'd by decorum,
Arrests of criminals, slights, adulterous offers made, acceptances,
rejections with convex lips,
I mind them or the show or resonance of them—I come and I
depart.[1]

9

The big doors of the country barn stand open and ready,
The dried grass of the harvest-time loads the slow-drawn
wagon,
The clear light plays on the brown gray and green intertinged,
The armfuls are pack'd to the sagging mow.[2]

I am there, I help, I came stretch'd atop of the load,
I felt its soft jolts, one leg reclined on the other,
I jump from the cross-beams and seize the clover and timothy,[3]
And roll head over heels and tangle my hair full of wisps.

10

Alone far in the wilds and mountains I hunt,
Wandering amazed at my own lightness and glee,[4]
In the late afternoon choosing a safe spot to pass the night,
Kindling a fire and broiling the fresh-kill'd game,
Falling asleep on the gather'd leaves with my dog and gun by my
side.

1. Cette série d'instantanés (images et sons) illustre parfaitement le paradoxe énoncé dans le premier poème de *Leaves of Grass* : « One's-Self I sing, a simple separate person / Yet utter the word Democratic, the word En-Masse. » Ce que « chante » ici le poète, c'est le pouvoir d'observation d'un Moi désincarné, œil omniprésent, ouïe infiniment réceptive aux signaux émis par la « Démocratie », mais aussi « personne séparée », capable de vivre l'intensité de chaque moment évoqué ici, de recevoir les « vibrations » multiples nées de tous ces « échos » : témoin, mais aussi acteur (cf. les deux premiers vers).

2. *Mow :* partie de la grange où l'on entasse le foin.

3. Fléole des prés (plante fourragère). Le « je » est ici à la fois à l'intérieur de la scène (puisqu'il y participe) et à l'extérieur (puisqu'il porte témoignage).

4. Le moissonneur se métamorphose en chasseur puis disparaît pour réapparaître sur un bateau : ectoplasme, ou instance onirique « stupéfaite de sa propre légèreté » ?

The Yankee clipper is under her sky-sails,[1] she cuts the sparkle and scud,[2]
My eyes settle the land, I bend at her prow or shout joyously from the deck.

The boatmen and clam-diggers arose early and stopt for me,
I tuck'd my trowser-ends in my boots and went and had a good time;
You should have been with us that day round the chowder-kettle.[3]

I saw the marriage of the trapper in the open air in the far west, the bride was a red girl,
Her father and his friends sat near cross-legged and dumbly smoking, they had moccasins to their feet and large thick blankets hanging from their shoulders,
On a bank lounged the trapper, he was drest mostly in skins, his luxuriant beard and curls protected his neck, he held his bride by the hand,
She had long eyelashes, her head was bare, her coarse straight locks descended upon her voluptuous limbs and reach'd to her feet.

The runaway slave came to my house and stopt outside,
I heard his motions crackling the twigs of the woodpile,
Through the swung half-door of the kitchen I saw him limpsy[4] and weak,
And went where he sat on a log and led him in and assured him,
And brought water and fill'd a tub for his sweated body and bruis'd feet,
And gave him a room that enter'd from my own, and gave him some coarse clean clothes,
And remember perfectly well his revolving eyes and his awkwardness,

1. Contre-cacatois (petite voile carrée située au-dessus du cacatois).
2. Crachin ou brume chassé(e) par le vent.
3. Cette familiarité subite rappelle tout à la fois la tradition du conte populaire et le début de *Moby Dick* : Whitman, comme Melville, cherche à impliquer le lecteur dans l'œuvre en recourant à des procédés familiers à tous les conteurs, mais étrangers aux codes du récit réaliste ou du poème narratif. On note le passage du présent au prétérite.
4. Sans énergie.

And remember putting plasters on the galls of his neck and ankles;
He staid with me a week before he was recuperated and pass'd north,
I had him sit next me at table, my fire-lock[1] lean'd in the corner.

Crossing Brooklyn Ferry[2]

1

Flood-tide below me! I see you face to face!
Clouds of the west—sun there half an hour high—I see you also face to face.

Crowds of men and women attired in the usual costumes, how curious you are to me!
On the ferry-boats the hundreds and hundreds that cross, returning home, are more curious to me than you suppose,
And you that shall cross from shore to shore years hence are more to me, and more in my meditations, than you might suppose.[3]

2

The impalpable sustenance of me from all things at all hours of the day,
The simple, compact, well-join'd scheme, myself disintegrated,[4] every one disintegrated yet part of the scheme,
The similitudes of the past and those of the future,
The glories strung like beads on my smallest sights and hearings, on the walk in the street and the passage over the river,
The current rushing so swiftly and swimming with me far away,
The others that are to follow me, the ties between me and them,
The certainty of others, the life, love, sight, hearing of others.

1. Fusil à pierre.

2. Publié pour la première fois dans la deuxième édition de 1856, ce poème a trouvé son titre définitif en 1860 et a été constamment remanié. Le texte est celui de 1892.

3. L'invocation au lecteur permet au poète, d'emblée, de franchir l'écart qui sépare le présent éphémère de l'écriture du présent éternel de la lecture : je et vous, présent et futur se fondent et se partagent la charge lyrique du poème.

4. Ce moi désintégré ressemble comme un frère à celui de « Song of Myself ».

Others will enter the gates of the ferry and cross from shore to shore,
Others will watch the run of the flood-tide,
Others will see the shipping of Manhattan north and west, and the heights of Brooklyn to the south and east,
Others will see the islands large and small;
Fifty years hence, others will see them as they cross, the sun half an hour high,
A hundred years hence, or ever so many hundred years hence, others will see them,
Will enjoy the sunset, the pouring-in of the flood-tide, the falling-back to the sea of the ebb-tide.

3

It avails not, time nor place—distance avails not,
I am with you, you men and women of a generation, or ever so many generations hence,
Just as you feel when you look on the river and sky, so I felt,
Just as any of you is one of a living crowd, I was one of a crowd,
Just as you are refresh'd by the gladness of the river and the bright flow, I was refresh'd,
Just as you stand and lean on the rail, yet hurry with the swift current, I stood yet was hurried,
Just as you look on the numberless masts of ships and the thickstemm'd pipes of steamboats, I look'd.[1]

I too many and many a time cross'd the river of old,
Watched the Twelfth-month[2] sea-gulls, saw them high in the air floating with motionless wings, oscillating their bodies,
Saw how the glistening yellow lit up parts of their bodies and left the rest in strong shadow,
Saw the slow-wheeling circles and the gradual edging toward the south,
Saw the reflection of the summer sky in the water,
Had my eyes dazzled by the shimmering track of beams,

1. Dérive du courant, dérive des temps : en deux strophes, le présent est devenu passé, le futur présent.

2. Les Quakers désignaient ainsi les mois de l'année. Ce « douzième mois » est celui de la désintégration, mais aussi celui qui porte en lui la promesse de l'année nouvelle.

Look'd at the fine centrifugal spokes of light round the shape of my
head in the sunlit water,
Look'd on the haze on the hills southward and south-westward,
Look'd on the vapor as it flew in fleeces tinged with violet,
Look'd toward the lower bay to notice the vessels arriving,
Saw their approach, saw aboard those that were near me,
Saw the white sails of schooners and sloops, saw the ships at
anchor,
The sailors at work in the rigging or out astride the spars,[1]
The round masts, the swinging motion of the hulls, the slender
serpentine pennants,[2]
The large and small steamers in motion, the pilots in their
pilot-houses,
The white wake left by the passage, the quick tremulous whirl of
the wheels,
The flags of all nations, the falling of them at sunset,
The scallop-edged waves in the twilight, the ladled cups, the
frolicsome crests and glistening,
The stretch afar growing dimmer and dimmer, the gray walls of
the granite storehouses by the docks,
On the river the shadowy group, the big steam-tug closely
flank'd on each side by the barges, the hay-boat, the
belated lighter,
On the neighboring shore the fires from the foundry chimneys
burning high and glaringly into the night,
Casting their flicker of black contrasted with wild red and yellow
light over the tops of houses, and down into the clefts of streets.

4

These and all else were to me the same as they are to you,
I loved well those cities, loved well the stately and rapid river,
The men and women I saw were all near to me,
Others the same—others who look back on me because I look'd
forward to them,
(The time will come, though I stop here to-day and to-night.)

1. Espars : toute pièce de bois utilisée comme mât, vergue, etc.
2. Flammes : drapeaux longs et étroits utilisés pour la signalisation et l'identification des bateaux.

5

What is it then between us?
What is the count of the scores or hundreds of years between us?

Whatever it is, it avails not—distance avails not, and place avails not,
I too lived, Brooklyn of ample hills was mine,
I too walk'd the streets of Manhattan island, and bathed in the waters around it,
I too felt the curious abrupt questionings stir within me,
In the day among crowds of people sometimes they came upon me,
In my walks home late at night or as I lay in my bed they came upon me,
I too had been struck from the float forever held in solution,
I too had receiv'd identity by my body,
That I was I knew was of my body, and what I should be I knew I should be of my body.

6

It is not upon you alone the dark patches fall,
The dark threw its patches down upon me also,
The best I had done seem'd to me blank and suspicious,
My great thoughts as I supposed them, were they not in reality meagre?
Nor is it you alone who know what it is to be evil,
I am he who knew what it was to be evil,[1]
I too knitted the old knot of contrariety,
Blabb'd, blush'd, resented, lied, stole, grudg'd,
Had guile, anger, lust, hot wishes I dared not speak,
Was wayward, vain, greedy, shallow, sly, cowardly, malignant,
The wolf, the snake, the hog, not wanting in me,
The cheating look, the frivolous word, the adulterous wish, not wanting,
Refusals, hates, postponements, meanness, laziness, none of these wanting,
Was one with the rest, the days and haps of the rest,

1. Dans « Song of Myself », la désintégration du moi préludait à une succession kaléidoscopique et triomphante de visions ; ici, elle permet au contraire la confession, l'aveu du manque et de la faute.

Was call'd by my nighest name by clear loud voices of young men
as they saw me approaching or passing,
Felt their arms on my neck as I stood, or the negligent leaning of
their flesh against me as I sat,
Saw many I loved in the street or ferry-boat or public assembly,
yet never told them a word,
Lived the same life with the rest, the same old laughing, gnawing,
sleeping,
Play'd the part that still looks back on the actor or actress,
The same old role, the role that is what we make it, as great as we
like,
Or as small as we like, or both great and small.

7

Closer yet I approach you,
What thought you have of me now, I had as much of you—I laid
in my stores in advance,
I consider'd long and seriously of you before you were born.

Who was to know what should come home to me?
Who knows but I am enjoying this?
Who knows, for all the distance, but I am as good as looking at you
now, for all you cannot see me?[1]

8

Ah, what can ever be more stately and admirable to me than
masthemm'd Manhattan?
River and sunset and scallop-edg'd waves of flood-tide?
The sea-gulls oscillating their bodies, the hay-boat in the twilight,
and the belated lighter?
What gods can exceed these that clasp me by the hand, and with
voices I love call me promptly and loudly by my nighest name
as I approach?
What is more subtle than this which ties me to the woman or man
that looks in my face?
Which fuses me into you now, and pours my meaning into you?

1. Retour du pouvoir visionnaire, passage du mode confessionnel au mode prophétique.

We understand then do we not?
What I promis'd without mentioning it, have you not accepted?
What the study could not teach—what the preaching could not accomplish is accomplish'd, is it not?

9

Flow on, river! flow with the flood-tide, and ebb with the ebb-tide![1]
Frolic on, crested and scallop-edg'd waves!
Gorgeous clouds of the sunset! drench with your splendor me, or the men and women generations after me!
Cross from shore to shore, countless crowds of passengers!
Stand up, tall masts of Mannahatta! stand up, beautiful hills of Brooklyn!
Throb, baffled and curious brain! throw out questions and answers!
Suspend here and everyhere, eternal float of solution!
Gaze, loving and thirsting eyes, in the house or street or public assembly!
Sound out, voices of young men! loudly and musically call me by my nighest name!
Live, old life! play the part that looks back on the actor or actress!
Play the old role, the tole that is great or small according as one makes it!
Consider, you who peruse me, whether I may not in unknown ways be looking upon you;
Be firm, rail over the river, to support those who lean idly, yet haste with the hasting current;
Fly on, sea-birds! fly sideways, or wheel in large circles high in the air;
Receive the summer sky, you water, and faithfully hold it till all downcast eyes have time to take it from you!
Diverge, fine spokes of light, from the shape of my head, or any one's head, in the sunlit water!
Come on, ships from the lower bay! pass up or down, white-sail'd schooners, sloops, lighters!

1. Le passage de la forme interrogative à la forme exclamative traduit à la fois le triomphe sur le temps et la victoire — par lecteur interposé — sur le doute et la culpabilité.

Flaunt away, flags of all nations! be duly lower'd at sunset!
Burn high your fires, foundry chimneys! cast black shadows at nightfall! cast red and yellow light over the tops of the houses!
Appearances, now or henceforth, indicate what you are,
You necessary film, continue to envelop the soul,
About my body for me, and your body for you, be hung our divinest aromas,
Thrive, cities—bring your freight, bring your shows, ample and sufficient rivers,
Expand, being than which none else is perhaps more spiritual,
Keep your places, objects than which none else is more lasting.

You have waited, you always wait, you dumb, beautiful ministers,
We receive you with free sense at last, and are insatiate henceforward,
Not you any more shall be able to foil us, or withhold yourselves from us,
We use you, and do not cast you aside—we plant you permanently within us,
We fathom you not—we love you—there is perfection in you also,
You furnish your parts toward eternity,
Great or small, you furnish your parts toward the soul.

Out of the Cradle Endlessly Rocking[1]

Out of the cradle endlessly rocking,
Out of the mocking-bird's throat, the musical shuttle,
Out of the Ninth-month midnight,[2]
Over the sterile sands and the fields beyond, where the child leaving his bed wander'd alone, bareheaded, barefoot,
Down from the shower'd halo,
Up from the mystic play of shadows twining and twisting as if they were alive,
Out from the patches of briers and blackberries,
From the memories of the bird that chanted to me,

1. Poème publié sous le titre « A Child's Reminiscence » le 24 décembre 1859 dans le *Saturday Press* de New York, puis inclus dans *Leaves of Grass* sous son titre actuel en 1871. Texte de la dernière édition.
2. Cf. « Crossing Brooklyn Ferry », n. 16.

From your memories sad brother, from the fitful risings and
    fallings I heard,
From under that yellow half-moon late-risen and swollen as if with
    tears,
From those beginning notes of yearning and love there in the
    mist,
From the thousand responses of my heart never to cease,
From the myriad thence-arous'd words,
From the word stronger and more delicious than any,
From such as now they start the scene revisiting,
As a flock, twittering, rising, or overhead passing,
Borne hither, ere all eludes me, hurriedly,
A man, yet by these tears a little boy again,
Throwing myself on the sand, confronting the waves,
I, chanter of pains and joys, uniter of here and hereafter,
Taking all hints to use them, but swiftly leaping beyond them,
A reminiscence sing.[1]

Once Paumanok,[2]
When the lilac-scent was in the air and Fifth-month grass was
    growing,
Up this seashore in some briers,
Two feather'd guests from Alabama, two together,
And their nest, and four light-green eggs spotted with brown,
And every day the he-bird to and fro near at hand,
And every day the she-bird crouch'd on her nest, silent, with
    bright eyes,
And every day I, a curious boy, never too close, never disturbing
    them,
Cautiously peering, absorbing, translating.[3]

Shine! shine! shine!
Pour down your warmth, great sun!
While we bask, we two together.

1. La structure très particulière de ces 22 vers est celle d'une phrase unique, qui se caractérise par l'inversion des termes et le rejet du verbe en position ultime : 15 vers pour le complément circonstanciel de lieu (origine de la « réminiscence »), 6 vers pour le sujet, assorti de divers épithètes et appositions, un vers — le plus court — pour le complément et (enfin) le verbe.

2. Nom indien pour Long Island, que Whitman affectionnait : voir le poème « Starting from Paumanok ».

3. Nouveau mouvement, nouvelle structure, fondée sur la coordination et l'omission du verbe.

Two together!
Winds blow south, or winds blow north,
Day come white, or night come black,
Home, or rivers and mountains from home,
Singing all time, minding no time,
While we two keep together.[1]

Till of a sudden,
May-be kill'd, unknown to her mate,
One forenoon the she-bird crouch'd not on the nest,
Nor return'd that afternoon, nor the next,
Nor ever appear'd again.

And thenceforward all summer in the sound of the sea,
And at night under the full of the moon in calmer weather,
Over the hoarse surging of the sea,
Or flitting from brier to brier by day,
I saw, I heard at intervals the remaining one, the he-bird,
The solitary guest from Alabama.

Blow! blow! blow!
Blow up sea-winds along Paumanok's shore;
I wait and I wait till you blow my mate to me.

Yes, when the stars glisten'd,
All night long on the prong of a moss-scallop'd stake,
Down almost amid the slapping waves,
Sat the lone singer wonderful causing tears.

He call'd on his mate,
He pour'd forth the meanings which I of all men know.

Yes my brother I know,
The rest might not, but I have treasur'd every note,
For more than once dimly down to the beach gliding,
Silent, avoiding the moonbeams, blending myself with the
shadows,

1. Les passages en *italiques*, qui « traduisent » le chant de l'oiseau, ont été constamment remaniés, d'édition en édition.

Recalling now the obscure shapes, the echoes, the sounds and sights after their sorts,
The white arms out in the breakers tirelessly tossing,
I, with bare feet, a child, the wind wafting my hair,
Listen'd long and long.

Listen'd to keep, to sing, now translating the notes,
Following you my brother.

Soothe! soothe! soothe!
Close on its wave soothes the wave behind,
And again another behind embracing and lapping, every one close,
But my love soothes not me, not me.

Low hangs the moon, it rose late,
It is lagging—O I think it is heavy with love, with love.

O madly the sea pushes upon the land,
With love, with love.

O night! do I not see my love fluttering out among the breakers?
What is that little black thing I see there in the white?

Loud! loud! loud!
Loud I call to you, my love!

High and clear I shoot my voice over the waves,
Surely you must know who is here, is here,
You must know who I am, my love.

Low-hanging moon!
What is that dusky spot in your brown yellow?
O it is the shape, the shape of my mate!
O moon do not keep her from me any longer.

Land! land! O land!
Whichever way I turn, O I think you could give me my mate back again if you only would,
For I am almost sure I see her dimly whichever way I look.

O rising stars!
Perhaps the one I want so much will rise, will rise with some of you.

O throat! O trembling throat!
Sound clearer through the atmosphere!
Pierce the woods, the earth,
Somewhere listening to catch you must be the one I want.

Shake out carols!
Solitary here, the night's carols!
Carols of lonesome love! death's carols!
Carols under that lagging, yellow, waning moon!
O under that moon where she droops almost down into the sea!
O reckless despairing carols.

But soft! sink low!
Soft! let me just murmur,
And do you wait a moment you husky-nois'd sea,
For somewhere I believe I heard my mate responding to me,
So faint, I must be still, be still to listen,
But not altogether still, for then she might not come immediately to me.

Hither my love!
Here I am! here!
With this just-sustain'd note I announce myself to you,
This gentle call is for you my love, for you.

Do not be decoy'd elsewhere,
That is the whistle of the wind, it is not my voice,
That is the fluttering, the fluttering of the spray,
Those are the shadows of leaves.

O darkness! O in vain!
O I am very sick and sorrowful.

O brown halo in the sky near the moon, drooping upon the sea!
O troubled reflection in the sea!
O throat! O throbbing heart!
And I singing uselessly, uselessly all the night.

O past! O happy life! O songs of joy!
In the air, in the woods, over fields,
Loved! loved! loved! loved! loved!
But my mate no more, no more whith me!
We two together no more.

The aria sinking,[1]
All else continuing, the stars shining,
The winds blowing, the notes of the bird continuous echoing,
With angry moans the fierce old mother incessantly moaning,
On the sands of Paumanok's shore gray and rustling,
The yellow half-moon enlarged, sagging down, drooping, the face of the sea almost touching,
The boy ecstatic, with his bare feet the waves, with his hair the atmosphere dallying,
The love in the heart long pent, now loose, now at last tumultuously bursting,
The aria's meaning, the ears, the soul, swiftly depositing,
The strange tears down the cheeks coursing,
The colloquy there, the trio, each uttering,
The undertone, the savage old mother incessantly crying,
To the boy's soul's questions sullenly timing, some drown'd secret hissing,
To the outsetting bard.[2]

Demon or bird! (said the boy's soul,)
Is it indeed toward your mate you sing? or is it really to me?
For I, that was a child, my tongue's use sleeping, now I have heard you,
Now in a moment I know what I am for, I awake,

1. Ce qui précède fait effectivement penser à une aria (mélodie accompagnée d'un ou de plusieurs instruments). On sait l'intérêt de Whitman pour le chant : ce passage traduit une tentative pour redonner tout son sens à l'expression « poésie lyrique », en créant à partir des seuls mots l'équivalent d'une mélodie, à l'aide de procédés récurrents : structures ternaires *(« Shine! shine! shine! »)*, échos et répétitions (ex. vers 75-78 : « *with love* »), invocations multiples, en particulier à la fin du mouvement, etc.

2. Nouvelle structure dont le principe organisateur est le participe présent. Les nombreux échos créés par cette répétition de formes en *-ing* donnent l'impression d'une rémanence, comme si le poète prenait le relais de l'oiseau. C'est donc bien à une métamorphose que nous assistons : grâce à l'oiseau, l'enfant devient « barde ».

And already a thousand singers, a thousand songs, clearer, louder
and more sorrowful than yours,
A thousand warbling echoes have started to life within me, never
to die.

O you singer solitary, singing by yourself, projecting me,
O solitary me listening, never more shall I cease perpetuating you,
Never more shall I escape, never more the reverberations,
Never more the cries of unsatisfied love be absent from me,
Never again leave me to be the peaceful child I was before what
there in the night,
By the sea under the yellow and sagging moon,
The messenger there arous'd, the fire, the sweet hell within,
The unknown want, the destiny of me.

O give me the clew! (it lurks in the night here somewhere,)
O if I am to have so much, let me have more!

A word then, (for I will conquer it,)
The word final, superior to all,
Subtle, sent up—what is it?—I listen;
Are you whispering it, and have been all the time, you sea-waves?
Is that it from your liquid rims and wet sands?

Whereto answering, the sea,
Delaying not, hurrying not,
Whisper'd me through the night, and very plainly before
day-break,
Lisp'd to me the low and delicious word death,
And again death, death, death, death,
Hissing melodious, neither like the bird nor like my arous'd child's
heart,
But edging near as privately for me rustling at my feet,
Creeping thence steadily up to my ears and laving me softly all
over,
Death, death, death, death, death.

Which I do not forget,
But fuse the song of my dusky demon and brother,
That he sang to me in the moonlight on Paumanok's gray beach,

With the thousand responsive songs at random,
My own songs awaked from that hour,
And with them the key, the word up from the waves,
The word of the sweetest song and all songs,
That strong and delicious word which, creeping to my feet,
(Or like some old crone rocking the cradle, swathed in sweet
garments, bending aside,)
The sea whisper'd me.

III – Les débuts de l'Amérique moderne, 1865-1920

La guerre de Sécession (1861-1865) marque sans doute une rupture décisive dans l'évolution historique et la vie littéraire des Etats-Unis. Aux signes avant-coureurs d'une crise politique, sociale et économique auxquels correspondaient de nouvelles œuvres littéraires ont succédé les violences du conflit entre l'Union et les Confédérés. Le déchirement se traduit par des conséquences économiques désastreuses et des effets tragiques sur les destins individuels. Les décennies qui suivent voient des bouleversements se produire dans tous les domaines de la vie et de la culture.

Avant la guerre de Sécession, la machine avait envahi le jardin de l'Amérique. Les écrivains de la Nouvelle-Angleterre s'étaient relativement peu alarmés de ses effets. Mais les progrès technologiques s'étendent après guerre à tout le pays. En 1869 est achevé le chemin de fer transcontinental et les cheminots font leurs premières grèves dans les années qui suivent. L'agitation ouvrière souvent violente et sanglante se poursuit jusqu'à la fin du siècle. A l'Age du Toc *(Gilded Age)*, selon les termes de Mark Twain, hommes d'affaires et politiciens concluent des alliances scélérates et s'enrichissent dans les cités de l'Est en plein essor. Ils contribuent aussi allégrement au pillage des ressources naturelles de l'Ouest, région désormais accessible grâce au développement du réseau ferroviaire que contrôlent souvent ces spéculateurs. Une douzaine de territoires de l'Ouest sont admis comme Etats de l'Union dans les trois décennies qui suivent la guerre de Sécession. Afin de frayer la voie de cette marche vers l'Ouest (le « destin manifeste » de l'homme blanc) les Indiens sont exterminés ou chassés de leurs terres, les forêts détruites et les troupeaux de bisons décimés. On sait que les clôtures de fil de fer barbelé et les colts ont joué un rôle déterminant dans la conquête de l'Ouest. Compte tenu des mouvements de population vers le Pacifique, la « Frontière » qui sépare la civilisation de l'état sauvage est virtuellement fermée après 1890. Le « Forest Reserve Act » de 1891 constitue la première disposition légale qui permette de sauver les ressources naturelles de l'exploitation industrielle forcenée.

Au sud, les Noirs libérés de l'esclavage, pendant et après la guerre, abandonnent souvent les régions rurales pour peupler les villes grouillantes du Nord. Ils s'ajoutent ainsi au flot des immigrants européens dans les ghettos urbains. Les Etats-Unis comptent 38 millions et demi d'habitants dès 1870, le double en 1900. Pour ceux des citadins qui peuvent bénéficier du progrès technologique, Alexander Graham Bell a inventé le téléphone en 1876 et Thomas Edison le phonographe (1878) ainsi que l'ampoule électrique (1879). Le tramway électrique fait son apparition à Baltimore en 1885 et la voiture à essence en 1893. La même année sont projetés les premiers films du cinématographe tant aux Etats-Unis qu'en France. Une décennie plus tard, l'ère moderne de la technologie trouve son élan le plus spectaculaire avec le vol du biplan des frères Wright.

Confrontés à la transformation brutale de l'Amérique en pays essentiellement industriel et urbain, les écrivains de l'après-guerre explorent de nouveaux modes littéraires, s'efforcent de décrire et, dans une certaine mesure, d'expliquer la déroutante variété des expériences de la modernité. Le pastoralisme littéraire auquel s'adjoignent les discours réalistes et naturalistes fournit aux auteurs un modèle explicatif et critique afin d'exprimer les valeurs traditionnelles de l'avant-guerre et d'interpréter les changements radicaux de la nouvelle ère.

1 – La machine, la cité et le pastoralisme littéraire

Le pastoralisme littéraire remonte aux *Idylles* grecques de Théocrite et aux *Eclogues* latines de Virgile. Il reparaît au travers des thèmes arcadiens de Shakespeare dans *As You Like It* et *The Tempest*. Pareil discours formule une dialectique critique entre un présent complexe et un passé à la fois simple et idéalisé. Chez les écrivains américains, c'est une synthèse qui, source d'espoir, se projette dans l'avenir et se résout en « paysage intermédiaire » selon la définition de Leo Marx dans *The Machine in the Garden* (1964). Si nos extraits se limitent à Mark Twain pour le début et Sherwood Anderson pour la phase ultime, d'autres auteurs de la période ont illustré dans leur fiction nombre d'aspects du pastoralisme, ou d'un antipastoralisme acerbe. Une liste partielle comprend W. D. Howells (*The Undiscovered Country*, 1880), Hamlin Garland (*Main-Travelled Roads*, 1891), Stephen Crane (« The Bride Comes to Yellow Sky », 1898), et Frank Norris (*The Octopus*, 1901). Les écrivains régionalistes tels que Harriet Beecher Stowe, Sarah Orne Jewett et Mary E. Wilkins Freeman ont également contribué au développement du genre. Chez tous ces auteurs, les conflits thématiques entre présent et passé s'inscrivent dans les schémas familiers du discours de la pastorale littéraire soit : ville/campagne, civilisation/nature, société/individu, machine/artisanat, changement/permanence, bruit/silence, tête/cœur, répression/liberté, sexualité polarisée / sympathie bisexuelle, domination de la femme / mystère féminin, vies désaxées / cérémonie et rituel, ambition étroite / rêves de dépassement de soi, expérience prosaïque / idéaux, isolement / solitude heureuse, mutisme desséchant / silence méditatif, verbosité / expression lyrique, religiosité confuse / foi religieuse, simple et sincère.

SAMUEL CLEMENS (MARK TWAIN), 1835-1910

Si l'expérience américaine de Mark Twain fut pour lui génératrice de tensions et de contradictions internes, le pastoralisme littéraire lui permit de les dissiper au moins partiellement. Après une enfance passée sur les bords du « majestueux, magnifique Mississippi » dans la relative simplicité du temps et de l'espace, Twain entend s'initier aux complexités d'une nation à ses débuts. Journaliste voué à l'errance, il s'aventure à l'est pour atteindre New York, puis il est pilote de bateau (1857-1861) et parcourt le Mississippi. Viennent ensuite cinq années passées à l'ouest comme prospecteur dans les mines d'argent et journaliste au Névada et en Californie. Il commence aussi une carrière littéraire avec « The Notorious Jumping Frog of Calaveras County » (1865), en s'inspirant de la tradition humoristique du Sud-Ouest. C'est dans cette même veine qu'il démontrera sa maîtrise en écrivant *Adventures of Huckleberry Finn* (1885). En 1870, il épouse une jeune fille de l'Est et, adoptant non sans frustration les manières plus distinguées de la région, devient gentleman et auteur à succès. Twain s'installe avec sa famille à Hartford, Connecticut, dans une somptueuse maison dont la forme rappelle volontairement celle des grands vapeurs du Mississippi de son enfance. Malgré sa circonspection vis-à-vis de l'âge industriel, il investit massivement dans une linotype à la fin des années quatre-vingt (« ce terrible miracle de la mécanique », dira-t-il) pour connaître un échec cuisant et y perdre une fortune. Accablé dans les vingt dernières années de sa vie par une santé déclinante et des deuils cruels, Twain devra entreprendre de longues tournées de conférences à travers le monde, afin notamment de payer ses dettes. Gagné par le pessimisme sur cette « maudite race humaine », il se livrera aussi à des diatribes de misanthrope. Sa « période sombre », selon ses propres termes, s'éclaire cependant par intermittence des honneurs rendus à l'homme et l'œuvre et de l'attachement indéfectible de son vieil et chaleureux ami W. D. Howells.

BIBLIOGRAPHIE SÉLECTIVE. — *The Works of Mark Twain*, Berkeley, University of California Press, 25 vol., 1972- ; Budd (Louis), *Mark Twain : Social Philosopher*, Bloomington, Indiana University Press, 1962 ; Cox (James), *Mark Twain : The Fate of Humor*, Princeton, NJ, Princeton University Press, 1966 ; Smith (Henry), *Mark Twain : The Development of a Writer*, Cambridge, Mass., Harvard University Press, 1962 ; Poli (Bernard), *Mark Twain, écrivain de l'Ouest*, Paris, PUF, 1965.

Old Times on the Mississippi[1]

III – THE CONTINUED PERPLEXITIES OF « CUB » PILOTING

En 1873, Twain est coauteur de The Gilded Age, *roman satirique sur la corruption du monde politique et des milieux économiques sous la présidence du général Grant. L'Ouest qui en est le lieu dramatique a pu raviver en Twain l'inspiration pastorale qui se traduit l'année suivante à propos de ses souvenirs d'enfance dans le Missouri avant la guerre de Sécession et de ses expériences de pilote sur le grand fleuve. Homme de l'Ouest comme Twain, et rédacteur de l'*Atlantic Monthly, *W. D. Howells publie avec enthousiasme les réminiscences de Twain sous le titre « Old Times on the Mississippi ». Cet extrait atteste que les images pastorales surgies de la mémoire de l'auteur relèvent à la fois du plaisir nostalgique propre au passager romantique et des regrets amers qui habitent le pilote, conscient du réel. L'impression d'une perte*

1. Le texte est tiré de l'*Atlantic Monthly*, XXXV (mars 1875), 288-289. Ce troisième chapitre réapparaît sous la forme des chap. VIII et IX de *Life on the Mississippi* (1883), volume qui incorpore les sept livraisons de « Old Times » et ajoute 45 chapitres supplémentaires que Twain écrivit après son retour du Mississippi en 1882. Ce voyage l'incita à terminer *Adventures of Huckleberry Finn.*

irrémédiable se substitue à la reconnaissance espérée de la vitalité du passé. On notera cependant que, paradoxalement, il déplore la beauté perdue du fleuve dans le souvenir plaisant d'un magnifique soleil couchant.

The face of the water, in time, became a wonderful book—a book that was a dead language to the uneducated passenger, but which told its mind to me without reserve, delivering its most cherished secrets as clearly as if it uttered them with a voice. And it was not a book to be read once and thrown aside, for it had a new story to tell every day. Throughout the long twelve hundred miles there was never a page that was void of interest, never one that you could leave unread without loss, never one that you would want to skip, thinking you could find higher enjoyment in some other thing. There never was so wonderful a book written by man; never one whose interest was so absorbing, so unflagging, so sparklingly renewed with every re-perusal. The passenger who could not read it was charmed with a peculiar sort of faint dimple on its surface (on the rare occasions when he did not overlook it altogether); but to the pilot that was an *italicized* passage; inded, it was more than that, it was a legend of the largest capitals, with a string of shouting exclamation points at the end of it; for it meant that a wreck or a rock was buried there that could tear the life out of the strongest vessel that ever floated. It is the faintest and simplest expression the water ever makes, and the most hideous to a pilot's eye. In truth, the passenger who could not read this book saw nothing but all manner of pretty pictures in it, painted by the sun and shaded by the clouds, whereas to the trained eye these were not pictures at all, but the grimmest and most dead-earnest of reading-matter.

Now when I had mastered the language of this water and had come to know every trifling feature that bordered the great river as familiarly as I knew the letters of the alphabet, I had made a valuable acquisition. But I had lost something, too. I had lost something which could never be restored to me while I lived. All the grace, the beauty, the poetry had gone out of the majestic river! I still keep in mind a certain wonderful sunset which I witnessed when steamboating was new to me. A broad expanse of the river was turned to blood; in the middle distance the red hue brightened into gold, through which a solitary log came floating, black and conspicuous; in one place a long, slanting mark lay sparkling upon the water; in another the surface was broken by boiling, tumbling rings, that were as many-tinted as an opal; where the ruddy flush was faintest, was a smooth spot that was covered with graceful circles and radiating lines, ever so delicately traced; the shore on our left was densely wooded, and the sombre shadow that fell from this forest was broken in one place by a long, ruffled trail that shone like silver; and high above the forest wall a clean-stemmed dead tree waved a single leafy bough that glowed like a flame in the unobstructed splendor that was flowing from the sun. There were graceful curves, reflected images, woody heights, soft distances; and over the whole scene, far and near, the dissolving lights drifted steadily, enriching it, every passing moment, with new marvels of coloring.

I stood like one bewitched. I drank it in, in a speechless rapture. The world was new to me, and I had never seen anything like this at home. But as I have said, a day came when I began to cease from noting the glories and the charms which the moon and the sun and the twilight wrought upon the river's face; another day came when I ceased altogether to note them. Then, if that sunset scene had been repeated, I should have looked upon it without rapture, and should have commented upon it, inwardly, after this fashion: This sun means that we are going to have wind to-morrow; that floating log means that the river is rising, small thanks to it; that slanting mark on the water refers to a bluff reef which is going to kill somebody's steamboat one of these nights, if it keeps on stretching out like that; those tumbling "boils" show a dissolving bar and a changing channel there; the lines and circles in the slick water over yonder are a warning that that troublesome place is shoaling up dangerously; that silver streak in the shadow of the forest is the "break" from a new snag, and he has located himself in the very best place he could have found to fish for steamboats; that tall dead tree, with a single living branch, is not going to last long, and then how is a body ever going to get through this blind place at night without the friendly old landmark?

No, the romance and the beauty were all gone from the river. All the value any feature of it had for me now was the amount of usefulness it could furnish toward compassing the safe piloting of a steamboat. Since those days, I have pitied doctors from my heart. What does the lovely flush in a beauty's cheek mean to a doctor but a "break" that ripples above some deadly disease? Are not all her visible charms sown thick with what are to him the signs and symbols of hidden decay? Does he ever see her beauty at all, or does n't he simply view her professionally, and comment upon her unwholesome condition all to himself? And does n't he sometimes wonder whether he has gained most or lost most by learning his trade?

Adventures of Huckleberry Finn[1]

(TOM SAWYER'S COMRADE)
SCENE: THE MISSISSIPPI
TIME: FORTY TO FIFTY YEARS AGO

NOTICE. — Persons attempting to find a motive in this narrative will be prosecuted; persons attempting to find a moral in it will be banished; persons attempting to find a plot in it will be shot.

BY ORDER OF THE AUTHOR
Per G. G., CHIEF OF ORDNANCE.

EXPLANATORY. — In this book a number of dialects are used, to wit: the Missouri negro dialect; the extremest form of the backwoods South-Western dialect; the ordinary "Pike-County" dialect; and four modified varieties of this last. The shadings have not been done in a hap-hazard fashion, or by guess-work; but pains-takingly, and with the trustworthy guidance and support of personal familiarity with these several forms of speech.
I make this explanation for the reason that without it many readers would suppose that all these characters were trying to talk alike and not succeeding.

THE AUTHOR

I

You don't know about me, without you have read a book by the name of "The Adventures of Tom Sawyer", but that ain't no matter. That book was made by Mr. Mark Twain, and he told the

1. En 1876, stimulé par les souvenirs de « Old Times » et le succès de *The Adventures of Tom Sawyer* (1876), Twain commença d'écrire ce qui, par à-coups, devait devenir *Adventures of Huckleberry Finn* neuf ans plus tard. Le texte est celui de la première édition américaine (1885).

truth, mainly. There was things which he stretched, but mainly he told the truth. That is nothing. I never seen anybody but lied, one time or another, without it was Aunt Polly, or the widow, or maybe Mary. Aunt Polly—Tom's Aunt Polly, she is—and Mary, and the Widow Douglas, is all told about in that book—which is mostly a true book; with some stretchers, as I said before.

Now the way that the book winds up, is this: Tom and me found the money that the robbers hid in the cave, and it made us rich. We got six thousand dollars apiece—all gold. It was an awful sight of money when it was piled up. Well, Judge Thatcher, he took it and put it out at interest, and it fetched us a dollar a day apiece, all the year round—more than a body could tell what to do with. The Widow Douglas, she took me for her son, and allowed she would sivilize me; but it was rough living in the house all the time, considering how dismal regular and decent the widow was in all her ways; and so when I couldn't stand it no longer, I lit out. I got into my old rags, and my sugar-hogshead again, and was free and satisfied. But Tom Sawyer, he hunted me up and said he was going to start a band of robbers, and I might join if I would go back to the widow and be respectable. So I went back.

The widow she cried over me, and called me a poor lost lamb, and she called me a lot of other names, too, but she never meant no harm by it. She put me in them new clothes again, and I couldn't do nothing but sweat and sweat, and feel all cramped up. Well, then, the old thing commenced again. The widow rung a bell for supper, and you had to come to time. When you got to the table you couldn't go right to eating, but you had to wait for the widow to tuck down her head and grumble a little over the victuals, though there warn't really anything the matter with them. That is, nothing only everything was cooked by itself. In a barrel of odds and ends it is different; things get mixed up, and the juice kind of swaps around, and the things go better.

After supper she got out her book and learned me about Moses and the Bulrushers; and I was in a sweat to find out all about him; but by-and-by she let it out that Moses had been dead a considerable long time; so then I didn't care no more about him; because I don't take no stock in dead people.

Pretty soon I wanted to smoke, and asked the widow to let me. But she wouldn't. She said it was a mean practice and wasn't clean, and I must try to not do it any more. That is just the way with some people. They get down on a thing when they don't know nothing about it. Here she was a bothering about Moses, which was no kin to her, and no use to anybody, being gone, you see, yet finding a power of fault with me for doing a thing that had some good in it. And she took snuff too; of course that was all right, because she done it herself.

Her sister, Miss Watson, a tolerable slim old maid, with goggles on, had just come to live with her, and took a set at me now, with a spelling-book. She worked me middling hard for about an hour, and then the widow made her ease up. I couldn't stood it much longer. Then for an hour it was deadly dull, and I was fidgety. Miss Watson would say, "Dont put your feet up there, Huckleberry;" and "dont scrunch up like that, Huckleberry—set up straight;" and pretty soon she would say, "Don't gap and stretch like that, Huckleberry—why don't you try to behave?" Then she told me all about the bad place, and I said I wished I was there. She got mad, then, but I didn't mean no harm. All I wanted was to go somewheres; all I wanted was a change, I warn't particular. She said it was wicked to say what I said; said she wouldn't say it for the whole world; *she* was going to live so as to go to the good place. Well, I couldn't see no advantage in going where she was going, so I made up my mind I wouldn't try for it. But I never said so, because it would only make trouble, and wouldn't do no good.

Now she had got a start, and she went on and told me all about the good place. She said all a body would have to do there was to go around all day long with a harp and sing, forever and ever. So I didn't think much of it. But I never said so. I asked her if she reckoned Tom Sawyer would go there, and, she said, not by a considerable sight. I was glad about that, because I wanted him and me to be together.

Miss Watson she kept pecking at me, and it got tiresome and lonesome. By-and-by they fetched the niggers in and had prayers, and then everybody was off to bed. I went up to my room with a piece of candle and put it on the table. Then I set down in a chair by the window and tried to think of something cheerful, but it warn't no use. I felt so lonesome I most wished I was dead. The stars was shining, and the leaves rustled in the woods ever so mournful; and I heard an owl, away off, who-whooing about somebody that was dead, and a whippowill and a dog crying about somebody that was going to die; and the wind was trying to whisper something to me and I couldn't make out what it was, and so it made the cold shivers run over me. Then away out in the woods I heard that kind of a sound that a ghost makes when it wants to tell about something that's on its mind and can't make itself understood, and so can't rest easy in its grave and has to go about that way every night grieving. I got so down-hearted and scared, I did wish I had some company. Pretty soon a spider went crawling up my shoulder, and I flipped it off and it lit in the candle; and before I could budge it was all shriveled up. I didn't need anybody to tell me that that was an awful bad sign and would fetch me some bad luck, so I was scared and most shook the clothes off of me. I got up and turned around in my tracks three times and crossed my breast every time; and then I tied up a little lock of my hair with a thread to keep witches away. But I hadn't no confidence. You do that when you've lost a horse-shoe that you've found, instead of nailing it up over the door, but I hadn't ever heard anybody say it was any way to keep off bad luck when you'd killed a spider.

I set down again, a shaking all over, and got out my pipe for a smoke; for the house was all as still as death, now, and so the widow wouldn't know. Well, after a long time I heard the clock away off in the town go boom—boom—boom—twelve licks—and all still again—stiller than ever. Pretty soon I heard a twig snap, down in the dark amongst the trees—something was a stirring. I set still and listened. Directly I could just barely hear a "*me-yow! me-yow!*" down there. That was good! Says I, "*me-yow, me-yow!*" as soft as I could, and then I put out the light and scrambled out of the window onto the shed. Then I slipped down to the ground and crawled in amongst the trees, and sure enough there was Tom Sawyer waiting for me.

IX

Séquestré par un père dégénéré, avide de son argent, Huck simule ensuite sa propre mort et trouve refuge à Jackson's Island sur le Mississippi. Il y rencontre l'esclave Jim qui, à l'annonce que sa propriétaire Miss Watson entendait le vendre, a lui aussi pris la fuite. Surgit à nouveau le thème pastoral : Huck et Jim sont tous deux prisonniers d'une civilisation chrétienne hypocrite dont ils s'échappent ensemble vers une nature libre et accueillante sur l'île inhabitée. C'est le regard innocent de Huck qui donne le jour à certaines des images parmi les plus originales et les plus lyriques de la prose de Twain.

[...] I wanted to go and look at a place right about the middle of the island, that I'd found when I was exploring; so we started, and soon got to it, because the island was only three miles long and a quarter of a mile wide.

This place was a tolerable long steep hill or ridge, about forty foot high. We had a rough time getting to the top, the sides was so steep and the bushes so thick. We tramped and clumb around all over it, and by-and-by found a good big cavern in the rock, most up to the top on the side towards Illinois. The cavern was as big as two or three rooms bunched together, and Jim could stand up straight in it. It was cool in there. Jim was for putting our traps in there, right away, but I said we didn't want to be climbing up and down there all the time.

Jim said if we had the canoe hid in a good place, and had all the traps in the cavern, we could rush there if anybody was to come to the island, and they would never find us without dogs. And besides, he said them little birds had said it was going to rain, and did I want the things to get wet?

So we went back and got the canoe and paddled up abreast the cavern, and lugged all the traps up there. Then we hunted up a place close by to hide the canoe in, amongst the thick willows. We took some fish off of the lines and set them again, and begun to get ready for dinner.

The door of the cavern was big enough to roll a hogshead in, and on one side of the door the floor stuck out a little bit and was flat and a good place to build a fire on. So we built it there and cooked dinner.

We spread the blankets inside for a carpet, and eat our dinner in there. We put all the other things handy at the back of the cavern. Pretty soon it darkened up and begun to thunder and lighten; so the birds was right about it. Directly it begun to rain, and it rained like all fury, too, and I never see the wind blow so. It was one of these regular summer storms. It would get so dark that it looked all blue-black outside, and lovely; and the rain would thrash along by so thick that the trees off a little ways looked dim and spider-webby; and here would come a blast of wind that would bend the trees down and turn up the pale underside of the leaves; and then a perfect ripper of a gust would follow along and set the branches to tossing their arms as if they was just wild; and next, when it was just about the bluest and blackest—*fst!* it was as bright as glory and you'd have a little glimpse of tree-tops a-plunging about, away off yonder in the storm, hundreds of yards further than you could see before; dark as sin again in a second, and now you'd hear the thunder let go with an awful crash and then go rumbling, grumbling, tumbling down the sky towards the under side of the world, like rolling empty barrels down stairs, where it's long stairs and they bounce a good deal, you know.

"Jim, this is nice," I says. "I wouldn't want to be nowhere else but here. Pass me along another hunk of fish and some hot corn-bread."

"Well, you wouldn't a ben here, 'f it hadn't a ben for Jim. You'd a ben down dah in de woods widout any dinner, en gittn' mos' drownded, too, dat you would, honey. Chickens knows when its gwyne to rain, en so do de birds, chile."

The river went on raising and raising for ten or twelve days, till at last it was over the banks. The water was three or four foot deep on the island in the low places and on the Illinois bottom. On that side it was a good many miles wide; but on the Missouri side it was the same old distance across—a half a mile—because the Missouri shore was just a wall of high bluffs.

Daytimes we paddled all over the island in the canoe. It was mighty cool and shady in the deep woods even if the sun was blazing outside. We went winding in and out amongst the trees; and sometimes the vines hung so thick we had to back away and go some other way. Well, on every old broken-down tree, you could see rabbits, and snakes, and such things; and when the island had been overflowed a day or two, they got so tame, on account of being hungry, that you could paddle right up and put your hand on them if you wanted to; but not the snakes and turtles—they would slide off in the water. The ridge our cavern was in, was full of them. We could a had pets enough if we'd wanted them.

One night we catched a little section of a lumber raft—nice pine planks. It was twelve foot wide and about fifteen or sixteen foot long, and the top stood above water six or seven inches, a solid level floor. We could see saw-logs go by in the daylight, sometimes, but we let them go; we didn't show ourselves in daylight.

Another night, when we was up at the head of the island, just before daylight, here comes a frame house down, on the west side. She was a two-story, and tilted over, considerable. We paddled out and got aboard—clumb in at an up-stairs window. But it was too dark to see yet, so we made the canoe fast and set in her to wait for daylight.

The light begun to come before we got to the foot of the island. Then we looked in at the window. We could make out a bed, and a table, and two old chairs, and lots of things around about on the floor; and there was clothes hanging against the wall. There was something laying on the floor in the far corner that looked like a man. So Jim says:

"Hello, you!"

But it didn't budge. So I hollered again, and then Jim says:

"De man ain't asleep—he's dead. You hold still—I'll go en see."

He went and bent down and looked, and says:

"It's a dead man. Yes, indeedy; naked, too. He's ben shot in de back. I reck'n he's ben dead two er three days. Come in, Huck, but doan' look at his face—it's too gashly."[1]

I didn't look at him at all. Jim throwed some old rags over him, but he needn't done it; I didn't want to see him. There was heaps of old greasy cards scattered around over the floor, and old whisky bottles, and a couple of masks made out of black cloth; and all over the walls was the ignorantest kind of words and pictures, made with charcoal. There was two old dirty calico dresses, and a sun-bonnet, and some women's under-clothes, hanging against the wall, and some men's clothing, too. We put the lot into the canoe; it might come good. There was a boy's old speckled straw hat on the floor; I took that too. And there was a bottle that had had milk in it; and it had a rag stopper for a baby to suck. We would a took the bottle, but it was broke. There was a seedy old chest, and an old hair trunk with the hinges broke. They stood open, but there warn't nothing left in them that was any account. The way things was scattered about, we reckoned the people left in a hurry and warn't fixed so as to carry off most of their stuff.

1. Jim identifie le cadavre comme étant celui du père de Huck et, de sa manière paternelle, entend protéger Huck de l'horrible vérité. Dans sa logique linguistique, Jim confond *gashly* et *ghastly*.

We got an old tin lantern, and a butcher-knife without any handle, and a bran-new Barlow knife[1] worth two bits[2] in any store, and a lot of tallow candles, and a tin candlestick, and a gourd, and a tin cup, and a ratty old bed-quilt off the bed, and a reticule with needles and pins and beeswax and buttons and thread and all such truck in it, and a hatchet and some nails, and a fish-line as thick as my little finger, with some monstrous hooks on it, and a roll of buckskin, and a leather dog-collar, and a horse-shoe, and some vials of medicine that didn't have no label on them; and just as we was leaving I found a tolerable good curry-comb, and Jim he found a ratty old fiddle-bow, and a wooden leg. The straps was broke off of it, but barring that, it was a good enough leg, though it was too long for me and not long enough for Jim, and we couldn't find the other one, though we hunted all around.

And so, take it all around, we made a good haul. When we was ready to shove off, we was a quarter of a mile below the island, and it was pretty broad day; so I made Jim lay down in the canoe and cover up with the quilt, because if he set up, people could tell he was a nigger a good ways off. I paddled over to the Illinois shore, and drifted down most a half a mile doing it. I crept up the dead water under the bank, and hadn't no accidents and didn't see nobody. We got home all safe.

XIX

Alors que Jim est recherché comme esclave fugitif et meurtrier présumé de Huck, tous deux s'échappent sur un radeau et descendent le fleuve. Ils vivent dans l'illusion pastorale puisque, selon Huck, « Other places do seem so cramped up and smothery », et « you feel mighty free and easy and comfortable on a raft ». Huck parle à Jim de la civilisation française et celui-ci répond en s'interrogeant sur le Français et son étrange langage, « Why doan he talk *like a man ? » Sur le radeau qui suit le cours du grand fleuve, ils demeurent insensibles au déterminisme des forces qui les entraînent au fil de l'eau. La machine constitue aussi un pouvoir hostile. Le radeau est brutalement abordé par un vapeur, accident qui provoque leur*

1. Couteau de poche du nom de son inventeur.
2. Pièces (ou « sous »).

séparation pour un temps. Dans le passage qui suit, ils sont de nouveau réunis après la douloureuse expérience que fait Huck sur la rive d'une vendetta sanglante chez des aristocrates du Sud. Huck s'extasie maintenant sur son retour à la liberté de la nature. Cette description mérite d'être comparée au passage de « Old Times » où Twain déplore que la connaissance scientifique du fleuve ait mis un terme au plaisir esthétique qu'il procurait. Par le regard de Huck, Twain fait reconnaître l'existence à la fois d'escrocs ambulants et de souches redoutables au ras de l'eau, ressentir aussi la liberté exaltante d'un jeune Adam américain qui s'éveille à l'aurore renaissante du monde naturel. Comme l'affirme le critique Leo Marx, Twain réconcilie par la voix de Huck le pilote réaliste et le passager romantique. Mais ce moment idyllique est brutalement interrompu par l'arrivée du Duc et du Roi, deux escrocs venus du monde civilisé, qui investissent immédiatement le radeau pour faire de Huck et Jim leurs esclaves. Désormais arraché à l'utopie d'une démocratie idéale, le radeau dérive dangereusement vers de nouvelles aventures dans le Sud profond des esclavagistes.

Two or three days and nights went by; I reckon I might say they swum by, they slid along so quiet and smooth and lovely. Here is the way we put in the time. It was a monstrous big river down there—sometimes a mile and a half wide; we run nights, and laid up and hid day-times; soon as night was most gone, we stopped navigating and tied up—nearly always in the dead water under a tow-head; and then cut young cottonwoods and willows and hid the raft with them. Then we set out the lines. Next we slid into the river and had a swim, so as to freshen up and cool off; then we set down on the sandy bottom where the water was about knee deep, and watched the daylight come. Not a sound, anywheres—perfectly still—just like the whole world was asleep, only sometimes the bull-frogs a-cluttering, maybe. The first thing to see, looking away over the water, was a kind of dull line—that was the woods on t'other side—you couldn't make nothing else out; then a pale place in the sky; then more paleness, spreading around; then the river softened up, away off, and warn't black any more, but gray; you could see little dark spots drifting along, ever so far away—trading scows, and such things; and long black streaks—rafts; sometimes you could hear a sweep screaking; or jumbled up voices, it was so still, and sounds come so far; and by-and-by you could see a streak on the water which you know by the look of the streak that there's a snag there in a swift current which breaks on it and makes that streak look that way; and you see the mist curl up off of the water, and the east reddens up, and the river, and you make out a log cabin in the edge of the woods, away on the bank on t'other side of the river, being a wood-yard, likely, and piled by them cheats so you can throw a dog through it anywheres; then the nice breeze springs up, and comes fanning you from over there, so cool and fresh, and sweet to smell, on account of the woods and the flowers; but sometimes not that way, because they've left dead fish laying around, gars, and such, and they do get pretty rank; and next you've got the full day, and everything smiling in the sun, and the song-birds just going it!

A little smoke couldn't be noticed, now, so we would take some fish off of the lines, and cook up a hot breakfast. And afterwards we would watch the lonesomeness of the river, and kind of lazy along, and by-and-by lazy off to sleep. Wake up, by-and-by, and look to see what done it, and maybe see a steamboat coughing along up stream, so far off towards the other side you couldn't tell nothing about her only whether she was stern-wheel or side-wheel; then for about an hour there wouldn't be nothing to hear nor nothing to see—just solid lonesomeness. Next you'd see a raft sliding by, away off yonder, and maybe a galoot on it chopping, because they're almost always doing it on a raft; you'd see the ax flash, and come down—you don't hear nothing; you see that ax go up again, and by the time it's above the man's head, then you hear the *k'chunk!*—it had took all that time to come over the water. So we would put in the day, lazying around, listening to the stillness. Once there was a thick fog, and the rafts and things that went by was beating tin pans so the steamboats wouldn't run over them. A scow or a raft went by so close we could hear them talking and cussing and laughing—heard them plain; but we couldn't see no sign of them; it made you feel crawly, it was like spirits carrying on that way in the air. Jim said he believed it was spirits; but I says:

"No, spirits wouldn't say, 'dern the dern[1] fog'. "

Soon as it was night, out we shoved; when we got her out to about the middle, we let her alone, and let her float wherever the current wanted her to; then we lit the pipes, and dangled our legs in the water and talked about all kinds of things—we was always

1. *Damned.*

naked, day and night, whenever the mosquitoes would let us—the new clothes Buck's folks made for me was too good to be comfortable, and besides I didn't go much on clothes, nohow.

Sometimes we'd have that whole river all to ourselves for the longest time. Yonder was the banks and the islands, across the water; and maybe a spark—which was a candle in a cabin window—and sometimes on the water you could see a spark or two—on a raft or a scow, you know; and maybe you could hear a fiddle or a song coming over from one of them crafts. It's lovely to live on a raft. We had the sky, up there, all speckled with stars, and we used to lay on our backs and look up at them, and discuss about whether they was made, or only just happened—Jim he allowed they was made, but I allowed they happened; I judged it would have took too long to *make* so many. Jim said the moon could a *laid* them; well, that looked kind of reasonable, so I didn't say nothing against it, because I've seen a frog lay most as many, so of course it could be done. We used to watch the stars that fell, too, and see them streak down. Jim allowed they'd got spoiled and was hove out of the nest.

Once or twice of a night we would see a steamboat slipping along in the dark, and now and then she would belch a whole world of sparks up out of her chimbleys,[1] and they would rain down in the river and look awful pretty; then she would turn a corner and her lights would wink out and her pow-wow shut off and leave the river still again; and by-and-by her waves would get to us, a long time after she was gone, and joggle the raft a bit, and after that you wouldn't hear nothing for you couldn't tell how long, except maybe frogs or something.

After midnight the people on shore went to bed, and then for two or three hours the shores was black—no more sparks in the cabin windows. These sparks was our clock—the first one that showed again meant morning was coming, so we hunted a place to hide and tie up, right away.

1. *Chimneys.*

SHERWOOD ANDERSON, 1876-1941

Ernest Hemingway a pu présenter *Huckleberry Finn* de Mark Twain comme la source de la littérature américaine moderne. Son jugement se renforce quand, recherchant les descendants de Huck, nous rencontrons d'abord le jeune narrateur à demi innocent dans la nouvelle de Sherwood Anderson « I Want to Know Why » (1918), puis le petit Joe, narrateur naïf de la nouvelle sportive « My Old Man » (1923) de Hemingway, enfin Holden Caulfield, narrateur à la première personne de *Catcher in the Rye* (1951) de J. D. Salinger. Moins reconnu dans la tradition pastorale est George Willard, le jeune observateur et écrivain en herbe de *Winesburg, Ohio* (1919), œuvre de Sherwood Anderson où le personnage s'identifie partiellement à son auteur. Après une vie riche d'expériences, Anderson entendait retrouver ses racines dans la bourgade américaine. A la différence de Mark Twain qui, au soir de sa vie, se livra à une satire pessimiste de la cupidité et de l'hypocrisie de la petite ville dans « The Man Who Corrupted Hadleyburg » (1899), Anderson perçut chez les victimes « grotesques » de l'Amérique rurale la quête d'un idéal pastoral de nature à donner un sens à leurs vies confuses. Typique est dans *Winesburg, Ohio* le conflit interne de Jesse Bentley, fermier proche de la nature. Ayant atteint l'âge adulte dans les années qui suivent la guerre de Sécession, il est comme les hommes de son temps, sous l'influence des courants profonds qui agitent l'Amérique quand s'ouvre l'ère industrielle moderne. Pour Anderson, le paysage intermédiaire entre vieille Amérique rurale et jeune Amérique urbaine n'est accessible que par la reconquête des valeurs villageoises. A cette fin, Anderson s'installe en 1925 dans une ferme proche de Marion en Virginie. A la recherche d'une vision équilibrée, il devient à la fois propriétaire et rédacteur en chef des journaux rivaux de la petite ville, l'un Démocrate, l'autre Républicain.

BIBLIOGRAPHIE SÉLECTIVE. — Anderson (David), *Sherwood Anderson : An Introduction and Interpretation*, New York, Holt, Rinehart and Winston, 1967 ; Bruyère (Claire), *Sherwood Anderson : L'impuissance créatrice*, Paris, Méridiens-Klincksieck, 1985 ; Howe (Irwing), *Sherwood Anderson*, New York, Sloane, 1951 ; Love (Glen), "Sherwood Anderson : Stilling the Machine", *New Americans : The Westerner and the Modern Experience in the American Novel*, Lewisburg, Pa., Bucknell University Press, 1982.

Hands[1]

Anderson a rappelé qu'il écrivit « Hands » à Chicago vers la fin de 1915. Il vivait alors dans un modeste meublé, s'acquittant d'une tâche qu'il détestait, la rédaction de réclames. Il s'assit un soir à sa table pour écrire « Hands » d'un trait. Quand ensuite, il descendit en ville il eut l'impression d'être réconcilié avec le monde urbain de son temps. (« I thought that the snow had suddenly made the city very beautiful. ») Comme les autres histoires de Winesburg, *« Hands » est « an idea grasped whole as one would pick an apple in an orchard ».*

Upon the half decayed veranda of a small frame house that stood near the edge of a ravine near the town of Winesburg, Ohio, a fat little old man walked nervously up and down. Across a long field that had been seeded for clover but that had produced only a dense crop of yellow mustard weeds, he could see the public highway along which went a wagon filled with berry pickers returning from the fields. The berry pickers, youths and maidens, laughed and shouted boisterously. A boy clad in a blue shirt leaped from the wagon and attempted to drag after him one of the maidens, who screamed and protested shrilly. The feet of the boy in the road kicked up a cloud of dust that floated across the face of the departing sun. Over the long field came a thin girlish voice. "Oh, you Wing Biddlebaum, comb you hair, it's falling into your eyes," commanded the voice to the man, who was bald and whose nervous little hands fiddled about the bare white forehead as though arranging a mass of tangled locks.

Wing Biddlebaum, forever frightened and beset by a ghostly band of doubts, did not think of himself as in any way a part of the life of the town where he had lived for twenty years. Among all the

1. Cette histoire et la suivante appartiennent à l'édition de *Winesburg* datant de 1919.

people of Winesburg but one had come close to him. With George Willard, son of Tom Willard, the proprietor of the New Willard House, he had formed something like a friendship. George Willard was the reporter on the *Winesburg Eagle* and sometimes in the evenings he walked out along the highway to Wing Biddlebaum's house. Now as the old man walked up and down on the veranda, his hands moving nervously about, he was hoping that George Willard would come and spend the evening with him. After the wagon containing the berry pickers had passed, he went across the field through the tall mustard weeds and climbing a rail fence peered anxiously along the road to the town. For a moment he stood thus, rubbing his hands together and looking up and down the road, and then, fear overcoming him, ran back to walk again upon the porch on his own house.

In the presence of George Willard, Wing Biddlebaum, who for twenty years had been the town mystery, lost something of his timidity, and his shadowy personality, submerged in a sea of doubts, came forth to look at the world. With the young reporter at his side, he ventured in the light of day into Main Street or strode up and down on the rickety front porch of his own house, talking excitedly. The voice that had been low and trembling became shrill and loud. The bent figure straightened. With a kind of wriggle, like a fish returned to the brook by the fisherman, Biddlebaum the silent began to talk, striving to put into words the ideas that had been accumulated by his mind during long years of silence.

Wing Biddlebaum talked much with his hands. The slender expressive fingers, forever active, forever striving to conceal themselves in his pockets or behind his back, came forth and became the piston rods of his machinery of expression.

The story of Wing Biddlebaum is a story of hands. Their restless activity, like unto the beating of the wings of an imprisoned bird, had given him his name. Some obscure poet of the town had thought of it. The hands alarmed their owner. He wanted to keep them hidden away and looked with amazement at the quiet inexpressive hands of other men who worked beside him in the fields, or passed, driving sleepy teams on country roads.

When he talked to George Willard, Wing Biddlebaum closed his fists and beat with them upon a table or on the walls of his house. The action made him more comfortable. If the desire to talk came to him when the two were walking in the fields, he sought out a stump or the top board of a fence and with his hands pounding busily talked with renewed ease.

The story of Wing Biddlebaum's hands is worth a book in itself. Sympathetically set forth it would tap many strange, beautiful qualities in obscure men. It is a job for a poet. In Winesburg the hands had attracted attention merely because of their activity. With them Wing Biddlebaum had picked a high as a hundred and forty quarts of strawberries in a day. They became his distinguishing feature, the source of his fame. Also they made more grotesque an already grotesque and elusive individuality. Winesburg was proud of the hands of Wing Biddlebaum in the same spirit in which it was proud of Banker White's new stone house and Wesley Moyer's bay stallion, Tony Tip, that had won the two-fifteen trot at the fall races in Cleveland.

As for George Willard, he had many times wanted to ask about the hands. At times an almost overwhelming curiosity had taken hold of him. He felt that there must be a reason for their strange activity and their inclination to keep hidden away and only a growing respect for Wing Biddlebaum kept him from blurting out the questions that were often in his mind.

Once he had been on the point of asking. The two were walking in the fields on a summer afternoon and had stopped to sit upon a grassy bank. All afternoon Wing Biddlebaum had talked as one inspired. By a fence he had stopped and beating like a giant woodpecker upon the top board had shouted at George Willard, condemning his tendency to be too much influenced by the people about him. "You are destroying yourself," he cried. "You have the inclination to be alone and to dream and you are afraid of dreams. You want to be like others in town here. You hear them talk and you try to imitate them."

On the grassy bank Wing Biddlebaum had tried again to drive his point home. His voice became soft and reminiscent, and with a sigh of contentment he launched into a long rambling talk, speaking as one lost in a dream.

Out of the dream Wing Biddlebaum made a picture for George Willard. In the picture men lived again in a kind of pastoral golden age. Across a green open country came clean-limbed young men, some afoot, some mounted upon horses. In crowds the young men came to gather about the feet of an old man who sat beneath a tree in a tiny garden and who talked to them.

Wing Biddlebaum became wholly inspired. For once he forgot the hands. Slowly they stole forth and lay upon George Willard's shoulders. Something new and bold came into the voice that talked. "You must try to forget all you have learned," said the old man. "You must begin to dream. From this time on you must shut your ears to the roaring of the voices."

Pausing in his speech, Wing Biddlebaum looked long and earnestly at George Willard. His eyes glowed. Again he raised the hands to caress the boy and then a look of horror swept over his face.

With a convulsive movement of his body, Wing Biddlebaum sprang to his feet and thrust his hands deep into his trousers pockets. Tears came to his eyes. "I must be getting along home. I can talk no more with you," he said nervously.

Without looking back, the old man had hurried down the hillside and across a meadow, leaving George Willard perplexed and frightened upon the grassy slope. With a shiver of dread the boy arose and went along the road toward town. "I'll not ask him about his hands," he thought, touched by the memory of the terror he had seen in the man's eyes. "There's something wrong, but I don't want to know what it is. His hands have something to do with his fear of me and of everyone."

And George Willard was right. Let us look briefly into the story of the hands. Perhaps our talking of them will arouse the poet who will tell the hidden wonder story of the influence for which the hands were but fluttering pennants of promise.

In his youth Wing Biddlebaum had been a school teacher in a town in Pennsylvania. He was not then known as Wing Biddlebaum, but went by the less euphonic name of Adolph Myers. As Adolph Myers he was much loved by the boys of his school.

Adolph Myers was meant by nature to be a teacher of youth. He was one of those rare, little-understood men who rule by a power so gentle that it passes as a lovable weakness. In their feeling for the boys under their charge such men are not unlike the finer sort of women in their love of men.

And yet that is but crudely stated. It needs the poet there. With the boys of his school, Adolph Myers had walked in the evening or had sat talking until dusk upon the schoolhouse steps lost in a kind of dream. Here and there went his hands, caressing the shoulders of the boys, playing about the tousled heads. As he talked his voice became soft and musical. There was a caress in that also. In a way the voice and the hands, the stroking of the shoulders and the touching of the hair were a part of the schoolmaster's effort to carry a dream into the young minds. By the caress that was in his fingers he expressed himself. He was one of those men in whom the force that creates life is diffused, not centralized. Under the caress of his hands doubt and disbelief went out of the minds of the boys and they began also to dream.

And then the tragedy. A half-witted boy of the school became enamored of the young master. In his bed at night he imagined unspeakable things and in the morning went forth to tell his dreams as facts. Strange, hideous accusations fell from his loose-hung lips. Through the Pennsylvania town went a shiver. Hidden, shadowy doubts that had been in men's minds concerning Adolph Myers were galvanized into beliefs.

The tragedy did not linger. Trembling lads were jerked out of bed and questioned. "He put his arms about me," said one. "His fingers were always playing in my hair," said another.

One afternoon a man of the town, Henry Bradford, who kept a saloon, came to the schoolhouse door. Calling Adolph Myers into the school yard he began to beat him with his fists. As his hard knuckles beat down into the frightened face of the schoolmaster, his wrath became more and more terrible. Screaming with dismay, the children ran here and there like disturbed insects. "I'll teach you to put your hands on my boy, you beast," roared the saloon keeper, who, tired of beating the master, had begun to kick him about the yard.

Adolph Myers was driven from the Pennsylvania town in the night. With lanterns in their hands a dozen men came to the door of the house where he lived alone and commanded that he dress and come forth. It was raining and one of the men had a rope in his hands. They had intended to hang the schoolmaster, but something in his figure, so small, white, and pitiful, touched their hearts and they let him escape. As he ran away into the darkness they repented of their weakness and ran after him, swearing and throwing sticks and great balls of soft mud at the figure that screamed and ran faster and faster into the darkness.

For twenty years Adolph Myers had lived alone in Winesburg. He was but forty but looked sixty-five. The name of Biddlebaum he got from a box of goods seen at a freight station as he hurried through an eastern Ohio town. He had an aunt in Winesburg, a black-toothed old woman who raised chickens, and with her he lived until she died. He had been ill for a year after the experience in Pennsylvania, and after his recovery worked as a day laborer in the fields, going timidly about and striving to conceal his hands. Although he did not understand what had happened he felt that the hands must be to blame. Again and again the fathers of the boys had talked of the hands. "Keep your hands to yourself," the saloon keeper had roared, dancing with fury in the schoolhouse yard.

Upon the veranda of his house by the ravine, Wing Biddlebaum continued to walk up and down until the sun had disappeared and the road beyond the filed was lost in the grey shadows. Going into his house he cut slices of bread and spread honey upon them. When the rumble of the evening train that took away the express cars loaded with the day's harvest of berries had passed and restored the silence of the summer night, he went again to walk upon the veranda. In the darkness he could not see the hands and they became quiet. Although he still hungered for the presence of the boy, who was the medium through which he expressed his love of man, the hunger became again a part of his loneliness and his waiting. Lighting a lamp, Wing Biddlebaum washed the few dishes soiled by his simple meal and, setting up a folding cot by the screen door that led to the porch, prepared to undress for the night. A few stray white bread crumbs lay on the cleanly washed floor by the table; putting the lamp upon a low stool he began to pick up the crumbs, carrying them to his mouth one by one with unbelievable rapidity. In the dense blotch of light beneath the table, the kneeling figure looked like a priest engaged in some service of his church. The nervous expressive fingers, flashing in and out of the light, might well have been mistaken for the fingers of the devotee going swiftly through decade after decade of his rosary.

Sophistication

C'est l'avant-dernière histoire de Winesburg *après la mort de la mère de George Willard. Elle faisait partie des personnages féminins inadaptés d'Anderson, l'une de ces « oversensitive women that... industrialism was to bring in such numbers into the world ». Avec une conscience plus mûre de la vie rurale, George rejoint la ville pour devenir l'écrivain qui, tel Anderson, tentera de transfigurer la vision de la campagne et de la cité dans le paysage futur de l'Amérique. De manière significative, Helen White revient dans cette histoire comme une jeune femme qui a mûri. Elle parachève ainsi le moment pastoral, réalisant une harmonie entre homme et femme qui s'accompagne d'une intense émotion.*

[...] On the veranda of Banker White's house Helen was restless and distraught. The instructor sat between the mother and daughter.[1] His talk wearied the girl. Although he had also been raised in an Ohio town, the instructor began to put on the airs of the city. He wanted to appear cosmopolitan. "I like the chance you have given me to study the background out of which most of our girls come," he declared. "It was good of you, Mrs. White, to have me down for the day." He turned to Helen and laughed. "Your life is still bound up with the life of this town?" he asked. "There are people here in whom you are interested?" To the girl his voice sounded pompous and heavy.

Helen arose and went into the house. At the door leading to a garden at the back she stopped and stood listening. Her mother began to talk. "There is no one here fit to associate with a girl of Helen's breeding," she said.

Helen ran down a flight of stairs at the back of the house and into the garden. In the darkness she stopped and stood trembling. It seemed to her that the world was full of meaningless people saying words. Afire with eagerness she ran through a garden gate and, turning a corner by the banker's barn, went into a little side street. "George! Where are you, George?" she cried, filled with nervous excitement. She stopped running, and leaned against a tree to laugh hysterically. Along the dark little street came George Willard, still saying words. "I'm going to walk right into her house. I'll go right in and sit down," he declared as he came up to

1. L'enseignant travaille à Cleveland, Ohio, dans le collège universitaire où Helen suit des cours.

her. He stopped and stared stupidly. "Come on," he said and took hold of her hand. With hanging heads they walked away along the street under the trees. Dry leaves rustled under foot. Now that he had found her George wondered what he had better do and say.

At the upper end of the Fair Ground, in Winesburg, there is a half decayed old grand-stand. It has never been painted and the boards are all warped out of shape. The Fair Ground stands on top of a low hill rising out of the valley of Wine Creek and from the grand-stand one can see at night, over a cornfield, the lights of the town reflected against the sky.

George and Helen climbed the hill to the Fair Ground, coming by the path past Waterworks Pond. The feeling of loneliness and isolation that had come to the young man in the crowded streets of his town was both broken and intensified by the presence of Helen. What he felt was reflected in her.

In youth there are always two forces fighting in people. The warm unthinking little animal struggles against the thing that reflects and remembers, and the older, the more sophisticated thing had possession of George Willard. Sensing his mood, Helen walked beside him filled with respect. When they got to the grand-stand they climbed up under the roof and sat down on one of the long bench-like seats.

There is something memorable in the experience to be had by going into a fair ground that stands at the edge of a Middle Western town on a night after the annual fair has been held. The sensation is one never to be forgotten. On all sides are ghosts, not of the dead, but of living people. Here, during the day just passed, have come the people pouring in from the town and the country around. Farmers with their wives and children and all the people from the hundreds of little frame houses have gathered within these board walls. Young girls have laughed and men with beards have talked of the affairs of their lives. The place has been filled to overflowing with life. It has itched and squirmed with life and now it is night and the life has all gone away. The silence is almost terrifying. One conceals oneself standing silently beside the trunk of a tree and what there is of a reflective tendency in his nature is intensified. One shudders at the thought of the meaninglessness of life while at the same instant, and if the people of the town are his people, one loves life so intensely that tears come into the eyes.

In the darkness under the roof of the grand-stand, George Willard sat beside Helen White and felt very keenly his own insignificance in the scheme of existence. Now that he had come out of town where the presence of the people stirring about, busy with a multitude of affairs, had been so irritating, the irritation was all gone. The presence of Helen renewed and refreshed him. It was as though her woman's hand was assisting him to make some minute readjustment of the machinery of his life. He began to think of the people in the town where he had always lived with something like reverence. He had reverence for Helen. He wanted to love and to be loved by her, but he did not want at the moment to be confused by her womanhood. In the darkness he took hold of her hand and when she crept close put a hand on her shoulder. A wind began to blow and he shivered. With all his strength he tried to hold and to understand the mood that had come upon him. In that high place in the darkness the two oddly sensitive human atoms held each other tightly and waited. In the mind of each was the same thought. "I have come to this lonely place and here is this other," was the substance of the thing felt.

In Winesburg the crowded day had run itself out into the long night of the late fall. Farm horses jogged away along lonely country roads pulling their portion of weary people. Clerks began to bring samples of goods in off the sidewalks and lock the doors of stores. In the Opera House a crowd had gathered to see a show and further down Main Street the fiddlers, their instruments tuned, sweated and worked to keep the feet of youth flying over a dance floor.

In the darkness in the grand-stand Helen White and George Willard remained silent. Now and then the spell that held them was broken and they turned and tried in the dim light to see into each other's eyes. They kissed but that impulse did not last. At the upper end of the Fair Ground a half dozen men worked over horses that had raced during the afternoon. The men had built a fire and were heating kettles of water. Only their legs could be seen as they passed back and forth in the light. When the wind blew the little flames of the fire danced crazily about.

George and Helen arose and walked away into the darkness. They went along a path past a field of corn that had not yet been cut. The wind whispered among the dry corn blades. For a moment during the walk back into town the spell that held them was broken. When they had come to the crest of Waterworks Hill they stopped by a tree and George again put his hands on the girl's shoulders. She embraced him eagerly and then again they drew quickly back from that impulse. They stopped kissing and stood a little apart. Mutual respect grew big in them. They were both embarrassed and to relieve their embarrassment dropped into the animalism of youth. They laughed and began to pull and haul at each other. In some way chastened and purified by the mood they had been in, they became, not man and woman, not boy and girl, but excited little animals.

It was so they went down the hill. In the darkness they played like two splendid young things in a young world. Once, running swiftly forward, Helen tripped George and he fell. He squirmed and shouted. Shaking with laughter, he rolled down the hill. Helen ran after thim. For just a moment she stopped in the darkness. There is no way of knowing what woman's thoughts went through her mind but, when the bottom of the hill was reached and she came up to the boy, she took his arm and walked beside him in dignified silence. For some reason they could not have explained they had both got from their silent evening together the thing needed. Man or boy, woman or girl, they had for a moment taken hold of the thing that makes the mature life of men and women in the modern world possible.

Les débuts de l'Amérique moderne

2 – Les écrivains réalistes décrivent la nouvelle ère

La seconde stratégie que conçoivent des écrivains américains pour dépeindre le nouvel âge industriel, le monde urbain et celui de la science, consiste à élaborer un mode littéraire réaliste. Essentiellement recherché comme une technique de nature à traduire fidèlement « things as they are », le réalisme devient une voie d'accès à la « vérité » dans la fiction et les œuvres critiques de nombreux auteurs après la guerre de Sécession, qu'ils soient régionalistes, humoristes, naturalistes, ou observateurs du comportement social et de la psychologie humaine. Le choix que nous proposons ici, de W. D. Howells, Henry James et Kate Chopin, s'accorde avec nombre d'idées que développe Howells dans ses essais séminaux sur le réalisme, examinant les indispensables éléments de complexité, de pragmatisme, de vraisemblance et d'exigence esthétique non moralisante. Howells énonce ces principes antiromantiques dans un éditorial consacré à la critique, « The Editor's Study », pour *Harper's Magazine* de 1886 à 1891, alors qu'il commente les œuvres littéraires des principaux auteurs américains et européens. Il rassemblera ensuite ses éditoriaux dans *Criticism and Fiction* (1891). En opposant le nouveau réalisme américain à un romantisme plus ancien et essentiellement anglais, Howells plaide pour des personnages d'Américains de tous les jours, néanmoins complexes et individualisés, par opposition à des Européens aristocratiques, conformes à des types littéraires. Pour tout ce qui a trait au milieu romanesque, ses préférences vont à l'Amérique contemporaine plutôt qu'à une Europe surannée et lointaine. L'intrigue, à son gré, devait s'attacher à des existences moyennes, plausibles, et éviter le sentimentalisme, le fantastique et l'horrible, autant que le sensationnalisme, en traitant des passions humaines du quotidien et des problèmes sociaux.

WILLIAM DEAN HOWELLS, 1837-1920

Comme son grand ami Mark Twain, Howells est venu de l'Ouest (Ohio) pour conquérir une célébrité littéraire à l'Est. Leur première rencontre a lieu à Boston où Twain rend visite au jeune Howells dans la salle de rédaction de l'*Atlantic Monthly* pour le remercier de la recension d'*Innocents Abroad* (1869). Par la suite, Howells accueillera les œuvres de son ami dans l'*Atlantic*, lira les épreuves de ses livres et le réconfortera dans les périodes difficiles. Pendant ce temps, Howells est l'auteur prolifique de fictions et de critiques, faisant campagne pour promouvoir un réalisme spécifiquement américain. Lorsqu'il passe à *Harper's Magazine* à la fin de 1885, la communauté littéraire de l'Est ressent que le foyer de la littérature américaine s'est déplacé de Boston à New York. Dans les trente-quatre années qui suivront, Howells jouera un rôle majeur comme romancier, critique et protecteur de jeunes écrivains, pour faire progresser la cause de la modernité littéraire. En jouant sur son second prénom, on dira de lui qu'il a acquis le statut de « Dean of American Letters ».

BIBLIOGRAPHIE SÉLECTIVE. — *Selected Edition of W. D. Howells*, 41 vol., Bloomington, Indiana University Press, 1968- ; Crowley (John), *The Black Heart's Truth: The Early Career of W. D. Howells*, Chapel Hill, University of North Carolina Press, 1985 ; Vanderbilt (Kermit), *The Achievement of William Dean Howells: A Reinterpretation*, Princeton, NJ, Princeton University Press, 1968 ; Rivière (Jean), *W. D. Howells*, Paris, Didier, 1972.

The Rise of Silas Lapham[1]

I

Ce premier passage de la dixième œuvre romanesque de Howells illustre la maturité de son talent dans le dialogue réaliste et l'exposition minimale. Il présente aussi une rapide introduction des personnages principaux, rassembant les thèmes majeurs dans une sorte d'ouverture d'opéra. Journaliste cynique, amateur d'entretiens, Bartley Hubbard est familier des lecteurs de A Modern Instance *(1882).*

When Bartley Hubbard went to interview Silas Lapham for the "Solid Men of Boston" series, which he undertook to finish up in "The Events," after he replaced their original projector on that newspaper, Lapham received him in his private office by previous appointment.

"Walk right in!" he called out to the journalist, whom he caught sight of through the door of the counting-room.

He did not rise from the desk at which he was writing, but he gave Bartley his left hand for welcome, and he rolled his large head in the direction of a vacant chair. "Sit down! I'll be with you in just half a minute."

"Take your time," said Bartley, with the ease he instantly felt. "I'm in no hurry." He took a note-book from his pocket, laid it on his knee, and began to sharpen a pencil.

"There!" Lapham pounded with his great hairy fist on the envelope he had been addressing. "William!" he called out, and he handed the letter to a boy who came to get it. "I want that to go right away. Well, sir," he continued, wheeling round in his leather-cushioned swivel-chair, and facing Bartley, seated so near that their knees almost touched, "so you want my life, death, and Christian sufferings, do you, young man?"

"That's what I'm after," said Bartley. "Your money or your life."

"I guess you wouldn't want my life without the money," said Lapham, as if he were willing to prolong these moments of preparation.

1. Ce texte est extrait du chap. I paru en feuilleton dans *Century Magazine* (novembre 1884) dans la forme la plus proche du manuscrit manquant et des intentions de l'auteur.

"Take 'em both," Bartley suggested. "Don't want your money without your life, if you come to that. But you're just one million times more interesting to the public than if you hadn't a dollar; and you know that as well as I do, Mr. Lapham. There's no use beating about the bush."

"No," said Lapham, somewhat absently. He put out his huge foot and pushed the ground-glass door shut between his little den and the book-keepers, in their larger den outside.

"In personal appearance," wrote Bartley in the sketch for which he now studied his subject, while he waited patiently for him to continue, "Silas Lapham is a fine type of the successful American. He has a square, bold chin, only partially concealed by the short, reddish-gray beard, growing to the edges of his firmly closing lips. His nose is short and straight; his forehead good, but broad rather than high; his eyes blue, and with a light in them that is kindly or sharp according to his mood. He is of medium height, and fills an average arm-chair with a solid bulk, which, on the day of our interview, was unpretentiously clad in a business suit of blue serge. His head droops somewhat from a short neck, which does not trouble itself to rise far from a pair of massive shoulders."

"I don't know as I know just where you want me to begin," said Lapham.

"Might begin with your birth; that's where most of us begin," replied Bartley.

A gleam of humorous appreciation shot into Lapham's blue eyes.

"I didn't know whether you wanted me to go quite so far back as that," he said. "But there's no disgrace in having been born, and I was born in the State of Vermont, pretty well up under the Canada line—so well up, in fact, that I came very near being an adoptive citizen; for I was bound to be an American of *some* sort, from the word Go! That was about—well, let me see!—pretty near sixty years ago: this is '75, and that was '20. Well, say I'm fifty-five years old; and I've *lived* 'em, too; not an hour of waste time about *me*, anywheres! I was born on a farm, and—"

"Worked in the fields summers and went to school winters: regulation thing?" Bartley cut in.

"Regulation thing," said Lapham, accepting this irreverent version of his history somewhat dryly.

"Parents poor, of course," suggested the journalist. "Any

barefoot business? Early deprivations of any kind, that would encourage the youthful reader to go and do likewise? Orphan myself, you know," said Bartley, with a smile of cynical good comradery.

Lapham looked at him silently, and then said with quiet self-respect, "I guess if you see these things as a joke, my life wont inter*est* you."

"Oh, yes, it will," returned Bartley, unabashed. "You'll see; it'll come out all right." And in fact it did so, in the interview which Bartley printed.

"Mr. Lapham," he wrote, "passed rapidly over the story of his early life, its poverty and its hardships, sweetened, however, by the recollections of a devoted mother, and a father who, if somewhat her inferior in education, was no less ambitious for the advancement of his children. They were quiet, unpretentious people, religious, after the fashion of that time, and of sterling morality, and they taught their children the simple virtues of the Old Testament and Poor Richard's Almanac."

Bartley could not deny himself this gibe; but he trusted to Lapham's unliterary habit of mind for his security in making it, and most other people would consider it sincere reporter's rhetoric.

"You know," he explained to Lapham, "that we have to look at all these facts as material, and we get the habit of classifying them. Sometimes a leading question will draw out a whole line of facts that a man himself would never think of." He went on to put several queries, and it was from Lapham's answers that he genralized the history of his childhood. "Mr. Lapham, although he did not dwell on his boyish trials and struggles, spoke of them with deep feeling and an abiding sense of their reality." This was what he added in the interview, and by the time he had got Lapham past the period where risen Americans are all pathetically alike in their narrow circumstances, their sufferings, and their aspirations, he had beguiled him into forgetfulness of the check he had received, and had him talking again in perfect enjoyment of his autobiography.

"Yes, sir," said Lapham, in a strain which Bartley was careful not to interrupt again, "a man never sees all that his mother has been to him till it's too late to let her know that he sees it. Why, *my* mother—" he stopped. "It gives me a lump in the throat," he said apologetically, with an attempt at a laugh. Then he went on: "She was a little, frail thing, not bigger than a good-sized intermediate school-girl; but she did the whole work of a family of boys, and boarded the hired men besides. She cooked, swept, washed, ironed, made and mended from daylight till dark—and from dark till daylight, I was going to say; for I don't know how she got any time for sleep. But I suppose she did. She got time to go to church, and to teach us to read the Bible, and to misunderstand it in the old way. She was *good*. But it aint her on her knees in church that comes back to me so much like the sight of an angel, as her on her knees before me at night, washing my poor, dirty little feet, that I'd run bare in all day, and making me decent for bed. There were six of us boys; it seems to me we were all of a size; and she was just so careful with all of us. I can feel her hands on my feet yet!" Bartley looked at Lapham's No. 10 boots and softly whistled through his teeth. "We were patched all over; but we wa'n't ragged. *I* don't know how she got through it. She didn't seem to think it was anything; and I guess it was no more than my father expected of her. *He* worked like a horse in doors and out—up at daylight, feeding the stock, and groaning round all day with his rheumatism, but not stopping."

Bartley hid a yawn over his note-book, and probably, if he could have spoken his mind, he would have suggested to Lapham that he was not there for the purpose of interviewing his ancestry. But Bartley had learned to practice a patience with his victims which he did not always feel, and to feign an interest in their digressions till he could bring them up with a round turn.

"I tell you," said Lapham, jabbing the point of his penknife into the writing-pad on the desk before him, "when I hear women complaining nowadays that their lives are stunted and empty, I want to tell 'em about my *mother's* life. *I* could paint it out for 'em."

Bartley saw his opportunity at the word paint, and cut in. "And you say, Mr. Lapham, that you discovered this mineral paint on the old farm yourself?"

Lapham acquiesced in the return to business. "*I* didn't discover it," he said, scrupulously. "My father found it one day, in a hole made by a tree blowing down. There it was, laying loose in the pit, and sticking to the roots that had pulled up a big cake of dirt with 'em. *I* don't know what give him the idea that there was money in it, but he did think so from the start. I guess, if they'd had the word in those days, they'd considered him pretty much of a crank about it. He was trying as long as he lived to get that paint introduced; but he couldn't make it go. The country was so poor they couldn't paint their houses with anything; and father hadn't any facilities. It got to be a kind of joke with us; and I guess that paint-mine[1] did as much as any one thing to make us boys clear out as soon as we got old enough. All my brothers went West and took up land; but I hung on to New England, and I hung on to the old farm, not because the paint-mine was on it, but because the old house was—and the graves. Well," said Lapham, as if unwilling to give himself too much credit, "there wouldn't been any market for it, anyway. You can go through that part of the State and buy more farms than you can shake a stick at for less money than it cost to build the barns on 'em. Of course, it's turned out a good thing. I keep the old house up in good shape, and we spend a month or so there every summer. M' wife kind of likes it, and the girls. Pretty place; sightly all round it. I've got a force of men at work there the whole time, and I've got a man and his wife in the house. Had a family meeting there last year; the whole connection from out West. There!" Lapham rose from his seat and took down a large warped, unframed photograph from the top of his desk, passing his hand over it, and then blowing vigorously upon it, to clear it of the dust. "There we are, *all* of us."

"I don't need to look twice at *you*," said Bartley, putting his finger on one of the heads.

"Well, that's Bill," said Lapham, with a gratified laugh. "He's about as brainy as any of us, I guess. He's one of their leading lawyers, out Dubuque way; been judge of the Common Pleas once or twice. That's his son—just graduated at Yale—alongside of my youngest girl. Good-looking chap, aint he?"

"*She's* a good-looking chap," said Bartley, with prompt irreverence. He hastened to add, at the frown which gathered between Lapham's eyes, "What a beautiful creature she is! What a lovely, refined, sensitive face! And she looks *good*, too."

"She *is* good," said the father, relenting.

"And, after all, that's about the best thing in a woman," said the potential reprobate. "If my wife wasn't good enough to keep both of us straight, I don't know what would become of me."

1. Composé à base de fer et d'huile de lin qui produit une peinture de qualité.

"My other daughter," said Lapham, indicating a girl with eyes that showed large, and a face of singular gravity. "Mis' Lapham," he continued, touching his wife's effigy with his little finger. "My brother Willard and his family—farm at Kankakee. Hazard Lapham and his wife—Baptist preacher in Kansas. Jim and his three girls—milling business at Minneapolis. Ben and his family—practicing medicine in Fort Wayne."

The figures were clustered in an irregular group in front of an old farm-house, whose original ugliness had been smartened up with a coat of Lapham's own paint and heightened with an incongruous piazza. The photographer had not been able to conceal the fact that they were all decent, honest-looking, sensible people, with a very fair share of beauty among the young girls; some of these were extremely pretty, in fact. He had put them into awkward and constrained attitudes, of course; and they all looked as if they had the instrument of torture which photographers call a head-rest under their occiputs. Here and there an elderly lady's face was a mere blur; and some of the younger children had twitched themselves into wavering shadows, and might have passed for spirit-photographs of their own little ghosts. It was the standard family-group photograph, in which most Americans have figured at some time or other; and Lapham exhibited a just satisfaction in it. "I presume," he mused aloud, as he put it back on top of his desk, "that we sha'n't soon get together again, all of us."

"And you say," suggested Bartley, "that you staid right along on the old place, when the rest cleared out West?"

"No-o-o-o," said Lapham, with a long, loud drawl; "I cleared out West too, first off. Went to Texas. Texas was all the cry in those days. But I got enough of the Lone Star in about three months, and I come back with the idea that Vermont was good enough for me."

"Fatted calf business?" queried Bartley, with his pencil poised above his note-book.

"I presume they were glad to see me," said Lapham, with dignity. "Mother," he added gently, "died that winter, and I staid on with father. I buried him in the spring; and then I came down to a little place called Lumberville, and picked up what jobs I could get. I worked round at the saw-mills, and I was ostler awhile at the hotel—I always *did* like a good horse. Well, I *wa'n't* exactly a college graduate, and I went to school odd times. I got to driving the stage after while, and by and by I *bought* the stage and run the business myself. Then I hired the tavern-stand, and—well, to make a long story short, then I got married. Yes," said Lapham, with pride, "I married the school-teacher. We did pretty well with the hotel, and my wife she was always at me to paint up. Well, I put it off, and *put* if off, as a man will, till one day I give in, and says I, 'Well, *let's* paint up. Why, Pert,'—m'wife's name's Persis,—'I've got a whole paint-mine out on the farm. Let's go out and look at it.' So we drove out. I'd let the place for seventy-five dollars a year to a shif'less kind of a Kanuck[1] that had come down that way; and I'd hated to see the house with him in it; but we drove out one Saturday afternoon, and we brought back about a bushel of the stuff in the buggy-seat, and I tried it crude, and I tried it burnt; and I liked it. M'wife she liked it, too. There wa'n't any painter by trade in the village, and I mixed it myself. Well, sir, that tavern's got that coat of paint on it yet, and it haint ever had any other, and I don't know's it ever will. Well, you know, I felt as if it was a kind of a harumscarum experiment, all the while; and I presume I shouldn't have tried it, but I kind of liked to do it because father'd always set so much store by his paint-mine. And when I'd got the first coat on,"—Lapham called it *cut*,—"I presume I must have set as much as half an hour, looking at it and thinking how he would have enjoyed it. I've had my share of luck in this world, and I aint a-going to complain on my *own* account, but I've noticed that most things get along too late for most people. It made me feel bad, and it took all the pride out my success with the paint, thinking of father. Seemed to me I might 'a' taken more interest in it when he was by to see; but we've got to live and learn. Well, I called my wife out,—I'd tried it on the back of the house, you know,—and she left her dishes,—I can remember she came out with her sleeves rolled up and set down alongside of me on the trestle,—and says I, 'What do you think, Persis?' And says she, 'Well, you haint got a paint-mine, Silas Lapham; you've got a *gold*-mine.' She always was just so enthusiastic about things. Well, it was just after two or three boats had burnt up out West, and a lot of lives lost, and there was a great cry about non-inflammable paint, and I guess that was what was in her mind. 'Well, I guess it aint any gold-mine, Persis,' says I; 'but I guess it *is* a paint-mine. I'm going to have it analyzed, and if it turns out what I think it is, I'm going to work it. And if

1. Canadien francophone.

father hadn't had such a long name, I should call it the Nehemiah Lapham Mineral Paint. But, any rate, every barrel of it, and every keg, and every bottle, and every package, big or little, has got to have the initials and figures N. L. f. 1835, S. L. t. 1855, on it. Father found it in 1835, and I tried it in 1855.' "

" 'S. T.—1860—X.' business," said Bartley.

"Yes," said Lapham, "but I hadn't heard of Plantation Bitters[1] then, and I hadn't seen any of the fellow's labels. I set to work and I got a man down from Boston; and I carried him out to the farm, and he analyzed it—made a regular job of it. Well, sir, we built a kiln, and we kept a lot of that paint-ore red-hot for forty-eight hours; kept the Kanuck and his family up, firing. The presence of iron in the ore showed with the magnet from the start; and when he came to test it, he found out that it contained about seventy-five per cent. of the peroxide of iron."

Lapham pronounced the scientific phrases with a sort of reverent satisfaction, as if awed through his pride by a little lingering uncertainty as to what peroxide was. He accented it as if it were purr-ox-*eyed*; and Bartley had to get him to spell it.

"Well, and what then?" he asked, when he had made a note of the percentage.

"What then?" echoed Lapham. "Well, then, the fellow set down and told me, 'You've got a paint here,' says he, 'that's going to drive every other mineral paint out of the market. Why,' says he, 'it'll drive 'em right into the Back Bay!'[2] Of course, *I* didn't know what the Back Bay was then; but I begun to open my eyes; thought I'd had 'em open before, but I guess I hadn't. Says he, 'That paint has got hydraulic cement in it, and it can stand fire and water and acids'; he named over a lot of things. Says he, 'It'll mix easily with linseed oil, whether you want to use it boiled or raw; and it aint a-going to crack nor fade any; and it aint a-going to scale. When you've got your arrangements for burning it properly, you're going to have a paint that will stand like the everlasting hills, in every climate under the sun.' Then he went into a lot of

1. Médicament alcalin bien connu en 1860.

2. Marais du fleuve Charles le long de Beacon Street, rue élégante de Boston. Il fut asséché après la guerre de Sécession pour édifier des constructions. Silas y a fait l'acquisition d'un terrain et s'apprête à construire une splendide maison qui reflétera sa situation de millionnaire. Quand la maison inachevée et non assurée est entièrement détruite par un incendie (chap. XXIV), Silas accomplit alors son « ascension » morale au milieu de cette catastrophe financière et sociale. Il quitte Boston et retourne à la vie rurale, simple et saine de sa ferme du Vermont.

particulars, and I begun to think he was drawing a long bow, and meant to make his bill accordingly. So I kept pretty cool; but the fellow's bill didn't amount to anything hardly—said I might pay him after I got going; young chap, and pretty easy; but every word he said was gospel. Well, I aint a-going to brag up my paint; I don't suppose you came here to hear me blow—"

"Oh, yes, I did," said Bartley. "That's what I want. Tell all there is to tell, and I can boil it down afterward. A man can't make a greater mistake with a reporter than to hold back anything out of modesty. It may be the very thing we want to know. What we want is the whole truth, and more; we've got so much modesty of our own that we can temper almost any statement."

Lapham looked as if he did not quite like this tone, and he resumed a little more quietly. "Oh, there isn't really very much more to say about the paint itself. But you can use it for almost anything where a paint is wanted, inside or out. It'll prevent decay, and it'll stop it, after it's begun, in tin or iron. You can paint the inside of a cistern or a bath-tub with it, and water wont hurt it; and you can paint a steam-boiler with it, and heat wont. You can cover a brick wall with it, or a railroad car, or the deck of a steam-boat, and you can't do a better thing for either."

"Never tried it on the human conscience, I suppose," suggested Bartley.

"No, sir," replied Lapham, gravely. "I guess you want to keep that as free from paint as you can, if you want much use of it. I never cared to try any of it on mine."

HENRY JAMES, 1843-1916

A l'image de Mark Twain, Henry James découvre en W. D. Howells son allié le plus déterminé pour servir la cause du réalisme. Ils font connaissance en 1866 et passent immédiatement de longues heures à parler de l'art du roman. Howells publie avec enthousiasme la fiction de James dans *The Atlantic*, ils font mutuellement des comptes rendus de leurs ouvrages et s'associent pour la vie dans une campagne dirigée contre les courants littéraires romantiques et victoriens. James a repris la distinction entre le réel et le romantique dans un passage mémorable : « The real represents to my perception the things we cannot *not* know, sooner or later, in one way or another. » « The romantic stands, on the other hand, for the things that... we never *can* directly know. » Initié à l'Europe dans sa jeunesse par des voyages et des études, il appartenait à une famille particulièrement douée qui comptait notamment son frère William, philosophe et théoricien du pragmatisme et de l'empirisme. James se préparait à offrir aux lecteurs une vision globale de la civilisation occidentale. Au-delà de 1870, il abandonnera à Howells le champ de l'expérience américaine et s'installera en Angleterre, trouvant dans la scène internationale un point de vue particulièrement stimulant pour observer attentivement la psychologie et le comportement social de ses concitoyens. C'est avant et après son séjour en Angleterre que James a produit les analyses de caractère les plus incisives de la fiction moderne. Des stylistes du XXe siècle aussi divers que Edith Wharton, Ernest Hemingway et F. Scott Fitzgerald ont manifesté leur admiration pour l'acuité, le professionnalisme et la technique littéraire de James.

BIBLIOGRAPHIE SÉLECTIVE. — *The Novels and Tales*, 24 vol., New York, Scribner's, 1907-1909 ; Anderson (Charles), *Person, Place, and Thing in Henry James's Novels*, Durham, North Carolina, Duke University Press, 1977 ; Fogel (Daniel), *Henry James and the Structure of the Romantic Imagination*, Baton Rouge, Louisiana State University Press, 1981 ; Matthiessen (F. O.), *Henry James : The Major Phase*, New York, Oxford University Press, 1944 ; Henry James, (N. Blake, C. Vieilledent, ed.), *Delta*, 15, 1982.

The Ambassadors[1]

LIVRE 12 — II

Mme Newsome qui emploie l'Américain Lambert Strether l'a envoyé à Paris pour sauver son fils Chad de l'emprise d'une Française, Mme Marie de Vionnet, de dix ans plus âgée que lui. Mais à Paris, Strether observe que leurs rapports semblent

1. Publié pour la première fois en 1903. Texte du vol. 22 de l'édition de New York (1907-1909).

platoniques. Chad est en outre devenu un homme du monde cultivé. C'est en apparence un « attachement vertueux ». Strether prolonge sa mission mais, lors d'un week-end à la campagne, éprouve un choc à la découverte de Marie et Chad en train de canoter non loin d'une auberge. Les soupçons de Mme Newsome sur leur intimité étaient en somme fondés. Dans ce chapitre, Marie espère regagner l'estime de Strether et éviter de perdre Chad. La tension monte au cours d'une vive discussion dans cette scène exemplaire de James qui révèle la subtilité de son réalisme psychologique.

"Oh, you're all right, you're all right," he almost impatiently declared; his impatience being moreover not for her pressure, but for her scruple. More and more distinct to him was the tune to which she would have had the matter out with Chad; more and more vivid for him the idea that she had been nervous as to what he might be able to "stand." Yes, it had been a question if he had "stood" what the scene on the river had given him, and, though the young man had doubtless opined in favour of his recuperation, her own last word must have been that she should feel easier in seeing for herself. That was it, unmistakeably; she *was* seeing for herself. What he could stand was thus, in these moments, in the balance for Strether, who reflected, as he became fully aware of it, that he must properly brace himself. He wanted fully to appear to stand all he might; and there was a certain command of the situation for him in this very wish not to look too much at sea. She was ready with everything, but so, sufficiently, was he; that is he was at one point the more prepared of the two, inasmuch as, for all her cleverness, she could n't produce on the spot—and it was surprising—an account of the motive of her note. He had the advantage that his pronouncing her "all right" gave him for an enquiry. "May I ask, delighted as I've been to come, if you've wished to say something special?" He spoke as if she might have seen he had been waiting for it—not indeed with discomfort, but with natural interest. Then he saw that she was a little taken aback, was even surprised herself at the detail she had neglected—the only one ever yet; having somehow assumed he would known, would recognise, would leave some things not to be said. She looked at him, however, an instant as if to convey that if he wanted them *all*—!

"Selfish and vulgar—that's what I must seem to you. You've done everything for me, and here I am as if I were asking for more. But it is n't," she went on, "because I'm afraid—though I *am* of course afraid, as a woman in my position always is. I mean it is n't because one lives in terror—it is n't because of that one is selfish, for I'm ready to give you my word to-night that I don't care; don't care what still may happen and what I may lose. I don't ask you to raise your little finger for me again, nor do I wish so much as to mention to you what we've talked of before, either my danger or my safety, or his mother, or his sister, or the girl he may marry, or the fortune he may make or miss, or the right or the wrong, of any kind, he may do. If after the help one has had from you one can't either take care of one's self or simply hold one's tongue, one must renounce all claim to be an object of interest. It's in the name of what I *do* care about that I've tried still to keep hold of you. How can I be indifferent," she asked, "to how I appear to you?" And as he found himself unable immediately to say: "Why, if you're going, *need* you, after all? It is impossible you should stay on—so that one may n't lose you?"

"Impossible I should live with you here instead of going home?"

"Not 'with' us, if you object to that, but near enough to us, somewhere, for us to see you—well," she beautifully brought out, "when we feel we *must*. How shall we not sometimes feel it? I've wanted to see you often when I could n't," she pursued, "all these last weeks. How shan't I then miss you now, with the sense of your being gone forever?" Then as if the straightness of this appeal, taking him unprepared, had visibly left him wondering: "Where *is* your 'home' moreover now—what has become of it? I've made a change in your life, I know I have; I've upset everything in your mind as well; in your sense of—what shall I call it?—all the decencies and possibilities. It gives me a kind of detestation—" She pulled up short.

Oh but he wanted to hear. "Detestation of what?"

"Of everything—of life."

"Ah that's too much," he laughed—"or too little!"

"Too little, precisely"—she was eager. "What I hate is myself—when I think that one has to take so much, to be happy, out of the lives of others, and that one is n't happy even then. One does it to cheat one's self and to stop one's mouth—but that's only at the best for a little. The wretched self is always there, always making one somehow a fresh anxiety. What it comes to is that it's not, that it's never, a happiness, any happiness at all, to *take*. The only safe thing is to give. It's what plays you least false." Interesting, touching, strikingly sincere as she let these things come from her, she yet puzzled and troubled him—so fine was the quaver of her quietness. He felt what he had felt before with her, that there was always more behind what she showed, and more and more again behind that. "You know so, at least," she added, "where you are!"

"*You* ought to know it indeed then; for is n't what you've been giving exactly what has brought us together this way? You've been making, as I've so fully let you know I've felt," Strether said, "the most precious present I've ever seen made, and if you can't sit down peacefully on that performance you *are*, no doubt, born to torment yourself. But you ought," he wound up, "to be easy."

"And not trouble you any more, no doubt—not thrust on you even the wonder and the beauty of what I've done; only let you regard our business as over, and well over, and see you depart in a peace that matches my own? No doubt, no doubt, no doubt," she nervously repeated—"all the more that I don't really pretend I believe you could n't, for yourself, *not* have done what you have. I don't pretend you feel yourself victimised, for this evidently is the way you live, and it's what—we're agreed—is the best way. Yes, as you say," she continued after a moment, "I ought to be easy and rest on my work. Well then here am I doing so. I *am* easy. You'll have it for your last impression. When is it you say you go?" she asked with a quick change.

He took some time to reply—his last impression was more and more so mixed a one. It produced in him a vague disappointment, a drop that was deeper even than the fall of his elation the previous night. The good of what he had done, if he had done so much, was n't there to enliven him quite to the point that would have been ideal for a grand gay finale. Women were thus endlessly absorbent, and to deal with them was to walk on water. What was at bottom the matter with her, embroider as she might and disclaim as she might—what was at bottom the matter with her was simply Chad himself. It was of Chad she was after all renewedly afraid; the strange strength of her passion was the very strength of her fear; she clung to *him*, Lambert Strether, as to a source of safety she had tested, and, generous graceful truthful as she might try to be, exquisite as she was, she dreaded the term of his being within reach. With this sharpest perception yet, it was like a chill in the air to him, it was almost appalling, that a creature so fine could be, by mysterious forces, a creature so exploited. For at the end of all things they *were* mysterious : she had but made Chad what he was—so why could she think she had made him infinite? She had made him better, she had made him best, she had made him anything one would; but it came to our friend with supreme queerness that he was none the less only Chad. Strether had the sense that *he*, a little, had made him too; his high appreciation had, as it were, consecrated her work. The work, however admirable, was nevertheless of the strict human order, and in short it was marvellous that the companion of mere earthly joys, of comforts, aberrations (however one classed them) within the common experience, should be so transcendently prized. It might have made Strether hot or shy, as such secrets of others brought home sometimes do make us; but he was held there by something so hard that it was fairly grim. This was not the discomposure of last night; that had quite passed—such discomposures were a detail; the real coercion was to see a man ineffably adored. There it was again—it took women, it took women; if to deal with them was to walk on water what wonder that the water rose? And it had never surely risen higher than round this woman. He presently found himself taking a long look from her, and the next thing he knew he had uttered all his thought. "You're afraid for your life!"

It drew out her long look, and he soon enough saw why. A spasm came into her face, the tears she had already been unable to hide overflowed at first in silence, and then, as the sound suddenly comes from a child, quickened to gasps, to sobs. She sat and covered her face with her hands, giving up all attempt at a manner. "It's how you see me, it's how you see me"—she caught her breath with it—"and it's as I *am*, and as I must take myself, and of course it's no matter." Her emotion was at first so incoherent that he could only stand there at a loss, stand with his sense of having upset her, though of having done it by the truth. He had to listen to her in a silence that he made no immediate effort to attenuate, feeling her doubly woeful amid all her dim diffused elegance; consenting to it as he had consented to the rest, and even conscious of some vague inward irony in the presence of such a fine free range of bliss and bale. He could n't say it was *not* no matter; for he was serving her to the end, he now knew, anyway—quite as if what he thought of her had nothing to do with it. It was actually moreover as if he did n't think of her at all, as if he could think of nothing but the passion, mature, abysmal, pitiful, she represented, and the possibilities she betrayed. She was older for him to-night, visibly less exempt from the touch of time; but she was as much as ever the finest and subtlest creature, the happiest apparition, it had been given him, in all his years, to meet; and yet he could see her there as vulgarly troubled, in very truth, as a maidservant crying for her young man. The only thing was that she judged herself as the maidservant would n't; the weakness of which wisdom too, the dishonour of which judgement, seemed but to sink her lower. Her collapse, however, no doubt, was briefer and she had in a manner recovered herself before he intervened. "Of course I'm afraid for my life. But that's nothing. It is n't that."

He was silent a little longer, as if thinking what it might be. "There's something I have in mind that I can still do."

But she threw off at last, with a sharp sad headshake, drying her eyes, what he could still do. "I don't care for that. Of course, as I've said, you're acting, in your wonderful way, for yourself; and what's for yourself is no more my business—though I may reach out unholy hands so clumsily to touch it—than if it were something in Timbuctoo. It's only that you don't snub me, as you've had fifty chances to do—it's only your beautiful patience that makes one forget one's manners. In spite of your patience, all the same," she went on, "you'd do anything rather than be with us here, even if that were possible. You'd do everything for us but be mixed up with us—which is a statement you can easily answer to the advantage of your own manners. You can say 'What's the use of talking of things that at the best are impossible?' What *is* of course the use? It's only my little madness. You'd talk if you were tormented. And I don't mean now about *him*. Oh for him—!" Positively, strangely, bitterly, as it seemed to Strether, she gave "him," for the moment, away. "You don't care what I think of you; but I happen to care what you think of me. And what you *might*," she added. "What you perhaps even did."

He gained time. "What I did—?"

"Did think before. Before this. *Did n't* you think—?"

But he had already stopped her. "I did n't think anything. I never think a step further than I'm obliged to."

"That's perfectly false, I believe," she returned—"except that you may, no doubt, often pull up when things become *too* ugly; or even, I'll say, to save you a protest, too beautiful. At any rate, even so far as it's true, we've thrust on you appearances that you've had to take in and that have therefore made your obligation. Ugly or beautiful—it does n't matter what we call them—you were getting on without them, and that's where we're detestable. We bore you—that's where we are. And we may well—for what we've cost you. All you can do *now* is not to think at all. And I who should have liked to seem to you—well, sublime!"

He could only after a moment re-echo Miss Barrace. "You're wonderful!"

"I'm old and abject and hideous"—she went on as without hearing him. "Abject above all. Or old above all. It's when one's old that it's worst. I don't care what becomes of it—let what *will*; there it is. It's a doom—I know it; you can't see it more than I do myself. Things have to happen as they will." With which she came back again to what, face to face with him, had so quite broken down. "Of course you would n't, even if possible, and no matter what may happen to you, be near us. But think of me, think of me—!" She exhaled it into air.

He took refuge in repeating something he had already said and that she had made nothing of. "There's something I believe I can still do." And he put his hand out for good-bye.

She again made nothing of it; she went on with her insistence. "That won't help you. There's nothing to help you."

"Well, it may help *you*," he said.

She shook her head. "There's not a grain of certainty in my future—for the only certainty is that I shall be the loser in the end."

She had n't taken his hand, but she moved with him to the door. "That's cheerful," he laughed, "for your benefactor!"

"What's cheerful for *me*," she replied, "is that we might, you and I, have been friends. That's it—that's it. You see how, as I say, I want everything. I've wanted you too."

"Ah but you've *had* me!" he declared, at the door, with an emphasis that made an end.

V

Strether a rencontré Chad et l'a pressé de ne pas quitter Marie. Dans ce dernier chapitre, il se prépare à regagner Woolett au Massachusetts pour affronter la colère de Mme Newsome. Mais sa confidente, Maria Gostrey, tombée amoureuse de Strether, lui suggère discrètement de rester avec elle. Strether est dans une totale confusion morale. Il a rejeté les contraintes puritaines de l'Amérique pour une ample expérience « à la française ». Il est alors desenchanté à double titre. Ce qui ressemble maintenant à ses valeurs morales a été l'objet de larges débats de la critique.

He had, however, within two days, another separation to face. He had sent Maria Gostrey a word early, by hand, to ask if he might come to breakfast; in consequence of which, at noon, she awaited him in the cool shade of her little Dutch-looking dining-room. This retreat was at the back of the house, with a view of a scrap of old garden that had been saved from modern ravage; and though he had on more than one other occasion had his legs under its small and peculiarly polished table of hospitality, the place had never before struck him as so sacred to pleasant knowledge, to intimate charm, to antique order, to a neatness that was almost august. To sit there was, as he had told his hostess before, to see life reflected for the time in ideally kept pewter; which was somehow becoming, improving to life, so that one's eyes were held and comforted. Strether's were comforted at all events now—and the more that it was the last time—with the charming effect, on the board bare of a cloth and proud of its perfect surface, of the small old crockery and old silver, matched by the more substantial pieces happily disposed about the room. The specimens of vivid Delf,[1] in particular, had the dignity of family portraits; and it was in the midst of them that our friend resignedly expressed himself. He spoke even with a certain philosophic humour. "There's nothing more to wait for; I seem to have done a good day's work. I've let them have it all round. I've seen Chad, who has been to London and come back. He tells me I'm 'exciting,' and I seem indeed pretty well to have upset every one. I've at any rate excited *him*. He's distinctly restless."

1. Porcelaine hollandaise (Delft).

"You've excited *me*," Miss Gostrey smiled. "*I'm* distinctly restless."

"Oh you were that when I found you. It seems to me I've rather got you out of it. What's this," he asked as he looked about him, "but a haunt of ancient peace?"

"I wish with all my heart," she presently replied, "I could make you treat it as a haven of rest." On which they fronted each other, across the table, as if things unuttered were in the air.

Strether seemed, in his way, when he next spoke, to take some of them up. "It would n't give me—that would be the trouble—what it will, no doubt, still give you. I'm not," he explained, leaning back in his chair, but with his eyes on a small ripe round melon—"in real harmony with what surrounds me. You *are*. I take it too hard. You *don't*. It makes—that's what it comes to in the end—a fool of me." Then at a tangent, "What has he been doing in London?" he demanded.

"Ah one may go to London," Maria laughed. "You know *I* did."

Yes—he took the reminder. "And you brought *me* back." He brooded there opposite to her, but without gloom. "Whom has Chad brought? He's full of ideas. And I wrote to Sarah,"[1] he added, "the first thing this morning. So I'm square. I'm ready for them."

She neglected certain parts of this speech in the interest of others. "Marie said to me the other day that she felt him to have the makings of an immense man of business."

"There it is. He's the son of his father!"

"But *such* a father!"

"Ah just the right one from that point of view! But it is n't his father in him," Strether added, "that troubles me."

"What is it then?" He came back to his breakfast; he partook presently of the charming melon, which she liberally cut for him; and it was only after this that he met her question. Then moreover it was but to remark that he'd answer her presently. She waited, she watched, she served him and amused him, and it was perhaps with this last idea that she soon reminded him of his having never

1. Mme Sarah Pocock est la sœur de Chad. Mrs Newsome l'a envoyée à Paris quand échoue le dessein de faire ramener Chad aux Etats-Unis par Strether.

even yet named to her the article produced at Woollett. "Do you remember our talking of it in London—that night at the play?" Before he could say yes, however, she had put it to him for other matters. Did he remember, did he remember—this and that of their first days? He remembered everything, bringing up with humour even things of which she professed no recollection, things she vehemently denied; and falling back above all on the great interest of their early time, the curiosity felt by both of them as to where he would "come out." They had so assumed it was to be in some wonderful place—they had thought of it as so very *much* out. Well, that was doubtless what it had been—since he had come out just there. He was out, in truth, as far as it was possible to be, and must now rather bethink himself of getting in again. He found on the spot the image of his recent history; he was like one of the figures of the old clock at Berne. *They* came out, on one side, at their hour, jigged along their little course in the public eye, and went in on the other side. He too had jigged his little course—him too a modest retreat awaited. He offered now, should she really like to know, to name the great product of Woollett. It would be a great commentary on everything. At this she stopped him off; she not only had no wish to know, but she would n't know for the world. She had done with the products of Woollett—for all the good she had got from them. She desired no further news of them, and she mentioned that Madame de Vionnet herself had, to her knowledge, lived exempt from the information he was ready to supply. She had never consented to receive it, though she would have taken it, under stress, from Mrs. Pocock. But it was a matter about which Mrs. Pocock appeared to have had little to say—never sounding the word—and it did n't signify now. There was nothing clearly for Maria Gostrey that signified now—save one sharp point, that is, to which she came in time. "I don't know whether it's before you as a possibility that, left to himself, Mr. Chad may after all go back. I judge that it *is* more or less so before you, from what you just now said of him."

Her guest had his eyes on her, kindly but attentively, as if foreseeing what was to follow this. "I don't think it will be for the money." And then as she seemed uncertain: "I mean I don't believe it will be for that he'll give her up."

"Then he *will* give her up?"

Strether waited a moment, rather slow and deliberate now,

drawing out a little this last soft stage, pleading with her in various suggestive and unspoken ways for patience and understanding. "What were you just about to ask me?"

"Is there anything he can do that would make you patch it up?"

"With Mrs. Newsome?"

Her assent, as if she had had a delicacy about sounding the name, was only in her face; but she added with it: "Or is there anything he can do that would make *her* try it?"

"To patch it up with me?" His answer came at last in a conclusive headshake. "There's nothing any one can do. It's over. Over for both of us."

Maria wondered, seemed a little to doubt. "Are you so sure for her?"

"Oh yes—sure now. Too much has happened. I'm different for her."

She took it in then, drawing a deeper breath. "I see. So that as she's different for *you*—"

"Ah but," he interrupted, "she's not." And as Miss Gostrey wondered again: "She's the same. She's more than ever the same. But I do what I did n't before—I *see* her."

He spoke gravely and as if responsibly—since he had to pronounce; and the effect of it was slightly solemn, so that she simply exclaimed "Oh!" Satisfied and grateful, however, she showed in her own next words an acceptance of his statement. "What then do you go home to?"

He had pushed his plate a little away, occupied with another side of the matter; taking refuge verily in that side and feeling so moved that he soon found himself on his feet. He was affected in advance by what he believed might come from her, and he would have liked to forestall it and deal with it tenderly; yet in the presence of it he wished still more to be—though as smoothly as possible—deterrent and conclusive. He put her question by for the moment; he told her more about Chad. "It would have been impossible to meet me more than he did last night on the question of the infamy of not sticking to her."

"Is that what you called it for him—'infamy'?"

"Oh rather! I described to him in detail the base creature he'd be, and he quite agrees with me about it."

"So that it's really as if you had nailed him?"

"Quite really as if—! I told him I should curse him."

"Oh," she smiled, "you *have* done it." And then having thought again: "You *can't* after that propose—!" Yet she scanned his face.

"Propose again to Mrs. Newsome?"

She hesitated afresh, but she brought it out. "I've never believed, you know, that you did propose. I always believed it was really she—and, so far as that goes, I can understand it. What I mean is," she explained, "that with such a spirit—the spirit of curses!—you breach is past mending. She has only to know what you've done to him never again to raise a finger."

"I've done," said Strether, "what I could—one can't do more. He protests his devotion and his horror. But I'm not sure I've saved him. He protests too much. He asks how one can dream of his being tired. But he has all life before him."

Maria saw what he meant. "He's formed to please."

"And it's our friend who has formed him." Strether felt in it the strange irony.

"So it's scarcely his fault!"

"It's at any rate his danger. I mean," said Strether, "it's hers. But she knows it."

"Yes, she knows it. And is your idea," Miss Gostrey asked, "that there was some other woman in London?"

"Yes. No. That is I *have* no ideas. I'm afraid of them. I've done with them." And he put out his hand to her. "Good-bye."

It brought her back to her unanswered question. "To what do you go home?"

"I don't know. There will always be something."

"To a great difference," she said as she kept his hand.

"A great difference—no doubt. Yet I shall see what I can make of it."

"Shall you make anything so good—?" But, as if remembering what Mrs. Newsome had done, it was as far as she went.

He had sufficiently understood. "So good as this place at this moment? So good as what *you* make of everything you touch?" He took a moment to say, for, really and truly, what stood about him there in her offer—which was as the offer of exquisite service, of lightened care, for the rest of his days—might well have tempted. It built him softly round, if roofed him warmly over, it rested, all so firm, on selection. And what ruled selection was beauty and knowledge. It was awkward, it was almost stupid, not to seem to prize such things; yet, none the less, so far as they made his opportunity they made it only for a moment. She'd moreover understand—she always understood.

That indeed might be, but meanwhile she was going on. "There's nothing, you know, I would n't do for you."

"Oh yes—I know."

"There's nothing," she repeated, "in all the world."

"I know. I know. But all the same I must go." He had got it at last. "To be right."

"To be right?"

She had echoed it in vague deprecation, but he felt it already clear for her. "That, you see, is my only logic. Not, out of the whole affair, to have got anything for myself."

She thought. "But with your wonderful impressions you'll have got a great deal."

"A great deal"—he agreed. "But nothing like *you*. It's you who would make me wrong!"

Honest and fine, she could n't greatly pretend she did n't see it. Still she could pretend just a little. "But why should you be so dreadfully right?"

"That's the way that—if I must go—you yourself would be the first to want me. And I can't do anything else."

So then she had to take it, though still with her defeated protest. "It is n't so much your *being* 'right'—it's your horrible sharp eye for what makes you so."

"Oh but you're just as bad yourself. You can't resist me when I point that out."

She sighed it at last all comically, all tragically, away. "I can't indeed resist you."

"Then there we are!" said Strether.

THE END

KATE CHOPIN, 1851-1904

Les auteurs régionalistes, adeptes de la couleur locale, furent des partisans appréciés de Howells et de son école réaliste. Les femmes figurent en bonne place parmi eux. Leur regard était attentif au détail descriptif et leur sympathie allait aux obscures destinées. Ces auteurs contribuèrent à enrichir la conscience collective d'une culture américaine marquée par la variété et la vitalité. Parmi ce groupe on relèvera les noms de Jewett, Freeman et Stowe (Nouvelle-Angleterre) déjà mentionnés, ainsi que d'Edward Eggleston (Middle West), Bret Harte (Far West) auxquels se joindra George W. Cable en Louisiane, enfin Kate Chopin, récemment redécouverte. Mariée à l'âge de dix-neuf ans, Kate Chopin quitte Saint-Louis pour la Louisiane où elle élève une nombreuse famille, tandis que la richesse culturelle du pays des bayous enflamme son imagination. Après la mort de son mari, elle retourne à Saint-Louis et commence sa carrière tardive d'audacieux auteur réaliste, pré-freudien. Elle estime trop édénique et complaisante l'approche régionaliste de ses homologues de la Nouvelle-Angleterre et du Middle West. Malheureusement, lecteurs et critiques de la fin du XIXe siècle sont unanimes à désapprouver la franchise qu'oppose Kate Chopin à pareille complaisance dans sa présentation hardie de la sexualité féminine, qu'évoque son héroïne réprimée et devenue adultère de *The Awakening* (1899). Kate Chopin peut aujourd'hui prétendre au panthéon littéraire américain, étant également reconnue pour son féminisme rebelle, son acuité psychologique et son art du roman.

BIBLIOGRAPHIE SÉLECTIVE. — *The Complete Works of Kate Chopin*, ed. Per Peyersted, 2 vol., Baton Rouge, Louisiana State University Press, 1969 ; Peyersted (Per), *Kate Chopin : A Critical Biography*, Baton Rouge, Louisiana University Press, 1969 ; voir Le Sud avant Faulkner, Etienne de Planchard, ed., *Caliban*, XXVI, 1989.

A Respectable Woman[1]

Mrs. Baroda was a little provoked to learn that her husband expected his friend, Gouvernail, up to spend a week or two on the plantation.

They had entertained a good deal during the winter; much of the time had also been passed in New Orleans in various forms of mild dissipation. She was looking forward to a period of unbroken rest, now, and undisturbed tête-à-tête with her husband, when he informed her that Gouvernail was coming up to stay a week or two.

This was a man she had heard much of but never seen. He had been her husband's college friend; was now a journalist, and in no sense a society man or "a man about town," which were, perhaps, some of the reasons she had never met him. But she had unconsciously formed an image of him in her mind. She pictured him tall, slim, cynical; with eye-glasses, and his hands in his pockets; and she did not like him. Gouvernail was slim enough, but he wasn't very tall nor very cynical; neither did he wear eye-glasses nor carry his hands in his pockets. And she rather liked him when he first presented himself.

But why she liked him she could not explain satisfactorily to herself when she partly attempted to do so. She could discover in him none of those brilliant and promising traits which Gaston, her husband, had often assured her that he possessed. On the contrary, he sat rather mute and receptive before her chatty eagerness to make him feel at home and in face of Gaston's frank and wordy hospitality. His manner was as courteous toward her as the most exacting woman could require; but he made no direct appeal to her approval or even esteem.

Once settled at the plantation he seemed to like to sit upon the wide portico in the shade of one of the big Corinthian pillars, smoking his cigar lazily and listening attentively to Gaston's experience as a sugar planter.

"This is what I call living," he would utter with deep satisfaction, as the air that swept across the sugar field caressed him with its warm and scented velvety touch. It pleased him also to get on familiar terms with the big dogs that came about him, rubbing

1. Extrait de *A Night in Acadie* (Way and Williams, 1897).

themselves sociably against his legs. He did not care to fish, and displayed no eagerness to go out and kill grosbecs when Gaston proposed doing so.

Gouvernail's personality puzzled Mrs. Baroda, but she liked him. Indeed, he was a lovable, inoffensive fellow. After a few days, when she could understand him no better than at first, she gave over being puzzled and remained piqued. In this mood she left her husband and her guest, for the most part, alone together. Then finding that Gouvernail took no manner of exception to her action, she imposed her society upon him, accompanying him in his idle strolls to the mill and walks along the batture. She persistently sought to penetrate the reserve in which he had unconsciously enveloped himself.

"When is he going—your friend?" she one day asked her husband. "For my part, he tires me frightfully."

"Not for a week yet, dear. I can't understand; he gives you no trouble."

"No. I should like him better if he did; if he were more like others, and I had to plan somewhat for his comfort and enjoyment."

Gaston took his wife's pretty face between his hands and looked tenderly and laughingly into her troubled eyes. They were making a bit of toilet sociably together in Mrs. Baroda's dressing-room.

"You are full of surprises, ma belle," he said to her. "Even I can never count upon how you are going to act under given conditions." He kissed her and turned to fasten his cravat before the mirror.

"Here you are," he went on, "taking poor Gouvernail seriously and making a commotion over him, the last thing he would desire or expect."

"Commotion!" she hotly resented. "Nonsense! How can you say such a thing? Commotion, indeed! But, you know, you said he was clever."

"So he is. But the poor fellow is run down by overwork now. That's why I asked him here to take a rest."

"You used to say he was a man of ideas," she retorted, unconciliated. "I expected him to be interesting, at least. I'm going to the city in the morning to have my spring gowns fitted. Let me know when Mr. Gouvernail is gone; I shall be at my Aunt Octavie's."

That night she went and sat alone upon a bench that stood beneath a live oak tree at the edge of the gravel walk.

She had never known her thoughts or her intentions to be so confused. She could gather nothing from them but the feeling of a distinct necessity to quit her home in the morning.

Mrs. Baroda heard footsteps crunching the gravel; but could discern in the darkness only the approaching red point of a lighted cigar. She knew it was Gouvernail, for her husband did not smoke. She hoped to remain unnoticed, but her white gown revealed her to him. He threw away his cigar and seated himself upon the bench beside her; without a suspicion that she might object to his presence.

"Your husband told me to bring this to you, Mrs. Baroda," he said, handing her a filmy, white scarf with which she sometimes enveloped her head and shoulders. She accepted the scarf from him with a murmur of thanks, and let it lie in her lap.

He made some commonplace observation upon the baneful effect of the night air at that season. Then as his gaze reached out into the darkness, he murmured, half to himself:

> " 'Night of south winds—night of the large few stars!
> Still nodding night—' "[1]

She made no reply to this apostrophe to the night, which indeed, was not addressed to her.

Gouvernail was in no sense a diffident man, for he was not a self-conscious one. His periods of reserve were not constitutional, but the result of moods. Sitting there beside Mrs. Baroda, his silence melted for the time.

He talked freely and intimately in a low, hesitating drawl that was not unpleasant to hear. He talked of the old college days when he and Gaston had been a good deal to each other; of the days of keen and blind ambitions and large intentions. Now there was left with him, at least, a philosophic acquiescence to the existing order—only a desire to be permitted to exist, with now and then a little whiff of genuine life, such as he was breathing now.

Her mind only vaguely grasped what he was saying. Her physical being was for the moment predominant. She was not

1. Cf. « Song of Myself » de Whitman, section 21. Le second vers se prolonge par « mad naked summer night ». Kate Chopin était une fervente de la poésie sensuelle et, selon l'Amérique victorienne, dégradante de Walt Whitman.

thinking of his words, only drinking in the tones of his voice. She wanted to reach out her hand in the darkness and touch him with the sensitive tips of her fingers upon the face or the lips. She wanted to draw close to him and whisper against his cheek—she did not care what—as she might have done if she had not been a respectable woman.

The stronger the impulse grew to bring herself near him, the further, in fact, did she draw away from him. As soon as she could do so without an appearance of too great rudeness, she rose and left him there alone.

Before she reached the house, Gouvernail had lighted a fresh cigar and ended his apostrophe to the night.

Mrs. Baroda was greatly tempted that night to tell her husband—who was also her friend—of this folly that had seized her. But she did not yield to the temptation. Beside being a respectable woman she was a very sensible one; and she knew there are some battles in life which a human being must fight alone.

When Gaston arose in the morning, his wife had already departed. She had taken an early morning train to the city. She did not return till Gouvernail was gone from under her roof.

There was some talk of having him back during the summer that followed. That is, Gaston greatly desired it; but this desire yielded to his wife's strenuous opposition.

However, before the year ended, she proposed, wholly from herself, to have Gouvernail visit them again. Her husband was surprised and delighted with the suggestion coming from her.

"I am glad, chère amie, to know that you have finally overcome your dislike for him; truly he did not deserve it."

"Oh," she told him, laughingly, after pressing a long, tender kiss upon his lips, "I have overcome everything! you will see. This time I shall be very nice to him."

3 – Les écrivains naturalistes interprètent la modernité

Des écrivains américains adoptèrent une troisième approche pour fournir de leur société en mutation à la fois une image dramatique et l'interprétation la plus explicite. Le naturalisme littéraire fut tributaire des découvertes scientifiques de Sir Charles Lyell en géologie, Auguste Comte en sociologie et Charles Darwin en biologie, son éloquent vulgarisateur Herbert Spencer ayant puissamment contribué à la vogue de Darwin. C'est Emile Zola qui dans *Le roman expérimental* (1880) énonce avec force l'application de ces découvertes dans la littérature moderne. Ce naturalisme scientifique tranche radicalement sur les principes du naturalisme transcendantal du temps d'Emerson. A l'être idéalisé libre et indépendant se substitue au mieux chez les héros de Stephen Crane et Frank Norris, ou même chez Silas Lapham et Huckleberry Finn, une figure ambiguë dont la présomption de liberté est constamment battue en brèche par les implications négatives de l'auteur. Moins ironique sera le naturalisme scientifique du zélé Theodore Dreiser. Sa compassion embarrassée face à l'environnement et au hasard aveugle rend ses portraits également équivoques. Seul le romancier et historien Henri Adams échappe tant à l'ironique doute religieux de Howells et Crane qu'à l'ardeur scientifique confuse de Dreiser. Il nie que la géologie de Lyell ou l'évolutionnisme de Darwin puissent proposer une loi scientifique irréfutable. Pour Adams, l'histoire de l'expérience humaine indique encore un état de « multiplicité » et de chaos, non l'unité scientifique et la cohérence. A l'évidence, la nouvelle pensée scientifique a un tel impact que tous les auteurs dignes de ce nom s'attaquent aux données qu'elle recèle en matière d'enchaînement logique, de personnages, d'actions et de décors. De date comparativement récente, le péché originel du vieil Adam s'oublie aisément au temps de Lyell, Comte et Darwin. Le comportement humain semble alors un peu mieux explicable à la lumière des connaissances acquises sur les forces de l'environnement (sociales, économiques ou géographiques), les impératifs et pulsions biologiques tels que la sexualité, la faim, la soif et la peur. Echappant au contrôle de l'individu existent aussi des contingences imputables aux impondérables. En fin de compte, l'homme paraît, à l'instar de l'animal, doté d'un certain instinct de survie, sans doute inégalement partagé, dans la mesure où il s'adapte à son environnement grâce aux réactions associatives en termes d'expérience passée et présente.

STEPHEN CRANE, 1871-1900

En dix ans d'une remarquable carrière qui s'est brutalement achevée sur sa mort à l'âge de vingt-huit ans, Stephen Crane a déconcerté ses critiques qui l'ont tour à tour désigné comme réaliste, romantique, symboliste, parodiste, impressionniste ou naturaliste. Né dans le New Jersey, quatorzième enfant d'un pasteur méthodiste, Crane en vient peu à peu à s'interroger sur la capacité des hommes d'Eglise et la bonne volonté qu'ils mettent à soulager la misère des masses urbaines. Il passe de brèves périodes dans les taudis de New York et écrit sous un pseudonyme à vingt et un ans, *Maggie : A Girl of the Streets* (1893). Cet ouvrage lui vaut immédiatement l'admiration et le soutien du puissant Howells. La dédicace qu'écrit Crane dans l'exemplaire d'Hamlin Garland suggère son indignation face à la société, et son naturalisme à la fois hésitant et ironique : « (The book) tries to show that environment is a tremendous thing in the world and frequently shapes lives regardless. If one proves that theory, one makes room in Heaven for all sorts of souls (notably an occasional street girl) who are not confidently expected to be there by many excellent people. » Servi par une brillante imagination et malgré son inexpérience, Crane dépeint ensuite dans *The Red Badge of Courage* (1895), son œuvre majeure, la féroce barbarie des hommes en guerre. Crane participe finalement comme correspondant de guerre à l'insurrection cubaine (1897), au conflit gréco-turc (1897) et à la Guerre de Cuba (1898). Dans un livre qui porte le titre ironique de *War is Kind* (1899), il décrit la vanité humaine dans un monde amoral : « A man said to the universe : / "Sir, I exist!" / "However," replied the universe, / "The fact has not created in me / A sense of obligation." » La même année Crane va vivre en Angleterre où il s'était auparavant pris d'amitié pour Henry James. L'année suivante il meurt de la tuberculose en Allemagne.

BIBLIOGRAPHIE SÉLECTIVE. — *University of Virginia Edition of the Works of Stephen Crane*, 10 vol., Charlottesville, University Press of Virginia, 1969-1976 ; Berryman (John), *Stephen Crane*, New York, Sloane, 1950 ; Cazemajou (Jean), *Stephen Crane (1871-1900) : écrivain-journaliste*, Paris, Didier, 1969 ; Cazemajou (Jean), Gonnaud (Maurice), Santraud (Jeanne-Marie), *Maggie, A Girl of The Streets, The Red Badge of Courage*, Paris, Armand Colin, 1969.

The Blue Hotel[1]

VII

Dans la première moitié du récit, un Suédois affligé d'une peur maladive est arrivé en train à Fort Romper, localité du Nebraska prise sous la neige. Il est conduit à l'hôtel peint en bleu de Scully, en compagnie d'un cowboy et d'un homme de l'Est. Pour dominer la crainte qu'il a d'être tué dans l'Ouest sauvage, le Suédois adopte une attitude pleine d'arrogance au dîner, défie tout le monde aux cartes, accuse Johnny, le fils de Scully, de tricher et fouette cruellement celui-ci au cours d'une violente rixe. Le Suédois s'apprête à reparaître avec sa valise.

1. Le texte est tiré de *The Monster and Other Stories* (1899).

(...) "I'd like to fight this here Dutchman myself," said the cowboy, breaking a long silence.

Scully wagged his head sadly. "No, that wouldn't do. It wouldn't be right. It wouldn't be right."

"Well, why wouldn't it?" argued the cowboy. "I don't see no harm in it."

"No," answered Scully with mournful heroism. "It wouldn't be right. It was Johnnie's fight, and now we mustn't whip the man just because he whipped Johnnie."

"Yes, that's true enough," said the cowboy; "but—he better not get fresh with me, because I couldn't stand no more of it."

"You'll not say a word to him," commanded Scully, and even then they heard the tread of the Swede on the stairs. His entrance was made theatric. He swept the door back with a bang and swaggered to the middle of the room. No one looked at him. "Well," he cried, insolently, at Scully. "I s'pose you'll tell me now how much I owe you?"

The old man remained stolid. "You don't owe me nothin'."

"Huh!" cried the Swede, "huh! Don't owe 'im nothin'."

The cowboy addressed the Swede. "Stranger, I don't see how you come to be so gay around here."

Old Scully was instantly alert. "Stop!" he shouted, holding his hand forth, fingers upward. "Bill, you shut up!"

The cowboy spat carelessly into the sawdust box. "I didn't say a word, did I?" he asked.

"Mr. Scully," called the Swede, "how much do I owe you?" It was seen that he was attired for departure, and that he had his valise in his hand.

"You don't owe me nothin'," repeated Scully in his same imperturbable way.

"Huh!" said the Swede. "I guess you're right. I guess if it was any way at all, you'd owe me somethin'. That's what I guess." He turned to the cowboy. " 'Kill him! Kill him! Kill him!' " he mimicked, and then guffawed victoriously. " 'Kill him!' " He was convulsed with ironical humor.

But he might have been jeering the dead. The three men were immovable and silent, staring with glassy eyes at the stove.

The Swede opened the door and passed into the storm, giving one derisive glance backward at the still group.

As soon as the door was closed, Scully and the cowboy leaped to their feet and began to curse. They trampled to and fro, waving their arms and smashing into the air with their fists. "Oh, but that was a hard minute!" wailed Scully. "That was a hard minute! Him there leerin' and scoffin'! One bang at his nose was worth forty dollars to me that minute! How did you stand it, Bill?"

"How did I stand it?" cried the cowboy in a quivering voice. "How did I stand it? Oh!"

The old man burst into sudden brogue. "I'd loike to take that Swade," he wailed, "and hould 'im down on a shtone flure and bate 'im to a jelly wid a shtick!"

The cowboy groaned in sympathy. "I'd like to git him by the neck and haammer him"—he brought his hand down on a chair with a noise like a pistol-shot—"hammer that there Dutchman until he couldn't tell himself from a dead coyote!"

"I'd bate 'im until he——"

"I'd show *him* some things——"

And then together they raised a yearning fanatic cry. "Oh-o-oh! if we only could——"

"Yes!"

"Yes!"

"And then I'd——"

"O-o-oh!"

VIII

The Swede, tightly gripping his valise, tacked across the face of the storm as if he carried sails. He was following a line of little naked gasping trees, which he knew must mark the way of the road. His face, fresh from the pounding of Johnnie's fists, felt more pleasure than pain in the wind and the driving snow. A number of square shapes loomed upon him finally, and he knew them as the houses of the main body of the town. He found a street and made travel along it, leaning heavily upon the wind whenever, at a corner, a terrific blast caught him.

He might have been in a deserted village. We picture the world as thick with conquering and elate humanity, but here, with the bugles of the tempest pealing, it was hard to imagine a peopled earth. One viewed the existence of man then as a marvel, and conceded a glamour of wonder to these lice which were caused to cling to a whirling, fire-smote, ice-locked, disease-stricken, space-lost bulb. The conceit of man was explained by this storm to be the very engine of life. One was a coxcomb not to die in it. However, the Swede found a saloon.

In front of it an indomitable red light was burning, and the snowflakes were made blood-color as they flew through the circumscribed territory of the lamp's shining. The Swede pushed open the door of the saloon and entered. A sanded expanse was before him, and at the end of it four men sat about a table drinking. Down one side of the room extended a radiant bar, and its guardian was leaning upon his elbows listening to the talk of the men at the table. The Swede dropped his valise upon the floor, and, smiling fraternally upon the barkeeper, said: "Gimme some whisky, will you?" The man placed a bottle, a whisky-glass, and a glass of ice-thick water upon the bar. The Swede poured himself an abnormal portion of whisky and drank it in three gulps. "Pretty bad night," remarked the bartender indifferently. He was making the pretension of blindness, which is usually a distinction of his class; but it could have been seen that he was furtively studying the half-erased bloodstains on the face of the Swede. "Bad night," he said again.

"Oh, it's good enough for me," replied the Swede, hardily, as he poured himself more whisky. The barkeeper took his coin and maneuvered it through its reception by the highly-nickeled cash-machine. A bell rang; a card labeled "20 cts." had appeared.

"No," continued the Swede, "this isn't too bad weather. It's good enough for me."

"So?" murmured the barkeeper languidly.

The copious drams made the Swede's eyes swim, and he breathed a trifle heavier. "Yes, I like this weather. I like it. It suits me." It was apparently his design to impart a deep significance to these words.

"So?" murmured the bartender again. He turned to gaze dreamily at the scroll-like birds and bird-like scrolls which had been drawn with soap upon the mirrors back of the bar.

"Well, I guess I'll take another drink," said the Swede presently. "Have something?"

"No, thanks; I'm not drinkin'," answered the bartender. Afterward he asked: "How did you hurt your face?"

The Swede immediately began to boast loudly. "Why, in a

fight. I thumped the soul out of a man down here at Scully's hotel."

The interest of the four men at the table was at last aroused.

"Who was it?" said one.

"Johnnie Scully," blustered the Swede. "Son of the man what runs it. He will be pretty near dead for some weeks, I can tell you. I made a nice thing of him, I did. He couldn't get up. They carried him in the house. Have a drink?"

Instantly the men in some subtle way incased themselves in reserve. "No, thanks," said one. The group was of curious formation. Two were prominent local business men; one was the district-attorney; and one was a professional gambler of the kind known as "square." But a scrutiny of the group would not have enabled an observer to pick the gambler from the men of more reputable pursuits. He was, in fact, a man so delicate in manner, when among people of fair class, and so judicious in his choice of victims, that in the strictly masculine part of the town's life he had come to be explicitly trusted and admired. People called him a thoroughbred. The fear and contempt with which his craft was regarded was undoubtedly the reason that his quiet dignity shone conspicuous above the quiet dignity of men who might be merely hatters, billiard-markers or grocery clerks. Beyond an occasional unwary traveler, who came by rail, this gambler was supposed to prey solely upon reckless and senile farmers, who, when flush with good crops, drove into town in all the pride and confidence of an absolutely invulnerable stupidity. Hearing at times in circuitous fashion of the despoilment of such a farmer, the important men of Romper invariably laughed in contempt of the victim, and if they thought of the wolf at all, it was a kind of pride at the knowledge that he would never dare think of attacking their wisdom and courage. Besides, it was popular that this gambler had a real wife and two real children in a neat cottage in a suburb, where he led an exemplary home life, and when any one even suggested a discrepancy in his character, the crowd immediately vociferated descriptions of this virtuous family circle. Then men who led exemplary home lives, and men who did not lead exemplary home lives, all subsided in a bunch, remarking that there was nothing more to be said.

However, when a restriction was placed upon him—as, for instance, when a strong clique of members of the new Pollywog

Club refused to permit him, even as a spectator, to appear in the rooms of the organization—the candor and gentleness with which he accepted the judgment disarmed many of his foes and made his friends more desperately partisan. He invariably distinguished between himself and a respectable Romper man so quickly and frankly that his manner actually appeared to be a continual broadcast compliment.

And one must not forget to declare the fundamental fact of his entire position in Romper. It is irrefutable that in all affairs outside of his business, in all matters that occur eternally and commonly between man and man, this thieving card-player was so generous, so just, so moral, that, in a contest, he could have put to flight the consciences of nine-tenths of the citizens of Romper.

And so it happened that he was seated in this saloon with the two prominent local merchants and the district-attorney.

The Swede continued to drink raw whisky, meanwhile babbling at the barkeeper and trying to induce him to indulge in potations. "Come on. Have a drink. Come on. What—no? Well, have a little one then. By gawd, I've whipped a man to-night, and I want to celebrate. I whipped him good, too. Gentlemen," the Swede cried to the men at the table, "have a drink?"

"Ssh!" said the barkeeper.

The group at the table, although furtively attentive, had been pretending to be deep in talk, but now a man lifted his eyes toward the Swede and said shortly: "Thanks. We don't want any more."

At this reply the Swede ruffled out his chest like a rooster. "Well," he exploded, "it seems I can't get anybody to drink with me in this town. Seems so, don't it? Well!"

"Ssh!" said the barkeeper.

"Say," snarled the Swede, "don't you try to shut me up. I won't have it. I'm a gentleman, and I want people to drink with me. And I want 'em to drink with me now. *Now*—do you understand?" He rapped the bar with his knuckles.

Years of experience had calloused the bartender. He merely grew sulky. "I hear you," he answered.

"Well," cried the Swede, "listen hard then. See those men over there? Well, they're going to drink with me, and don't you forget it. Now you watch."

"Hi!" yelled the barkeeper, "this won't do!"

"Why won't it?" demanded the Swede. He stalked over to the table, and by chance laid his hand upon the shoulder of the gambler. "How about this?" he asked, wrathfully. "I asked you to drink with me."

The gambler simply twisted his head and spoke over his shoulder. "My friend, I don't know you."

"Oh, hell!" answered the Swede, "come and have a drink."

"Now, my boy," advised the gambler kindly, "take your hand off my shoulder and go 'way and mind your own business." He was a little slim man, and it seemed strange to hear him use this tone of heroic patronage to the burly Swede. The other men at the table said nothing.

"What? You won't drink with me, you little dude! I'll make you then! I'll make you!" The Swede had grasped the gambler frenziedly at the throat, and was dragging him from his chair. The other men sprang up. The barkeeper dashed around the corner of his bar. There was a great tumult, and then was seen a long blade in the hand of the gambler. It shot forward, and a human body, this citadel of virtue, wisdom, power, was pierced as easily as if it had been a melon. The Swede fell with a cry of supreme astonishment.

The prominent merchants and the district-attorney must have at once tumbled out of the place backward. The bartender found himself hanging limply to the arm of a chair and gazing into the eyes of a murderer.

"Henry," said the latter, as he wiped his knife on one of the towels that hung beneath the bar-rail, "you tell 'em where to find me. I'll be home, waiting for 'em." Then he vanished. A moment afterward the barkeeper was in the street dinning through the storm for help, and, moreover, companionship.

The corpse of the Swede, alone in the saloon, had its eyes fixed upon a dreadful legend that dwelt a-top of the cash-machine. "This registers the amount of your purchase."

IX

Months later, the cowboy was frying pork over the stove of a little ranch near the Dakota line, when there was a quick thud of hoofs outside, and presently, the Easterner entered with the letters and the papers.

"Well," said the Easterner at once, "the chap that killed the Swede has got three years. Wasn't much, was it?"

"He has? Three years?" The cowboy poised his pan of pork, while he ruminated upon the news. "Three years. That ain't much."

"No. It was a light sentence," replied the Easterner as he unbuckled his spurs. "Seems there was a good deal of sympathy for him in Romper."

"If the bartender had been any good," observed the cowboy thoughtfully, "he could have gone in and cracked that there Dutchman on the head with a bottle in the beginnin' of it and stopped all this here murderin'."

"Yes, a thousand things might have happened," said the Easterner tartly.

The cowboy returned his pan of pork to the fire, but his philosophy continued. "It's funny, ain't it? If he hadn't said Johnnie was cheatin' he'd be alive this minute. He was an awful fool. Game played for fun, too. Not for money. I believe he was crazy."

"I feel sorry for that gambler," said the Easterner.

"Oh, so do I," said the cowboy. "He don't deserve none of it for killin' who he did."

"The Swede might not have been killed if everything had been square."

"Might not have been killed?" exclaimed the cowboy. "Everythin' square? Why, when he said that Johnnie was cheatin' and acted like such a jackass? And then in the saloon he fairly walked up to git hurt?" With these arguments the cowboy browbeat the Easterner and reduced him to rage.

"You're a fool!" cried the Easterner viciously. "You're a bigger jackass than the Swede by a million majority. Now let me tell you one thing. Let me tell you something. Listen! Johnnie *was* cheating!"

" 'Johnnie,' " said the cowboy blankly. There was a minute of silence, and then he said robustly: "Why, no. The game was only for fun."

"Fun or not," said the Easterner, "Johnnie was cheating. I saw him. I know it. I saw him. And I refused to stand up and be a man. I let the Swede fight it out alone. And you—you were simply puffing around the place and wanting to fight. And then old Scully himself! We are all in it! This poor gambler isn't even a noun. He is kind of an adverb. Every sin is the result of a collaboration. We, five of us, have collaborated in the murder of this Swede. Usually there are from a dozen to forty women really involved in every murder, but in this case it seems to be only five men—you, I, Johnnie, old Scully, and that fool of an unfortunate gambler came merely as a culmination, the apex of a human movement, and gets all the punishment."

The cowboy, injured and rebellious, cried out blindly into this fog of mysterious theory. "Well, I didn't do anything', did I?"

THEODORE DREISER, 1871-1945

Né la même année que Crane, Theodore Dreiser, autre écrivain du Middle West après la guerre de Sécession, a grandi dans une famille catholique de l'Indiana. Il a lu les récits d'Horatio Alger sur le thème de la réussite individuelle et le classique *Self-Help* (1859) de Samuel Smiles. Parce que sa mère, à laquelle il est profondément attaché, appartenait à une famille de Moraves, l'Eglise tergiverse sur son inhumation dans un cimetière catholique. Aussi Dreiser renie-t-il le catholicisme autant que Crane contestait les soucis humanitaires des institutions religieuses. D'abord manœuvre puis journaliste, Dreiser se met à douter du mythe américain du succès. Quand il arrive à New York en 1894, il voit des épaves humaines sur les bancs de parcs, dans le décor de l'empire financier de Wall Street. Six années plus tard, les implacables inégalités de la vie américaine resurgissent lugubrement dans la défaite du héros de *Sister Carrie*. Avant ce premier roman, Dreiser qui a lu Herbert Spencer s'est imprégné de la logique du darwinisme social et a tenté de formuler une interprétation scientifique de l'homme moderne. Son trouble transparaît au travers des brefs essais dispersés dans *Sister Carrie*. « We see man far removed out of the lairs of the jungle », écrit-il dans le chapitre VIII, « his innate instincts dulled by too near an approach to free will, his free will scarcely sufficiently developed to replace his instincts and afford him perfect guidance ». Mesurés à l'aune de la logique philosophique, de tels énoncés confinent cependant au non-sens. Chez Crane et Howells, l'écrivain dramatise de surcroît les questions controversées de la liberté et de la vanité humaines, y ajoutant une pointe d'ironie naturaliste. Non que Dreiser fasse preuve d'un médiocre sens artistique. Dans *Sister Carrie*, il tisse un réseau d'images fonctionnelles où figurent marées, tempêtes, ports, animaux, cavernes, tours de magie et faux-semblants, argent, vêtements et plus encore. Il exprime ainsi avec talent et dans une veine poétique sa vision quasi naturaliste de l'homme et de la femme, broyés par les forces du capitalisme américain. A un âge avancé il s'inscrira au Parti communiste. Mais il publiera aussi *The Bulwark* (1946) dont le héros est un homme d'affaires quaker humblement soumis aux actes mystérieux de la nature et respectueux des desseins cosmiques du divin.

BIBLIOGRAPHIE SÉLECTIVE. — Lehan (Richard), *Theodore Dreiser : His World and His Novels*, Carbondale, Southern Illinois University Press, 1969 ; Matthiessen (F. O.), *Theodore Dreiser*, New York, Sloane, 1951 ; Pizer (Donald), *The Novels of Theodore Dreiser : A Critical Study*, Minneapolis, University of Minnesota Press, 1976.

Sister Carrie[1]

XXXIX

La scène se passe dans la seconde partie du roman, centrée sur New York. George Hurstwood a pris le nom de Wheeler après s'être enfui avec plus de 10 000 dollars du saloon de Chicago dont il était le patron. A Chicago, il a obtenu de Carrie, une jeune femme fraîchement débarquée de sa campagne mais fort accommodante, qu'elle parte avec lui. A New York, il a été

1. Ce texte appartient à la première édition de 1900, alors censurée pour offense à la morale et retirée des librairies sur la demande de la femme de l'éditeur Doubleday. Dreiser révisa le roman pour une nouvelle publication en 1907.

copropriétaire d'un bar, mais l'affaire n'a pas marché. Le bail lui a été retiré et il s'avère incapable de trouver une autre affaire ou même un emploi. Dans ce chapitre, il se tourne vers le poker en croyant à sa chance. Mais le jeune adversaire de Hurstwood/Wheeler est un beau mâle qui lui révèle impitoyablement son inaptitude grandissante à survivre dans la métropole où tout lui est étranger. Comme l'écrit Dreiser, Hurstwood n'est qu'une goutte d'eau impalpable dans un océan comme New York, « already full of whales. A common fish must needs disappear wholly from view, remain unseen ». En d'autres termes, « Hurstwood was nothing ».

[...] He knew of several poker rooms down town. A few acquaintances he had in down-town resorts and about the city hall. It was a change to see them and exchange a few friendly commonplaces.

"Hello, Wheeler, how are you?"

"Oh, very fair."

"You're looking. What news?"

"Oh, nothing much."

Such little things as these made the world still tolerable, though they profited him nothing.

He had once been accustomed to hold a pretty fair hand at poker. Many a friendly game had netted him a hundred dollars or more at the time when that sum was merely sauce to the dish of the game—not the all in all. Now, on such a fair day as this, he would think somewhat of playing.

"I might win a couple of hundred. I'm not out of practise."

It is but fair to say that this thought had occurred to him several times before he acted upon it.

The poker room which he first invaded was over a saloon which he knew, in West Street, near one of the ferries. He had been there before. Several games were going on at the time. These he watched for a time and noticed that the pots were quite large for the ante involved.

"Deal me a hand," he said, at the beginning of a new shuffle. He pulled up a chair and studied his cards. Those playing made that quiet study of him which is so unapparent and yet invariably so searching.

Poor fortune was with him at first. He received a mixed collection without progression or pairs.

"I pass," he said.

On the strength of this he was content to lose his ante. The deals did fairly by him in the long run, causing him to come away with a few dollars to the good.

A little success, like a little wisdom, is certainly a dangerous thing. The very next afternoon he was back again, seeking amusement and profit. This time he followed up three of a kind to his doom. There was a better hand across the table, held by a pugnacious Irish youth, who was a political hanger-on of the Tammany district in which they were located. Hurstwood was surprised at the persistence of this individual, whose bets came with a sang-froid which, if a bluff, was excellent art. Hurstwood began to doubt, but kept, or thought to keep at least, the cool demeanor with which, in olden times, he deceived those psychic students of the gaming table who seem to read thoughts and moods, rather than exterior evidences, however subtle. He could not down the cowardly thought that this man had something better and would stay to the end, drawing his last dollar into the pot, should he choose to go so far. Still he hoped to win much—his hand was excellent. Why not raise it five more?

"I raise you three," said the youth.

"Make it five," said Hurstwood, fishing out his chips.

"Come again," said the youth, pushing out a small pile of reds.

"Let me have some more chips," said Hurstwood to the keeper in charge, taking out a bill.

A cynical grin lit up the face of his youthful opponent. When the chips were laid out, Hurstwood met the raise.

"Five again," said the youth.

Hurstwood's brow was wet. He was deep in now—very deep for him. Sixty dollars of his good money was up. He was ordinarily no coward, but the thought of losing so much weakened him. Finally he gave way. He would not trust to this fine hand any longer.

"I call," he said.

"Hearts straight," said the youth, showing a flush progression of high cards.

Hurstwood's hand dropped.

"I thought I had you," he said weakly.

The youth raked in his chips and Hurstwood came away, not without first stopping to count his remaining cash on the stair.

"Three hundred and forty dollars," he said.

With this loss and ordinary expenses, so much had already gone.

Back in the flat he decided he would play no more, and that he would look for something to do. The fact was, however, that pride stopped him—a keen remembrance of former days. He did go out, but a little aimless walking took the nerve out of him and made him as apathetic as before. He returned home and occupied his chair in the corner.

XLV

Tandis que Hurstwood s'achemine vers la déchéance, Carrie s'est adaptée au monde du théâtre new-yorkais. Voyant son étoile monter, elle répugne à entretenir Hurstwood, décide d'habiter chez une amie actrice et déménage l'appartement lorsque Hurstwood est parti en promenade.

[...] When he reached the flat by half-past five, it was still dark. He knew that Carrie not there, not only because there was no light showing through the transom, but because the evening papers were stuck between the outside knob and the door frame. He opened with his key and went in. Everything was still dark. Lighting the gas he sat down, proposing to wait a little while. Even if Carrie did come now, dinner would be late. He read until six, then got up to fix something for himself.

As he did so, he noticed that the room seemed a little queer. What was it? He looked around, as if he missed something, and then saw an envelope right near where he had been sitting. It spoke for itself, almost without further action on his part.

Reaching over he took it, a sort of chill settling upon him even while he reached. The crackle of the envelope in his hands was loud. Green paper money lay soft within the note.

"Dear George," he read, crunching the money in one hand. "I am going away. I'm not coming back any more. It's no use trying to keep up the flat. I can't do it. I wouldn't mind helping you if I could, but I can't support us both and pay the rent. I need what little I make to pay for my clothes. I'm leaving twenty dollars. It's all I have just now. You can do whatever you like with the furniture. I won't want it. Carrie."

He dropped the note and looked quietly round. Now he knew what he missed. It was the little ornamental clock, which was hers. It had gone from the mantel-piece. He went into the front room—his bed-room, the parlor, lighting the gas as he went. From the chiffonier had gone the knick-knacks of silver and plate. From the table top, the lace coverings. He opened the wardrobe—no clothes of hers. He opened the drawers—nothing of hers. Her trunk was gone from its accustomed place. Back in his own room hung his old clothes, just as he had left them. Nothing else was gone.

He stopped in the parlor and waited for he knew not what. The silence grew oppressive. The little flat seemed wonderfully deserted. He wholly forgot that he was hungry, that it was only dinner-time. It seemed later in the night.

Suddenly he found that the money was still in his hands. There was twenty dollars in all, as she had said. Now he walked back, leaving the lights ablaze and feeling as if the flat were empty.

"I'll get out of this," he said to himself.

Then the sheer loneliness of his situation rushed upon him in full.

"Left me," he muttered and repeated, "left me."

The place that had been so comfortable, where he had spent so many days of warmth, was now a memory. Something colder and chillier confronted him. He sank down in his chair, resting his chin in his hand, mere sensation, without thought, holding him.

Then something like bereaved affection and self-pity swept over him.

"She needn't have gone away," he said. "I'd have got something." He sat a long while without rocking, and then added, quite clearly to himself—"I tried, didn't I?"

At midnight he was still rocking, staring at the floor.

L

[...] One day in the middle of the winter, the sharpest spell of the season set in. It broke gray and cold on the first day and on the second snowed. Poor luck pursuing him, he had secured but ten cents by nightfall, and this he had spent for food. At evening he found himself at the Boulevard and 67th Street, where he finally turned his face Bowery-ward. Especially fatigued because of the wandering propensity which had seized him in the morning, he now half dragged his wet feet, slopping the soles upon the sidewalk. An old, thin coat was turned up about his red ears—his cracked derby hat was pulled down until it turned the same hearing organs outward. His hands were in his pockets.

"I'll just go down Broadway," he said to himself.

When he reached 42nd Street, the fire signs were already blazing bright. Crowds were hastening to dine. Through bright windows at every corner might be seen gay companies in luxuriant restaurants. There were coaches, and crowded cable cars.

In his weary and hungry state he should never have come here. The contrast was too sharp. Even he was recalled keenly to better things.

"What's the use," he thought. "It's all up with me. I'll quit this."

People turned to look after him, so uncouth was his shambling figure. Several officers followed him with their eyes to see that he did not beg of anybody.

Once he paused in an aimless, incoherent sort of way and looked through the windows of an imposing restaurant, before which blazed a fire sign and through the large plate windows of which could be seen the red and gold decorations, the palms, the white napery and shiny glassware, and above all, the comfortable crowd. Weak as his mind had become, his hunger was sharp enough to show the importance of his. He stopped stock still, his frayed pants soaking in the slush, and peered foolishly in.

"Eat," he mumbled. "That's right, eat. Nobody else wants any."

Then his voice dropped even lower and his mind half lost the fancy it had.

"It's mighty cold," he said. "Awful cold."

At Broadway and 39th Street was blazing, in incandescent fire, Carrie's name. "Carrie Madenda," it read, "and the Casino Company." All the wet, snowy sidewalk was bright with this radiated fire. It was so bright that it attracted Hurstwood's gaze. He looked up, and then at a large gilt-framed poster-board on which was a fine lithograph of Carrie, life-size.

Hurstwood gazed at it a moment, snuffling and hunching one shoulder as if something were scratching him. He was so run-down however, that his mind was not exactly clear.

"That's you," he said at last, addressing her. "Wasn't good enough for you, was I? Huh."

He lingered, trying to think logically. This was no longer possible with him.

"She's got it," he said, incoherently, thinking of money. "Let her give me some."

He started around to the side door. Then he forgot what he was going for and paused, pushing his hands deeper to warm the wrists. Suddently it returned. The stage door! That was it.

He approached that entrance and went in.

"Well," said the attendant, staring at him. Seeing him pause he went over and shoved him. "Get out of here," he said.

"I want to see Miss Madenda," he said.

"You do, eh!" the other said, almost tickled at the spectacle. "Get out of here," and he shoved him again.

Hurstwood had no strength to resist.

"I want to see Miss Madenda," he tried to explain, even as he was being hustled away. "I'm all right. I—"

The man gave him at last push and closed the door. As he did so Hurstwood slipped and fell in the snow. It hurt him and some old vague sense of shame returned. He began to cry and swear follishly.

"God damned dog!" he said. "Damned old cur," wiping the slush from his worthless coat. "I—I hired such people as you once."

Now a fierce feeling against Carrie welled up—just one fierce, angry thought before the whole thing slipped out of his mind.

"She owes me something to eat", he said. "She owes it to me."

Hopelessly he turned back into Broadway again and slopped onward, and away, begging, crying, losing track of this thoughts, one after another, as a mind decayed and disjointed is wont to do.

It was a truly wintry evening a few days later when his one distinguished mental decision was reached. Already at four o'clock the sombre hue of night was thickening the air. A heavy snow was falling—a fine, picking, whipping snow, borne forward by a swift wind in long, thin lines. The streets were bedded with it, six inches of cold, soft carpet, churned to a dirty brown by the crush of teams and the feet of men. Along Broadway, men picked their way in ulsters and umbrellas. Along the Bowery, men slouched through it with collars up and hats pulled over their ears.

In the former thoroughfare, business men and travellers were making for comfortable hotels. In the latter, crowds on cold errands shifted past dingy stores, in the deep recesses of which lights were already gleaming. There were early lights in the cable cars, whose usual clatter was reduced by the mantle about the wheels. The whole city was muffled by its fast-thickening mantle.

In her comfortable chambers at the Waldorf, Carrie was reading, at this time, "Père Goriot," which Ames[1] had recommended to her. It was so strong, and Ames's mere commendation had so aroused her interest, that she caught nearly the full sympathetic significance of it. For the first time it was being borne in upon her how silly and worthless had been her earlier reading, as a whole. Becoming wearied, however, she yawned and came to the window, looking out upon the old unending procession of carriages rolling up Fifth Avenue.

"Isn't it bad," she observed to Lola.

"Terrible," said that little lady, joining her. "I hope it snows enough to go sleigh riding."

"Oh, dear," said Carrie, with whom the sufferings of father Goriot were still keen. "That's all you think of. Aren't you sorry for the people who haven't got anything tonight?"

"Of course I am," said Lola, "but what can I do? I haven't got anything."

Carrie smiled.

"You wouldn't care if you had," she returned.

"I would too," said Lola. "But people never gave me any thing when I was hard up."

"Isn't it just awful," said Carrie, studying the winter's storm.

"Look at that man over there," laughed Lola, who had caught sight of someone falling down. "How sheepish men look when they fall, don't they?"

"We'll have to take a coach tonight," answered Carrie absently.

In the lobby of the Imperial, Mr. Charles Drouet [2] was just arriving, shaking the snow from a very handsome ulster. Bad weather had driven him home early and stirred his desires for those

1. Bob Ames est un jeune intellectuel que Carrie a rencontré à New York.

2. Charles Drouet, voyageur de commerce. Il a rencontré Carrie pour la première fois dans le train qu'elle avait pris au Wisconsin pour aller à Chicago. Ils ont ensuite vécu ensemble. Il a présenté Carrie à son ami Hurstwood et ainsi a commencé leur fatale liaison.

pleasures which shut out the snow and gloom of life. A good dinner, the company of a young woman, and an evening at the theatre were the chief things for him.

"Why hello, Harry," he said, addressing a lounger in one of the comfortable lobby chairs—"how are you?"

"Oh, about six and six," said the other.

"Rotten weather, isn't it."

"Well, I should say," said the other. "I've been just sitting here, thinking where I'd go tonight."

"Come along with me," said Drouet. "I can introduce you to something dead swell."

"Who is it?" said the other.

"Oh, a couple of girls over here in 40th Street. We could have a dandy time. I was just looking for you."

"Supposing we get 'em and take 'em out to dinner."

"Sure," said Drouet. "Wait'll I go upstairs and change my clothes."

"Well, I'll be in the barber shop," said the other. "I want to get a shave."

"All right," said Drouet, creaking off in his good shoes toward the elevator. The old butterfly was a light on the wing as ever.

On an incoming vestibuled Pullman, speeding at forty miles an hour through the snow of the evening, were three others, all related.

"First call for dinner in the dining car," a Pullman servitor was announcing, as he hastened through the aisle in snow-white apron and jacket.

"I don't believe I want to play any more," said the youngest, a black-haired beauty (turned supercilious by fortune) as she pushed a euchre hand away from her.

"Shall we go in to dinner?" inquired her husband, who was all that fine rainment can make.

"Oh, not yet," she answered. "I don't want to play any more, though."

"Jessica,"[1] said her mother, who was also a study in what good clothing can do for age, "push that pin down in your tie—it's coming up."

Jessica obeyed, incidentally touching at her lovely hair, and

1. Jessica est la fille de Hurstwood. Il est toujours légalement l'époux de Mme Hurstwood.

looking at a little jewel-faced watch. Her husband studied her, for beauty, even cold, is fascinating from one point of view.

"Well, we won't have much more of this weather," he said. "It only takes two weeks to get to Rome."

Mrs. Hurstwood nestled comfortably in her corner and smiled. It was so nice to be mother-in-law of a rich young man—one whose financial state had borne her personal inspection.

"Do you suppose the boat will sail promptly," asked Jessica, "if it keeps up like this?"

"Oh, yes," answered her husband. "This won't make any difference."

Passing down the aisle came a very fair-haired banker's son, also of Chicago, who had long eyed this supercilious beauty. Even now he did not hesitate to glance at her, and she was conscious of it. With a specially conjured show of indifference she turned her pretty face wholly away. It was not wifely modesty at all. By so much was her pride satisfied.

The last of this small and once partially united company, however, was elsewhere, having reached a distinguished decision. Before a dirty four-story building in a side street quite near the Bowery, whose one-time coat of buff had been changed by soot and rain, he mingled with a significant crowd of men—a crowd which had been and was still gathering by degrees. It began with the approach of two or three who hung about the closed wooden doors and beat their feet to keep them warm. They had on faded derby hats with dents in them. Their misfit coats were heavy with melted snow and turned up at the collars. Their trousers were mere bags, frayed at the bottoms and wobbling over big, soppy shoes, torn at the sides and worn almost to shreds. They made no effort to go in but shifted ruefully about, digging their hands deep in their pockets and leering at the crowd and the increasing lamps. With the minutes increased the numbers. There were old men with grizzled beards and sunken eyes, men who were comparatively young but shrunken by diseases, men who were middle-aged. None was fat. There was a face in the thick of the collection which was as white as drained veal. There was another red as brick. Some came with thin, rounded shoulders; others with wooden legs; still others with frames so lean that clothes only flapped about them. There were great ears, swollen noses, thick lips, and above all, red, bloodshot eyes. Not a normal, healthy face in the whole mass; not a straight figure; not a straightforward, steady glance.

In the drive of the wind and sleet they pushed in on one another. There were wrists, unprotected by coat or pocket, which were red with cold. There were ears, half-covered by every conceivable semblance of a hat, which still looked stiff and bitten. In the snow they shifted, now one foot, now another, almost rocking in unison.

With the growth of the crowd about the door came a murmur. It was not conversation but a running comment directed at anyone in general. It contained oaths and slang phrases.

"By damn, I wisht they'd hurry up."

"Jesus."

"Look at the copper watchin'."

"Maybe it ain't winter, nuther."

"I wisht I was in Sing Sing."[1]

Now a sharper lash of wind cut down and they huddled closer. It was an edging, shifting, pushing throng. There was no anger, no pleading, no threatening words. It was all sullen endurance, unlightened by either wit or good fellowship.

A carriage went jingling by with some reclining figure in it. One of the members nearest the door saw it.

"Look at the bloke, ridin'."

"He ain't so cold!"

"Eh! Eh! Eh!" yelled another, the carriage having long since passed out of hearing.

Little by little the night crept on. Along the walk a crowd turned out on its way home. Men and shop girls went by with quick steps. The cross-town cars began to be crowded. The gas lamps were blazing and every window bloomed ruddy with steady flames. Still the crowd hung about the door, unwavering.

"Ain't they ever goin' to open up?" queried a hoarse voice suggestively.

This seemed to renew general interest in the closed door, and many gazed in that direction. They looked at it as dumb brutes look, as dogs paw and whine and study the knob. They shifted and blinked and muttered, now a curse, now a comment. Still they waited and still the snow whirled and cut them with biting flakes.

1. Sing-Sing est une prison de l'Etat de New York.

On the old hats and peaked shoulders it was piling it gathered in little heaps and curves and no one brushed it off. In the centre of the crowd the warmth and steam melted it, and water trickled off hat-rims and down noses, which the owners could not reach to scratch. On the outer rim the piles remained unmelted. Those who could not get in the centre lowered their heads to the weather and bent their forms.

A light appeared through the transom overhead. It sent a thrill of possibility through the watchers. There was a murmur of recognition. At last the bars grated inside and the crowd pricked up its ears. Footsteps shuffled within and it murmured again. Some one called: "Slow up there now," and then the door opened. It was push and jam for a minute, with grim, beast silence to prove its quality, and then it melted inward, like logs floating, and disappeared. There were wet hats and wet shoulders, a cold, shrunken, disgruntled mass pouring in between bleak walls. It was just six o'clock and there was supper in every hurrying pedestrian's face. And yet no supper was provided here—nothing but beds. Of these, Hurstwood was claiming one.

He laid down his fifteen cents and crept off with weary steps to his allotted room. It was a dingy affair, wooden, dusty, hard. A small gas jet furnished sufficient light for so rueful a corner.

"Hm," he said, clearing his throat and locking the door.

Now he began leisurely to take off his clothes, but stopped first with his coat and tucked it along the crack under the door. His vest he arranged in the same place. His old wet, cracked hat he laid softly upon the table. Then he pulled off his shoes and lay down.

It seemed as if he thought awhile for now he arose and turned the gas out, standing calmly in the blackness, hidden from view. After a few moments in which he reviewed nothing, but merely hesitated, he turned the gas on again, but applying no match. Even then he stood there, hidden wholly in that kindness which is night, while the uprising fumes filled the room. When the odor reached his nostrils he quit his attitude and fumbled for the bed.

"What's the use," he said wearily, as he stretched himself to rest.[1]

1. La version originale se termine ici. Dans l'édition révisée de 1907, Dreiser ajouta un chapitre décrivant, sans la condamner, une Carrie, qui, triomphante, reste toutefois solitaire et désenchantée.

4 – Nouvelles voix de poètes au temps de la prose

A l'orée de ce siècle, Ezra Pound se lamentait sur la poésie américaine dont l'état déplorable se prolongeait depuis les décennies antérieures jusqu'à son époque. Son double poétique, Hugh Selwyn Mauberley, « born/In a half savage country, out of date », s'était efforcée « to resuscitate the dead art/Of poetry » en un temps où dominait la prose. Pendant un demi-siècle, la poésie américaine avait tout juste survécu parmi une cohorte de versificateurs mineurs, dont nombreux étaient les imitateurs de Longfellow et de son école de gentils rimeurs, qui célébraient l'âtre et la maison, les oiseaux et les fleurs et la promesse d'un ordre moral universel. Il apparaît aujourd'hui que seul Walt Whitman manifesta une réelle vitalité poétique dans les années qui suivirent la guerre de Sécession. En 1867, il publia une quatrième édition augmentée de *Leaves of Grass* dont il avait poursuivi la rédaction avec de splendides poèmes de guerre. Il contemplait alors les années à venir avec un optimisme frémissant.. Mais il renonça à son ambition d'écrire des poèmes visionnaires, porteurs de nouvelles promesses pour ses lecteurs américains, quand ses capacités déclinèrent après une attaque en 1873. Sa contemporaine, Emily Dickinson qui partageait son esprit de rébellion, aurait pu remplir le vide de ces années-là mais seuls huit de ses quelque mille huit cents poèmes furent publiés avant sa mort en 1886. Au tournant du siècle le temps était au progrès et la poésie américaine n'était plus tout à fait l' « art défunt » dont se lamentait Pound. De nouveaux poètes réagissaient aux réalités mouvantes de la vie moderne. S'appuyant sur les œuvres publiées ici et tirées de Robinson, Frost, Eliot et Sandburg, comme de Whitman et Emily Dickinson, le lecteur pourra avec profit associer divers poèmes aux sélections en prose décrivant des préoccupations similaires de la même période historique. Romanciers et poètes étaient ensemble confrontés aux forces vives et déroutantes qui transformaient irrévocablement le paysage tant rural qu'urbain de l'Amérique. Ces auteurs étaient ainsi soucieux de l'évolution des sensibilités que provoquait l'impact de ces forces, quel que fût le mode de vie des Américains.

WALT WHITMAN, 1819-1892

Après la publication en 1860 de la troisième édition de *Leaves of Grass*, Walt Whitman semble perdre l'enthousiasme qui accompagnait sa carrière proclamée de « barde américain ». Puis vient la guerre de Sécession. Quand son frère est blessé en 1862, Whitman prend la direction du Sud pour le soigner en Virginie. Le reste de la guerre, il demeure à Washington où il s'occupe des blessés, est employé par le gouvernement fédéral et retrouve l'intensité débordante de son inspiration poétique. Ses poèmes de la guerre de Sécession, qui incluent des œuvres sur la mort du Président Lincoln, figurent dans la quatrième édition de *Leaves of Grass* (1867). Mais son idéalisme du temps de guerre est durement éprouvé par la flagrante immoralité qu'il observe dans l'Amérique *post-bellum*. La corruption qui règne dans les affaires et la politique s'étend comme un cancer à tous les aspects de la culture (voir *Democratic Vistas*, 1871). Il lui reste cependant l'espoir ténu que, dans le Nouveau Monde, la démocratie au service de l'homme du peuple pourra renaître dans l'Ouest encore peu peuplé. En dépit de son attaque de 1873, Whitman continue de nourrir son imagination poétique de la passion que lui inspirent les nouvelles merveilles technologiques et la beauté fruste encore visible des régions de l'Ouest sauvage. Les deux poèmes qui suivent illustrent une bonne humeur revenue, que rendent d'autant plus remarquable son déclin physique et sa conscience déçue devant la relative indifférence des lecteurs américains à l'égard de son rugueux vers libre.

BIBLIOGRAPHIE SÉLECTIVE. — *Voir page 209.*

To a Locomotive in Winter[1]

Thee for my recitative,
Thee in the driving storm even as now, the snow, the winter-day declining,
Thee in thy panoply, thy measur'd dual throbbing and thy beat convulsive.
Thy black cylindric body, golden brass and silvery steel,
Thy ponderous side-bars, parallel and connecting rods, gyrating, shuttling at thy sides,
Thy metrical, now swelling pant and roar, now tapering in the distance,
Thy great protruding head-light fix'd in front,
Thy long, pale, floating vapor-pennants, tinged with delicate purple,
The dense and murky clouds out-belching from thy smoke-stack,
Thy knitted frame, thy springs and valves, the tremulous twinkle of thy wheels,
Thy train of cars behind, obedient, merrily following,
Through gale or calm, now swift, now slack, yet steadily careering;
Type of the modern—emblem of motion and power—pulse of the continent,
For once come serve the Muse and merge in verse, even as here I see thee,
With storm and buffeting gusts of wind and falling snow,
By day thy warning ringing bell to sound its notes,
By night thy silent signal lamps to swing.

1. Ce poème fut d'abord publié en 1876 pour être ensuite incorporé dans la septième édition de *Leaves of Grass* (1881).

Fierce-throated beauty!
Roll through my chant with all thy lawless music, thy swinging
 lamps at night,
Thy madly-whistled laughter, echoing, rumbling like an
 earthquake, rousing all,
Law of thyself complete, thine own track firmly holding,
(No sweetness debonair of tearful harp or glib piano thine,)
Thy trills of shrieks by rocks and hills return'd,
Launch'd o'er the prairies wide, across the lakes,
To the free skies unpent and glad and strong.

Spirit That Form'd This Scene[1]

Written in Platte Cañon, Colorado.

Spirit that form'd this scene,
These tumbled rock-piles grim and red,
These reckless heaven-ambitious peaks,
These gorges, turbulent-clear streams, this naked freshness,
These formless wild arrays, for reasons of their own,
I know thee, savage spirit—we have communed together,
Mine too such wild arrays, for reasons of their own;
Was't charged against my chants they had forgotten art?
To fuse within themselves its rules precise and delicatesse?
The lyrist's measur'd beat, the wrought-out temple's
 grace—column and polish'd arch forgot?
But thou that revelest here—spirit that form'd this scene,
They have remember'd thee.

1. Whitman voyagea dans l'Ouest en 1879. Ce poème parut pour la première fois dans la septième édition de *Leaves of Grass*.

EMILY DICKINSON, 1830-1886

Communément admirée aujourd'hui pour avoir été l'une des voix majeures de la rébellion poétique et féministe contre la piété et la pruderie endémiques de l'Amérique, Emily Dickinson était inconnue du monde littéraire avant la publication initiale d'une partie de son œvre, quatre ans après sa mort. Ses écrits les plus prolifiques datent des années de la guerre de Sécession, lorsque vivant dans sa retraite d'Amherst au Massachusetts, elle s'habillait de blanc avec excentricité. Ils traduisent avec une remarquable densité l'expérience d'émotions intenses, allant des souffrances du temps de guerre aux amours déçues du passé. La poésie d'Emily Dickinson préfigure celle des auteurs qui dépeindront la psychologie tourmentée de l'Amérique moderne. On l'a présentée comme l'héritière des Puritains pour son intériorité et la morbidité présumée des images qu'elle offre de la culpabilité, de la douleur et de la mort. Une lecture attentive permet cependant de déceler dans ses œuvres l'esprit des poètes métaphysiques, l'évocation mordante de la réticence néo-anglaise et la subtilité d'un écrivain dont Henry James a dit « upon whom nothing is lost ». Pourtant circonscrite à son jardin d'Amherst, l'expérience d'Emily Dickinson est à vrai dire illimitée, et au sens où l'entend James, le produit intime d'une imagination qui « takes to itself the faintest hints of life (that) converts the very pulses of the air into revelations » (*The Art of Fiction*, 1884). Les poèmes présentés ici décrivent les phases complexes des sentiments et émotions quotidiennes tels que les définit le génie dickinsonien. Même le premier poème qui paraît s'harmoniser avec la célébration de la locomotive chez Whitman, révèle un locuteur peut-être inconscient que ses images poétiques trahissent une réaction ambivalente au « cheval de fer » qui serpente dans le jardin américain.

BIBLIOGRAPHIE SÉLECTIVE. — Anderson (Charles), *Emily Dickinson's Poetry : Stairway to Surprise*, New York, Holt, Rinehart and Winston, 1960 ; Diehl (Joanne), *Dickinson and the Romantic*

Imagination, Princeton, NJ, Princeton University Press, 1981 ; Gelpi (Albert), *Emily Dickinson : The Mind of the Poet*, Cambridge, Mass., Harvard University Press, 1965 ; Delphy (Françoise), *Emily Dickinson*, Paris, Didier, 1984.

585[1]

I like to see it lap the Miles—
And lick the Valleys up—
And stop to feed itself at Tanks—
And then—prodigious step

Around a Pile of Mountains—
And supercilious peer
In Shanties—by the sides of Roads—
And then a Quarry pare

To fit it's sides
And crawl between
Complaining all the while
In horrid—hooting stanza—
Then chase itself down Hill-

And neigh like Boanerges—[2]
Then—prompter than a Star
Stop—docile and omnipotent
At it's own stable door—

1862/1891

254

"Hope" is the thing with feathers—
That perches in the soul—
And sings the tune without the words—
And never stops—at all—

1. Tel qu'il a été établi en 1955 par Thomas H. Johnson dans son édition en trois volumes des *Poems of Emily Dickinson* (Cambridge, Massachusetts, Harvard University Press), le texte de ce poème témoigne, comme les autres, de la ponctuation originale et souvent capricieuse d'Emily Dickinson. Johnson a également attribué des nombres à ces poèmes sans titre selon l'apparente chronologie de leur composition. Les deux années qui suivent chacun des poèmes indiquent la date connue ou supposée de cette composition ainsi que l'année de publication.

2. « Sons of Thunder », le surnom que donna le Christ aux frères Jacques et Jean après qu'ils eurent voulu détruire un village samaritain inhospitalier. Voir Marc 3, 17 et Luc 9, 51-56. Les trois vers suivants font écho avec une égale audace au Nouveau Testament.

And sweetest—in the Gale—is heard—
And sore must be the storm—
That could abash the little Bird—
That kept so many warm—

I've heard it in the chillest land—
And on the strangest Sea—
Yet, never, in Extremity,
It asked a crumb—of Me.

1861/1891

258

There's a certain Slant of light,
Winter Afternoons—
That oppresses, like the Heft
Of Cathedral Tunes—

Heavenly Hurt, it gives us—
We can find no scar,
But internal difference,
Where the Meanings, are—

None may teach it—Any—
'Tis the Seal Despair—
An imperial affliction
Sent us of the Air—

When it comes, the Landscape listens—
Shadows—hold their breath—
When it goes, 'tis like the Distance
On the look of Death—

1861/1890

341

After great pain, a formal feeling comes—
The Nerves sit ceremonious, like Tombs—
The stiff Heart questions was it He, that bore,
And Yesterday, or Centuries before?

The Feet, mechanical, go round—
Of Ground, or Air, or Ought—[1]
A Wooden way
Regardless grown,
A Quartz contentment, like a stone—

This is the Hour of Lead—
Remembered, if outlived,
As Freezing persons, recollect the Snow—
First—Chill—then Stupor—then the letting go—

1862/1929

465

I heard a Fly buzz—when I died—
The Stillness in the Room
Was like the Stillness in the Air—
Between the Heaves of Storm—

The Eyes around—had wrung them dry—
And Breaths were gathering firm
For that last Onset—when the King
Be witnessed—in the Room—

I willed my Keepsakes—Signed away
What portion of me be
Assignable—and then it was
There interposed a Fly—

With Blue—uncertain stumbling Buzz—
Between the light—and me—
And then the Windows failed—and then
I could not see to see—

1862/1896

1540

As imperceptibly as Grief
The Summer lapsed away—
Too imperceptible at last

1. Zéro.

To seem like Perfidy—
A Quietness distilled
As Twilight long begun,
Or Nature spending with herself
Sequestered Afternoon—
The Dusk drew earlier in—
The Morning foreign shone—
A courteous, yet harrowing Grace,
As Guest, that would be gone—
And thus, without a Wing
Or service of a Keel
Our Summer made her light escape
Into the Beautiful.

1882/1891

EDWIN ARLINGTON ROBINSON, 1869-1935

De son vivant, Edwin Arlington Robinson fit l'expérience de la diversité du monde extérieur et du drame intérieur que connaissaient ses contemporains quand la vieille Amérique cédait la place à la nouvelle. Il connut la vitalité déclinante de l'Amérique rurale au cours d'une jeunesse passée à Gardiner dans le Maine, qu'il rebaptisa Tilbury Town dans ses plus vigoureux poèmes. Ses personnages mémorables dont la vie est un échec préfigurent plus nettement les villageois angoissés du Middle West dépeints dans *Spoon River Anthology* (1915) d'Edgar Lee Masters que les « grotesques » du *Winesburg* de Sherwood Anderson. (Malgré la dette qu'Anderson reconnut envers Masters, Winesburg réalise à travers le personnage de Willard, l'espérance qu'on associe communément au pastoralisme littéraire.) Egalement contemporain de Dreiser à New York, Robinson comprendra le désespoir qui accable un Hurstwood rendu suicidaire par ses malheurs financiers. (Le frère de Robinson se suicida effectivement.) Occupant des emplois sans intérêt en ville, Robinson est alors stimulé par la communauté littéraire de New York et publie ses œuvres poétiques les plus marquantes avant 1920. Il fait entrer dans ses vers le monde contemporain que décrivent les romanciers. Aussi Robinson capte-t-il le discours pastoral, rendant compte de la « réalité » psychologique du citoyen ordinaire dans le langage particulier de la conversation, et explorant comme les Naturalistes l'influence de l'environnement et du hasard sur le destin des Américains, dans sa brillante galerie de portraits miniatures.

BIBLIOGRAPHIE SÉLECTIVE. — *Collected Poems*, New York, Macmillan, 1937 ; Cestre (Charles), *An Introduction to Edwin Arlington Robinson*, New York, Macmillan, 1930 ; Robinson (W. R.), *Edwin Arlington Robinson : A Poetry of the Act*, Cleveland, Ohio, The Press of Western Reserve University, 1967.

Richard Cory[1]

Whenever Richard Cory went down town,
We people on the pavement looked at him:
He was a gentleman from sole to crown,
Clean favored, and imperially slim.

And he was always quietly arrayed,
And he was always human when he talked;
But still he fluttered pulses when he said,
"Good-morning," and he glittered when he walked.

And he was rich—yes, richer than a king—
And admirably schooled in every grace:
In fine, we thought that he was everything
To make us wish that we were in his place.

So on we worked, and waited for the light,
And went without the meat, and cursed the bread;
And Richard Cory, one calm summer night,
Went home and put a bullet through his head.

1897

1. Ces quatre poèmes ont paru pour la première fois aux années indiquées dans les volumes suivants : *Children of the Night* (1897), *The Man Against the Sky* (1916) et *The Three Taverns* (1920).

Bewick Finzer

Time was when his half million drew
  The breath of six per cent;
But soon the worm of what-was-not
  Fed hard on his content;
And something crumbled in his brain
  When his half million went.

Time passed, and filled along with his
  The place of many more:
Time came, and hardly one of us
  Had credence to restore,
From what appeared one day, the man
  Whom we had known before.

The broken voice, the withered neck,
  The coat worn out with care,
The cleanliness of indigence,
  The brilliance of despair,
The fond imponderable dreams
  Of affluence,—all were there.

Poor Finzer, with his dreams and schemes,
  Fares hard now in the race,
With heart and eye that have a task
  When he looks in the face
Of one who might so easily
  Have been in Finzer's place.

He comes unfailing for the loan
  We give and then forget;
He comes, and probably for years
  Will he be coming yet,—
Familiar as an old mistake,
  And futile as regret.

1916

The Mill

The miller's wife had waited long,
  The tea was cold, the fire was dead;
And there might yet be nothing wrong
  In how he went and what he said:
"There are no millers any more,"
  Was all that she had heard him say;
And he had lingered at the door
  So long that it seemed yesterday.

Sick with a fear that had no form
  She knew that she was there at last;
And in the mill there was a warm
  And mealy fragrance of the past.
What else there was would only seem
  To say again what he had meant;
And what was hanging from a beam
  Would not have heeded where she went.

And if she thought it followed her,
  She may have reasoned in the dark
That one way of the few there were
  Would hide her and would leave no mark:
Black water, smooth above the weir[1]
  Like starry velvet in the night,
Though ruffled once, would soon appear
  The same as ever to the sight.

1920

Firelight

Ten years together without yet a cloud,
They seek each other's eyes at intervals
Of gratefulness to firelight and four walls
For love's obliteration of the crowd.
Serenely and perennially endowed

1. Barrage de moulin.

And bowered as few may be, their joy recalls
No snake, no sword; and over them there falls
The blessing of what neither says aloud.

Wiser for silence, they were not so glad
Were she to read the graven tale of lines
On the wan face of one somewhere alone;
Nor were they more content could he have had
Her thoughts a moment since of one who shines
Apart, and would be hers if he had known.

1920

ROBERT FROST, 1874-1963

Robert Frost affecta d'être un simple habitant de la Nouvelle-Angleterre rurale dont les vers traduisaient la même simplicité du terroir dans une langue qui exprimait davantage le familier que l'envolée poétique. Frost a vécu en fait les onze premières années de sa vie à San Francisco. Après ses études secondaires au Massachusetts, il se marie, passe deux années à Harvard où il s'intéresse particulièrement à la philosophie, et s'achète ensuite une ferme dans le New Hampshire avec l'argent légué par son grand-père. Père de cinq enfants en 1906, Frost enseigne et écrit des poèmes. Après avoir vainement attendu d'être publié pendant cinq ans, il vend sa ferme et s'embarque pour l'Angleterre. Il y trouve presque immédiatement un éditeur pour ses poèmes qu'on juge alors distinctement américains. Quand éclate la Première Guerre, il revient aux Etats-Unis. Cette fois, un éditeur américain republie ses deux premiers volumes et accepte de prendre les œuvres à venir. Pour la plus grande partie de sa vie ultérieure, Frost subviendra à ses besoins grâce à des postes associés de « poet-in-residence » dans différentes universités, tout en cultivant son autre image de fermier yankee. Très productif dans les années vingt et après, il poursuit alors son œuvre dans cette même veine de trompeuse simplicité qui lui avait donné sa réputation initiale. Il confère une valeur dramatique aux questions platoniciennes de l'essence et de la substance, de la nature et de l'esprit, aux implications darwiniennes du comportement humain et animal, aux graves enjeux du libre arbitre, du déterminisme et du nihilisme anti-chrétien. Parmi les plus populaires des poètes américains majeurs, Frost a su enrober une âpre matière, du lyrisme sans apprêt de poèmes « parlés », selon sa modeste définition, d'où émergent ses thèmes « in parables and in hints and in indirections ».

BIBLIOGRAPHIE SÉLECTIVE. — *Complete Poems,* New York, Holt, Rinehart and Winston, 1962 ; Kemp (John), *Robert Frost and New England : The Poet as Regionalist,* Princeton, N.J., Princeton University Press, 1979 ; Poirier (Richard), *Robert Frost : The Work of Knowing,* New York, Oxford University Press, 1977.

Mending Wall[1]

Something there is that doesn't love a wall,
That sends the frozen-ground-swell under it,
And spills the upper boulders in the sun;
And makes gaps even two can pass abreast.
The word of hunters is another thing:
I have come after them and made repair
Where they have left not one stone on a stone,
But they would have the rabbit out of hiding,
To please the yelping dogs. The gaps I mean,
No one has seen them made or heard them made,
But at spring mending-time we find them there.
I let my neighbor know beyond the hill;
And on a day we meet to walk the line
And set the wall between us once again.
We keep the wall between us as we go.
To each the boulders that have fallen to each.
And some are loaves and some so nearly balls
We have to use a spell to make them balance:
"Stay where you are until our backs are turned!"

1. Ce quartet de poèmes parut pour la première fois aux années indiquées dans *North of Boston* (1914) et *Mountain Interval* (1916).

We wear our fingers rough with handling them.
Oh, just another kind of outdoor game.
One on a side. It comes to little more:
There where it is we do not need the wall:
He is all pine and I am apple orchard.
My apple trees will never get across
And eat the cones under his pines, I tell him.
He only says, "Good fences make good neighbors."
Spring is the mischief in me, and I wonder
If I could put a notion in his head:
"Why do they make good neighbors? Isn't it
Where there are cows? But here there are no cows.
Before I built a wall I'd ask to know
What I was walling in or walling out,
And to whom I was like like to give offense.
Something there is that doesn't love a wall,
That wants it down." I could say "Elves" to him,
But it's not elves exactly, and I'd rather
He said it for himself. I see him there
Bringing a stone grasped firmly by the top
In each hand, like an old-stone savage armed.
He moves in darkness as it seems to me,
Not of woods only and the shade of trees.
He will not go behind his father's saying,
And he likes having thought of it so well
He says again, "Good fences make good neighbors."

1914

After Apple-Picking

My long two-pointed ladder's sticking through a tree
Toward heaven still,
And there's a barrel that I didn't fill
Beside it, and there may be two or three
Apples I didn't pick upon some bough.
But I am done with apple-picking now.
Essence of winter sleep is on the night,
The scent of apples: I am drowsing off.
I cannot rub the strangeness from my sight

I got from looking through a pane of glass
I skimmed this morning from the drinking trough
And held against the work of hoary grass.
It melted, and I let it fall and break.
But I was well
Upon my way to sleep before it fell,
And I could tell
What form my dreaming was about to take.
Magnified apples appear and disappear,
Stem end and blossom end,
And every fleck of russet showing clear.
My instep arch not only keeps the ache,
It keeps the pressure of a ladder-round.
I feel the ladder sway as the boughs bend.
And I keep hearing from the cellar bin
The rumbling sound
Of load on load of apples coming in.
For I have had too much
Of apple-picking: I am overtired
Of the great harvest I myself desired.
There were ten thousand thousand fruit to touch,
Cherish in hand, lift down, and not let fall.
For all
That struck the earth,
No matter if not bruised or spiked with stubble,
Went surely to the cider-apple heap
As of no worth.
One can see what will trouble
This sleep of mine, whatever sleep it is.
Were he not gone,
The woodchuck could say whether it's like his
Long sleep, as I describe its coming on,
Or just some human sleep.

1914

The Road Not Taken

Two roads diverged in a yellow wood,
And sorry I could not travel both

And be one traveler, long I stood
And looked down one as far as I could
To where it bent in the undergrowth;

Then took the other, as just as fair,
And having perhaps the better claim,
Because it was grassy and wanted wear;
Though as for that the passing there
Had worn them really about the same,

And both that morning equally lay
In leaves no step had trodden black.
Oh, I kept the first for another day!
Yet knowing how way leads on to way,
I doubted if I should ever come back.

I shall be telling this with a sigh
Somewhere ages and ages hence:
Two roads diverged in a wood, and I—
I took the one less traveled by,
And that has made all the difference.

1916

The Oven Bird[1]

There is a singer everyone has heard,
Loud, a mid-summer and a mid-wood bird,
Who makes the solid tree trunks sound again.
He says that leaves are old and that for flowers
Mid-summer is to spring as one to ten.
He says the early petal-fall is past
When pear and cherry bloom went down in showers
On sunny days a moment overcast;
And comes that other fall we name the fall.
He says the highway dust is over all.

1. Oiseau chanteur d'Amérique du Nord qui construit un nid en forme de four dans le sol des bois. Le son qu'il émet suggère *teacher*, aussi est-il appelé *teacher bird*. Avec une pointe de nihilisme, Frost l'imagine bavard, sombre et moralisant, comme un vrai professeur.

The bird would cease and be as other birds
But that he knows in singing not to sing.
The question that he frames in all but words
Is what to make of a diminished thing.

1916

T(HOMAS) S(TEARNS) ELIOT, 1888-1965

Comme ses contemporains de l'époque moderne, T. S. Eliot écarta la délicate poésie qui était servie aux menus littéraires de dames chlorotiques « allant et venant, parlant de Michel-Ange » (« The Love Song of J. Alfred Prufrock », 1915), dans leurs salons distingués. Eliot eut un plus long chemin à parcourir que Mark Twain en arrivant de son Missouri natal. Revenu dans la Nouvelle-Angleterre de ses ancêtres, il fréquente Harvard où, poète précoce (il y écrit son « Prufrock ») il prépare ensuite une thèse de Ph.D. En 1914, il fait des études en Europe. L'année suivante, il épouse une Anglaise et choisit de résider en Angleterre à titre permanent, y travaillant comme enseignant, puis employé de banque, fondateur et rédacteur en chef du *Criterion*, enfin directeur chez l'éditeur Faber and Faber. Dans l'intervalle, il s'efforce de structurer sa vision de la civilisation occidentale en tant que *waste land*. Son modernisme complexe qu'influence et parraine fortement l'Américain Ezra Pound, inclut des mythes éternels, la littérature référentielle du passé et une vue cyclique de l'Histoire. Après son poème *The Waste Land* paru en 1922 et qui exercera une influence déterminante, Eliot abandonnera lentement son humanisme agnostique pour se convertir en 1927 à l'anglicanisme. Par la suite, ses variations sur le conflit permanent entre scepticisme et croyance deviendront l'inébranlable préoccupation de sa poésie et de son théâtre. Moins nombreux sont alors les vers qui méritent une mention, à la différence de ses premières œuvres, mais ils lui suffiront pour obtenir le prix Nobel de Littérature de 1948. En définitive, Eliot reconnaît dans l'Amérique ses racines et la source de ses émotions. Son retour au Missouri natal se traduira en 1950 par son introduction révélatrice à une nouvelle édition de *Huckleberry Finn*. Le poème urbain ci-dessous, écrit au début de sa carrière, montre son plus ample champ d'inspiration au travers de sa compassion, proche de celle de Dreiser, pour des travailleurs délaissés et saisis par le découragement dans l'aliénation et la solitude d'une cité moderne déshumanisée.

BIBLIOGRAPHIE SÉLECTIVE. — Hay (Eloise), *T. S. Eliot's Negative Way*, Cambridge, Mass., Harvard University Press, 1982 ; Kenner (Hugh), *The Invisible Poet : T. S. Eliot*, New York, McDowell, Obolensky, 1959 ; Matthiessen (F. O.), *The Achievement of T. S. Eliot*, New York, Oxford University Press, 1935.

Preludes[1]

I

The winter evening settles down
With smell of steaks in passageways.
Six o'clock.
The burnt-out ends of smoky days.
And now a gusty shower wraps
The grimy scraps
Of withered leaves about your feet
And newspapers from vacant lots;
The showers beat
On broken blinds and chimney-pots,
And at the corner of the street
A lonely cab-horse steams and stamps.

And then the lighting of the lamps.

1. Ce poème sur la banlieue de Boston fut publié pour la première fois par Wyndham Lewis dans son *Blast* de Londres en 1915. Il fut republié dans *Prufrock and Other Observations* (1917).

II

The morning comes to consciousness
Of faint stale smells of beer
From the sawdust-trampled street
With all its muddy feet that press
To early coffee-stands.

With the other masquerades
That time resumes,
One thinks of all the hands
That are raising dingy shades
In a thousand furnished rooms.

III

You tossed a blanket from the bed,
You lay upon your back, and waited;
You dozed, and watched the night revealing
The thousand sordid images
Of which your soul was constituted;
They flickered against the ceiling.
And when all the world came back
And the light crept up between the shutters
And you heard the sparrows in the gutters,
You had such a vision of the street
As the street hardly understands;
Sitting along the bed's edge, where
You curled the papers from your hair,
Or clasped the yellow soles of feet
In the palms of both soiled hands.

IV

His soul stretched tight across the skies
That fade behind a city block,
Or trampled by insistent feet
At four and five and six o'clock;
And short square fingers stuffing pipes,
And evening newspapers, and eyes
Assured of certain certainties,
The conscience of a blackened street
Impatient to assume the world.

I am moved by fancies that are curled
Around these images, and cling;
The notion of some infinitely gentle
Infinitely suffering thing.

Wipe your hand across your mouth, and laugh;
The worlds revolve like ancient women
Gathering fuel in vacant lots.

CARL SANDBURG, 1878-1967

Les gens de Chicago évoqués par Carl Sandburg rappellent plus les New-Yorkais exubérants de Walt Whitman que les survivants désespérés de Dreiser, ou même que l'humanité fractionnée des populations urbaines du monde moderne, décrites par Eliot. La « City of the Big Shoulders » de Sandburg manifeste une confiance juvénile et joyeuse dans la vigueur de la vie démocratique. Aux moments les plus calmes, le chatoiement de sa beauté lunaire suggère l' « Ashcan School » des peintres américains contemporains, attentifs à la valeur picturale de ces sites et voies urbaines dont se désespérait le locuteur des « Preludes » d'Eliot. L'attitude de Sandburg à l'égard de la vie du peuple américain émane de sa ferme adhésion aux valeurs socialistes. Ne fut-il pas membre actif du syndicat révolutionnaire IWW (International Workers of the World) ? Il a connu l'Amérique profonde comme voyageur de commerce, conférencier, chanteur folklorique, ou encore simple « hobo », occupé à « brûler le dur ». Journaliste à Chicago pendant de nombreuses années, il reconstitue son expérience américaine dans un vers libre continuellement prolifique, qui évoque Whitman par la souplesse de la structure prosodique. C'est avec une rigueur plus conventionnelle qu'il exprime sa foi démocratique dans une biographie d'un co-résident de l'Illinois, Abraham Lincoln. Les quatre volumes lui vaudront le prix Pulitzer en 1940. Dans ses dernières années, il sera comme Robert Frost, le vénérable poète chenu d'une autre ère, honoré de nombreuses distinctions, mais candidat toujours malheureux au prix Nobel de littérature.

BIBLIOGRAPHIE SÉLECTIVE. — *Complete Poems,* New York, Harcourt, Brace, 1950 ; Allen (Gay), *Carl Sandburg,* Minneapolis, University of Minnesota Press, 1972 ; Crowder (Richard), *Carl Sandburg,* New York, Twayne, 1964.

Chicago[1]

Hog Butcher for the World,
Tool Maker, Stacker of Wheat,
Player with Railroads and the Nation's Freight Handler;
Stormy, husky, brawling,
City of the Big Shoulders:
They tell me you are wicked and I believe them, for I have seen your painted women under the gas lamps luring the farm boys.
And they tell me you are crooked and I answer: Yes, it is true I have seen the gunman kill and go free to kill again.
And they tell me you are brutal and my reply is: On the faces of women and children I have seen the marks of wanton hunger.
And having answered so I turn once more to those who sneer at this my city, and I give them back the sneer and say to them:
Come and show me another city with lifted head singing so proud to be alive and coarse and strong and cunning.
Flinging magnetic curses amid the toil of piling job on job, here is a tall bold slugger set vivid against the little soft cities;
Fierce as a dog with tongue lapping for action, cunning as a savage pitted against the wilderness,
Bareheaded,
Shoveling,
Wrecking,
Planning,
Building, breaking, rebuilding,

1. Ce poème parut d'abord dans la nouvelle et importante revue de Harriet Monroe, *Poetry : A Magazine of Verse,* publiée à Chicago, en 1914. Il fut reproduit dans *Chicago Poems* (1916).

Under the smoke, dust all over his mouth, laughing with white
 teeth,
Under the terrible burden of destiny laughing as a young man
 laughs,
Laughing even as an ignorant fighter laughs who has never lost a
 battle,
Bragging and laughing that under his wrist is the pulse, and under
 his ribs the heart of the people,
  Laughing!
Laughing the stormy, husky, brawling laughter of Youth,
 half-naked, sweating, proud to be Hog Butcher, Tool Maker,
 Stacker of Wheat, Player with railroads and Freight Handler
 to the Nation.

Nocturne in a Deserted Brickyard[1]

  Stuff of the moon
Runs on the lapping sand
Out to the longest shadows.
Under the curving willows,
And round the creep of the wave line,
Fluxions[2] of yellow and dusk on the waters
Make a wide dreaming pansy of an old pond in the night.

1. De *Chicago Poems* (1916).
2. Mouvements chatoyants.

IV – Les années d'ébranlement culturel : séismes nationaux et internationaux, 1920-1945

Trois événements historiques majeurs ont influé sur le cours de la littérature américaine du XXe siècle. La Première Guerre produisit des ondes de choc culturelles, nationales et internationales, qui déferlèrent dans les années vingt. Elles furent encore ressenties par Hemingway à la fin de la décennie, lorsqu'il fixa sa perspective pour écrire son roman de la Grande Guerre, *A Farewell to Arms* (1929). Puis en octobre 1929, après le boom du capitalisme sous les présidences de Coolidge et Hoover, la Bourse de Wall Street s'effondra, plongeant le pays dans la Grande Dépression des années trente. Connaissant l'aliénation, les auteurs américains des années vingt, anciens combattants pour certains, étaient devenus des esthètes, vivant en exil volontaire à Paris. Ils revinrent alors aux Etats-Unis pour s'engager politiquement et socialement. Des écrivains comme Dos Passos et Hemingway se tournèrent de nouveau vers la scène internationale quand sévit l'oppression fasciste au temps de la guerre d'Espagne. La fièvre qui s'était emparée à l'étranger des communautés artistiques de l'après-guerre, et l'euphorie correspondant en Amérique à l'affranchissement des mœurs puritaines au cours des Années folles, s'effacèrent dans les années trente devant une réalité moins exaltante : le capitalisme de la libre entreprise avait trahi la nation et l'économie internationale. Quelles que fussent les causes du krach de Wall Street, on en ressentit les effets dans les banqueroutes en séries, dans la ruine des entreprises grandes et petites, la saisie des fermes hypothéquées, outre un chômage désastreux. Les suicides étaient courants. Les gens sans emploi et sans toit firent la queue devant les soupes populaires. Il n'est pas surprenant que les écrivains et les intellectuels se soient alors interrogés sur l'alternative offerte par le communisme soviétique et le socialisme, tandis que le Président Roosevelt faisait passer des mesures législatives massives pour apporter le soutien du gouvernement aux banques, mines, fermes et syndicats. Il tentait aussi de nommer à la Cour suprême des juges prêts à approuver la constitutionnalité de son programme progressiste.

En littérature, romanciers, poètes et essayistes s'affrontèrent aux causes immédiates et aux vastes implications idéologiques de la crise nationale. Certains écrivains insistèrent avec éloquence sur le déconcertant échec d'une grande nation démocratique à satisfaire ses idéaux humanitaires, fraternels et communautaires. D'autres s'attachèrent aux résultats observables de cet échec. Thomas Wolfe disait avec tristesse dans *Of Time and The River* (1935) : « We are so lost, so naked and lonely in America. Immense and cruel skies bend over us, and all of us are driven on forever and we have no home. » Sherwood Anderson lui faisait écho l'année suivante dans *Kit Brandon* : « There is something that separates people, curiously, persistently in America. » Et John Dos Passos laissait exploser sa colère de romancier dans sa trilogie *USA*, en représentant l'Américain comme un vagabond désabusé, faisant de l'auto-stop sans destination connue. Plus révélateur de la littérature des années de la Dépression est le thème constant de l'esprit d'endurance, individuel et communautaire qui défie les forces dominatrices et oppressives, et arrache finalement la victoire. Les textes proposés ci-dessous reflètent quelques-unes de ces œuvres significatives.

Tard dans l'été de 1939, deux événements de portée internationale se produisirent virtuellement en une semaine. Ils détournèrent ainsi l'attention des vicissitudes économiques de la nation et précipitèrent l'Amérique dans une nouvelle crise d'ampleur historique. Le 23 août 1939, la Russie et l'Allemagne signèrent un pacte de non-agression à la consternation mêlée d'incrédulité des écrivains et intellectuels américains qui s'en étaient remis au Petit Père des Peuples (malgré les purges staliniennes des années trente) pour conduire le monde vers plus d'égalité et de justice sociale. Avec le pacte germano-soviétique, la critique du capitalisme et la revendication d'un Etat prolétarien perdirent leur aura révolutionnaire en un après-midi. L'invasion de la Pologne par l'Allemagne le 1er septembre 1939 ramena au dur sens des réalités.

Si comme la Guerre de 14-18, la Deuxième Guerre mondiale eut une influence vitale sur la littérature américaine, ce fut non pas durant le conflit, mais dans l'effondrement de l'idéalisme qui s'ensuivit. Au cours des années de guerre, de 1941 à 1945, le chauvinisme, le goût du slogan et le sentimentalisme eurent, comme il fallait s'y attendre, une voix prépondérante dans le pays. Il est vrai que Tennessee Williams connut son premier succès en 1944 avec *The Glass Menagerie,* drame qui, prenant pour décor un logement des ruelles de Saint-Louis, dessine les ombres inquiétantes de la Deuxième Guerre, depuis le massacre de Guernica par les Franquistes jusqu'aux concessions de Chamberlain à Munich et à l'apogée d'Hitler à Berchtesgaden. Plus typique encore est le cas de John Steinbeck dont la grande épopée de la Dépression, *The Grapes of Wrath,* fut suivie de *The Moon is Down* (1942), roman de guerre de second ordre qui traite médiocrement de l'invasion nazie en Norvège. Aussi peut-on ici généraliser sans risque : au cours des conflits majeurs, les muses prononcent un moratoire qui s'applique, au moins en Amérique, à la grande littérature de l'imaginaire.

1 – Les années vingt : désillusions d'après guerre et réévaluations culturelles

Peu avant la Première Guerre, le nouvel esprit qui soufflait puissamment dans la poésie américaine s'accompagnait d'une critique tout aussi vigoureuse de la moralité puritaine et de l'*establishment* socio-économique. Après la guerre, le réexamen des valeurs culturelles atteint plus profondément mœurs et institutions. Ezra Pound et T. S. Eliot emploient leur talent critique et poétique à écrire des vers incisifs et dévastateurs sur le désert culturel et spirituel des deux rives de l'Atlantique. Journaliste volontiers fielleux, H. L. Mencken déboulonne avec délice puritanisme, bon ton et médiocrité littéraire que vénère la « booboisie » américaine. Dans le roman, Sinclair Lewis procure au public de Mencken le portrait satirique des cousins de province du gogo, qui poursuivent leurs ambitions à l'ombre des clochers de Gopher Prairie et de Zénith, dans le Middle West. Parallèlement, E. E. Cummings et Wallace Stephens pourfendent les mêmes valeurs rances de leurs concitoyens au moyen de traits poétiques inattendus, voire scandaleux qu'ils destinent aux « réalités » conventionnelles. F. Scott Fitzgerald offre une chronique des Années folles, avec ses réceptions extravagantes, son alcool clandestin du temps de la Prohibition, ses robes courtes et son émancipation sexuelle. C'est toutefois dans le réexamen critique du Rêve américain de l'idéal du moi qu'il a laissé le véritable legs de ses romans. Puisant dans une veine plus existentielle, Ernest Hemingway a ciselé un style de nature à exprimer la lutte individuelle tendue vers ce qu'il appelle l'authentique « grace under pressure », cette forme d'intégrité intime qui s'oppose aux fausses valeurs et rituels factices de l'Américain moyen.

EZRA POUND, 1885-1972

Personne n'a fait plus qu'Ezra Pound au début de ce siècle pour promouvoir la littérature américaine. Après ses études universitaires, il vit pendant douze ans (1908-1920) en Angleterre au milieu d'écrivains et de peintres, tandis qu'il élabore un nouvel « imagisme » afin de servir la poésie américaine moderne. Il préconise un langage poétique de communication plus intense, des rythmes plus libres, des sujets plus audacieux et surtout le recours à l'image vive et évocatrice comme véhicule de la substance poétique. En 1914, il rencontre T. S. Eliot en Angleterre et découvre en lui un autodidacte moderne. Eliot s'en remet pourtant à Pound en matière de goût et de souci de la densité, appréciant de surcroît le soutien que Pound lui apporte dans ses efforts de longue haleine. Pound aide Eliot à se trouver des éditeurs, obtient de mécènes l'argent qui permettra à celui-ci d'écrire librement et surtout joue un rôle déterminant dans la révision du manuscrit de *The Waste Land* (1922). Eliot dédie alors le poème à Pound, « Il miglior fabbro » (Le meilleur écrivain), compliment dithyrambique jugé, selon les exégètes, d'une humilité excessive. Plus tard, ils comprendront l'admiration sincère d'Eliot. Pound est déjà l'auteur d'une poésie faite de jugements critiques pénétrants. Eliot a justement désigné *Hugh Selwyn Mauberley* (1920) comme « a document of an epoch ». Plus impressionnants et surprenants dans leur perspective épique sont les *Cantos* de Pound (109 terminés et 8 inachevés à sa mort). Ce panorama de la civilisation occidentale, fourmillant de références instructives sur les enseignements de Confucius, reflète des convictions inébranlables, sources de polémiques. Pound est en outre notoirement antisémite. Publié alors que paraissaient les premiers Cantos *Mauberley* partage une semblable vision critique des Etats-Unis.

BIBLIOGRAPHIE SÉLECTIVE. — Jackson (Thomas), *The Early Poetry of Ezra Pound,* Cambridge, Mass., Harvard University Press, 1968 ; Kenner (Hugh), *The Pound Era,* Berkeley, University of California Press, 1971 ; Witemeyer (Hugh), *The Poetry of Ezra Pound : Forms and Renewal, 1908-1920,* Berkeley, University of California Press, 1969 ; Veza (Laurette), *La poésie américaine de 1910 à 1940,* Paris, Didier, 1972.

Hugh Selwyn Mauberley[1]

II

The age demanded an image
Of its accelerated grimace,
Something for the modern stage,
Not, at any rate, an Attic grace;[2]

Not, not certainly, the obscure reveries
Of the inward gaze;
Better mendacities
Than the classics in paraphrase!

The "age demanded" chiefly a mould in plaster,
Made with no loss of time,
A prose kinema, not, not assuredly, alabaster
Or the "sculpture" of rhyme.

IV

These fought in any case,
and some believing,
　　　　pro domo,[3] in any case . . .

Some quick to arm,
some for adventure,

1. *Hugh Selwyn Mauberley : Life and Contacts* fut publié en 1920.
2. Elégance athénienne : écho de « Ode on a Grecian Urn » de John Keats.
3. Pour leur patrie.

some from fear of weakness,
some from fear of censure,
some for love of slaughter, in imagination,
learning later . . .
some in fear, learning love of slaughter;

Died some, pro patria,
          non "dulce" non "et decor"[1] . . .
walked eye-deep in hell
believing in old men's lies, then unbelieving
came home, home to a lie,
home to many deceits,
home to old lies and new infamy;
usury age-old and age-thick
and liars in public places.

Daring as never before, wastage as never before.
Young blood and high blood,
fair cheeks, and fine bodies;

fortitude as never before

frankness as never before,
disillusions as never told in the old days,
hysterias, trench confessions,
laughter out of dead bellies.

V

There died a myriad,
And of the best, among them,
For an old bitch gone in the teeth,
For a botched civilization,

Charm, smiling at the good mouth,
Quick eyes gone under earth's lid,

For two gross of broken statues,
For a few thousand battered books.

1. Déni satirique du patriotisme latin d'Horace : « Dulce et decorum est pro patria mori », « il est doux et juste de mourir pour son pays » (*Odes,* III, ii, 13).

T. S. ELIOT, 1888-1965

Voir l'introduction, p. 328.

The Waste Land

II – A GAME OF CHESS[1]

[. . .]
When Lil's husband got demobbed,[2] I said—
I didn't mince my words, I said to her myself,
HURRY UP PLEASE ITS TIME[3]
Now Albert's coming back, make yourself a bit smart.
He'll want to know what you done with that money he gave you
To get yourself some teeth. He did, I was there.
You have them all out, Lil, and get a nice set,
He said, I swear, I can't bear to look at you.
And no more can't I, I said, and think of poor Albert,
He's been in the army four years, he wants a good time,
And if you don't give it him, there's others will, I said.
Oh is there, she said. Something o' that, I said.
Then I'll know who to thank, she said, and give me a straight look.
HURRY UP PLEASE ITS TIME
If you don't like it you can get on with it, I said.
Others can pick and choose if you can't.
But if Albert makes off, it won't be for lack of telling.

1. Dans cette seconde partie, Eliot vient de décrire le désespoir d'une aristocrate qui ressemble à Ophélie ainsi que la lassitude de son Hamlet, intellectuel d'aujourd'hui. Apparaissent aussi des réminiscences ironiques d'*Antoine et Cléopâtre*. Le jeu d'échecs occupe une partie de leur existence stérile. Eliot évoque ensuite la même absence d'amour dans un bar de la banlieue ouvrière de Londres lorsqu'on surprend une voix de femme perfide qui fait des commérages sur le mariage de Lil et Albert.

2. Démobilisé de l'armée britannique pendant la Première Guerre. On reconnaît ici l'une des nombreuses suggestions verbales apportées par Ezra Pound dans le manuscrit.

3. Valeur polysémique sur 1 / l'annonce par le patron du bar de l'heure de fermeture ; 2 / l'annonce qu'il est temps d'agir de manière significative dans ce désert spirituel. Thème lancinant que l'on retrouve dans « The Love Song of J. Alfred Prufrock ».

You ought to be ashamed, I said, to look so antique.
(And her only thirty-one.)
I can't help it, she said, pulling a long face,
It's them pills I tooks, to bring it off, she said.
(She's had five already, and nearly died of young George.)
The chemist said it would be all right, but I've never been the same.
You *are* a proper fool, I said.
Well, if Albert won't leave you alone, there it is, I said,
What you get married for if you don't want children ?
HURRY UP PLEASE ITS TIME
Well, that Sunday Albert was home, they had a hot gammon,[1]
And they asked me in to dinner, to get the beauty of it hot—
HURRY UP PLEASE ITS TIME
HURRY UP PLEASE ITS TIME
Goonight Bill. Goonight Lou. Goonight May. Goonight.
Ta ta. Goonight. Goonight.
Good night, ladies, good night, sweet ladies, good night, good night.[2]

III – THE FIRE SERMON[3]

[. . .]
At the violet hour, when the eyes and back
Turn upward from the desk, when the human engine waits
Like a taxi throbbing waiting,
I Tiresias, though blind, throbbing between two lives,[4]
Old man with wrinkled female breasts, can see
At the violet hour, the evening hour that strives

1. Jambon braisé ou fumé.

2. Evocation des derniers mots d'Ophélie, prise de folie dans *Hamlet* (IV, v, 72-74). Ces mots rappellent la femme désespérée, voir n. 1, *supra*. « Good night, ladies », dans la chanson à boire familière, se poursuit par « Merrily we roll along... » (fort éloigné de l'humeur des personnages d'Eliot de ce poème).

3. La note d'Eliot sur le titre se réfère au Sermon sur le Feu de Bouddah qui met en garde contre les flammes de la luxure.

4. Dans une autre note, Eliot explique que ce prophète de la tragédie grecque, parce qu'il fut autrefois bisexuel, est un spectateur idéal de la rencontre sordide entre la dactylo blasée et l'employé au visage pustuleux. Typiquement, Eliot fait allusion dans ce passage aux œuvres de divers auteurs, incluant les poètes anglais Robert Louis Stevenson, John Keats, Oliver Goldsmith, ainsi que le poète latin Ovide et le mythe de Tirésias dans ses *Métamorphoses*.

Homeward, and brings the sailor home from sea,
The typist home at teatime, clears her breakfast, lights
Her stove, and lays out food in tins.
Out of the window perilously spread
Her drying combinations touched by the sun's last rays,
On the divan are piled (at night her bed)
Stockings, slippers, camisoles, and stays.
I Tiresias, old man with wrinkled dugs
Perceived the scene, and foretold the rest—
I too awaited the expected guest.
He, the young man carbuncular, arrives,
A small house agent's clerk, with one bold stare,
One of the low on whom assurance sits
As a silk hat on a Bradford millionaire.
The time is now propitious, as he guesses,
The meal is ended, she is bored and tired,
Endeavours to engage her in caresses
Which still are unreproved, if undesired.
Flushed and decided, he assaults at once;
Exploring hands encounter no defence;
His vanity requires no response,
And makes a welcome of indifference.
(And I Tiresias have foresuffered all
Enacted on this same divan or bed;
I who have sat by Thebes below the wall
And walked among the lowest of the dead.)
Bestows one final patronising kiss,
And gropes his way, finding the stairs unlit . . .

She turns and looks a moment in the glass,
Hardly aware of her departed lover;
Her brain allows one half-formed thought to pass:
"Well now that's done: and I'm glad it's over."
When lovely woman stoops to folly and
Paces about her room again, alone,
She smoothes her hair with automatic hand,
And puts a record on the gramophone.

V – WHAT THE THUNDER SAID[1]

[. . .]
Then spoke the thunder
DA
Datta: what have we given?
My friend, blood shaking my heart
The awful daring of a moment's surrender
Which an age of prudence can never retract
By this, and this only, we have existed
Which is not to be found in our obituaries
Or in memories draped by the beneficent spider
Or under seals broken by the lean solicitor
In our empty rooms
DA
Dayadhvam: I have heard the key
Turn in the door once and turn once only
We think of the key, each in his prison
Thinking of the key, each confirms a prison
Only at nightfall, aethereal rumours
Revive for a moment a broken Coriolanus[9]
DA
Damyata : The boat responded
Gaily, to the hand expert with sail and oar
The sea was calm, your heart would have responded
Gaily, when invited, beating obedient
To controlling hands

. . . .

Datta. Dayadhvam. Damyata.
        Shantih shantih shantih[10]

1. Dans cette partie finale, le locuteur d'Eliot, tel un chevalier en quête du Graal, traverse le pays dévasté (1) sur la route d'Emmaüs prise par le Christ ressuscité (2) dans l'Europe apocalyptique moderne de Herman Hesse. A la traditionnelle Chapelle périlleuse, sa quête de réponses porteuses de rédemption semble désespérée, avant que ne commence à tomber la pluie et que le tonnerre n'énonce en sanscrit le message universel aux hommes du Brihadaranyaka-Upanishad hindou : Datta : (donne), Dayadhvam (accorde ta sympathie) et Damyata (contrôle).

2. Général romain orgueilleux et félon dans la pièce de Shakespeare. La mort de Coriolan suscite à la fin la sympathie de ses meurtriers.

3. Ce dernier vers (434) constitue la fin obligée d'un Upanishad. Eliot explique dans sa note « The Peace which passeth understanding is our equivalent to this word ».

H(ENRY) L(OUIS) MENCKEN, 1880-1956

Tandis qu'Eliot et Pound organisent leur approche critique de la culture dominante dans un large contexte historique ou international, H. L. Mencken centre essentiellement son discours sur les folies du présent. En 1922, Mencken publie la troisième série de ses truculents *Prejudices* au moment où *The Waste Land* étonne l'intelligentsia européenne et américaine. Ce sont les gogos des Etats-Unis ses cibles préférées : professeurs collet monté, réformateurs puritains, vieilles filles jouant aux arbitres des élégances, hommes d'affaires vulgaires et, pour couronner le tout, politiciens hypocrites et leurs dupes, à savoir la masse stupide des électeurs. N'ayant pas accédé comme étudiant à l'enseignement supérieur, Mencken manifesta son dépit vis-à-vis des universitaires quand il ridiculisa l'enseignement de haut niveau. Il eut aussi la faiblesse coupable de vouloir surcompenser son sentiment d'infériorité en prônant une aristocratie du goût et de l'intelligence qui eût fait pièce à la vulgarité d'une nation de troisième ordre composée d'immigrants. Malgré tout, Mencken eut de nombreux lecteurs et sut mettre en joie ses adversaires dont beaucoup étaient sensibles à ses vastes dons de journaliste professionnel et de linguiste érudit. *The American Language* (1919), revu et augmenté dans plusieurs éditions jusqu'à 1948, est un classique reconnu. *The American Mercury*, dont il fut le fondateur en 1923 et rédacteur en chef pendant dix ans, constitua la plus vivante des revues satiriques et littéraires des années vingt. Mencken prit fait et cause pour Dreiser, Sandburg, Anderson, Sinclair Lewis et ses contemporains allergiques aux dames trop distinguées, et aux professeurs guindés. Dans la sélection qui suit, Mencken brocarde un bon nombre de ses souffre-douleur préférés parmi les Américains.

BIBLIOGRAPHIE SÉLECTIVE. — Fisher (Charles), *Mencken : A Study of His Thought*, New York, Knopf, 1978 ; Stenerson (Douglas), *H. L. Mencken : Iconoclast from Baltimore*, Chicago, University of Chicago Press, 1971 ; Forgue (Guy J.), *H. L. Mencken, l'homme, l'œuvre, l'influence*, U. de Nice, 1967.

On Being an American[1]

[. . .] Third-rate men, of course, exist in all countries, but it is only here that they are in full control of the state, and with it of all the national standards. The land was peopled, not by the hardy adventurers of legend, but simply by incompetents who could not get on at home, and the lavishness of nature that they found here, the vast ease with which they could get livings, confirmed and augmented their native incompetence. No American colonist, even in the worst days of the Indian wars, ever had to face such hardships as ground down the peasants of Central Europe during the Hundred Years War, nor even such hardships as oppressed the English lower classes during the century before the Reform Bill of 1832. In most of the colonies, indeed, he seldom saw any Indians at all: the one thing that made life difficult for him was his congenital dunderheadedness. The winning of the West, so rhetorically celebrated in American romance, cost the lives of fewer men than the single battle of Tannenberg, and the victory was much easier and surer. The immigrants who have come in since those early days have been, if anything, of even lower grade than their forerunners. The old notion that the United States is peopled by the offspring of brave, idealistic and liberty loving minorities, who revolted against injustice, bigotry and mediævalism at home—this notion is fast succumbing to the alarmed study that has been given of late to the immigration of recent years. The truth is that the majority of non-Anglo-Saxon immigrants since the Revolution, like the majority of Anglo-Saxon immigrants before the Revolution, have been, not the superior men of their native lands, but the botched and unfit: Irishmen starving to death in Ireland, Germans unable to weather the *Sturm und Drang* of the post-Napoleonic reorganization, Italians weed-grown on exhausted soil, Scandinavians run to all bone and no brain, Jews too incompetent to swindle even the barbarous peasants of Russia, Poland and Roumania. Here and there among the immigrants, of course, there may be a bravo, or even a superman—*e. g.*, the ancestors of Volstead, Ponzi, Jack

1. Dans *Prejudices : Third Series* (1922). Ce volume eut sept éditions en quatre ans et fut suivi de trois « séries » supplémentaires.

Dempsey, Schwab, Daugherty, Debs, Pershing[1]—but the average newcomer is, and always has been simply a poor fish.

Nor is there much soundness in the common assumption, so beloved of professional idealists and wind-machines, that the people of America constitute "the youngest of the great peoples." The phrase turns up endlessly; the average newspaper editorial writer would be hamstrung if the Postoffice suddenly interdicted it, as it interdicted "the right to rebel" during the war. What gives it a certain specious plausibility is the fact that the American Republic, compared to a few other existing governments, is relatively young. But the American Republic is not necessarily identical with the American people; they might overturn it to-morrow and set up a monarchy, and still remain the same people. The truth is that, as a distinct nation, they go back fully three hundred years, and that even their government is older than that of most other nations, *e. g.*, France, Italy, Germany, Russia. Moreover, it is absurd to say that there is anything properly describable as youthfulness in the American outlook. It is not that of young men, but that of old men. All the characteristics of senescence are in it: a great distrust of ideas, an habitual timorousness, a harsh fidelity to a few fixed beliefs, a touch of mysticism. The average American is a prude and a Methodist under his skin, and the facts is never more evident than when he is trying to disprove it. His vices are not those of a healthy boy, but those of an ancient paralytic escaped from the *Greisenheim.*[2] If you would penetrate to the causes thereof, simply go down to Ellis Island and look at the next shipload of immigrants. You will not find the spring

1. Dans sa liste d'Américains hauts en couleur, Mencken mêle comme à l'habitude des héros légitimes aux coquins qui ont mystifié leurs stupides compatriotes. *A. J. Volstead* (1860-1947) fit voter en 1919 la législation qui interdit la vente de l'alcool. La « Prohibition » fut abrogée par le 18e Amendement à la Constitution en 1933. *Charles Ponzi* (1877-1949) organisa une escroquerie de plusieurs millions de dollars à Boston en 1920, en promettant aux investisseurs de doubler leur mise en quatre-vingt-dix jours. Il soutira l'argent des derniers investisseurs pour régler les gros bénéfices des premiers dont l'argent réinvesti servit à payer leurs prédécesseurs et ainsi de suite, jusqu'à la découverte de l'escroquerie et de la foule des victimes. Affaire connue sous le nom de « The Ponzi Scheme ». *Jack Dempsey* (1895-1983), champion de boxe poids lourd de 1919 à 1926. Célèbre en France pour son combat contre Georges Carpentier. *Charles M. Schwab* (1862-1939) fut un magnat de l'acier et profiteur de guerre. *Harry M. Daugherty* (1860-1941) fut sous la présidence de Harding un ministre de la Justice (Attorney General) de moralité douteuse (1921-1924). *Eugène Debs* (1855-1926), leader syndical et militant socialiste, fut cinq fois candidat à la présidence des Etats-Unis. *John J. Pershing* (1860-1948) fut commandant en chef du Corps expéditionnaire de la Première Guerre.

2. Home du troisième âge.

of youth in their step; you will find the shuffling of exhausted men. From such exhausted men the American stock has sprung. It was easier for them to survive here than it was where they came from, but that ease, though it made them feel stronger, did not actually strengthen them. It left them what they were when they came: weary peasants, eager only for the comfortable security of a pig in a sty. Out of that eagerness has issued many of the noblest manifestations of American *Kultur*: the national hatred of war, the pervasive suspicion of the aims and intents of all others nations, the short way with heretics and disturbers of the peace, the unshakable belief in devils, the implacable hostility to every novel idea and point of view.

All these ways of thinking are the marks of the peasant—more, of the peasant long ground into the mud of his wallow, and determined at last to stay there—the peasant who has definitely renounced any lewd desire he may have ever had to gape at the stars. The habits of mind of this dull, sempiternal *fellah*—the oldest man in Christendom—are, with a few modifications, the habits of mind of the American people. The peasant has a great practical cunning, but he is unable to see any further than the next farm. He likes money and knows how to amass property, but his cultural development is but little above that of the domestic animals. He is intensely and cocksurely moral, but his morality and his self-interest are crudely identical. He is emotional and easy to scare, but his imagination cannot grasp an abstraction. He is a violent nationalist and patriot, but he admires rogues in office and always beats the tax-collector if he can. He has immovable opinions about all the great affairs of state, but nine-tenths of them are sheer imbecilities. He is violently jealous of what he conceives to be his rights, but brutally disregardful of the other fellow's. He is religious, but his religion is wholly devoid of beauty and dignity. This man, whether city or country bred, is the normal Americano—the 100 per cent. Methodist, Odd Fellow, Ku Kluxer, and Know Nothing.[1] He exists in all countries, but here alone he rules—here alone his anthropoid fears and rages are accepted gravely as logical ideas, and dissent from them is

1. The Odd Fellows est un club réservé aux hommes (loge) fondé en Angleterre au XVIIIe siècle. Le Ku Klux Klan fut créé par des fanatiques protestants de race blanche après la guerre de Sécession. Les « Know Nothings » constituèrent après 1850 une organisation secrète qui s'opposa à l'élection aux mandats politiques de candidats nés à l'étranger.

punished as a sort of public offense. Around every one of his principal delusions—of the sacredness of democracy, of the feasibility of sumptuary law, of the incurable sinfulness of all other peoples, of the menace of ideas, of the corruption lying in all the arts—there is thrown a barrier of taboos, and woe to the anarchist who seeks to break it down!

The multiplication of such taboos is obviously not characteristic of a culture that is moving from a lower plane to a higher—that is, of a culture still in the full glow of its youth. It is a sign, rather, of a culture that is slipping downhill—one that is reverting to the most primitive standards and ways of thought. The taboo, indeed, is the trade-mark of the savage, and wherever it exists it is a relentless and effective enemy of civilized enlightenment. The savage is the most meticulously moral of men; there is scarcely an act of his daily life that is not conditioned by unyielding prohibitions and obligations, most of them logically unintelligible. The mob-man, a savage set amid civilization, cherishes a code of the same draconian kind. He believes firmly that right and wrong are immovable things—that they have an actual and unchangeable existence, and that any challenge of them, by word or act, is a crime against society. And with the concept of wrongness, of course, he always confuses the concept of mere differentness—to him the two are indistinguishable. Anything strange is to be combatted; it is of the Devil. The mob-man cannot grasp ideas in their native nakedness. They must be dramatized and personalized for him, and provided with either white wings or forked tails. All discussion of them, to interest him, must take the form of a pursuit and scotching of demons. He cannot think of a heresy without thinking of a heretic to be caught, condemned, and burned.

. . . .

All the while I have been forgetting the third of my reasons for remaining so faithful a citizen of the Federation, despite all the lascivious inducements from expatriates to follow them beyond the seas, and all the surly suggestions from patriots that I succumb.[1] It is the reason which grows out of my mediæval

1. Mencken fournit d'emblée trois raisons pour rester aux Etats-Unis. Il préférait être « a / Well-fed, unhounded by sordid cares, at ease in Zion ; b / Full of a comfortable feeling of superiority to the masses of my fellowmen ; c / Delicately and unceasingly amused according to my taste ».

but unashamed taste for the bizarre and indelicate, my congenital weakness for comedy of the grosser varieties. The United States, to my eye, is incomparably the greatest show on earth. It is a show which avoids diligently all the kinds of clowning which tire me most quickly—for example, royal ceremonials, the tedious hocus-pocus of *haut politique,* the taking of politics seriously—and lays chief stress upon the kinds which delight me unceasingly—for example, the ribald combats of demagogues, the exquisitely ingenious operations of master rogues, the pursuit of witches and heretics, the desperate struggles of inferior men to claw their way into Heaven. We have clowns in constant practice among us who are as far above the clowns of any other great state as a Jack Dempsey is above a paralytic—and not a few dozen or score of them, but whole droves and herds. Human enterprises which, in all other Christian countries, are resigned despairingly to an incurable dullness—things that seem devoid of exhilarating amusement by their very nature—are here lifted to such vast heights of buffoonery that contemplating them strains the midriff almost to breaking. I cite an example: the worship of God. Everywhere else on earth it is carried on in a solemn and dispiriting manner; in England, of course, the bishops are obscene, but the average man seldom gets a fair chance to laugh at them and enjoy them. Now come home. Here we not only have bishops who are enormously more obscene than even the most gifted of the English bishops; we have also a huge force of lesser specialists in ecclesiastical mountebankery—tin-horn Loyolas, Savonarolas and Xaviers of a hundred fantastic rites, each performing untiringly and each full of a grotesque and illimitable whimsicality. Every American town, however small, has one of its own: a holy clerk with so fine a talent for introducing the arts of jazz into the salvation of the damned that his performance takes on all the gaudiness of a four-ring circus, and the bald announcement that he will raid Hell on such and such a night is enough to empty all the town blind-pigs and bordellos and pack his sanctuary to the doors. And to aid him and inspire him there are traveling experts to whom he stands in the relation of a wart to the Matterhorn—stupendous masters of theological imbecility, contrivers of doctrines utterly preposterous, heirs to the Joseph Smith, Mother Eddy and John Alexander Dowie tradition—Bryan, Sunday, and their like.[1] These are the eminences of the American Sacred College. I delight in them. Their proceedings make me a happier American.

Turn, now, to politics. Consider, for example, a campaign for the Presidency. Would it be possible to imagine anything more uproariously idiotic—a deafening, nerve-wracking battle to the death between Tweedledum and Tweedledee, Harlequin and Sganarelle, Gobbo and Dr. Cook[2]—the unspeakable, with fearful snorts, gradually swallowing the inconceivable? I defy any one to match it elsewhere on this earth. In other lands, at worst, there are at least intelligible issues, coherent ideas, salient personalities. Somebody says something, and somebody replies. But what did Harding say in 1920, and what did Cox reply? Who was Harding, anyhow, and who was Cox?[3] Here, having perfected democracy, we lift the whole combat to symbolism, to transcendentalism, to metaphysics. Here we load a pair of palpably tin cannon with blank cartridges charged with talcum powder, and so let fly. Here one may howl over the show without any uneasy reminder that it is serious, and that some one may be hurt. I hold that this elevation of politics to the plane of undiluted comedy is peculiarly American, that nowhere else on this disreputable ball has the art of the sham-battle been developed to such fineness. Two experiences are in point. During the Harding-Cox combat of bladders an article of mine, dealing with some of its more melodramatic phases, was translated into German and reprinted by a Berlin paper. At the head of it the editor was careful to insert a preface

1. *Joseph Smith* (1805-1844) fut le fondateur de l'Eglise des Mormons (1830), *Mary Baker Eddy* (1821-1910), fondatrice de la doctrine de la Christian Science (1875), de la Church of Christ Scientist (1879). *John A. Dowie* (1847-1907), guérisseur par la foi, fondateur de la Christian Catholic Apostolic Church in Zion (Chicago, 1896). *William Jennings Bryan* (1860-1925), membre du Congrès et trois fois candidat à l'élection présidentielle, fut un fondamentaliste religieux. Voué longuement au discrédit après avoir mis en accusation le professeur du Tennessee John T. Scopes, traduit en justice en 1925 parce qu'il avait enseigné à ses élèves l'évolutionnisme de Darwin. *Billy Sunday* (1863-1935), évangéliste populaire, brocardé par Carl Sandburg dans le poème « To a Contemporary Bunk-Shooter » (1914).

2. Les trois duos de personnages de répertoire appartenant au genre comique universel et allant par paire, respectivement dans *Through the Looking Glass* de Lewis Carroll, dans la comédie italienne et Molière, dans *Le Marchand de Venise* de Shakespeare et la vie américaine. (*Frederick A. Cook* prétendit avoir découvert le pôle Nord mais des Esquimaux déclarèrent que ses photographies du pôle avaient été prises à des centaines de kilomètres au sud. Cook alla en prison pour détournement de courrier en 1923).

3. *Warren G. Harding* (1865-1923), sénateur de l'Ohio, fut élu Président en 1921. Son gouvernement fut sans doute le plus corrompu de l'Histoire américaine. Son adversaire en 1920 était *James M. Cox* (1870-1957), gouverneur de l'Ohio.

explaining to his readers, but recently delivered to democracy, that such contests were not taken seriously by intelligent Americans, and warning them solemnly against getting into sweats over politics. At about the same time I had dinner with an Englishman. From cocktails to bromo seltzer he bewailed the political lassitude of the English populace—its growing indifference to the whole partisan harliquinade. Here were two typical foreign attitudes: the Germans were in danger of making politics too harsh and implacable, and the English were in danger of forgetting politics altogether. Both attitudes, it must be plain, make for bad shows. Observing a German campaign, one is uncomfortably harassed and stirred up; observing an English campaign (at least in times of peace), one falls asleep. In the United States the thing is done better. Here politics is purged of all menace, all sinister quality, all genuine significance, and stuffed with such gorgeous humors, such inordinate farce that one comes to the end of a campaign with one's ribs loose, and ready for "King Lear," or a hanging, or a course of medical journals.

But feeling better for the laugh. *Ridi si sapis*, said Martial. Mirth is necessary to wisdom, to comfort, above all, to happiness. Well, here is the land of mirth, as Germany is the land of metaphysics and France is the land of fornication. Here the buffoonery never stops. What could be more delightful than the endless struggle of the Puritan to make the joy of the minority unlawful and impossible? The effort is itself a greater joy to one standing on the side-lines than any or all of the carnal joys that it combats. Always, when I contemplate an uplifter at his hopeless business, I recall a scene in an old-time burlesque show, witnessed for hire in my days as a dramatic critic. A chorus girl executed a fall upon the stage, and Rudolph Krausemeyer, the Swiss comedian, rushed to her aid. As he stooped painfully to succor her, Irving Rabinovitz, the Zionist comedian, fetched him a fearful clout across the cofferdam with a slap-stick. So the uplifter, the soul-saver, the Americanizer, striving to make the Republic fit for Y. M. C. A. secretaries. He is the eternal American, ever moved by the best of intentions, ever running *a la* Krausemeyer to the rescue of virtue, and ever getting his pantaloons fanned by the Devil. I am naturally sinful, and such spectacles caress me. If the slap-stick were a sash-weight the show would be cruel, and I'd probably complain to the *Polizei*. As it is, I know that the uplifter is not really hurt, but simply shocked. The blow, in fact, does him good, for it helps to get him into Heaven, as exegetes prove from Matthew V, 11: *Heureux serez-vous, lorsqu'on vous outragera, qu'on vous persécutera,* and so on. As for me, it makes me a more contented man, and hence a better citizen. One man prefers the Republic because it pays better wages than Bulgaria. Another because it has laws to keep him sober and his daughter chaste. Another because the Woolworth Building is higher than the cathedral at Chartres. Another because, living here, he can read the New York *Evening Journal*. Another because there is a warrant out for him somewhere else. Me, I like it because it amuses me to my taste. I never get tired of the show. It is worth every cent it costs.

That cost, it seems to me is very moderate. Taxes in the United States are not actually high. I figure, for example, that my private share of the expense of maintaining the Hon. Mr. Harding in the White House this year will work out to less than 80 cents. Try to think of better sport for the money: in New York it has been estimated that it costs $8 to get comfortably tight, and $17.50, on an average, to pinch a girl's arm. The United States Senate will cost me perhaps $11 for the year, but against that expense set the subscription price of the *Congressional Record,* about $15, which, as a journalist, I receive for nothing. For $4 less than nothing I am thus entertained as Solomon never was by his hooch dancers. Col. George Brinton McClellan Harvey costs me but 25 cents a year; I get Nicholas Murray Butler free.[1] Finally, there is young Teddy Roosevelt, the naval expert.[2] Teddy costs me, as I work it out, about 11 cents a year, or less than a cent a month. More, he entertains me doubly for the money, first as naval expert, and secondly as a walking, *attentat* upon democracy, a devastating proof that there is nothing, after all, in that superstition. We Americans subscribe to the doctrine of human equality—and the Rooseveltii reduce it to an absurdity as brilliantly as the sons of Veit Bach.[3] Where is your equal opportunity now? Here in this Eden of clowns, with the highest rewards of clowning theoretically open to every poor boy—here in the very citadel of democracy we found and cherish a clown *dynasty*!

1. *Harvey* (1864-1928), éditeur et engagé à droite chez les Républicains. Il contribua à l'élection de Harding. Il fut récompensé par le poste d'ambassadeur à Londres. *Butler* était aussi un Républicain résolu, président de Columbia University (New York) de 1902 à 1945.

2. *Theodore Roosevelt Jr* (1887-1944), fils de l'ancien Président (1901-1909) et secrétaire d'Etat à la Marine de 1921 à 1924.

3. Trisaïeul du compositeur allemand *Jean-Sebastien Bach* (1685-1750).

SINCLAIR LEWIS, 1885-1951

C'est un troisième événement littéraire qui, en 1922, accompagne *The Waste Land* d'Eliot et *Prejudices* de Mencken. Dans son roman *Babbitt,* Sinclair Lewis, autre écrivain du Middle West des débuts du XXe siècle, dépeint au travers de cette région une civilisation plus morne que ne l'avait représentée Whitman ou connue Sherwood Anderson. Whitman espérait que l'idéal américain serait sauvé de la disparition et recréé « in some western settlement or town, where a couple of hundred best men and women, of ordinary worldly status, have by luck been drawn together, with nothing extra of genius, or wealth, but virtuous, chaste, industrious, cheerful, resolute, friendly and devout. » Mais les vies étroites et frustrées de Gopher Prairie ont été dans *Main Street* (1920) de Sinclair Lewis, envahies par le virus provincial d'un matérialisme mesquin et vide de sens. Tout aussi hypocrite, stérile et pathétique est dans *Babbitt* la vie du gros agent immobilier George F. Babbitt et des autres hommes d'affaires de la ville de Zenith. Dans ces deux romans, la fiction satirique de Lewis semble à tous égards illustrer les conclusions sarcastiques de Mencken sur ce spécimen moderne qu'est le *boobus Americanus.* Lewis trouve néanmoins dans *Dodsworth* (1929) des raisons d'admirer le dirigeant d'entreprise américain. L'année suivante il est le premier Américain à recevoir le prix Nobel de littérature. Bien que prolifique par la suite, il ne pourra renouer avec la vigueur, l'acuité, le talent mimétrique et la sympathie complexe qui caractérisent ses premiers romans.

BIBLIOGRAPHIE SÉLECTIVE. — Dooley (D. J.), *The Art of Sinclair Lewis,* Lincoln, University of Nebraska Press, 1967 ; Kazin (Alfred), The New Realism : Anderson and Lewis, *On Native Grounds,* New York, Reynal and Hitchcock, 1942 ; Love (Glen), Sinclair Lewis : New Pioneering on the Prairies, *New Americans : The Westerner and the Modern Experience in the American Novel,* Lewisburg, Pa., Bucknell University Press, 1982 ; Silhol (Robert), *Les tyrans tragiques,* Paris, PUF, 1969.

Babbitt[1]

IV

His morning was not sharply marked into divisions. Interwoven with correspondence and advertisement-writing were a thousand nervous details: calls from clerks who were incessantly and hopefully seeking five furnished rooms and bath at sixty dollars a month; advice to Mat Penniman on getting money out of tenants who had no money.

Babbitt's virtues as a real-estate broker—as the servant of society in the department of finding homes for families and shops for distributors of food—were steadiness and diligence. He was conventionally honest, he kept his records of buyers and sellers complete, he had experience with leases and titles and an excellent memory for prices. His shoulders were broad enough, his voice deep enough, his relish of hearty humor strong enough, to establish him as one of the ruling caste of Good Fellows. Yet his eventual importance to mankind was perhaps lessened by his large and complacent ignorance of all architecture save the types of houses turned out by speculative builders; all landscape gardening save the use of curving roads, grass, and six ordinary shrubs; and all the commonest axioms of economics. He serenely believed that the one purpose of the real-estate business was to make money for George F. Babbitt. True, it was a good advertisement at Boosters' Club lunches, and all the varieties of Annual Banquets to which Good Fellows were invited, to speak sonorously of Unselfish Public Service, the Broker's Obligation to Keep Inviolate the Trust of His Clients, and a thing called Ethics, whose nature was confusing but if you had it you were a High-class Realtor and if you hadn't you were a shyster, a piker, and a fly-by-night. These virtues awakened Confidence, and enabled you to handle Bigger Propositions. But they didn't imply that you were to be impractical and refuse to take twice the value of a house if a buyer was such an idiot that he didn't jew you down on the asking-price.

1. Publié en 1922. Ces deux extraits offrent l'exemple des traits caractéristiques qui ont tôt fait de *babbittry* un nouveau terme du lexique américain pour décrire l'homme d'affaires : matérialisme égocentrique, racisme subtil, humanitarisme de pacotille, conservatisme politique, pharisaïsme, lâcheté morale, fausse bonhomie, ascension sociale dérisoire, vocabulaire lardé de poncifs rassurants. Vue ici comme une entreprise lucrative, l'Eglise servira plus tard de cadre au portrait comique de l'évangéliste opportuniste dans *Elmer Gantry* (1927).

Babbitt spoke well—and often—at these orgies of commercial righteousness about the "realtor's function as a seer of the future development of the community, and as a prophetic engineer clearing the pathway for inevitable changes"—which meant that a real-estate broker could make money by guessing which way the town would grow. This guessing he called Vision.

In an address at the Boosters' Club he had admitted, "It is at once the duty and the privilege of the realtor to know everything about his own city and its environs. Where a surgeon is a specialist on every vein and mysterious cell of the human body, and the engineer upon electricity in all its phases, or every bolt of some great bridge majestically arching o'er a mighty flood, the realtor must know his city, inch by inch, and all its faults and virtues."

Though he did know the market-price, inch by inch, of certain districts of Zenith, he did not know whether the police force was too large or too small, or whether it was in alliance with gambling and prostitution. He knew the means of fireproofing buildings and the relation of insurance-rates to fireproofing, but he did not know how many firemen there were in the city, how they were trained and paid, or how complete their apparatus. He sang eloquently the advantages of proximity of school-buildings to rentable homes, but he did not know—he did not know that it was worth while to know—whether the city schoolrooms were properly heated, lighted, ventilated, furnished; he did not know how the teachers were chosen; and though he chanted "One of the boasts of Zenith is that we pay our teachers adequately," that was because he had read the statement in the *Advocate-Times*. Himself, he could not have given the average salary of teachers in Zenith or anywhere else.

He had heard it said that "conditions" in the County Jail and the Zenith City Prison were not very "scientific;" he had, with indignation at the criticism of Zenith, skimmed through a report in which the notorious pessimist Seneca Doane, the radical lawyer, asserted that to throw boys and young girls into a bull-pen crammed with men suffering from syphilis, delirium tremens, and insanity was not the perfect way of educating them. He had controverted the report by growling, "Folks that think a jail ought to be a bloomin' Hotel Thornleigh make me sick. If people don't like a jail, let 'em behave 'emselves and keep out of it. Besides, these reform cranks always exaggerate." That was the beginning and quite completely the end of his investigations into Zenith's charities and corrections; and as to the "vice districts" he brightly expressed it, "Those are things that no decent man monkeys with. Besides, smatter fact, I'll tell you confidentially: it's a protection to our daughters and to decent women to have a district where tough nuts can raise Cain. Keeps 'em away from our own homes."

As to industrial conditions, however, Babbitt had thought a great deal, and his opinions may be coördinated as follows:

"A good labor union is of value because it keeps out radical unions, which would destroy property. No one ought to be forced to belong to a union, however. All labor agitators who try to force men to join a union should be hanged. In fact, just between ourselves, there oughtn't to be any unions allowed at all; and as it's the best way of fighting the unions, every business man ought to belong to an employers' association and to the Chamber of Commerce. In union there is strength. So any selfish hog who doesn't join the Chamber of Commerce ought to be forced to."

In nothing—as the expert on whose advice families moved to new neighborhoods to live there for a generation—was Babbitt more splendidly innocent than in the science of sanitation. He did not know a malaria-bearing mosquito from a bat; he knew nothing about tests of drinking water; and in the matters of plumbing and sewage he was as unlearned as he was voluble. He often referred to the excellence of the bathrooms in the houses he sold. He was fond of explaining why it was that no European ever bathed. Some one had told him, when he was twenty-two, that all cesspools were unhealthy, and he still denounced them. If a client impertinently wanted him to sell a house which had a cesspool, Babbitt always spoke about it—before accepting the house and selling it.

When he laid out the Glen Oriole acreage development, when he ironed woodland and dipping meadow into a glenless, orioleless, sunburnt flat prickly with small boards displaying the names of imaginary streets, he righteously put in a complete sewage-system. It made him feel superior; it enabled him to sneer privily at the Martin Lumsen development, Avonlea, which had a cesspool; and it provided a chorus for the full-page advertisements in which he announced the beauty, convenience, cheapness, and supererogatory healthfulness of Glen Oriole. The only flaw was that the Glen Oriole sewers had insufficient outlet, so that waste remained in them, not very agreeably, while the Avonlea cesspool was a Waring septic tank.

The whole of the Glen Oriole project was a suggestion that Babbitt, though he really did hate men recognized as swindlers, was not too unreasonably honest. Operators and buyers prefer that brokers should not be in competition with them as operators and buyers themselves, but attend to their clients' interests only. It was supposed that the Babbitt-Thompson Company were merely agents for Glen Oriole, serving the real owner, Jake Offut, but the fact was that Babbitt and Thompson owned sixty-two per cent. of the Glen, the president and purchasing agent of the Zenith Street Traction Company owned twenty-eight per cent., and Jake Offutt (a gang-politician, a small manufacturer, a tobacco-chewing old farceur who enjoyed dirty politics, business diplomacy, and cheating at poker) had only ten per cent., which Babbitt and the Traction officials had given to him for "fixing" health inspectors and fire inspectors and a member of the State Transportation Commission.

But Babbitt was virtuous. He advocated, though he did not practise, the prohibition of alcohol; he praised, though he did not obey, the laws against motor-speeding; he paid his debts; he contributed to the church, the Red Cross, and the Y. M. C. A.; he followed the custom of his clan and cheated only as it was sanctified by precedent; and he never descended to trickery—though, as he explained to Paul Riesling:

"Course I don't mean to say that every ad I write is literally true or that I always believe everything I say when I give some buyer a good strong selling-spiel. You see—you see it's this: In the first place, maybe the owner of the property exaggerated when he put it into my hands, and it certainly isn't my place to go proving my principal a liar! And then most folks are so darn crooked themselves that they expect a fellow to do a little lying, so if I was fool enough to never whoop the ante I'd get the credit for lying anyway! In self-defense I got to toot my own horn, like a lawyer defending a client—his bounden duty, ain't it, to bring out the poor dub's good points? Why, the Judge himself would bawl out a lawyer that didn't, even if they both knew the guy was guilty! But even so, I don't pad out the truth like Cecil Rountree or Thayer or the rest of these realtors. Fact, I think a fellow that's willing to deliberately up and profit by lying ought to be shot!"

XVI

1

The certainty that he was not going to be accepted by the McKelveys made Babbitt feel guilty and a little absurd. But he went more regularly to the Elks; at a Chamber of Commerce luncheon he was oratorical regarding the wickedness of strikes; and again he saw himself as a Prominent Citizen.

His clubs and associations were food comfortable to his spirit.

Of a decent man in Zenith it was required that he should belong to one, preferably two or three, of the innumerous "lodges" and prosperity-boosting lunch-clubs; to the Rotarians, the Kiwanis, or the Boosters; to the Old Fellows, Moose, Masons, Red Men, Woodmen, Owls, Eagles, Maccabees, Knights of Pythias, Knights of Columbus, and other secret orders characterized by a high degree of heartiness, sound morals, and reverence for the Constitution. There were four reasons for joining these orders: It was the thing to do. It was good for business, since lodge-brothers frequently became customers. It gave to Americans unable to become Geheimräte Commendatori such unctuous honorifics as High Worthy Recording Scribe and Grand Hoogow to add to the commonplace distinctions of Colonel, Judge, and Professor. And it permitted the swaddled American husband to stay away from home for one evening a week. The lodge was his piazza, his pavement café. He could shoot pool and talk man-talk and be obscene and valiant.

Babbitt was what he called a "joiner" for all these reasons.

Behind the gold and scarlet banner of his public achievements was the dun background of office-routine: leases, sales-contracts, lists of properties to rent. The evenings of oratory and committees and lodges stimulated him like brandy, but every morning he was sandy-tongued. Week by week he accumulated nervousness. He was in open disagreement with his outside salesman, Stanley Graff; and once, though her charms had always kept him nickeringly polite to her, he snarled at Miss McGoun for changing his letters.

But in the presence of Paul Riesling he relaxed. At least once a week they fled from maturity. On Saturday they played golf, jeering, "As a golfer, you're a fine tennis-player," or they motored all Sunday afternoon, stopping at village lunchrooms to sit on high stools at a counter and drink coffee from thick cups. Sometimes Paul came over in the evening with his violin, and even Zilla was silent as the lonely man who had lost his way and forever crept down unfamiliar roads spun out his dark soul in music.

2

Nothing gave Babbitt more purification and publicity than his labors for the Sunday School.

His church, the Chatham Road Presbyterian, was one of the largest and richest, one of the most oaken and velvety, in Zenith. The pastor was the Reverend John Jennison Drew, M.A., D.D., LL.D. (The M.A. and the D.D. were from Elbert University, Nebraska, the LL.D. from Waterbury College, Oklahoma.) He was eloquent, efficient, and versatile. He presided at meetings for the denunciation of unions or the elevation of domestic service, and confided to the audiences that as a poor boy he had carried newspapers. For the Saturday edition of the *Evening Advocate* he wrote editorials on "The Manly Man's Religion" and "The Dollars and Sense Value of Christianity," which were printed in bold type surrounded by a wiggly border. He often said that he was "proud to be known as primarily a business man" and that he certainly was not going to "permit the old Satan to monopolize all the pep and punch." He was a thin, rustic-faced young man with gold spectacles and a bang of dull brown hair, but when he hurled himself into oratory he glowed with power. He admitted that he was too much the scholar and poet to imitate the evangelist, Mike Monday, yet he had once awakened his fold to new life, and to larger collections, by the challenge, "My brethren, the real cheap skate is the man who won't lend to the Lord!"

He had made his church a true community center. It contained everything but a bar. It had a nursery, a Thursday evening supper with a short bright missionary lecture afterward, a gymnasium, a fortnightly motion-picture show, a library of technical books for young workmen—though, unfortunately, no young workman ever entered the church except to wash the windows or repair the furnace—and a sewing-circle which made short little pants for children of the poor while Mrs. Drew read aloud from earnest novels.

Though Dr. Drew's theology was Presbyterian, his church-building was gracefully Episcopalian. As he said, it had the "most perdurable features of those noble ecclesiastical monuments of grand Old England which stand as symbols of the eternity of faith, religious and civil." It was built of cheery iron-spot brick in an improved Gothic style, and the main auditorium had indirect lighting from electric globes in lavish alabaster bowls.

On a December morning when the Babbitts went to church, Dr. John Jennison Drew was unusually eloquent. The crowd was immense. Ten brisk young ushers, in morning coats with white roses, were bringing folding chairs up from the basement. There was an impressive musical program, conducted by Sheldon Smeeth, educational director of the Y.M.C.A., who also sang the offertory. Babbitt cared less for this, because some misguided person had taught young Mr. Smeeth to smile, smile, smile while he was singing, but with all the appreciation of a fellow-orator he admired Dr. Drew's sermon. It had the intellectual quality which distinguished the Chatham Road congregation from the grubby chapels on Smith Street.

"At this abundant harvest-time of all the year," Dr. Drew chanted, "when, though stormy the sky and laborious the path to the drudging wayfarer, yet the hovering and bodiless spirit swoops back o'er all the labors and desires of the past twelve months, oh, then it seems to me there sounds behind all our apparent failures the golden chorus of greeting from those passed happily on; and lo! on the dim horizon we see behind dolorous clouds the mighty mass of mountains—mountains of melody, mountains of mirth, mountains of might!"

"I certainly do like a sermon with culture and thought in it," meditated Babbitt.

At the end of the service he was delighted when the pastor, actively shaking hands at the door, twittered, "Oh, Brother Babbitt, can you wait a jiffy? Want your advice."

"Sure, doctor! You bet!"

"Drop into my office. I think you'll like the cigars there." Babbitt did like the cigars. He also liked the office, which was distinguished from other offices only by the spirited change of the familiar wall-placard to "This is the Lord's Busy Day." Chum Frink came in, then William W. Eathorne.

Mr. Eathorne was the seventy-year-old president of the First State Bank of Zenith. He still wore the delicate patches of side-whiskers which had been the uniform of bankers in 1870. If Babbitt was envious of the Smart Set of the McKelveys, before William Washington Eathorne he was reverent. Mr. Eathorne had nothing to do with the Smart Set. He was above it. He was the great-grandson of one of the five men who founded Zenith, in 1792, and he was of the third generation of bankers. He could examine credits, make loans, promote or injure a man's business. In his presence Babbitt breathed quickly and felt young.

The Reverend Dr. Drew bounced into the room and flowered into speech:

"I've asked you gentlemen to stay so I can put a proposition before you. The Sunday School needs bucking up. It's the fourth largest in Zenith, but there's no reason why we should take anybody's dust. We ought to be first. I want to request you, if you will, to form a committee of advice and publicity for the Sunday School; look it over and make any suggestions for its betterment, and then, perhaps, see that the press gives us some attention—give the public some really helpful and constructive news instead of all these murders and divorces."

"Excellent," said the banker.

Babbitt and Frink were enchanted to join him.

WALLACE STEVENS, 1879-1955

Les aspirations et cocasseries du Babbitt américain ne cadrent guère avec Wallace Stevens qui fut directeur de compagnie d'assurances. Comme Robinson, Frost et T. S. Eliot, Stevens fait ses études à Harvard où il est particulièrement redevable au professeur de philosophie George Santayana. Il jette ainsi les bases d'une carrière poétique dont la préoccupation dominante sera la nature du réel et les structures de l'imaginaire qui s'y attachent. Soucieux de garder un contact quotidien avec son métier, Stevens communique au lecteur la vision sensuelle, libératrice, non transcendante d'un monde d'objets édénique. Il affirme en vérité que le poète « gives to life the supreme fictions without which we are unable to conceive it ». Dans les poèmes ci-dessous, publiés dans *Harmonium* (1923), Stevens se gausse du Puritain américain sur un ton plus badin que Mencken ou Lewis. Il enjoint à la femme chrétienne d'abandonner ses mornes fantasmes du sublime pour les images poétiques païennes qui impriment aux représentations et rituels telluriques un élan cosmique. Et dans les deux autres de ses poèmes les plus connus, il entend faire percevoir la richesse fugitive et la beauté du monde matériel que découvre et informe l'imagination tellurique.

BIBLIOGRAPHIE SÉLECTIVE. — *The Collected Poems,* New York, Knopf, 1968 ; Blessing (Richard), *Wallace Stevens' « Whole Harmonium »,* Syracuse, NY, Syracuse University Press, 1970 ; Bloom (Harold), *Wallace Stevens : The Poems of Our Climate,* Ithaca, NY, Cornell University Press, 1977.

A High-Toned Old Christian Woman

Poetry is the supreme fiction, madame.
Take the moral law and make a nave of it
And from the nave build haunted heaven. Thus,
The conscience is converted into palms,
Like windy citherns hankering for hymns.
We agree in principle. That's clear. But take
The opposing law and make a peristyle,
And from the peristyle project a masque
Beyond the planets. Thus, our bawdiness,
Unpurged by epitaph, indulged at last,
Is equally converted into palms,
Squiggling like saxophones. And palm for palm,
Madame, we are where we began.[1] Allow,
Therefore, that in the planetary scene
Your disaffected flagellants, well-stuffed,

1. Stevens dit sans doute que la haute conscience morale de la femme et l'imagination « fictive » du poète exigent l'une et l'autre des images concrètes pour prendre leur essor, qu'elles s'élèvent des nefs d'églises ou des péristyles païens. La nef d'église suggère autant des mains levées en prière *(palms)* que des palmiers au vent *(windy citherns)*. Depuis la colonnade païenne, le poète s'abandonne cependant aux « palmes » beaucoup plus vibrantes, et représente un rituel beaucoup plus allègre « in the planetary scene ».

Smacking their muzzy bellies in parade,
Proud of such novelties of the sublime,
Such tink and tank and tunk-a-tunk-tunk,
May, merely may, madame, whip from themselves
A jovial hullabaloo among the spheres.
This will make widows wince. But fictive things
Wink as they will. Wink most when widows wince.

The Emperor of Ice-Cream

Call the roller of big cigars,
The muscular one, and bid him whip
In kitchen cups concupiscent curds.
Let the wenches dawdle in such dress
As they are used to wear, and let the boys
Bring flowers in last month's newspapers.
Let be be finale of seem.
The only emperor is the emperor of ice-cream.[1]

Take from the dresser of deal,[2]
Lacking the three glass knobs, that sheet
On which she embroidered fantails[3] once
And spread it so as to cover her face.
If her horny feet protrude, they come
To show how cold she is, and dumb.
Let the lamp affix its beam.
The only emperor is the emperor of ice-cream.

Anecdote of the Jar

I placed a jar in Tennessee,
And round it was, upon a hill.
It made the slovenly wilderness
Surround that hill.

1. Que l'existence et la réalité des plaisirs évanescents (tels que la crème glacée) prévalent sur la mort et sur les illusions d'une veillée rituelle.

2. Bois tendre, peu coûteux, d'usage limité.

3. Pigeons.

The wilderness rose up to it,
And sprawled around, no longer wild.
The jar was round upon the ground
And tall and of a port in air.

It took dominion everywhere.
The jar was gray and bare.
It did not give of bird or bush,
Like nothing else in Tennessee.

E(DWARD) E(STLIN) CUMMINGS, 1894-1962

E. E. Cummings vient grossir le groupe des écrivains de la Nouvelle-Angleterre, composé pour une bonne part d'anciens étudiants de Harvard, qui rallièrent la cohorte des écrivains américains du XXe siècle. Cummings fait également partie des nombreux combattants de la Première Guerre qui revinrent aux Etats-Unis avec une moisson d'expériences personnelles, le talent littéraire pour en tirer parti, et à la suite d'un apprentissage temporaire à Paris, pour affûter ce talent. En raison de ses variations enjouées sur l'expression poétique et l'orthodoxie de la ponctuation, ses pieds de nez irrévérencieux aux traditionnalistes et ses désopilants poèmes antimilitaristes, Cummings est depuis longtemps l'enfant chéri des cours de littérature, bien que relégué par la critique à un rang inférieur derrière ses contemporains plus « sérieux ». Cummings mérite cependant un meilleur sort. Il apporte à la poésie américaine l'esprit satirique acéré de Mencken et de Lewis, l'indignation morale de Pound, Eliot et Hemingway, outre la fraîcheur d'un émerveillement poétique face au monde naturel, au moins égale à celle, plus philosophique, de Stevens.

BIBLIOGRAPHIE SÉLECTIVE. — *Complete Poems : 1913-1962*, New York, Harcourt Brace Jovanovich, 1972 ; Friedman (Norman), *E. E. Cummings : The Growth of a Writer*, Carbondale, Southern Illinois University Press, 1964 ; Kidder (Rushworth), *E. E. Cummings : An Introduction to the Poetry*, New York, Columbia University Press, 1979.

The Cambridge ladies who live in furnished souls[1]

the Cambridge ladies who live in furnished souls
are unbeautiful and have comfortable minds
(also, with the church's protestant blessings
daughters, unscented shapeless spirited)
they believe in Christ and Longfellow, both dead,
are invariably interested in so many things—
at the present writing one still finds
delighted fingers knitting for the is it Poles?
perhaps. While permanent faces coyly bandy
scandal of Mrs. N and Professor D
. . . the Cambridge ladies do not care, above
Cambridge if sometimes in its box of
sky lavender and cornerless, the
moon rattles like a fragment of angry candy

O sweet spontaneous

O sweet spontaneous
earth how often have
the
doting

          fingers of
prurient philosophers pinched
and
poked

thee
, has the naughty thumb
of science prodded
thy

1. Comme l'indique la référence à Longfellow, le Cambridge de Cummings est ici la ville américaine, non l'anglaise, et le siège au Massachusetts de l'Université de Harvard. Ce poème et les suivants sont tirés de *Tulips and Chimneys* (1923).

beauty . how
often have religions taken
thee upon their scraggy knees
squeezing and

buffeting thee that thou mightest conceive
gods
(but
true

to the incomparable
couch of death thy
rhythmic
lover

thou answerest

them only with

spring)

Come, gaze with me upon this dome[1]

come, gaze with me upon this dome
of many coloured glass,[2] and see
his mother's pride, his father' joy,
unto whom duty whispers low

"thou must!" and who replies "I can!"[3]
—yon clean upstanding well dressed boy
that with his peers full oft hath quaffed
the wine of life and found it sweet—

a tear within his stern blue eye,
upon his firm white lips a smile,
one thought alone: to do or die
for God for country and for Yale

1. De *Is 5* (1926) Cummings explique le titre de son livre par la liberté du poète de nier « the undeniable fact that two times two is four ».
2. Non la pure boule de crystal de l'habituelle diseuse de bonne aventure.
3. La citation moralisante sur le devoir est du poème d'Emerson « Voluntaries » (1867).

above his blond determined head
the sacred flag of truth unfurled,
in the bright heyday of his youth
the upper class American

unsullied stands, before the world:
with manly heart and conscience free,
upon the front steps of her home
by the high minded pure young girl

much kissed, by loving relatives
well fed, and fully photographed
the son of man goes forth to war
with trumpets clap[1] and syphilis

"Next to of course god america i"[2]

"next to of course god america i
love you land of the pilgrims's and so forth oh
say can you see by the dawn's early my
country 'tis of centuries come and go
and are no more what of it we should worry
in every language even deafanddumb
thy sons acclaim your glorious name by gorry
by jingo by gee by gosh by gum
why talk of beauty what could be more beautiful
than these heroic happy dead
who rushed like lions to the roaring slaughter
they did not stop to think they died instead
then shall the voice of liberty be mute?"

He spoke. And drank rapidly a glass of water

1. 1 / Applaudissements ; 2 / gonorrhée.

2. Egalement tiré de *Is 5* (1926). Le pastiche des clichés patriotiques, incluant des phrases d'hymnes américains constitue la parodie héroï-comique de l'éloquence guerrière du combattant homérique.

ERNEST HEMINGWAY, 1899-1961

Ernest Hemingway allie l'idéalisme critique de ses contemporains de l'après-guerre à la recherche de l'ordre que conduit Wallace Stevens dans le chaos du monde naturel. Né à Oak Park dans l'Illinois, il subit l'influence inhibante d'une mère abusive, pétrie d'esprit victorien, qui dans son enfance l'a habillé en petite fille. Médecin, pêcheur et chasseur, le père s'efforça en compensation de développer la virilité de son fils. Père et fils se suicidèrent par balle. A cause d'une blessure à l'œil qu'il a reçue au cours d'une leçon de boxe au collège, Hemingway est déclaré inapte à servir dans la Première Guerre et, ainsi que le fera son héros de *A Farewell to Arms*, il se porte alors volontaire comme ambulancier de l'armée italienne. En tant que correspondant de guerre, il frôlera encore la mort dans la guerre d'Espagne entre 1937 et 1938 et sur la fin de la Deuxième Guerre mondiale. Après sa blessure et le traumatisme de la Première Guerre, Hemingway recherche un exutoire à la peur de la mort en poursuivant une quête philosophique de la « grace under pressure ». Ce périple le mène à Paris où il s'initie à l'essentiel du métier d'auteur soucieux d'intégrité. Il a paradoxalement pour principaux maîtres ses concitoyens Gertrude Stein et Ezra Pound. Sherwood Anderson lui fournit aussi un modèle de simplicité stylistique tandis que F. Scott Fitzgerald lui fait d'utiles remarques d'ailleurs récusées sur les fautes de goût du manuscrit de *The Sun Also Rises* (1926). A l'époque, Hemingway a déjà publié sa première collection de nouvelles et défini le noyau central de sa vie et de sa fiction. Bien qu'il doive beaucoup à une foule de ses prédécesseurs en littérature comme Flaubert, Tourgueniev, Twain, James, Crane, Eliot et bien d'autres, Hemingway affine avec soin le style d'une prose originale qui concilie recherche de la sincérité et courage dans un monde essentiellement dépourvu d'ordre et de sens. « Grace under pressure » correspond à sa célèbre définition du cran, une manière de résister aux pressions qu'il dramatise diversement dans ses romans : le nihilisme de « A Clean, Well-Lighted Place », le désordre de la société dans « The Killers », les fausses valeurs de l'Amérique dans « Soldier's Home », et les désastres de la guerre dans différentes histoires comme surtout *A Farewell to Arms* (1929). Les voies de la « grâce » ouvertes aux héros tourmentés et qu'indiquent souvent des guides qui sont eux-mêmes en proie à l'angoisse, conduisent aux rituels de la convivialité, aux règles immuables du sport et du langage, à la définition de codes moraux individuels et à l'effort pour retrouver et exprimer des émotions intimes authentiquement éprouvées. Ce code personnel est au cœur de ses deux derniers romans à succès, *For Whom the Bell Tolls* (1940) et *The Old Man and the Sea* (1952). Ce dernier roman renouvellera brièvement sa gloire littéraire, lui valant le prix Nobel de littérature en 1954.

BIBLIOGRAPHIE SÉLECTIVE. — Benson (Jack), *Hemingway : The Writer's Art of Self-Defense*, Minneapolis, University of Minnesota Press, 1969 ; Hovey (Richard), *Hemingway : The Inward Terrain*, Seattle, University of Washington Press, 1968 ; Young (Philip), *Ernest Hemingway : A Reconsideration*, University Park, Pennsylvania State University Press, 1966 ; Hily-Mane (Geneviève), *Le style d'Ernest Hemingway. La plume et le masque*, Paris, PUF, 1983 ; Méral (Jean), *Paris dans la littérature américaine*, Paris, CNRS, 1983.

Soldier's Home[1]

Krebs went to the war from a Methodist college in Kansas. There is a picture which shows him among his fraternity brothers, all of them wearing exactly the same height and style collar. He enlisted in the Marines in 1917 and did not return to the United States until the second division returned from the Rhine in the summer of 1919.

There is a picture which shows him on the Rhine with two German girls and another corporal. Krebs and the corporal look too big for their uniforms. The German girls are not beautiful. The Rhine does not show in the picture.

By the time Krebs returned to his home town in Oklahoma the

1. Tiré de *In Our Time* (1925).

greeting of heroes was over. He came back much too late. The men from the town who had been drafted had all been welcomed elaborately on their return. There had been a great deal of hysteria. Now the reaction had set in. People seemed to think it was rather ridiculous for Krebs to be getting back so late, years after the war was over.

At first Krebs, who had been at Belleau Wood, Soissons, the Champagne, St. Mihiel and in the Argonne, did not want to talk about the war at all. Later he felt the need to talk but no one wanted to hear about it. His town had heard too many atrocity stories to be thrilled by actualities. Krebs found that to be listened to at all he had to lie, and after he had done this twice he, too, had a reaction against the war and against talking about it. A distaste for everything that had happened to him in the war set in because of the lies he had told. All of the times that had been able to make him feel cool and clear inside himself when he thought of them; the times so long back when he had done the one thing, the only thing for a man to do, easily and naturally, when he might have done something else, now lost their cool, valuable quality and then were lost themselves.

His lies were quite unimportant lies and consisted in attributing to himself things other men had seen, done or heard of, and stating as facts certain apocryphal incidents familiar to all soldiers. Even his lies were not sensational at the pool room. His acquaintances, who had heard detailed accounts of German women found chained to machine-guns in the Argonne forest and who could not comprehend, or were barred by their patriotism from interest in, any German machine-gunners who were not chained, were not thrilled by his stories.

Krebs acquired the nausea in regard to experience that is the result of untruth or exaggeration, and when he occasionally met another man who had really been a soldier and they talked a few minutes in the dressing room at a dance he fell into the easy pose of the old soldier among other soldiers: that he had been badly, sickeningly frightened all the time. In this way he lost everything.

During this time, it was late summer, he was sleeping late in bed, getting up to walk down town to the library to get a book, eating lunch at home, reading on the front porch until he became bored and then walking down through the town to spend the hottest hours of the day in the cool dark of the pool room. He loved to play pool.

In the evening he practised on his clarinet, strolled down town, read and went to bed. He was still a hero to his two young sisters. His mother would have given him breakfast in bed if he had wanted it. She often came in when he was in bed and asked him to tell her about the war, but her attention always wandered. His father was non-committal.

Before Krebs went away to the war he had never been allowed to drive the family motor car. His father was in the real estate business and always wanted the car to be at his command when he required it to take clients out into the country to show them a piece of farm property. The car always stood outside the First National Bank building where his father had an office on the second floor. Now, after the war, it was still the same car.

Nothing was changed in the town except that the young girls had grown up. But they lived in such a complicated world of already defined alliances and shifting feuds that Krebs did not feel the energy or the courage to break into it. He liked to look at them, though. There were so many good-looking young girls. Most of them had their hair cut short. When he went away only little girls wore their hair like that or girls that were fast. They all wore sweaters and shirt waists with round Dutch collars. It was a pattern. He liked to look at them from the front porch as they walked on the other side of the street. He liked to watch them walking under the shade of the trees. He liked the round Dutch collars above their sweaters. He liked their silk stockings and flat shoes. He liked their bobbed hair and the way they walked.

When he was in town their appeal to him was not very strong. He did not like them when he saw them in the Greek's ice cream parlour. He did not want them themselves really. They were too complicated. There was something else. Vaguely he wanted a girl but he did not want to have to work to get her. He would have liked to have a girl but he did not want to have to spend a long time getting her. He did not want to get into the intrigue and the politics. He did not want to have to do any courting. He did not want to tell any more lies. It wasn't worth it.

He did not want any consequences. He did not want any consequences ever again. He wanted to live along without consequences. Besides he did not really need a girl. The army had taught him that. It was all right to pose as though you had to have a girl. Nearly everybody did that. But it wasn't true. You did not need a girl. That was the funny thing. First a fellow boasted how girls meant nothing to him, that he never thought of them, that they could not touch him. Then a fellow boasted that he could not get along without girls, that he had to have them all the time, that he could not go to sleep without them.

That was all a lie. It was all a lie both ways. You did not need a girl unless you thought about them. He learned that in the army. Then sooner or later you always got one. When you were really ripe for a girl you always got one. You did not have to think about it. Sooner or later it would come. He had learned that in the army.

Now he would have liked a girl if she had come to him and not wanted to talk. But here at home it was all too complicated. He knew he could never get through it all again. It was not worth the trouble. That was the thing about French girls and German girls. There was not all this talking. You couldn't talk much and you did not need to talk. It was simple and you were friends. He thought about France and then he began to think about Germany. On the whole he had liked Germany better. He did not want to leave Germany. He did not want to come home. Still, he had come home. He sat on the front porch.

He liked the girls that were walking along the other side of the street. He liked the look of them much better than the French girls or the German girls. But the world they were in was not the world he was in. He would like to have one of them. But it was not worth it. They were such a nice pattern. He liked the pattern. It was exciting. But he would not go through all the talking. He did not want one badly enough. He liked to look at them all, though. It was not worth it. Not now when things were getting good again.

He sat there on the porch reading a book on the war. It was a history and he was reading about all the engagements he had been in. It was the most interesting reading he had ever done. He wished there were more maps. He looked forward with a good feeling to reading all the really good histories when they would come out with good detail maps. Now he was really learning about the war. He had been a good soldier. That made a difference.

One morning after he had been home about a month his mother came into his bedroom and sat on the bed. She smoothed her apron.

"I had a talk with your father last night, Harold," she said, "and he is willing for you to take the car out in the evenings."

"Yeah?" said Krebs, who was not fully awake. "Take the car out? Yeah?"

"Yes. Your father has felt for some time that you should be able to take the car out in the evenings whenever you wished, but we only talked it over last night."

"I'll bet you made him," Krebs said.

"No. It was your father's suggestion that we talk the matter over."

"Yeah. I'll bet you made him," Krebs sat up in bed.

"Will you come down to breakfast, Harold?" his mother said.

"As soon as I get my clothes on," Krebs said.

His mother went out of the room and he could hear her frying something downstairs while he washed, shaved and dressed to go down into the dining-room for breakfast. While he was eating breakfast his sister brought in the mail.

"Well, Hare," she said. "You old sleepy-head. What do you ever get up for?"

Krebs looked at her. He liked her. She was his best sister.

"Have you got the paper?" he asked.

She handed him *The Kansas City Star* and he shucked off its brown wrapper and opened it to the sporting page. He folded *The Star* open and propped it against the water pitcher with his cereal dish to steady it, so he could read while he ate.

"Harold," his mother stood in the kitchen doorway, "Harold, please don't muss up the paper. Your father can't read his *Star* if it's been mussed."

"I won't muss it," Krebs said.

His sister sat down at the table and watched him while he read.

"We're playing indoor over at school this afternoon," she said. "I'm going to pitch."

"Good," said Krebs. "How's the old wing?"

"I can pitch better than lots of the boys. I tell them all you taught me. The other girls aren't much good."

"Yeah?" said Krebs.

"I tell them all you're my beau. Aren't you my beau, Hare?"

"You bet."

"Couldn't your brother really be your beau just because he's your brother?"

"I don't know."

"Sure you know. Couldn't you be my beau, Hare, if I was old enough and if you wanted to?"

"Sure. You're my girl now."

"Am I really your girl?"

"Sure."

"Do you love me?"

"Uh, huh."

"Will you love me always?"

"Sure."

"Will you come and watch me play indoor?"

"Maybe."

"Aw, Hare, you don't love me. If you loved me, you'd want to come over and watch me play indoor."

Krebs's mother came into the dining-room from the kitchen. She carried a plate of two fried eggs and some crisp bacon on it and a plate of buckwheat cakes.

"You run along, Helen," she said. "I want to talk to Harold."

She put the eggs and bacon down in front of him and brought in a jug of maple syrup for the buckwheat cakes. Then she sat down across the table from Krebs.

"I wish you'd put down the paper a minute, Harold," she said.

Krebs took down the paper and folded it.

"Have you decided what you are going to do yet, Harold?" his mother said, taking off her glasses.

"No," said Krebs.

"Don't you think it's about time?" His mother did not say this in a mean way. She seemed worried.

"I hadn't thought about it," Krebs said.

"God has some work for everyone to do," his mother said. "There can be no idle hands in His Kingdom."

"I'm not in His Kingdom," Krebs said.

"We are all of us in His Kingdom."

Krebs felt embarrassed and resentful as always.

"I've worried about you so much, Harold," his mother went on. "I know the temptations you must have been exposed to. I know how weak men are. I know what your own dear grandfather, my own father, told us about the Civil War, and I have prayed for you. I pray for you all day long, Harold."

Krebs looked at the bacon fat hardening on his plate.

"Your father is worried, too," his mother went on. "He thinks you have lost your ambition, that you haven't got a definite aim in life. Charley Simmons, who is just your age, has a good job and is going to be married. The boys are all settling down; they're all determined to get somewhere; you can see that boys like Charley Simmons are on their way to being really a credit to the community."

Krebs said nothing.

"Don't look that way, Harold," his mother said. "You know we love you and I want to tell you for your own good how matters stand. Your father does not want to hamper your freedom. He thinks you should be allowed to drive the car. If you want to take some of the nice girls out riding with you, we are only too pleased. We want you to enjoy yourself. But you are going to have to settle down to work, Harold. Your father doesn't care what you start in at. All work is honourable as he says. But you've got to make a start at something. He asked me to speak to you this morning and then you can stop in and see him at his office."

"Is that all?" Krebs said.

"Yes. Don't you love your mother, dear boy?"[1]

"No," Krebs said.

His mother looked at him across the table. Her eyes were shiny. She started crying.

"I don't love anybody," Krebs said.

It wasn't any good. He couldn't tell her, he couldn't make her see it. It was silly to have said it. He had only hurt her. He went over and took hold of her arm. She was crying with her head in her hands.

"I didn't mean it," he said. "I was just angry at something. I didn't mean I didn't love you."

His mother went on crying. Krebs put his arm on her shoulder.

"Can't you believe me, mother?"

His mother shook her head.

"Please, please, mother. Please believe me."

"All right," his mother said chokily. She looked up at him. "I believe you, Harold."

Krebs kissed her hair. She put her face up to him.

1. La mère de Krebs l'a initié aux formes de piété les plus exécrables aux yeux de Hemingway : autorité religieuse, « work ethic », abstinence sexuelle et amour contraint d'une mère.

"I'm your mother," she said. "I held you next to my heart when you were a tiny baby."

Krebs felt sick and vaguely nauseated.

"I know, Mummy," he said. "I'll try to be a good boy for you."

"Would you kneel and pray with me, Harold?" his mother asked.

They knelt down beside the dining-room table and Krebs's mother prayed.

"Now, you pray, Harold," she said.

"I can't," Krebs said.

"Try, Harold."

"I can't."

"Do you want me to pray for you?"

"Yes."

So his mother prayed for him and then they stood up and Krebs kissed his mother and went out of the house. He had tried so to keep his life from being complicated. Still, none of it had touched him. He had felt sorry for this mother and she had made him lie. He would go to Kansas City and get a job and she would feel all right about it. There would be one more scene maybe before he went away. He would not go down to his father's office. He would miss that one. He wanted his life to go smoothly. It had just gotten going that way. Well, that was all over now, anyway. He would go over to the schoolyard and watch Helen play indoor baseball.

A Farewell to Arms[1]

XI

Ambulancier américain dans l'armée italienne pendant la Première Guerre, Frederic Henry vient d'être blessé au combat et reçoit la visite de l'aumônier à l'hôpital. Leur conversation rappelle les voies de la grâce que recherche Frederic : 1 / idéalisme dans la participation à une cause patriotique (magnifié pour un infirmier volontaire dans un autre pays) ; 2 / conviction religieuse, comme en donne l'exemple précaire le prêtre « fatigué » ; 3 / approche

1. Publié pour la première fois en 1929.

mécaniste de la vie, désir assouvi, alcool et sommeil mis en pratique par le Dr Rinaldi ; 4 / amour de la femme qui va au-delà du désir et de l'érotisme partagé pour s'élever jusqu'à l'agapé d'essence quasi divine et 5 / le témoignage des cinq sens en éveil aux révélations du monde naturel. A propos d'amour, Frederic s'est épris d'une infirmière britannique, Catherine Barkley. Il est ensuite transféré dans un hôpital de Milan avec Catherine. Plus tard, il retourne au combat, déserte au cours d'une retraite et s'enfuit en Suisse avec elle. Il éprouve brièvement avec Catherine le don de soi de l'agapé avant qu'elle ne meure en couches.

It was dusk when the priest came. They had brought the soup and afterward taken away the bowls and I was lying looking at the rows of beds and out the window at the tree-top that moved a little in the evening breeze. The breeze came in through the window and it was cooler with the evening. The flies were on the ceiling now and on the electric light bulbs that hung on wires. The lights were only turned on when some one was brought in at night or when something was being done. It made me feel very young to have the dark come after the dusk and then remain. It was like being put to bed after early supper. The orderly came down between the beds and stopped. Some one was with him. It was the priest. He stood there small, brown-faced, and embarrassed.

"How do you do?" he asked. He put some packages down by the bed, on the floor.

"All right, father."

He sat down in the chair that had been brought for Rinaldi and looked out of the window embarrassedly. I noticed his face looked very tired.

"I can only stay a minute," he said. "It is late."

"It's not late. How is the mess?"

He smiled. "I am still a great joke," he sounded tired too. "Thank God they are all well."

"I am so glad you are all right," he said. "I hope you don't suffer." He seemed very tired and I was not used to seeing him tired.

"Not any more."

"I miss you at the mess."

"I wish I were there. I always enjoyed our talking."

"I brought you a few little things," he said. He picked up the packages, "This is mosquito netting. This is a bottle of vermouth. You like vermouth? These are English papers."

"Please open them."

He was pleased and undid them. I held the mosquito netting in my hands. The vermouth he held up for me to see and then put it on the floor beside the bed. I held up one of the sheaf of English papers. I could read the headlines by turning it so the half-light from the window was on it. It was *The News of the World.*

"The others are illustrated," he said.

"It will be a great happiness to read them. Where did you get them?"

"I sent for them to Mestre. I will have more."

"You were very good to come, father. Will you drink a glass of vermouth?"

"Thank you. You keep it. It's for you."

"No, drink a glass."

"All right. I will bring you more then."

The orderly brought the glasses and opened the bottle. He broke off the cork and the end had to be shoved down into the bottle. I could see the priest was disappointed but he said, "That's all right. It's no matter."

"Here's to your health, father."

"To your better health."

Afterward he held the glass in his hand and we looked at one another. Sometimes we talked and were good friends but to-night it was difficult.

"What's the matter, father? You seem very tired."

"I am tired but I have no right to be."

"It's the heat."

"No. This is only the spring. I feel very low."

"You have the war disgust."

"No. But I hate the war."

"I don't enjoy it," I said. He shook his head and looked out of the window.

"You do not mind it. You do not see it. You must forgive me. I know you are wounded."

"That is an accident."

"Still even wounded you do not see it. I can tell. I do not see it myself but I feel it a little."

"When I was wounded we were talking about it. Passini was talking."[1]

The priest put down the glass. He was thinking about something else.

"I know them because I am like they are," he said.

"You are different though."

"But really I am like they are."

"The officers don't see anything."

"Some of them do. Some are very delicate and feel worse than any of us."

"They are mostly different."

"It is not education or money. It is something else. Even if they had education or money men like Passini would not wish to be officers. I would not be an officer."

"You rank as an officer. I am an officer."

"I am not really. You are not even an Italian. You are a foreigner. But you are nearer the officers than you are to the men."

"What is the difference?"

"I cannot say it easily. There are people who would make war. In this country there are many like that. There are other people who would not make war."

"But the first ones make them do it."

"Yes."

"And I help them."

"You are a foreigner. You are a patriot."

"And the ones who would not make war? Can they stop it?"

"I do not know."

He looked out of the window again. I watched his face.

"Have they ever been able to stop it?"

"They are not organized to stop things and when they get organized their leaders sell them out."

"Then it's hopeless?"

"It is never hopeless. But sometimes I cannot hope. I try always to hope but sometimes I cannot."

"Maybe the war will be over."

"I hope so."

"What will you do then?"

"If it is possible I will return to the Abruzzi."

1. Il s'agit de l'un des ambulanciers de Frederic. Il s'était plaint du bellicisme des officiers italiens juste avant d'être tué par l'obus autrichien qui a blessé Frederic.

His brown face was suddenly very happy.

"You love the Abruzzi?"

"Yes, I love it very much."

"You ought to go there then."

"I would be too happy. If I could live there and love God and serve Him."

"And be respected," I said.

"Yes and be respected. Why not?"

"No reason not. You should be respected."

"It does not matter. But there in my country it is understood that a man may love God. It is not a dirty joke."

"I understand."

He looked at me and smiled.

"You understand but you do not love God."

"No."

"You do not love Him at all?" he asked.

"I am afraid of Him in the night sometimes."

"You should love Him."

"I don't love much."

"Yes," he said "you do. What you tell me about in the nights. That is not love. That is only passion and lust. When you love, you wish to do things for. You wish to sacrifice for. You wish to serve."

"I don't love."

"You will. I know you will. Then you will be happy."

"I'm happy. I've always been happy."

"It is another thing. You cannot know about it unless you have it."

"Well," I said. "If I ever get it I will tell you."

"I stay too long and talk too much." He was worried that he really did.

"No. Don't go. How about loving women? If I really loved some woman would it be like that?"

"I don't know about that. I never loved any woman."

"What about your mother?"

"Yes, I must have loved my mother."

"Did you always love God?"

"Ever since I was a little boy."

"Well," I said. I did not know what to say. "You are a fine boy," I said.

"I am a boy," he said. "But you call me father."

"That's politeness."

He smiled.

"I must go, really," he said. "You do not want me for anything?" he asked hopefully.

"No. Just to talk."

"I will take your greetings to the mess."

"Thank you for the many fine presents."

"Nothing."

"Come and see me again."

"Yes. Good-by," he patted my hand.

"So long," I said in dialect.

"Ciaou," he repeated.

It was dark in the room and the orderly, who had sat by the foot of the bed, got up and went out with him. I liked him very much and I hoped he would get back to the Abruzzi some time. He had a rotten life in the mess and he was fine about it but I thought how he would be in his own country. At Capracotta, he had told me, there were trout in the stream below the town. It was forbidden to play the flute at night. When the young men serenaded only the flute was forbidden. Why, I had asked. Because it was bad for the girls to hear the flute at night. The peasants all called you "Don" and when you met them they took off their hats. His father hunted every day and stopped to eat at the houses of peasants. They were always honored. For a foreigner to hunt he must present a certificate that he had never been arrested. There were bears on the Gran Sasso D'Italia but it was a long way. Aquila was a fine town. It was cool in the summer at night and the spring in Abruzzi was the most beautiful in Italy. But what was lovely was the fall to go hunting through the chestnut woods. The birds were all good because they fed on grapes and you never took a lunch because the peasants were always honored if you would eat with them at their houses. After a while I went to sleep.

F(RANCIS) SCOTT FITZGERALD, 1896-1940

F. Scott Fitzgerald remplissait toutes les conditions pour devenir le chroniqueur romanesque de l'âge du jazz. Son éducation au Minnesota, dans une famille autrefois prospère et encore attachée aux valeurs de la haute société, lui permit de mesurer l'importance culturelle d'une Nouvelle-Angleterre vieillissante à l'aune de la rude et récente histoire des pionniers de l'Ouest comme à celle des années folles à New York. Quand parut *The Great Gatsby*, en 1925, T. S. Eliot félicita Fitzgerald en le désignant comme l'héritier de Henry James qui était lui-même pour Eliot un historien des mœurs dans la tradition de Hawthorne. Fitzgerald comprit que le « Rêve américain » ne consistait pas seulement à rechercher puis préserver fortune et rang social, mais représentait la conscience d'une liberté individuelle en devenir, recherchant dans le Nouveau Monde l'accomplissement de soi selon l'idéal platonicien. Bien que Fitzgerald eût fait ses études à l'Université en vogue de Princeton et gaspillé son énergie d'écrivain à payer le coût de ses frasques à New York, il couvait sa haine des riches, surtout les héritiers oisifs, cyniques et snobs de fortunes familiales. Les Américains authentiques, restés chez lui adolescents d'esprit, s'éblouissent des infinies possibilités qu'offre l'expérience américaine. Le style de Fitzgerald irradie la resplendissante sensualité du langage lorsqu'il imagine ses rêveurs tels que John Unger dans « The Diamond as Big as the Ritz », Dexter Green dans « Winter Dreams » et l'incomparable héros de *Great Gatsby*.

BIBLIOGRAPHIE SÉLECTIVE. — Lehan (Richard), *F. Scott Fitzgerald and the Craft of Fiction*, Carbondale, Southern Illinois University Press, 1966 ; Miller (James), *F. Scott Fitzgerald : His Art and His Technique*, New York, New York University Press, 1964 ; Way (Brian), *F. Scott Fitzgerald and the Art of Social Fiction*, New York, St. Martin's, 1980 ; Le Vot (André), *F. Scott Fitzgerald*, Paris, Julliard, 1979 ; Le Vot (André), Poli (Bernard), *The Great Gatsby*, Paris, Colin, 1979.

The Diamond as Big as the Ritz[1]

Jeune homme du Middle West, John Unger a rencontré le riche Percy Washington, issu d'une célèbre famille américaine, dans un collège huppé de la Nouvelle-Angleterre, Saint-Midas. Le nom suggère la vision puritaine de la fortune comme signe de la grâce.

1. De *Tales of the Jazz Age* (1922).

Très doué, John Unger vient d'une ville ingrate du Mississippi, qui a pour nom Hades. Percy invite John à visiter le domaine familial dans l'Ouest, où la génération des Washington, héritière des pionniers, vit dans le luxe sur une montagne de diamant « plus gros que l'hôtel Ritz-Carlton », selon Percy. Alors que Percy et John arrivent au Montana, Fitzgerald compose une scène particulièrement forte, qui, par des allusions au Nouveau Testament, suggère le désert spirituel de la modernité dans l'Ouest, désormais fermé aux pionniers et livré au pillage. La « vallée des cendres », proche des résidences de milliardaires, constituera à nouveau le même paysage moral dans The Great Gatsby.

The Montana sunset lay between two mountains like a gigantic bruise from which dark arteries spread themselves over a poisoned sky. An immense distance under the sky crouched the village of Fish, minute, dismal, and forgotten. There were twelve men, so it was said, in the village of Fish, twelve sombre and inexplicable souls who sucked a lean milk from the almost literally bare rock upon which a mysterious populatory force had begotten them. They had become a race apart, these twelve men of Fish, like some species developed by an early whim of nature, which on second thought had abandoned them to struggle and extermination.

Out of the blue-black bruise in the distance crept a long line of moving lights upon the desolation of the land, and the twelve men of Fish gathered like ghosts at the shanty depot to watch the passing of the seven o'clock train, the Transcontinental Express from Chicago. Six times or so a year the Transcontinental Express, through some inconceivable jurisdiction, stopped at the village of Fish, and when this occurred a figure or so would disembark, mount into a buggy that always appeared from out of the dusk, and drive off toward the bruised sunset. The observation of this pointless and preposterous phenomenon had become a sort of cult among the men of Fish. To observe, that was all; there remained in them none of the vital quality of illusion which would make them wonder or speculate, else a religion might have grown up around these mysterious visitations. But the men of Fish were beyond all religion—the barest and most savage tenets of even Christianity could gain no foothold on that barren rock—so there was no altar, no priest, no sacrifice; only each night at seven the silent concourse by the shanty depot, a congregation who lifted up a prayer of dim, anæmic wonder.

On this June night, the Great Brakeman, whom, had they deified any one, they might well have chosen as their celestial protagonist, had ordained that the seven o'clock train should leave its human (or inhuman) deposit at Fish. At two minutes after seven Percy Washington and John T. Unger disembarked, hurried past the spellbound, the agape, the fearsome eyes of the twelve men of Fish, mounted into a buggy which had obviously appeared from nowhere, and drove away.

After half an hour, when the twilight had coagulated into dark, the silent negro who was driving the buggy hailed an opaque body somewhere ahead of them in the gloom. In response to his cry, it turned upon them a luminous disk which regarded them like a malignant eye out of the unfathomable night. As they came closer, John saw that it was the tail-light of an immense automobile, larger and more magnificent than any he had ever seen. Its body was of gleaming metal richer than nickel and lighter than silver, and the hubs of the wheels were studded with irridescent geometric figures of green and yellow—John did not dare to guess whether they were glass or jewel.

Two negroes, dressed in glittering livery such as one sees in pictures of royal processions in London, were standing at attention beside the car and as the two young men dismounted from the buggy they were greeted in some language which the guest could not understand, but which seemed to be an extreme form of the Southern negro's dialect.

"Get in," said Percy to his friend, as their trunks were tossed to the ebony roof of the limousine. "Sorry we had to bring you this far in that buggy, but of course it wouldn't do for the people on the train or those Godforsaken fellas in Fish to see this automobile."

"Gosh! What a car!!" This ejaculation was provoked by its interior. John saw that the upholstery consisted of a thousand minute and exquisite tapestries of silk, woven with jewels and embroideries, and set upon a background of cloth of gold. The two armchair seats in which the boys luxuriated were covered with stuff that resembled duvetyn, but seemed woven in numberless colors of the ends of ostrich feathers.

"What a car!" cried John again, in amazement.

"This thing?" Percy laughed. "Why, it's just an old junk we use for a station wagon."

By this time they were gliding along throught the darkness toward the break between the two mountains.

"We'll be there in an hour and a half," said Percy, looking at the clock. "I may as well tell you it's not going to be like anything you ever saw before."

If the car was any indication of what John would see, he was prepared to be astonished indeed. The simple piety prevalent in Hades has the earnest worship of and respect for riches as the first article of its creed—had John felt otherwise than radiantly humble before them, his parents would have turned away in horror at the blasphemy.

They had now reached and were entering the break between the two mountains and almost immediately the way became much rougher.

"If the moon shone down here, you'd see that we're in a big gulch," said Percy, trying to peer out of the window. He spoke a few words into the mouthpiece and immediately the footman turned on a searchlight and swept the hillsides with an immense beam.

"Rocky, you see. An ordinary car would be knocked to pieces in half an hour. In fact, it'd take a tank to navigate it unless you knew the way. You notice we're going uphill now."

They were obviously ascending, and within a few minutes the car was crossing a high rise, where they caught a glimpse of a pale moon newly risen in the distance. The car stopped suddenly and several figures took shape out of the dark beside it—these were negroes also. Again the two young men were saluted in the same dimly recognizable dialect; then the negroes set to work and four immense cables dangling from overhead were attached with hooks to the hubs of the great jeweled wheels. At a resounding "Hey-yah!" John felt the car being lifted slowly from the ground—up and up—clear of the tallest rocks on both sides—then higher, until he could see a wavy, moonlit valley stretched out before him in sharp contrast to the quagmire of rocks that they had just left. Only on one side was there still rock—and then suddenly there was no rock beside them or anywhere around.

It was apparent that they had surmounted some immense knife-blade of stone, projecting perpendicularly into the air. In a moment they were going down again, and finally with a soft bump they were landed upon the smooth earth.

"The worst is over," said Percy, squinting out the window.

"It's only five miles from here, and our own road—tapestry brick—all the way. This belongs to us. This is where the United States ends, father says."

"Are we in Canada?"

"We are not. We're in the middle of the Montana Rockies. But you are now on the only five square miles of land in the country that's never been surveyed."

"Why hasn't it? Did they forget it?"

"No," said Percy, grinning, "they tried to do it three times. The first time my grandfather corrupted a whole department of the State survey; the second time he had the official maps of the United States tinkered with—that held them for fifteen years. The last time was harder. My father fixed it so that their compasses were in the strongest magnetic field ever artificially set up. He had a whole set of surveying instruments made with a slight defection that would allow for this territory not to appear, and he substituted them for the ones that were to be used. Then he had a river deflected and he had what looked like a village built up on its banks—so that they'd see it, and think it was a town ten miles farther up the valley. There's only one thing my father's afraid of," he concluded, "only one thing in the world that could be used to find us out."

"What's that?"

Percy sank his voice to a whisper.

"Aeroplanes," he breathed. "We've got half a dozen anti-aircraft guns and we've arranged it so far—but there've been a few deaths and a great many prisoners. Not that we mind *that*, you know, father and I, but it upsets mother and the girls, and there's always the chance that some time we won't be able to arrange it."

Shreds and tatters of chinchilla, courtesy clouds in the green moon's heaven, were passing the green moon like precious Eastern stuffs paraded for the inspection of some Tartar Khan. It seemed to John that it was day, and that he was looking at some lads sailing above him in the air, showering down tracts and patent medicine circulars, with their messages of hope for despairing, rockbound hamlets. It seemed to him that he could see them look down out of the clouds and stare—and stare at whatever there was to stare at in this place whither he was bound—What then? Were they induced to land by some insidious device there to be immured far from patent medicines and from tracts until the judgment day—or, should they fail to fall into the trap, did a quick puff of smoke and the sharp round of a splitting shell bring them drooping to earth—and "upset" Percy's mother and sisters. John shook his head and the wraith of a hollow laugh issued silently from his parted lips. What desperate transaction lay hidden here? What a moral expedient of a bizarre Crœsus? What terrible and golden mystery? . . .

The chinchilla clouds had drifted past now and outside the Montana night was bright as day. The tapestry brick of the road was smooth to the tread of the great tires as they rounded a still, moonlit lake; they passed into darkness for a moment, a pine grove, pungent and cool, then they came out into a broad avenue of lawn and John's exclamation of pleasure was simultaneous with Percy's taciturn "We're home."

Full in the light of the stars, an exquisite château rose from the borders of the lake, climbed in marble radiance half the height of an adjoining mountain, then melted in grace, in perfect symmetry, in translucent feminine languor, into the massed darkness of a forest of pine. The many towers, the slender tracery of the sloping parapets, the chiselled wonder of a thousand yellow windows with their oblongs and hectagons and triangles of golden light, the shattered softness of the intersecting planes of star-shine and blue shade, all trembled on John's spirit like a chord of music. On one of the towers, the tallest, the blackest at its base, an arrangement of exterior lights at the top made a sort of floating faiyland—and as John gazed up in warm enchantment the faint acciaccare sound of violins drifted down in a rococo harmony that was like nothing he had ever heard before. Then in a moment the car stopped before wide, high marble steps around which the night air was fragrant with a host of flowers. At the top of the steps two great doors swung silently open and amber light flooded out upon the darkness, silhouetting the figure of an exquisite lady with black, high-piled hair, who held out her arms toward them.

"Mother," Percy was saying, "this is my friend, John Unger, from Hades."

Afterward John remembered that first night as a daze of many colors, of quick sensory impressions, of music soft as a voice in love, and of the beauty of things, lights and shadows, and motions and faces. There was a white-haired man who stood drinking a many-hued cordial from a crystal thimble set on a golden stem. There was a girl with a flowery face, dressed like Titania with braided sapphires in her hair. There was a room where the solid, soft gold of the walls yielded to the pressure of his hand, and a room that was like a platonic conception of the ultimate prison—ceiling, floor, and all, it was lined with an unbroken mass of diamonds, diamonds of every size and shape, until, lit with tall violet lamps in the corners, it dazzled the eyes with a whiteness that could be compared only with itself, beyond human wish or dream.

The Great Gatsby[1]

VI

Nick Carraway, le narrateur, tente de comprendre le caractère et la carrière du gangster Jay Gatsby, son voisin de Long Island, New York, dans l'été de 1922. Nick a organisé un rendez-vous secret entre Gatsby et Mme Tom (Daisy) Buchanan en les invitant un après-midi à prendre le thé. Daisy est la cousine de Nick dont Gatsby est tombé amoureux cinq ans auparavant. Nick rassemble maintenant de nouveaux fragments biographiques de la carrière notoirement douteuse de Gatsby qui est cependant pénétré d'un profond idéalisme.

[...] About this time an ambitious young reporter from New York arrived one morning at Gatsby's door and asked him if he had anything to say.

"Anything to say about what?" inquired Gatsby politely.

"Why—any statement to give out."

It transpired after a confused five minutes that the man had heard Gatsby's name around his office in a connection which he either wouldn't reveal or didn't fully understand. This was his day off and with laudable initiative he had hurried out "to see."

It was a random shot, and yet the reporter's instinct was right. Gatsby's notoriety, spread about by the hundreds who had accepted his hospitality and so become authorities upon his past, had increased all summer until he fell just short of being news.

1. Première édition en 1925.

Contemporary legends such as the "underground pipe-line to Canada" attached themselves to him, and there was one persistent story that he didn't live in a house at all, but in a boat that looked like a house and was moved secretly up and down the Long Island shore. Just why these inventions were a source of satisfaction of James Gatz of North Dakota isn't easy to say.

James Gatz—that was really, or at least legally, his name. He had changed it at the age of seventeen and at the specific moment that witnessed the beginning of his career—when he saw Dan Cody's yacht drop anchor over the most insidious flat on Lake Superior. It was James Gatz who had been loafing along the beach that afternoon in a torn green jersey and a pair of canvas pants, but it was already Jay Gatsby who borrowed a rowboat, pulled out to the *Tuolomee*, and informed Cody that a wind might catch him and break him up in half an hour.

I suppose he'd had the name ready for a long time, even then. His parents were shiftless and unsuccessful farm people—his imagination had never really accepted them as his parents at all. The truth was that Jay Gatsby of West Egg, Long Island, sprang from his Platonic conception of himself. He was a son of God—a phrase which, if it means anything, means just that—and he must be about His Father's business, the service of a vast, vulgar, and meretricious beauty. So he invented just the sort of Jay Gatsby that a seventeen-year-old boy would be likely to invent, and to this conception he was faithful to the end.

For over a year he had been beating his way along the south shore of Lake Superior as a clam-digger and a salmon-fisher or in any other capacity that brought him food and bed. His brown, hardening body lived naturally through the half-fierce, half-lazy work of the bracing days. He knew women early, and since they spoiled him he became contemptuous of them, of young virgins because they were ignorant, of the others because they were hysterical about things which in his overwhelming self-absorption he took for granted.

But his heart was in a constant, turbulent riot. The most grotesque and fantastic conceits haunted him in his bed at night. A universe of ineffable gaudiness spun itself out in his brain while the clock ticked on the washstand and the moon soaked with wet light his tangled clothes upon the floor. Each night he added to the pattern of his fancies until drowsiness closed down upon some vivid scene with an oblivious embrace. For a while these reveries provided an outlet for his imagination; they were a satisfactory hint of the unreality of reality, a promise that the rock of the world was founded securely on a fairy's wing.

An instinct toward his future glory had led him, some months before, to the small Lutheran college of St. Olaf in southern Minnesota. He stayed there two weeks, dismayed at its ferocious indifference to the drums of his destiny, to destiny itself, and despising the janitor's work with which he was to pay his way through. Then he drifted back to Lake Superior, and he was still searching for something to do on the day that Dan Cody's yacht dropped anchor in the shallows alongshore.

Cody was fifty years old then, a product of the Nevada silver fields, of the Yukon, of every rush for metal since seventy-five. The transactions in Montana copper that made him many times a millionaire found him physically robust but on the verge of solft-mindedness, and, suspecting this, an infinite number of women tried to separate him from his money. The none too savory ramifications by which Ella Kaye, the newspaper woman, played Madame de Maintenon to his weakness and sent him to sea in a yacht, were common knowledge to the turgid sub-journalism of 1902. He had been coasting along all too hospitable shores for five years when he turned up as James Gatz's destiny in Little Girl Bay.

To young Gatz, resting on his oars and looking up at the railed deck, that yacht represented all the beauty and glamour in the world. I suppose he smiled at Cody—he had probably discovered that people liked him when he smiled. At any rate Cody asked him a few questions (one of them elicited the brand new name) and found that he was quick and extravagantly ambitious. A few days later he took him to Duluth and bought him a blue coat, six pairs of white duck trousers, and a yachting cap. And when the *Tuolomee* left for the West Indies and the Barbary Coast Gatsby left too.

He was employed in a vague personal capacity—while he remained with Cody he was in turn steward, mate, skipper, secretary, and even jailor, for Dan Cody sober knew what lavish doings Dan Cody drunk might soon be about, and he provided for such contingencies by reposing more and more trust in Gatsby. The arrangement lasted five years, during which the boat went three times around the Continent. It might have lasted indefinitely except for the fact that Ella Kaye came on board one night in Boston and a week later Dan Cody inhospitably died.

I remember the portrait of him up in Gatsby's bedroom, a gray, florid man with a hard, empty face—the pioneer debauchee, who during one phase of American life brought back to the Eastern seaboard the savage violence of the frontier brothel and saloon. It was indirectly due to Cody that Gatsby drank so little. Sometimes in the course of gay parties women used to rub champagne into his hair; for himself he formed the habit of letting liquor alone.

IX

Après la mort de Gatsby que tue par erreur le mari de la maîtresse de Tom Buchanan, Nick rencontre le père de Gatsby le jour des obsèques. Il aide Nick a compléter le portrait spirituel du Gatsby américain : image composite du cowboy héroïque (Hopalong Cassidy) mêlée de « self-made man » du XVIIIe siècle (le parcours de Gatsby est modelé sur celui de Benjamin Franklin dans son Autobiographie), et enfin de l'explorateur hollandais du XVIIe siècle qui avait jadis contemplé avec émerveillement « the fresh, green breast » de Long Island.

[... Mr. Gatz] pulled from his pocket a ragged old copy of a book called *Hopalong Cassidy.*

"Look here, this is a book he had when he was a boy. It just shows you."

He opened it at the back cover and turned it around for me to see. On the last fly-leaf was printed the word schedule, and the date September 12, 1906. And underneath:

Rise from bed	6.00	A.M.
Dumbbell exercise and wall-scaling.........	6.15–6.30	—
Study electricity, etc.....................	7.15–8.15	—
Work	8.30–4.30	P.M.
Baseball and sports......................	4.30–5.00	—
Practice elocution, poise and how to attain it	5.00–6.00	—
Study needed inventions	7.00–9.00	—

GENERAL RESOLVES

No wasting time at Shafters or [a name, indecipherable]
No more smokeing or chewing
Bath every other day
Read one improving book or magazine per week
Save $5.00 [crossed out] $3.00 per week
Be better to parents

"I come across this book by accident," said the old man. "It just shows you, don't it?"

"It just shows you."

"Jimmy was bound to get ahead. He always had some resolves like this or something. Do you notice what he's got about improving his mind? He was always great for that. He told me I et like a hog once, and I beat him for it."

He was reluctant to close the book, reading each item aloud and then looking eagerly at me. I think he rather expected me to copy down the list for my own use.

. . . .

On the last night, with my trunk packed and my car sold to the grocer, I went over and looked at that huge incoherent failure of a house once more. On the white steps an obscene word, scrawled by some boy with a piece of brick, stood out clearly in the moonlight, and I erased it, drawing my shoe raspingly along the stone. Then I wandered down to the beach and sprawled out on the sand.

Most of the big shore places were closed now and there were hardly any lights except the shadowy, moving glow of a ferry-boat across the Sound. And as the moon rose higher the inessential houses began to melt away until gradually I became aware of the old island here that flowered once for Dutch sailors' eyes—a fresh, green breast of the new world. Its vanished trees, the trees that had made way for Gatsby's house, had once pandered in whispers to the last and greatest of all human dreams; for a transitory enchanted moment man must have held his breath in the presence of this continent, compelled into an æsthetic contemplation he neither understood nor desired, face to face for the last time in history with something commensurate to his capacity for wonder.

And as I sat there brooding on the old, unknown world, I thought of Gatsby's wonder when he first picked out the green light at the end of Daisy's dock. He had come a long way to this blue lawn, and his dream must have seemed so close that he could hardly fail to grasp it. He did not know that it was already behind him, somewhere back in that vast obscurity beyond the city, where the dark fields of the republic rolled on under the night.

Gatsby believed in the green light, the orgiastic future that year by year recedes before us. It eluded us then, but that's no matter—tomorrow we will run faster, stretch out our arms farther. . . . And one fine morning—

So we beat on, boats against the current, borne back ceaselessly into the past.

2 – La foi en l'homme resurgit lors de la Grande Dépression

La nation est à l'orée des années trente plus troublée qu'à toute autre époque antérieure de son Histoire depuis la guerre de Sécession. Le krach de Wall Street traduit, après octobre 1929, l'effondrement du système capitaliste américain, dont la cupidité et les profits exorbitants des années vingt conduisaient inéluctablement à cette catastrophe tant morale qu'économique. L'idéalisme de l'opulent Gatsby devient soudain une incroyable fiction. Rares sont les écrivains alors enclins à brosser du *businessman* américain une image flatteuse. Le capitalisme est désormais ressenti comme au-delà du bien et du mal, évoqué comme une gigantesque abstraction, anonyme et insondable, une force opaque et secrète échappant au contrôle moral et économique de tout agent humain. John Steinbeck reproduit dans le chapitre 5 de *The Grapes of Wrath* (1939) la réaction de gens frustrés et désemparés. Un métayer spolié de l'Oklahoma, qui menace de tirer sur le représentant du propriétaire foncier, se rend bientôt compte que le propriétaire est en réalité un monstre tentaculaire appelé la Banque ou la Firme, qui à son tour « gets orders from the East ». La leçon est implacable : cela ne sert à rien de tirer sur une banque. Steinbeck glisse en outre un trait révélateur dans le défi qui, naissant de l'esprit de résistance individuel et collectif, engage l'agriculteur en lutte à proclamer la dignité humaine par ces mots : « We've got a bad thing made by men, and by God that's something we can change. »

Rejoignant Steinbeck pour défendre la même cause, Carl Sandburg publie peu avant *The People, Yes* (1936), titre significatif d'une œuvre qui est l'équivalent poétique de *The Grapes of Wrath*. Dans le Sud profond, Faulkner écrit sa version régionale de l'histoire morale qui, ultimement reconnue et honorée à la fin des années quarante, lui vaudra le prix Nobel pour, selon ses propres mots, « a life's work in the agony and sweat of the human spirit. » D'autres écrivains attachés au prolétariat dans leur fiction tels que John Dos Passos, James T. Farrell et Richard Wright, parmi les plus influents, dépeignent avec une égale sympathie l'individu en lutte avec les puissances économiques, sociales et politiques.

Appartenant à un groupe d'auteurs de nouvelles, Katherine Anne Porter inaugure la décennie avec la publication de « Flowering Judas », où, pressentant les défis de la Dépression, elle célèbre la volonté humaine. Elle se livre à une allégorie de la répression exercée sur l'individu et mise au service de la discipline communiste ou de la stratégie nihiliste au nom d'intérêts supérieurs. Inspirée de la scène politique mexicaine, peu avant la débâcle de Wall Street, l'histoire de cette héroïne secrètement rebelle préfigure le courant humaniste qui sous-tendra nombre d'œuvres littéraires. Il faudrait également citer William Carlos Williams et « The Use of Force », fable politique dans laquelle un docteur amoureux se déchaîne soudain contre une patiente de neuf ans et, s'appuyant sur une rhétorique totalitariste, justifie ses fins par des moyens violents. Mais l'enfant demeure intraitable face à l'usurpation de ses droits. Dans « The Eighty-Yard Run », Irwin Shaw imagine un athlète finalement sans illusion devant les autorités universitaires qui, négligeant son éducation, le laissent vulnérable dans le New York des années trente. Et Nelson Algren, comme Steinbeck, invoque l'empathie démocratique de Withman dans « A Bottle of Milk for Mother », en décrivant un *punk* du ghetto de Chicago qui comprend comment la police et les puissances d'argent qu'elle soutient l'ont trompé sur les promesses infinies du Rêve américain. Parmi tous ces ouvrages, c'est la nouvelle de Katherine Anne Porter que nous reproduisons pour la valeur de son dessein prophétique, ainsi que le conte de Williams qui lui sert de parallèle.

WILLIAM FAULKNER, 1897-1962

William Faulkner grandit à Oxford dans le Mississippi, lieu privilégié où un futur romancier pouvait apprendre des vieux conteurs l'art des humoristes de la Frontière dont avait hérité Mark Twain en le perfectionnant dans *Huckleberry Finn*. Au sein de ce monde traditionnel de stéréotypes locaux, fait d'indolence et de rudesse, résonnant de dialectes ruraux, Faulkner a soumis au regard un panorama historique du Sud, sur le fond de paysage mythique du Yoknapatawpha County (vieille appellation des Indiens Chickasaw signifiant « eau qui coule lentement dans le plat pays »). Roman après roman, de 1929 à 1962, il persévère, souvent sous la pression de ceux qu'il désigne comme ses « démons » intimes, avant que Malcolm Cowley ne propose chronologiquement dans *The Portable Faulkner* (1946) différents extraits de ses œuvres. Le Faulkner de Cowley se présente davantage comme un solide historien des mœurs du Sud qu'un romancier à sensations morbides tenant la chronique d'une région sur le déclin, dont les habitants sont en proie aux rapports sexuels interraciaux, à l'inceste, au viol, au suicide, à la zoophilie et au meurtre. La troisième facette de son génie littéraire apparaît dans son discours de réception du prix Nobel de littérature à Stockholm (1950). Il insiste alors sur la portée *universelle* de sa fiction régionaliste, exposant ses thèmes obsédants de « love and honor and pity and pride and compassion and sacrifice. » Le lecteur attentif pourra aisément ajouter à cette liste. Naturellement le comité de sélection du prix Nobel avait déjà retenu la dimension universelle. L'abondante critique faulknérienne a ensuite interprété les vices et vertus profonds attachés à ses personnages récurrents aux prodigieuses ramifications familiales, de *Sartoris* et *The Sound and the Fury* (1929) à *Go Down, Moses* (1942) et après, avec les Sartoris, Compson, Bundren, Sutpen, Snopes et McCaslin. Le meilleur moyen de comprendre le génie faulknérien exige de reconnaître les quatre niveaux de sa richesse : la vigoureuse technique narrative, la densité régionale et historique, le lacis métaphorique procédant d'un inconscient individuel ou collectif et les vérités universelles qui en émergent, traduisant une indéfectible foi en l'homme.

BIBLIOGRAPHIE SÉLECTIVE. — Brooks (Cleanth), *William Faulkner : Toward Yoknapatawpha and Beyond*, New Haven, Conn., Yale University Press, 1978 ; Kartiganer (Donald), *The Fragile Thread : The Meaning of Form in Faulkner's Novels*, Amherst, University of Massachusetts Press, 1979 ; Waggoner (Hyatt), *William Faulkner : From Jefferson to the World*, Lexington, University Press of Kentucky, 1960 ; Bleikasten (André), *Parcours de Faulkner*, Paris, Ophrys, 1982 ; Gresset (Michel), *Faulkner ou la fascination*, Paris, Klinsieck, 1982 ; Pitavy (François), *William Faulkner, romancier (1929-1939)*, Paris, Didier, 1981 ; Rouberol (Jean), *L'esprit du Sud dans l'œuvre de Faulkner*, Paris, Didier, 1982.

Barn Burning[1]

The store in which the Justice of the Peace's court was sitting smelled of cheese. The boy, crouched on his nail keg at the back of the crowded room, knew he smelled cheese, and more: from where he sat he could see the ranked shelves close-packed with the solid, squat, dynamic shapes of tin cans whose labels his stomach read, not from the lettering which meant nothing to his mind but from the scarlet devils and the silver curve of fish—this, the cheese which he knew he smelled and the hermetic meat which his intestines believed he smelled coming in intermittent gusts momentary and brief between the other constant one, the smell and sense just a little of fear because mostly of despair and grief, the old fierce pull of blood. He could not see the table where the Justice sat and before which his father and his father's enemy (*our enemy* he

1. Paru pour la première fois dans *Harper's*, en juin 1939, et republié dans *Collected Stories* (1950). Cette nouvelle ne fut pas incluse dans *The Hamlet* (1940) avec d'autres sur la famille Snopes, lignée de *rednecks*, petites gens sans scrupule d'après la guerre de Sécession. Le garçon, Sarty, est le plus honnête de tous les Snopes. Son nom suggère le conflit qui porte sur la continuité souhaitée d'une tradition entre la vieille plantation (colonel Sartoris) et la nouvelle et vigoureuse génération des Snopes. L'incendiaire de grange, Ab Snopes, ne sera pas tué dans cette histoire, mais ni lui ni Sarty ne figureront dans la saga future de la famille. A leur place, Flem, brièvement mentionné comme *older brother* dans « Barn Burning », devient le chef de la famille. Faulkner compléta la trilogie des Snopes avec *The Town* (1957) et *The Mansion* (1959), le troisième roman révélant l'immoral Flem en heureux propriétaire de la résidence de Major de Spain.

thought in that despair; *ourn! mine and hisn both! He's my father!*) stood, but he could hear them, the two of them that is, because his father had said no word yet:

"But what proof have you, Mr. Harris?"

"I told you. The hog got into my corn. I caught it up and sent it back to him. The next time I put the hog in my pen. When he came to get it I gave him enough wire to patch up his pen. The next time I put the hog up and kept it. I rode down to his house and saw the wire I gave him still rolled on to the spool in his yard. I told him he could have the hog when he paid me a dollar pound fee. That evening a nigger came with the dollar and got the hog. He was a strange nigger. He said, 'He say to tell you wood and hay kin burn.' I said, 'What?' 'That whut he say to tell you,' the nigger said. 'Wood and hay kin burn.' That night my barn burned. I got the stock out but I lost the barn."

"Where is the nigger? Have you got him?"

"He was a strange nigger, I tell you. I don't know what became of him."

"But that's not proof. Don't you see that's not proof?"

"Get that boy up here. He knows." For a moment the boy thought too that the man meant his older brother until Harris said, "Not him. The little one. The boy," and, crouching, small for his age, small and wiry like his father, in patched and faded jeans even too small for him, with straight, uncombed, brown hair and eyes gray and wild as storm scud, he saw the men between himself and the table part and become a lane of grim faces, at the end of which he saw the Justice, a shabby, collarless, graying man in spectacles, beckoning him. He felt no floor under his bare feet; he seemed to walk beneath the palpable weight of the grim turning faces. His father stiff in his black Sunday coat donned not for the trial but for the moving, did not even look at him. *He aims for me to lie*, he thought, again with that frantic grief and despair. *And I will have to do hit.*

"What's your name, boy?" the Justice said.

"Colonel Sartoris Snopes," the boy whispered.

"Hey?" the Justice said. "Talk louder. Colonel Sartoris? I reckon anybody named for Colonel Sartoris in this country can't help but tell the truth, can they?" The boy said nothing. *Enemy! Enemy!* he thought; for a moment he could not even see, could not see that the Justice's face was kindly nor discern that his voice was troubled when he spoke to the man named Harris: "Do you want me to question this boy?" But he could hear, and during those subsequent long seconds while there was absolutely no sound in the crowded little room save that of quiet and intent breathing it was as if he had swung outward at the end of a grape vine, over a ravine, and at the top of the swing had been caught in a prolonged instant of mesmerized gravity, weightless in time.

"No!" Harris said violently, explosively. "Damnation! Send him out of here!" Now time, the fluid world, rushed beneath him again, the voices coming to him again through the smell of cheese and sealed meat, the fear and despair and the old grief of blood:

"This case is closed. I can't find against you, Snopes, but I can give you advice. Leave this country and don't come back to it."

His father spoke for the first time, his voice cold and harsh, level, without emphasis: "I aim to. I don't figure to stay in a country among people who . . ." he said something unprintable and vile, addressed to no one.

"That'll do," the Justice said. "Take your wagon and get out of this country before dark. Case dismissed."

His father turned, and he followed the stiff black coat, the wiry figure walking a little stiffly from where a Confederate provost's man's musket ball had taken him in the heel on a stolen horse thirty years ago, followed the two backs now, since his older brother had appeared from somewhere in the crowd, no taller than the father but thicker, chewing tobacco steadily, between the two lines of grim-faced men and out of the store and across the worn gallery and down the sagging steps and among the dogs and half-grown boys in the mild May dust, where as he passed a voice hissed:

"Barn burner!"

Again he could not see, whirling; there was a face in a red haze, moonlike, bigger than the full moon, the owner of it half again his size, he leaping in the red haze toward the face, feeling no blow, feeling no shock when his head struck the earth, scrabbling up and leaping again, feeling no blow this time either and tasting no blood, scrabbling up to see the other boy in full flight and himself already leaping into pursuit as his father's hand jerked him back, the harsh, cold voice speaking above him: "Go get in the wagon."

It stood in a grove of locusts and mulberries across the road. His two hulking sisters in their Sunday dresses and his mother and her sister in calico and sunbonnets were already in it, sitting on and among the sorry residue of the dozen and more movings which even the boy could remember—the battered stove, the broken beds and chairs, the clock inlaid with mother-of-pearl, which would not run, stopped at some fourteen minutes past two o'clock of a dead and forgotten day and time, which had been his mother's dowry. She was crying, though when she saw him she drew her sleeve across her face and began to descend from the wagon. "Get back," the father said.

"He's hurt. I got to get some water and wash his . . ."

"Get back in the wagon," his father said. He got in too, over the tail-gate. His father mounted to the seat where the older brother already sat and struck the gaunt mules two savage blows with the peeled willow, but without heat. It was not even sadistic; it was exactly that same quality which in later years would cause his descendants to over-run the engine before putting a motor car into motion, striking and reining back in the same movement. The wagon went on, the store with its quiet crowd of grimly watching men dropped behind; a curve in the road hid it. *Forever* he thought. *Maybe he's done satisfied now, now that he has* . . . stopping himself, not to say it aloud even to himself. His mother's hand touched his shoulder.

"Does hit hurt?" she said.

"Naw," he said. "Hit don't hurt. Lemme be."

"Can't you wipe some of the blood off before it dries?"

"I'll wash to-night," he said. "Lemme be, I tell you."

The wagon went on. He did not know where they were going. None of them ever did or ever asked, because it was always somewhere, always a house of sorts waiting for them a day or two days or even three days away. Likely his father had already arranged to make a crop on another farm before he . . . Again he had to stop himself. He (the father) always did. There was something about his wolflike independence and even courage when the advantage was at least neutral which impressed strangers, as if they got from his latent ravening ferocity not so much a sense of dependability as a feeling that his ferocious conviction in the rightness of his own actions would be of advantage to all whose interest lay with his.

That night they camped, in a grove of oaks and beeches where a spring ran. The nights were still cool and they had a fire against it, of a rail lifted from a nearby fence and cut into lengths—a small fire, neat, niggard almost, a shrewd fire; such fires were his father's habit and custom always, even in freezing weather. Older, the boy might have remarked this and wondered why not a big one; why should not a man who had not only seen the waste and extravagance of war, but who had in his blood an inherent voracious prodigality with material not his own, have burned everything in sight? Then he might have gone a step farther and thought that that was the reason: that niggard blaze was the living fruit of nights passed during those four years in the woods hiding from all men, blue or gray, with his strings of horses (captured horses, he called them). And older still, he might have divined the true reason: that the element of fire spoke to some deep mainspring of his father's being, as the element of steel or of powder spoke to other men, as the one weapon for the preservation of integrity, else breath were not worth the breathing, and hence to be regarded with respect and used with discretion.

But he did not think this now and he had seen those same niggard blazes all his life. He merely ate his supper beside it and was already half asleep over his iron plate when his father called him, and once more he followed the stiff back, the stiff and ruthless limp, up the slope and on to the starlit road where, turning, he could see his father against the stars but without face or depth—a shape black, flat, and bloodless as though cut from tin in the iron folds of the frockcoat which had not been made for him, the voice harsh like tin and without heat like tin:

"You were fixing to tell them. You would have told him." He didn't answer. His father struck him with the flat of his hand on the side of the head, hard but without heat, exactly as he had struck the two mules at the store, exactly as he would strike either of them with any stick in order to kill a horse fly, his voice still without heat or anger: "You're getting to be a man. You got to learn. You got to learn to stick to your own blood or you ain't going to have any blood to stick to you. Do you think either of them, any man there this morning, would? Don't you know all they wanted was a chance to get at me because they knew I had them beat? Eh?" Later, twenty years later, he was to tell himself, "If I had said they wanted only truth, justice, he would have hit me again." But now he said nothing. He was not crying. He just stood there. "Answer me," his father said.

"Yes," he whispered. His father turned.

"Get on to bed. We'll be there tomorrow."

To-morrow they were there. In the early afternoon the wagon stopped before a paintless two-room house identical almost with the dozen others it had stopped before even in the boy's ten years, and again, as on the other dozen occasions, his mother and aunt got down and began to unload the wagon, although his two sisters and his father and brother had not moved.

"Likely hit ain't fitten for hawgs," one of the sisters said.

"Nevertheless, fit it will and you'll hog it and like it," his father said. "Get out of them chairs and help your Ma unload."

The two sisters got down, big, bovine, in a flutter of cheap ribbons; one of them drew from the jumbled wagon bed a battered lantern, the other a worn broom. His father handed the reins to the older son and began to climb stiffly over the wheel. "When they get unloaded, take the team to the barn and feed them." Then he said, and at first the boy thought he was still speaking to his brother: "Come with me."

"Me?" he said.

"Yes," his father said. "You."

"Abner," his mother said. His father paused and looked back—the harsh level stare beneath the shaggy, graying, irascible brows.

"I reckon I'll have a word with the man that aims to begin to-morrow owning me body and soul for the next eight months."

They went back up the road. A week ago—or before last night, that is—he would have asked where they were going, but not now. His father had struck him before last night but never before had he paused afterward to explain why; it was as if the blow and the following calm, outrageous voice still rang, repercussed, divulging nothing to him save the terrible handicap of being young, the light weight of his few years, just heavy enough to prevent his soaring free of the world as it seemed to be ordered but not heavy enough to keep him footed solid in it, to resist it and try to change the course of its events.

Presently he could see the grove of oaks and cedars and the other flowering trees and shrubs and where the house would be, though not the house yet. They walked beside a fence massed with honeysuckle and Cherokee roses and came to a gate swinging open between two brick pillars, and now, beyond a sweep of drive, he saw the house for the first time and at that instant he forgot his father and the terror and despair both, and even when he remembered his father again (who had not stopped) the terror and despair did not return. Because, for all the twelve movings, they had sojourned until now in a poor country, a land of small farms and fields and houses, and he had never seen a house like this before. *Hit's big as a courthouse* he thought quietly, with a surge of peace and joy whose reason he could not have thought into words, being too young for that: *They are safe from him. People whose lives are a part of this peace and dignity are beyond his touch, he no more to them than a buzzing wasp: capable of stinging for a little moment but that's all; the spell of this peace and dignity rendering even the barns and stable and cribs which belong to it impervious to the puny flames he might contrive* . . . this, the peace and joy, ebbing for an instant as he looked again at the stiff black back, the stiff and implacable limp of the figure which was not dwarfed by the house, for the reason that it had never looked big anywhere and which now, against the serene columned backdrop, had more than ever that impervious quality of something cut ruthlessly from tin, depthless, as though, sidewise to the sun, it would cast no shadow. Watching him, the boy remarked the absolutely undeviating course which his father held and saw the stiff foot come squarely down in a pile of fresh droppings where a horse had stood in the drive and which his father could have avoided by a simple change of stride. But it ebbed only for a moment, though he could not have thought this into words either, walking on in the spell of the house, which he could even want but without envy, without sorrow, certainly never with that ravening and jealous rage which unknown to him walked in the ironlike black coat before him: *Maybe he will feel it too. Maybe it will even change him now from what maybe he couldn't help but be.*

They crossed the portico. Now he could hear his father's stiff foot as it came down on the boards with clocklike finality, a sound out of all proportion to the displacement of the body it bore and which was not dwarfed either by the white door before it, as though it had attained to a sort of vicious and ravening minimum not to be dwarfed by anything—the flat, wide, black hat, the formal coat of broadcloth which had once been black but which had now that friction-glazed greenish cast of the bodies of old house flies, the lifted sleeve which was too large, the lifted hand like a curled claw. The door opened so promptly that the boy knew the

Negro must have been watching them all the time, an old man with neat grizzled hair, in a linen jacket, who stood barring the door with his body, saying, "Wipe yo foots, white man, fo you come in here? Major ain't home nohow."

"Get out of my way, nigger," his father said, without heat too, flinging the door back and the Negro also and entering, his hat still on his head. And now the boy saw the prints of the stiff foot on the doorjamb and saw them appear on the pale rug behind the machinelike deliberation of the foot which seemed to bear (or transmit) twice the weight which the body compassed. The Negro was shouting "Miss Lula! Miss Lula!" somewhere behind them, then the boy, deluged as though by a warm wave by a suave turn of carpeted stair and a pendant glitter of chandeliers and a mute gleam of gold frames, heard the swift feet and saw her too, a lady—perhaps he had never seen her like before either—in a gray, smooth gown with lace at the throat and an apron tied at the waist and the sleeves turned back, wiping cake or biscuit dough from her hands with a towel as she came up the hall, looking not at his father at all but at the tracks on the blond rug with an expression of incredulous amazement.

"I tried," the Negro cried. "I tole him to . . ."

"Will you please go away?" she said in a shaking voice. "Major de Spain is not at home. Will you please go away?"

His father had not spoken again. He did not speak again. He did not even look at her. He just stood stiff in the center of the rug, in his hat, the shaggy irony-gray brows twitching slightly above the pebble-colored eyes as he appeared to examine the house with brief deliberation. Then with the same deliberation he turned; the boy watched him pivot on the good leg and saw the stiff foot drag round the arc of the turning, leaving a final long and fading smear. His father never looked at it, he never once looked down at the rug. The Negro held the door. It closed behind them, upon the hysteric and indistinguishable woman-wail. His father stopped at the top of the steps and scraped his boot clean on the edge of it. At the gate he stopped again. He stood for a moment, planted stiffly on the stiff foot, looking back at the house. "Pretty and white, ain't it?" he said. "That's sweat. Nigger sweat. Maybe it ain't white enough yet to suit him. Maybe he wants to mix some white sweat with it."

Two hours later the boy was chopping wood behind the house within which his mother and aunt and the two sisters (the mother and aunt, not the two girls, he knew that; even at this distance and muffled by walls the flat loud voices of the two girls emanated an incorrigible idle inertia) were setting up the stove to prepare a meal, when he heard the hooves and saw the linen-clad man on a fine sorrel mare, whom he recognized even before he saw the rolled rug in front of the Negro youth following on a fat bay carriage horse—a suffused, angry face vanishing, still at full gallop, beyond the corner of the house where his father and brother were sitting in the two tilted chairs; and a moment later, almost before he could have put the axe down, he heard the hooves again and watched the sorrel mare go back out of the yard, already galloping again. Then his father began to shout one of the sisters' names, who presently emerged backward from the kitchen door dragging the rolled rug along the ground by one end while the other sister walked behind it.

"If you ain't going to tote, go on and set up the wash pot," the first said.

"You, Sarty!" the second shouted. "Set up the wash pot!" His father appeared at the door, framed against that shabbiness, as he had been against that other bland perfection, impervious to either, the mother's anxious face at his shoulder.

"Go on," the father said. "Pick it up." The two sisters stooped, broad, lethargic; stooping, they presented an incredible expanse of pale cloch and a flutter of tawdry ribbons.

"If I though enough of a rug to have to git hit all the way from France I wouldn't keep hit where folks coming in would have to tromp on hit," the first said. They raised the rug.

"Abner," the mother said. "Let me do it."

"You go back and git dinner," his father said. "I'll tend to this."

From the woodpile through the rest of the afternoon the boy watched them, the rug spread flat in the dust beside the bubbling wash-pot, the two sisters stooping over it with that profound and lethargic reluctance, while the father stood over them in turn, implacable and grim, driving them though never raising his voice again. He could smell the harsh homemade lye they were using; he saw his mother come to the door once and look toward them with an expression not anxious now but very like despair; he saw his father turn, and he fell to with the axe and saw from the corner of his eye his father raise from the ground a flattish fragment of field stone and examine it and return to the pot, and this time his mother actually spoke: "Abner. Abner. Please don't. Please, Abner."

Then he was done too. It was dusk; the whippoorwills had already begun. He could smell coffee from the room where they would presently eat the cold food remaining from the mid-afternoon meal, though when he entered the house he realized they were having coffee again probably because there was a fire on the hearth, before which the rug now lay spread over the backs of the two chairs. The tracks of his father's foot were gone. Where they had been were now long, water-cloudy scoriations resembling the sporadic course of a lilliputian mowing machine.

It will hung there while they ate the cold food and then went to bed, scattered without order or claim up and down the two rooms, his mother in one bed, where his father would later lie, the older brother in the other, himself, the aunt, and the two sisters on pallets on the floor. But his father was not in bed yet. The last thing the boy remembered was the depthless, harsh silhouette of the hat and coat bending over the rug and it seemed to him that he had not even closed his eyes when the silhouette was standing over him, the fire almost dead behind it, the stiff foot prodding him awake. "Catch up the mule," his father said.

When he returned with the mule his father was standing in the black door, the rolled rug over his shoulder. "Ain't you going to ride?" he said.

"No. Give me your foot."

He bent his knee into this father's hand, the wiry, surprising power flowed smoothly, rising, he rising with it, on to the mule's bare back (they had owned a saddle once; the boy could remember it though not when or where) and with the same effortlessness his father swung the rug up in front of him. Now in the starlight they retraced the afternoon's path, up the dusty road rife with honeysuckle, through the gate and up the black tunnel of the drive to the lightless house, where he sat on the mule and felt the rough warp of the rug drag across his thighs and vanish.

"Don't you want me to help?" he whispered. His father did not answer and now he heard again that stiff foot striking the hollow portico with that wooden and clocklike deliberation, that outrageous overstatement of the weight it carried. The rug, hunched, not flung (the boy could tell that even in the darkness) from his father's shoulder, struck the angle of wall and floor with a sound unbelievably loud, thunderous, then the foot again, unhurried and enormous; a light came on in the house and the boy sat, tense, breathing steadily and quietly and just a little fast, though the foot itself did not increase its beat at all, descending the steps now; now the boy could see him.

"Don't you want to ride now?" he whispered. "We kin both ride now," the light within the house altering now, flaring up and sinking. *He's coming down the stairs now*, he thought. He had already ridden the mule up beside the horse block; presently his father was up behind him and he doubled the reins over and slashed the mule across the neck, but before the animal could begin to trot the hard, thin arm came round him, the hard, knotted hand jerking the mule back to a walk.

In the first red rays of the sun they were in the lot, putting plow gear on the mules. This time the sorrel mare was in the lot before he heard it at all, the rider collarless and even bareheaded, trembling, speaking in a shaking voice as the woman in the house had done, his father merely looking up once before stooping again to the hame he was buckling, so that the man on the mare spoke to his stooping back:

"You must realize you have ruined that rug. Wasn't there anybody here, any of your women . . ." he ceased, shaking, the boy watching him, the older brother leaning now in the stable door, chewing, blinking slowly and steadily at nothing apparently. "It cost a hundred dollars. But you never had a hundred dollars. You never will. So I'm going to charge you twenty bushels of corn against your crop. I'll add it in your contract and when you come to the commissary you can sign it. That won't keep Mrs. de Spain quiet but maybe it will teach you to wipe your feet off before you enter her house again."

Then he was gone. The boy looked at his father, who still had not spoken or even looked up again, who was now adjusting the logger-head in the hame.

"Pap," he said. His father looked at him—the inscrutable face, the shaggy brows beneath which the gray eyes glinted coldly. Suddenly the boy went toward him, fast, stopping as suddenly. "You done the best you could" he cried. "If he wanted hit done different why didn't he wait and tell you how? He won't git no twenty bushels! He won't git none! We'll gether hit and hide hit! I kin watch . . ."

"Did you put the cutter back in that straight stock like I told you?"

"No, sir," he said.

"Then go do it."

That was Wednesday. During the rest of that week he worked steadily, at what was within his scope and some which was beyond it, with an industry that did not need to be driven nor even commanded twice; he had this from his mother, with the difference that some at least of what he did he liked to do, such as splitting wood with the half-size axe which his mother and aunt had earned, or saved money somehow, to present him with at Christmas. In company with the two older women (and on one afternoon, even one of the sisters), he built pens for the shoat and the cow which were a part of his father's contract with the landlord, and one afternoon, his father being absent, gone somewhere on one of the mules, he went to the field.

They were running a middle buster now, his brother holding the plow straight while he handled the reins, and walking beside the straining mule, the rich black soil shearing cool and damp against his bare ankles, he thought *Maybe this is the end of it. Maybe even that twenty bushels that seems hard to have to pay for just a rug will be a cheap price for him to stop forever and always from being what he used to be;* thinking, dreaming now, so that his brother had to speak sharply to him to mind the mule: *Maybe he even won't collect the twenty bushels. Maybe it will all add up and balance and vanish—corn, rug, fire; the terror and grief, the being pulled two ways like between two teams of horses—gone, done with for ever and ever.*

Then it was Saturday; he looked up from beneath the mule he was harnessing and saw his father in the black coat and hat. "Not that," his father said. "The wagon gear." And then, two hours later, sitting in the wagon bed behind his father and brother on the seat, the wagon accomplished a final curve, and he saw the weathered paintless store with its tattered tobacco- and patent-medicine posters and the tethered wagons and saddle animals below the gallery. He mounted the gnawed steps behind his father and brother, and there again was the lane of quiet, watching faces for the three of them to walk through. He saw the man in spectacles sitting at the plank table and he did not need to be told this was a Justice of the Peace; he sent one glare of fierce, exultant, partisan defiance at the man in collar and cravat now, whom he had seen but twice before in his life, and that on a galloping horse, who now wore on his face an expression not of rage but of amazed unbelief which the boy could not have known was at the incredible circumstance of being sued by one of his own tenants, and came and stood against his father and cried at the Justice: "He ain't done it! He ain't burnt..."

"Go back to the wagon," his father said.

"Burnt?" the Justice said. "Do I understand this rug was burned too?"

"Does anybody here claim it was?" his father said. "Go back to the wagon." But he did not, he merely retreated to the rear of the room, crowded as that other had been, not to sit down this time, instead, to stand pressing among the motionless bodies, listening to the voices:

"And you claim twenty bushels of corn is too high for the damage you did to the rug?"

"He brought the rug to me and said he wanted the tracks washed out of it. I washed the tracks out and took the rug back to him."

"But you didn't carry the rug back to him in the same condition it was in before you made the tracks on it."

His father did not answer, and now for perhaps half a minute there was no sound at all save that of breathing, the faint, steady suspiration of complete and intent listening.

"You decline to answer that, Mr. Snopes?" Again his father did not answer. "I'm going to find against you, Mr. Snopes. I'm going to find that you were responsible for the injury to Major de Spain's rug and hold you liable for it. But twenty bushels of corn seems a little high for a man in your circumstances to have to pay. Major de Spain claims it cost a hundred dollars. October corn will be worth about fifty cents. I figure that if Major de Spain can stand a ninety-five-dollar loss on something he paid cash for, you can stand a five-dollar loss you haven't earned yet. I hold you in damages to Major de Spain to the amount of ten bushels of corn over and above your contract with him, to be paid to him out of your crop at gathering time. Court adjourned."

It had taken no time hardly, the morning was but half begun. He thought they would return home and perhaps back to the field, since they were late, far behind all other farmers. But instead his father passed on behind the wagon, merely indicating with his hand for the older brother to follow with it, and crossed the road toward the blacksmith shop opposite, pressing on after his father, overtaking him, speaking, whispering up at the harsh, calm face beneath the weathered hat: "He won't git no ten bushels neither. He won't git one. We'll . . ." until his father glanced for an instant down at him, the face absolutely calm, the grizzled eyebrows tangled above the cold eyes, the voice almost pleasant, almost gentle:

"You think so? Well, we'll wait till October anyway."

The matter of the wagon—the setting of a spoke or two and the tightening of the tires—did not take long either, the business of the tires accomplished by driving the wagon into the spring branch behind the shop and letting it stand there, the mules nuzzling into the water from time to time, and the boy on the seat with the idle reins, looking up the slope and through the sooty tunnel of the shed where the slow hammer rang and where his father sat on an upended cypress bolt, easily, either talking or listening, still sitting there when the boy brought the dripping wagon up out of the branch and halted it before the door.

"Take them on to the shade and hitch," his father said. He did so and returned. His father and the smith and a third man squatting on his heels inside the door were talking, about crops and animals; the boy, squatting too in the ammoniac dust and hoof-parings and scales of rust, heard his father tell a long and unhurried story out of the time before the birth of the older brother even when he had been a professional horsetrader. And then his father came up beside him where he stood before a tattered last year's circus poster on the other side of the store, gazing rapt and quiet at the scarlet horses, the incredible poisings and convolutions of tulle and tights and the painted leers of comedians, and said "It's time to eat."

But not at home. Squatting beside his brother against the front wall, he watched his father emerge from the store and produce from a paper sack a segment of cheese and divide it carefully and deliberately into three with his pocket knife and produce crackers from the same sack. They all three squatted on the gallery and ate, slowly, without talking; then in the store again, they drank from a tin dipper tepid water smelling of the cedar bucket and of living beech trees. And still they did not go home. It was a horse lot this time, a tall rail fence upon and along which men stood and sat and out of which one by one horses were led, to be walked and trotted and then cantered back and forth along the road while the slow swapping and buying went on and the sun began to slant westward, they—the three of them—watching and listening, the older brother with his muddy eyes and his steady, inevitable tobacco, the father commenting now and then on certain of the animals, to no one in particular.

It was after sundown when they reached home. They ate supper by lamplight, then, sitting on the doorstep, the boy watched the night fully accomplish, listening to the whippoorwills and the frogs, when he heard his mother's voice: "Abner! No! No! Oh, God. Oh, God. Abner!" and he rose, whirled, and saw the altered light through the door where a candle stub now burned in a bottle neck on the table and his father, still in the hat and coat, at once formal and burlesque as though dressed carefully for some shabby and ceremonial violence, emptying the reservoir of the lamp back into the five-gallon kerosene can from which it had been filled, while the mother tugged at his arm until he shifted the lamp to the other hand and flung her back, not savagely or viciously, just hard, into the wall, her hands flung out against the wall for balance, her mouth open and in her face the same quality of hopeless despair as had been in her voice. Then his father saw him standing in the door.

"Go to the barn and get that can of oil we were oiling the wagon with," he said. The boy did not move. Then he could speak.

"What . . ." he cried. "What are you . . ."

"Go get that oil," his father said. "Go."

Then he was moving, running, outside the house, toward the stable: this is the old habit, the old blood which he had not been permitted to choose for himself, which had been bequeathed him willy nilly and which had run for so long (and who knew where, battening on what of outrage and savagery and lust) before it came to him. *I could keep on*, he thought. *I could run on and on and never look back, never need to see his face again. Only I can't. I can't*, the rusted can in his hand now, the liquid sploshing in it as he ran back to the house and into it, into the sound of his mother's weeping in the next room, and handed the can to his father.

"Ain't you going to even send a nigger?" he cried. "At least you sent a nigger before!"

This time his father didn't strike him. The hand came even faster than the blow had, the same hand which had set the can on the table with almost excruciating care flashing from the can toward him too quick for him to follow it, gripping him by the back of his shirt and on to tipetoe before he had seen it quit the can, the face stooping at him in breathless and frozen ferocity, the cold, dead voice speaking over him to the older brother who leaned against the table, chewing with that steady, curious, sidewise motion of cows:

"Empty the can into the big one and go on. I'll catch up with you."

"Better tie him up to the bedpost," the brother said.

"Do like I told you," the father said. Then the boy was moving, his bunched shirt and the hard, bony hand between his shoulder-blades, his toes just touching the floor, across the room and into the other one, past the sisters sitting with spread heavy thighs in the two chairs over the cold hearth, and to where his mother and aunt sat side by side on the bed, the aunt's arms about his mother's shoulders.

"Hold him," the father said. The aunt made a startled movement. "Not you," the father said. "Lennie. Take hold of him. I want to see you do it." His mother took him by the wrist. "You'll hold him better than that. If he gets loose don't you know what he is going to do? He will go up yonder." He jerked his head toward the road. "Maybe I'd better tie him."

"I'll hold him," his mother whispered.

"See you do then." Then his father was gone, the stiff foot heavy and measured upon the boards, ceasing at last.

Then he began to struggle. His mother caught him in both arms, he jerking and wrenching at them. He would be stronger in the end, he knew that. But he had no time to wait for it. "Lemme go!" he cried. "I don't want to have to hit you!"

"Let him go!" the aunt said. "If he don't go, before God, I am going there myself!"

"Don't you see I can't!" his mother cried. "Sarty! Sarty! No! No! Help me, Lizzie!"

Then he was free. His aunt grasped at him but it was too late. He whirled, running, his mother stumbled forward on to her knees behind him, crying to the nearer sister: "Catch him, Net! Catch him!" But that was too late too, the sister (the sisters were twins, born at the same time, yet either of them now gave the impression of being, encompassing as much living meat and volume and weight as any other two of the family) not yet having begun to rise from the chair, her head, face, alone merely turned, presenting to him in the flying instant an astonishing expanse of young female features untroubled by any surprise even, wearing only an expression of bovine interest. Then he was out of the room, out of the house, in the mild dust of the starlit road and the heavy rifeness of honeysuckle, the pale ribbon unspooling with terrific slowness under his running feet, reaching the gate at last and turning in, running, his heart and lungs drumming, on up the drive toward the lighted house, the lighted door. He did not knock, he burst in, sobbing for breath, incapable for the moment of speech; he saw the astonished face of the Negro in the linen jacket without knowing when the Negro had appeared.

"De Spain!" he cried, panted. "Where's . . ." then he saw the white man too emerging from a white door down the hall. "Barn!" he cried. "Barn!"

"What?" the white man said. "Barn?"

"Yes!" the boy cried. "Barn!"

"Catch him!" the white man shouted.

But it was too late this time too. The Negro grasped his shirt, but the entire sleeve, rotten with washing, carried away, and he was out that door too and in the drive again, and had actually never ceased to run even while he was screaming into the while man's face.

Behind him the white man was shouting, "My horse! Fetch my horse!" and he thought for an instant of cutting across the park and climbing the fence into the road, but he did not know the park nor how high the vine-massed fence might be and he dared not risk it. So he ran on down the drive, blood and breath roaring; presently he was in the road again though he could not see it. He could not hear either: the galloping mare was almost upon him before he heard her, and even then he held his course, as if the very urgency of his wild grief and need must in a moment more find him wings, waiting until the ultimate instant to hurl himself aside and into the weed-choked roadside ditch as the horse thundered past and on, for an instant in furious silhouette against the stars, the tranquil early summer night sky which, even before the shape of the horse and rider vanished, stained abruptly and violently upward: a long, swirling roar incredible and soundless, blotting the stars, and he springing up and into the road again, running again, knowing it was too late yet still running even after he heard the shot and, an instant later, two shots, pausing now without knowing he had ceased to run, crying "Pap! Pap!", running again before he knew he had begun to run, stumbling, tripping over something and scrabbling up again without ceasing to run, looking backward over his shoulder at the glare as he got up, running on among the invisible trees, panting, sobbing, "Father! Father!"

At midnight he was sitting on the crest of a hill. He did not know it was midnight and he did not know how far he had come. But there was no glare behind him now and he sat now, his back toward what he had called home for four days anyhow, his face toward the dark woods which he would enter when breath was strong again, small, shaking steadily in the chill darkness, hugging himself into the remainder of his thin, rotten shirt, the grief and despair now no longer terror and fear but just grief and despair. *Father. My father*, he thought. "He was brave!" he cried suddenly, aloud but not loud, no more than a whisper: "He was! He was in the war! He was in Colonel Sartoris' cav'ry!" not knowing that his father had gone to that war a private in the fine old European sense, wearing no uniform, admitting the authority of and giving fidelity to no man or army or flag, going to war as Malbrouck himself did: for booty—it meant nothing and less than nothing to him if it were enemy booty or his own.

The slow constellations wheeled on. It would be dawn and then sun-up after a while and he would be hungry. But that would be to-morrow and now he was only cold, and walking would cure that. His breathing was easier now and he decided to get up and go on, and then he found that he had been asleep because he knew it was almost dawn, the night almost over. He could tell that from the whippoorwills. They were everywhere now among the dark trees below him, constant and inflectioned and ceaseless, so that, as the instant for giving over to the day birds drew nearer and nearer, there was no interval at all between them. He got up. He was a little stiff, but walking would cure that too as it would the cold, and soon there would be the sun. He went on down the hill, toward the dark woods within which the liquid silver voices of the birds called unceasing—the rapid and urgent beating of the urgent and quiring heart of the late spring night. He did not look back.

KATHERINE ANNE PORTER, 1890-1980

Dans les dernières années, les critères littéraires qui accordaient la prééminence aux auteurs masculins sur leurs homologues féminins ont été vigoureusement battus en brèche, surtout par la critique féministe. Mais dès 1965, le critique Louis Auchinloss vit dans un groupe de femmes-écrivains les pionnières et garantes de la littérature américaine. Figuraient sur sa liste Katherine Anne Porter ainsi que Sarah Orne Jewett, Edith Wharton, Willa Cather, Jean Stafford, Carson McCullers et plusieurs autres. Katherine Anne Porter présente peut-être la garantie la plus scrupuleuse sur l'art qu'elle partage avec ses consœurs. Le champ d'inspiration de cette Texane d'origine est relativement réduit. Ses histoires du Sud et du Mexique valent par la force des personnages et du décor. De toutes ses œuvres de fiction qui incluent cinq romans et trois collections de contes, seul un roman, *Ship of Fools*, a pu lui acquérir la faveur d'un large public, grâce en partie à la version cinématographique pourtant édulcorée qui suivit sa publication. Ses préoccupations sont généralement sociales plus que strictement politiques. Dans les sombres années trente, elle vécut en Europe, trouvant plus d'intérêt dans l'Allemagne hitlérienne que dans l'Amérique de Roosevelt. Malgré tout, son « Flowering Judas », écrit à la veille de la Dépression, offrit aux écrivains prolétariens de l'époque un paradigme de l'individu en lutte pour préserver une identité personnelle en butte au pouvoir institutionnel et à l'oppression idéologique, fût-ce le communisme, le capitalisme ou le fascisme.

BIBLIOGRAPHIE SÉLECTIVE. — Hendrick (George), *Katherine Anne Porter*, New York, Twayne, 1965 ; Nance (William), *Katherine Anne Porter and the Art of Rejection*, Chapel Hill, University of North Carolina Press, 1964.

Flowering Judas[1]

Braggioni sits heaped upon the edge of a straight-backed chair much too small for him, and sings to Laura in a furry, mournful voice. Laura has begun to find reasons for avoiding her own house until the latest possible moment, for Braggioni is there almost every night. No matter how late she is, he will be sitting there with a surly, waiting expression, pulling at his kinky yellow hair, thumbing the strings of his guitar, snarling a tune under his breath. Lupe the Indian maid meets Laura at the door, and says with a flicker of a glance towards the upper room, "He waits."

Laura wishes to lie down, she is tired of her hairpins and the feel of her long tight sleeves, but she says to him, "Have you a new song for me this evening?" If he says yes, she asks him to sing it. If he says no, she remembers his favorite one, and asks him to sing it again. Lupe brings her a cup of chocolate and a plate of rice, and Laura eats at the small table under the lamp, first inviting Braggioni, whose answer is always the same: "I have eaten, and besides, chocolate thickens the voice."

Laura says, "Sing, then," and Braggioni heaves himself into song. He scratches the guitar familiarly as thought it were a pet animal, and sings passionately off key, taking the high notes in a prolonged painful squeal. Laura, who haunts the markets listening to the ballad singers, and stops every day to hear the blind boy playing his reed-flute in Sixteenth of September street,[2] listens to Braggioni with pitiless courtesy, because she dares not smile at his miserable performance. Nobody dares to smile at him. Braggioni is cruel to everyone, with a kind of specialized insolence, but he is so vain of his talents, and so sensitive to slights, it would require a cruelty and vanity greater than his own to lay a finger on the vast cureless wound of his self-esteem. It would require courage, too, for it is dangerous to offend him, and nobody has this courage.

Braggioni loves himself with such tenderness and amplitude and eternal charity that his followers—for he is a leader of men, a

1. Première publication dans *Flowering Judas and Other Stories* (1930). Le titre rappelle l'arbre auquel s'est pendu Judas après avoir trahi le Christ (Mathieu 27, 5). Selon la légende le sang de Judas fit éclore des fleurs rouges. L'héroïne se voit ici comme traître à sa religion chrétienne et au mouvement communiste.

2. Le décor est Mexico.

skilled revolutionist, and his skin has been punctured in honorable warfare—warm themselves in the reflected glow, and say to each other: "He has a real nobility, a love of humanity raised above mere personal affections." The excess of this self-love has flowed out, inconveniently for her, over Laura, who, with so many others, owes her comfortable situation and her salary to him. When he is in a very good humor, he tells her, "I am tempted to forgive you for being a *gringa. Gringita!*"[1] and Laura, burning, imagines herself leaning forward suddenly, and with a sound back-handed slap wiping the suety smile from his face. If he notices her eyes at these moments he gives no sign.

She knows what Braggioni would offer her, and she must resist tenaciously without appearing to resist, and if she could avoid it she would not admit even to herself the slow drift of his intention. During these long evenings which have spoiled a long month for her, she sits in her deep chair with an open book on her knees, resting her eyes on the consoling rigidity of the printed page when the sight and sound of Braggioni singing threaten to identify themselves with all her remembered afflictions and to add their weight to her uneasy premonitions of the future. The gluttonous bulk of Braggioni has become a symbole of her many disillusions, for a revolutionist should be lean, animated by heroic faith, a vessel of abstract virtues. This is nonsense, she knows it now and is ashamed of it. Revolution must have leaders, and leadership is a career for energetic men. She is, her comrades tell her, full of romantic error, for what she defines as cynicism in them is merely "a developed sense of reality." She is almost too willing to say, "I am wrong, I suppose I don't really understand the principles," and afterward she makes a secret truce with herself, determined not to surrender her will to such expedient logic. But she cannot help feeling that she has been betrayed irreparably by the disunion between her way of living and her feeling of what life should be, and at times she is almost contented to rest in this sense of grievance as a private store of consolation. Sometimes she wishes to run away, but she stays. Now she longs to fly out of this room, down the narrow stairs, and into the street where the houses lean together like conspirators under a single mottled lamp, and leave Braggioni singing to himself.

1. Petit étranger.

Instead she looks at Braggioni, frankly and clearly, like a good child who understands the rules of behavior. Her knees cling together under sound blue serge, and her round white collar is not purposely nun-like. She wears the uniform of an idea, and has renounced vanities. She was born Roman Catholic, and in spite of her fear of being seen by someone who might make a scandal of it, she slips now and again into some crumbling little church, kneels on the chilly stone, and says a Hail Mary on the gold rosary she bought in Tehuantepec. It is no good and she ends by examining the altar with its tinsel flowers and ragged brocades, and feels tender about the battered doll-shape of some male saint whose white, lace-trimmed drawers hang limply around his ankles below the hieratic dignity of his velvet robe. She has encased herself in a set of principles derived from her early training, leaving no detail of gesture or of personal taste untouched, and for this reason she will not wear lace made on machines. This is her private heresy, for in her special group the machine is sacred, and will be the salvation of the workers. She loves fine lace, and there is a tiny edge of fluted cobweb on this collar, which is one of twenty precisely alike, folded in blue tissue paper in the upper drawer of her clothes chest.

Braggioni catches her glance solidly as if he had been waiting for it, leans forward, balancing his paunch between his spread knees, and sings with tremendous emphasis, weighing his words. He has, the song relates, no father and no mother, nor even a friend to console him; lonely as a wave of the sea he comes and goes, lonely as a wave. His mouth opens round and yearns sideways, his balloon cheeks grow oily with the labor of song. He bulges marvelously in his expensive garments. Over his lavender collar, crushed upon a purple necktie, held by a diamond hoop: over his ammunition belt of tooled leather worked in silver, buckled cruelly around his gasping middle: over the tops of his glossy yellow shoes Braggioni swells with ominous ripeness, his mauve silk hose stretched taut, his ankles bound with the stout leather thongs of his shoes.

When he stretches his eyelids at Laura she notes again that his eyes are the true tawny yellow cat's eyes. He is rich, not in money, he tells her, but in power, and this power brings with it the blameless ownership of things, and the right to indulge his love of small luxuries. "I have a taste for the elegant refinements," he said once, flourishing a yellow silk handkerchief before her nose.

"Smell that? It is Jockey Club, imported from New York." Nonetheless he is wounded by life. He will say so presently. "It is true everything turns to dust in the hand, to gall on the tongue." He sighs and his leather belt creaks like a saddle girth. "I am disappointed in everything as it comes. Everything." He shakes his head. "You, poor thing, you will be disappointed too. You are born for it. We are more alike than you realize in some things. Wait and see. Some day you will remember what I have told you, you will know that Braggioni was your friend."

Laura feels a slow chill, a purely physical sense of danger, a warning in her blood that violence, mutilation, a shocking death, wait for her with lessening patience. She has translated this fear into something homely, immediate, and sometimes hesitates before crossing the street. "My personal fate is nothing, except as the testimony of a mental attitude," she reminds herself, quoting from some forgotten philosophic primer, and is sensible enough to add, "Anyhow, I shall not be killed by an automobile if I can help it."

"It may be true I am as corrupt, in another way, as Braggioni," she thinks in spite of herself, "as callous, as incomplete," and if this is so, any kind of death seems preferable. Still she sits quietly, she does not run. Where could she go? Uninvited she has promised herself to this place; she can no longer imagine herself as living in another country, and there is no pleasure in remembering her life before she came here.

Precisely what is the nature of this devotion, its true motives, and what are its obligations? Laura cannot say. She spends part of her days in Xochimilco, near by, teaching the Indian children to say in English, "The cat is on the mat." When she appears in the classroom they crowd about her with smiles on their wise, innocent, clay-colored faces, crying, "Good morning, my titcher!" in immaculate voices, and they make of her desk a fresh garden of flowers every day.

During her leisure she goes to union meetings and listens to busy important voices quarreling over tactics, methods, internal politics. She visits the prisoners of her own political faith in their cells, where they entertain themselves with counting cockroaches, repenting of their indiscretions, composing their memoirs, writing out manifestos and plans for their comrades who are still walking about free, hands in pockets, sniffing fresh air. Laura brings them food and cigarettes and a little money, and she brings messages disguised in equivocal phrases from the men outside who dare not set foot in the prison for fear of disappearing into the cells kept empty for them. If the prisoners confuse night and day, and complain, "Dear little Laura, time doesn't pass in this infernal hole, and I won't know when it is time to sleep unless I have a reminder," she brings them their favorite narcotics, and says in a tone that does not wound them with pity, "Tonight will really be night for you," and though her Spanish amuses them, they find her comforting, useful. If they lose patience and all faith, and curse the slowness of their friends in coming to their rescue with money and influence, they trust her not to repeat everything, and if she inquires, "Where do you think we can find money, or influence?" they are certain to answer, "Well, there is Braggioni, why doesn't he do something?"

She smuggles letters from headquarters to men hiding from firing squads in back streets in mildewed houses, where they sit in tumbled beds and talk bitterly as if all Mexico were at their heels, when Laura knows positively they might appear at the band concert in the Alameda on Sunday morning, and no one would notice them. But Braggioni says, "Let them sweat a little. The next time they may be careful. It is very restful to have them out of the way for a while." She is not afraid to knock on any door in any street after midnight, and enter in the darkness, and say to one of these men who is really in danger: "They will be looking for you—seriously—tomorrow morning after six. Here is some money from Vicente. Go to Vera Cruz and wait."

She borrows money from the Roumanian agitator to give to his bitter enemy the Polish agitator. The favor of Braggioni is their disputed territory, and Braggioni holds the balance nicely, for he can use them both. The Polish agitator talks love to her over café tables, hoping to exploit what he believes is her secret sentimental preference for him, and he gives her misinformation which he begs her to repeat as the solemn truth to certain persons. The Roumanian is more adroit. He is generous with his money in all good causes, and lies to her with an air of ingenuous candor, as if he were her good friend and confidant. She never repeats anything they may say. Braggioni never asks questions. He has other ways to discover all that he wishes to know about them.

Nobody touches her, but all praise her gray eyes, and the soft, round under lip which promises gayety, yet is always grave, nearly always firmly closed: and they cannot understand why she is in Mexico. She walks back and forth on her errands, with puzzled eyebrows, carrying her little folder of drawings and music and school papers. No dancer dances more beautifully than Laura walks, and she inspires some amusing, unexpected ardors, which cause little gossip, because nothing comes of them. A young captain who had been a soldier in Zapata's army[1] attempted, during a horseback ride near Cuernavaca, to express his desire for her with the noble simplicity befitting a rude folk-hero: but gently, because he was gentle. This gentleness was his defeat, for when he alighted, and removed her foot from the stirrup, and essayed to draw her down into his arms, her horse, ordinarily a tame one, shied fiercely, reared and plunged away. The young hero's horse careered blindly after his stable-mate, and the hero did not return to the hotel until rather late that evening. At breakfast he came to her table in full charro dress, gray buckskin jacket and trousers with strings of silver buttons down the leg, and he was in a humorous, careless mood. "May I sit with you?" and "You are a wonderful rider. I was terrified that you might be thrown and dragged. I should never have forgiven myself. But I cannot admire you enough for your riding!"

"I learned to ride in Arizona," said Laura.

"If you ride with me again this morning, I promise you a horse that will not shy with you," he said. But Laura remembered that she must return to Mexico City at noon.

Next morning the children made a celebration and spent their playtime writing on the blackboard, "We lov ar ticher," and with tinted chalks they drew wreaths of flowers around the words. The young hero wrote her a letter: "I am a very foolish, wasteful, impulsive man. I should have first said I love you, and then you would not have run away. But you shall see me again." Laura thought, "I must send him a box of colored crayons," but she was trying to forgive herself for having spurred her horse at the wrong moment.

A brown, shock-haired youth came and stood in her patio one night and sang like a lost soul for two hours, but Laura could think

1. Emiliano Zapata (*ca.* 1879-1919) dirigea une bande de paysans révolutionnaires dans diverses attaques contre le gouvernement en place au cours de la deuxième décennie de ce siècle.

of nothing to do about it. The moonlight spread a wash of gauzy silver over the clear spaces of the garden, and the shadows were cobalt blue. The scarlet blossoms of the Judas tree were dull purple, and the names of the colors repeated themselves automatically in her mind, while she watched not the boy, but his shadow, fallen like a dark garment across the fountain rim, trailing in the water. Lupe came silently and whispered expert counsel in her ear: "If you will throw him one little flower, he will sing another song or two and go away." Laura threw the flower, and he sang a last song and went away with the flower tucked in the band of his hat. Lupe said, "He is one of the organizers of the Typographers Union, and before that he sold corridos[1] in the Merced market, and before that, he came from Guanajuato, where I was born. I would not trust any man, but I trust least those from Guanajuato."

She did not tell Laura that he would be back again the next night, and the next, nor that he would follow her at a certain fixed distance around the Merced market, through the Zócolo, up Francisco I. Madero Avenue, and so along the Paseo de la Reforma to Chapultepec Park, and into the Philosopher's Footpath, still with that flower withering in his hat, and an indivisible attention in his eyes.

Now Laura is accustomed to him, it means nothing except that he is nineteen years old and is observing a convention with all propriety, as though it were founded on a law of nature, which in the end it might well prove to be. He is beginning to write poems which he prints on a wooden press, and he leaves them stuck like handbills in her door. She is pleasantly disturbed by the abstract, unhurried watchfulness of his black eyes which will in time turn easily towards another object. She tells herself that throwing the flower was a mistake, for she is twenty-two years old and knows better; but she refuses to regret it, and persuades herself that her negation of all external events as they occur is a sign that she is gradually perfecting herself in the stoicism she strives to cultivate against that disaster she fears, though she cannot name it.

She is not at home in the world. Every day she teaches children who remain strangers to her, though she loves their tender round hands and their charming opportunist savagery. She knocks at

1. Ballades.

unfamiliar doors not knowing whether a friend or a stranger shall answer, and even if a known face emerges from the sour gloom of that unknown interior, still it is the face of a stranger. No matter what this stranger says to her, nor what her message to him, the very cells of her flesh reject knowledge and kinship in one monotonous word. No. No. No. She draws her strength from this one holy talismanic word which does not suffer her to be led into evil. Denying everything, she may walk anywhere in safety, she looks at everything without amazement.

No, repeats this firm unchanging voice of her blood; and she looks at Braggioni without amazement. He is a great man, he wishes to impress this simple girl who covers her great round breasts with thick dark cloth, and who hides long, invaluably beautiful legs under a heavy skirt. She is almost thin except for the incomprehensible fullness of her breasts, like a nursing mother's, and Braggioni, who considers himself a judge of women, speculates again on the puzzle of her notorious virginity, and takes the liberty of speech which she permits without a sign of modesty, indeed, without any sort of sign, which is disconcerting.

"You think you are so cold, *gringita*! Wait and see. You will surprise yourself some day! May I be there to advise you!" He stretches his eyelids at her, and his ill-humored cat's eyes waver in a separate glance for the two points of light marking the opposite ends of a smoothly drawn path between the swollen curve of her breasts. He is not put off by that blue serge, nor by her resolutely fixed gaze. There is all the time in the world. His cheeks are bellying with the wind of song. "O girl with the dark eyes," he sings, and reconsiders. "But yours are not dark. I can change all that. O girl with the green eyes, you have stolen my heart away!" then his mind wanders to the song, and Laura feels the weight of his attention being shifted elsewhere. Singing thus, he seems harmless, he is quite harmless, there is nothing to do but sit patiently and say "No," when the moment comes. She draws a full breath, and her mind wanders also, but not far. She dares not wander too far.

Not for nothing has Braggioni taken pains to be a good revolutionist and a professional lover of humanity. He will never die of it. He has the malice, the cleverness, the wickedness, the sharpness of wit, the hardness of heart, stipulated for loving the world profitably. *He will never die of it.* He will live to see himself kicked out from his feeding trough by other hungry world-saviors. Traditionally he must sing in spite of his life which drives him to bloodshed, he tells Laura, for his father was a Tuscany peasant who drifted to Yucatan and married a Maya woman: a woman of race, an aristocrat. They gave him the love and knowledge of music, thus: and under the rip of his thumbnail, the strings of the instrument complain like exposed nerves.

Once he was called Delgadito[1] by all the girls and married women who ran after him; he was so scrawny all his bones showed under his thin cotton clothing, and he could squeeze his emptiness to the very blackbone with his two hands. He was a poet and the revolution was only a dream then; too many women loved him and sapped away his youth, and he could never find enough to eat anywhere, anywhere! Now he is a leader of men, crafty men who whisper in his ear, hungry men who wait for hours outside his office for a word with him, emaciated men with wild faces who waylay him at the street gate with a timid, "Comrade, let me tell you . . ." and they blow the foul breath from their empty stomachs in his face.

He is always sympathetic. He gives them handfuls of small coins from his own pocket, he promises them work, there will be demonstrations, they must join the unions and attend the meetings, above all they must be on the watch for spies. They are closer to him than his own brothers, without them he can do nothing—until tomorrow, comrade!

Until tomorrow. "They are stupid, they are lazy, they are treacherous, they would cut my throat for nothing," he says to Laura. He has good food and abundant drink, he hires an automobile and drives in the Paseo on Sunday morning, and enjoys plenty of sleep in a soft bed beside a wife who dares not disturb him; and he sits pampering his bones in easy billows of fat, singing to Laura, who knows and thinks these things about him. When he was fifteen, he tried to drown himself because he loved a girl, his first love, and she laughed at him. "A thousand women have paid for that," and his tight little mouth turns down at the corners. Now he perfumes his hair with Jockey Club, and confides to Laura: "One woman is really as good as another for me, in the dark. I prefer them all."

1. Petit garçon malingre.

His wife organizes unions among the girls in the cigarette factories, and walks in picket lines, and even speaks at meetings in the evening. But she cannot be brought to acknowledge the benefits of true liberty. "I tell her I must have my freedom, net. She does not understand my point of view." Laura has heard this many times. Braggioni scratches the guitar and meditates. "She is an instinctively virtuous woman, pure gold, no doubt of that. If she were not, I should lock her up, and she knows it."

His wife, who works so hard for the good of the factory girls, employs part of her leisure lying on the floor weeping because there are so many women in the world, and only one husband for her, and she never knows where nor when to look for him. He told her: "Unless you can learn to cry when I am not here, I must go away for good." That day he went away and took a room at the Hotel Madrid.

It is this month of separation for the sake of higher principles that has been spoiled not only for Mrs. Braggioni, whose sense of reality is beyond criticism, but for Laura, who feels herself bogged in a nightmare. Tonight Laura envies Mrs. Braggioni, who is alone, and free to weep as much as she pleases about a concrete wrong. Laura has just come from a visit to the prison, and she is waiting for tomorrow with a bitter anxiety as if tomorrow may not come, but time may be caught immovably in this hour, with herself transfixed, Braggioni singing on forever, and Eugenio's body not yet discovered by the guard.

Braggioni says: "Are you going to sleep?" Almost before she can shake her head, he begins telling her about the May-day disturbances coming on in Morelia, for the Catholics hold a festival in honor of the Blessed Virgin, and the Socialists celebrate their martyrs on that day. "There will be two independent processions, starting from either end of town, and they will march until they meet, and the rest depends . . ." He asks her to oil and load his pistols. Standing up, he unbuckles his ammunition belt, and spreads it laden across her knees. Laura sits with the shells slipping through the cleaning cloth dipped in oil, and he says again he cannot understand why she works so hard for the revolutionary idea unless she loves some man who is in it. "Are you not in love with someone?" "No," says Laura. "And no one is in love with you?" "No." "Then it is your own fault. No woman need go begging. Why, what is the matter with you? The legless beggar woman in the Alameda has a perfectly faithful lover. Did you know that?"

Laura peers down the pistol barrel and says nothing, but a long, slow faintness rises and subsides in her; Braggioni curves his swollen fingers around the throat of the guitar and softly smothers the music out of it, and when she hears him again he seems to have forgotten her, and is speaking in the hypnotic voice he uses when talking in small rooms to a listening, close-gathered crowd. Some day this world, now seemingly so composed and eternal, to the edges of every sea shall be merely a tangle of gaping trenches, of crashing walls and broken bodies. Everything must be torn from its accustomed place where it has rotted for centuries, hurled skyward and distributed, cast down again clean as rain, without separate identity. Nothing shall survive that the stiffened hands of poverty have created for the rich and no one shall be left alive except the elect spirits destined to procreate a new world cleansed of cruelty and injustice, ruled by benevolent anarchy: "Pistols are good, I love them, cannons are even better, but in the end I pin my faith to good dynamite," he concludes, and strokes the pistol lying in her hands. "Once I dreamed of destroying the city, in case it offered resistance to General Ortíz, but it fell into his hands like an overripe pear."

He is made restless by his own words, rises and stands waiting. Laura holds up the belt to him: "Put that on, and go kill somebody in Morelia, and you will be happier," she says softly. The presence of death in the room makes her bold. "Today, I found Eugenio going into a stupor. He refused to allow me to call the prison doctor. He had taken all the tablets I brought him yesterday. He said he took them because he was bored."

"He is a fool, and his death is his own business," says Braggioni, fastening his belt carefully.

"I told him if he had waited only a little while longer, you would have got him set free," says Laura. "He said he did not want to wait."

"He is a fool and we are well rid of him," says Braggioni, reaching for his hat.

He goes away. Laura knows his mood has changed, she will not see him any more for a while. He will send word when he needs her to go on errands into strange streets, to speak to the strange faces that will appear, like clay masks with the power of human speech, to mutter their thanks to Braggioni for his help. Now she is free, and she thinks, I must run while there is time. But she does not go.

Braggioni enters his own house where for a month his wife has spent many hours every night weeping and tangling her hair upon her pillow. She is weeping now, and she weeps more at the sight of him, the cause of all her sorrows. He looks about the room. Nothing is changed, the smells are good and familiar, he is well acquainted with the woman who comes toward him with no reproach except grief on her face. He says to her tenderly: "You are so good, please don't cry any more, you dear good creature." She says, "Are you tired, my angel? Sit here and I will wash your feet." She brings a bowl of water, and kneeling, unlaces his shoes, and when from her knees she raises her sad eyes under her blackened lids, he is sorry for everything, and bursts into tears. "Ah, yes, I am hungry, I am tired, let us eat something together," he says, between sobs. His wife leans her head on his arm and says, "Forgive me!" and this time he is refreshed by the solemn, endless rain of her tears.

Laura takes off her serge dress and puts on a white linen nightgown and goes to bed. She turns her head a little to one side, and lying still, reminds herself that it is time to sleep. Numbers tick in her brain like little clocks, soundless doors close of themselves around her. If you would sleep, you must not remember anything, the children will say tomorrow, good morning, my teacher, the poor prisoners who come every day bringing flowers to their jailor. 1-2-3-4-5—it is monstrous to confuse love with revolution, night with day, life with death—ah, Eugenio!

The tolling of the midnight bell is a signal, but what does it mean? Get up, Laura, and follow me: come out of your sleep, out of your bed, out of this strange house. What are you doing in this house? Without a word, without fear she rose and reached for Eugenio's hand, but he eluded her with a sharp, sly smile and drifted away. This is not all, you shall see—Murderer, he said, follow me, I will show you a new country, but it is far away and we must hurry. No, said Laura, not unless you take my hand, no; and she clung first to the stair rail, and then to the topmost branch of the Judas tree that bent down slowly and set her upon the earth, and then to the rocky ledge of a cliff, then to the jagged wave of a sea that was not water but a desert of crumbling stone. Where are you taking me, she asked in wonder but without fear. To death, and it is a long way off, and we must hurry, said Eugenio. No, said Laura, not unless you take my hand. Then eat these flowers, poor prisoner, said Eugenio in a voice of pity, take and eat: and from the Judas tree he stripped the warm bleeding flowers, and held them to her lips. She saw that his hand was fleshless, a cluster of small white petrified branches, and his eye sockets were without light, but she ate the flowers greedily for they satisfied both hunger and thirst. Murderer! said Eugenio, and Cannibal! This is my body and my blood.[1] Laura cried No! and at the sound of her own voice, she awoke trembling, and was afraid to sleep again.

WILLIAM CARLOS WILLIAMS, 1883-1963

Wallace Stevens ne fut pas le seul poète américain moderne à occuper par ailleurs une situation prospère dans une profession non littéraire. Son ami, William Carlos Williams, pédiatre au New Jersey, faisait souvent une pause dans sa journée de travail, pour griffonner quelques vers au dos d'une ordonnance. Outre son ultime legs poétique qui trouve son apogée dans cinq livraisons d'un poème épique sur Paterson dans le New Jersey, Williams produira de nombreuses œuvres de fiction dont quatre romans. C'est aussi un observateur de la culture de son temps. *In the American Grain* est une série d'essais critiques originaux, d'une facture très personnelle, qui le désigne comme chef de file de la tradition néo-whitmanienne. Williams rejette expressément l'intellectualisme d'Eliot en faveur d'une poésie du terroir écrite dans la langue américaine populaire. « No ideas but

1. Le rêve coupable de Laura est difficile à décoder car il s'y mêle les éléments chrétiens et communistes déjà présents dans l'histoire. Le paysage onirique ressemble à l'holocauste de Braggioni avant que ne naisse le « monde nouveau » du communisme. Dans le cauchemar, le communiste Eugenio conduit Laura sur cette scène dévastée, faisant écho aux mots prononcés par Jésus-Christ au cours de la Cène (Mathieu 26, 26-27), et Laura est ainsi un Judas chrétien-communiste dont la trahison peut causer sa mort en prison. Mais le fait qu'elle mange les fleurs ensanglantées de l'arbre de Judas change l'identité d'Eugenio qui devient lui aussi le traître Judas. Finalement, Eugenio peut être aussi le substitut déguisé de Braggioni dans le subconscient coupable de Laura. La représentation de Braggioni en communiste fait aussi allusion au Christ et à la trahison de Judas.

in things » constitue la philosophie pratique de son œuvre. Quand il aborde la nouvelle avec « The Use of Force », les qualités intrinsèques du poète resurgissent au travers de la sensibilité sociale et politique, du prosaïsme factuel qui s'élève à la hauteur d'une fable implicite, et de la concision avec laquelle il met sobrement en lumière les moments privilégiés d'une existence de pédiatre submergé de travail. Le protagoniste est une jeune fille petite mais volontaire. Le docteur, malgré son amour et son respect pour les enfants, succombe à la tentation perverse d'une force supérieure pour devenir un méprisable tyran qui opprime sa patiente au nom de la « nécessité sociale ».

BIBLIOGRAPHIE SÉLECTIVE. — Breslin (James), *William Carlos Williams : An American Artist*, New York, Oxford University Press, 1970 ; Coles (Robert), *William Carlos Williams : The Knack of Survival in America*, New Brunswick, NJ, Rutgers University Press, 1975 ; Ollier (Jacqueline), *William Carlos Williams*, Paris, Les Belles-Lettres, 1979.

The Use of Force[1]

They were new patients to me, all I had was the name, Olson. Please come down as soon as you can, my daughter is very sick.

When I arrived I was met by the mother, a big startled looking woman, very clean and apologetic who merely said, Is this the doctor? and let me in. In the back, she added. You must excuse us, doctor, we have her in the kitchen where it is warm. It is very damp here sometimes.

The child was fully dressed and sitting on her father's lap near the kitchen table. He tried to get up, but I motioned for him not to bother, took off my overcoat and started to look things over. I could see that they were all very nervous, eyeing me up and down distrustfully. As often, in such cases, they weren't telling me more than they had to, it was up to me to tell them; that's why they were spending three dollars on me.

The child was fairly eating me up with her cold, steady eyes, and no expression to her face whatever. She did not move and

1. Première édition dans le *Blast*, revue publiée aux Etats-Unis (1933) et réédité dans *Life Along the Passaic River* (1938).

seemed, inwardly, quiet; an unusually attractive little thing, and as strong as a heifer in appearance. But her face was flushed, she was breathing rapidly, and I realized that she had a high fever. She had magnificent blonde hair, in profusion. One of those picture children often reproduced in advertising leaflets and the photogravure sections of the Sunday papers.

She's had a fever for three days, began the father and we don't know what it comes from. My wife has given her things, you know, like people do, but it don't do no good. And there's been a lot of sickness around. So we tho't you'd better look her over and tell us what is the matter.

As doctors often do I took a trial shot at it as a point of departure. Has she had a sore throat?

Both parents answered me together, No . . . No, she says her throat don't hurt her.

Does your throat hurt you? added the mother to the child. But the little girl's expression didn't change nor did she move her eyes from my face.

Have you looked?

I tried to, said the mother, but I couldn't see.

As it happens we had been having a number of cases of diphtheria in the school to which this child went during that month and we were all, quite apparently, thinking of that, though no one had as yet spoken of the thing.

Well, I said, suppose we take a look at the throat first. I smiled in my best professional manner and asking for the child's first name I said, come on, Mathilda, open your mouth and let's take a look at your throat.

Nothing doing.

Aw, come on, I coaxed, just open your mouth wide and let me take a look. Look, I said opening both hands wide, I haven't anything in my hands. Just open up and let me see.

Such a nice man, put in the mother. Look how kind he is to you. Come on, do what he tells you to. He won't hurt you.

At that I ground my teeth in disgust. If only they wouldn't use the word "hurt" I might be able to get somewhere. But I did not allow myself to be hurried or disturbed but speaking quietly and slowly I approached the child again.

As I moved my chair a little nearer suddenly with one catlike movement both her hands clawed instinctively for my eyes and she almost reached them too. In fact she knocked my glasses flying and they fell, though unbroken, several feet away from me on the kitchen floor.

Both the mother and father almost turned themselves inside out in embarrassment and apology. You bad girl, said the mother, taking her and shaking her by one arm. Look what you've done. The nice man . . .

For heaven's sake, I broke in. Don't call me a nice man to her. I'm here to look at her throat on the chance that she might have diphtheria and possibly die of it. But that's nothing to her. Look here, I said to the child, we're going to look at your throat. You're old enough to understand what I'm saying. Will you open it now by yourself or shall we have to open it for you?

Not a move. Even her expression hadn't changed. Her breaths however were coming faster and faster. Then the battle began. I had to do it. I had to have a throat culture for her own protection. But first I told the parents that it was entirely up to them. I explained the danger but said that I would not insist on a throat examination so long as they would take the responsibility.

If you don't do what the doctor says you'll have to go to the hospital, the mother admonished her severely.

Oh yeah? I had to smile to myself. After all, I had already fallen in love with the savage brat, the parents were contemptible to me. In the ensuing struggle they grew more and more abject, crushed, exhausted while she surely rose to magnificent heights of insane fury of effort bred of her terror of me.

The father tried his best, and he was a big man but the fact that she was his daughter, his shame at her behavior and his dread of hurting her made him release her just at the critical moment several times when I had almost achieved success, till I wanted to kill him. But his dread also that she might have diphtheria made him tell me to go on, go on though he himself was almost fainting, while the mother moved back and forth behind us raising and lowering her hands in an agony of apprehension.

Put her in front of you on your lap, I ordered, and hold both her wrists.

But as soon as he did the child let out a scream. Don't, you're hurting me. Let go of my hands. Let them go I tell you. Then she shrieked terrifyingly, hysterically. Stop it! Stop it! You're killing me!

Do you think she can stand it, doctor! said the mother.

You get out, said the husband to his wife. Do you want her to die of diphtheria?

Come on now, hold her, I said.

Then I grasped the child's head with my left hand and tried to get the wooden tongue depressor between her teeth. She fought, with clenched teeth, desperately! But now I also had grown furious—at a child. I tried to hold myself down but I couldn't. I know how to expose a throat for inspection. And I did my best. When finally I got the wooden spatula behind the last teeth and just the point of it into the mouth cavity, she opened up for an instant but before I could see anything she came down again and gripping the wooden blade between her molars she reduced it to splinters before I could get it out again.

Aren't you ashamed, the mother yelled at her. Aren't you ashamed to act like that in front of the doctor?

Get me a smooth-handled spoon of some sort, I told the mother. We're going through with this. The child's mouth was already bleeding. Her tongue was cut and she was screaming in wild hysterical shrieks. Perhaps I should have desisted and come back in an hour or more. No doubt it would have been better. But I have seen at least two children lying dead in bed of neglect in such cases, and feeling that I must get a diagnosis now or never I went at it again. But the worst of it was that I too had got beyond reason. I could have torn the child apart in my own fury and enjoyed it. It was a pleasure to attack her. My face was burning with it.

The damned little brat must be protected against her own idiocy, one says to one's self at such times. Others must be protected against her It is social necessity. And all these things are true. But a blind fury, a feeling of adult shame, bred of a longing for muscular release are the operatives. One goes on to the end.

In a final unreasoning assault I overpowered the child's neck and jaws. I forced the heavy silver spoon back of her teeth and down her throat till she gagged. And there it was—both tonsils covered with membrane. She had fought valiantly to keep me from knowing her secret. She had been hiding that sore throat for three days at least and lying to her parents in order to escape just such an outcome as this.

Now truly she *was* furious. She had been on the defensive before but now she attacked. Tried to get off her father's lap and fly at me while tears of defeat blinded her eyes.

CARL SANDBURG, 1879-1967

Introduction à Sandburg, p. 331.

The People Will Live on[1]

The people will live on.
The learning and blundering people will live on.
They will be tricked and sold and again sold
And go back to the nourishing earth for rootholds,
The people so peculiar in renewal and comeback,
You can't laugh off their capacity to take it.
The mammoth rests between his cyclonic dramas.

The people so often sleepy, weary, enigmatic,
is a vast huddle with many units saying:
"I earn my living.
I make enough to get by
and it takes all my time.
If I had more time
I could do more for myself
and maybe for others.
I could read and study
and talk things over
and find out about things.
It takes time.
I wish I had the time."

1. De *The People, Yes* (1936).

The people is a tragic and comic two-face:
hero and hoodlum: phantom and gorilla twist-
ing to moan with a gargoyle mouth: "They
buy me and sell me . . . it's a game . . .
sometime I'll break loose . . ."

Once having marched
Over the margins of animal necessity,
Over the grim line of sheer subsistence
Then man came
To the deeper rituals of his bones,
To the lights lighter than any bones,
To the time for thinking things over,
To the dance, the song, the story,
Or the hours given over to dreaming,
Once having so marched.

Between the finite limitations of the five senses
and the endless yearnings of man for the beyond
the people hold to the humdrum bidding of work and food
while reaching out when it comes their way
for lights beyond the prisms of the five senses,
for keepsakes lasting beyond any hunger or death.
This reaching is alive.
The panderers and liars have violated and smutted it.
Yet this reaching is alive yet
for lights and keepsakes.

The people know the salt of the sea
and the strength of the winds
lashing the corners of the earth.
The people take the earth
as a tomb of rest and a cradle of hope.
Who else speaks for the Family of Man?
They are in tune and step
with constellations of universal law.

The people is a polychrome,
a spectrum and a prism
held in a moving monolith,

a console organ of changing themes,
a clavilux of color poems
wherein the sea offers fog
and the fog moves off in rain
and the labrador sunset shortens
to a nocturne of clear stars
serene over the shot spray
of northern lights.

The steel mill sky is alive.
The fire breaks white and zigzag
shot on a gun-metal gloaming.
Man is a long time coming.
Man will yet win.
Brother may yet line up with brother:

This old anvil laughs at many broken hammers.
There are men who can't be bought.
The fireborn are at home in fire.
The stars make no noise.
You can't hinder the wind from blowing.
Time is a great teacher.
Who can live without hope?

In the darkness with a great bundle of grief
 the people march.
In the night, and overhead a shovel of stars for
 keeps, the people march:
  "Where to? what next?"

JOHN STEINBECK, 1902-1968

C'est *The Grapes of Wrath* (1939) du Californien John Steinbeck le chef-d'œuvre littéraire de la Dépression, toujours incontesté, un demi-siècle après sa parution. L'adaptation cinématographique (1940) égale d'ailleurs en puissance son modèle romanesque. Cette épopée américaine pétrie de références implicites aux mythes de la Frontière, à l'exode biblique et à l'aspiration transcendantale du moi américain, a singulièrement éclipsé le reste de son œuvre. Ainsi Steinbeck est tenu pour l'auteur d'un livre qui émerge d'un ensemble indistinct de créations littéraires de second ordre, antérieures et postérieures à une inexplicable œuvre maîtresse. Lorsque fut décerné à Steinbeck le prix Nobel de littérature en 1962, ses détracteurs firent ironiquement observer que l'œuvre de sa vie s'était achevée vingt-trois années auparavant sur un superbe roman. La gloire littéraire de celui-ci est en partie redevable au génie qu'il manifeste, dans la diversité de l'expérience et la fermeté de l'engagement social, à puiser aux sources de l'individualisme américain quand le Rêve était exposé à des dangers sans précédent. Whitman avait entrepris d'écrire son récit épique « Song of Myself », en définissant trois étapes du développement individuel : bien-être physique dans le contact étroit avec la terre, perception aiguë d'une identité génétique dans le sentiment filial, conscience progressive d'une appartenance à l'*oversoul* émersonienne et à la famille humaine. C'est ce même triptyque que l'on décèle dans l'évolution de Tom Joad, à travers les principaux extraits qui suivent. En faisant accéder Tom à l'individualisme d'Emerson et de Whitman, Steinbeck signifie dans son roman le triomphe de l'esprit humain sur la tyrannie multiforme du capitalisme. Celui-ci a trahi les idéaux démocratiques traditionnels de l'homme du peuple contre qui se sont dressés les milieux de la finance, les grandes exploitations agricoles et autres pouvoirs disposant, face aux travailleurs, de moyens illégaux ou paramilitaires.

BIBLIOGRAPHIE SÉLECTIVE. — French (Warren), *John Steinbeck*, New York, Twayne, 1961 ; Lisca (Peter), *The Wide World of John Steinbeck*, New Brunswick, NJ, Rutgers University Press, 1958 ; voir aussi, sur un autre romancier de la peinture sociale : Muraire (André), *Polémique et littérature chez Upton Sinclair*, Paris, Didier, 1982.

The Grapes of Wrath[1]

III

Tom Joad vient de purger une peine de quatre ans pour homicide et il retourne à sa ferme de l'Oklahoma pour découvrir qu'elle a été dévastée par les tourbillons de poussières qui sévissent dans les années trente, et que la banque l'a reprise. En route, il rencontre Jim Casy, un pasteur qu'il a connu autrefois (ses initiales suggéreront des parallèles avec Jésus-Christ). Tom est un être sain et réaliste qui au début du roman ne comprend ni le sentiment de culpabilité sexuelle chez Casy, ni sa vision nouvelle, émersonienne et whitmanienne, d'une humanité transcendantale au sein d'une oversoul *cosmique.*

[... Casy said,] "Tell you what—I use ta get the people jumpin' an' talkin' in tongues, an' glory-shoutin' till they just fell down an' passed out. An' some I'd baptize to bring 'em to. An' then—you know what I'd do? I'd take one of them girls out in the grass, an' I'd lay with her. Done it ever' time. Then I'd feel bad, an' I'd pray an' pray, but it didn't do no good. Come the nex' time, them an' me was full of the sperit, I'd do it again. I figgered there just wasn't no hope for me, an'I was a damned ol' hypocrite. But I didn't mean to be."

Joad smiled and his long teeth parted and he licked his lips. "There ain't nothing like a good hot meetin' for pushin' 'em over," he said. "I done that myself."

Casy leaned forward excitedly. "You see," he cried, "I seen it was that way, an' I started thinkin'." He waved his bony big-knuckled hand up and down in a patting gesture. "I got to thinkin' like this—'Here's me preachin' grace. An' here's them people gettin' grace so hard they're jumpin' an' shoutin'. Now they say layin' up with a girl comes from the devil. But the more grace a girl got in her, the quicker she wants to go out in the grass.' An' I got to thinkin' how in hell, s'cuse me, how can the devil get in when a girl is so full of the Holy Sperit that it's spoutin' out of her

1. Première publication en 1939. Le titre vient d'un chant de la guerre de Sécession, « The Battle Hymn of the Republic » (1862) de Julia Ward Howe (1819-1910) : « Mine eyes have seen the glory of the coming of the Lord / He is trampling out the vintage where the grapes of wrath are stored... » Sur la source biblique, voir Jérémie 25, 30, « The Lord shall roar from on high..., he shall give a shout, as they that tread *the grapes*, against all the inhabitants of the earth ».

nose an' ears. You'd think that'd be one time when the devil didn't stand a snowball's chance in hell. But there it was." His eyes were shining with excitement. He worked his cheeks for a moment and then spat into the dust, and the gob of spit rolled over and over, picking up dust until it looked like a round dry little pellet. The preacher spread out his hand and looked at his palm as though he were reading a book. "An' there's me," he went on softly. "There's me with all them people's souls in my han'—responsible an' feelin' my responsibility—an' ever' time, I lay with one of them girls." He looked over at Joad and his face looked helpless. His expression asked for help.

Joad carefully drew the torso of a woman in the dirt, breasts, hips, pelvis. "I wasn't never a preacher," he said. "I never let nothin' get by when I could catch it. An' I never had no idears about it except I was goddamn glad when I got one."

"But you wasn't a preacher," Casy insisted. "A girl was just a girl to you. They wasn't nothin' to you. But to me they was holy vessels. I was savin' their souls. An' here with all that responsibility on me I'd just get 'em frothin' with the Holy Sperit, an' then I'd take 'em out in the grass."

"Maybe I should of been a preacher," said Joad. He brought out his tobacco and papers and rolled a cigarette. He lighted it and squinted through the smoke at the preacher. "I been a long time without a girl," he said. "It's gonna take some catchin' up."

Casy continued, "It worried me till I couldn't get no sleep. Here I'd go to preachin' and I'd say, 'By God, this time I ain't gonna do it.' And right while I said it, I knowed I was."

"You should a got a wife," said Joad. "Preacher an' his wife stayed at our place one time. Jehovites they was. Slep' upstairs. Held meetin's in our barnyard. Us kids would listen. That preacher's missus took a godawful poundin' after ever' night meetin'."

"I'm glad you tol' me," said Casy. "I use to think it was jus' me. Finally it give me such pain I quit an' went off by myself an' give her a damn good thinkin' about." He doubled up his legs and scratched between his dry dusty toes. "I says to myself, 'What's gnawin' you? Is it the screwin'?'[1] An' I says, 'No, it's the sin.' An' I says, 'Why is it that when a fella ought to be just about mule-ass

1. Argot pour désigner l'acte sexuel.

proof against sin, an' all full up of Jesus, why is it that's the time a fella gets fingerin' his pants buttons?' " He laid two fingers down in his palm in rhythm, as though he gently placed each word there side by side. "I says, 'Maybe it ain't a sin. Maybe it's just the way folks is. Maybe we been whippin' the hell out of ourselves for nothin'.' An' I thought how some sisters took to beatin' theirselves with a three-foot shag of bobwire. An' I thought how maybe they liked to hurt themselves, an' maybe I liked to hurt myself. Well, I was layin' under a tree when I figured that out, and I went to sleep. And it come night, an' it was dark when I come to. They was a coyote squawkin' near by. Before I knowed it, I was sayin' out loud, 'The hell with it! There ain't no sin and there ain't no virtue. There's just stuff people do. It's all part of the same thing. And some of the things folks do is nice, and some ain't nice, but that's as far as any man got a right to say.' " He paused and looked up from the palm of his hand, where he had laid down the words.

Joad was grinning at him, but Joad's eyes were sharp and interested, too. "You give her a goin'-over," he said. "You figured her out."

Casy spoke again, and his voice rang with pain and confusion. "I says, 'What's this call, this sperit?' An' I says, 'It's love. I love people so much I'm fit to bust, sometimes.' An' I says, 'Don't you love Jesus?' Well, I thought an' thought, an' finally I says, 'No, I don't know nobody name' Jesus. I know a bunch of stories, but I only love people. An' sometimes I love 'em fit to bust, an' I want to make 'em happy, so I been preachin' somepin I thought would make 'em happy.' An' then—I been talkin' a hell of a lot. Maybe you wonder about me using bad words. Well, they ain't bad to me no more. They're jus' words folks use, an' they don't mean nothing bad with 'em. Anyways, I'll tell you one more thing I thought out; an' from a preacher it's the most unreligious thing, and I can't be a preacher no more because I thought it an' I believe it."

"What's that?" Joad asked.

Casy looked shyly at him. "If it hits you wrong, don't take no offense at it, will you?"

"I don't take no offense 'cept a bust in the nose," said Joad. "What did you figger?"

"I figgered about the Holy Sperit and the Jesus road. I figgered, 'Why do we got to hang it on God or Jesus? Maybe,' I figgered, 'maybe it's all men an' all women we love; maybe that's the Holy Sperit—the human sperit—the whole shebang. Maybe all men got one big soul ever'body's a part of.' Now I sat there thinkin' it, an' all of a suddent—I knew it. I knew it so deep down that it was true, and I still know it."

Joad's eyes dropped to the ground, as though he could not meet the naked honesty in the preacher's eyes. "You can't hold no church with idears like that," he said. "People would drive you out of the country with idears like that. Jumpin' an' yellin'. That's what folks like."

XVIII

Après différentes épreuves subies dans leur « vieille bagnole » surchargée, sur la route qui va de l'Oklahoma en Californie, et la mort du grand-père et de la grand-mère, les Joad ont traversé le désert Mohave. Dans ce passage se poursuivent les évocations bibliques, suggérant l'arrivée de Moïse (Tom) et de ses disciples sur le mont Pisgah qui domine la Terre promise (Deutéronome III, 27). Faisant écho à l'annonce faite par Moïse que la jeune génération de Josué héritera d'Israël, Tom déclare « who's really seein' it is Ruthie and Winfiel ». Cette nouvelle conscience des liens familiaux révèle que Tom est arrivé à la deuxième étape de l'individualisme whitmanien.

They drove through Tehachapi in the morning glow, and the sun came up behind them, and then—suddenly they saw the great valley below them. Al Jammed on the brake and stopped in the middle of the road, and, "Jesus Christ! Look!" he said. The vineyards, the orchards, the great flat valley, green and beautiful, the trees set in rows, and the farm houses.

And Pa said, "God Almighty!" The distant cities, the little towns in the orchard land, and the morning sun, golden on the valley. A car honked behind them. Al pulled to the side of the road and parked.

"I want ta look at her." The grain fields gloden in the morning, and the willow lines, the eucalyptus trees in rows.

Pa sighed, "I never knowed they was anything like her." The peach trees and the walnut groves, and the dark green patches of oranges. And red roofs among the trees, and barns—rich barns. Al got out and stretched his legs.

He called, "Ma—come look. We're there!"

Ruthie and Winfield scrambled down from the car, and then they stood, silent and awestruck, embarrassed before the great valley. The distance was thinned with haze, and the land grew softer and softer in the distance. A windmill flashed in the sun, and its turning blades were like a little heliograph, far away? Ruthie and Winfield looked at it, and Ruthie whispered, "It's California."

Winfield moved his lips silently over the syllables. "There's fruit," he said aloud.

Casy and Uncle John, Connie and Rose of Sharon climbed down. And they stood silently. Rose of Sharon had started to brush her hair back, when she caught sight of the valley and her hand dropped slowly to her side.

Tom said, "Where's Ma? I want Ma to see it. Look, Ma! Come here, Ma." Ma was climbing slowly, stiffly, down the back board. Tom looked at her. "My God, Ma, you sick?" Her face was stiff and putty-like, and her eyes seemed to have sunk deep into her head, and the rims were red with weariness. Her feet touched the ground and she braced herself by holding the truck-side.

Her voice was a croak. "Ya say we're acrost?"

Tom pointed to the great valley. "Look!"

She turned her head, and her mouth opened a little. Her fingers went to her throat and gathered a little pinch of skin and twisted gently. "Thank God!" she said. "The fambly's here." Her knees buckled and she sat down on the running board.

"You sick, Ma?"

"No, jus' tar'd."

"Didn' you get no sleep?"

"No."

"Was Granma bad?"

Ma looked down at her hands, lying together like tired lovers in her lap. "I wisht I could wait an' not tell you. I wisht it could be all—nice."

Pa said, "Then Granma's bad."

Ma raised her eyes and looked over the valley. "Granma's dead."

They looked at her, all of them, and Pa asked, "When?"

"Before they stopped us las' night."

"So that's why you didn' want 'em to look."

"I was afraid we wouldn' get acrost," she said. "I tol' Grandma we couldn' he'p her. The fambly had ta get acrost. I tol' her, tol' her when she was a-dyin'. We couldn' stop in the desert. There was the young ones—an' Rosasharn's baby. I tol' her." She put up her hands and covered her face for a moment. "She can get buried in a nice green place," Ma said softly. "Trees aroun' an' a nice place. She got to lay her head down in California."

The family looked at Ma with a little terror at her strength.

Tom said, "Jesus Christ! You layin' there with her all night long!"

"The fambly hadda get acrost," Ma said miserably.

Tom moved close to put his hand on her shoulder.

"Don't touch me," she said. "I'll hol' up if you don' touch me. That'd get me."

Pa said, "We got to go on now. We got to go on down."

Ma looked up at him. "Can—can I set up front? I don' wanna go back there no more—I'm tar'd. I'm awful tar'd."

They climbed back on the load, and they avoided the long stiff figure covered and tucked in a comforter, even the head covered and tucked. They moved to their places and tried to keep their eyes from it—from the hump on the comfort that would be the nose, and the steep cliff that would be the jut of the chin. They tried to keep their eyes away, and they could not. Ruthie and Winfield, crowded in a forward corner as far away from the body as they could get, stared at the tucked figure.

And Ruthie whispered, "Tha's Granma, an' she's dead."

Winfield nodded solemnly. "She ain't breathin' at all. She's awful dead."

And Rose of Sharon said softly to Connie, "She was adyin' right when we—"

"How'd we know?" he reassured her.

Al climbed on the load to make room for Ma in the seat. And Al swaggered a little because he was sorry. He plumped down beside Casy and Uncle John. "Well, she was ol'. Guess her time was up," Al said. "Ever'body got to die." Casy and Uncle John turned eyes expressionlessly on him and looked at him as though he were a curious talking bush. "Well, ain't they?" he demanded. And the eyes looked away, leaving Al sullen and shaken.

Casy said in wonder, "All night long, an' she was alone." And he said, "John, there's a woman so great with love—she scares me. Makes me afraid an' mean."

John asked, "Was it a sin? Is they any part of it you might call a sin?"

Casy turned on him in astonishment, "A sin? No, there ain't no part of it that's a sin."

"I ain't never done nothin' that wasn't part sin," said John, and he looked at the long wrapped body.

Tom and Ma and Pa got into the front seat. Tom let the truck roll and started on compression. And the heavy truck moved, snorting and jerking and popping down the hill. The sun was behind them, and the valley golden and green before them. Ma shook her head slowly from side to side. "It's purty," she said. "I wisht they could of saw it."

"I wisht so too," said Pa.

Tom patted the steering wheel under his hand. "They was too old," he said. "They wouldn't of saw nothin' that's here. Grampa would a been a-seein' the Injuns an' the prairie country when he was a young fella. An' Granma would a remembered an' seen the first home she lived in. They was too ol'. Who's really seein' it is Ruthie an' Winfiel'."

Pa said, "Here's Tommy talkin' like a growed-up man, talkin' like a preacher almos'."

And Ma smiled sadly. "He is. Tommy's growed way up—way up so I can't get aholt of 'im sometimes."

They popped down the mountain, twisting and looping, losing the valley sometimes, and then finding it again. And the hot breath of the valley came up to them, with hot green smells on it, and with resinous sage and tarweed smells. The crickets crackled along the road. A rattlesnake crawled across the road and Tom hit it and broke it and left it squirming.

Tom said, "I guess we got to go to the coroner, wherever he is. We got to get her buried decent. How much money might be lef', Pa?"

" 'Bout forty dollars," said Pa.

Tom laughed. "Jesus, are we gonna start clean! We sure ain't bringin' nothin' with us." He chuckled a moment, and then his face straightened quickly. He pulled the visor of his cap down low over his eyes. And the truck rolled down the mountain into the great valley.

XXVIII

Les Joad ont eu des hauts et des bas dans leur recherche d'un travail agricole en Californie. Ils font un bref séjour dans des baraquements de secours du type « Hooverville », tels qu'ils ont été conçus par le Président Hoover pour venir en aide aux sans-abris pendant son désastreux mandat de 1929 à 1932. Ils font ensuite halte dans l'un des camps du gouvernement qui, pour Steinbeck, sert de modèle d'Etat socialiste en miniature. Puis ils arrivent dans une exploitation de pêchers paralysée par la grève où Casy est tué après être apparu comme l'ami « communiste » des travailleurs. Tom tue l'homme qui a abattu Casy. Dans la plantation de coton où Tom s'est réfugié, il rencontre Ma pour la dernière fois. Les réflexions de Tom indiquent qu'il a enfin compris la troisième phase du moi transcendantal de Whitman, que Casy avait exprimée plus tôt dans le roman.

[...] "Hm-m," [Tom] said. "Lookie, Ma. I been all day an' all night hidin' alone. Guess who I been thinkin' about? Casy! He talked a lot. Used ta bother me. But now I been thinkin' what he said, an' I can remember—all of it. Says one time he went out in the wilderness to find his own soul, an' he foun' he didn' have no soul that was his'n. Says he foun' he jus' got a little piece of a great big soul. Says a wilderness ain't no good, 'cause his little piece of a soul wasn't no good 'less it was with the rest, an' was whole. Funny how I remember. Didn' think I was even listenin'. But I know now a fella ain't no good alone."

"He was a good man," Ma said.

Tom went on, "He spouted out some Scripture once, an' it didn' soun' like no hell-fire Scripture. He tol' it twicet, an' I remember it. Says it's from the Preacher."

"How's it go, Tom?"

"Goes, 'Two are better than one, because they have a good reward for their labor. For if they fall, the one will lif' up his fellow, but woe to him that is lone when he falleth, for he hath not another to help him up.' That's part of her."

"Go on," Ma said. "Go on, Tom."

"Jus' a little bit more. 'Again, if two lie together, then they have heat: but how can one be warm alone? And if one prevail against him, two shall withstand him, and a three-fold cord is not quickly broken.' "

"An' that's Scripture?"

"Casy said it was. Called it the Preacher."[1]

"Hush—listen."

"On'y the wind, Ma. I know the wind. An' I got to thinkin', Ma—most of the preachin' is about the poor we shall have always with us, an' if you got nothin', why, jus' fol' your hands an' to hell with it, you gonna git ice cream on gol' plates when you're dead. An' then this here Preacher says two get a better reward for their work."

"Tom," she said. "What you aimin' to do?"

He was quiet for a long time. "I been thinkin' how it was in that gov'ment camp, how our folks took care a theirselves, an' if they was a fight they fixed it theirself; an' they wasn't no cops[2] wagglin' their guns, but they was better order than them cops ever give. I been a-wonderin' why we can't do that all over. Throw out the cops that ain't our people. All work together for our own thing—all farm our own lan'."

"Tom," Ma repeated, "what you gonna do?"

"What Casy done," he said.

"But they killed him."

"Yeah," said Tom. "He didn' duck quick enough. He wasn' doing nothin' against the law, Ma. I been thinkin' a hell of a lot, thinkin' about our people livin' like pigs, an' the good rich lan' layin' fallow, or maybe one fella with a million acres, while a hunderd thousan' good farmers is starvin'. An' I been wonderin' if all our folks got together an' yelled, like them fellas yelled, only a few of 'em at the Hooper ranch—"

Ma said, "Tom, they'll drive you, an' cut you down like they done to young Floyd."

"They gonna drive me anyways. They drivin' all our people."

"You don't aim to kill nobody, Tom?"

"No. I been thinkin', long as I'm a outlaw anyways, maybe I could—Hell, I ain't thought it out clear, Ma. Don' worry me now. Don' worry me."

They sat silent in the coal-black cave of vines. Ma said, "How'm I gonna know 'bout you? They might kill ya an' I wouldn' know. They might hurt ya. How'm I gonna know?"

1. De l'Ecclesiaste, 4, 9-10.
2. Flics.

Tom laughed uneasily, "Well, maybe like Casy says, a fella ain't got a soul of his own, but on'y a piece of a big one—an' then—"

"Then what, Tom?"

"Then it don' matter. Then I'll be all aroun' in the dark. I'll be ever'where—wherever you look. Wherever they's a fight so hungry people can eat, I'll be there. Wherever they's a cop beatin' up a guy, I'll be there. If Casy knowed, why, I'll be in the way guys yell when they're mad an'—I'll be in the way kids laugh when they're hungry an' they know supper's ready. An' when our folks eat the stuff they raise an' live in the houses they build—why, I'll be there. See? God, I'm talkin' like Casy. Comes of thinkin' about him so much. Seems like I can see him sometimes."

"I don' un'erstan'," Ma said. "I don' really know."

"Me neither," said Tom. "It's jus' stuff I been thinkin' about. Get thinkin' a lot when you ain't movin' aroun'. You got to get back, Ma."

"You take the money then."

He was silent for a moment. "Awright," he said.

"An', Tom, later—when it's blowed over, you'll come back. You'll find us?"

"Sure," he said. "Now you better go. Here, gimme your han'." He guided her toward the entrance. Her fingers clutched his wrist. He swept the vines aside and followed her out. "Go up to the field till you come to a sycamore on the edge, an' then cut acrost the stream. Good-by."

"Good-by," she said, and she walked quickly away. Her eyes were wet and burning, but she did not cry.

3 – La Deuxième Guerre mondiale : interim littéraire

Les mesures législatives novatrices du New Deal de Franklin Roosevelt ne réussissent pas totalement à dissiper les conséquences économiques de la Dépression des années trente. Comme les adversaires républicains le dénoncent avec raison au cours de la campagne présidentielle de 1940, agriculture et main-d'œuvre souffrent encore d'une économie en mauvaise santé. (En 1937-1938, le pays a subi une nouvelle crise économique.) Mais Roosevelt est élu pour un troisième mandat, fait sans précédent dans l'histoire des Etats-Unis, au moment où la nation affronte de nouveaux périls liés à son engagement militaire aux côtés de ses alliés traditionnels, en guerre avec l'Allemagne. Les usines d'armement accomplissent en vérité ce que le programme de Roosevelt n'a pu réaliser dans les années trente. Dès 1941, la production de matériel militaire sort la nation de la Dépression.

En littérature, les débuts de la nouvelle décennie voient aussi se prolonger l'idéalisme social du New Deal au milieu des préoccupations quotidiennes. Mais la prise de conscience du temps de guerre contribue à balayer de tels soucis. Faulkner élabore et compose sa saga des Snopes et des McCaslin dans respectivement *The Hamlet* (1940) et *Go Down, Moses* (1942) mais ne publie plus rien d'autre pendant les hostilités.

En 1940, Hemingway fait paraître son roman de la guerre d'Espagne, *For Whom the Bell Tolls,* et participe ensuite à sa troisième guerre, cette fois encore comme correspondant. Le quatrième roman de Thomas Wolfe, *You Can't Go Home Again* (1940) complète à titre posthume sa longue odyssée solitaire en quête de l'identité américaine.

Richard Wright publie son plus grand roman, *Native Son,* en 1940. A la fin de la guerre, il parviendra de nouveau à s'exprimer avec éloquence sur la colère et le désespoir des Noirs américains dans *Black Boy* (1945). Ailleurs, la fièvre patriotique trouble la lucide sérénité de toute écriture littéraire digne de ce nom. Critique et érudition révèlent une identique discrétion. Le témoignage silencieux de pareil déclin littéraire apparaît dans la liste des noms relativement indistincts des lauréats du prix Pulitzer pour la littérature dans les années de guerre. Pour le roman : en 1941, non décerné ; 1942, Ellen Glasgow ; 1943, Upton Sinclair ; 1944, Martin Flavin ; et 1945, John Hersey. Pour le théâtre de ces cinq années : 1941, Robert E. Sherwood ; 1942, non décerné ; 1943, Thornton Wilder ; 1944, non décerné et en 1945, Mary Chase. En poésie les prix allèrent chronologiquement à Leonard Bacon, William Rose Benet, Robert Frost, Stephen Vincent Benet et Karl Shapiro. En 1946, nulle récompense ne fut accordée pour la fiction ou la poésie de l'année précédente, la dernière de la guerre.

Bien qu'écarté de ces prix, Tennessee Williams apparaît pourtant comme un jeune dramaturge promis au succès. Le 26 décembre 1944, est créée à Chicago *The Glass Menagerie* que l'on joue ensuite 561 fois à New York avant son interruption le 3 août 1946. Williams sait traduire avec intensité l'atmosphère qui entoure ses personnages américains, vivant sous la menace de plus en plus précise d'une conflagration. L'action du temps de guerre mettra fin à la vie de son poète-héros. A la fin des hostilités, la vive appréhension des Wingfield à Saint-Louis correspond à ce que T. S. Eliot aurait appelé le « corrélatif objectif » ou l'équivalent dramatique de l'état d'une nation ou du monde entier, « waiting for the sunrise » et pressentant des bombardements.

TENNESSEE WILLIAMS, 1911-1983

Le plus poétique des dramaturges américains, Tennessee Williams est né dans le Mississippi de Faulkner. Comme celui-ci, il hérite de la conscience d'un passé qui déborde sur le présent et constitue un legs à la fois familial et régional. Le trio mémorable des Wingfield dans *The Glass Menagerie,* outre le père absent, se compose de portraits sortis tout droit de la famille de Williams et d'un roman de Faulkner. Sa famille vit en effet à Saint-Louis quand Williams a douze ans. La Dépression abrège ses études à l'Université du Missouri, et comme son ambitieux poète Tom Wingfield, Williams tente d'écrire tout en occupant un emploi rebutant dans un dépôt de chaussures. Redevenu étudiant en 1936, Williams confirme ses débuts prometteurs comme dramaturge avec plusieurs pièces à succès, produites en milieu universitaire. En 1939, il adopte le pseudonyme de Tennessee pour des raisons encore confuses. La précarité de l'emploi le contraint à chercher du travail, de La Nouvelle-Orléans jusqu'en Californie. A la mobilisation de 1940, il est réformé pour insuffisance cardiaque. En même temps, sa carrière d'écrivain prend le chemin de la réussite bien qu'un scénario de *The Glass Menagerie* soit rejeté en 1942. Sans se décourager, il récrit le texte pour la scène. Le grand succès de la pièce en 1945 fait découvrir à l'Amérique son second véritable dramaturge après Eugène O'Neill qui a pris de l'âge. Durant plus de quinze ans, la carrière de Williams prospère grâce au succès qu'obtient presque chaque année l'une de ses nouvelles pièces, bientôt suivie d'une adaptation à Hollywood. Sa dépendance grandissante vis-à-vis de l'alcool et de la drogue le conduit au déclin dans les années soixante et soixante-dix, et à la mort en 1983.

BIBLIOGRAPHIE SÉLECTIVE. — Jackson (Esther), *The Broken World of Tennessee Williams,* Madison, University of Wisconsin Press, 1965 ; Weales (Gerald), *Tennessee Williams,* Minneapolis, University of Minnesota Press, 1965 ; Fayard (Jeanne), *Tennessee Williams,* Paris, Seghers, 1972 ; *Tennessee Williams,* George M. Sarotte, éd., Paris, Album Masques, 1979.

The Glass Menagerie[1]

Dans chacune des sept scènes effectivement transparentes de la pièce, intrigue et évolution des personnages s'insèrent dans une impeccable logique. Dans la première partie (scène 1 à 5), on comprend le trouble d'Amanda qui vit à la fois dans un passé sudiste romantique et un présent terre à terre. La scène 2 appartient à Laura qui est infirme et à son univers d'introvertie au milieu de sa ménagerie de verre. La scène 3 révèle en Tom le poète frustré et l'ouvrier de l'entrepôt. Dans la scène 4, Amanda demande à Tom de présenter à Laura un homme de bien qui puisse subvenir aux besoins de la famille quand Tom sera appelé à servir dans les garde-côtes. Dans la scène 5 Tom annonce la venue d'un sauveur, son camarade de travail Jim O'Connor. La seconde partie (scènes 6 et 7) inclut le dîner offert à Jim (mais Laura est trop inquiète pour y participer) et finalement après dîner, la scène entre Jim et Laura qui valsent avant qu'ils ne brisent la corne de la licorne de verre, incident que Laura appelle « a blessing in disguise », car (comme elle ?) la licorne désormais amputée peut avoir une nouvelle vie et « feel less - freakish ». Le reste de la scène 7 est donné ici dans le dernier extrait.

Nobody, not even the rain, has such small hands.
E. E. Cummings[2]

Characters:

AMANDA WINGFIELD, *the mother*
LAURA WINGFIELD, *her daughter*
TOM WINGFIELD, *her son*
JIM O'CONNOR, *the gentleman caller*

SCENE: AN ALLEY IN ST. LOUIS
PART I. Preparation for a Gentleman Caller.
PART II. The Gentleman calls.
TIME: Now and the Past.

1. Ce texte est la version autorisée par Williams en 1945.

2. Cette citation est de Cummings (« somewhere i have never travelled ») (1931), en éloge de « the power of intense fragility » dans l'univers de la femme. Sans doute une analogie avec l'intense Laura et sa ménagerie de fragiles animaux de verre.

SCENE ONE[1]

[*The Wingfield apartment is in the rear of the building, one of those vast hive-like conglomerations of cellular living-units that flower as warty growths in overcrowded urban centers of lower middle-class population and are symptomatic of the impulse of this largest and fundamentally enslaved section of American society to avoid fluidity and differentiation and to exist and function as one interfused mass of automatism.*

The apartment faces an alley and is entered by a fire-escape, a structure whose name is touch of accidental poetic truth, for all of these huge buildings are always burning with the slow and implacable fires of human desperation. The fire-escape is included in the set—that is, the landing of it and steps descending from it.

The scene is memory and is therefore nonrealistic. Memory takes a lot of poetic license. It omits some details; others are exaggerated, according to the emotional value of the articles it touches, for memory is seated predominantly in the heart. The interior is therefore rather dim and poetic.

At the rise of the curtain, the audience is faced with the dark, grim rear wall of the Wingfield tenement. This building, which runs parallel to the footlights, is flanked on both sides by dark, narrow alleys which run into murky canyons of tangled clotheslines, garbage cans and the sinister lattice-work of neighboring fire-escapes. It is up and down these side alleys that exterior entrances and exists are made, during the play. At the end of Tom's *opening commentary, the dark tenement wall slowly reveals (by means of a transparency) the interior of the ground floor Wingfield apartment.*

Downstage is the living room, which also serves as a sleeping room for Laura, *the sofa unfolding to make her bed. Upstage, center, and divided by a wide arch or second proscenium with transparent faded portieres (or second curtain), is the dining room. In an old-fashioned what-not in the living room are seen scores of transparent glass animals. A blown-up photograph of the father hangs on the wall of the living room, facing the audience, to the left of the archway. It is the face of a very handsome young man in a doughboy's First World War cap. He is gallantly smiling, ineluctably smiling, as if to say, "I will be smiling forever."*

The audience hears and sees the opening scene in the dining-room

1. La description entre parenthèses qui suit fut donnée par Williams.

through both the transparent fourth wall of the building and the transparent gauze portieres of the dining-room arch. It is during this revealing scene that the fourth wall slowly ascends, out of sight. This transparent exterior wall is not brought down again until the very end of the play, during TOM'S *final speech.*

The narrator is an undisguised convention of the play. He takes whatever license with dramatic convention as is convenient to his purposes.

TOM *enters dressed as a merchant sailor from alley, stage left, and strolls across the front of the stage to the fire-escape. There he stops and lights a cigarette. He addresses the audience.*]

TOM. — Yes, I have tricks in my pocket, I have things up my sleeve. But I am the opposite of a stage magician. He gives you illusion that has the appearance of truth. I give you truth in the pleasant disguise of illusion. To begin with, I turn back time. I reverse it to that quaint period, the thirties, when the huge middle class of America was matriculating in a school for the blind. Their eyes had failed them, or they had failed their eyes, and so they were having their fingers pressed forcibly down on the fiery Braille alphabet of a dissolving economy. In Spain there was revolution. Here there was only shouting and confusion. In Spain there was Guernica.[1] Here there were disturbances of labor, sometimes pretty violent, in otherwise peaceful cities such as Chicago, Cleveland, Saint Louis . . . This is the social background of the play.

[MUSIC.]

The play is memory. Being a memory play, it is dimly lighted, it is sentimental, it is not realistic. In memory everything seems to happen to music. That explains the fiddle in the wings. I am the narrator of the play, and also a character in it. The other characters are my mother, Amanda, my sister, Laura, and a gentleman caller who appears in the final scenes. He is the most realistic character in the play, being an emissary from a world of reality that we were somehow set apart from. But since I have a poet's weakness for symbols, I am using this character also as a symbol; he is the long delayed but always expected something that we live for. There is a fifth character in the play who doesn't

1. La guerre d'Espagne éclata le 18 juillet 1936. Le 26 avril 1937, des avions allemands en soutien des Franquistes bombardèrent la ville sans défense de Guernica. La guerre se termina sur la reddition des Loyalistes à Madrid et Valence le 28 mars 1939. La guerre coûta environ 745 000 vies humaines.

appear except in this larger-than-life photograph over the mantel. This is our father who left us a long time ago. He was a telephone man who fell in love with long distances; he gave up his job with the telephone company and skipped the light fantastic out of town . . . The last we heard of him was a picture post-card from Mazatlan, on the Pacific coast of Mexico, containing a message of two words—"Hello—Good-bye!" and no address. I think the rest of the play will explain itself. . . .[5]

SCÈNE 1

Tom réapparaît de manière caractéristique comme narrateur et observateur culturel vers le début de la scène 5, pour créer un climat d'attente aussi bien à Saint-Louis que dans le monde extérieur. Après ce monologue, il parlera à sa mère de la venue possible et espérée d'un gentleman qui doit rencontrer Laura au dîner.

[DANCE MUSIC: "ALL THE WORLD IS WAITING FOR THE SUNRISE!"][2]

TOM [*to the audience*]. — Across the alley from us was the Paradise Dance Hall. On evenings in spring the windows and doors were open and the music came outdoors. Sometimes the lights were turned out except for a large glass sphere that hung from the ceiling. It would turn slowly about and filter the dusk with delicate rainbow colors. The the orchestra played a waltz or a tango, something that had a slow and sensuous rhythm. Couples would come outside, to the relative privacy of the alley. You could see them kissing behind ash-pits and telephone poles. This was the compensation for lives that passed like mine, without any change or adventure. Adventure and change were imminent in this year. They were waiting around the corner for all these kids. Suspended in the mist over Berchtesgaden, caught in the folds of Chamberlain's umbrella—[3] In Spain there was Guernica! But

1. En fait, Tom joue le rôle de commentateur de l'action dramatique à cinq reprises.

2. Ce sont les paroles d'un populaire chant d'espoir de la Dépression. « Sunrise » est remplacé par « bombardements » à la fin du monologue de Tom. L'espérance pascale est également impliquée par « spring » et « Paradise ».

3. Berchtesgaden fut la retraite de Hitler dans les Alpes bavaroises. Le 15 septembre 1938, le Premier Ministre britannique y rencontra le Führer pour discuter de la volonté allemande d'annexer des territoires, autorisant ainsi davantage d'*espace vital*. Deux semaines plus tard à Munich ils signèrent l'accord selon lequel l'Allemagne n'annexerait que la Tchécoslovaquie.

here there was only hot swing music and liquor, dance halls, bars, and movies, and sex that hung in the gloom like a chandelier and flooded the world with brief, deceptive rainbows. . . . All the world was waiting for bombardments!

SCÈNE 7

Le comportement de Jim envers Laura après dîner suscite une grave question pour Amanda. Jim serait-il un beau parleur qui s'amuserait de Laura et aurait inventé l'histoire d'une fiancée, Betty ?

JIM. — Your eyes—your hair—are pretty! Your hands are pretty! [*He catches hold of her hand.*] You think I'm making this up because I'm invited to dinner and have to be nice. Oh, I could do that! I could put on an act for you, Laura, and say lots of things without being very sincere. But this time I am. I'm talking to you sincerely. I happened to notice you had this inferiority complex that keeps you from feeling comfortable with people. Somebody needs to build your confidence up and make you proud instead of shy and turning away and—blushing—Somebody ought to—Ought to—*kiss* you, Laura! [*His hand slips slowly up her arm to her shoulder.*] [MUSIC SWELLS TUMULTUOUSLY.] [*He suddenly turns her about and kisses her on the lips.*] [*When he releases her* LAURA *sinks on the sofa with a bright, dazed look.*] [JIM *backs away and fishes in his pocket for a cigarette.*] [LEGEND ON SCREEN: "SOUVENIR."][1] Stumble-john! [*He lights the cigarette, avoiding her look.*] [*There is a peal of girlish laughter from* AMANDA *in the kitchen.*] [LAURA *slowly raises and opens her hand. It still contains the little broken glass animal. She looks at it with a tender, bewildered expression.*] Stumble-john! I shouldn't have done that—That was way off the beam. You don't smoke, do you? [*She looks up, smiling, not hearing the question.*] [*He sits beside her a little*

1. Dans « PRODUCTION NOTES » à la fin de la pièce, Williams dit qu'il eut pour projet initial « the use of a screen on which were projected magic-lantern slides bearing images or titles ». Bien qu'elles ne fussent pas utilisées, il fournit le contenu de ces images fixes dans le manuscrit publié. Particulièrement intéressantes sont celles qui font ironiquement allusion au Messie de la tradition chrétienne.

Il y a une image de Jim qui, participant à un débat de lycéens porte « a silver cup » (calice). En outre, la légende « Annunciation » apparaît quand Tom (l'ange Gabriel) dit à Amanda (Mary) que Jim O'Connor arrive, et la mission religieuse se renforce par l'autoportrait de Jim en « Superman » portant un candélabre et du vin à Laura. La cérémonie comprend aussi le don qu'il lui fait d'une pastille de menthe (« Life-Saver »). Mais il disparaît de nouveau dans son univers de matérialisme scientifique, tel en somme, un Messie factice.

gingerly. She looks at him speechlessly—waiting.] [*He coughs decorously and moves a little farther aside as he considers the situation and senses her feelings, dimly, with perturbation.*] [*Gently.*] Would you—care for a—mint? [*She doesn't seem to hear him but her look grows brighter even.*] Peppermint—Life Saver? My pocket's a regular drug store—wherever I go . . . [*He pops a mint in his mouth. Then gulps and decides to make a clean breast of it. He speaks slowly and gingerly.*] Laura, you know, if I had a sister like you, I'd do the same thing as Tom. I'd bring out fellows and—introduce her to them. The right type of boys of a type to—appreciate her. Only—well— he made a mistake about me. Maybe I've got no call to be saying this. That may not have been the idea in having me over. But what if it was? There's nothing wrong about that. The only trouble is that in my case—I'm not in a situation to—do the right thing. I can't take down your number and say I'll phone. I can't call up next week and—ask for a date. I thought I had better explain the situation in case you misunderstood it and—hurt your feelings. . . . [*Pause.*] [*Slowly, very slowly,* LAURA'S *look changes, her eyes returning slowly from his to the ornament in her palm.*]

[AMANDA *utters another gay laugh in the kitchen.*]

LAURA [*faintly*]. — You—won't—call again?

JIM. — No, Laura, I can't. [*He rises from the sofa.*] As I was just explaining, I've—got strings on me, Laura, I've—been going steady! I go out all the time with a girl named Betty. She's a home-girl like you, and Catholic, and Irish, and in a great many ways we—get along fine. I met her last summer on a moonlight boat trip up the river to Alton, on the *Majestic*. Well—right away from the start it was—love! [LEGEND: LOVE!] [LAURA *sways slightly forward and grips the arm of the sofa. He fails to notice, now enrapt in his own confortable being.*] Being in love has made a new man of me! [*Leaning stiffly forward, clutching the arm of the sofa,* LAURA *struggles visibly with her storm. But* JIM *is oblivious, she is a long way off.*] The power of love is really pretty tremendous! Love is something that—changes the whole world, Laura! [*The storm abates a little and* LAURA *leans back. He notices her again.*] It happened that Betty's aunt took sick, she got a wire and had to go to Centralia. So Tom—when he asked me to dinner—I naturally just accepted the invitation, not knowing that you—that he—that I— [*He stops awkwardly.*] Huh—I'm a stumble-john! [*He flops back on the sofa.*]

[*The holy candles in the altar of* LAURA'S *face have been snuffed out. There is a look of almost infinite desolation.*] [JIM *glances at her uneasily.*] I wish that you would—say something. [*She bites her lip which was trembling and then bravely smiles. She opens her hand again on the broken glass ornament. Then she gently takes his hand and raises it level with her own. She carefully places the unicorn in the palm of his hand, then pushes his fingers closed upon it.*] What are you—doing that for? You want me to have him?—Laura? [*She nods.*] What for?

LAURA. — A—souvenir...

[*She rises unsteadily and crouches beside the victrola to wind it up.*]

[LEGEND ON SCREEN: "THINGS HAVE A WAY OF TURNING OUT SO BADLY!"]

[OR IMAGE: "GENTLEMAN CALLER WAVING GOODBYE!—GAILY."]

[*At this moment* AMANDA *rushes brightly back in the front room. She bears a pitcher of fruit punch in an old-fashioned cut-glass pitcher and a plate of macaroons. The plate has a gold border and poppies painted on it.*]

AMANDA. — Well, well, well! Isn't the air delightful after the shower? I've made you children a little liquid refreshment. [*Turns gaily to the gentleman caller.*] Jim, do you know that song about lemonade?

"Lemonade, lemonade
Made in the shade and stirred with a spade—
Good enough for any old maid!"

JIM. [*uneasily*]. — Ha-ha! No—I never heard it.

AMANDA. — Why, Laura! You look so serious!

JIM. — We were having a serious conversation.

AMANDA. — Good! Now you're better acquainted!

JIM. [*uncertainly*]. — Ha-ha! Yes.

AMANDA. — You modern young people are much more serious-minded than my generation. I was so gay as a girl!

JIM. — You haven't changed, Mrs. Wingfield.

AMANDA. — Tonight I'm rejuvenated! The gaiety of the occasion, Mr. O'Connor! [*She tosses her head with a pearl of laughter. Spills lemonade.*] Oooo! I'm baptizing myself!

JIM. — Here—let me—

AMANDA. — [*setting the pitcher down*]. There now. I discovered we had some maraschino cherries. I dumped them in, juice and all!

JIM. — You shouldn't have gone to that trouble, Mrs. Wingfield.

AMANDA. — Trouble, trouble? Why it was loads of fun! Didn't you hear me cutting up in the kitchen? I bet your ears were burning! I told Tom how outdone with him I was for keeping you to himself so long a time! He should have brought you over much, much sooner! Well, now that you've found your way, I want you to be a very frequent caller! Not just occasional but all the time. Oh, we're going to have a lot of gay times together! I see them coming! Mmm, just breathe that air! So fresh, and the moon's so pretty! I'll skip back out—I know where my place is when young folks are having a—serious conversation!

JIM. — Oh, don't go out, Mrs. Wingfield. The fact of the matter is I've got to be going.

AMANDA. — Going, now? You're joking! Why, it's only the shank of the evening, Mr. O'Connor!

JIM. — Well, you know how it is.

AMANDA. — You mean you're a young workingman and have to keep workingmen's hours. We'll let you off early tonight. But only on the condition that next time you stay later. What's the best night for you? Isn't Saturday night the best night for you workingmen?

JIM. — I have a couple of time-clocks to punch, Mrs. Wingfield. One at morning, another one at night!

AMANDA. — My, but you *are* ambitious! You work at night, too?

JIM. — No, Ma'am, not work but—Betty! [*He crosses deliberately to pick up his hat. The band at the Paradise Dance Hall goes into a tender waltz.*]

AMANDA. — Betty? Betty? Who's—Betty! [*There is an ominous cracking sound in the sky.*]

JIM. — Oh, just a girl. The girl I go steady with! [*He smiles charmingly. The sky falls.*]

[LEGEND: "THE SKY FALLS."]

AMANDA [*a long-drawn exhalation*]. — Ohhhh . . . Is it a serious romance, Mr. O'Connor?

JIM. — We're going to be married the second Sunday in June.

AMANDA. — Ohhhh—how nice! Tom didn't mention that you were engaged to be married.

JIM. — The cat's not out of the bag at the warehouse yet. You know how they are. They call you Romeo and stuff like that. [*He stops at the oval mirror to put on his hat. He carefully shapes the brim and the crown to give a discreetly dashing effect.*] It's been a wonderful evening, Mrs. Wingfield. I guess this is what they mean by Southern hospitality.

AMANDA. — It really wasn't anything at all.

JIM. — I hope a don't seem like I'm rushing off. But I promised Betty I'd pick her up at the Wabash depot, an' by the time I get my jalopy down there her train'll be in. Some women are pretty upset if you keep 'em waiting.

AMANDA. — Yes, I known—The tyranny of women! [*Extends her hand.*] Good-bye, Mr. O'Connor. I wish you luck—and happiness—and success! All three of them, and so does Laura!—Don't you, Laura?

LAURA. — Yes!

JIM [*taking her hand*]. — Good-bye, Laura. I'm certainly going to treasure that souvenir. And don't you forget the good advice I gave you. [*Raises his voice to a cheery shout.*] So long, Shakespeare! Thanks again, ladies—Good night!

[*He grins and ducks jauntily out.*]

[*Still bravely grimacing,* AMANDA *closes the door on the gentleman caller. Then she turns back to the room with a puzzled expression. She and* LAURA *don't dare to face each other.* LAURA *crouches beside the victrola to wind it.*]

AMANDA [*faintly*]. — Things have a way of turning out so badly. I don't believe that I would play the victrola. Well, well—well—Our gentleman caller was engaged to be married! Tom!

TOM [*from back*]. — Yes, Mother?

AMANDA. — Come in here a minute. I want to tell you something awfully funny.

TOM [*enters with macaroon and a glass of the lemonade*]. — Has the gentleman caller gotten away already?

AMANDA. — The gentleman caller has made an early departure. What a wonderful joke you played on us!

TOM. — How do you mean?

AMANDA. — You didn't mention that he was engaged to be married.

TOM. — Jim? Engaged?

AMANDA. — That's what he just informed us.

TOM. — I'll be jiggered! I didn't know about that.

AMANDA. — That seems very peculiar.

TOM. — What's peculiar about it?

AMANDA. — Didn't you call him your best friend down at the warehouse?

TOM. — He is, but how did I know?

AMANDA. — It seems extremely peculiar that you wouldn't know your best friend was going to be married!

TOM. — The warehouse is where I work, not where I know things about people!

AMANDA. — You don't know things anywhere! You live in a dream; you manufacture illusions! [*He crosses to door.*] Where are you going?

TOM. — I'm going to the movies.

AMANDA. — That's right, now that you've had us make such fools of ourselves. The effort, the preparations, all the expense! The new floor lamp, the rug, the clothes for Laura! All for what? To encertain some other girl's fiancé! Go to the movies, go! Don't think about us, a mother deserted, an unmarried sister who's crippled and has no job! Don't let anything interfere with your selfish pleasure! Just go, go, go—to the movies!

TOM. — All right, I will! The more you shout about my selfishness to me the quicker I'll go, and I won't go to the movies!

AMANDA. — Go, then! Then go to the moon—you selfish dreamer!

[TOM *smashes his glass on the floor. He plunges out on the fire-escape, slamming the door.* LAURA *screams—cut by door.*]

[*Dance-hall musicup.* TOM *goes to the rail and grips it desperately, lifting his face in the chill white moonlight penetrating the narrow abyss of the alley.*]

[LEGEND ON SCREEN: "AND SO GOOD-BYE . . ."]

[TOM'S *closing speech is timed with the interior pantomime. The interior scene is played as though viewed through soundproof glass.* AMANDA *appears to be making a comforting speech to* LAURA *who is huddled upon the sofa. Now that we cannot hear the mother's speech, her silliness is gone and she has dignity and tragic beauty.* LAURA'S *dark hair hides her face until at the end of the speech she lifts it to smile at her mother.* AMANDA'S *gestures are slow and graceful, almost dancelike, as she comforts the daughter. At the end of her speech she glances a moment at the father's picture—then withdraws through the portieres. At close of* TOM'S *speech,* LAURA *blows out the candles, ending the play.*]

TOM. — I didn't go to the moon, I went much further—for time is the longest distance between two places—Not long after that I was fired for writing a poem on the lid of a shoe-box. I left Saint Louis. I descended the steps of this fire-escape for a last time and followed, from then on, in my father's footsteps, attempting to find in motion what was lost in space—I traveled around a great deal. The cities swept about me like dead leaves, leaves that were brightly colored but torn away from the branches. I would have stopped, but I was pursued by something. It always came upon me unawares, taking me altogether by surprise. Perhaps it was a familiar bit of music. Perhaps it was only a piece of transparent glass—Perhaps I am walking along a street at night, in some strange city, before I have found companions. I pass the lighted window of a shop where perfume is sold. The window is filled with pieces of colored glass, tiny transparent bottles in delicate colors, like bits of a shattered rainbow. Then all at once my sister touches my shoulder. I turn around and look into her eyes . . . Oh, Laura, Laura, I tried to leave you behind me, but I am more faithful than I intended to be! I reach for a cigarette, I cross the street, I run into the movies or a bar, I buy a drink, I speak to the nearest stranger—anything that can blow your candles out! [LAURA *bends over the candles.*]—for nowadays the world is lit by lightning! Blow out your candles, Laura—and so good-bye. . . .

[*She blows the candles out.*]

THE SCENE DISSOLVES

V – Nouvelles approches culturelles et expériences littéraires depuis 1945

En 1782, alors que l'union s'était pratiquement faite entre les colonies au moment où s'achevait leur guerre révolutionnaire, le voyageur français St. Jean de Crèvecœur s'enquit, avec sa clairvoyance habituelle, de l'identité des habitants du Nouveau Monde. Ainsi fut formulée la question « qu'est-ce qu'un Américain ? ». A la suite de plusieurs autres guerres, pareille interrogation a été réitérée, mais sans jamais susciter de réponses aussi provocatrices que celles proposées par auteurs et critiques depuis 1945. « Au-delà de l'innocence », tel est le titre qui pourrait s'appliquer au thème omniprésent des œuvres historiques de l'après-guerre. L'Amérique n'était plus l'enfant en bas âge des nations du monde. Elle avait été éprouvée par la vilenie de Pearl Harbour, le génocide nazi et la perte tragique de centaines de milliers de soldats américains tués ou blessés dans une guerre moderne dominée par la technologie. La culpabilité des Américains dans ce carnage fut peut-être égale et sans doute plus effroyable quand leurs forces aériennes larguèrent des bombes atomiques sur les populations civiles de Hiroshima et Nagasaki en août 1945.

Si les Etats-Unis avaient désormais dit adieu à l'état d'innocence, étaient-ils toujours en mesure de préserver l'idéalisme rayonnant du passé, signe d'espoir pour le monde, aux termes des graves et douloureux réexamens de l'après-guerre ? La littérature américaine a joué un rôle primordial dans cette évolution culturelle jusque dans les années cinquante, faisant ainsi écho à la décennie qui suivit le premier conflit mondial. La guerre fut d'abord le thème de romans d'aventures dont les auteurs eux-mêmes étaient souvent des anciens combattants. Les plus intéressantes et durables de ces œuvres firent du champ de bataille le lieu d'une initiation pour le soldat qui cherchait la vérité au milieu des combats. Parmi les premières, deux d'entre elles sont devenues des classiques mineurs : la pièce d'Arthur Miller *All My Sons* (1947) et le roman-fleuve de Norman Mailer, *The Naked and the Dead* (1948). Par ailleurs, *All the King's Men* (1946) de Robert Penn Warren amplifia le thème de l'initiation dans un roman politique majeur. Des poètes méditèrent aussi sur la dérobade morale au combat, ou encore, dans le cas de Robert Lowell, sur les conséquences éthiques que peut avoir à l'arrière l'attitude de l'objecteur de conscience. Certaines de ces œuvres figureront dans notre dernière partie.

Les Etats-Unis assumèrent alors une plus grande maturité parmi les autres nations, en prenant conscience des évolutions sociales, des courants de pensée et des mouvements littéraires européens. Des anciens combattants ayant servi sur les théâtres d'opérations extérieurs tirèrent parti des mesures prises par le gouvernement au titre de la « GI Bill ». Ils poursuivirent assidûment des études et découvrirent avec d'autres des idées stimulantes dans l'existentialisme de Kierkegaard et de Sartre, les romanciers russes et des écrivains américains relativement sous-estimés comme Melville, James et Faulkner, dont la fiction prit une valeur très contemporaine. Existentialisme et nihilisme pénétrèrent les œuvres d'auteurs tels que Ralph Ellison et John Barth. Ellison associa en outre cette vision à l'aliénation du Noir américain et ne fut pas le seul à lier pareil statut à maints aspects du « pluralisme culturel ». L'idéal consacré d'un *melting pot* d'immigrants assimilés fut contrecarré par la notion d'une identité hybride plus complexe, qu'exprime notamment le trait d'union dans Italien-Américain, Polonais-Américain ou Norvégien-Américain, etc. C'est la nouvelle quête du sujet authentique, inscrit dans des origines tant nationales qu'étrangères, qu'entreprirent en particulier les écrivains juifs américains pour découvrir un riche potentiel dans leur culture d'immigrants, l'histoire de leur race et l'oppression nazie. Saul Bellow, Bernard Malamud, Philip Roth et, dans une certaine mesure,

J. D. Salinger, constituent le noyau impressionnant de cette école d'auteurs à succès. Une pression comparable s'exerça aussi dans la littérature régionaliste pour remettre en question l'idée d'une identité américaine indifférenciée. En 1987, *A Literary History of the American West* fit le bilan culturel d'une région dans un volume de 1 400 pages.

L'accession de John F. Kennedy à la présidence en 1960 augurait, dans l'optimisme retrouvé, d'une « nouvelle frontière » de progrès social à l'intérieur, et d'audacieuse exploration de l'espace. Kennedy et son entourage apportèrent charme et intelligence au « Camelot » de Washington, où, 150 artistes ayant été invités à son inauguration, Robert Frost dit son poème patriotique « The Gift Outright ». Le pays était néanmoins troublé par les incertitudes nées de son nouveau rôle de superpuissance. A la crise des missiles soviétiques de Cuba, succéda l'engagement irréfléchi au Sud Viêt-nam, suivi sous la présidence de Johnson d'une escalade qui se termina par un fiasco militaire en Asie du Sud-Est, et creusa dans le pays un fossé profond entre faucons et colombes. Chez les écrivains, ces années de prise de conscience sans précédent se traduisirent par de nouvelles et vastes perspectives. Ils rencontrèrent un large public de lecteurs sensibles aux œuvres qui contestaient non seulement l'esprit militariste, mais aussi le racisme, le sexisme et le puritanisme. Ce renouveau de l'idéalisme américain traditionnel contribua à faire revenir les soldats au pays et créa le climat moral qui força le Président Nixon à démissionner en 1974, après ses faux pas et sa vaine tentative pour étouffer le scandale du Watergate. Faut-il s'étonner que les étudiants des campus aient regretté dans les années quatre-vingt d'être nés trop tard pour participer aux années soixante, pétries d'idéalisme ? Dans cette époque récente, l'esprit de lucre fut élevé au rang de vertu nationale par l'Administration de Ronald Reagan, ex-acteur devenu millionnaire en dollars.

John Barth et quelques autres romanciers pressentirent que l'intensité des remous sociaux et l'hyperactivité littéraire des années soixante conduisaient à « a literature of exhaustion ». Le modèle ontologique et esthétique du réalisme traditionnel semblait ainsi dépassé. Barth et Vladimir Nabokov avaient pris la tête d'expérimentateurs « postmodernes » dont le mouvement esthétique fit éclater, de la fin des années soixante aux années quatre-vingt, le cadre désuet de la « représentation » pour affirmer, comme le dit Barth, « the artificial element in art ». Ils raillèrent ouvertement, ou ignorèrent parfois délibérément, l'illusion dramatique et la causalité sociale d'un « réalisme » suranné.

Pareils efforts ont été soutenus par des critiques américains redevables à la sémiotique de Roland Barthes et au déconstructionnisme de Jacques Derrida. A la fin des années quatre-vingt, il est cependant hasardeux de se prononcer sur la durable vitalité de l'expérimentation littéraire et de l'ingéniosité critique des postmodernistes. L'héritage de Hawthorne, Howells, James et Hemingway d'une part, et de Whitman, Dickinson, Eliot et Stevens d'autre part.,reste bien vivant parmi les nombreux écrivains qui, aujourd'hui, représentent les générations successives depuis 1945.

1 – Au-delà de l'innocence : aliénation, existentialisme et pluralisme culturel dans les années cinquante

Tel qu'il se dégage des œuvres de fiction les plus représentatives, le climat moral de l'après-guerre est soumis à des turbulences qu'il est possible de décrire sommairement : dénonciation virulente de ceux qui ont trahi l'idéal national, maturité des efforts pour sauvegarder ce qui reste de l'innocence, quitte à la retrouver dans les aspects les plus sombres de la réalité présente. Dans *All My Sons,* le héros de Arthur Miller est un ancien combattant idéaliste en proie au soupçon que son père a été un cynique profiteur de guerre. Dans le dénouement, digne de la catharsis d'une tragédie grecque, Miller laisse au public l'impression que les hommes d'affaires américains auront davantage le sens de la dignité humaine en temps de paix. Les protagonistes de J. D. Salinger sont également des idéalistes meurtris, notamment Holden Caulfield dans *The Catcher in the Rye* (1951) qui a connu une immense popularité. Le personnage central en est un adolescent de seize ans. Dans son rêve pastoral, il fantasme sur un champ de seigle qui amortira la chute d'enfants innocents quand, tombant d'une falaise, ils sombreront dans l'expérience des adultes. Si Holden est en fin de compte réconcilié avec le monde des adultes américains, ce n'est pas le cas de Salinger. Il refuse en effet d'autoriser ses éditeurs « à utiliser ses écrits de quelle que manière que ce soit, à l'exception des transcriptions en braille ».

Le héros noir et anonyme de Ralph Ellison se guérit dans *Invisible Man* d'une innocente adhésion à l'optimisme émersonien que la vie a mise à rude épreuve. Il fait l'expérience d'une nouvelle identité et se prépare à retourner aux complexités de son milieu social. Flannery O'Connor conduit ses personnages de Sudistes imprévoyants jusqu'aux confins du mal. Sombre et dévastatrice, sa fiction a provoqué chez les lecteurs américains des années cinquante quelques chocs douloureux alors que le pays recherchait un réconfort moral dans la présidence d'Eisenhower. Enfin, Bernard Malamud fait le portrait d'un Juif américain qui, ayant appris avec horreur l'existence des chambres à gaz dans l'Allemagne de Hitler, trouve l'occasion salutaire de commencer une nouvelle vie et de connaître l'amour dans le ghetto américain.

ARTHUR MILLER, 1915-

Les deux premières influences notables exercées sur Arthur Miller ont été les mauvaises affaires de son père après le krach de 1929 et les encouragements que, jeune dramaturge, il reçut à l'Université du Michigan. Elles ne sont pas étrangères au fait qu'il est devenu auteur célèbre et critique social passionné dans la tradition de Henrik Ibsen. L'adaptation que fit Miller de *The Enemy of the People* fut montée en 1951. Marié en 1940, il put ainsi échapper à l'incorporation au cours de la Deuxième Guerre, bien que ses visites de camps militaires l'eussent familiarisé avec l'atmosphère réelle de l'armée pour écrire son scénario de *The Story of G. I. Joe* (1944) et restituer la camaraderie des soldats dans *All My Sons* (1947). La pièce reçut le prix du New York Drama Critics Circle et révéla pour la première fois son impressionnante maîtrise des personnages et son aisance dans l'art difficile du dialogue. *Death of a Salesman* (1949) constitua une critique encore plus accentuée de la civilisation mercantile en Amérique. Ce fut suivi de *The Crucible* (1953), pièce dans laquelle Miller mit férocement en parallèle les procès de sorcières par les Puritains dans la colonie du Massachusetts, avec la chasse aux sorcières organisée contre les communistes par le sénateur Joseph McCarthy au temps de la Guerre froide. En raison des opinions politiques avancées dont il avait témoigné aussi bien antérieurement qu'à la même époque, Miller fut convoqué en 1956 devant la Commission de la Chambre des Représentants sur les activités anti-américaines. Mais les journalistes se préoccupèrent davantage de photographier sa nouvelle épouse Marilyn Monroe. Refusant de donner les noms de ceux qu'il avait vus lors de réunions du Parti communiste, Miller fut jugé coupable d'outrage au Congrès, mais on cassa le jugement en appel. Il a poursuivi ensuite sa carrière d'écrivain sans être toutefois prolifique. Depuis la mort de Tennessee Williams, Miller est le doyen des dramaturges américains, statut de souverain que confirme son inévitable et récente autobiographie.

BIBLIOGRAPHIE SÉLECTIVE. — Murray (Edward), *Arthur Miller : Dramatist*, New York, Fredrich Ungar, 1967 ; Welland (Dennis), *Miller The Playwright*, London, Methuen, 1983 ; Pasquier (Marie-Claire), *Le théâtre américain d'aujourd'hui*, Paris, PUF, 1978 ; sur le théâtre contemporain, voir aussi Kerjan (Liliane), *Le théâtre d'Edward Albee*, Paris, Klincksieck, 1978.

All My Sons[1]

ACTE II

Intrigues du temps de guerre et du temps de paix se combinent ici en 1947. Steve (« Herb ») Deever et Joe Keller étaient partenaires dans une usine d'armement où ils fabriquaient des culasses pour les avions de chasse P-40. Quand un jour furent produites des pièces défectueuses, Joe resta à la maison, prétendant qu'il avait la grippe et il appela Herb au téléphone pour qu'il les livre malgré tout. Vingt et un pilotes se tuèrent. Herb est toujours en prison, mais Joe a été innocenté. Peu de temps après, le pilote Larry Keller est porté disparu bien qu'il ne fût pas aux commandes d'un P-40. Sa fiancée Ann Deever est retournée dans une ville de l'Ohio espérant épouser Chris Keller, un ancien combattant aussi idéaliste que Larry. Son frère George est aussi présent après la visite qu'il a rendue à leur père

1. Première édition en 1947.

en prison. Celui-ci a déclaré que Joe était complice du crime. George, un avocat, sait qu'il ne peut prouver la culpabilité de Joe à partir d'un simple coup de téléphone, mais Kate, la femme de Joe, dit par inadvertance à George que son mari n'est pas malade depuis quinze ans. L'erreur de Kate bouleverse les données de la situation. La réunion amicale s'interrompt sur le brutal départ de George, tandis que Chris s'affronte violemment à son père dans cette scène proche de la fin de l'acte II.

MOTHER. — [*To* CHRIS, *but not facing them.*] Your brother's alive, darling, because if he's dead, your father killed him. Do you understand me now? As long as you live, that boy is alive. God does not let a son be killed by his father. Now you see, don't you? Now you see. [*Beyond control, she hurries up and into house.*]

KELLER [CHRIS *has not moved. He speaks insinuatingly, questioningly*]. — She's out of her mind.

CHRIS [*a broken whisper*]. — Then . . . you did it?

KELLER [*the beginning of plea in his voice*]. — He never flew a P-40—

CHRIS [*struck. Deadly*]. — But the others.

KELLER [*insistently*]. — She's out of her mind. [*He takes a step toward* CHRIS, *pleadingly.*]

CHRIS [*unyielding*]. — Dad . . . you did it?

KELLER. — He never flew a P-40, what's the matter with you?

CHRIS [*still asking, and saying*]. — Then you did it. To the others.

[*Both hold their voices down.*]

KELLER [*afraid of him, his deadly insistence*]. — What's the matter with you? What the hell is the matter with you?

CHRIS [*quietly, incredibly*]. — How could you do that? How?

KELLER. — What's the matter with you?

CHRIS. — Dad . . . Dad, you killed twenty-one men!

KELLER. — What, killed?

CHRIS. — You killed them, you murdered them.

KELLER [*as though throwing his whole nature open before* CHRIS]. — How could I kill anybody?

CHRIS. — Dad! Dad!

KELLER [*trying to hush him*]. — I didn't kill anybody!

CHRIS. — Then explain it to me. What did you do? Explain it to me or I'll tear you to pieces!

KELLER [*horrified at his overwhelming fury*]. — Don't Chris, don't . . .

CHRIS. — I want to know what you did, now what did you do? You had a hundred and twenty cracked engine-heads, now what did you do?

KELLER. — If you're going to hang me then I . . .

CHRIS. — I'm listening, God Almighty, I'm listening!

KELLER [*their movements now are those of subtle pursuit and escape.* KELLER *keeps a step out of* CHRIS' *range as he talks*]. — You're a boy, what could I do! I'm in business, a man is in business; a hundred and twenty cracked, you're out of business; you got a process, the process don't work you're out of business; you don't know how to operate, your stuff is no good; they close you up, they tear up your contracts, what the hell's it to them? You lay forty years into a business and they knock you out in five minutes, what could I do, let them take forty years, let them take my life away? [*His voice cracking.*] I never thought they'd install them. I swear to God. I thought they'd stop 'em before anybody took off.

CHRIS. — Then why'd you ship them out?

KELLER. — By the time they could spot them I thought I'd have the process going again, and I could show them they needed me and they'd let it go by. But weeks passed and I got no kick-back, so I was going to tell them.

CHRIS. — Then why didn't you tell them?

KELLER. — It was too late. The paper, it was all over the front page, twenty-one went down, it was too late. They came with handcuffs into the shop, what could I do? [*He sits on bench at center.*] Chris . . . Chris, I did it for you, it was a chance and I took it for you. I'm sixty-one years old, when would I have another chance to make something for you? Sixty-one years old you don't get another chance, do ya?

CHRIS. — You even knew they wouldn't hold up in the air.

KELLER. — I didn't say that . . .

CHRIS. — But you were going to warn them not to use them . . .

KELLER. — But that don't mean . . .

CHRIS. — It means you knew they'd crash.

KELLER. — It don't mean that.

CHRIS. — Then you *thought* they'd crash.

KELLER. — I was afraid maybe . . .

CHRIS. — You were afraid maybe! God in heaven, what kind of

a man are you? Kids were hanging in the air by those heads. You knew that!

KELLER. — For you, a business for you!

CHRIS [*with burning fury*]. — For me! Where do you live, where have you come from? For me!—I was dying every day and you were killing my boys and you did it for me? What the hell do you think I was thinking of, the Goddam business? Is that as far as your mind can see, the business? What is that, the world—the business? What the hell do you mean, you did it for me? Don't you have a country? Don't you live in the world? What the hell are you? You're not even an animal, no animal kills his own, what are you? What must I do to you? I ought to tear the tongue out of your mouth, what must I do? [*With his fist he pounds down upon his father's shoulder. He stumbles away, covering his face as he weeps.*] What must I do, Jesus God, what must I do?

KELLER. — Chris . . . My Chris . . .

ACTE III

Chris est allé au parc pour s'interroger sur un possible châtiment de son père. Il revient après qu'Ann eut choqué Kate en lui montrant une lettre de Larry juste avant son accident d'avion. Dans cette tragique scène finale, Chris lit alors la lettre à haute voix.

[KELLER *enters from house.* CHRIS *sees him, goes down right near arbor.*]

KELLER. — What's the matter with you? I want to talk to you.

CHRIS. — I've got nothing to say to you.

KELLER [*taking his arm*]. — I want to talk to you!

CHRIS [*pulling violently away from him*]. — Don't do that, Dad. I'm going to hurt you if you do that. There's nothing to say, so say it quick.

KELLER. — Exactly what's the matter? What's the matter? You got too much money? Is that what bothers you?

CHRIS [*with an edge of sarcasm*]. — It bothers me.

KELLER. — If you can't get used to it, then throw it away. You hear me? Take every cent and give it to charity, throw it in the sewer. Does that settle it? In the sewer, that's all. You think I'm kidding? I'm tellin' you what to do, if it's dirty then burn it. It's your money, that's not my money. I'm a dead man, I'm an old dead man, nothing's mine. Well, talk to me!—what do you want to do!

CHRIS. — It's not what I want to do. It's what you want to do.

KELLER. — What should I want to do? [CHRIS *is silent.*] Jail? You want me to go jail? If you want me to go, say so! Is that where I belong?—then tell me so! [*Slight pause.*] What's the matter, why can't you tell me? [*Furiously.*] You say everything else to me, say that! [*Slight pause.*] I'll tell you why you can't say it. Because you know I don't belong there. Because you know! [*With growing emphasis and passion, and a persistent tone of desperation.*] Who worked for nothin' in that war? When they work for nothin', I'll work for nothin'. Did they ship a gun or a truck outa Detroit before they got their price? Is that clean? It's dollars and cents, nickels and dimes; war and peace, it's nickels and dimes, what's clean? Half the Goddamn country is gotta go if I go! That's why you can't tell me.

CHRIS. — That's exactly why.

KELLER. — Then . . . why am *I* bad?

CHRIS. — *I* know you're no worse than most men but I thought you were better. I never saw you as a man. I saw you as my father. [*Almost breaking.*] I can't look at you this way, I can't look at myself! [*He turns away unable to face* KELLER. ANN *goes quickly to* MOTHER, *takes letter from her and starts for* CHRIS. MOTHER *instantly rushes to intercept her.*]

MOTHER. — Give me that!

ANN. — He's going to read it! [*She thrusts letter into* CHRIS' *hand.*] Larry. He wrote it to me the day he died. . . .

KELLER. — Larry!?

MOTHER. — Chris, it's not for you. [*He starts to read.*] Joe . . . go away . . .

KELLER [*mystified, frightened*]. — Why'd she say, Larry, what . . .?

MOTHER. [*She desperately pushes him toward alley, glancing at* CHRIS.] — Go to the street Joe, go to the street! [*She comes down beside* KELLER.] Don't, Chris . . . [*Pleading from her whole soul.*] Don't tell him . . .

CHRIS [*quietly*]. — Three and one half years . . . talking, talking. Now you tell me what you must do. . . . This is how he died, now tell me where you belong.

KELLER [*pleading*]. — Chris, a man can't be a Jesus in this world!

CHRIS. — I know all about the world. I know the whole crap story. Now listen to this, and tell me what a man's got to be! [*Reads*]. "My dear Ann: . . ." You listening? He wrote this the day he died. Listen, don't cry . . . listen! "My dear Ann: It is impossible to put down the things I feel. But I've got to tell you something. Yesterday they flew in a load of papers from the States and I read about Dad and your father being convicted. I can't express myself. I can't tell you how I feel—I can't bear to live any more. Last night I circled the base for twenty minutes before I could bring myself in. How could he have done that? Every day three or four men never come back and he sits back there doing business. . . . I don't know how to tell you what I feel . . . I can't face anybody . . . I'm going out on a mission in a few minutes. They'll probably report me missing. If they do, I want you to know that you mustn't wait for me. I tell you, Ann, if I had him here now I could kill him—" [KELLER *grabs letter from* CHRIS' *hand and reads it.*] [*After a long pause.*] Now blame the world. Do you understand that letter?

KELLER [*he speaks almost inaudibly*]. — I think I do. Get the car, I'll put on my jacket. [*He turns and starts slowly for the house.* MOTHER *rushes to intercept him.*]

MOTHER. — Why are you going? You'll sleep, why are you going?

KELLER. — I can't sleep here. I'll feel better if I go.

MOTHER. — You're so foolish. Larry was your son too, wasn't he? You know he'd never tell you to do this.

KELLER [*looking at letter in his hand*]. — Then what is this if it isn't telling me? Sure, he was my son. But I think to him they were all my sons. And I guess they were, I guess they were. I'll be right down. [*Exits into house.*]

MOTHER [*to* CHRIS, *with determination*]. — You're not going to take him!

CHRIS. — I'm taking him.

MOTHER. — It's up to you, if you tell him to stay he'll stay. Go and tell him!

CHRIS. — Nobody could stop him now.

MOTHER. — You'll stop him! How long will he live in prison?—are you trying to kill him?

CHRIS [*holding out letter*]. — I thought you read this!

MOTHER [*of Larry, the letter*]. — The war is over! Didn't you hear?—it's over!

CHRIS. — Then what was Larry to you? A stone that fell into the water? It's not enough for him to be sorry. Larry didn't kill himself to make you and Dad sorry.

MOTHER. — What more can we be!

CHRIS. — You can be better! Once and for all you can know there's a universe of people outside and you're responsible to it, and unless you know that you threw away your son because that's why he died.

[*A shot is heard in the house. They stand frozen for a brief second.* CHRIS *starts for porch, pauses at step, turns to* ANN.]

CHRIS. — Find Jim! [*He goes on into the house and* ANN *runs up driveway.* MOTHER *stands alone, transfixed.*]

MOTHER [*softly, almost moaning*]. — Joe . . . Joe . . . Joe . . . Joe . . . [CHRIS *comes out of house, down to* MOTHER'S *arms.*]

CHRIS [*almost crying*]. — Mother, I didn't mean to . . .

MOTHER. — Don't dear. Don't take it on yourself. Forget now. Live. [CHRIS *stirs as if to answer.*] Shhh . . . [*She puts his arms down gently and moves towards porch.*] Shhh . . . [*As she reaches porch steps she begins sobbing, as the curtain falls.*]

RALPH ELLISON, 1914-

Il est patent aujourd'hui que la littérature noire des Etats-Unis a une longue et impressionnante histoire. Mais quand parut *Invisible Man* de Ralph Waldo Ellison en 1952, l'événement fut généralement considéré comme la première révélation d'un génie littéraire parmi ceux que l'Amérique désignait alors sous le terme de *negro*, terme auquel s'est substitué aujourd'hui celui de *black*. Presque homonyme de Ralph Waldo Emerson, l'auteur de *Invisible Man* a donné au monde une œuvre cruciale qui, rappelant Dostoïevsky par sa complexité humaine et sa ténébreuse puissance, élève à une dignité supérieure l'image intellectuelle et l'expression littéraire de sa race. Paul Lawrence Dunbar, Langston Hughes (figure importante de la Renaissance de Harlem dans les années vingt) et Richard Wright, qui exerça sur Ellison une influence déterminante, furent alors découverts et lus plus attentivement. Ellison prépara en somme le terrain pour le succès que rencontra, l'année suivante, le premier roman de James Baldwin, *Go Tell it on the Mountain*. *Invisible Man* reçut rapidement le National Book Award. Même treize ans après, alors qu'on attendait toujours le second roman d'Ellison (et on l'attend encore à la fin des années quatre-vingt), *Invisible Man* se vit attribuer de nouveaux lauriers puisqu'un groupe d'auteurs, de journalistes et de critiques le désigna comme « the most distinguished single work » publié depuis la Deuxième Guerre. Cette opinion fut loin d'être partagée par les leaders noirs en colère, à la fin des années soixante. Ellison était pour eux un Oncle Tom conciliant et son roman une contestation veule du « pouvoir noir » militant. Ils marquèrent aussi leur désapprobation envers l'essai publié par Ellison en 1970 dans l'*Atlantic Monthly* et dans lequel il engageait les Noirs, qu'ils fussent auteurs ou lecteurs, à se considérer comme des Américains doublement bénis. Ils étaient selon Ellison les détenteurs privilégiés d'une culture noire américaine qu'il opposait radicalement à la mode du retour aux sources africaines, et les heureux héritiers des ressources créatrices de la culture commune à tous les Américains.

BIBLIOGRAPHIE SÉLECTIVE. — Gottesman (Ronald), ed., *Studies in « Invisible Man »*, Columbus, Ohio, Charles E. Merrill, 1971 ; O'Meally (Robert), *The Craft of Ralph Ellison*, Cambridge, Mass., Harvard University Press, 1980 ; Fabre (Michel), *La rive noire, de Harlem à la Seine*, Paris, Lieu commun, 1985 ; Ralph Ellison, (M. Fabre, éd.), *Delta*, 18, avril 1984.

Invisible Man[1]

XVI

Le narrateur noir anonyme (« homme invisible ») qui est un étudiant monté à New York, porte innocemment sur lui des lettres de recommandation présumées du président d'une université noire du

1. Première édition en 1952.

Sud, richement subventionnée par un Blanc du Nord. Le président est un « Oncle Tom », type du Noir docile de Uncle Tom's Cabin *(1852), roman classique de Harriet Beecher Stowe sur l'esclavage. Il désapprouve l'esprit d'indépendance du narrateur. Quand l'homme invisible découvre qu'il n'est pas vraiment en possession de lettres de recommandation, il est partiellement guéri de son innocence. Il tombe cependant dans un piège politique quand on le recrute pour son éloquence dans un mouvement marxiste « fraternel » de Noirs et de Blancs. Les leaders, principalement un Blanc appelé « Brother Jack », se préoccupent de la discipline et emploient tous les moyens pour s'arroger le pouvoir politique. Le narrateur présume à tort qu'ils s'intéressent prioritairement à la liberté existentielle des Noirs, à la vraie fraternité et à la prise de parole, gage de dignité humaine. Avec son premier discours public pour le mouvement fraternel au cours d'un meeting dans le quartier noir de Harlem, il reçoit sa deuxième leçon de cynisme racial en politique.*

Someone pulled on my coat sleeve—my turn had come. I went toward the microphone where Brother Jack himself waited, entering the spot of light that surrounded me like a seamless cage of stainless steel. I halted. The light was so strong that I could no longer see the audience, the bowl of human faces. It was as though a semi-transparent curtain had dropped between us, but through which they could see me—for they were applauding—without themselves being seen. I felt the hard, mechanical isolation of the hospital machine and I didn't like it. I stood, barely hearing Brother Jack's introduction. Then he was through and there was an encouraging burst of applause. And I thought, They remember; some of them were there.

The microphone was strange and unnerving. I approached it incorrectly, my voice sounding raspy and full of air, and after a few words I halted, embarrassed. I was getting off to a bad start, something had to be done. I leaned toward the vague audience closest to the platform and said, "Sorry, folks. Up to now they've kept me so far away from these shiny electric gadgets I haven't learned the technique . . . And to tell you the truth, it looks to me like it might bite! Just look at it, it looks like the steel skull of man! Do you think he died of dispossession?"

It worked and while they laughed someone came and made an adjustment. "Don't stand too close," he advised.

"How's that?" I said, hearing my voice boom deep and vibrant over the arena. "Is that better?"

There was a ripple of applause.

"You see, all I needed was a chance. You've granted it, now it's up to me!"

The applause grew stronger and from down front a man's far-carrying voice called out, "We with you, Brother. You pitch 'em we catch 'em!"

That was all I needed, I'd made a contact, and it was as though his voice was that of them all. I was wound up, nervous. I might have been anyone, might have been trying to speak in a foreign language. For I couldn't remember the correct words and phrases from the pamphlets. I had to fall back upon tradition and since it was a political meeting, I selected one of the political techniques that I'd heard so often at home: The old down-to-earth, I'm-sick-and-tired-of-the-way-they've-been-treating-us approach. I couldn't see them so I addressed the microphone and the co-operative voice before me.

"You know, there are those who think we who are gathered here are dumb," I shouted. "Tell me if I'm right."

"That's a strike, Brother," the voice called. "You pitched a strike."

"Yes, they think we're dumb. They call us the 'common people.' But I've been sitting here listening and looking and trying to understand what's so *common* about us. I think they're guilty of a gross mis-statement of fact—we are the uncommon people—"

"Another strike," the voice called in the thunder, and I paused holding up my hand to halt the noise.

"Yes, we're the uncommon people—and I'll tell you why. They call us dumb and they treat us dumb. And what do they do with dumb ones? Think about it, look around! They've got a slogan and a policy, they've got what Brother Jack would call a 'theory and a practice.' It's 'Never give a sucker an even break!' It's dispossess him! Evict him! Use his empty head for a spittoon and his back for a door mat! It's break him! Deprive him of his wages! It's use his protest as a sounding brass to frighten him into silence, it's beat his ideas and his hopes and homely aspirations into a tinkling cymbal! A small, cracked cymbal to tinkle on the Fourth of July! Only muffle it! Don't let it sound too loud! Beat it in stoptime, give the dumb bunnies the solft-shoe dance! The Big

Wormy Apple, the Chicago Get Away, the Shoo Fly Don't Bother Me!"

"And do you know what makes us so uncommon?" I whispered hoarsely. "*We let them do it!*"

The silence was profound. The smoke boiled in the spotlight.

"Another strike," I heard the voice call sadly. "Ain't no use to protest the decision!" And I thought, Is he with me or against me?

"Dispossession! *Dis*-possession is the word!" I went on. "They've tried to dispossess us of our manhood and womanhood! Of our childhood and adolescence—You heard the sister's statistics on our infant mortality rate. Don't you know you're lucky to be uncommonly born? Why, they even tried to dispossess us of *our dislike of being dispossessed!* And I'll tell you something else—if we don't resist, pretty soon they'll succeed! These are the days of dispossession, the season of homelessness, the time of evictions. We'll be dispossessed of the very brains in our heads! And we're so *un*-common that we can't even see it! Perhaps we're too polite. Perhaps we don't care to look at unpleasantness. They think we're blind—*un*-commonly blind. And I don't wonder. Think about it, they've dispossessed us each of one eye from the day we're born. So now we can only see in straight white lines. We're a nation of one-eyed mice—Did you ever see such a sight in your life? Such an *un*-common sight!"

"An' ain't a farmer's wife in the house," the voice called through the titters of bitter laughter.[1] "It's another strike!"

I leaned forward. "You know, if we aren't careful, they'll slip up on our blind sides and—*plop!* out goes our last good eye and we're blind as bats! Someone's afraid we'll see something. Maybe that's why so many of our fine friends are present tonight—blue steel pistols and blue serge suits and all!—but I believe one eye is enough to lose without resistance and I think that's your belief. So let's get together. Did you ever notice, my dumb one-eyed brothers, how two totally blind men can get together and help one another along? They stumble, they bump into things, but they avoid dangers too; they get along. Let's get together, uncommon people. With both our eyes we may see what makes us so uncommon, we'll see *who* makes us so uncommon! Up to now

1. La ronde populaire dit « Three blind mice... / See how they run... / They all ran after the farmer's wife, / She cut off their tails with a carving knife, / Did ever you see such a sight in your life?...

we've been like a couple of one-eyed men walking down opposite sides of the street. Someone starts throwing bricks and we start blaming each other and fighting among ourselves. But we're mistaken! Because there's a third party present. There's a smooth, oily scoundrel running down the *middle* of the wide gray street throwing stones—He's the one! He's doing the damage! He claims he needs the space—he calls it his *freedom.* And he knows he's got us on our blind side and he's been popping away till he's got us silly—*uncommonly* silly! In fact, *his* freedom has got us damn-nigh blind! Hush now, don't call no names!" I called, holding up my palm. "I say to hell with this guy! I say come on, cross over! Let's make an alliance! I'll look out for you, and you look out for me! I'm good at catching and I've got a damn good pitching arm!"

"You don't pitch no balls, Brother! Not a single one!"

"Let's make a miracle," I shouted. "Let's take back our pillaged eyes! Let's reclaim our sight; let's combine and spread our vision. Peep around the corner, there's a storm coming. Look down the avenue, there's only one enemy. Can't you see his face?"

It was a natural pause and there was applause, but as it burst I realized that the flow of words had stopped. What would I do when they started to listen again? I leaned forward, straining to see through the barrier of light. They were mine, out there, and I couldn't afford to lose them. Yet I suddenly felt naked, sensing that the words were returning and that something was about to be said that I shouldn't reveal.

"Look at me!" The words ripped from my solar plexus. "I haven't lived here long. Times are hard, I've known despair. I'm from the South, and since coming here I've known eviction. I'd come to distrust the world . . . But look at me now, something strange is happening. I'm here before you. I must confess . . ."

And suddenly Brother Jack was beside me, pretending to adjust the microphone. "Careful now", he whispered. "Don't end your usefulness before you've begun."

"I'm all right," I said, leaning toward the mike.

"May I confess?" I shouted. "You are my friends. We share a common disinheritance, and it's said that confession is good for the soul. Have I your permission?"

"You batting .500, Brother," the voice called.

There was a stir behind me. I waited until it was quiet and hurried on.

"Silence is consent," I said, "so I'll have it out, I'll confess it!" My shoulders were squared, my chin thrust forward and my eyes focused straight into the light. "*Something strange and miraculous and transforming is taking place in me right now . . . as I stand here before you!*"

I could feel the words forming themselves, slowly falling into place. The light seemed to boil opalescently, like liquid soap shaken gently in a bottle.

"Let me describe it. It is something odd. It's something that I'm sure I'd never experience anywhere else in the world. I feel your eyes upon me. I hear the pulse of your breathing. And now, at this moment, with your black and white eyes upon me, I feel . . . I feel . . ."

I stumbled in a stillness so complete that I could hear the gears of the huge clock mounted somewhere on the balcony gnawing upon time.

"What is it, son, what do you feel?" a shrill voice cried.

My voice fell to a husky whisper, "I feel, I feel suddenly that I have become *more human.* Do you understand? More human. Not that I have become a man, for I was born a man. But that I am more human. I feel strong, I feel able to get things done! I feel that I can see sharp and clear and far down the dim corridor of history and in it I can hear the footsteps of militant fraternity! No, wait, let me confess . . . I feel the urge to affirm my feelings . . . I feel that here, after a long and desperate and uncommonly blind journey, I have come home . . . Home! With your eyes upon me I feel that I've found my true family! My true people! My true country! I am a new citizen of the country of your vision, a native of your fraternal land. I feel that here tonight, in this old arena, the new is being born and the vital old revived. In each of you, in me, in us all.

"SISTERS! BROTHERS!

"WE ARE THE TRUE PATRIOTS! THE CITIZENS OF TOMORROW'S WORLD!

"WE'LL BE DISPOSSESSED NO MORE!"

The applause struck like a clap of thunder. I stood transfixed, unable to see, my body quivering with the roar. I made an indefinite movement. What should I do—wave to them? I faced the shouts, cheers, shrill whistling, my eyes burning from the light. I felt a large tear roll down my face and I wiped it away with embarrassment. Others were starting down. Why didn't someone help me get out of the spot before I spoiled everything? But with the tears came an increase of applause and I lifted my head, surprised, my eyes streaming. The sound seemed to roar up in waves. They had begun to stomp the floor and I was laughing and bowing my head now unashamed. It grew in volume, the sound of splitting wood came from the rear. I grew tired, but still they cheered until, finally, I gave up and started back toward the chairs. Red spots danced before my eyes. Someone took my hand, and leaned toward my ear.

"You did it, goddamnit! You did it!" And I was puzzled by the hot mixture of hate and admiration bursting through his words as I thanked him and removed my hand from his crushing grasp.

"Thanks," I said, "but the others had raised them to the right pitch."

I shuddered; he sounded as though he would like to throttle me. I couldn't see and there was much confusion and suddenly someone spun me around, pulling me off balance, and I felt myself pressed against warm feminine softness, holding on.

"Oh, Brother, Brother!" a woman's voice cried into my ear, "Little Brother!" and I felt the hot moist pressure of her lips upon my cheek.

Blurred figures bumped about me. I stumbled as in a game of blindman's buff. My hands were shaken, my back pounded. My face was sprayed with the saliva of enthusiasm, and I decided that the next time I stood in the spotlight it would be wise to wear dark glasses.

It was a deafening demonstration. We left them cheering, knocking over chairs, stomping the floor. Brother Jack guided me off the platform. "It's time we left," he shouted. "Things have truly begun to move. All that energy must be organized!"

He guided me through the shouting crowd, hands continuing to touch me as I stumbled along. Then we entered the dark passage and when we reached the end the spots faded from my eyes and I began to see again. Brother Jack paused at the door.

"Listen to them," he said. "Just waiting to be told what to do!" And I could still hear the applause booming behind us. Then several of the others broke off their conversation and faced us, as the applause muffled down behind the closing door.

"Well, what do you think?" Brother Jack said enthusiastically. "How's that for a starter?"

There was a tense silence. I looked from face to face, black and white, feeling swift panic. They were grim.

"Well?" Brother Jack said, his voice suddenly hard.

I could hear the creaking of someone's shoes.

"Well?" he repeated.

Then the man with the pipe spoke up, a swift charge of tension building with his words.

"It was a most unsatisfactory beginning," he said quietly, punctuating the "unsatisfactory" with a stab of his pipe. He was looking straight at me and I was puzzled. I looked at the others. Their faces were noncommittal, stolid.

"Unsatisfactory!" Brother Jack exploded. "And what alleged process of thought led to that brilliant pronouncement?"

"This is no time for cheap sarcasm, Brother," the brother with the pipe said.

"Sarcasm? You made the sarcasm. No, it isn't a time for sarcasms nor for imbecilities. Nor for plain damn-fooleries! This is a key moment in the struggle, things have just begun to move—and suddenly you are unhappy. You are afraid of success? What's wrong? Isn't this just what we've been working for?"

"Again, ask yourself. You are the great leader. Look into your crystal ball."

Brother Jack swore.

"Brothers!" someone said.

Brother Jack swore and swung to another brother. "You," he said to the husky man. "Have you the courage to tell me what's going on here? Have we become a street-corner gang?"

Silence. Someone shuffled his feet. The man with the pipe was looking now at me.

"Did I do somethingw wrong?" I said.

"The worst you could have done," he said coldly.

Stunned, I looked at him wordlessly.

"Never mind," Brother Jack said, suddenly calm. "Just what is the problem, Brother? Let's have it out right here. Just what is your complaint?"

"Not a complaint, an opinion. If we are still allowed to express our opinions," the brother with the pipe said.

"Your opinion, then," Brother Jack said.

"In my opinion the speech was wild, hysterical, politically irresponsible and dangerous," he snapped. "And worse than that, it was *incorrect!*" He pronounced "incorrect" as though the term described the most heinous crime imaginable, and I stared at him openmouthed, feeling a vague guilt.

"Soooo," Brother Jack said, looking from face to face, "there's been a caucus and decisions have been made. Did you take minutes, Brother Chairman? Have you recorded your wise disputations?"

"There was no caucus and the opinion still holds," the brother with the pipe said.

"No meeting, but just the same there has been a caucus and decisions have been reached even before the event is finished."

"But, Brother," someone tried to intervene.

"A most brilliant operation," Brother Jack went on, smiling now. "A consummate example of skilled theoretical Nijinskys leaping ahead of history. But come down, Brothers, come down or you'll land on your dialectics; the stage of history hasn't built that far. The month after next, perhaps, but not yet. And what do you think, Brother Wrestrum?" he asked, pointing to a big fellow of the shape and size of Supercargo.

"I think the brother's speech was backward and reactionary!" he said.

I wanted to answer but could not. No wonder his voice had sounded so mixed when he congratulated me. I could only stare into the broad face with its hate-burning eyes.

"And you," Brother Jack said.

"I liked the speech," the man said, "I thought it was quite effective."

"And you?" Brother Jack said to the next man.

"I am of the opinion that it was a mistake."

"And just why?"

"Because we must strive to reach the people through their intelligence . . ."

"Exactly," the brother with the pipe said. "It was the antithesis of the scientific approach. Ours is a reasonable point of view. We are champions of a scientific approach to society, and such a speech as we've identified ourselves with tonight destroys everything that has been said before. The audience isn't thinking, it's yelling its head off."

"Sure, it's acting like a mob," the big black brother said.

Brother Jack laughed. "And this mob," he said, "is it a mob *against* us, or is it a mob *for* us—how do our muscle-bound scientists answer that?"

But before they could answer he continued, "Perhaps you're right, perhaps it is a mob; but if it is, then it seems to be a mob that's simply boiling over to come along with us. And I shouldn't have to tell you theoreticians that science bases its judgments upon *experiment!* You're jumping to conclusions before the experiment has run its course. In fact, what's happening here tonight represents only one step in the experiment. The *initial* step, the release of energy. I can understand that it should make you timid—you're afraid of carrying through to the next step—because it's up to you to organize that energy. Well, it's going to be organized and not by a bunch of timid sideline theoreticians arguing in a vacuum, but by getting out and leading the people!"

He was fighting mad, looking from face to face, his red head bristling, but no one answered his challenge.

"It's disgusting," he said, pointing to me. "Our new brother has succeeded by instinct where for two years your 'science' has failed, and now all you can offer is destructive criticism."

"I beg to differ," the brother with the pipe said. "To point out the dangerous nature of his speech isn't destructive criticism. Far from it. Like the rest of us, the new brother must learn to speak scientifically. He must be trained!"

"So at last it occurs to you," Brother Jack said, pulling down the corners of his mouth. "*Training*. All is not lost. There's hope that our wild but effective speaker may be tamed. The scientists perceive a possibility! Very well, it has been arranged; perhaps not scientifically but arranged nevertheless. For the next few months our new brother is to undergo a period of intense study and indoctrination under the guidance of Brother Hambro. That's right," he said, as I started to speak. "I meant to tell you later."

"But that's a long time," I said. "How am I going to live?"

"Your salary will continue," he said. "Meanwhile, you'll be guilty of no further unscientific speeches to upset our brothers' scientific tranquillity. In fact, you are to stay completely out of Harlem. Perhaps then we'll see if you brothers are as swift at organizing as you are at criticizing. It's your move, Brothers."

ÉPILOGUE

Après son discours dans l'arène politique le narrateur reçoit une initiation complémentaire aux subtilités de la conquête du pouvoir. Les leaders de la Fraternité s'efforcent surtout de discréditer un groupe rival de militants noirs. La stratégie consiste à ralentir le développement de la Fraternité à Harlem (l'éloquent narrateur est transféré au centre de New York) afin de permettre aux rivaux de fomenter une émeute raciale vouée à l'échec, mais qui aurait l'avantage politique de se solder par un bain de sang des Noirs de Harlem. Le narrateur s'échappe de l'émeute et se réfugie dans une pièce en sous-sol où il a illégalement branché le courant pour allumer 1 369 ampoules électriques.

[. . .] How had it all happened? And I asked myself if it were only a joke and I couldn't answer. Since then I've sometimes been overcome with a passion to return into that "heart of darkness" across the Mason-Dixon line,[1] but then I remind myself that the true darkness lies within my own mind, and the idea loses itself in the gloom. Still the passion persists. Sometimes I feel the need to reaffirm all of it, the whole unhappy territory and all the things loved and unlovable in it, for all of it is part of me. Till now, however, this is as far as I've ever gotten, for all life seen from the hole of invisibility is absurd.

So why do I write, torturing myself to put it down? Because in spite of myself I've learned some things. Without the possibility of action, all knowledge comes to one labeled "file and forget," and I can neither file nor forget. Nor will certain ideas forget me; they keep filing away at my lethargy, my complacency. Why should I be the one to dream this nightmare? Why should I be dedicated and set aside—yes, if not to at least *tell* a few people about it? There seems to be no escape. Here I've set out to throw my anger into the world's face, but now that I've tried to put it all down the old fascination with playing a role returns, and I'm drawn upward again. So that even before I finish I've failed (maybe my anger is too heavy; perhaps, being a talker, I've used too many words). But I've failed. The very act of trying to put it all down has confused me and negated some of the anger and some of the

1. La ligne fut tracée en 1767 par les arpenteurs anglais Mason et Dixon comme la limite sud séparant l'Etat libre de Pennsylvanie des Etats esclavagistes du Maryland et de Virginie. Cette latitude est devenue la frontière traditionnelle entre le nord et le sud des Etats-Unis.

bitterness. So it is that now I denounce and defend, or feel prepared to defend. I condemn and affirm, say no and say yes, say yes and say no. I denounce because though implicated and partially responsible, I have been hurt to the point of abysmal pain, hurt to the point of invisibility. And I defend because in spite of all I find that I love. In order to get some of it down I *have* to love. I sell you no phony forgiveness, I'm a desperate man—but too much of your life will be lost, its meaning lost, unless you approach it as much through love as through hate. So I approach it through division. So I denounce and I defend and I hate and I love.

Perhaps that makes me a little bit as human as my grandfather. Once I thought my grandfather incapable of thoughts about humanity, but I was wrong. Why should an old slave use such a phrase as, "This and this or this has made me more human," as I did in my arena speech? Hell, he never had any doubts about his humanity—that was left to his "free" offspring. He accepted his humanity just as he accepted the principle. It was his, and the principle lives on in all its human and absurd diversity. So now having tried to put it down I have disarmed myself in the process. You won't believe in my invisibility and you'll fail to see how any principle that applies to you could apply to me. You'll fail to see it even though death waits for both of us if you don't. Nevertheless, the very disarmament has brought me to a decision. The hibernation is over. I must shake off the old skin and come up for breath. There's a stench in the air, which, from this distance underground, might be the smell either of death or of spring—I hope of spring. But don't let me trick you, there *is* a death in the smell of spring and in the smell of thee as in the smell of me. And if nothing more, invisibility has taught my nose to classify the stenches of death.

In going underground, I whipped it all except the mind, the *mind*. And the mind that has conceived a plan of living must never lose sight of the chaos against which that pattern was conceived. That goes for societies as well as for individuals. Thus, having tried to give pattern to the chaos which lives within the pattern of your certainties, I must come out, I must emerge. And there's still a conflict within me: With Louis Armstrong[1] one half of me says,

1. Comme Louis Armstrong (1900-1971), Ellison est aussi un trompettiste de jazz.

"Open the window and let the foul air out," while the other says, "It was good green corn before the harvest." Of course Louie was kidding, *he* wouldn't have thrown old Bad Air out, because it would have broken up the music and the dance, when it was the good music that came from the bell of old Bad Air's horn that counted. Old Bad Air is still around with his music and his dancing and his diversity, and I'll be up and around with mine. And, as I said before, a decision has been made. I'm shaking off the old skin and I'll leave it here in the hole. I'm coming out, no less invisible without it, but coming out nevertheless. And I suppose it's damn well time. Even hibernations can be overdone, come to think of it. Perhaps that's my greatest social crime, I've overstayed my hibernation, since there's a possibility that even an invisible man has a socially responsible role to play.

"Ah," I can hear you say, "so it was all a build-up to bore us with his buggy jiving. He only wanted us to listen to him rave!" But only partially true: Being invisible and without substance, a disembodied voice, as it were, what else could I do? What else but try to tell you what was really happening when your eyes were looking through? And it is this which frightens me:

Who knows but that, on the lower frequencies, I speak for you?

FLANNERY O'CONNOR, 1925-1964

Connue et estimée dans la première décennie de l'après-guerre, l'œuvre de Flannery O'Connor est parcourue par les thèmes obsédants du mal et de l'innocence, mais puise encore aux sources littéraires, sociales et spirituelles des premières décennies du siècle. Née en Géorgie, elle partage avec Faulkner l'héritage du Sud, sa tradition d'humour du terroir, ses conventions sociales et ses cloisonnements de classes, ses inadaptés moraux et sociaux, et les tensions entre bien et mal qui génèrent les comportements grotesques, la violence et les fulgurances de la révélation spirituelle. Elle subvertit le cliché pastoral des bons paysans et lui substitue l'ignorance des rustauds et les mystères de la dépravation. C'est dans les replis ténébreux de ce Sud qu'elle se découvre des affinités avec l'Américain Reinold Niehbuhr, le Suisse Karl Barth et l'Allemand Paul Tillich qui exposent dans leur théologie les éléments tragiques de l'expérience humaine. Catholique, Flannery O'Connor est particulièrement influencée par Teilhard de Chardin, bien qu'elle ait pris ses distances avec son mysticisme scientique que dénonça le Vatican en 1963. Ecartant toute allégeance à l'égard du naturalisme littéraire, elle revient aux mystères qu'ont explorés par différentes voies Hawthorne, Poe, Melville, Faulkner et T. S. Eliot : péché, mal, peur, souffrance, grâce, rédemption et transcendance. Ses modèles européens vont de Dostoïevsky à Proust.

BIBLIOGRAPHIE SÉLECTIVE. — Stephens (Martha), *The Question of Flannery O'Connor,* Baton Rouge, Louisiana State University Press, 1973 ; Asals (Frederick), *Flannery O'Connor : The Imagination of Extremity,* Athens, University of Georgia Press, 1982 ; Rougé (Jean-Robert), *L'inquiétude religieuse dans le roman américain moderne,* Paris, Klincksieck, 1973.

A Good Man is Hard to Find[1]

The grandmother didn't want to go to Florida. She wanted to visit some of her connections in east Tennessee and she was seizing at every chance to change Bailey's mind. Bailey was the son she lived with, her only boy. He was sitting on the edge of his chair at the table, bent over the orange sports section of the *Journal.* "Now look here, Bailey," she said, "see here, read this," and she stood with one hand on her thin hip and the other rattling the newspaper at his bald head. "Here this fellow that calls himself the Misfit is aloose from the Federal Pen and headed toward Florida and you read here what it says he did to these people. Just you read it. I wouldn't take my children in any direction with a criminal like that aloose in it. I couldn't answer to my conscience if I did."

Bailey didn't look up from his reading so she wheeled around then and faced the children's mother, a young woman in slacks, whose face was as broad and innocent as a cabbage and was tied

1. Première édition dans *The Berkeley Book of Modern Writing* (1953). C'est la première nouvelle dans la collection *A Good Man is Hard to Find* (1955).

around with a green head-kerchief that had two points on the top like rabbit's ears. She was sitting on the sofa, feeding the baby his apricots out of a jar. "The children have been to Florida before," the old lady said. "You all ought to take them somewhere else for a change so they would see different parts of the world and be broad. They never have been to east Tennessee."

The children's mother didn't seem to hear but the eight-year-old boy, John Wesley, a stocky child with glasses, said, "If you don't want to go to Florida, why dontcha stay at home?" He and the little girl, June Star, were reading the funny papers on the floor.

"She wouldn't stay at home to be queen for a day," June Star said without raising her yellow head.

"Yes and what would you do if this fellow, The Misfit, caught you?" the grandmother asked.

"I'd smack his face," John Wesley said.

"She wouldn't stay at home for a million bucks," June Star said. "Afraid she'd miss something. She has to go everywhere we go."

"All right, Miss, " the grandmother said. "Just remember that the next time you want me to curl your hair."

June Star said her hair was naturally curly.

The next morning the grandmother was the first one in the car, ready to go. She had her big black valise that looked like the head of a hippopotamus in one corner, and underneath it she was hiding a basket with Pitty Sing, the cat, in it. She didn't intend for the cat to be left alone in the house for three days because he would miss her too much and she was afraid he might brush against one of the gas burners and accidentally asphyxiate himself. Her son, Bailey, didn't like to arrive at a motel with a cat.

She sat in the middle of the back seat with John Wesley and June Star on either side of her. Bailey and the children's mother and the baby sat in front and they left Atlanta at eight forty-five with the mileage on the car at 55890. The grandmother wrote this down because she thought it would be interesting to say how many miles they had been when they got back. It took them twenty minutes to reach the outskirts of the city.

The old lady settled herself comfortably, removing her white cotton gloves and putting them up with her purse on the shelf in front of the back window. The children's mother still had on slacks and still had her head tied up in a green kerchief, but the grandmother had on a navy blue straw sailor hat with a bunch of white violets on the brim and a navy blue dress with a small white dot in the print. Her collars and cuffs were white organdy trimmed with lace and at her neckline she had pinned a purple spray of cloth violets containing a sachet. In case of an accident, anyone seeing her dead on the highway would know at once that she was a lady.

She said she thought it was going to be a good day for driving, neither too hot nor too cold, and she cautioned Bailey that the speed limit was fifty-five miles an hour and that the patrolmen hid themselves behind billboards and small clumps of trees and sped out after you before you had a chance to slow down. She pointed out interesting details of the scenery: Stone Mountain; the blue granite that in some places came up to both sides of the highways; the brilliant red clay banks slightly streaked with purple; and the various crops that made rows of green lace-work on the ground. The trees were full of silver-white sunlight and the meanest of them sparkled. The children were reading comic magazines and their mother had gone back to sleep.

"Let's go through Georgia fast so we won't have to look at it much," John Wesley said.

"If I were a little boy," said the grandmother, "I wouldn't talk about my native state that way. Tennessee has the mountains and Georgia has the hills."

"Tennessee is just a hillbilly dumping ground," John Wesley said, "and Georgia is a lousy state too."

"You said it," June Star said.

"In my time," said the grandmother, folding her thin veined fingers, "children were more respectful of their native states and their parents and everything else. People did right then. Oh look at the cute little pickaninny!" she said and pointed to a Negro child standing in the door of a shack. "Wouldn't that make a picture, now?" she asked and they all turned and looked at the little Negro out of the back window. He waved.

"He didn't have any britches on," June Star said.

"He probably didn't have any," the grandmother explained. "Little niggers in the country don't have things like we do. If I could paint, I'd paint that picture," she said.

The children exchanged comic books.

The grandmother offered to hold the baby and the children's

mother passed him over the front seat to her. She set him on her knee and bounced him and told him about the things they were passing. She rolled her eyes and screwed up her mouth and stuck her leathery thin face into his smooth bland one. Occasionally he gave her a faraway smile. They passed a large cotton field with five or six graves fenced in the middle of it, like a small island. "Look at the graveyard!" the grandmother said, pointing it out. "That was the old family burying ground. That belonged to the plantation."

"Where's the plantation?" John Wesley asked.

"Gone With the Wind,"[1] said the grandmother. "Ha. Ha."

When the children finished all the comic books they had brought, they opened the lunch and ate it. The grandmother ate a peanut butter sandwich and an olive and would not let the children throw the box and the paper napkins out the window. When there was nothing else to do they played a game by choosing a cloud and making the other two guess what shape it suggested. John Wesley took one the shape of a cow and June Star guessed a cow and John Wesley said, no, an automobile, and June Star said he didn't play fair, and they began to slap each other over the grandmother.

The grandmother said she would tell them a story if they would keep quiet. When she told a story, she rolled her eyes and waved her head and was very dramatic. She said once when she was a maiden lady she had been courted by a Mr. Edgar Atkins Teagarden from Jasper, Georgia. She said he was a very good-looking man and a gentleman and that he brought her a watermelon every Saturday afternoon with his initials cut in it, E. A. T. Well, one Saturday, she said, Mr. Teagarden brought the watermelon and there was nobody at home and he left it on the front porch and returned in his buggy to Jasper, but she never got the watermelon, she said, because a nigger boy ate it when he saw the initials, E. A. T.! This story tickled John Wesley's funny bone and he giggled and giggled but June Star didn't think it was any good. She said she wouldn't marry a man that just brought her a watermelon on Saturday. The grandmother said she would have done well to marry Mr. Teagarden because he was a gentleman and had bought Coca-Cola stock when it first came out and that he had died only a few years ago, a very wealthy man.

1. Titre du roman de Margaret Mitchell (1936). C'est l'histoire romanesque d'une plantation de Géorgie pendant et après la guerre de Sécession. Le livre s'est immédiatement vendu par millions. Le film de 1939 avec Clark Gable et Vivien Leigh reste immensément populaire.

They stopped at The Tower for barbecued sandwiches. The Tower was a part stucco and part wood filling station and dance hall set in a clearing outside of Timothy. A fat man named Red Sammy Butts ran it and there were signs stuck here and there on the building and for miles up and down the highway saying, TRY RED SAMMY'S FAMOUS BARBECUE. NONE LIKE FAMOUS RED SAMMY'S! RED SAM! THE FAT BOY WITH THE HAPPY LAUGH. A VETERAN! RED SAMMY'S YOUR MAN!

Red Sammy was lying on the bare ground outside The Tower with his head under a truck while a gray monkey about a foot high, chained to a small chinaberry tree, chattered nearby. The monkey sprang back into the tree and got on the highest limb as soon as he saw the children jump out of the car and run toward him.

Inside, The Tower was a long dark room with a counter at one end and tables at the other and dancing space in the middle. They all sat down at a board table next to the nickelodeon and Red Sam's wife, a tall burnt-brown woman with hair and eyes lighter than her skin, came and took their order. The children's mother put a dime in the machine and played "The Tennessee Waltz," and the grandmother said that tune always made her want to dance. She asked Bailey if he would like to dance but he only glared at her. He didn't have a naturally sunny disposition like she did and trips made him nervous. The grandmother's brown eyes were very bright. She swayed her head from side to side and pretended she was dancing in her chair. June Star said play something she could tap to so the children's mother put in another dime and played a fast number and June Star stepped out onto the dance floor and did her tap routine.

"Ain't she cute?" Red Sam's wife said, leaning over the counter. "Would you like to come be my little girl?"

"No I certainly wouldn't," June Star said. "I wouldn't live in a broken-down place like this for a million bucks!" and she ran back to the table.

"Ain't she cute?" the woman repeated, stretching her mouth politely.

"Arn't you ashamed?" hissed the grandmother.

Red Sam came in and told his wife to quit lounging on the counter and hurry up with these people's order. His khaki trousers reached just to his hip bones and his stomach hung over them like a sack of meal swaying under his shirt. He came over and sat down at a table nearby and let out a combination sigh and a yodel. "You can't win," he said. "You can't win," and he wiped his sweating red face off with a gray handkerchief. "These days you don't know who to trust," he said. "Ain't that the truth?"

"People are certainly not nice like they used to be," said the grandmother.

"Two fellers come in here last week," Red Sammy said, "driving a Chrysler. It was a old beat-up car but it was a good one and these boys looked all right to me. Said they worked at the mill and you know I let them fellers charge the gas they bought? Now why did I do that?"

"Because you're a good man!" the grandmother said at once.

"Yes'm, I suppose so," Red Sam said as if he were struck with this answer.

His wife brought the orders, carrying the five plates all at once without a tray, two in each hand and one balanced on her arm. "It isn't a soul in this green world of God's that you can trust," she said. "And I don't count nobody out of that, not nobody," she repeated, looking at Red Sammy.

"Did you read about that criminal, The Misfit, that's escaped?" asked the grandmother.

"I wouldn't be a bit surprised if he didn't attact this place right here," said the woman. "If he hears about it being here, I wouldn't be none surprised to see him. If he hears it's two cent in the cash register, I wouldn't be a tall surprised if he . . ."

"That'll do," Red Sam said. "Go bring these people their Co'-Colas," and the woman went off to get the rest of the order.

"A good man is hard to find," Red Sammy said. "Everything is getting terrible. I remember the day you could go off and leave your screen door unlatched. Not no more."

He and the grandmother discussed better times. The old lady said that in her opinion Europe was entirely to blame for the way things were now. She said the way Europe acted you would think we were made of money and Red Sam said it was no use talking about it, she was exactly right. The children ran outside into the white sunlight and looked at the monkey in the lacy chinaberry tree. He was busy catching fleas on himself and biting each one carefully between his teeth as if it were a delicacy.

They drove off again into the hot afternoon. The grandmother took cat naps and woke up every few minutes with her own snoring. Outside of Toombsboro she woke up and recalled an old plantation that she had visited in this neighborhood once when she was a young lady. She said the house had six white columns across the front and that there was an avenue of oaks leading up to it and two little wooden trellis arbors on either side in front where you sat down with your suitor after a stroll in the garden. She recalled exactly which road to turn off to get to it. She knew that Bailey would not be willing to lose any time looking at an old house, but the more she talked about it, the more she wanted to see it once again and find out if the little twin arbors were still standing. "There was a secret panel in this house," she said craftily, not telling the truth but wishing that she were, "and the story went that all the family silver was hidden in it when Sherman came through but it was never found . . ."

"Hey!" John Wesley said. "Let's go see it! We'll find it! We'll poke all the woodwork and find it! Who lives there? Where do you turn off at? Hey Pop, can't we turn off there?"

"We never have seen a house with a secret panel!" June Star shrieked. "Let's go to the house with the secret panel! Hey Pop, can't we go see the house with the secret panel!"

"It's not far from here, I know," the grandmother said. "It wouldn't take over twenty minutes."

Bailey was looking straight ahead. His jaw was as rigid as a horseshoe. "No," he said.

The children began to yell and scream that they wanted to see the house with the secret panel. John Wesley kicked the back of the front seat and June Star hung over her mother's shoulder and whined desperately into her ear that they never had any fun even on their vacation, that they could never do what THEY wanted to do. The baby began to scream and John Wesley kicked the back of the seat so hard that his father could feel the blows in his kidney.

"All right!" he shouted and drew the car to a stop at the side of the road. "Will you all shut up? Will you all just shut up for one second? I you don't shut up, we won't go anywhere."

"It would be very educational for them," the grandmother murmured.

"All right," Bailey said, "but get this: this is the only time we're going to stop for anything like this. This is the one and only time."

"The dirt road that you have to turn down is about a mile back," the grandmother directed. "I marked it when we passed."

"A dirt road," Bailey groaned.

After they had turned around and were headed toward the dirt road, the grandmother recalled other points about the house, the beautiful glass over the front doorway and the candle-lamp in the hall. John Wesley said that the secret panel was probably in the fireplace.

"You can't go inside this house," Bailey said. "You don't know who lives there."

"While you all talk to the people in front, I'll run around behind and get in a window," John Wesley suggested.

"We'll all stay in the car," his mother said.

They turned onto the dirt road and the car raced roughly along in a swirl of pink dust. The grandmother recalled the times when there were no paved roads and thirty miles was a day's journey. The dirt road was hilly and there were sudden wahes in it and sharp curves on dangerous embankments. All at once they would be on a hill, looking down over the blue tops of trees for miles around, then the next minute, they would be in a red depression with the dustcoated trees looking down on them.

"This place had better turn up in a minute," Bailey said, "or I'm going to turn around."

The road looked as if no one had traveled on it in months.

"It's not much father," the grandmother said and just as she said it, a horrible thought came to her. The thought was so embarrassing that she turned red in the face and her eyes dilated and her feet jumped up, upsetting her valise in the corner. The instant the valise moved, the newspaper top she had over the basket under it rose with a snarl and Pitty Sing, the cat, sprang onto Bailey's shoulder.

The children were thrown to the floor and their mother, clutching the baby, was thrown out the door onto the ground; the old lady was thrown into the front seat. The car turned over once and landed right-side-up in a gulch off the side of the road. Bailey remained in the driver's seat with the cat—gray-striped with a broad white face and an orange nose—clinging to his neck like a caterpillar.

As soon as the children saw they could move their arms and legs, they scrambled out of the car, shouting, "We've had an

ACCIDENT!" The grandmother was curled up under the dashboard, hoping she was injured so that Bailey's wrath would not come down on her all at once. The horrible thought she had had before the accident was that the house she had remembered so vividly was not in Georgia but in Tennessee.

Bailey removed the cat from his neck with both hands and flung it out the window against the side of a pine tree. Then he got out of the car and started looking for the children's mother. She was sitting against the side of a red gutted ditch, holding the screaming baby, but she only had a cut down her face and a broken shoulder. "We've had an ACCIDENT!" the children screamed in a frenzy of delight.

"But nobody's killed," June Star said with disappointment as the grandmother limped out of the car, her hat still pinned to her head but the broken front brim standing up at a jaunty angle and the violet spray hanging off the side. They all sat down in the ditch, except the children, to recover from the shock. They were all shaking.

"Maybe a car will come along," said the children's mother hoarsely.

"I believe I have injured an organ," said the grandmother, pressing her side, but no one answered her. Bailey's teeth were clattering. He had on a yellow sport shirt with bright blue parrots designed in it and his face was as yellow as the shirt. The grandmother decided that she would not mention that the house was in Tennessee.

The road was about ten feet above and they could see only the tops of the trees on the other side of it. Behind the ditch they were sitting in there were more woods, tall and dark and deep. In a few minutes they saw a car some distance away on top of a hill, coming slowly as if the occupants were watching them. The grandmother stood up and waved both arms dramatically to attract their attention. The car continued to come on slowly, disappeared around a bend and appeared again, moving even slower, on top of the hill they had gone over. It was a big black battered hearse-like automobile. There were three men in it.

It came to a stop just over them and for some minutes, the driver looked down with a steady expressionless gaze to where they were sitting, and didn't speak. Then he turned his head and muttered something to the other two and they got out. One was a fat boy in black trousers and a red sweat shirt with a silver stallion embossed on the front of it. He moved around on the right side of them and stood staring, his mouth partly open in a kind of loose grin. The other had on khaki pants and a blue striped coat and a gray hat pulled down very low, hiding most of his face. He came around slowly on the left side. Neither spoke.

The driver got out of the car and stood by the side of it, looking down at them. He was an older man than the other two. His hair was just beginning to gray and he wore silver-rimmed spectacles that gave him a scholarly look. He had a long creased face and didn't have on any shirt or undershirt. He had on blue jeans that were too tight for him and he was holding a black hat and a gun. The two boys also had guns.

"We've had an ACCIDENT!" the children screamed.

The grandmother had the peculiar feeling that the bespectacled man was someone she knew. His face was as familiar to her as if she had known him all her life but she could not recall who he was. He moved away from the car and began to come down the embankment, placing his feet carefully so that he wouldn't slip. He had on tan and white shoes and no socks, and his ankles were red and thin. "Good afternoon," he said. "I see you all had you a little spill."

"We turned over twice!" said the grandmother.

"Oncet," he corrected. "We seen it happen. Try their car and see will it run, Hiram," he said quietly to the boy with the gray hat.

"What you got that gun for?" John Wesley asked. "Whatcha gonna do with that gun?"

"Lady," the man said to the children's mother, "would you mind calling them children to sit down by you? Children make me nervous. I want all you all to sit down right together there where your're at."

"What are you telling US what to do for?" June Star asked.

Behind them the line of woods gaped like a dark open mouth. "Come here," said the mother.

"Look here now," Bailey began suddenly, "we're in a predicament! We're in . . ."

The grandmother shrieked. She scrambled to her feet and stood staring. "You're The Misfit!" she said. "I recognized you at once!"

"Yes'm," the man said, smiling slightly as if he were pleased in spite of himself to be known, "but it would have been better for all of you, lady, if you hadn't of reckernized me."

Bailey turned his head sharply and said something to his mother that shocked even the children. The old lady began to cry and The Misfit reddened.

"Lady," he said, "don't you get upset. Sometimes a man says things he don't mean. I don't reckon he meant to talk to you that-away."

"You wouldn't shoot a lady, would you?" the grandmother said and removed a clean handkerchief from her cuff and began to slap at her eyes with it.

The Misfit pointed the toe of his shoe into the ground and made a little hole and then covered it up again. "I would hate to have to," he said.

"Listen," the grandmother almost screamed, "I know you're a good man. You don't look a bit like you have common blood. I know you must come from nice people!"

"Yes mam," he said, "finest people in the world." When he smiled he showed a row of strong white teeth. "God never made a finer woman than my mother and my daddy's heart was pure gold," he said. The boy with the red sweat shirt had come around behind them and was standing with his gun at his hip. The Misfit squatted down on the ground. "Watch them children, Bobby Lee," he said. "You know they make me nervous." He looked at the six of them huddled together in front of him and he seemed to be embarrassed as if he couldn't think of anything to say. "Ain't a cloud in the sky," he remarked, looking up at it. "Don't see no sun but don't see no cloud neither."

"Yes, it's a beautiful day," said the grandmother. "Listen," she said, "you shouldn't call yourself The Misfit because I know you're a good man at heart. I can just look at you and tell."

"Hush!" Bailey yelled. "Hush! Everybody shut up and let me handle this!" He was squatting in the position of a runner about to sprint forward but he didn't move.

"I pre-chate[1] that, lady," The Misfit said and drew a little circle in the ground with the butt of his gun.

1. *Appreciate*. O'Connor montre que la langue de l'inadapté appartient à la classe inférieure, si bien que l'allusion faite par la grand-mère à son statut social (« you must come from nice people ») relève de la flatterie.

"It'll take a half a hour to fix this here car," Hiram called, looking over the raised hood of it.

"Well, first you and Bobby Lee get him and that little boy to step over yonder with you," The Misfit said, pointing to Bailey and John Wesley. "The boys want to ast you something," he said to Bailey. "Would you mind stepping back in them woods there with them?"

"Listen," Bailey began, "we're in a terrible predicament! Nobody realizes what this is," and his voice cracked. His eyes were as blue and intense as the parrots in his shirt and he remained perfectly still.

The grandmother reached up to adjust her hat brim as if she were going to the woods with him but it came off in her hand. She stood staring at it and after a second she let it fall on the ground. Hiram pulled Bailey up by the arm as if he were assisting an old man. John Wesley caught hold of his father's hand and Bobby Lee followed. They went off toward the woods and just as they reached the dark edge, Bailey turned and supporting himself against a gray naked pine trunk, he shouted, "I'll be back in a minute, Mamma, wait on me!"

"Come back this instant!" his mother shrilled but they all disappeared into the woods.

"Bailey Boy!" the grandmother called in a tragic voice but she found she was looking at The Misfit squatting on the ground in front of her. "I just know you're a good man," she said desperately. "You're not a bit common!"

"Nome, I ain't a good man," The Misfit said after a second as if he had considered her statement carefully, "but I ain't the worst in the world neither. My daddy said I was a different breed of dog from my brothers and sisters. 'You know,' Daddy said, 'it's some that can live their whole life out without asking about it and it's others has to know why it is, and this boy is one of the latters. He's going to be into everything!' " He put on his black hat and looked up suddenly and then away deep into the woods as if he were embarrassed again. "I'm sorry I don't have on a shirt before you ladies," he said, hunching his shoulders slightly. "We buried our clothes that we had on when we escaped and we're just making do until we can get better. We borrowed these from some folks we met," he explained.

"That's perfectly all right," the grandmother said. "Maybe Bailey has an extra shirt in his suitcase."

"I'll look and see terrectly," The Misfit said.

"Where are you taking him?" the children's mother screamed.

"Daddy was a card himself," The Misfit said. "You couldn't put anything over on him. He never got in trouble with the Authorities though. Just had the knack of handling them."

"You could be honest too if you'd only try," said the grandmother. "Think how wonderful it would be to settle down and live a comfortable life and not have to think about somebody chasing you all the time."

The Misfit kept scratching in the ground with the butt of his gun as if he were thinking about it. "Yes'm, somebody is always after you," he murmured.

The grandmother noticed how thin his shoulder blades were just behind his hat because she was standing up looking down on him. "Do you ever pray?" she asked.

He shook his head. All she saw was the black hat wiggle between his shoulder blades. "Nome," he said.

There was a pistol shot from the woods, followed closely by another. Then silence. The old lady's head jerked around. She could hear the wind move through the tree tops like a long satisfied insuck of breath. "Bailey Boy!" she called.

"I was a gospel singer for a while," The Misfit said. "I been most everything. Been in the arm service, both land and sea, at home and abroad, been twict married, been an undertaker, been with the railroads, plowed Mother Earth been in a tornado, seen a man burnt alive oncet," and he looked up at the children's mother and the little girl who were sitting close together, their faces white and their eyes glassy; "I even seen a woman flogged," he said.

"Pray, pray," the grandmother began, "pray, pray . . ."

"I never was a bad boy that I remember of," The Misfit said in an almost dreamy voice, "but somewheres along the line I done something wrong and got sent to the penitentiary. I was buried alive," and he looked up and held her attention to him by a steady stare.

"That's when you should have started to pray," she said, "What did you do to get sent to the penitentiary that first time?"

"Turn to the right, it was a wall," The Misfit said, looking up again at the cloudless sky. "Turn to the left, it was a wall. Look up it was a ceiling, look down it was a floor. I forget what I done, lady. I set there and set there, trying to remember what it was I done and I ain't recalled it to this day. Oncet in a while, I would think it was coming to me, but it never come."

"Maybe they put you in by mistake," the old lady said vaguely.

"Nome," he said. "It wasn't no mistake. They had the papers on me."

"You must have stolen something," she said.

The Misfit sneered slightly. "Nobody had nothing I wanted," he said. "It was a head-doctor at the penitentiary said what I had done was kill my daddy but I known that for a lie. My daddy died in nineteen ought nineteen of the epidemic flu and I never had a thing to do with it. He was buried in the Mount Hopewell Baptist churchyard and you can go there and see for yourself."

"If you would pray," the old lady said, "Jesus would help you."

"That's right," The Misfit said.

"Well then, why don't you pray?" she asked trembling with delight suddenly.

"I don't want no hep," he said. "I'm doing all right by myself."

Bobby Lee and Hiram came ambling back from the woods. Bobby Lee was dragging a yellow shirt with bright blue parrots in it.

"Thow me that shirt, Bobby Lee," The Misfit said. The shirt came flying at him and landed on his shoulder and he put it on. The grandmother couldn't name what the shirt reminded her of. "No, lady," The Misfit said while he was buttoning it up, "I found out the crime don't matter. You can do one thing or you can do another, kill a man or take a tire off his car, because sooner or later you're going to forget what it was you done and just be punished for it."

The children's mother had begun to make heaving noises as if she couldn't get her breath. "Lady," he asked, "would you and that little girl like to step off yonder with Bobby Lee and Hiram and join your husband?"

"Yes, thank you," the mother said faintly. Her left arm dangled helplessly and she was holding the baby, who had gone to sleep, in the other. "Hep that lady up, Hiram," The Misfit said as she struggled to climb out of the ditch, "and Bobby Lee, you hold onto that little girl's hand."

"I don't want to hold hands with him," June Star said, "He reminds me of a pig."

The fat boy blushed and laughed and caught her by the arm and pulled her off into the woods after Hiram and her mother.

Alone with The Misfit, the grandmother found that she had lost her voice. There was not a cloud in the sky nor any sun. There was nothing around her but woods. She wanted to tell him that he must pray. She opened and closed her mouth several times before anything came out. Finally she found herself saying, "Jesus. Jesus," meaning, Jesus will help you, but the way she was saying it, it sounded as if she might be cursing.

"Yes'm," The Misfit said as if he agreed. "Jesus thown everything off balance. It was the same case with Him as with me except He hadn't committed any crime and they could prove I had committed one because they had the papers on me. Of course," he said, "they never shown me my papers. That's why I sign myself now. I said long ago, you get you a signature and sign everything you do and keep a copy of it. Then you'll know what you done and you can hold up the crime to the punishment and see do they match and in the end you'll have something to prove you ain't been treated right. I call myself The Misfit," he said, "because I can't make what all I done wrong fit what all I gone through in punishment."

There was a piercing scream from the woods, followed closely by a pistol report. "Does it seem right to you, lady, that one is punished a heap and another ain't punished at all?"

"Jesus!" the old lady cried. "You've got good blood! I know you wouldn't shoot a lady! I know you come from nice people! Pray! Jesus, you ought not to shoot a lady. I'll give you all the money I've got!"

"Lady," The Misfit said, looking beyond her far into the woods, "there never was a body that give the undertaker a tip."

There were two more pistol reports and the grandmother raised her head like a parched old turkey hen crying for water and called, "Bailey Boy, Bailey Boy!" as if her heart would break.

"Jesus was the only One that ever raised the dead," The Misfit continued, "and He shouldn't have done it. He thown everything off balance. If He did what He said, then it's nothing for you to do but thow away everything and follow Him, and if He didn't, then it's nothing for you to do but enjoy the few minutes you got left the best way you can—by killing somebody or burning down his house or doing some other meanness to him. No pleasure but meanness," he said and his voice had become almost a snarl.

"Maybe He didn't raise the dead," the old lady mumbled, not knowing what she was saying and feeling so dizzy that she sank down in the ditch with her legs twisted under her.

"I wasn't there so I can't say He didn't," The Misfit said. "I wisht I had of been there," he said, hitting the ground with his fist. "It ain't right I wasn't there because if I had of been there I would of known. Listen lady," he said in a high voice, "if I had of been there I would of known and I wouldn't be like I am now." His voice seemed about to crack and the grandmother's head cleared for an instant. She saw the man's face twisted close to her own as if he were going to cry and she murmured, "Why you're one of my babies. You're one of my own children!" She reached out and touched him on the shoulder. The Misfit sprang back as if a snake had bitten him and shot her three times through the chest. Then he put his gun down on the ground and took off his glasses and began to clean them.

Hiram and Bobby Lee returned from the woods and stood over the ditch, looking down at the grandmother who half sat and half lay in a puddle of blood with her legs crossed under her like a child's and her face smiling up at the cloudless sky.

Without his glasses, The Misfit's eyes were red-rimmed and pale and defenseless-looking. "Take her off and thow her where you thown the others," he said, picking up the cat that was rubbing itself against his leg.

"She was a talker, wasn't she?" Bobby Lee said, sliding down the ditch with a yodel.

"She would of been a good woman," The Misfit said, "if it had been somebody there to shoot her every minute of her life."

"Some fun!" Bobby Lee said.

"Shut up, Bobby Lee," The Misfit said. "It's no real pleasure in life."

BERNARD MALAMUD, 1914-1986

La carrière d'écrivain et les sujets de Bernard Malamud sont indissociablement liés aux lieux et aux gens qui ont marqué sa vie. Son père était épicier et conteur. Pendant la Dépression, Malamud suivit les cours de deux universités new-yorkaises. Ses œuvres les plus récentes sont discrètement tissées d'allusions à ses vastes lectures. Tout aussi utiles pour un auteur furent les enseignements qu'il tira de son observation directe des efforts et des souffrances de Juifs en proie aux difficultés économiques de la Dépression. La leçon humaine qui lui fut donnée tenait aussi à la force de l'esprit de famille et de la solidarité humaine qui appartiennent à la tradition juive. Au début des années quarante, Malamud commença, à l'âge de vingt-sept ans, d'écrire des nouvelles tout en assurant des cours du soir dans un établissement secondaire. Après la guerre, son imagination littéraire prit en compte la dimension européenne, à la suite de l'horrible révélation de l'holocauste de six millions de Juifs. Ce crime nazi contre l'humanité et le poids plus lourd de l'histoire juive ont hanté les pages de sa fiction dans les années cinquante et après. N'étant pas enclin à écrire rapidement, il a maintenu sa production à un niveau uniformément élevé durant sa carrière. Avec *The Assistant,* il publie en 1957 son premier véritable roman juif et réunit l'année suivante sa collection de nouvelles des années cinquante dans *The Magic Barrel,* volume qui lui vaut son premier prix littéraire, le National Book Award. Emerge alors la structure habituelle des récits de Malamud : 1 / le protagoniste vit dans le trouble spirituel, souvent à l'intérieur de la « prison » d'un ghetto, nourrissant l'espoir du succès matériel pour lui-même ou ses enfants (fausse conception du Rêve américain). Il éprouve en outre le besoin d'acquérir plus de générosité humaine et une sagesse morale supérieure ; 2 / un « messager » fait son entrée, portant sur lui-même tout le poids de l'expérience du passé, et éveille le personnage central à la conscience qu'il doit être une source vive d'humanité ; 3 / le héros subit des épreuves successives en crescendo jusqu'au moment de la révélation finale. Des images d'effondrement, de dégel ou de cassure accompagnent généralement ces pages terminales.

BIBLIOGRAPHIE SÉLECTIVE. — Guttmann (Allen), *The Jewish Writer in America : Assimilation and the Crisis of Identity*, New York, Oxford University Press, 1971 ; Richman (Sidney), *Bernard Malamud*, New York, Twayne, 1966.

The First Seven Years[1]

Feld, the shoemaker, was annoyed that his helper, Sobel, was so insensitive to his reverie that he wouldn't for a minute cease his fanatic pounding at the other bench. He gave him a look, but Sobel's bald head was bent over the last as he worked and he didn't notice. The shoemaker shrugged and continued to peer through the partly frosted window at the near-sighted haze of falling February snow. Neither the shifting white blur outside, nor the sudden deep remembrance of the snowy Polish village where he had wasted his youth could turn his thoughts from Max the college boy, (a constant visitor in the mind since early that morning when Feld saw him trudging through the snowdrifts on his way to school) whom he so much respected because of the sacrifices he had made throughout the years—in winter or direst heat—to further his education. An old wish returned to haunt the shoemaker: that he had had a son instead of a daughter, but this blew away in the snow for Feld, if anything, was a practical man. Yet he could not help but contrast the diligence of the boy, who was a peddler's son, with Miriam's unconcern for an education. True, she was always with a book in her hand, yet when the opportunity arose for a college education, she had said no she would rather find a job. He had begged her to go, pointing out how many fathers could not afford to send their children to college, but she said she wanted to be independent. As for education, what was it, she asked, but books, which Sobel, who diligently read the classics, would as usual advise her on. Her answer greatly grieved her father.

1. Première édition dans *Partisan Review* (septembre-octobre 1950). Figure dans la collection de nouvelles intitulée *The Magic Barrel* (1958).

A figure emerged from the snow and the door opened. At the counter the man withdrew from a wet paper bag a pair of battered shoes for repair. Who he was the shoemaker for a moment had no idea, then his heart trembled as he realized, before he had thoroughly discerned the face, that Max himself was standing there, embarrassedly explaining what he wanted done to his old shoes. Though Feld listened eagerly, he couldn't hear a word, for the opportunity that had burst upon him was deafening.

He couldn't exactly recall when the thought had occurred to him, because it was clear he had more than once considered suggesting to the boy that he go out with Miriam. But he had not dared speak, for if Max said no, how would he face him again? Or suppose Miriam, who harped so often on independence, blew up in anger and shouted at him for his meddling? Still, the chance was too good to let by: all it meant was an introduction. They might long ago have become friends had they happened to meet somewhere, therefore was it not his duty—an obligation—to bring them together, nothing more, a harmless connivance to replace an accidental encounter in the subway, let' say, or a mutual friend's introduction in the street? Just let him once see and talk to her and he would for sure be interested. As for Miriam, what possible harm for a working girl in an office, who met only loud-mouthed salesmen and illiterate shipping clercks, to make the acquaintance of a fine scholarly boy? Maybe he would awaken in her a desire to go to college; if not—the shoemaker's mind at last came to grips with the truth—let her marry an educated man and live a better life.

When Max finished describing what he wanted done to his shoes, Feld marked them, both with enormous holes in the soles which he pretended not to notice, with large white-chalk x's, and the rubber heels, thinned to the nails, he marked with o's, though it troubled him he might have mixed up the letters. Max inquired the price, and the shoemaker cleared his throat and asked the boy, above Sobel's insistent hammering, would he please step through the side door there into the hall. Though surprised, Max did as the shoemaker requested, and Feld went in after him. For a minute they were both silent, because Sobel had stopped banging, and it seemed they understood neither was to say anything until the noise began again. When it did, loudly, the shoemaker quickly told Max why he had asked to talk to him.

"Ever since you went to high school," he said, in the dimly-lit hallway, "I watched you in the morning go to the subway to school, and I said to myself, this is a fine boy that he wants so much an education."

"Thanks," Max said, nervously alert. He was tall and grotesquely thin, with sharply cut features, particularly a beak-like nose. He was wearing a loose, long slushy overcoat that hung down to his ankles, looking like a rug draped over his bony shoulders, and a soggy, old brown hat, as battered as the shoes he had brought in.

"I am a business man," the shoemaker abruptly said to conceal his embarrassment, "so I will explain you right away why I talk to you. I have a girl, my daughter Miriam—she is nineteen—a very nice girl and also so pretty that everybody looks on her when she passes by in the street. She is smart, always with a book, and I thought to myself that a boy like you, an educated boy—I thought maybe you will be interested sometime to meet a girl like this." He laughed a bit when he had finished and was tempted to say more but had the good sense not to.

Max stared down like a hawk. For an uncomfortable second he was silent, then he asked, "Did you say nineteen?"

"Yes."

"Would it be all right to inquire if you have a picture of her?"

"Just a minute." The shoemaker went into the store and hastily returned with a snapshot that Max held up to the light.

"She's all right," he said.

Feld waited.

"And is she sensible—not the flighty kind?"

"She is very sensible."

After another short pause, Max said it was okay with him if he met her.

"Here is my telephone," said the shoemaker, hurriedly handing him a slip of paper. "Call her up. She comes home from work six o'clock."

Max folded the paper and tucked it away into his worn leather wallet.

"About the shoes," he said. "How much did you say they will cost me?"

"Don't worry about the price."

"I just like to have an idea."

"A dollar—dollar fifty. A dollar fifty," the shoemaker said.

At once he felt bad, for he usually charged two twenty-five for this kind of job. Either he should have asked the regular price or done the work for nothing.

Later, as he entered the store, he was startled by a violent clanging and looked up to see Sobel pounding with all his might upon the naked last. It broke, the iron striking the floor and jumping with a thump against the wall, but before the enraged shoemaker could cry out, the assistant had torn his hat and coat from the hook and rushed out into the snow.

So Feld, who had looked forward to anticipating how it would go with his daughter and Max, instead had a great worry on his mind. Without his temperamental helper he was a lost man, especially since it was years now that he had carried the store alone. The shoemaker had for an age suffered from a heart condition that threatened collapse if he dared exert himself. Five years ago, after an attack, it had appeared as though he would have either to sacrifice his business upon the auction block and live on a pittance thereafter, or put himself at the mercy of some unscrupulous employee who would in the end probably ruin him. But just at the moment of his darkest despair, this Polish refugee, Sobel, appeared one night from the street and begged for work. He was a stocky man, poorly dressed, with a bald head that had once been blond, a severely plain face and soft blue eyes prone to tears over the sad books he read, a young man but old—no one would have guessed thirty. Though he confessed he knew nothing of shoemaking, he said he was apt and would work for a very little if Feld taught him the trade. Thinking that with, after all, a landsman, he would have less to fear than from a complete stranger, Feld took him on and within six weeks the refugee rebuilt as good a shoe as he, and not long thereafter expertly ran the business for the thoroughly relieved shoemaker.

Feld could trust him with anything and did, frequently going home after an hour or two at the store, leaving all the money in the till, knowing Sobel would guard every cent of it. The amazing thing was that he demanded so little. His wants were few; in money he wasn't interested—in nothing but books, it seemed—which he one by one lent to Miriam, together with his profuse, queer written comments, manufactured during his lonely rooming house evenings, thick pads of commentary which the shoemaker peered at and twitched his shoulders over as his daughter, from her fourteenth year, read page by sanctified page, as if the word of God were inscribed on them. To protect Sobel, Feld himself had to see that he received more than he asked for. Yet his conscience bothered him for not insisting that the assistant accept a better wage than he was getting, though Feld had honestly told him he could earn a handsome salary if he worked elsewhere, or maybe opened a place of his own. But the assistant answered, somewhat ungraciously, that he was not interested in going elsewhere, and though Feld frequently asked himself what keeps him here? why does he stay? he finally answered it that the man, no doubt because of his terrible experiences as a refugee, was afraid of the world.

After the incident with the broken last, angered by Sobel's behavior, the shoemaker decided to let him stew for a week in the rooming house, although his own strength was taxed dangerously and the business suffered. However, after several sharp nagging warnings from both his wife and daughter, he went finally in search of Sobel, as he had once before, quite recently, when over some fancied slight—Feld had merely asked him not to give Miriam so many books to read because her eyes were strained and red—the assistant had left the place in a huff, an incident which, as usual, came to nothing for he had returned after the shoemaker had talked to him, and taken his seat at the bench. But this time, after Feld had plodded through the snow to Sobel's house—he had thought of sending Miriam but the idea became repugnant to him—the burly landlady at the door informed him in a nasal voice that Sobel was not at home, and though Feld knew this was a nasty lie, for where had the refugee to go? still for some reason he was not completely sure of—it may have been the cold and his fatigue—he decided not to insist on seeing him. Instead he went home and hired a new helper.

Having settled the matter, though not entirely to his satisfaction, for he had much more to do than before, and so, for example, could no longer lie late in bed mornings because he had to get up to open the store for the new assistant, a speechless, dark man with an irritating rasp as he worked, whom he would not trust with the key as he had Sobel. Furthermore, this one, though able to do a fair repair job, knew nothing of grades of leather or prices, so Feld had to make his own purchases; and every night at closing time it was necessary to count the money in the till and lock up. However, he was not dissatisfied, for he lived much in his thoughts of Max and Miriam. The college boy had called her, and they had arranged a meeting for this coming Friday night. The shoemaker would personally have preferred Saturday, which he felt would make it a date of the first magnitude, but he learned Friday was Miriam's choice, so he said nothing. The day of the week did not matter. What mattered was the aftermath. Would they like each other and want to be friends? He sighed at all the time that would have to go by before he knew for sure. Often he was tempted to talk to Miriam about the boy, to ask whether she thought she would like his type—he had told her only that he considered Max a nice boy and had suggested he call her—but the one time he tried she snapped at him—justly—how should she know?

At last Friday came. Feld was not feeling particularly well so he stayed in bed, and Mrs. Feld thought it better to remain in the bedroom with him when Max called. Miriam received the boy, and her parents could hear their voices, his throaty one, as they talked. Just before leaving, Miriam brought Max to the bedroom door and he stood there a minute, a tall, slightly hunched figure wearing a thick, droopy suit, and apparently at ease as he greeted the shoemaker and his wife, which was surely a good sign. And Miriam, although she had worked all day, looked fresh and pretty. She was a large-framed girl with a well-shaped body, and she had a fine open face and soft hair. They made, Feld thought, a first-class couple.

Miriam returned after 11:30. Her mother was already asleep, but the shoemaker got out of bed and after locating his bathrobe went into the kitchen, where Miriam, to his surprise, sat at the table, reading.

"So where did you go?" Feld asked pleasantly.

"For a walk," she said, not looking up.

"I advised him," Feld said, clearing his throat, "he shouldn't spend so much money."

"I didn't care."

The shoemaker boiled up some water for tea and sat down at the table with a cupful and a thick slice of lemon.

"So how," he sighed after a sip, "did you enjoy?"

"It was all right."

He was silent. She must have sensed his disappointment, for she added, "You can't really tell much the first time."

"You will see him again?"

Turning a page, she said that Max had asked for another date.

"For when?"

"Saturday."

"So what did you say?"

"What did I say?" she asked, delaying for a moment—"I said yes."

Afterwards she inquired about Sobel, and Feld, without exactly knowing why, said the assistant had got another job. Miriam said nothing more and began to read. The shoemaker's conscience did not trouble him; he was satisfied with the Saturday date.

During the week, by placing here and there a deft question, he managed to get from Miriam some information about Max. It surprised him to learn that the boy was not studying to be either a doctor or lawyer but was taking a business course leading to a degree in accountancy. Feld was a little disappointed because he thought of accountants as bookkeepers and would have preferred "a higher profession." However, it was not long before he had investigated the subject and discovered that Certified Public Accountants were highly respected people, so he was thoroughly content as Saturday approached. But because Saturday was a busy day, he was much in the store and therefore did not see Max when he came to call for Miriam. From his wife he learned there had been nothing especially revealing about their meeting. Max had rung the bell and Miriam had got her coat and left with him—nothing more. Feld did not probe, for his wife was not particularly observant. Instead, he waited up for Miriam with a newspaper on his lap, which he scarcely looked at so lost was he in thinking of the future. He awoke to find her in the room with him, tiredly removing her hat. Greeting her, he was suddenly inexplicably afraid to ask anything about the evening. But since she volunteered nothing he was at last forced to inquire how she had enjoyed herself. Miriam began something non-committal but apparently changed her mind, for she said after a minute, "I was bored."

When Feld had sufficiently recovered from his anguished disappointment to ask why, she answered without hesitation, "Because he's nothing more than a materialist."

"What means this word?"

"He has no soul. He's only interested in things."

He considered her statement for a long time but then asked, "Will you see him again?"

"He didn't ask."

"Suppose he will ask you?"

"I won't see him."

He did not argue; however, as the days went by he hoped increasingly she would change her mind. He wished the boy would telephone, because he was sure there was more to him than Miriam, with her inexperienced eye, could discern. But Max didn't call. As a matter of fact he took a different route to school, no longer passing the shoemaker's store, and Feld was deeply hurt.

Then one afternoon Max came in and asked for his shoes. The shoemaker took them down from the shelf where he had placed them, apart from the other pairs. He had done the work himself and the soles and heels were well built and firm. The shoes had been highly polished and somehow looked better than new. Max's Adam's apple went up once when he saw them, and his eyes had little lights in them.

"How much?" he asked, without directly looking at the shoemaker.

"Like I told you before," Feld answered sadly. "One dollar fifty cents."

Max handed him two crumpled bills and received in return a newly-minted silver half dollar.

He left. Miriam had not been mentioned. That night the shoemaker discovered that his new assistant had been all the while stealing from him, and he suffered a heart attack.

Though the attack was very mild, he lay in bed for three weeks. Miriam spoke of going for Sobel, but sick as he was Feld rose in wrath against the idea. Yet in his heart he knew there was no other way, and the first weary day back in the shop thoroughly convinced him, so that night after supper he dragged himself to Sobel's rooming house.

He toiled up the stairs, though he knew it was bad for him, and at the top knocked at the door. Sobel opened it and the shoemaker entered. The room was a small, poor one, with a single window facing the street. It contained a narrow cot, a low table and several stacks of books piled haphazardly around on the floor along the wall, which made him think how queer Sobel was, to be uneducated and read so much. He had once asked him, Sobel, why you read so much? and the assistant could not answer him. Did you ever study in a college someplace? he had asked, but Sobel shook his head. He read, he said, to know. But to know what, the shoemaker demanded, and to know, why? Sobel never explained, which proved he read much because he was queer.

Feld sat down to recover his breath. The assistant was resting on his bed with his heavy back to the wall. His shirt and trousers were clean, and his stubby fingers, away from the shoemaker's bench, were strangely pallid. His face was thin and pale, as if he had been shut in this room since the day he had bolted from the store.

"So when you will come back to work?" Feld asked him.

To his surprise, Sobel burst out, "Never."

Jumping up, he strode over to the window that looked out upon the miserable street, "Why should I come back?" he cried.

"I will raise your wages."

"Who cares for your wages!"

The shoemaker, knowing he didn't care, was at a loss what else to say.

"What do you want from me, Sobel,"

"Nothing."

"I always treated you like you was my son."

Sobel vehemently denied it. "So why you look for strange boys in the street they should go out with Miriam? Why you don't think of me?"

The shoemaker's hands and feet turned freezing cold. His voice became so hoarse he couldn't speak. At last he cleared his throat and croaked, "So what has my daughter got to do with a shoemaker thirty-five years old who works for me?"

"Why do you think I worked so long for you?" Sobel cried out. "For the stingy wages I sacrificed five years of my life so you could have to eat and drink and where to sleep?"

"Then for what?" shouted the shoemaker.

"For Miriam," he blurted—"for her."

The shoemaker, after a time, managed to say, "I pay wages in cash, Sobel," and lapsed into silence. Though he was seething with excitement, his mind was coldly clear, and he had to admit to himself he had sensed all along that Sobel felt this way. He had never so much as thought it consciously, but he had felt it and was afraid.

"Miriam knows?" he muttered hoarsely.

"She knows."

"You told her?"

"No."

"Then how does she know?"

"How does she know?" Sobel said, "because she knows. She knows who I am and what is in my heart."

Feld had a sudden insight. In some devious way, with his books and commentary, Sobel had given Miriam to understand that he loved. The shoemaker felt a terrible anger at him for his deceit.

"Sobel, you are crazy," he said bitterly. "She will never marry a man so old and ugly like you."

Sobel turned black with rage. He cursed the shoemaker, but then, though he trembled to hold it in, his eyes filled with tears and he broke into deep sobs. With his back to Feld, he stood at the window, fists clenched, and his shoulders shook with his choked sobbing.

Watching him, the shoemaker's anger diminished. His teeth were on edge with pity for the man, and his eyes grew moist. How strange and sad that a refugee, a grown man, bald and old with his miseries, who had by the skin of his teeth escaped Hitler's incinerators, should fall in love, when he had got to America, with a girl less than half his age. Day after day, for five years he had sat at his bench, cutting and hammering away, waiting for the girl to become a woman, unable to ease his heart with speech, knowing no protest but desperation.

"Ugly I didn't mean," he said half aloud.

Then he realized that what he had called ugly was not Sobel but Miriam's life if she married him. He felt for his daughter a strange and gripping sorrow, as if she were already Sobel's bride, the wife, after all, of a shoemaker, and had in her life no more than her mother had had. And all his dreams for her—why he had slaved and destroyed his heart with anxiety and labor—all these dreams of a better life were dead.

The room was quiet. Sobel was standing by the window reading, and it was curious that when he read he looked young.

"She is only nineteen," Feld said brokenly. "This is too young yet to get married. Don't ask her for two years more, till she is twenty-one, then you can talk to her."

Sobel didn't answer. Feld rose and left. He went slowly down the stairs but once outside, though it was an icy night and the crisp falling snow whitened the street, he walked with a stronger stride.

But the next morning, when the shoemaker arrived, heavy-hearted, to open the store, he saw he needn't have come, for his assistant was already seated at the last, pounding leather for his love.

2 – *Les bouleversements des années soixante*

La richesse de la littérature américaine des années soixante exigerait toute une anthologie à elle seule. Les étudiants contestataires du campus de Berkeley sonnèrent avec le « Free Speech Movement » le ralliement d'une génération prête, en 1964, à se battre pour la libre expression dans tous les secteurs de la vie américaine. En littérature, des écrivains confirmés trouvèrent l'inspiration pour produire certaines de leurs meilleures œuvres, tandis que des auteurs encore méconnus s'imposèrent avec éclat à un public acquis aux libertés d'un langage littéraire débridé comme à la musique de Bob Dylan ou à celle des Beatles qui soulevèrent l'hystérie lors de leurs tournées américaines.

A l'orée de la décennie, le portrait que fait le jeune John Updike de Harry « Rabbit » Angstrom en rebelle des classes moyennes lui vaut un succès notoire. Updike décrit ainsi la confusion d'une Amérique privée d'autorité morale, pressentant les bouleversements culturels qui s'annoncent à l'horizon. L'humour noir de l'absurde préfigure dans *Catch 22* (1961) de Joseph Heller une rébellion imminente, cette fois contre le « complexe militairo-industriel américain ». James Baldwin renouvelle ses analyses pénétrantes de l'agitation raciale qui s'amplifie en 1966 dans le front uni de la colère du « Black Power ». Enfin, Norman Mailer retrouve l'esprit de H. L. Mencken comme « New Journalist », pour évaluer la force de l'opposition à la guerre du

Viêt-nam lors d'une marche de manifestants sur le Pentagone en 1967. Reproduites ici, ses conclusions eussent sans doute été encore plus pessimistes au terme de cinq nouvelles années de guerre. Des 2 700 000 Américains qui allèrent au Viêt-nam, 47 244 furent tués et 306 653 blessés.

JOHN UPDIKE, 1932-

Diplômé de Harvard et étudiant en lettres à Oxford, John Updike commença de se faire une réputation dans le monde littéraire au milieu des années cinquante pour des nouvelles de jeunesse. Non moins évidents étaient ses dons critiques. Son talent fut pleinement reconnu après la publication en 1960 de *Rabbit, Run,* son deuxième roman. Protestant luthérien pratiquant, cas rare chez un auteur américain, et chroniqueur du milieu ouvrier, il allie les deux intérêts dans le portrait de Harry (« Rabbit ») Angstrom, personnage sans culture ni prétention intellectuelle. Les trois noms indiquent les trois niveaux de l'identité chez Kierkegaard, philosophe sur lequel Updike a écrit avec autorité. Le passage du premier stade de l'homme esthétique-sensuel, au stade éthique et enfin au stade religieux explique 1 / le lapin (connotation sexuelle en anglais), 2 / l'angoisse du juste et du faux *(angst)* et 3 / son aspiration à la lumière *(angstrom)*. Pareilles implications philosophiques sont réapparues dans les suites, *Rabbit Redux* (1971) et *Rabbit is Rich* (1981). Dans les années quatre-vingt, cet auteur prolifique a entrepris d'écrire une trilogie inspirée des dilemmes chrétiens du roman de Hawthorne, *The Scarlet Letter.* Dans les extraits qui suivent, les notes suggèrent comment ces dilemmes ont été inscrits dans le premier des *Rabbit.*

BIBLIOGRAPHIE SÉLECTIVE. — Greiner (Donald), *The Other John Updike,* Athens, Ohio University Press, 1981 ; Taylor (Larry), *Pastoral and Anti-Pastoral Patterns in John Updike's Fiction,* Carbondale, Southern Illinois University Press, 1971 ; Dommergues (Pierre), *L'aliénation dans le roman américain contemporain,* Paris, « 10-18 », 1976.

Rabbit, Run[1]

I, 5[2]

Ayant quitté sa femme Janice et s'étant installé dans l'appartement de Ruth Leonard, Rabbit Anstrom joue au golf avec le Révérend Jack Eccles. Le nom fait ironiquement écho à l'Ecclésiaste et au prêcheur, dans la mesure où Jack est un pasteur pathétique qui a perdu la foi. Le « it » *que recherche Rabbit tant bien que mal, est le troisième state du moi chez Kierkegaard, la découverte de l'extase et de la grâce dans l'irrationnel « saut de la foi » de l'homme religieux. Cette rare « lumière » est suggérée dans « angstrom », unité affinée de mesure de la lumière.*

Eccles sinks his [putt]. The ball wobbles up and with a glottal rattle bobbles in. The minister looks up with the light of triumph in his eyes. "Harry," he asks, sweetly yet boldly, "why have you left her? You're obviously deeply involved with her."

"I *told* ja. There was this thing that wasn't there."

"What thing? Have you ever seen it? Are you sure it exists?"

Harry's two-foot putt dribbles short and he picks up the ball with trembling fingers. "Well if you're not sure it exists don't ask me. It's right up your alley. If you don't know nobody does."

"No," Eccles cries in the same strained voice in which he told his wife to keep her heart open for Grace. "Christianity isn't looking for a rainbow. If it were what you think it is we'd pass out opium at services. We're trying to *serve* God, not *be* God."

They pick up their bags and walk the way a wooden arrow tells them.

Eccles goes on, explanatorily, "This was all settled centuries ago, in the heresies of the early Church."

"I tell you, I know what it is."

"What is it? What *is* it? Is it hard or soft? Harry. Is it blue? Is it red? Does it have polka dots?"

It hits Rabbit depressingly that he really wants to be told. Underneath all this I-know-more-about-it-than-you heresies-of-the-early-Church business he really wants to be told about it, wants to be told that it is there, that he's not lying to all those

1. Première édition en 1960.

2. Le numéro du chapitre est fourni. Updike n'a utilisé que l'espacement sur la page pour indiquer comment il divise parties et chapitres, sans titre ni numéro.

people every Sunday. As if it's not enough to be trying to get some sense out of this crazy game you have to carry around this madman trying to swallow your soul. The hot strap of the bag gnaws his shoulder.

"The truth is," Eccles tells him with womanish excitement, in a voice agonized by embarrassment, "you're monstrously selfish. You're a coward. You don't care about right or wrong; you worship nothing except your own worst instincts."[1]

They reach the tee, a platform of turf beside a hunchbacked fruit tree offering fists of taut pale buds. "I better go first," Rabbit says. "'Til you calm down." His heart is hushed, held in mid-beat, by anger. He doesn't care about anything except getting out of this mess. He wishes it would rain. In avoiding looking at Eccles he looks at the ball, which sits high on the tee and already seems free of the ground. Very simply he brings the clubhead around his shoulder into it. The sound has a hollowness, a singleness he hasn't heard before. His arms force his head up and his ball is hung way out, lunarly pale against the beautiful black blue of storm clouds, his grandfather's color stretched dense across the east. It recedes along a line straight as a ruler-edge. Stricken; sphere, star, speck. It hesitates, and Rabbit thinks it will die, but he's fooled, for the ball makes his hesitation the ground of a final leap: with a kind of visible sob takes a last bite of space before vanishing in falling. "That's *it!*" he cries and, turning to Eccles with a smile of aggrandizement, repeats, "That's it."

III, 1

Rabbit revient chez sa femme quand elle a un enfant, mais ils s'affrontent et il la quitte de nouveau. En état d'ivresse, Janice noie accidentellement le bébé. Ici, Rabbit est chez ses parents. Tothero, son vieil entraîneur de basketball, qui vient d'avoir une attaque et qui, moralement, ne sait plus très bien où il en est. Les remarques de Tothero rendent confuse la notion de l'homme éthique de Kierkegaard qui apprend par la souffrance, la terreur, l'angoisse et le douloureux choix moral. Ce passage se termine sur la même note religieuse que le passage précédent.

1. Eccles dit effectivement que Rabbit ne se soucie nullement du second stade éthique de Kierkegaard (qui inclut *angst* ou angoisse) et qu'il est seulement l'homme sensuel, esthétique du premier stade.

[Rabbit] gets up and walks a few steps forward to greet the man coming into the room, Tothero, leaning on a cane and his face half-paralyzed; but talking, walking, alive. And the baby dead. "Hi! Gee, how are you?"

"Harry." With the hand that is not on the cane he grips Harry's arm. He brings a long look to bear on Harry's face; his mouth is tweaked downward on one side and the skin over his eye on this side is dragged down diagonally so it nearly curtains the glitter. The gouging grip of his fingers trembles.

"Let's sit down," Rabbit says, and helps him into an easy chair. Tothero knocks off a doily in arranging his arms. Rabbit brings over a straight chair and sits close so he won't have to raise his voice. "Should you be running around?" he asks when Tothero says nothing.

"My wife brought me. In the car. Outside, Harry. We heard your terrible news. Didn't I warn you?" Already his eyes are bulging with water.

"When?"

"When?" The stricken side of his face is turned away, perhaps consciously, into shadow, so his smile seems wholly alive, wise, and sure. "That first night. I said go back. I begged you."

"I guess you did. I've forgotten."

"No you haven't. No you haven't, Harry." His breath chuffs on the "Ha" of "Harry." "Let me tell you something. Will you listen?"

"Sure."

"Right and wrong," he says, and stops; his big head shifts, and the stiff downward lines of his mouth and bad eye show. "Right and wrong aren't dropped from the sky. We. We make them. Against misery. Invariably, Harry, invariably"—he grows confident of his ability to negotiate long words—"misery follows their disobedience. Not our own, often at first not our own. Now you've had an example of that in your own life." Rabbit wonders when the tear-trails appeared on Tothero's cheeks; there they are, like snail-tracks. "Do you believe me?"

"Sure. Sure. Look, I know this has been my fault. I've felt like a, like an insect ever since that thing happened."

Tothero's tranquil smile deepens; a faint rasping purr comes out of his face. "I warned you," he says, "I warned you, Harry, but youth is deaf. Youth is careless."

Harry blurts, "But what can I do?"

Tothero doesn't seem to hear. "Don't you remember? My begging you to go back?"

"I don't know, I guess so."

"Good. Ah. You're still a fine man. Harry. You have a healthy body. When I'm dead and gone, remember how your old coach told you to avoid suffering. Remember." The last word is intoned coyly, with a little wag of the head; on the thrust of this incongruous vivacity he rises from his chair, and prevents himself from pitching forward by quick use of his cane. Harry jumps up in alarm, and the two of them stand for the moment very close. The old man's big head breathes a distressing scent, not so much medicine as a sweet vegetable staleness. "You young people," he says with a rising intonation, a schoolteacher's tone, scolding yet sly, "tend to forget. Don't you? Now don't you?"

He wants this admission mysteriously much. "Sure," Rabbit says, praying he'll go.

Harry helps him to his car, a '57 blue-and-cream Dodge waiting in front of the orange fire hydrant. Mrs. Tothero offers, rather coolly, her regrets at the death of his infant daughter. She looks harried and noble. Gray hair straggles down across her finely wrinkled silver temple. She wants to get away from him, away with her prize. Beside her on the front seat Tothero looks like a smirking gnome, brainlessly stroking the curve of his cane. Rabbit returns to the house feeling depressed and dirtied by the visit. Tothero's revelation chilled him. He wants to believe in the sky as the source of all things.

III, 2

A la fin du roman, après l'enterrement du bébé, Rabbit fuit Janice, son fils Nelson et Ruth Leonard, maintenant enceinte. Aspirant toujours aux stades éthique et religieux, mais sans le secours de quelqu'un qui aurait la qualité de guide moral ou spirituel dans la société américaine, il demeure intrinsèquement un lapin sensuel qui court toujours.

Outside in the air his fears condense. Globes of ether, pure nervousness, slide down his legs. The sense of outside space scoops at his chest. Standing on the step he tries to sort his worries, tries to analyze the machinery behind him in the house, put his finger on what makes it so loud. Two thoughts comfort him, let a little light through the dense pack of impossible alternatives. Ruth has parents, and she will let his baby live; two thoughts that are perhaps the same thought, the vertical order of parenthood, a kind of thin tube upright in time in which our solitude is somewhat diluted. Ruth and Janice both have parents: with this thought he dissolves both of them. Nelson remains: here is a hardness he must carry with him. On this small fulcrum he tries to balance the rest, weighing opposites against each other: Janice and Ruth, Eccles and his mother, the right way and the good way, the way to the delicatessen—gaudy with stacked fruit lit by a naked bulb—and the other way, down Summer Street to where the city ends. He tries to picture how it will end, with an empty baseball field, a dark factory, and then over a brook into a dirt road, he doesn't know. He pictures a huge vacant field of cinders and his heart goes hollow.

Afraid, really afraid, he remembers what once consoled him by seeming to make a hole where he looked through into underlying brightness, and lifts his eyes to the church window. It is, because of church poverty or the late summer nights or just carelessness, unlit, a dark circle in a stone façade.

There is light, though, in the streetlights; muffled by trees their mingling cones retreat to the unseen end of Summer Street. Nearby, to his left, directly under one, the rough asphalt looks like dimpled snow. He decides to walk around the block, to clear his head and pick his path. Funny, how what makes you move is so simple and the field you must move in is so crowded. His legs take strength from the distinction, scissor along evenly. Goodness lies inside, there is nothing outside, those things he was trying to balance have no weight. He feels his inside as very real suddenly, a pure blank space in the middle of a dense net. *I don't know,* he kept telling Ruth; he doesn't know, what to do, where to go, what will happen, the thought that he doesn't know seems to make him infinitely small and impossible to capture. Its smallness fills him like a vastness. It's like when they heard you were great and put two men on you and no matter which way you turned you bumped into one of them and the only thing to do was pass. So you passed and the ball belonged to the others and your hands were empty and the men on you looked foolish because in effect there was nobody there.

Rabbit comes to the curb but instead of going to his right and around the block he steps down, with as big a feeling as if this little side-street is a wide river, and crosses. He wants to travel to the next patch of snow. Although this block of brick three-stories is just like the one he left, something in it makes him happy; the steps and window sills seem to twitch and shift in the corner of his eye, alive. This illusion trips him. His hands lift of their own and he feels the wind on his ears even before, his heels hitting heavily on the pavement at first but with an effortless gathering out of a kind of sweet panic growing lighter and quicker and quieter, he runs. Ah: runs. Runs.

JAMES BALDWIN, 1924-1987

Né à Harlem, James Baldwin se distingua très jeune par son talent d'écrivain. Sensible et intelligent, il lui resta toujours en mémoire le choc qu'il ressentit en prenant conscience qu'il n'était pas blanc. Au cours des huit années d'exil qu'il passa ensuite à Paris, il s'exprima avec force sur le « negro » (même dans les années soixante, il préféra « negro » à « black ») et sur l'expérience du racisme que fait un natif de couleur au pays de la liberté. De retour aux Etats-Unis en 1957, il s'éveille au mouvement des droits civiques qui s'était amplifié pendant son absence sous l'impulsion du Révérend Martin Luther King. En 1954, la Cour suprême avait aboli la ségrégation dans les écoles publiques, l'intégration fut ordonnée dans les bus de l'Alabama en 1956, et l'année suivante, le Président Eisenhower envoya des troupes fédérales à Little Rock dans l'Arkansas, où le gouverneur Faubus avait interdit l'accès des Noirs aux établissements secondaires des Blancs. La Commission sur les droits civiques fut également créée en 1957. Baldwin se rendit alors aux points chauds et devint l'essayiste, le romancier et le dramaturge le plus incisif et talentueux du mouvement noir des années soixante. Le Roi Jones qui prit le nom de Imamu Amiri

Baraka, en fut le poète le plus expressif. Nombre des thèmes d'élection de Baldwin apparaissent dans le discours prononcé en 1946 et qui figure ci-dessous. 1965 fut l'année du meurtre de Malcolm X par les Black Muslims dont il faisait partie, des émeutes raciales du quartier de Watts à Los Angeles, et de la violence policière contre les manifestants de Selma dans l'Alabama. En 1966, un jeune Noir charismatique, Stokely Carmichael fit entendre le cri de guerre du « pouvoir noir ». Des émeutes raciales suivirent à Newark, Detroit et dans d'autres villes des Etats-Unis.

BIBLIOGRAPHIE SÉLECTIVE. — O' Daniel (Therman), ed., *James Baldwin : A Critical Evaluation,* Washington, DC, Howard University Press, 1977; Pratt (Louis), *James Baldwin,* Boston, Twayne, 1978; Julien (Claude), Et si l'on restait chacun chez soi, *Revue française d'Etudes américaines,* 29, mai 1986, p. 327-343 ; Sarotte (Georges M.), *Comme un frère, comme un amant,* Paris, Flammarion, 1974.

The American Dream and the American Negro[1]

I find myself, not for the first time, in the position of a kind of Jeremiah. It would seem to me that the question before the house is a proposition horribly loaded, that one's response to that question depends on where you find yourself in the world, what your sense of reality is. That is, it depends on assumptions we hold so deeply as to be scarcely aware of them.

The white South African or Mississippi sharecropper or Alabama sheriff has at bottom a system of reality which compels them really to believe when they face the Negro that this woman, this man, this child must be insane to attack the system to which he owes his entire identity. For such a person, the proposition which we are trying to discuss here does not exist.

On the other hand, I have to speak as one of the people who have been most attacked by the western system of reality. It comes from Europe. That is how it got to America. It raises the question

1. Discours devant la Cambridge Union Society de l'Université de Cambridge en février 1965. D'abord publié dans *The New York Times Magazine* du 7 mai 1965. Republié dans *The Price of the Ticket : Collected Nonfiction,* 1948-1985 (1985).

of whether or not civilizations can be considered equal, or whether one civilization has a right to subjugate—in fact, to destroy—another.

Now, leaving aside all the physical factors one can quote—leaving aside the rape or murder, leaving aside the bloody catalogue of oppression which we are too familiar with anyway—what the system does to the subjugated is to destroy his sense of reality. It destroys his father's authority over him. His father can no longer tell him anything because his past has disappeared.

In the case of the American Negro, from the moment you are born every stick and stone, every face, is white. Since you have not yet seen a mirror, you suppose you are too. It comes as a great shock around the age of five, six, or seven to discover that the flag to which you have pledged allegiance, along with everybody else, has not pledged allegiance to you. It comes as a great shock to see Gary Cooper killing off the Indians, and, although you are rooting for Gary Cooper, that the Indians are you.

It comes as a great shock to discover that the country which is your birthplace and to which you owe your life and identity has not, in its whole system of reality, evolved any place for you. The disaffection and the gap between people, only on the basis of their skins, begins there and accelerates throughout your whole lifetime. You realize that you are thirty and you are having a terrible time. You have been through a certain kind of mill and the most serious effect is again not the catalogue of disaster—the policeman, the taxi driver, the waiters, the landlady, the banks, the insurance companies, the millions of details twenty-four hours of every day which spell out to you that you are a worthless human being. It is not that. By that time you have begun to see it happening in your daughter, your son or your niece or your nephew. You are thirty by now and nothing you have done has helped you escape the trap. But what is worse is that nothing you have done, and as far as you can tell nothing you *can* do, will save your son or your daughter from having the same disaster and from coming to the same end.

We speak about expense. There are several ways of addressing oneself to some attempt to find out what the word means here. From a very literal point of view, the harbors and the ports and the railroads of the country—the economy, especially in the

South—could not conceivably be what they are if it had not been (and this is still so) for cheap labor. I am speaking very seriously, and this is not an overstatement: I picked cotton, I carried it to the market, I built the railroads under someone else's whip for nothing. For nothing.

The Southern oligarchy which has still today so very much power in Washington, and therefore some power in the world, was created by my labor and my sweat and the violation of my women and the murder of my children. This in the land of the free, the home of the brave. None can challenge that statement. It is a matter of historical record.

In the Deep South you are dealing with a sheriff or a landlord or a landlady or the girl at the Western Union desk. She doesn't know quite whom she is dealing with—by which I mean, if you are not part of a town and if you are a northern nigger, its shows in millions of ways. She simply knows that it is an unknown quantity and she wants nothing to do with it. You have to wait a while to get your telegram. We have all been through it. By the time you get to be a man it is fairly easy to deal with.

But what happens to the poor white man's, the poor white woman's mind? It is this: they have been raised to believe, and by now they helplessly believe, that no matter how terrible some of their lives may be and no matter what disaster overtakes them, there is one consolation like a heavenly revelation—at least they are not black. I suggest that of all the terrible things that could happen to a human being that is one of the worst. I suggest that what has happened to the white southerner is in some ways much worse than what has happened to the Negroes there.

Sheriff Clark in Selma, Alabama, cannot be dismissed as a total monster; I am sure he loves his wife and children and likes to get drunk. One has to assume that he is a man like me. But he does not know what drives him to use the club, to menace with the gun and to use the cattle prod. Something awful must have happened to a human being to be able to put a cattle prod against a woman's breasts. What happens to the woman is ghastly. What happens to the man who does it is in some ways much, much worse. Their moral lives have been destroyed by the plague called color.

This is not being done one hundred years ago, but in 1965 and in a country which is pleased with what we call prosperity, with a certain amount of social coherence, which calls itself a civilized nation and which espouses the notion of freedom in the world. If it were white people being murdered, the government would find some way of doing something about it. We have a civil rights bill now. We had the Fifteenth Amendment nearly one hundred years ago. If it was not honored then, I have no reason to believe that the civil rights bill will be honored now.[1]

The American soil is full of the corpses of my ancestors, through four hundred years and at least three wars. Why is my freedom, my citizenship, in question now? What one begs the American people to do, for all our sakes, is simply to accept our history.

It seems to me when I watch Americans in Europe that what they don't know about Europeans is what they don't know about me. They were not trying to be nasty to the French girl, rude to the French waiter. They did not know that they hurt their feelings; they didn't have any sense that this particular man and woman were human beings. They walked over them with the same sort of bland ignorance and condescension, the charm and cheerfulness, with which they had patted me on the head and which made them upset when I was upset.

When I was brought up I was taught in American history books that Africa had no history and that neither had I. I was a savage about whom the least said the better, who had been saved by Europe and who had been brought to America. Of course, I believed it. I didn't have much choice. These were the only books there were. Everyone else seemed to agree. If you went out of Harlem the whole world agreed. What you saw was much bigger, whiter, cleaner, safer. The garbage was collected, the children were happy. You would go back home and it would seem, of course, that this was an act of God. You belonged where white people put you.

It is only since World War II that there has been a counter-image in the world. That image has not come about because of any legislation by any American government, but because Africa was suddenly on the stage of the world and Africans had to be dealt with in a way they had never been dealt with

1. La loi sur les droits civiques de 1964 mit hors la loi la discrimination et la ségrégation dans tout établissement privé destiné au public. C'était une partie de la législation sur la « Grande Société » du Président Lyndon Johnson, programme que brocarda Baldwin dans ses écrits des années soixante. Le XVe amendement à la Constitution fut promulgué le 30 mars 1870, assurant le droit de vote aux Noirs américains.

before. This gave the American Negro, for the first time, a sense of himself not as a savage. It has created and will create a great many conundrums.

One of the things the white world does not know, but I think I know, is that black people are just like everybody else. We are also mercenaries, dictators, murderers, liars. We are human, too. Unless we can establish some kind of dialogue between those people who enjoy the American dream and those people who have not achieved it, we will be in terrible trouble. This is what concerns me most. We are sitting in this room and we are all civilized; we can talk to each other, at least on certain levels, so that we can walk out of here assuming that the measure of our politeness has some effect on the world.

I remember when the ex-Attorney General Mr. Robert Kennedy said it was conceivable that in forty years in America we might have a Negro President.[1] That sounded like a very emancipated statement to white people. They were not in Harlem when this statement was first heard. They did not hear the laughter and the bitterness and scorn with which this statement was greeted. From the point of view of the man in the Harlem barber shop, Bobby Kennedy only got here yesterday and now he is already on his way to the Presidency. We were here for four hundred years and now he tells us that maybe in forty years, if you are good, we may let you become President.

Perhaps I can be reasoned with, but I don't know—neither does Martin Luther King[2]—none of us knows how to deal with people whom the white world has so long ignored, who don't believe anything the white worlds says and don't entirely believe anything I or Martin say. You can't blame them.

It seems to me that the City of New York has had, for example, Negroes in it for a very long time. The City of New York was able in the last fifteen years to reconstruct itself, to tear down buildings and raise great new ones, and has done nothing whatever except build housing projects, mainly in the ghettoes, for the Negroes. And of

1. Frère du Président John F. Kennedy, Robert fit campagne en 1968 pour être le candidat désigné des Démocrates à la présidence des Etats-Unis en 1968. Il fut assassiné en juin 1968.

2. King, disciple de la non-violence du Mahatma Gandhi, fut assassiné par un raciste blanc en mars 1968. Les violences raciales éclatèrent ensuite dans de nombreuses villes.

course the Negroes hate it. The children can't bear it. They want to move out of the ghettoes. If American pretensions were based on more honest assessments of life, it would not mean for Negroes that when someone says "urban renewal" some Negroes are going to be thrown out into the streets, which is what it means now.

It is a terrible thing for an entire people to surrender to the notion that one-ninth of its population is beneath them. Until the moment comes when we, the Americans, are able to accept the fact that my ancestors are both black and white, that on that continent we are trying to forge a new identity, that we need each other, that I am not a ward of America, I am not an object of missionary charity, I am one of the people who built the country—until this moment comes there is scarcely any hope for the American dream. If the people are denied participation in it, by their very presence they will wreck it. And if that happens it is a very grave moment for the West.

NORMAN MAILER, 1923-

Qui aura été l'homme de notre époque ? Haut en couleur et égotiste invétéré, Norman Mailer se désignerait sans doute lui-même aux suffrages. Beaucoup s'accordent à penser que Mailer est généralement là où il se passe quelque chose. Né dans le New Jersey, il grandit dans le milieu confortable d'un « petit juif bien sage » et reçoit une éducation « néo-victorienne », comme il le confie avec réticence dans *The Armies of the Night* (1967). Après Harvard où il est lauréat d'un prix littéraire, il combat dans le Pacifique au cours de la Deuxième Guerre. Par la suite, ses romans et écrits autobiographiques se lisent comme l'histoire morale et culturelle d'une époque. Il nous fait passer en effet de la guerre dans *The Naked and the Dead* (1948), à Hollywood, à l'univers de la sexualité et du divorce (avec des réminiscences de son aîné Henry Miller), au mouvement « Beat » de Allen Ginsberg et Jack Kerouac, et enfin aux années soixante où « New Journalist » il est en digne compagnie avec Truman

Capote et Tom Wolfe. Dans ce dernier dosage de reportage et de fiction, subjectivité du romancier et techniques narratives apparaissent comme une résurgence naturelle du « modernisme » littéraire. La représentation du réel à travers le point de vue d'un observateur central fait largement écho à Henry James. Mailer est devenu la conscience critique des grands faits de société comme successivement, l'opposition à la guerre du Viêt-nam, les manifestations violentes à la Convention démocrate de 1968 et le vol habité vers la Lune. Il a aussi écrit sur des célébrités telles que Muhammad Ali et Marilyn Monroe. Animé d'une prodigieuse énergie, il a été également candidat à la mairie de New York, a souvent choqué des téléspectateurs au cours d'émissions de variétés et fustigé le mouvement de libération de la femme. Dans les années quatre-vingt, il a réalisé de nouveaux prodiges littéraires suffisamment rémuné- rateurs pour verser des pensions alimentaires à ses ex-épouses.

BIBLIOGRAPHIE SÉLECTIVE. — Bailey (Jennifer), *Norman Mailer : Quick-Change Artist,* New York, Barnes and Noble, 1980 ; Begiebing (Robert), *Acts of Regeneration : Allegory and Archetype in the Works of Norman Mailer,* Columbia, University of Missouri Press, 1980 ; Deflaux (Pierre), *Aspects idéologiques du roman américain de la Deuxième Guerre mondiale,* Paris, Didier, 1984.

The Armies of the Night[1]

BOOK 1 – HISTORY AS A NOVEL : THE STEPS OF THE PENTAGON

III : SATURDAY MATINEE

CHAPTER 1 : THE NEXT STEP

Avant le passage qui suit, sont intervenus trois événements préliminaires à la marche sur le Pentagone du samedi. Le jeudi soir, 19 octobre 1967, à l'Ambassador Theatre de Washington,

1. Le texte est de l'édition de 1968. Le titre fait écho aux vers de Matthew Arnold dans « Dover Beach » (1867) : « ... we are here as on a darkling plain / Swept with confused alarms of struggle and flight, / Where ignorant armies clash by night ».

D. C. Mailer, observateur non engagé et en état d'ivresse, présenta le poète Robert Lowell, déchaînant l'enthousiasme des pacifistes. Le vendredi après-midi, la foule marcha sur le bâtiment du ministère de la Justice où les protestataires rendirent leurs livrets militaires. Avec une exaltation grandissante, Mailer prononça un discours sur l'« obscène » guerre du Viêt-nam. Au dîner du vendredi soir, Mailer, Lowell et un critique engagé, Dwight Macdonald, discutèrent de l'opportunité de passionner le débat sans éluder les avantages que présenterait leur mise en arrestation éventuelle le jour suivant. On est maintenant au matin du samedi, jour fatidique.

[...] No conclusion was reached that night. Over breakfast they were ready to take it up again. It was evident that none had thought about it too much; also obvious there was nothing particularly to think about. Over the years they had all been bored by speeches, polemics and political programmings which invariably detailed the sound-as-brickwork logic of the next step in some hard new Left program. Existentially, it hardly mattered whether the logic came from a Communist, Trotskyist, Splinter Marxist, union organizer, or plain Social Democrat. While the ideals of such speakers were sometimes as separated as a flush in one hand is from a full house in the other, there was dependably a false but uxorious confidence in the adenoidal whine of the speaker as he shifted gears in his larynx the better to drive the certain efficacy of the program into the ears of his audience. Thus, at their worst, had Communist speakers used these gears of the larynx to defend the Moscow-Berlin pact in 1939. So had Trotskyists worked in and out of the knots of the thesis of the degenerated worker's state—a thesis which seemed less absurd to Mailer in 1967 than to Sidney Hook[1] in 1947, but the Trotskyists had been as full of the unbreakable logic of the next step as the Communists, so they had succeeded in smashing the bones of their own movement into the hundred final slivers of American Marxism, miniscule radical sects complete each with their own special martyred genius of a Marxicologist. There had been the enlightened polemics of the cultivated socialism of the Committee for Cultural Freedom wich had been brought by the sound-as-brickwork-logic-of-the-next-step in good Socialist

1. Hook (1902-1989), intellectuel américain qui rompit avec le communisme après les années trente.

Anti-Communism to so incisive an infestation by the CIA that it now called up pictures of the cockroaches in a slum sink; not all the wines of the Waldorf[1] could wash out a drop of that! Yes, and the labor movement, and the confidence once held by Communists and Trotskyists, Splinterites, and Reutherites,[2] that the labor union would prove the strong back to jack the country up from the Depression to that luminous plane where Peace and Justice, Equality and Freedom would reign. The labor movement lifted the country and carried it to a field of plenty, but it was a football field where professionals played, and America watched on Sunday full of Peace before the rainbow of the color set, feeling Justice when their side won, knowing Equality since everyone presumably had an unimpeded view of his own set, and Freedom in abundance for a man could always turn his set off, yes, the labor unions now sat closer to the Mafia than to Marx.

Well, Macdonald, Lowell, and Mailer knew all this, they did not have to talk or argue, they had learned what politics they had, each in his own separate way, and so they did not need to discuss the sound-as-brickwork-logic-of-the-next-step. The March tomorrow would more or less work or not work. If it didn't, the Left would always find a new step—the Left never left itself unemployed (that much must be said for the conservative dictum that a man who wants to, can always find work) if the March did more or less succeed, one knew it would be as a result of episodes one had never anticipated, and the results might lead you in directions altogether unforeseen. And indeed how could one measure success or failure in a venture so odd and unprecedented as this? One did not march on the Pentagon and look to get arrested as a link in a master scheme to take over the bastions of the Republic step by step, no, that sort of sound-as-brickwork-logic was left to the FBI.[3] Rather, one marched on the Pentagon because . . . because . . . and here the reasons became so many and so curious and so vague, so political and so primitive, that there was no need, or perhaps no possibility to talk about it yet, one

1. Waldorf Astoria, hôtel de luxe à New York.

2. Walter Reuther (1907-1970), leader ouvrier des années trente. Il fut président du syndicat United Auto Workers et du Congress of Industrial Organizations (CIO) qui fusionna en 1955 avec l'American Federation of Labor pour devenir l'AFL-CIO.

3. Federal Bureau of Investigation of crime dirigé de 1924 à 1972 par le puissant J. Edgar Hoover connu pour ses opinions conservatrices.

could only ruminate over the morning coffee. What possibly they shared now between them at the morning table of the Hay-Adams was the unspoken happy confidence that politics had again become mysterious, had begun to partake of Mystery; that gave life to a thought the gods were back in human affairs. A generation of the American young had come along different from five previous generations of the middle class. The new generation believed in technology more than any before it, but the generation also believed in LSD, in witches, in tribal knowledge, in orgy, and revolution. It had no respect whatsoever for the unassailable logic of the next step: belief was reserved for the revelatory mystery of the happening where you did not know what was going to happen next; that was what was good about it. Their radicalism was in their hate for the authority—the authority was manifest of evil to this generation. It was the authority who had covered the land with those suburbs where they stifled as children while watching the adventures of the West in the movies, while looking at the guardians of dull genial celebrity on television; they had had their minds jabbed and poked and twitched and probed and finally galvanized into surrealistic modes of response by commercials cutting into dramatic narratives, and parents flipping from network to network—they were forced willy-nilly to build their idea of the space-time continuum (and therefore their nervous system) on the jumps and cracks and leaps and breaks which every phenomenon from the media seemed to contain within it.

The authority had operated on their brain with commercials, and washed their brain with packaged education, packaged politics. The authority had presented itself as honorable, and it was corrupt, corrupt as payola on television, and scandals concerning the safety of automobiles, and scandals concerning the leasing of aviation contracts—the real scandals as everyone was beginning to sense were more intimate and could be found in all the products in all the suburban homes which did not work so well as they should have worked, and broke down too soon for mysterious reasons. The shoddiness was buried in the package, buried somewhere in the undiscoverable root of all those modern factories with their sanitize daisles and automated machines; perhaps one place the shoddiness was buried was in the hangovers of a working class finally alienated from any remote interest or attention in the process of the work itself. Work was shoddy everywhere. Even in the Warren Commission.[1]

Finally, this new generation of the Left hated the authority, because the authority lied. It lied through the teeth of corporation executives as Cabinet officials and police enforcement officers and newspaper editors and advertising agencies, and in its mass magazines, where the subtlest apologies for the disasters of the authority (and the neatest deformations of the news) were grafted in the best possible style into the ever-open mind of the walking American lobotomy: the corporation office worker and his high school son.

The New Left was drawing its political aesthetic from Cuba. The revolutionary idea which the followers of Castro had induced from their experience in the hills was that you created the revolution first and learned from it, learned of what your revolution might consist and where it might go out of the intimate truth of the way it presented itself to your experience. Just as the truth of his material was revealed to a good writer by the cutting edge of his style (he could thus hope his style was in each case the most appropriate tool for the material of the experience) so a revolutionary began to uncover the nature of his true situation by trying to ride the beast of his revolution. The idea behind these ideas was then obviously that the future of the revolution existed in the nerves and cells of the people who created it and lived with it, rather than in the sanctity of the original idea.

Castro's Cuba was of course a mystery to Mailer. He had eard much in its favor, much he could hardly enjoy. That was not necessarily to the point. Revolutions could fail as well by Castro's method as by the most inflexible Comintern program; what seemed significant here, was the idea of a revolution which preceded ideology; the New Left had obviously adopted the idea for this March.

The aesthetic of the New Left now therefore began with the notion that the authority could not comprehend nor contain nor finally manage to control any political action whose end was unknown. They could attack it, beat it, jail it, misrepresent it, and

1. Dirigé par le Chief Justice de la Cour suprême, Earl Warren, cette commission fut désignée par le Président Johnson en novembre 1963, après l'assassinat de John Kennedy, afin de déterminer si l'assassin présumé Lee Harvey Oswald avait agi seul. En septembre 1964, la commission écarta la présomption de complot et fut ensuite critiquée en raison des lacunes et carences du rapport.

finally abuse it, but they could not feel a sense of victory because they could not understand a movement which inspired thousands and hundreds of thousands to march without a coordinated plan. The bureaucrats of the Old Left had not been alone in their adoration of the solid-as-brickwork-logic-of-the-next-step; no, the bureaucrats of the American Center, now liked it as much, and were as aghast at any political activity which ignored it.

These Leviathan ruminations and meditations on the nature of the March coming up, and the reasons for their participation without much discussion now completed, ch-ch-ch-click! in the touch of the tea cup on Mailer's lip, let us move on to the event concerning us—that first major battle of a war which may go on for twenty years; let us even consider there is one interesting chance (one chance of a thousand) that in fifty years the day may loom in our history large as the ghosts of the Union[1] dead.

BOOK 1

IV : SATURDAY NIGHT AND ALL OF SUNDAY

CHAPTER 3 : GRANDMA WITH ORANGE HAIR

Vers la fin de la marche du samedi après-midi, Mailer a défié la police militaire pour qu'elle l'arrête. Il est finalement mis dans un bus pour être conduit dans une prison de Virginie. Comme d'autres manifestants arrêtés montent à bord, Mailer a le temps de méditer sur l'âme perdue de l'Amérique des bourgades, telle qu'elle peut se lire confusément sur le visage des policiers sauveurs de la patrie et autres vils partisans de la guerre.

The gang of Marshals now studied outside the bus were enough to firm up any fading loyalty to his own cause: they had the kind of faces which belong to the bad guys in a Western. Some were fat, some were too thin, but nearly all seemed to have those subtle anomalies of the body which come often to men from small towns who have inherited strong features, but end up, by their own

1. L'armée des Etats-Unis, par opposition aux forces des Confédérés. Mailer développe le thème des divisions intérieures créées par la guerre du Viêt-nam et correspondant à une seconde guerre de Sécession.

measure, in failure. Some would have powerful chests, but abrupt paunches, the skinny ones would have a knob in the shoulder, or a hitch in their gait, their foreheads would have odd cleaving wrinkles, so that one man might look as if an ax had struck him between the eyes, another paid tithe to ten parallel deep lines rising in ridges above his eye brows. The faces of all too many had a low cunning mixed with a stroke of rectitude: if the mouth was slack, the nose was straight and severe; should the lips be tight, the nostrils showed an outsize greed. Many of them looked to be ex-First Sergeants, for they liked to stand with the heels of their hands on the top of their hips, or they had that way of walking, belly forward, which a man will promote when he is in comfortable circumstances with himself and packing a revolver in a belt holster. The toes turn out; the belly struts. They were older men than he might have expected, some in their late thirties, more in their forties, a few looked to be over fifty, but then that may have been why they were here to receive prisoners rather than out on the line—in any case they emitted a collective spirit which, to his mind, spoke of little which was good, for their eyes were blank and dull, that familiar small-town cast of eye which speaks of apathy rising to fanaticism only to subside in apathy again. (Mailer had wondered more than once at that curious demand of small-town life which leaves something good and bright in the eyes of some, is so deadening for others—it was his impression that people in small towns had eyes which were generally livelier or emptier than the more concentrated look of city vision.) These Marshals had the dead eye and sour cigar, that sly shuffle of propriety and rut which so often comes out in a small-town sheriff as patriotism and the sweet stink of a crooked dollar. Small-town sheriffs sidled over to a crooked dollar like a High Episcopalian hooked on a closet queen. If one could find the irredeemable madness of America (for we are a nation where weeds will breed in the gilding tank) it was in those late afternoon race track faces coming into the neon lights of the parimutuel windows, or those early morning hollows in the eye of the soul in places like Vegas where the fevers of America go livid in the hum of the night, and Grandmother, the church-goer, orange hair burning bright now crooned over the One-Arm Bandit, pocketbook open, driving those half-dollars home, home to the slot.

"Madame, we are burning children in Vietnam."

"Boy, you just go get yourself lost. Grandma's about ready for a kiss from the jackpot."

The burned child is brought into the gaming hall on her hospital bed.

"Madame, regard our act in Vietnam."

"I hit! I hit! Hot deedy, I hit. Why, you poor burned child—you just brought me luck. Here, honey, here's a lucky half-dollar in reward. And listen sugar, tell the nurse to change your sheets. Those sheets sure do stink. I hope you ain't got gangrene. Hee hee, hee hee. I get a supreme pleasure mixing with gooks in Vegas."

One did not have to look for who would work in the concentration camps and the liquidation centers—the garrison would be filled with applicants from the pages of a hundred American novels, from *Day of the Locust* and *Naked Lunch* and *The Magic Christian,*[1] one could enlist half the Marshals outside this bus, simple, honest, hard-working government law-enforcement agents, yeah! There was something at loose now in American life, the poet's beast slinking to the marketplace. The country had always been wild. It had always been harsh and hard, it had always had a fever—when life in one American town grew insupportable, one could travel, the fever to travel was in the American blood, so said all, but now the fever had left the blood, it was in the cells, the cells traveled, and the cells were as insane as Grandma with orange hair. The small towns were disappearing in the bypasses and the supermarkets and the shopping centers, the small town in America was losing its sense of the knuckle, the herb, and the root, the walking sticks were no longer cut from trees, nor were they cured, the schools did not have crazy old teachers now but teaching aids, and in the libraries, *National Geographic* gave way to *TV Guide*. Enough of the old walled town had once remained in the American small town for gnomes and dwarfs and knaves and churls (yes, and owls and elves and crickets) to live in the constellated cities of the spiders below the eaves in the old leaning barn which—for all one knew—had been a secret ear to the fevers of the small town, message center for the inhuman dreams which passed through the town at night in sleep and came to tell their insane tale of the old barbarian lust to slaughter villages and drink

1. Les trois œuvres satiriques, maintenant des classiques mineurs sont de Nathanael West (en 1939), William Burroughs (1959) et Terry Southern (1960).

their blood, yes who knew which ghosts, and which crickets, with which spider would commune—which prayers and whose witch's curses would travel those subterranean trails of the natural kingdom about the town, who knows which fevers were forged in such communion and returned on the blood to the seed, it was an era when the message came by the wind and not by the wire (for the town gossip began to go mad when the telephone tuned its buds to the tip of her tongue) the American small town grew out of itself, and grew out of itself again and again, harmony between communication and the wind, between lives and ghosts, insanity, the solemn reaches of nature where insanity could learn melancholy (and madness some measure of modesty) had all been lost now, lost to the American small town. It had grown out of itself again and again, its cells traveled, worked for government, found security through wars in foreign lands, and the nightmares which passed on the winds in the old small towns now traveled on the nozzle tip of the flame thrower, no dreams now of barbarian lusts, slaughtered villages, battles of blood, no, nor any need for them—technology had driven insanity out of the wind and out of the attic, and out of all the lost primitive places: one had to find it now wherever fever, force, and machines could come together, in Vegas, at the race track, in pro football, race riots for the Negro, suburban orgies—none of it was enough—one had to find it in Vietnam; that was where the small town had gone to get its kicks.

That was on the faces of the Marshals. It was a great deal to read on the limited evidence before him, but he had known these faces before—they were not so different from the cramped, mean, stern, brave, florid, bestial, brutish, narrow, calculating, incurious, hardy, wily, leathery, simple, good, stingy, small-town faces he had once been familiar with in his outfit overseas, all those Texans from all those small towns, it was if he could tell—as at a college reunion—the difference these more than twenty years had made. If it were legitimate to read the change in American character by the change in the faces of one's classmates, then he could look at these Marshals like men he had known in the Army, but now revisited, and something had gone out of them, something had come in. If there was a common unattractive element to the Southern small-town face, it was in that painful pinch between their stinginess and their greed. No excess of love seemed ever to come off a poor white Southerner, no fats, no riches, no sweets, just the avidity for such wealth. But there had been sadness attached to this in the old days, a sorrow; in the pinch of their cheeks was the kind of abnegation and loneliness which spoke of what was tender and what was lost forever. So they had dignity. Now the hollows in their faces spoke of men who were rabid and toothless, the tenderness had turned corrosive, the abnegation had been replaced by hate, dull hate, cloud banks of hate, the hatred of failures who had not lost their greed. So he was reminded of a probability he had encountered before: that, nuclear bombs all at hand, the true war party of America was in all the small towns, even as the peace parties had to collect in the cities and the suburbs. Nuclear warfare was dividing the nation. The day of power for the small-town mind was approaching—who else would be left when atomic war was done would reason the small-town mind, and in measure to the depth of their personal failure, would love Vietman, for Vietnam was the secret hope of a bigger war, and that bigger war might yet clear the air of races, faces, in fact—technologies—all that alienation they could not try to comprehend.

BOOK 2 – THE NOVEL AS HISTORY : THE BATTLE OF THE PENTAGON

CHAPTER 9 : THE AESTHETIC FORGED

A la fin du livre 1, Mailer rappelait son emprisonnement du samedi soir et sa mise en liberté du dimanche après paiement d'une amende de 50 dollars assortie d'une condamnation à cinq jours de détention (il y aura un non-lieu en appel). Dans le livre 2, Mailer s'efforce de relater à nouveau son expérience en historien, mais perd son objectivité et revient à l'amalgame du factuel et de l' « esthétique ». Vers la fin, il conclut que l'esthétique symbolique de la manifestation et les brutalités des militaires sont devenues pour les jeunes manifestants un « rite de passage » personnel d'une profonde signification.

[...] Yes, the passage through the night against every temptation to leave—the cold, the possibility of new, more brutal, and more overwhelming attacks, the boredom, the middle-class terror of excess (if one has done two or three good acts in a row, it is time to cash them in) the fear of moral vertigo (one courageous action resolutely following another without compromise and without cease must end in the whirlpool of death) yes, even the fear that if they remained through the night, they would be obliged to remain through the morning, the afternoon, and the evening of the next night, and even then! would there be ever an end? yes, the passage through the night brought every temptation to leave including the thundering schisms of muttered political argument in the dark—the proud advertisements of the new resistance had been ground back to the old masochistic tramping grounds of the sit-in—an argument which was undeniable, and could have prevailed, except if they left, and no one was at the Pentagon then but the soldiers through the night, well what unseen burning torch of which unknown but still palpably felt spirit might expire? no, this passage through the night was a rite of passage, and these disenchanted heirs of the Old Left, this rabble of American Vietcong, and hippies, and pacifists, and whoever else was left were afloat on a voyage whose first note had been struck with the first sound of the trumpet Mailer had heard crossing Washington Monument in the morning. "Come here, come here, come here," the trumpet had said, and now eighteen hours later, in the false dawn, the echo of far greater rites of passage in American history, the light reflected from the radiance of greater more heroic hours may have come nonetheless to shine along the inner space and the caverns of the freaks, some hint of a glorious future may have hung in the air, some refrain from all the great American rites of passage when men and women manacled themselves to a lost and painful principle and survived a day, a night, a week, a month, a year, a celebration of Thanksgiving—the country had been founded on a rite of passage. Very few had not emigrated here without the echo of that rite, even if it were no more (and no less!) than eight days in the stink, bustle, fear, and propinquity of steerage on an ocean crossing (or the eighty days of dying on a slave ship) each generation of Americans had forged their own rite, in the forest of the Alleghenies and the Adirondacks, at Valley Forge, at New Orleans in 1812, with Rogers and Clark or a Sutter's Mill, at Gettysburg, the Alamo, the Klondike, the Argonne, Normandy, Pusan[1]—the engagement at the Pentagon was a pale rite of

1. Mailer a dressé la liste en ordre approximativement chronologique, des guerres et conflits territoriaux liés à l'expansion, depuis les combats des pionniers contre les Indiens jusqu'à la guerre de Corée de 1950-1953.

passage next to these, and yet it was probably a true one, for it came to the spoiled children of a dead de-animalized middle class who had chosen most freely, out of the incomprehensible mysteries of moral choice, to make an attack and then hold a testament before the most authoritative embodiment of the principle that America was right, America was might, America was the true religious war of Christ against the Communist. So it became a rite of passage for these tender drug-vitiated jargon-mired children, they endured through a night, a black dark night which began in joy, near foundered in terror, and dragged on through empty apathetic hours while glints of light came to each alone. Yet the rite of passage was invoked, the moral ladder was climbed, they were forever different in the morning than they had been before the night, which is the meaning of a rite of passage, one has voyaged through a channel of shipwreck and temptation, and so some of the vices carried from another nether world into life itself (on the day of one's birth) may have departed, or fled, or quit: some part of the man has been born again, and is better, just as some hardly so remarkable area of the soul may have been in some miniscule sweet fashion reborn on the crossing of the marchers over Arlington Memorial Bridge, for the worst of them and the most timid were moving nonetheless to a confrontation they could only fear, they were going to the land of the warmakers. Not so easy for the timid when all is said.

3 – Depuis les années soixante : expériences post-modernes dans la fiction

Les turbulentes années soixante se terminèrent sur une floraison d'estimables best-sellers dont les auteurs s'efforçaient de discerner la signification de la forme et du mouvement dans la pensée activiste, la violence, mais aussi les incertitudes de la période précédente. Révolte des minorités, manifestations, brutalités policières, lutte anti-drogue et libération sexuelle s'amalgamaient en effet dans la mémoire immédiate de l'Amérique. Une liste partielle de ces œuvres, entre les années soixante et soixante-dix, inclurait *Confessions of Nat Turner* de William Styron (sur le leader d'une révolte d'esclaves noirs en 1831), *Mr Sammler's Planet* de Saul Bellow, *The Electric Kool-Aid Acid Test* du « New Journalist » Tom Wolfe, *Rabbit Redux* de John Updike, *The Tenants* de Bernard Malamud (sur l'antagonisme entre Noirs et Juifs), *Slaughterhouse-Five* de Kurt Vonnegut et *Our Gang*, de Philip Roth, qui est une charge contre Nixon. Ces œuvres reflètent dans l'ensemble l'impression trouble d'une fin prochaine. Elles mettent un terme à ce qui reste de l'esprit militant et de l'espoir d'affranchissement. Ainsi se traduit un vague sentiment expiatoire où se mêlent attente impuissante et résignation. Comme le suggèrent ces auteurs, les Etats-Unis sont arrivés, non pas à l'orée d'une solution ou d'un nouveau consensus, mais au contraire à un état de stase morale et d'épuisement. La nation attend maintenant « la nouvelle étape ». Bien que tous ces écrivains continuent de consacrer leur expérience de créateur à une vision des « réalités » culturelles de la modernité, l'un d'eux, Kurt Vonnegut, s'est quelquefois mis en retrait, joignant ainsi ses forces à un nouveau groupe d'expérimentateurs « post-modernes » de nouvelles techniques. Ces experts en fabulation et parafiction mettent en doute le caractère observable et vérifiable des réalités traditionnelles, « *out there* ». Ils ont ensuite pris John Barth pour mentor. Celui-ci avait déjà fondé dans les années soixante son nouvel « antiréalisme » en réaction aux carences de la « représentation » en littérature. D'autres exemples ont suivi avec le « supra-réalisme » de William Pynchon, l'« irréalisme » latino-américain conçu par Borgès ou le « réalisme magique » de Marquez. Les années quatre-vingt ont vu aussi émerger le « super-réalisme » d'Ann Beattie. Ces auteurs et d'autres, tels que Donald Barthelme, Robert Coover et Raymond Carver, pourraient aisément prendre à leur compte ce jugement de William Gass : « my fictions are, by and large, experimental constructions ».

JOHN BARTH, 1930-

Comme Norman Mailer, John Barth a commencé sa carrière de romancier avec les perspectives et techniques modernistes explorées par les réalistes de la fin du XIXe siècle. Après des études littéraires et son apprentissage de l'écriture à l'Université Johns Hopkins de son Maryland natal, Barth a subvenu à ses besoins comme professeur d'université tout en écrivant ses deux premiers romans. *The Floating Opera* (1956) et *The End of The Road* (1958) ont une forme traditionnelle tout en proposant une sombre vision du monde (Barth imaginait que son idée de l'absurde lui était propre avant de lire Sartre). Il abandonne ensuite le techniques du réalisme littéraire, ne sachant plus ce que signifie la « réalité ». Dans *The Sotweed Factor* (1960) et *Giles Goat-Boy* (1966), il parodie le roman passé de mode, en prélude à sa troisième prise de position, bientôt désignée sous le nom de « post-moderniste ». A ce nouveau stade, il rompt les liens entre art du roman et sens de l'expérience, entre conventions dramatiques ou narratives et présomptueuses illusions du réel. A cet égard, « Lost in the Funhouse » est devenu, depuis les années soixante-dix, l'un des points de repère sur le nouveau terrain de la littérature post-moderniste. Durant cette dernière période, chacune des nouvelles œuvres de Barth s'est distinguée par sa puissance intellectuelle, son esprit et quelquefois sa stupéfiante innovation technique.

BIBLIOGRAPHIE SÉLECTIVE. — Morrell (David), *John Barth : An Introduction,* University Park, Pennsylvania State University Press, 1976 ; Tharpe (Jac), *John Barth : The Comic Sublimity of Paradox,* Carbondale, Southern Illinois University Press, 1974 ; Safer (Elaine B.), *The Contemporary American Comic Epic,* Wayne State U. Press, 1988 ; Chenetier (Marc), *Au-delà du soupçon, la nouvelle fiction américaine de 1960 à nos jours,* Paris, Seuil, 1989.

Lost in the Funhouse[1]

For whom is the funhouse fun? Perhaps for lovers. For Ambrose it is *a place of fear and confusion.* He has come to the seashore with his family for the holiday, *the occasion of their visit is Independence Day, the most important secular holiday of the United States of America.* A single straight underline is the manuscript mark for italic type, *which in turn* is the printed equivalent to oral emphasis of words and phrases as well as the customary type for titles of complete works, not to mention. Italics are also employed, in fiction stories especially, for "outside," intrusive, or artificial voices, such as radio announcements, the texts of telegrams and newspaper articles, et cetera. They should be used *sparingly.* If passages originally in roman type are italicized by someone repeating them, it's customary to acknowledge the fact. *Italics mine.*

Ambrose was "at that awkward age." His voice came out high-pitched as a child's if he let himself get carried away; to be on the safe side, therefore, he moved and spoke with *deliberate calm* and *adult gravity.* Talking soberly of unimportant or irrelevant matters and listening consciously to the sound of your own voice are useful habits for maintaining control in this difficult interval. *En route* to

1. Tiré de *Lost in the Funhouse : Fiction for Print, Tape, Live Voice* (1968).

Ocean City he sat in the back seat of the family car with his brother Peter, age fifteen, and Magda G——, age fourteen, a pretty girl an exquisite young lady, who lived not far from them on B—— Street in the town of D——, Maryland. Initials, blanks, or both were often substituted for proper names in nineteenth-century fiction to enhance the illusion of reality. It is as if the author felt it necessary to delete the names for reasons of tact or legal liability. Interestingly, as with other aspects of realism, it is an *illusion* that is being enhanced, by purely artificial means. Is it likely, does it violate the principle of verisimilitude, that a thirteen-year-old boy could make such a sophisticated observation? A girl of fourteen is *the psychological coeval* of a boy of fifteen or sixteen; a thirteen-year-old boy, therefore, even one precocious in some other respects, might be three years *her emotional junior*.

Thrice a year—on Memorial, Independence, and Labor Days—the family visits Ocean City for the afternoon and evening. When Ambrose and Peter's father was their age, the excursion was made by train, as mentioned in the novel *The 42nd Parallel* by John Dos Passos. Many families from the same neighborhood used to travel together, with dependent relatives and often with Negro servants; schoolfuls of children swarmed through the railway cars; everyone shared everyone else's Maryland fried chicken, Virginia ham, deviled eggs, potato salad, beaten biscuits, iced tea. Nowadays (that is, in 19—, the year of our story) the journey is made by automobile—more comfortably and quickly though without the extra fun though without the *camaraderie* of a general excursion. It's all part of the deterioration of American life, their father declares; Uncle Karl supposes that when the boys take *their* families to Ocean City for the holidays they'll fly in Autogiros. Their mother, sitting in the middle of the front seat like Magda in the second, only with her arms on the seat-back behind the men's shoulders, wouldn't want the good old days back again, the steaming trains and stuffy long dresses; on the other hand she can do without Autogiros, too, if she has to become a grandmother to fly in them.

Description of physical appearance and mannerisms is one of several standard methods of characterization used by writers of fiction. It is also important to "keep the senses operating"; when a detail from one of the five senses, say visual, is "crossed" with a detail from another, say auditory, the reader's imagination is oriented to the scene, perhaps unconsciously. This procedure may be compared to the way surveyors and navigators determine their positions by two or more compass bearings, a process known as triangulation. The brown hair on Ambrose's mother's forearms gleamed in the sun like. Though right-handed, she took her left arm from the seat-back to press the dashboard cigar lighter for Uncle Karl. When the glass bead in its handle glowed red, the lighter was ready for use. The smell of Uncle Karl's cigar smoke reminded one of. The fragrance of the ocean came strong to the picnic ground where they always stopped for lunch, two miles inland from Ocean City. Having to pause for a full hour almost within sound of the breakers was difficult for Peter and Ambrose when they were younger; even at their present age it was not easy to keep their anticipation, *stimulated by the briny spume,* from turning into short temper. The Irish author James Joyce, in his unusual novel entitled *Ulysses,* now available in this country, uses the adjectives *snot-green* and *scrotum-tightening* to describe the sea. Visual, auditory, tactile, olfactory, gustatory. Peter and Ambrose's father, while steering their black 1936 LaSalle sedan with one hand, could with the other remove the first cigarette from a white pack of Lucky Strikes and, more remarkably, light it with a match forefingered from its book and thumbed against the flint paper without being detached. The match-book cover merely advertised U. S. War Bonds and Stamps. A fine metaphor, simile, or other figure of speech, in addition to its obvious "first-order" relevance to the thing it describes, will be seen upon reflection to have a second order of significance: it may be drawn from the *milieu* of the action, for example, or be particularly appropriate to the sensibility of the narrator, even hinting to the reader things of which the narrator is unaware; or it may cast further and subtler lights upon the thing it describes, sometimes ironically qualifying the more evident sense of the comparison.

To say that Ambrose's and Peter's mother was *pretty* is to accomplish nothing; the reader may acknowledge the proposition, but his imagination is not engaged. Besides, Magda was also pretty, yet in an altogether different way. Although she lived on B—— Street she had very good manners and did better than average in school. Her figure was very well developed for her age. Her right hand lay casually on the plush upholstery of the seat, very near Ambrose's left leg, on which his own hand rested. The space between their legs, between her right and his left leg, was out of the line of sight of anyone sitting on the other side of Magda, as well as anyone glancing into the rear-view mirror. Uncle Karl's face resembled Peter's—rather, vice versa. Both had dark hair and eyes, short husky statures, deep voices. Magda's left hand was probably in a similar position on her left side. The boy's father is difficult to describe; no particular feature of his appearance or manner stood out. He wore glasses and was principal of a T—— County grade school. Uncle Karl was a masonry contractor.

Although Peter must have known as well as Ambrose that the latter, because of his position in the car, would be the first to see the electrical towers of the power plant at V——, the halfway point of their trip, he leaned forward and slightly toward the center of the car and pretended to be looking for them through the flat pinewoods and tuckahoe creeks along the highway. For as long as the boys could remember, "looking for the Towers" had been a feature of the first half of their excursions to Ocean City, "looking for the standpipe" of the second. Though the game was childish, their mother preserved the tradition of rewarding the first to see the Towers with a candy-bar or piece of fruit. She insisted now that Magda play the game; the prize, she said, was "something hard to get nowadays." Ambrose decided not to join in; he sat far back in his seat. Magda, like Peter, leaned forward. Two sets of straps were discernible through the shoulders of her sun dress; the inside right one, a brassiere-strap, was fastened or shortened with a small safety pin. The right armpit of her dress, presumably the left as well, was damp with perspiration. The simple strategy for being first to espy the Towers, which Ambrose had understood by the age of four, was to sit on the right-hand side of the car. Whoever sat there, however, had also to put up with the worst of the sun, and to Ambrose, without mentioning the matter, chose sometimes the one and sometimes the other. Not impossibly Peter had never caught on to the trick, or thought that his brother hadn't simply because Ambrose on occasion preferred shade to a Baby Ruth or tangerine.

The shade-sun situation didn't apply to the front seat, owing to the windshield; if anything the driver got more sun, since the person on the passenger side not only was shaded below by the door and dashboard but might swing down his sunvisor all the way too.

"Is that them?" Magda asked. Ambrose's mother teased the boys for letting Magda win, insinuating that "somebody [had] a girlfriend." Peter and Ambrose's father reached a long thin arm across their mother to butt his cigarette in the dashboard ashtray, under the lighter. The prize this time for seeing the Towers first was a banana. Their mother bestowed it after chiding their father for wasting a half-smoked cigarette when everything was so scarce. Magda, to take the prize, moved her hand from so near Ambrose's that he could have touched it as though accidentally. She offered to share the prize, things like that were so hard to find; but everyone insisted it was hers alone. Ambrose's mother sang an iambic trimeter couplet from a popular song, femininely rhymed:

> "*What's good is in the Army;*
> *What's left will never harm me.*"

Uncle Karl tapped his cigar ash out the ventilator window; some particles were sucked by the slipstream back into the car through the rear window on the passenger side. Magda demonstrated her ability to hold a banana in one hand and peel it with her teeth. She still sat forward; Ambrose pushed his glasses back onto the bridge of his nose with his left hand, which he then negligently let fall to the seat cushion immediately behind her. He even permitted the single hair, gold, on the second joint of his thumb to brush the fabric of her skirt. Should she have sat back at that instant, his hand would have been caught under her.

Plush upholstery prickles uncomfortably through gabardine slacks in the July sun. The function of the *beginning* of a story is to introduce the principal characters, establish their initial relationships, set the scene for the main action, expose the background of the situation if necessary, plant motifs and foreshadowings where appropriate, and initiate the first complication or whatever of the "rising action." Actually, if one imagines a story called "The Funhouse," or "Lost in the Funhouse," the details of the drive to Ocean City don't seem especially relevant. The *beginning* should recount the events between Ambrose's first sight of the funhouse early in the afternoon and his entering it with Magda and Peter in the evening. The *middle* would narrate all relevant events from the time he goes in to the time he loses his way; middles have the double and contradictory function of delaying the climax while at the same time preparing the reader for it and fetching him to it. Then the *ending* would tell what Ambrose does while he's lost, how he finally finds his way out, and what everybody makes of the experience. So far there's been no real dialogue, very little sensory detail, and nothing in the way of a *theme*. And a long time has gone by already without anything happening; it makes a person wonder. We haven't even reached Ocean City yet: we will never get out of the funhouse.

The more closely an author identifies with the narrator, literally or metaphorically, the less advisable it is, as a rule, to use the first-person narrative viewpoint. Once three years previously the young people *afore-mentioned* played Niggers and Masters in the backyard; when it was Ambrose's turn to be Master and theirs to be Niggers Peter had to go serve his evening papers; Ambrose was afraid to punish Magda alone, but she led him to the whitewashed Torture Chamber between the woodshed and the privy in the Slaves Quarters; there she knelt sweating among bamboo rakes and dusty Mason jars, pleadingly embraced his knees, and while bees droned in the lattice as if on an ordinary summer afternoon, purchased clemency at a surprising price set by herself. Doubtless she remembered nothing of this event; Ambrose on the other hand seemed unable to forget the least detail of his life. He even recalled how, standing beside himself with awed impersonality in the reeky heat, he'd stared the while at an empty cigar box in which Uncle Karl kept stone-cutting chisels: beneath the words *El Producto,* a laureled, loose-toga'd lady regarded the sea from a marble bench; beside her, forgotten or not yet turned to, was a five-stringed lyre. Her shin reposed on the back of her right hand; her left depended negligently from the bench-arm. The lower half of scene and lady was peeled away; the words EXAMINED BY —— were inked there into the wood. Nowadays cigar boxes are made of pasteboard. Ambrose wondered what Magda would have done, Ambrose wondered what Magda would do when she sat back on his hand as he resolved she should. Be angry. Make a teasing joke of it. Give no sign at all. For a long time she leaned forward, playing cow-poker with Peter against Uncle Karl and Mother and watching for the first sign of Ocean City. At nearly the same instant, picnic ground and Ocean City standpipe hove into view; an Amoco filling station on their side of the road cost Mother and Uncle Karl fifty cows and the game; Magda bounced back, clapping her right hand on Mother's right arm; Ambrose moved clear "in the nick of time."

At this rate our hero, at this rate our protagonist will remain in the funhouse forever. Narrative ordinarily consists of alternating dramatization and summarization. One sympton of nervous tension, paradoxically, is repeated and violent yawning; neither Peter nor Magda nor Uncle Karl nor Mother reacted in this manner. Although they were no longer small children, Peter and Ambrose were each given a dollar to spend on board-walk amusements in addition to what money of their own they'd brought along. Magda too, though she protested she had ample spending money. The boy's mother made a little scene out of distributing the bills; she pretended that her sons and Magda were small children and cautioned them not to spend the sum too quickly or in one place. Magda promised with a merry laugh and, having both hands free, took the bill with her left. Peter laughed also and pledged in a falsetto to be a good boy. His imitation of a child was not clever. The boys' father was tall and thin, balding, fair-complexioned. Assertions of that sort are not effective; the reader may acknowledge the proposition, but. We should be much farther along than we are; something has gone wrong; not much of this preliminary rambling seems relevant. Yet everyone begins in the same place; how is it that most go along without difficulty but a few lose their way?

KURT VONNEGUT, 1922-

Ce fut après ses études supérieures de chimie et d'anthropologie que Kurt Vonnegut aborda l'écriture romanesque. Pendant le dernier conflit mondial, il était prisonnier des Allemands à Dresde quand cette ville ouverte fut écrasée sous les bombardements alliés en février 1945. Ce fait de guerre traumatisant (et difficilement reconnu) inspira à Vonnegut *Slaughterhouse-Five* (1969), roman qui lui valut son premier succès financier. Avant cela, il avait écrit cinq romans, trois d'entre eux de science-fiction et recelant une vigoureuse critique sous-jacente des valeurs culturelles. Mais comme Barth, Vonnegut s'était lancé dans les expériences post-modernes dès la fin des années soixante. La vision radicale et l'innovation technique de *Slaughterhouse-Five* ne pouvaient que combler d'aise le nombre croissant de ses lecteurs au cours des années de protestation contre la guerre du Viêt-nam. Et ce n'était qu'un début. Vonnegut révéla en effet que toute sa verve satirique ne s'était pas déployée dans ce roman. Aussi la reporta-t-il sur *Breakfast of Champions* (1973), prenant pour cibles maints aspects de la scène américaine tels que l'obsession dévorante de la sexualité, la discrimination raciale, les snacks sur le pouce, les désastres écologiques, l'automation et l'alcool (« the breakfast of champions »). Après ce best-seller, Vonnegut déclara qu'il se préparait à écrire des textes plus positifs voire utopistes sur les Etats-Unis. Dans une large mesure, *Jailbird* (1979) a répondu à cette promesse. Mais dans ses romans des années quatre-vingt, Vonnegut est revenu à un pessimisme de fin du monde, allié à cette satire venimeuse qui lui apporta sa popularité initiale.

BIBLIOGRAPHIE SÉLECTIVE. — Klinkowitz (Jerome), *Kurt Vonnegut*, London, Methuen, 1982 ; Vanderbilt (Kermit), Kurt Vonnegut's American Nightmares and Utopias, *The Utopian Vision*, Sullivan (E. D. S.), ed., San Diego, Calif., San Diego State University Press, 1983.

Breakfast of Champions[1]

ÉPILOGUE

L'action simple imaginée par Vonnegut est composée en alternance : 1 / de chapitres sur le voyage vers l'Ouest de l'auteur de science-fiction Kilgore Trout. Ceci le conduit des prostituées et agresseurs de New York au « Midland City Arts Festival », sur « a planet which was dying fast », 2 / de chapitres sur le comportement morbide de Dwayne Hoover, vendeur de voitures Pontiac à Midland City. Les actions se rejoignent quand Hoover devient fou furieux après sa rencontre avec Trout, alors que son attitude se conforme au modèle pernicieux que lui a donné Trout

1. Première édition en 1973.

dans sa science-fiction. Hoover adhère avec violence à l'idée exprimée dans le livre de Trout et selon laquelle le lecteur immédiat a la maîtrise du monde, car le reste de la population des Etats-Unis est soumis comme des machines au conditionnement social, leur corps et leur esprit sont ainsi pollués par des produits chimiques. Dans sa folle escapade, Hoover brutalise hommes et femmes, envoie onze d'entre eux à l'hôpital y compris Trout. Vonnegut subvertit le point de vue à la manière des post-modernistes en s'insérant lui-même dans le roman en tant qu'auteur en vie, et ceci en compagnie de ses personnages. Ce faisant, il démasque sa propre fiction et la fait apparaître comme le véhicule artificiel d'un faux-semblant transparent. L'épilogue est un bon exemple de la rupture de Vonnegut avec le réalisme traditionnel du roman.

The Midland City Festival of the Arts was postponed because of madness. Fred T. Barry, its chairman, came to the hospital in his limousine, dressed like a Chinaman, to offer his sympathy to Beatrice Keedsler and Kilgore Trout. Trout could not be found anywhere. Beatrice Keedsler had been put to sleep with morphine.

Kilgore Trout assumed that the Arts Festival would still take place that night. He had no money for any form of transportation, so he set out on foot. He began the five mile walk down Fairchild Boulevard—toward a tiny amber dot at the other end. The dot was the Midland City Center for the Arts. He would make it grow by walking toward it. When his walking had made it big enough, it would swallow him up. There would be food inside.

I was waiting to intercept him, about six blocks away. I sat in a Plymouth *Duster* I had rented from *Avis* with my *Diners' Club* card. I had a paper tube in my mouth. It was stuffed with leaves. I set it on fire. It was a *soigné* thing to do.

My penis was three inches long and five inches in diameter. Its diameter was a world's record as far as I knew.[1] It slumbered now in my *Jockey Shorts*. And I got out of the car to stretch my legs, which was another soigné thing to do. I was among factories and warehouses. The streetlights were widely-spaced and feeble. Parking lots were vacant, except for night watchmen's cars which were here and there. There was no traffic on Fairchild Boulevard,

1. Vonnegut fait allusion à l'obsédante curiosité de ses concitoyens pour la pornographie, les prouesses sexuelles et l'activité glandulaire.

which had once been the aorta of the town. The life had all been drained out of it by the Interstate and by the Robert F. Kennedy Inner Belt Expressway, which was built on the old right-of-way of the Monon Railroad. The Monon was defunct.

Defunct.

Nobody slept in that part of town. Nobody lurked there. It was a system of forts at night, with high fences and alarms, and with prowling dogs. They were killing machines.

When I got out of my Plymouth *Duster,* I feared nothing. That was foolish of me. A writer off-guard, since the materials with which he works are so dangerous, can expect agony as quick as a thunderclap.

I was about to be attacked by a Doberman pinscher. He was a leading character in an earlier version of this book.

Listen: That Doberman's name was *Kazak.* He patrolled the supply yard of the Maritimo Brothers Construction Compagny at night. Kazak's trainers, the people who explained to him what sort of a planet he was on and what sort of an animal he was, taught him that the Creator of the Universe wanted him to kill anything he could catch, and to *eat* it, too.

In an earlier version of this book, I had Benjamin Davis, the black husband of Lottie Davis, Dwayne Hoover's maid, take care of Kazak. He threw raw meat down into the pit where Kazak lived in the daytime. He dragged Kazak into the pit at sunrise. He screamed at him and threw tennis balls at him at sundown. Then he turned him loose.

Benjamin Davis was first trumpet with the Midland City Symphony Orchestra, but he got no pay for that, so he needed a real job. He wore a thick gown made of war-surplus mattresses and chicken wire, so Kazak could not kill him. Kazak tried and tried. There were chunks of mattress and swatches of chicken wire all over the yard.

And Kazak did his best to kill anybody who came too close to the fence which enclosed his planet. He leaped at people as though the fence weren't there. The fence bellied out toward the sidewalk everywhere. It looked as though somebody had been shooting cannonballs at it from inside.

I should have noticed the queer shape of the fence when I got out of my automobile, when I did the *soigné* thing of lighting a cigarette. I should have known that a character as ferocious as Kazak was not easily cut out of a novel.

Kazak was crouching behind a pile of bronze pipe which the Maritimo Brothers had bought cheap from a hijacker earlier that day. Kazak meant to kill and *eat* me.

I turned my back to the fence, took a deep puff of my cigarette. *Pall Malls* would kill me by and by. And I mooned philosophically at the murky battlements of the old Keedsler Mansion, on the other side of Fairchild Boulevard.

Beatrice Keedsler had been raised in there. The most famous murders in the city's history had been committed there. Will Fairchild, the war hero, and the maternal uncle of Beatrice Keedsler, appeared one summer night in 1926 with a Springfield rifle. He shot and killed five relatives, three servants, two policemen, and all the animals in the Keedsler's private zoo. Then he shot himself through his heart.

When an autopsy was performed on him, a tumor the size of a piece of birdshot was found in his brain. This was what *caused* the murders.

After the Keedslers lost the mansion at the start of the Great Depression, Fred T. Barry and his parents moved in. The old place was filled with the sounds of British birds. It was silent property of the city now, and there was talk of making it into a museum where children could learn the history of Midland City—as told by arrowheads and stuffed animals and white men's early artifacts.

Fred T. Barry had offered to donate half a million dollars to the proposed museum, on one condition: that the first *Robo-Magic*[1] and the early posters which advertised it be put on display.

And he wanted the exhibit to show, too, how machines evolved just as animals did, but with much greater speed.

I gazed at the Keedsler mansion, never dreaming that a volcanic dog was about to erupt behind me. Kilgore Trout came nearer. I was almost indifferent to his approach, although we had momentous things to say to one another about my having created him.

1. Machine à laver.

I thought instead of my paternal grandfather, who had been the first licensed architect in Indiana. He had designed some dream houses for *Hoosier* millionaires. They were mortuaries and guitar schools and cellar holes and parking lots now. I thought of my mother, who drove me around Indianapolis one time during the Great Depression, to impress me with how rich and powerful my maternal grandfather had been. She showed me where his brewery had been, where some of his dream houses had been. Every one of the monuments was a cellar hole.

Kilgore Trout was only half a block from his Creator now, and slowing down. I worried him.

I turned toward him, so that my sinus cavities, where all telepathic messages were sent and received, were lined up symmetrically with his. I told him this over and over telepathically: "I have good news for you."

Kazak sprung.

I saw Kazak out of the corner of my right eye. His eyes were pinwheels. His teeth were white daggers. His slobber was cyanide. His blood was nitroglycerine.

He was floating toward me like a zeppelin, hanging lazily in air.

My eyes told my mind about him.

My mind sent a message to my hypothalamus, told it to release the hormone CRF into the short vessels connecting my hypothalamus and my pituitary gland.

The CRF inspired my pituitary gland to dump the hormone ACTH into my bloodstream. My pituitary had been making and storing ACTH for just such an occasion. And nearer and nearer the zeppelin came.

And some of the ACTH in my bloodstream reached the outer shell of my adrenal gland, which had been making and storing glucocorticoids for emergencies. My adrenal gland added the glucocorticoids to my bloodstream. They went all over my body, changing glycogen into glucose. Glucose was muscle food. It would help me fight like a wildcat or run like a deer.

And nearer and nearer the zeppelin came.

My adrenal gland gave me a shot of adrenaline, too. I turned purple as my blood pressure skyrocketed. The adrenaline made my heart go like a burglar alarm. It also stood my hair on end. It also caused coagulants to pour into my bloodstream, so, in case I was wounded, my vital juices wouldn't drain away.

Everything my body had done so far fell within normal operating procedures for a human machine. But my body took one defensive measure which I am told was without precedent in medical history. It may have happened because some wire short-circuited or some gasket blew. At any rate, I also retracted my testicles into my abdominal cavity, pulled them into my fuselage like the landing gear of an airplane. And now they tell me that only surgery will bring them down again.

Be that as it may, Kilgore Trout watched me from half a block away, not knowing who I was, not knowing about Kazak and what my body had done about Kazak so far.

Trout had had a full day already, but it wasn't over yet. Now he saw his Creator leap completely over an automobile.

I landed on my hands and knees in the middle of Fairchild Boulevard.

Kazak was flung back by the fence. Gravity took charge of him as it had taken charge of me. Gravity slammed him down on concrete. Kazak was knocked silly.

Kilgore Trout turned away. He hastened anxiously back toward the hospital. I called out to him, but that only made him walk faster.

So I jumped into my car and chased him. I was still high as a kite on adrenaline and coagulants and all that. I did not know yet that I had retracted my testicles in all the excitement. I felt only vague discomfort down there.

Trout was cantering when I came alongside. I clocked him at eleven miles an hour, which was excellent for a man his age. He, too, was now full of adrenaline and coagulants and glucocorticoids.

My windows were rolled down, and I called this to him: "Whoa! Whoa! Mr. Trout! Whoa! Mr. Trout!"

It slowed him down to be called by name.

"Whoa! I'm a friend!" I said. He shuffled to a stop, leaned in panting exhaustion against a fence surrounding an appliance warehouse belonging to the General Electric Company. The company's monogram and motto hung in the night sky behind Kilgore Trout, whose eyes were wild. The motto was this:

PROGRESS IS OUR MOST IMPORTANT PRODUCT

"Mr. Trout," I said from the unlighted interior of the car, "you have nothing to fear. I bring you tidings of great joy."

He was slow to get his breath back, so he wasn't much of a conversationalist at first. "Are—are you—from the—the Arts Festival?" he said. His eyes rolled and rolled.

"I am from the *Everything* Festival," I replied.

"The what?" he said.

I thought it would be a good idea to let him have a good look at me, and so attempted to flick on the dome light. I turned on the windshield washers instead. I turned them off again. My view of the lights of the County Hospital was garbled by beads of water. I pulled at another switch, and it came away in my hand. It was a cigarette lighter. So I had no choice but to continue to speak from darkness.

"Mr. Trout," I said, "I am a novelist, and I created you for use in my books."

"Pardon me?" he said.

"I'm your Creator," I said. "You're in the middle of a book right now—close to the end of it, actually."

"Um," he said.

"Are there any questions you'd like to ask?"

"Pardon me?" he said.

"Feel free to ask anything you want—about the past, about the future," I said. "There's a Nobel Prize in your future."

"A what?" he said.

"A Nobel Prize in medicine."

"Huh," he said. It was a noncommittal sound.

"I've also arranged for you to have a reputable publisher from now on. No more beaver books[1] for you."

"Um," he said.

"If I were in your spot, I would certainly have lots of questions," I said.

"Do you have a gun?" he said.

I laughed there in the dark, tried to turn on the light again, activated the windshield washer again. "I don't need a gun to control you, Mr. Trout. All I have to do is write down something about you, and that's it."

1. Publication pornographique bon marché.

"Are you *crazy*?" he said.

"No," I said. And I shattered his power to doubt me. I transported him to the Taj Mahal and then to Venice and then to Dar es Salaam and then to the surface of the Sun, where the flames could not consume him—and then back to Midland City again.

The poor old man crashed to his knees. He reminded me of the way my mother and Bunny Hoover's mother used to act whenever somebody tried to take their photographs.

As he cowered there, I transported him to the Bermuda of his childhood, had him contemplate the infertile egg of a Bermuda Ern. I took him from there to the Indianapolis of my childhood. I put him in a circus crowd there. I had him see a man with *locomotor ataxia* and a woman with a goiter as big as a zucchini.

I got out of my rented car. I did it noisily, so his ears would tell him a lot about his *Creator*, even if he was unwilling to use his eyes. I slammed the car door firmly. As I approached him from the driver's side of the car, I swiveled my feet some, so that my footsteps were not only deliberate but *gritty*, too.

I stopped with the tips of my shoes on the rim of the narrow field of his downcast eyes. "Mr. Trout, I love you," I said gently. "I have broken your mind to pieces. I want to make it whole. I want you to feel a wholeness and inner harmony such as I have never allowed you to feel before. I want you to raise your eyes, to look at what I have in my hand."

I had nothing in my hand, but such was my power over Trout that he would see in it whatever I wished him to see. I might have shown him a Helen of Troy, for instance, only six inches tall.

"Mr. Trout—*Kilgore*—" I said, "I hold in my hand a symbol of wholeness and harmony and nourishment. It is Oriental in its simplicity, but we are *Americans*, Kilgore, and not Chinamen. We Americans require symbols which are richly colored and three-dimensional and juicy. Most of all, we hunger for symbols which have not been poisoned by great sins our nation has committed, such as slavery and genocide and criminal neglect, or by tinhorn commercial greed and cunning."

"Look up, Mr. Trout," I said, and I waited patiently. "Kilgore—?"

The old man looked up, and he had my father's wasted face when my father was a widower—when my father was an old old man.

He saw that I held an apple in my hand.

"I am approaching my fiftieth birthday, Mr. Trout," I said. "I am cleansing and renewing myself for the very different sorts of years to come. Under similar spiritual conditions, Count Tolstoi freed his serfs. Thomas Jefferson freed his slaves. I am going to set at liberty all the literary characters who have served me so loyally during my writing career."

"You are the only one I am telling. For the others, tonight will be a night like any other night. Arise, Mr. Trout, you are free, you are *free.*"

He arose shamblingly.

I might have shaken his hand, but his right hand was injured, so our hands remained dangling at our sides.

"*Bon voyage,*" I said. I disappeared.

I somersaulted lazily and pleasantly through the void, which is my hiding place when I dematerialize. Trout's cries to me faded as the distance between us increased.

His voice was my father's voice. I *heard* my father—and I *saw* my mother in the void. My mother stayed far, far away, because she had left me a legacy of suicide.

A small hand mirror floated by. It was a *leak*[1] with a mother-of-pearl handle and frame. I captured it easily, held it up to my own right eye, which looked like this:

1. L'écrivain de science-fiction Trout a imaginé que les miroirs sont des trous qui permettent de glisser dans un autre univers, faisant ainsi écho à *Through the Looking-Glass* de Lewis Carroll.

Here was what Kilgore Trout cried out to me in my father's voice: "*Make me young, make me young, make me young!*"

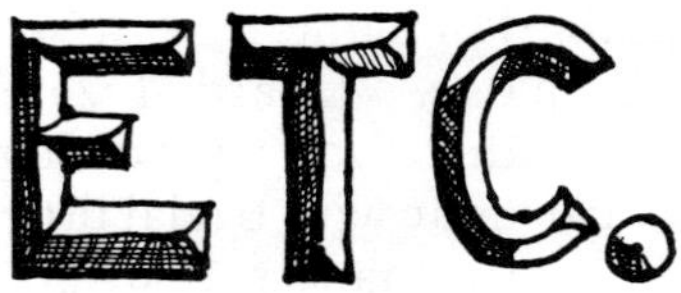

DONALD BARTHELME, 1931-1989

Une foule inattendue d'écrivains de talent, étudiants comme enseignants de *creative writing,* est apparue sur la scène universitaire dans les deux dernières décennies Donald Barthelme est l'un des dignes représentants de ces auteurs qui se sont fait une réputation modeste mais solide. Depuis ses premiers succès dans les années soixante, il travailla dans la perspective post-moderne de Barth et Vonnegut. Barthelme s'était justifié en réfutant avec verve les principes traditionnels de la fiction, disant que dans son œuvre « unlike things are stuck together to make, in the best case, a new reality ». Ses excellentes nouvelles ont illustré avec audace cette nouvelle littérature expérimentale, bien que son champ limité ne lui ait pas permis d'acquérir la stature de contemporains tels que Updike, Mailer, Malamud, Bellow, ou encore Styron et Heller qui font maintenant leur retour.

BIBLIOGRAPHIE SÉLECTIVE. — Klinkowitz (Jerome), *Literary Disruptions,* Urbana, University of Illinois Press, 1975 ; McCaffery (Larry), *The Metafictional Muse,* Pittsburgh, Pa., University of Pittsburgh Press, 1982 ; Couturier (Maurice), Durand (Régis), *Donald Barthelme,* New York, Methuen, 1982.

Rebecca[1]

Rebecca Lizard was trying to change her ugly, reptilian, thoroughly unacceptable last name.

"Lizard," said the judge. "Lizard, Lizard, Lizard, Lizard. There's nothing wrong with it if you say it enough times. You can't clutter up the court's calendar with trivial little minor irritations. And there have been far too many people changing their names lately. Changing your name countervails the best interests of the telephone company, the electric company, and the United States government. Motion denied."

Lizard in tears.

Lizard led from the courtroom. A chrysanthemum of Kleenex held under her nose.

"Shaky lady," said a man, "are you a schoolteacher?"

Of course she's a schoolteacher, you idiot. Can't you see the poor woman's all upset? Why don't you leave her alone?

"Are you a homosexual lesbian? Is that why you never married?"

Christ, yes, she's a homosexual lesbian, as you put it. *Would you please shut your face?*

Rebecca went to the damned dermatologist (a new damned dermatologist), but he said the same thing the others had said. "Greenish," he said, "slight greenishness, genetic anomaly, nothing to be done, I'm afraid, Mrs. Lizard."

"Miss Lizard."

"Nothing to be done, Miss Lizard."

"Thank you, Doctor. Can I give you a little something for your trouble?"

"Fifty dollars."

When Rebecca got home the retroactive rent increase was waiting for her, coiled in her mailbox like a pupil about to strike.

Must get some more Kleenex. Or a Ph.D. No other way.

She thought about sticking her head in the oven. But it was an electric oven.

Rebecca's lover, Hilda, came home late.

"How'd it go?" Hilda asked, referring to the day.

"Lousy."

1. Nouvelle tirée de *Amateurs* (1976).

"Hmmm," Hilda said, and quietly mixed strong drinks of busthead[1] for the two of them.

Hilda is a very good-looking woman. So is Rebecca. They love each other—an incredibly dangerous and delicate business, as we know. Hilda has long blond hair and is perhaps a shade the more beautiful. Of course Rebecca has a classic and sexual figure which attracts huge admiration from every beholder.

"You're late," Rebecca said. "Where were you?"

"I had a drink with Stephanie."

"Why did you have a drink with Stephanie?"

"She stopped by my office and said let's have a drink."

"Where did you go?"

"The Barclay."

"How is Stephanie?"

"She's fine."

"Why did you have to have a drink with Stephanie?"

"I was ready for a drink."

"Stephanie doesn't have a slight greenishness, is that it? Nice, pink Stephanie."

Hilda rose and put an excellent C & W[2] album on the record player. It was David Rogers's "Farewell to the Ryman," Atlantic SD 7283. It contains such favorites as "Blue Moon of Kentucky," "Great Speckled Bird," "I'm Movin' On," and "Walking the Floor Over You." Many great Nasville personnel appear on this record.

"Pinkness is not everything," Hilda said. "And Stephanie is a little bit boring. You know that."

"Not so boring that you don't go out for drinks with her."

"I am not interested in Stephanie."

"As I was leaving the courthouse," Rebecca said, "a man unzipped my zipper."

David Rogers was singing "Oh please release me, let me go."

"What were you wearing?"

"What I'm wearing now."

"So he had good taste," Hilda said, "for a creep." She hugged Rebecca, on the sofa. "I love you," she said.

"Screw that," Rebecca said plainly, and pushed Hilda away. "Go hang out with Stephanie Sasser."

1. Boisson alcoolisée bon marché.
2. « Country-Western ».

"I am not interested in Stephanie Sasser," Hilda said for the second time.

Very often one "pushes away" the very thing that one most wants to grab, like a lover. This is a common, although distressing, psychological mechanism, having to do (in my opinion) with the fact that what is presented is not presented "purely," that there is a tiny little canker or grim place in it somewhere. However, worse things can happen.

"Rebecca," said Hilda, "I really don't like your slight greenishness."

The term "lizard" also includes geckos, iguanas, chameleons, slowworms, and monitors. Twenty existing families make up the order, according to the *Larousse Encyclopedia of Animal Life,* and four others are known only from fossils. There are about twenty-five hundred species, and they display adaptations for walking, running, climbing, creeping, or burrowing. Many have interesting names, such as the Bearded Lizard, the Collared Lizard, the Flap-Footed Lizard, the Frilled Lizard, the Girdle-Tailed Lizard, and the Wall Lizard.

"I have been overlooking it for these several years, because I love you, but I really don't like it so much," Hilda said. "It's slightly—"

"Knew it", said Rebecca.

Rebecca went into the bedroom. The color television set was turned on, for some reason. In a greenish glow, a film called *Green Hell* was unfolding.

I'm ill, I'm ill.

I will become a farmer.

Our love, our sexual love, our ordinary love!

Hilda entered the bedroom and said, "Supper is ready."

"What is it?"

"Pork with red cabbage."

"I'm drunk," Rebecca said.

Too many of our citizens are drunk at times when they should be sober—suppertime, for example. Drunkenness leads to forgetting where you have put your watch, keys, or money clip, and to a decreased sensitivity to the needs and desires and calm good health of others. The causes of overuse of alcohol are not as clear as the results. Psychiatrists feel in general that alcoholism is a serious problem but treatable, in some cases. AA is said to be both popular and effective. At base, the question is one of willpower.

"Get up," Hilda said. "I'm sorry I said that."

"You told the truth," said Rebecca.

"Yes, it was the truth," Hilda admitted.

"You didn't tell me the truth in the beginning. In the beginning, you said it was beautiful."

"I was telling you the truth, in the beginning. I did think it was beautiful. Then."

This "then," the ultimate word in Hilda's series of three brief sentences, is one of the most pain-inducing words in the human vocabulary, when used in this sense. Departed time! And the former conditions that went with it! How is human pain to be measured? But remember that Hilda, too . . . It is correct to feel for Rebecca in this situation, but, reader, neither can Hilda's position be considered an enviable one, for truth, as Bergson knew, is a hard apple, whether one is throwing it or catching it.

"What remains?" Rebecca said stonily.

"I can love you *in spite of*—"

Do *I* want to be loved *in spite of*? Do you? Does anyone? But aren't we all, to some degree? Aren't there important parts of all of us which must be, so to say, gazed past? I turn a blind eye to that aspect of you, and you turn a blind eye to that aspect of me, and with these blind eyes eyeball-to-eyeball, to use an expression from the early 1960s, we continue our starched and fragrant lives. Of course it's also called "making the best of things," which I have always considered a rather soggy idea for an American ideal. But my criticisms of this idea must be tested against those of others—the late President McKinley,[1] for example, who maintained that maintaining a good, if not necessarily sunny, disposition was the one valuable and proper course.

Hilda placed her hands on Rebecca's head.

"The snow is coming," she said. "Soon it will be snow time. Together then as in other snow times. Drinking busthead round the fire. Truth is a locked room that we knock the lock off from time to time, and then board up again. Tomorrow you will hurt me,

1. William McKinley, Président des Etats-Unis, élu en 1896, réélu en 1900. Assassiné en 1901 par l'anarchiste Léon Czolgosz à Buffalo. Ici, Barthelme plaisante car McKinley ne fut pas un grand président.

and I will inform you that you have done so, and so on and so on. To hell with it. Come, viridian[1] friend, come and sup with me."

They sit down together. The pork with red cabbage steams before them. They speak quietly about the McKinley Administration, which is being revised by revisionist historians. The story ends. It was written for several reasons. Nine of them are secrets. The tenth is that one should never cease considering human love, which remains as grisly and golden as ever, no matter what is tattooed upon the warm tympanic page.

ANN BEATTIE, 1947-

Afin de se faire un nom distinct parmi la légion d'écrivains d'aujourd'hui (ou de toute autre époque), il faut avoir un sujet de valeur et une maîtrise technique susceptible d'organiser efficacement ses données. Ann Beattie a su à l'évidence répondre à cette double exigence. Auteur virtuellement autodidacte puisqu'elle se détourna des études littéraires à l'université, elle a reconnu son intérêt précoce pour un seul auteur, Hemingway.

Donald Barthelme est devenu l'un de ses écrivains préférés. Mais Ann Beattie fait preuve d'originalité. Elle écrit rapidement dans le jaillissement d'un art spontané. Bien qu'elle ait produit trois romans, elle préfère les nouvelles et, dans ce genre, Ann Beattie est apparue comme le chroniqueur de la nouvelle génération des *baby boomers,* formée de Yuppies *(young urban professionals)*. Nés dans les quinze à vingt années d'explosion démographique qui ont suivi la Deuxième Guerre, ce sont les jeunes adultes élégants et « branchés » mais inquiets, des années quatre-vingt. Dans les œuvres d'Ann Beattie, l'univers se compose de personnages centraux qui sont, selon le cas, des couples préoccupés de leur carrière, de jeunes parents divorcés (remariés ou vivant avec un partenaire qui vient de divorcer), des bisexuels, des ex-amants, des couples vivant librement, des partenaires homosexuels infidèles, et ainsi de suite. Victimes de ces

1. Couleur oxyde bleu-vert utilisée en peinture et teinture.

personnages sont les enfants en avance sur leur âge qui vivent parmi eux. Le cadre des récits peut être les bureaux des métropoles de l'Est, les centres commerciaux, les bars, les trains de banlieue, les appartements de New York, les quartiers résidentiels du Connecticut, les maisons de campagne. Tous sont dessinés de traits nets et vigoureux qui mettent en évidence les détails d'objets contemporains, la nourriture, la boisson, la drogue et la musique pop. La banalité de ces vies prend des formes diverses dans l'écroulement des rêves de jeunesse et des ambitions romantiques. Les rapports se détériorent mais les couples ne peuvent se séparer. A l'image de la « tranche de vie » des anciens réalistes, les histoires que nous raconte Ann Beattie fournissent rarement une solution. « I don't expect answers of anyone », a-t-elle dit, « other than a medical doctor ». Son narrateur est fréquemment une femme anonyme qui s'exprime à la première personne. Comme Updike, Ann Beattie apprécie l'immédiateté que traduit le verbe au présent. Ses phrases ont souvent une facture qui rappelle Hemingway. Elles sont brèves et simples, dans la mesure où elles relèvent davantage de la coordination que de la subordination. Ses nouvelles les plus réussies ont l'épure d'un plan photographique ou d'un tableau moderne de David Hockney, l'un des peintres préférés d'Ann Beattie, où la vision « superréaliste » émane de l'effet déconcertant d'une apparente reproduction qui n'a jamais eu de modèle original, inerte ou vivant.

BIBLIOGRAPHIE SÉLECTIVE. — McCaffery (Larry), ed., An Interview with Ann Beattie, *Alive and Writing,* Urbana, University of Illinois Press, 1987.

Afloat[1]

ANNIE BRINGS A HAND-DELIVERED LETTER TO HER FATHER. They stand together on the deck that extends far over the grassy lawn that slopes to the lake, and he reads and she looks off at the water. When she was a little girl she would stand on the metal table

1. Nouvelle publiée dans le *New Yorker* (21 septembre 1981) et reproduite dans *The Burning House* (1982).

pushed to the front of the deck and read the letters aloud to her father. If he sat, she sat. Later, she read them over his shoulder. Now she is sixteen, and she gives him the letter and stares at the trees or the water or the boat bobbing at the end of the dock. It has probably never occurred to her that she does not have to be there when he reads them.

Dear Jerome,

Last week the bottom fell out of the birdhouse you hung in the tree the summer Annie was three. Or something gnawed at it and the bottom came out. I don't know. I put the wood under one of the big clay pots full of pansies, just to keep it for old times' sake. (I've given up the fountain pen for a felt-tip. I'm really not a romantic.) I send to you for a month our daughter. She still wears bangs, to cover that little nick in her forehead from the time she fell out of the swing. The swing survived until last summer when—or maybe I told you in last year's letter—Marcy Smith came by with her "friend" Hamilton, and they were so taken by it that I gave it to them, leaving the ropes dangling. I mean that I gave them the old green swing seat, with the decals of roses even uglier than the scraggly ones we grew. Tell her to pull her bangs back and show the world her beautiful widow's peak. She now drinks spritzers. For the first two weeks she's gone I'll be in Ogunquit with Zack. He is younger than you, but no one will ever duplicate the effect of your slow smile. Have a good summer together. I will be thinking of you at unexpected times (unexpected to me, of course).

Love,
Anita

He hands the letter on to me, and then pours club soda and Chablis into a tall glass for Annie and fills his own glass with wine alone. He hesitates while I read, and I know he's wondering whether the letter will disturb me—whether I'll want club soda or wine. "Soda," I say. Jerome and Anita have been divorced for ten years.

In these first few days of Annie's visit, things aren't going very well. My friends think that it's just about everybody's summer story. Rachel's summers are spent with her ex-husband, and with his daughter by his second marriage, the daughter's boyfriend, and the boyfriend's best friend. The golden retriever isn't there this summer, because last summer he drowned. No one knows how. Jean is letting her optometrist, with whom she once had an affair, stay in her house in the Hamptons on weekends. She stays in town, because she is in love with a chef. Hazel's the exception. She teaches summer school, and when it ends she and her husband and their son go to Block Island for two weeks, to the house they always rent. Her husband has his job back, after a year in A. A. I study her life and wonder how it works. Of the three best friends I have, she blushes the most easily, is the worst dressed, is the least politically informed, and prefers AM rock stations to FM classical music. Our common denominator is that none of us was married in a church and all of us worried about the results of the blood test we had before we could get a marriage license. But there are so many differences. Say their names to me and what comes to mind is that Rachel cried when she heard Dylan's *Self Portrait* album, because, to her, that meant that everything was over; Jean fought off a man in a supermarket parking lot who was intent on raping her, and still has nightmares about the arugula she was going to the store to get; Hazel can recite Yeats's "The Circus Animals' Desertion" and bring tears to your eyes.

Sitting on the deck, I try to explain to Annie that there *should* be solidarity between women, but that when you look for a common bond you're really looking for a common denominator, and you can't do that with women. Annie puts down *My Mother/My Self* and looks out at the water.

Jerome and I, wondering when she will ever want to swim, go about our days as usual. She's gone biking with him, so there's no hostility. She has always sat at the foot of the bed while Jerome was showering at night and talked nonsense with me while she twisted the ends of her hair, and she still does. At her age, it isn't important that she's not in love, and she was once before anyway. When she pours for herself, it's sixty-forty white wine and club soda. Annie—the baby pushed in a swing. The bottom fell out of the birdhouse. Anita really knows how to hit below the belt.

Jerome is sulky at the end of the week, floating in the Whaler.

"Do you ever think that Anita's thinking of you?" I ask.

"Telepathy, you mean?" he says. He has a good tan. A scab by his elbow. Somehow, he's hurt himself. His wet hair is drying in curly strands. He hasn't had a haircut since we came to the summer house.

"No. Do you ever wonder if she just might be thinking about you?"

"I don't think about her," he says.

"You read the letter Annie brings you every year."

"I'm curious."

"Just curious for that one brief minute?"

Yes, he nods. "Notice that I'm always the one that opens the junk mail, too," he says.

According to Jerome, he and Anita gradually drifted apart. Or, at times when he blames himself, he say it's because he was still a child when he married her. He married her the week of his twentieth birthday. He says that his childhood wounds still weren't healed; Anita was Mama, she was the person he always felt he had to prove himself to—the stuff any psychiatrist will run down for you, he says now, trailing his hand in the water. "It's like there was a time in your life when you believed in paste," he says. "Think how embarrassed you'd be to go buy paste today. Now it's rubber cement. Or at least Elmer's glue. When I was young I just didn't know things."

I never had any doubt when things ended with my first husband. We knew things were wrong; we were going to a counselor and either biting our tongues or arguing because we'd loosened them with too much alcohol, trying to pretend that it didn't matter that I couldn't have a baby. One weekend Dan and I went to Saratoga, early in the spring, to visit friends. It was all a little too sun-dappled. Too *House Beautiful,* the way the sun, in the early morning, shone through the lace curtains and paled the walls to polka dots of light. The redwood picnic table on the stone-covered patio was as bright in the sunlight as if it had been waxed. We were drinking iced tea, all four of us out in the yard early in the morning, amazed at what a perfect day it was, how fast the garden was growing, how huge the heads of the peonies were. Then some people stopped by, with their little girl—people new to Saratoga, who really had no friends there yet. The little girl was named Alison, and she took a liking to Dan—came up to him without hesitation, the way a puppy that's been chastised will instantly choose someone in the room to cower by, or a bee will zero in on one member of a group. She came innocently, the way a child would come, fascinated by . . . by his curly hair? The way the sunlight reflected off the rims of his glasses? The wedding ring on his hand as he rested his arm on the picnic table? And then, as the rest of us talked, there was a squealing game, with the child suddenly climbing from the ground to his lap, some whispering, some laughing, and then the child, held around her middle, raised above his head, parallel to the ground. The game went on and on, with cries of "Again!" and "Higher!" until the child was shrill and Dan complained of numb arms, and for a second I looked away from the conversation the rest of us were having and I saw her raised above him, smiling down, and Dan both frowning and amused—that little smile at the edge of his lips—and the child's mouth, wide with delight, her long blond hair flopped forward. He was keeping her raised off the ground, and she was hoping that it would never end, and in that second I knew that for Dan and me it was over.

We took a big bunch of pink peonies back to the city with us, stuck in a glass jar with water in the bottom that I held wedged between my feet. I had on a skirt, and the flowers flopped as we went over the bumpy road and the sensation I felt was amazing: it wasn't a tickle, but a pain. When he stopped for gas I went into the bathroom and cried and washed my face and dried it on one of those brown paper towels that smell more strongly than any perfume. I combed my hair. When I was sure I looked fine I came back to the car and sat down, putting one foot on each side of the jar. He started to drive out of the gas station, and then he just drifted to a stop. It was still sunny. Late afternoon. We sat there with the sun heating us and other cars pulling around our car, and he said, "You are impossible. You are so emotional. After a perfect day, what have you been crying about?" Then there were tears, and since I said nothing, eventually he started to drive: out into the merging lane, then onto the highway, speeding all the way back to New York in silence. It was already over. The only other thing I remember about that day is that down by Thirty-fourth Street we saw the same man who had been there the week before, selling roses guaranteed to smell sweet and to be everlasting. There he was, in the same place, his roses on a stand behind him.

We swim, and gradually work our way back to the gunwale of the Whaler: six hands, white-knuckled, holding the rim. I slide along, hand over hand, then move so that my body touches

Jerome's from behind. With my arms around his chest, I kiss his neck. He turns and smiles and kisses me. Then I kick away and go to where Annie is holding on to the boat, her cheek on her hands, staring at her father. I swim up to her, push her wet bangs to one side, and kiss her forehead. She looks aggravated, and turns her head away. Just as quickly, she turns it back. "Am I interrupting you two getting it on out here?" she says.

"I kissed both of you," I say, between them again, feeling the weightlessness of my legs dangling as I hold on.

She continues to stare at me. "Girls kissing girls is so dumb," she says. "It's like the world's full of stupid hostesses who graduated from Sweet Briar."

Jerome looks at her silently for a long time.

"I guess your mother's not very demonstrative," he says.

"Were you ever?" she says. "Did you love Anita when you had me?"

"Of course I did," he says. "Didn't you know that?"

"It doesn't matter what I know," she says, as angry and petulant as a child. "How come you don't feed me birdseed?" she says. "How come you don't feed the carrier pigeon?"

He pauses until he understands what she is talking about. "The letters just go one ways," he says.

"Do you have too much *dignity* to answer them, or is it too risky to reveal anything?"

"Honey," he says, lowering his voice, "I don't have anything to say."

"That you loved her and now you don't?" she says. "That's what isn't worth saying?"

He's brought his knees up to his chin. The scab by his elbow is pale when he clasps his arm around his knees.

"Well, I think that's bullshit," she says. She looks at me. "And I think you're bullshit, too. You don't care about the bond between women. You just care about hanging on to him. When you kissed me, it was patronizing."

There are tears now. Tears that are ironic, because there is so much water everywhere. Today she's angry and alone, and I float between them knowing exactly how each one feels and, like the little girl Alison suspended above Dan's head, knowing that desire that can be more overwhelming than love—the desire, for one brief minute, simply to get off the earth.

4 – Poètes de l'engagement et de la confidence

Les poètes américains modernes ont considérablement raffiné leur technique, mais aucun d'entre eux ne domine la scène littéraire depuis la guerre. Rares ont été les poèmes spontanément gardés en mémoire ou les exemples d'éblouissante innovation. Seuls Robert Lowell, Theodore Roethke et le vénérable Robert Pen Warren ont été les émules des grands poètes du passé, cités dans les pages antérieures. Les membres de cette génération de l'après-guerre ont néanmoins composé des poèmes isolés qui par intermittence se distinguent nettement de l'ensemble. Lorsqu'on rassemble les œuvres de ces différents auteurs selon les thèmes culturels qui s'identifient à la période, beaucoup d'entre eux font entendre une voix et révèlent une communauté de valeurs dont on retrouve parfois les équivalences en prose. Dans ce groupe de poètes, les femmes affirment de plus en plus nettement leur présence. C'est l'esprit moderne et le modèle esthétique de la toujours jeune Eudora Welty qui semblent à maints égards inspirer cette pléiade de femmes-écrivains. Les écrits de Joyce Carol Oates, Alice Walker, Nora Ephron, Louise Erdrich, Toni Morrison, Mary Robison et bien d'autres, viennent à l'esprit quand on lit les vers de ces femmes qui leur font écho depuis le milieu du siècle et que nous présentons dans cette dernière partie de l'anthologie.

BIBLIOGRAPHIE SÉLECTIVE. — Greiner (Donald), ed., *American Poets Since World War II,* 2 vol., Detroit, Gale, 1980 ; Mills (Ralph), *Contemporary American Poetry,* New York, Random House, 1965 ; Rosenthal (M. L.) and Gall (Sally), *The Modern Poetic Sequence : The Genius of Modern Poetry,* New york, Oxford University Press, 1983 ; Hocquard (E.), Royet-Journoux (C.), American Poets Today, *Delta,* Montpellier, 1986 ; Les femmes-écrivains aux Etats-Unis, *Revue française d'Etudes américaines,* 30, novembre 1986 (articles de Ginette Castro, Elisabeth Béranger, Rolande Diot, Marc Chénetier) ; Pitavy-Souques (Danièle), Le Sud, territoire des femmes, *Revue française d'Etudes américaines,* février 1985, p. 25-50.

THE DARK LEGACY OF WORLD WAR II[1]

Randall Jarrell, 1914-1965[2]

THE DEATH OF THE BALL TURRET GUNNER

From my mother's sleep I fell into the State,
And I hunched in its belly till my wet fur froze.
Six miles from earth, loosed from its dream of life,
I woke to black flak and the nightmare fighters.
When I died they washed me out of the turret with a hose.

(1945)

1. La date des poèmes de cette partie, comme des autres sélections ci-dessous, se réfère à l'année de leur première publication dans un volume des œuvres de l'auteur. Les notes correspondent consécutivement à tous les poèmes d'un même groupe thématique.

Les intertitres en anglais de ce choix de poèmes et qui désignent les thèmes centraux sont de la rédaction.

2. A la différence du poète du passé, assimilé à un personnage romantique, vivant d'un travail ingrat, du moins s'il en trouvait un, ou condamné à la pauvreté en essayant d'écrire, Jarrell ressemble à la plupart des poètes de l'après-guerre publiés ici. Ils s'assurent une carrière bien rémunérée en exerçant des activités complémentaires. Ils font des lectures publiques, ou bien, en tant que *poet-in-residence* associé ou titulaire, ils enseignent les nombreux cours de *creative writing* dans presque toutes les grandes universités. L'intérêt biographique particulier qui s'attache aux cinq poètes de cette première partie réside dans leurs états de service pendant la guerre. Bien que Jarrell soit l'auteur des vers célèbres sur le mitrailleur à bord d'un bombardier, il échoua à son examen de sortie de l'école d'aviation pendant la guerre, période à laquelle il fut affecté aux Etats-Unis.

William Stafford, 1914-[1]

AT THE BOMB TESTING SITE

At noon in the desert a panting lizard
waited for history, its elbows tense,
watching the curve of a particular road
as if something might happen.

It was looking at something farther off
than people could see, an important scene
acted in stone for little selves
at the flute end of consequences.

There was just a continent without much on it
under a sky that never cared less.
Ready for a change, the elbows waited.
The hands gripped hard on the desert.

(1960)

Richard Hugo, 1923-1982[2]

G.I. GRAVES IN TUSCANY

They still seem G.I., the uniform lines
of white crosses, the gleam that rolls
white drums over the lawn. Machines
that cut the grass left their maneuvers plain.
Our flag doesn't seem silly though plainly
it flies only because there is wind.

Let them go by. I don't want to turn in.
After ten minutes I'd be sick of their names
or the names of their towns. Then
some guide would offer a tour
for two thousand lire, smiling the places

1. Stafford était un objecteur de conscience pendant la guerre.
2. Hugo fut bombardier dans le US Army Air Corps et eut pour base l'Italie.

of battle, feigning hate for the Krauts.
I guess visitors come. A cross here and there
is rooted in flowers. Maybe in Scranton
a woman is saving. Maybe in books
what happened and why is worked out.

The loss is so damn gross. I remember
a washtub of salad in basic, blacktop acres
of men waiting to march, passing three hours
of bombers, en route to Vienna, and bombing
and passing two hours of planes, coming back.
Numbers are vulgar. If I stayed
I'd count the men in years of probable loss.

I'm a liar. I'm frightened to stop.
Afraid of a speech I might make,
corny over some stone with a name
that indicates Slavic descent—you there,
you must be first generation,
I'm third. The farm, I'm told, was hard
but it all means something. Think
of Jefferson, of the Constitution,
not of these children
beside me, bumming a smoke and laughing.

(1969)

Donald Hall, 1928-[1]

THE MAN IN THE DEAD MACHINE

High on a slope in New Guinea
the Grumman Hellcat
lodges among bright vines
as thick as arms. In nineteen-forty-three,
the clenched hand of a pilot
glided it here
where no one has ever been.

1. Hall était trop jeune pour servir durant la Deuxième Guerre. Il s'opposa fermement à la guerre du Viêt-nam.

In the cockpit the helmeted
skeleton sits
upright, held
by dry sinews at neck
and shoulder, and by webbing
that straps the pelvic cross
to the cracked
leather of the seat, and the breastbone
to the canvas cover
of the parachute.

Or say that the shrapnel
missed me, I flew
back to the carrier, and every morning
take the train, my pale
hands on a black case, and sit
upright, held
by the firm webbing.

(1969)

Gerald Stern, 1925-[1]

THE WAR AGAINST THE JEWS

Look how peaceful these wooden figures are, going to their death.
How happy they were to go instead of me.
They love to march back and forth under the iron clock.
One tips his hat endlessly to a mother and her three children.
One dries his tears in front of the water fountain.
They bump their heads as they bend down to drink.

Over there a German soldier is blowing his whistle.
He was carved while he still could remember his mother's garden.
How glad he was to go to Poland.
How young he felt in his first pair of boots.

1. Stern servit dans le US Army Air Corps après la Deuxième Guerre.

I would give anything to bring them back:
to let them sit again on the polished benches;
to let them see the great glass roof again;
to rush through the noisy crowd screaming
"Stop! It's a dream! It's a dream!
Go back to your shuls.[1] Go back to your mother's garden.
O wooden figures, go back, go back."

(1981)

NATURE AND SELFHOOD

Elizabeth Bishop, 1911-1979

THE FISH

I caught a tremendous fish
and held him beside the boat
half out of water, with my hook
fast in a corner of his mouth.
He didn't fight.
He hadn't fought at all.
He hung a grunting weight,
battered and venerable
and homely. Here and there
his brown skin hung in strips
like ancient wallpaper,
and its pattern of darker brown
was like wallpaper:
shapes like full-blown roses
stained and lost through age.
He was speckled with barnacles,
fine rosettes of lime,
and infested
with tiny white sea-lice,

1. Synagogues.

and underneath two or three
rags of green weed hung down.
While his gills were breathing in
the terrible oxygen
—the frightening gills,
fresh and crisp with blood,
that can cut so badly—
I thought of the coarse white flesh
packed in like feathers,
the big bones and the little bones,
the dramatic reds and blacks
of his shiny entrails,
and the pink swim-bladder
like a big peony.
I looked into his eyes
which were far larger than mine
but shallower, and yellowed,
the irises backed and packed
with tarnished tinfoil
seen through the lenses
of old scratched isinglass.
They shifted a little, but not
to return my stare.
—It was more like the tipping
of an object toward the light.
I admired his sullen face,
the mechanism of his jaw,
and then I saw
that from his lower lip
—if you could call it a lip—
grim, wet, and weaponlike,
hung five old pieces of fish-line,
or four and a wire leader
with the swivel still attached,
with all their five big hooks
grown firmly in his mouth.
A green line, frayed at the end
where he broke it, two heavier lines,
and a fine black thread
still crimped from the strain and snap

when it broke and he got away.
Like medals with their ribbons
frayed and wavering,
a five-haired beard of wisdom
trailing from his aching jaw.
I stared and stared
and victory filled up
the little rented boat,
from the pool of bilge
where oil had spread a rainbow
around the rusted engine
to the bailer rusted orange,
the sun-cracked thwarts,
the oarlocks on their strings,
the gunnels—until everything
was rainbow, rainbow, rainbow!
And I let the fish go.

(1946)

Robert Lowell, 1917-1978

SKUNK HOUR

(for Elizabeth Bishop)

Nautilus Island's hermit
heiress still lives through winter in her Spartan cottage;[1]
her sheep still graze above the sea.
Her son's a bishop. Her farmer
is first selectman in our village;
she's in her dotage.

Thirsting for
the hierarchic privacy
of Queen Victoria's century,
she buys up all
the eyesores facing her shore,
and lets them fall.

1. Nautilus Island est dans le Maine.

The season's ill—
we've lost our summer millionaire,
who seemed to leap from an L. L. Bean[1]
catalogue. His nine-knot yawl
was auctioned off to lobstermen.
A red fox stain covers Blue Hill.

And now our fairy
decorator brightens his shop for fall;
his fishnet's filled with orange cork,
orange, his cobbler's bench and awl;
there is no money in his work,
he'd rather marry.

One dark night,
my Tudor Ford climbed the hill's skull;
I watched for love-cars. Lights turned down,
they lay together, hull to hull,
where the graveyard shelves on the town. . . .
My mind's not right.

A car radio bleats,
"Love, O careless Love. . . ." I hear
my ill-spirit sob in each blood cell,
as if my hand were at its throat. . . .
I myself am hell;
nobody's here—

only skunks, that search
in the moonlight for a bite to eat.
They march on their soles up Main Street:
white stripes, moonstruck eyes' red fire
under the chalk-dry and spar spire
of the Trinitarian Church.

1. Maison d'achat par correspondance du Maine qui vend du matériel de chasse et des équipements de plein air.

I stand on top
of our back steps and breathe the rich air—
a mother skunk with her column of kittens swills the garbage
pail.
She jabs her wedge-head in a cup
of sour cream, drops her ostrich tail,
and will not scare.

(1959)

James Wright, 1971-1980

A BLESSING

Just off the highway to Rochester, Minnesota,
Twilight bounds softly forth on the grass.
And the eyes of those two Indian ponies
Darken with kindness.
They have come gladly out of the willows
To welcome my friend and me.
We step over the barbed wire into the pasture
Where they have been grazing all day, alone.
They ripple tensely, they can hardly contain their happiness
That we have come.
They bow shyly as wet swans. They love each other.
There is no loneliness like theirs.
At home once more,
They begin munching the young tufts of spring in the
darkness.
I would like to hold the slenderer one in my arms,
For she has walked over to me
And nuzzled my left hand.
She is black and white,
Her mane falls wild on her forehead,
And the light breeze moves me to caress her long ear
That is delicate as the skin over a girl's wrist.
Suddenly I realize
That if I stepped out of my body I would break
Into blossom.

(1962)

Philip Levine, 1928-

ANIMALS ARE PASSING FROM OUR LIVES

It's wonderful how I jog
on four honed-down ivory toes
my massive buttocks slipping
like oiled parts with each light step.

I'm to market. I can smell
the sour, grooved block, I can smell
the blade that opens the hole
and the pudgy white fingers

that shake out the intestines
like a hankie. In my dreams
the snouts drool on the marble,
suffering children, suffering flies,

suffering the consumers
who won't meet their steady eyes
for fear they could see. The boy
who drives me along believes

that any moment I'll fall
on my side and drum my toes
like a typewriter or squeal
and shit like a new housewife

discovering television,
or that I'll turn like a beast
cleverly to hook his teeth
with my teeth. No. Not this pig.

(1968)

HARROWING EXISTENCE PRECEDES ESSENCE

Theodore Roethke, 1908-1963

THE WAKING

I wake to sleep, and take my waking slow.
I feel my fate in what I cannot fear.
I learn by going where I have to go.

We think by feeling. What is there to know?
I hear my being dance from ear to ear.
I wake to sleep, and take my waking slow.

Of those so close beside me, which are you?
God bless the Ground! I shall walk softly there,
And learn by going where I have to go.

Light takes the Tree; but who can tell us how?
The lowly worm climbs up a winding stair;
I wake to sleep, and take my waking slow.

Great Nature has another thing to do
To you and me; so take the lively air,
And, lovely, learn by going where to go.

This shaking keeps me steady. I should know.
What falls away is always. And is near.
I wake to sleep, and take my waking slow.
I learn by going where I have to go.

(1953)

IN A DARK TIME

In a dark time, the eye begins to see,
I meet my shadow in the deepening shade;
I hear my echo in the echoing wood—
A lord of nature weeping to a tree.
I live between the heron and the wren,
Beasts of the hill and serpents of the den.

What's madness but nobility of soul
At odds with circumstance? The day's on fire!
I know the purity of pure despair,
My shadow pinned against a sweating wall.
That place among the rocks—is it a cave,
Or winding path? The edge is what I have.

A steady storm of correspondences!
A night flowing with birds, a ragged moon,
And in broad day the midnight come again!
A man goes far to find out what he is—
Death of the self in a long, tearless night,
All natural shapes blazing unnatural light.

Dark, dark my light, and darker my desire.
My soul, like some heat-maddened summer fly,
Keeps buzzing at the sill. Which I is *I*?
A fallen man, I climb out of my fear.
The mind enters itself, and God the mind,
And one is One, free in the tearing wind.

(1964)

Richard Wilbur, 1921-

LOVE CALLS US TO THE THINGS OF THIS WORLD

The eyes open to a cry of pulleys,
And spirited from sleep, the astounded soul
Hangs for a moment bodiless and simple
As false dawn.
Outside the open window
The morning air is all awash with angels.

Some are in bed-sheets, some are in blouses,
Some are in smocks: but truly there they are.
Now they are rising together in calm swells
Of halcyon feeling, filling whatever they wear
With the deep joy of their impersonal breathing;

Now they are flying in place, conveying
The terrible speed of their omnipresence, moving
And staying like white water; and now of a sudden
They swoon down into so rapt a quiet
That nobody seems to be there.
The soul shrinks

From all that it is about to remember,
From the punctual rape of every blessed day,
And cries,
"Oh, let there be nothing on earth but laundry,
Nothing but rosy hands in the rising steam
And clear dances done in the sight of heaven."

Yet, as the sun acknowledges
With a warm look the world's hunks and colors,
The soul descends once more in bitter love
To accept the waking body, saying now
In a changed voice as the man yawns and rises,

"Bring them down from their ruddy gallows.
Let there be clean linen for the backs of thieves;
Let lovers go fresh and sweet to be undone,
And the heaviest nuns walk in a pure floating
Of dark habits,
keeping their difficult balance."

(1956)

Louis Simpson, 1923-

IN THE SUBURBS

There's no way out.
You were born to waste your life.
You were born to this middleclass life

As others before you
Were born to walk in procession
To the temple, singing.

(1963)

THE POET ENGAGÉ

Allen Ginsberg, 1926-

HOWL[1]

for Carl Solomon[2]

I

I saw the best minds of my generation destroyed by madness, starving hysterical naked,
dragging themselves through the negro streets at dawn looking for an angry fix,
angelheaded hipsters burning for the ancient heavenly connection to the starry dynamo in the machinery of night,
who poverty and tatters and hollow-eyed and high sat up smoking in the supernatural darkness of cold-water flats floating across the tops of cities contemplating jazz,

1. Ce poème de 112 vers proclama en 1956 l'esprit de la contre-culture du mouvement *beatnik* parmi les contestataires de la société américaine qui adoptèrent un langage, des vêtements et une chevelure non conventionnels en même temps que la drogue et l'amour libre. Les romans *On the Road* (1957) de Jack Kerouac et *The Naked Lunch* (1959) de William Burroughs accompagnèrent l'assaut de *Howl* contre la culture dominante.

2. Un malade à l'hôpital psychiatrique Rockland de New York. Toute la partie III du poème (vers 94-112) s'adresse à Solomon, chaque vers commençant par « I'm with you in Rockland ».

who bared their brains to Heaven under the El[1] and saw
    Mohammedan angels staggering on tenement roofs
    illuminated,
who passed through universities with radiant cool eyes
    hallucinating Arkansas and Blake-light tragedy among the
    scholars of war,
who were expelled from the academies for crazy & publishing
    obscene odes on the windows of the skull,
who cowered in unshaven rooms in underwear, burning their
    money in wastebaskets and listening to the Terror through the
    wall,
who got busted in their pubic beards returning through Laredo[2]
    with a belt of marijuana for New York,
who ate fire in paint hotels or drank turpentine in Paradise Alley,[3]
    death, or purgatoried their torsos night after night
with dreams, with drugs, with waking nightmares, alcohol and
    cock and endless balls,
incomparable blind streets of shuddering cloud and lightning in
    the mind leaping toward poles of Canada & Paterson,[4]
    illuminating all the motionless world of Time between,
Peyote solidities of halls, backyard green tree cemetery dawns,
    wine drunkenness over the rooftops, storefront boroughs of
    teahead joyride neon blinking traffic light, sun and moon and
    tree vibrations in the roaring winter dusks of Brooklyn, ashcan
    rantings and kind king light of mind,
who chained themselves to subways for the endless ride from
    Battery to holy Bronx[5] on benzedrine until the noise of wheels
    and children brought them down shuddering mouth-wracked
    and battered bleak of brain all drained of brilliance in the drear
    light of Zoo,
who sank all night in submarine light of Bickford's[6] floated out and
    sat through the stale beer afternoon in desolate Fugazzi's,[7]
    listening to the crack of doom on the hydrogen jukebox,

1. El : *elevated streetcar.*
2. Ville du Texas sur la frontière mexicaine.
3. Quartier de taudis dans le « Lower East side » de New York.
4. Ville du New Jersey proche de New York.
5. Battery est un parc du sud de Manhattan. Le Bronx est le quartier le plus au nord de New York et l'emplacement d'un célèbre zoo. Chacun de ces lieux est un terminus d'une ligne de métro.
6. Cafétéria de New York.
7. Bar de Greenwich Village.

who talked continuously seventy hours from park to pad to bar to
  Bellevue[1] to museum to the Brooklyn Bridge,
a lost battalion of platonic conversationalists jumping down the
  stoops off fire escapes off windowsills off Empire State[2] out of the
  moon,
yacketayakking screaming vomiting whispering facts and
  memories and anecdotes and eyeball kicks and shocks of
  hospitals and jails and wars,
whole intellects disgorged in total recall for seven days and nights
  with brilliant eyes, meat for the Synagogue cast on the
  pavement,
who vanished into nowhere Zen New Jersey leaving a trail of
  ambiguous picture postcards of Atlantic City Hall,
suffering Eastern sweats and Tangerian bone-grindings and
  migraines of China under junk-withdrawal in Newark's bleak
  furnished room,
who wandered around and around at midnight in the railroad
  yard wondering where to go, and went, leaving no broken
  hearts,
who lit cigarettes in boxcars boxcars boxcars racketing through
  snow toward lonesome farms in grandfather night,
who studied Plotinus Poe St. John of the Cross telepathy and bop
  kaballa[3] because the cosmos instinctively vibrated at their feet
  in Kansas,
who loned it through the streets of Idaho seeking visionary indian
  angels who were visionary indian angels,
who thought they were only mad when Baltimore gleamed in
  supernatural ecstasy,
who jumped in limousines with the Chinaman of Oklahoma on the
  impulse of winter midnight streetlight smalltown rain,
who lounged hungry and lonesome through Houston seeking jazz
  or sex or soup, and followed the brilliant Spaniard to converse
  about America and Eternity, a hopeless task, and so took ship
  to Africa,

1. Hôpital psychiatrique de New York.

2. Gratte-ciel de Manhattan.

3. Le Bop fut un rythme de jazz des années quarante et cinquante, développé par Dizzy Gillespie (trompette) et Charlie Parker (Saxo alto) ; kaballa est une approche mystique hébraïque des Saintes Ecritures.

who disappeared into the volcanoes of Mexico leaving behind
nothing but the shadow of dungarees and the lava and ash of
poetry scattered in fireplace Chicago,
who reappeared on the West Coast investigating the FBI[1] in beards
and shorts with big pacifist eyes sexy in their dark skin passing
out incomprehensible leaflets,
who burned cigarette holes in their arms protesting the narcotic
tobacco haze of Capitalism,
who distributed Supercommunist pamphlets in Union Square[2]
weeping and undressing while the sirens of Los Alamos[3] wailed
them down, and wailed down Wall,[4] and the Staten Island
ferry also wailed,
who broke down crying in white gymnasiums naked and
trembling before the machinery of other skeletons,
who bit detectives in the neck and shrieked with delight in
policecars for committing no crime but their own wild cooking
pederasty and intoxication,
who howled on their knees in the subway and were dragged off the
roof waving genitals and manuscripts. [. . .]

(1956)

Lawrence Ferlinghetti, 1919-[5]

I AM WAITING

I am waiting for my case to come up
and I am waiting
for a rebirth of wonder

1. Le Federal Bureau of Investigation est chargé des crimes au-delà des frontières d'Etat. Dans les années cinquante, après que le sénateur Joseph McCarthy eut estimé que les communistes complotaient pour renverser le gouvernement des Etats-Unis, le FBI surveilla les citoyens qui exprimaient des idées « anti-américaines ».

2. Lieu de réunions publiques où s'expriment librement les opinions.

3. Ville du Nouveau-Mexique où fut mise au point la première bombe atomique en 1945.

4. Wall Street est le quartier financier de New York. Jeu de mots possible de Ginsberg sur le « Mur des Lamentations (« Wailing Wall ») de Jérusalem.

5. Ferlinghetti mérite une attention particulière comme cofondateur influent (1952), propriétaire et directeur depuis 1953 de la maison d'édition City Lights Books de San Francisco. Il a publié les œuvres de nombreux poètes de la « San Francisco Renaissance » et de la « Beat Generation » des années cinquante, qui incluent *Howl* de Ginsberg. Son poème de 169 vers « I Am Waiting » est à la fois engagé et drôle. C'est une sorte de psalmodie telle qu'elle était chantée par les bardes beatniks dans les cafés, et qu'accompagnaient souvent les bongos.

and I am waiting for someone
to really discover America
and wail
and I am waiting
for the discovery
of a new symbolic western frontier
and I am waiting
for the American Eagle
to really spread its wings
and straighten up and fly right
and I am waiting
for the Age of Anxiety
to drop dead[1]
and I am waiting
for the war to be fought
which will make the world safe
for anarchy[2]
and I am waiting
for the final withering away
of all governments
and I am perpetually awaiting
a rebirth of wonder
I am waiting for the Second Coming
and I am waiting
for a religious revival
to sweep thru the state of Arizona
and I am waiting
for the Grapes of Wrath to be stored
and I am waiting
for them to prove
that God is really American
and I am seriously waiting
for Billy Graham and Elvis Presley
to exchange roles seriously
and I am waiting

1. *The Age of Anxiety* (1947) de W. H. Auden reçut le prix Pulitzer pour la poésie. Anglais de naissance, Auden fut naturalisé américain en 1946.

2. Référence ironique à la déclaration du président Woodrow Wilson, le 2 avril 1917, selon laquelle les Etats-Unis devaient entrer en guerre car « the world must be made safe for democracy ». Dans les quatre jours, le Congrès déclara la guerre à l'Allemagne.

to see God on television
piped onto church altars
if only they can find
the right channel
to tune in on
and I am waiting
for the Last Supper to be served again
with a strange new appetizer
and I am perpetually awaiting
a rebirth of wonder [. . .]

(1958)

Donald Justice, 1925-

THE ASSASSINATION
[of Robert Kennedy][1]

It begins again, the nocturnal pulse.
It courses through the cables laid for it.
It mounts to the chandeliers and beats there, hotly.
We are too close. Too late, we would move back.
We are involved with the surge.

Now it bursts. Now it has been announced.
Now it is being soaked up by newspapers.
Now it is running through the streets.
The crowd had it. The woman selling carnations
And the man in the straw hat stand with it in their shoes.

Here is the red marquee it sheltered under,
Here is the ballroom, here
The sadly various orchestra led
By a single gesture. My arms open.
It enters. Look, we are dancing.

June 5, 1968

(1973)

1. Robert Kennedy, ministre de la Justice (Attorney General) sous la présidence de son frère, fut assassiné à Los Angeles en juin 1968 alors qu'il faisait campagne pour être désigné comme le candidat démocrate à l'élection présidentielle.

THE SECOND CIVIL WAR - VIETNAM FALLOUT

Robert Bly, 1923-

COUNTING SMALL-BONED BODIES

Let's count the bodies over again.[1]

If we could only make the bodies smaller,
The size of skulls,
We could make a whole plain white with skulls in the moonlight!

If we could only make the bodies smaller,
Maybe we could get
A whole year's kill in front of us on a desk!

If we could only make the bodies smaller,
We could fit
A body into a finger-ring, for a keepsake forever.

(1967)

Denise Levertov, 1923-

THE ALTARS IN THE STREET

On June 17th, 1966, The New York Times reported that, as part of the Buddhist campaign of non-violent resistance, Viet-Namese children were building altars in the streets of Saigon and Hue, effectively jamming traffic.

Children begin at green dawn nimbly to build
topheavy altars, overweighted with prayers,
thronged each instant more densely

1. Pendant la guerre du Viêt-nam, au journal télévisé du soir, le gouvernement américain annonçait fièrement (et quelquefois grossissait) le nombre des tués appartenant au Viet Cong, afin de persuader les citoyens que les Etats-Unis étaient en train de gagner la guerre.

with almost-visible ancestors.
Where tanks have cracked the roadway
the frail altars shake; here a boy

with red stumps for hands steadies a corner,
here one adjusts with his crutch the holy base.
The vast silence of Buddha overtakes

and overrules the oncoming roar
of tragic life that fills alleys and avenues;
it blocks the way of pedicabs, police, convoys.

The hale and maimed together
hurry to construct for the Buddha
a dwelling at each intersection. Each altar

made from whatever stones, sticks, dreams, are at hand,
is a facet of one altar; by noon
the whole city in all its corruption,

all its shed blood the monsoon cannot wash away,
has become a temple,
fragile, insolent, absolute.

(1967)

Adrienne Rich, 1929-

FOR THE RECORD

The clouds and the stars didn't wage this war
the brooks gave no information
if the mountain spewed stones of fire into the river
it was not taking sides
the raindrop faintly swaying under the leaf
had no political opinions

and if here or there a house
filled with backed-up raw sewage
or poisoned those who lived there

with slow fumes, over years
the houses were not at war
nor did the tinned-up buildings

intend to refuse shelter
to homeless old women and roaming children
they had no policy to keep them roaming
or dying, no, the cities were not the problem
the bridges were non-partisan
the freeways burned, but not with hatred

Even the miles of barbed-wire
stretched around crouching temporary huts
designed to keep the unwanted
at a safe distance, out of sight
even the boards that had to absorb
year upon year, so many human sounds

so many depths of vomit, tears
slow-soaking blood
had not offered themselves for this
The trees didn't volunteer to be cut into boards
nor the thorns for tearing flesh
Look around at all of it

and ask whose signature
is stamped on the orders, traced
in the corner of the building plans
Ask where the illiterate, big-bellied
women were, the drunks and crazies,
the ones you fear most of all: ask where you were.

(1986)

BLACK EXPERIENCE

Gwendolyn Brooks, 1917-

WE REAL COOL

The Pool Players.
Seven at the Golden Shovel.

We real cool. We
Left school. We

Lurk late. We
Strike straight. We

Sing sin. We
Thin gin. We

Jazz June. We
Die soon.

(1960)

Robert Hayden, 1913-1980

THOSE WINTER SUNDAYS

Sundays too my father got up early
and put his clothes on in the blueblack cold,
then with cracked hands that ached
from labor in the weekday weather made
banked fires blaze. No one ever thanked him.

I'd wake and hear the cold splintering, breaking.
When the rooms were warm, he'd call,
and slowly I would rise and dress,
fearing the chronic angers of that house,

Speaking indifferently to him,
who had driven out the cold
and polished my good shoes as well.
What did I know, what did I know
of love's austere and lonely offices?

(1962)

THE PRISONERS

Steel doors—guillotine gates—
of the doorless house closed massively.
We were locked in with loss.

Guards frisked us, marked our wrists,
then let us into the drab Rec Hall—
splotched green walls, high windows barred—

where the dispossessed awaited us.
Hands intimate with knife and pistol,
hands that had cruelly grasped and throttled

clasped ours in welcome. I sensed the plea
of men denied: Believe us human
like yourselves, who but for Grace. . . .

We shared reprieving Hidden Words
revealed by the Godlike imprisoned
One, whose crime was truth.

And I read poems I hoped were true.
It's like you been there, brother, been there,
the scarred young lifer said.

(1978)

Lucille Clifton, 1936-

ADMONITIONS

boys
i don't promise you nothing
but this
what you pawn
i will redeem
what you steal
i will conceal
my private silence to
your public guilt
is all i got

girls
first time a white man
opens his fly
like a good thing
we'll just laugh
laugh real loud my
black women

children
when they ask you
why is your mama so funny
say
she is a poet
she don't have no sense

(1969)

[COME HOME FROM THE MOVIES]

Come home from the movies,
Black girls and boys,
the picture be over and the screen
be cold as our neighborhood.
Come home from the show,
don't be the show.
Take off some flowers and plant them,

pick us some papers and read them,
stop making some babies and raise them.
Come home from the movies
Black girls and boys,
show our fathers how to walk like men,
they already know how to dance.

(1974)

VARIETIES OF SEXUALITY AND LOVE

Theodore Roethke, 1908-1963

I KNEW A WOMAN

I knew a woman, lovely in her bones,
When small birds sighed, she would sigh back at them;
Ah, when she moved, she moved more ways than one:
The shapes a bright container can contain!
Of her choice virtues only gods should speak,
Or English poets who grew up on Greek
(I'd have them sing in chorus, cheek to cheek).

How well her wishes went! She stroked my chin,
She taught me Turn, and Counter-turn, and Stand;
She taught me Touch, that undulant white skin;
I nibbled meekly from her proffered hand;
She was the sickle; I, poor I, the rake,
Coming behind her for her pretty sake
(But what prodigious mowing we did make).

Love likes a gander, and adores a goose:[1]
Her full lips pursed, the errant note to seize;
She played it quick, she played it light and loose;
My eyes, they dazzled at her flowing knees;

1. Deux jeux de mots ici : *gander* signifie (1) le jars, (2) un coup d'œil ; *goose* est (1) l'oie, (2) un coup donné dans l'arrière-train pour s'amuser.

Her several parts could keep a pure repose,
Or one hip quiver with a mobile nose
(She moved in circles, and those circles moved).

Let seed be grass, and grass turn into hay:
I'm martyr to a motion not my own;
What's freedom for? To know eternity.
I swear she cast a shadow white as stone.
But who would count eternity in days?
These old bones live to learn her wanton ways:
(I measure time by how a body sways).

(1958)

Robert Lowell, 1917-1978

"TO SPEAK OF WOE THAT IS IN MARRIAGE"[1]

"It is the future generation that presses into being by means of these exuberant feelings and supersensible soap bubbles of ours."

Schopenhauer

"The hot night makes us keep our bedroom windows open.
Our magnolia blossoms. Life begins to happen.
My hopped up husband drops his home disputes,
and hits the streets to cruise for prostitutes,
free-lancing out along the razor's edge.
This screwball might kill his wife, then take the pledge.
Oh the monotonous meanness of his lust. . . .
It's the injustice . . . he is so unjust—
whiskey-blind, swaggering home at five.
My only thought is how to keep alive.
What makes him tick? Each night now I tie
ten dollars and his car key to my thigh. . . .
Gored by the climacteric of his want,
he stalls above me like an elephant."

(1959)

1. Les mots appartiennent à la femme expérimentée de Bath dans le prologue des *Contes de Cantorbéry* de Chaucer.

Anne Sexton, 1928-1974

THE FARMER'S WIFE

From the hodge porridge
of their country lust,
their local life in Illinois,
where all their acres look
like a sprouting broom factory,
they name just ten years now
that she has been his habit;
as again tonight he'll say
honey bunch let's go
and she will not say how there
must be more to living
than this brief bright bridge
of the raucous bed or even
the slow braille touch of him
like a heavy god grown light,
that old pantomime of love
that she wants although
it leaves her still alone,
built back again at last,
mind's apart from him, living
her own self in her own words
and hating the sweat of the house
they keep when they finally lie
each in separate dreams
and then how she watches him,
still strong in the blowzy bag
of his usual sleep while
her young years bungle past
their same marriage bed
and she wishes him cripple, or poet,
or even lonely, or sometimes,
better, my lover, dead.

(1960)

James Dickey, 1923-

ADULTERY

We have all been in rooms
We cannot die in, and they are odd places, and sad.
Often Indians are standing eagle-armed on hills

In the sunrise   open wide to the Great Spirit
Or gliding in canoes   or cattle are browsing on the walls
Far away   gazing down with the eyes of our children

Not far away   or there are men driving
The last railspike, which has turned
Gold in their hands. Gigantic forepleasure lives

Among such scenes, and we are alone with it
At last. There is always some weeping
Between us   and someone is always checking

A wrist watch by the bed to see how much
Longer we have left. Nothing can come
Of this   nothing can come

Of us: of me with my grim techniques
Or you who have sealed your womb
With a ring of convulsive rubber:

Although we come together,
Nothing will come of us. But we would not give
It up, for death is beaten

By praying Indians   by distant cows   historical
Hammers   by hazardous meetings that bridge
A continent. One could never die here

Never die   never die
While crying. My lover, my dear one
I will see you next week

When I'm in town. I will call you
If I can. Please get hold of please don't
Oh God, Please don't any more I can't bear . . . Listen:

We have done it again we are
Still living. Sit up and smile,
God bless you. Guilt is magical.

(1967)

WOMAN'S IDENTITY

Adrienne Rich, 1929-

AUNT JENNIFER'S TIGERS

Aunt Jennifer's tigers prance across a screen,
Bright topaz denizens of a world of green.
They do not fear the men beneath the tree;
They pace in sleek chivalric certainty.

Aunt Jennifer's fingers fluttering through her wool
Find even the ivory needle hard to pull.
The massive weight of Uncle's wedding band
Sits heavily upon Aunt Jennifer's hand.

When Aunt is dead, her terrified hands will lie
Still ringed with ordeals she was mastered by.
The tigers in the panel that she made
Will go on prancing, proud and unafraid.

(1951)

Isabella Gardner, 1915-1981

SUMMERS AGO

For Edith Sitwell

The Ferryman fairied us out to sea
Gold gold gold sang the apple-tree

Children I told you I tell you our sun was a hail of gold!
I say that sun stoned, that sun stormed our tranquil, our blue bay
bellsweet saltfresh water (bluer than tongue-can-tell, daughter)
and dazed us, darlings, and dazzled us, I say that sun crazed
(that sun clove) our serene as ceramic selves and our noon glazed cove,
and children all that grew wild by the wonderful water shot tall
as tomorrow, reeds suddenly shockingly green had sprouted like sorrow
and crimson explosions of roses arose in that flurry of Danaean glory
while at night we did swoon ah we swanned to a silverer moonlight than listen or lute,
we trysted in gondolas blown from glass and kissed in fluted Venetian bliss.

Sister and brother I your mother
Once was a girl in skirling weather
Though summer and swan must alter, falter,
I waltzed on the water once, son and daughter.

(1955)

Sylvia Plath, 1932-1963

DADDY

You do not do, you do not do
Any more, black shoe
In which I have lived like a foot
For thirty years, poor and white,
Barely daring to breathe or Achoo.

Daddy, I have had to kill you.
You died before I had time—
Marble-heavy, a bag full of God,
Ghastly statue with one grey toe
Big as a Frisco seal

And a head in the freakish Atlantic
Where it pours bean green over blue
In the waters off beautiful Nauset.
I used to pray to recover you.
Ach, du.

In the German tongue, in the Polish town
Scraped flat by the roller
Of wars, wars, wars.
But the name of the town is common.
My Polack friend

Says there are a dozen or two.
So I never could tell where you
Put your foot, your root,
I never could talk to you.
The tongue stuck in my jaw.

It stuck in a barb wire snare.
Ich, ich, ich, ich,
I could hardly speak.
I thought every German was you.
And the language obscene

An engine, an engine
Chuffing me off like a Jew.
A Jew to Dachau, Auschwitz, Belsen.
I began to talk like a Jew.
I think I may well be a Jew.

The snows of the Tyrol, the clear beer of Vienna
Are not very pure or true.
With my gypsy ancestress and my weird luck
And my Taroc pack and my Taroc pack
I may be a bit of a Jew.

I have always been scared of *you*,
With your Luftwaffe, your gobbledygoo.
And your neat moustache
And your Aryan eye, bright blue.
Panzer-man, panzer-man, O You—

Not God but a swastika
So black no sky could squeak through.
Every woman adores a Fascist,
The boot in the face, the brute
Brute heart of a brute like you.

You stand at the blackboard, daddy,
In the picture I have of you,
A cleft in your chin instead of your foot
But no less a devil for that, no not
Any less the black man who

Bit my pretty red heart in two.
I was ten when they buried you.
At twenty I tried to die
And get back, back, back to you.
I thought even the bones would do.

But they pulled me out of the sack,
And they stuck me together with glue.
And then I knew what to do.
I made a model of you,
A man in black with a Meinkampf look

And a love of the rack and the screw.
And I said I do, I do.
So daddy, I'm finally through.
The black telephone's off at the root,
The voices just can't worm through.

If I've killed one man, I've killed two—
The vampire who said he was you
And drank my blood for a year,
Seven years, if you want to know.
Daddy, you can lie back now.

There's a stake in your fat black heart
And the villagers never liked you.
They are dancing and stamping on you.
They always *knew* it was you.
Daddy, daddy, you bastard, I'm through.

(1965)

Carolyn Kizer, 1925-

PRO FEMINA

I will speak about women of letters, for I'm in the racket.
Our biggest successes to date? Old maids to a woman.
And our saddest conspicuous failures? The married spinsters
On loan to the husbands they treated like surrogate fathers.
Think of that crew of self-pitiers, not-very-distant,
Who carried the torch for themselves and got first-degree burns.
Or the sad sonneteers, toast-and-teasdales[1] we loved at thirteen;
Middle-aged virgins seducing the puerile anthologists
Through lust-of-the-mind; barbiturate-drenched Camilles
With continuous periods, murmuring softly on sofas
When poetry wasn't a craft but a sickly effluvium,
The air thick with incense, musk, and emotional blackmail.

I suppose they reacted from an earlier womanly modesty
When too many girls were scabs to their stricken sisterhood,
Impugning our sex to stay in good with the men,
Commencing their insecure bluster. How they must have swaggered
When women themselves indorsed their own inferiority!
Vestals, vassals and vessels, rolled into several,
They took notes in rolling syllabics, in careful journals,
Aiming to please a posterity that despises them.
But we'll always have traitors who swear that a woman surrenders
Her Supreme Function, by equating Art with aggression
And failure with Femininity. Still it's just as unfair
To equate Art with Femininity, like a prettily-packaged commodity

[1] Jeu de mot sur Sara Teasdale. Née en 1884 et auteur de poésies lyriques mineures, elle se suicida à New York en 1933.

When we are the custodians of the world's best-kept secret:
Merely the private lives of one-half of humanity.

But even with masculine dominance, we mares and mistresses
Produced some sleek saboteuses, making their cracks
Which the porridge-brained males of the day were too thick to perceive,
Mistaking young hornets for perfectly harmless bumblebees.
Being thought innocuous rouses some women to frenzy;
They try to be ugly by aping the ways of the men
And succeed. Swearing, sucking cigars and scorching the bedspread,
Slopping straight shots, eyes blotted, vanity-blown
In the expectation of glory: *she writes like a man!*
This drives other women mad in a mist of chiffon
(one poetess draped her gauze over red flannels, a practical feminist).

But we're emerging from all that, more or less,
Except for some lady-like laggards and Quarterly priestesses
Who flog men for fun, and kick women to maim competition.
Now, if we struggle abnormally, we may almost seem normal;
If we submerge our self-pity in disciplined industry;
If we stand up and be hated, and swear not to sleep with editors;
If we regard ourselves formally, respecting our true limitations
Without making an unseemly show of trying to unfreeze our assets;
Keeping our heads and our pride while remaining unmarried;
And if wedded, kill guilt in its tracks when we stack up the dishes
And defect to the typewriter. And if mothers, believe in the luck of our children,
Whom we forbid to devour us, whom we shall not devour,
And the luck of our husbands and lovers, who keep free women.

(1965)

Marge Piercy, 1936-

BARBIE DOLL

This girlchild was born as usual
and presented dolls that did pee-pee

and miniature GE[1] stoves and irons
and wee lipsticks the color of cherry candy.
Then in the magic of puberty, a classmate said:
You have a great big nose and fat legs.

She was healthy, tested intelligent,
possessed strong arms and back,
abundant sexual drive and manual dexterity.
She went to and fro apologizing.
Everyone saw a fat nose on thick legs.

She was advised to play coy,
exhorted to come on hearty,
exercise, diet, smile and wheedle.
Her good nature wore out
like a fan belt.
So she cut off her nose and her legs
and offered them up.

In the casket displayed on satin she lay
with the undertaker's cosmetics painted on,
a turned-up putty nose,
dressed in a pink and white nightie.
Doesn't she look pretty? everyone said.
Consummation at last.
To every woman a happy ending.

(1973)

1. La General Electric fabrique des appareils ménagers.

Tableau chronologique

Histoire

1606 Chartes accordées à la Compagnie de Londres et à la Compagnie de Plymouth pour établir des colonies entre le 34ᵉ et le 45ᵉ parallèle

1607 Fondation de Jamestown en Virginie
Prisonnier du chef indien Powhatan, John Smith est libéré grâce à la princesse Pocahontas

1609 Henry Hudson remonte le fleuve auquel il donnera son nom

1619 Arrivée des premiers esclaves noirs en Virginie

1620 Arrivée des pèlerins près du cap Cod, sur le *Mayflower*, signature du *Mayflower Compact*

1621 William Bradford devient gouverneur de la colonie de Plymouth
La plantation de Plymouth s'allie aux Wampanoags contre les Narragansetts

1626 Fondation de New Amsterdam sur l'île de Manhattan achetée aux Indiens

1630 Arrivée de l'*Arbella* et fondation de la colonie de la Baie au Massachusetts

1637 Conflit avec les Pequods dans le Connecticut

1643 Cambridge Platform. Confédération de la Nouvelle-Angleterre

Littérature

Thomas Hariot, *A Brief and True Report of the New Found Land of Virginia*	1588
John Smith, *A True Relation*	1608
John Smith, *A Description of New England*	1616
William Bradford, *Of Plymouth Plantation*, Annales depuis 1620	publié en 1856
John Smith, *The General Historie of Virginia, New England and the Summer Isles*	1624
John Smith, *The True Travels*	1630
John Winthrop, *Christian Charitie*	1630
John Winthrop, *A Journal of the Transactions and Occurrences in the Settlement of Massachusetts (1630-1649)*	publié en 1790
William Wood, *New England's Prospects*	1634
Thomas Morton, *The New English Canaan*	1637
Thomas Shepard, *The Sincere Convert*	1640
John Cotton, *The Way of Life*	1641
Nathaniel Ward, *Body of Liberties of Massachusetts Bay*	1641
Roger Williams, *The Bloody Tenent of Persecution*	1644
John Cotton, *The Bloody Tenent, Washed*	1647
Nathaniel Ward, *The Simple Cobler of Aggawam*	1647
Thomas Hooker, *A Survey of the Summe of Church-Discipline*	1648
Anne Bradstreet, *The Tenth Muse*	1650
Edward Johnson, *The Wonder-Working Providence of Sion's Saviour in New England*	(1653-1654)
John Cotton, *The Covenant of Grace*	1655
John Hammond, *Leah and Rachel; or The Two Fruitfull Sisters, Virginia and Maryland*	1656

Histoire

1663 Navigation Act

1664 Les Anglais prennent New Amsterdam qu'ils appellent New York

1675 Guerre du roi Philip (Metacomet), chef des Wampanoags
Rébellion de Nathaniel Bacon en Virginie

1682 Le Quaker William Penn fonde la Pennsylvanie
Fondation de la Louisiane française

1686 Rapport du Révérend John Clayton sur la culture du tabac en Virginie

1692 Procès de sorcières à Salem

1700 Nantucket est devenu un port de baleiniers

1732-1733 Nouvelles mesures coercitives de l'Angleterre contre les intérêts économiques des colons

1756 Début de la Guerre française et indienne

1763 Proclamation Act
Traité de Paris. La France abandonne à la Couronne britannique le Canada et les territoires à l'est du Mississippi

1764 James Otis manifeste son opposition à la « taxation sans représentation »

1765 Stamp Act

1770 « Massacre de Boston » où quelques manifestants sont abattus par les troupes britanniques

Littérature

Michael Wigglesworth, *The Day of Doom*	1662
George Alsop, *A Character of the Province of Maryland*	1666
John Eliot, *Indian Dialogues for the Instruction in the Knowledge of God*	1671
Samuel Sewall, *The Diary (1674-1729)*	publié en 1878-1882
Benjamin Tompson, *New England's Crisis*	1676
William Hubbard, *A Narrative of the Troubles with the Indians in New England*	1677
Mary Rowlandson, *A Narrative of the Captivity and Restoration of Mrs Mary Rowlandson*	1682
Increase Mather, *An Arrow Against Profane and Promiscuous Dancing*	1684
Increase Mather, *An Essay for the Recording Illustrious of Providences*	1684
Edward Taylor, Achèvement de *God's Determinations*	1690
Cotton Mather, *The Wonders of the Invisible World*	1692
Samuel Sewall, *The Selling of Joseph*	1700
Cotton Mather, *Magnalia Christi Americana*	1702
Robert Beverley, *The History and Present State of Virginia*	1705
Ebenezer Cook, *The Sot-Weed Factor*	1708
Cadwallader Colden, *The History of the Five Indian Nations*	1727
William Byrd II, *The History of the Dividing Line*	1728-1736, publié 1841
Richard Lewis, *Journey from Patapsco to Annapolis*	1731
Benjamin Franklin, *Poor Richard's Almanac*	1732
Jonathan Edwards, *Sinners in the Hands of an Angry God*	1741
John Woolman, *Some Considerations on the Keeping of Negroes*	1754
Thomas Hutchinson, *History of the Colony of Massachusetts Bay*	1764
Jonathan Mayhew, *The Snare Broken*	1766
Phillis Wheatley, *An Elegiac Poem on the Death of George Whitefield*	1770
Benjamin Franklin, début de la rédaction de l'*Autobiographie*	1771

Histoire

1773 « Boston Tea Party ». Cargaisons de thé précipitées dans le port de Boston par des manifestants déguisés en Indiens

1774 Premier Congrès continental à Philadelphie

1775 Bataille de Bunker Hill à Boston

1776 Déclaration d'Indépendance

1777 George Washington (commandant de l'Armée continentale), à Valley Forge

1778 Daniel Boone explore le Kentucky

1780 Abolition de l'esclavage en Pennsylvanie

1781 Articles de la Confédération
Victoire des troupes franco-américaines sur les Anglais à Yorktown

1783 Traité de Paris
L'esclavage est aboli au Massachusetts

1786 Rébellion de Daniel Shays à la tête de fermiers du Massachusetts

1787 Ordonnance du Nord-Ouest (législation, interdiction de l'esclavage et vente des territoires de l'Ouest)
Vote de la Constitution, ratifiée ensuite par les Etats

1789 George Washington, premier Président des Etats-Unis
Bill of Rights

1790 Guerre contre les Indiens dans le Nord-Ouest

1794 Eli Whitney connaît le succès avec sa machine à égrener le coton *(cotton gin)*

1796 Election de John Adams à la Présidence

1801 Thomas Jefferson devient le troisième Président, le premier Virginien et le premier Républicain après les années d'hégémonie fédéraliste

1803 Achat de la Louisiane à Napoléon
Expédition de Lewis et Clark dans le Nord-Ouest

1804 Réélection de Jefferson

1806 La marine marchande et les armateurs de la Nouvelle-Angleterre sont victimes de l'embargo anglais sur le commerce des Etats-Unis

1808 James Madison, deuxième Président virginien

1811 Victoire de Harrison sur le chef indien Tecumseh à Tippecanoe, Indiana

Littérature

John Woolman, *Journal*	1774
Thomas Paine, *Common Sense*	1776
Francis Hopkinson, *The Battle of the Kegs*	1778
Michel-Guillaume Jean de Crèvecœur, *Letters from an American Farmer*	1782
Philip Freneau, *Poems*	1786
Royall Tyler, *The Contrast*	1787
William Bartram, *Travels*	1791
Thomas Paine, *The Rights of Man*	1791-1792
Hugh Henry Brackenridge, *Modern Chivalry*	1792-1797
Thomas Paine, *The Age of Reason*	1794-1795
Royall Tyler, *The Algerine Captive*	1797
Charles Brockden Brown, *Wieland*	1798
Joel Barlow, *The Columbiad*	1807
Washington Irving, *A History of New York*	1809

Histoire

1812 Guerre avec L'Angleterre

1815 Victoire des troupes américaines sous la conduite d'Andrew Jackson sur les Britanniques à la Nouvelle-Orléans

1816 James Monroe, homme d'Etat de Virginie, élu Président

1820 Compromis du Missouri
Second mandat de Monroe

1821 Indépendance du Mexique
Développement de la vallée du Mississippi

1823 Affirmation de la doctrine Monroe sur la place des Etats-Unis dans le monde

1825 Election de John Quincy Adams à la Présidence consacrant le retour d'un patricien de la Nouvelle-Angleterre

1826 Expédition de Jerediah Smith en Californie

1828 Andrew Jackson, symbole de l'Amérique des pionniers de l'Ouest, élu à la Présidence

1830 Indian Removal Act

1831 William Lloyd Garrison dirige *The Liberator*

1832 Nullification. Les tarifs douaniers jugés nuls et non avenus par la Caroline du Sud. Réaction énergique d'Andrew Jackson qui affirme l'autorité de l'exécutif fédéral

1836 Martin Van Buren élu Président
Chute de Fort Alamo; victoire de San Jacinto et proclamation de la République du Texas

1838 Déportation des Cherokees dans le Territoire indien (Oklahoma) (The Trail of Tears)

1839 Fondation du Parti de la liberté qui fait entrer les abolitionnistes dans la vie politique

1841 Mort du président William Harrison (« Old Tippicanoe ») auquel succède John Tyler

1844 Election à la Présidence de James Polk

1845 Le Texas est admis dans l'Union

1846-1848 Guerre du Mexique et affirmation réitérée du « Destin manifeste »

Littérature

Washington Irving, *The Sketchbook*	**1819-1820**
James Fenimore Cooper, *The Pioneers*	**1823**
Washington Irving, *Tales of a Traveller*	**1824**
James Fenimore Cooper, *The Last of the Mohicans*	**1826**
James Fenimore Cooper, *The Prairie*	**1827**
John P. Kennedy, *Swallow Barn*	**1832**
Ralph Waldo Emerson, *Nature*	**1836**
Nathaniel Hawthorne, *Twice-Told Tales*	**1837**
Edgar Allan Poe, *The Narrative of Arthur Gordon Pym*	**1838**
James Fenimore Cooper, *The American Democrat*	**1838**
James Fenimore Cooper, *The Pathfinder*	**1840**
Edgar Allan Poe, *Tales of the Grotesque and Arabesque*	**1840**
James Fenimore Cooper, *The Deerslayer*	**1841**
Ralph Waldo Emerson, *Essays*, 1st series	**1841**
Ralph Waldo Emerson, *Essays*, 2nd series	**1844**
Edgar Allan Poe, « The Raven and Other Poems »	**1845**
Nathaniel Hawthorne, *Mosses from an Old Manse*	**1846**
Herman Melville, *Typee*	**1846**

Histoire

1848	Election du général Zachary Taylor à la Présidence Cession aux Etats-Unis des territoires mexicains au nord du Rio Grande
1849	Ruée vers l'or en Californie
1850	Millard Fillmore succède à Taylor à la Présidence Compromis de 1850. Admission de la Californie comme Etat libre et loi sur les esclaves fugitifs
1852	Franklin Pierce élu Président
1854	Kansas-Nebraska Act
1856	Election de James Buchanan à la Présidence
1857	Jugement de la Cour suprême favorable à l'esclavage dans l'affaire Dred Scott - Sanford
1859	Raid de l'abolitionniste John Brown à Harper's Ferry. Il sera jugé et exécuté en décembre
1860	Abraham Lincoln élu Président Sécession de la Caroline du Sud
1861	Jefferson Davis, président de la Confédération Attaque de Fort Sumter par les Sudistes
1863	Emancipation des esclaves par Lincoln Bataille de Gettysburg
1864	Incendie d'Atlanta par les troupes du général Sherman
1865	Robert E. Lee capitule à Appomatox Fin de la guerre de Sécession Assassinat de Lincoln, Andrew Johnson devient Président Début de la Reconstruction Abolition de l'esclavage par le 13e amendement à la Constitution
1866	Vote du 14e amendement (droits civiques) Organisation du Ku Klux Klan
1867	Lois de Reconstruction qui régissent le Sud
1868	Election de Ulysses Grant à la Présidence
1869	Développement spectaculaire des voies ferrées à l'ouest

Littérature

James Russell Lowell, *The Biglow Papers*, 1st series	1846-1848
Henry Wadsworth Longfellow, *Evangeline*	1847
Herman Melville, *Redburn*	1847
Francis Parkman, *The Oregon Trail*	1849
Herman Melville, *Moby Dick*	1850
Nathaniel Hawthorne, *The Scarlet Letter*	1850
Nathaniel Hawthorne, *The House of the Seven Gables*	1851
Ralph Waldo Emerson, *Representative Men*	1851
Harriet Beecher Stower, *Uncle Tom's Cabin*	1851-1852
Henry David Thoreau, *Walden*	1854
Henry Wadsworth Longfellow, *Hiawatha*	1855
Walt Whitman, *Leaves of Grass*	1855
Herman Melville, *Piazza Tales*	1856
Herman Melville, *The Confidence Man*	1857
Nathaniel Hawthorne, *The Marble Faun*	1860
Henry David Thoreau, *The Maine Woods*	1864
John Greenleaf Whittier, « Snow Bound »	1866
Walt Whitman, *Democratic Vistas*	1871

Histoire

1872 Grant est réélu

1873 Panique à la Bourse de New York
L'argent métal est démonétisé. Mesure préjudiciable aux agriculteurs de l'Ouest

1875 Scandales financiers
Agitation ouvrière et violences des « Molly Maguires » en Pennsylvanie

1876 Guerres indiennes. Défaite du général Custer à Little Big Horn

1877 Fin de la Reconstruction
Election de Rutherford Hayes à la Présidence

1880 James Garfield élu Président

1881 Garfield meurt dans un attentat. Chester Arthur devient Président

1882 Fondation de la Standard Oil par John Rockefeller

1884 Election de Grover Cleveland à la Présidence

1886 Immigration massive. Erection de la statue de la Liberté dans le port de New York
Agitation ouvrière à Chicago
Fondation de l'American Federation of Labor

1887 Dawes Act sur les réserves indiennes

1888 Election de Benjamin Harrison à la Présidence

1890 Au recensement, la Frontière est déclarée fermée compte tenu de la densité de la population à l'ouest
Sherman Anti-Trust Act
Fondation du mouvement populiste
Massacre de Sioux à Wounded Knee

1891 Formation du Parti populiste

1892 Grèves ouvrières

1893 Krach à Wall Street

1894 Grève des chemins de fer sous l'impulsion de Eugene Debs

1896 Découverte de l'or dans le Klondyke (Alaska)
La ségrégation *(separate but equal)* est justifiée par la Cour suprême dans l'affaire Plessy-Ferguson
William Jennings Bryan, candidat démocrate soutenu par les populistes, est battu aux élections par William McKinley qui devient Président

1898 Guerre de Cuba contre l'Espagne qui, vaincue, cède Porto Rico et les Philippines aux Etats-Unis

Littérature

Samuel L. Clemens (Mark Twain), *The Gilded Age* (with C. D. Warner)	1873
Samuel L. Clemens, *The Adventures of Tom Sawyer*	1876
Henry James, *The Portrait of a Lady*	1881
Samuel L. Clemens (Mark Twain), *Adventures of Huckleberry Finn*	1884
William Dean Howells, *The Rise of Silas Lapham*	1885
Henry James, *The Bostonians*	1886
Samuel L. Clemens, *A Connecticut Yankee in King Arthur's Court*	1889
Emily Dickinson, *Poems and Poems : Second Series*	1890-1891
Stephen Crane, *Maggie, a Girl of the Streets*	1893
Edwin Arlington Robinson, *Children of the Night*	1897
Frank Norris, *McTeague*	1899
Theodore Dreiser, *Sister Carrie*	1900

Histoire

1901 Amendement Platt (Cuba)
Theodore Roosevelt devient Président à la mort de McKinley

1904 Theodore Roosevelt élu Président
Corollaire de Theodore Roosevelt à la doctrine Monroe *(speak softly and carry a big stick)*

1907 Tour du monde de la flotte américaine
Panique à la Bourse de New York, crise économique

1908 Election de William Taft à la Présidence

1910 Rupture entre Taft et Roosevelt qui propose le programme du « nouveau nationalisme »

1912 Woodrow Wilson élu Président contre Theodore Roosevelt

1914 Incidents avec le Mexique après la révolte de 1910 contre le dictateur Diaz

1915 Le paquebot britannique *Lusitania* est coulé par un sous-marin allemand. De nombreux passagers américains trouvent la mort

1916 Incursion du révolutionnaire Pancho Villa au Nouveau-Mexique

1917 Le Congrès déclare la guerre à l'Allemagne
Les troupes du général Pershing arrivent en France

1918 Loi sur la sédition. Début de la « Red Scare » après la Révolution d'Octobre en Russie
Participation des Américains aux grandes batailles contre les forces allemandes
Proclamation des « quatorze points » par Wilson

1919 Conférence de la Paix

1920 Société des nations proposée par Wilson, rejetée par le Congrès
Arrestation de Nicola Sacco et Bartolomeo Vanzetti accusés de hold up et de meurtre à Boston
Début de la Prohibition (19e amendement)

1921 « Retour à la normale » après le programme progressiste de Wilson
Warren Harding est Président (Républicain)

1923 Scandales et corruption. Calvin Coolidge succède à Harding

1924 Coolidge élu Président
Loi restrictive sur l'immigration (quotas)

1925 Procès de John Scopes *(monkey trial)* sur l'enseignement de l'évolutionnisme. Bryan accuse Scopes au nom des « créationnistes »
Spéculation foncière (Floride)

Littérature

Edith Wharton, *The House of Mirth*	1905
Upton Sinclair, *The Jungle*	1906
Henry Adams, *The Education of Henry Adams*	1907
Jack London, *Martin Eden*	1909
Willa Cather, *O Pioneers*	1913
Robert Frost, *North of Boston*	1914
Carl Sandburg, *Chicago Poems*	1916
T. S. Eliot, *Prufrock and Other Observations*	1917
Sherwood Anderson, *Winesburg, Ohio*	1919
Ezra Pound, *Hugh Selwyn Mauberley*	1920
T. S. Eliot, *The Waste Land*	1922
Wallace Stevens, *Harmonium*	1923
Theodore Dreiser, *An American Tragedy*	1925
Ezra Pound, *Cantos*	1925
F. Scott Fitzgerald, *The Great Gatsby*	1925

Histoire

1927 Exécution de Sacco et Vanzetti

1928 Discours de Herbert Hoover qui proclame les bienfaits de « l'individualisme forcené ». Il est élu à la Présidence

1929 Massacre de la saint Valentin à Chicago
Krach (Jeudi noir) à Wall Street

1930 Début de la Grande Dépression

1931 Emeutes de fermiers et grèves de mineurs. Les mesures prises par Hoover ne parviennent pas à enrayer la crise (5 millions de chômeurs)

1932 Election de Franklin Delano Roosevelt à la Présidence

1933 Mise en œuvre de la politique du New Deal (NIRA, WPA, CCC, AAA, TVA, etc.)

1934 Dévaluation du dollar

1935 La Cour suprême déclare inconstitutionnels le NIRA et l'AAA

1936 Réélection de Roosevelt
National Labor Relations Act (Wagner Act)
Formation de la centrale syndicale « Committee for Industrial Organization »
Neutrality Act

1937 Le Congrès s'oppose à Roosevelt qui entend s'inféoder la Cour suprême

1938 Récession économique

1939 Proclamation de l'état d'urgence limité

1940 Réélection de Roosevelt

1941 Discours sur les quatre libertés fondamentales
Fourniture de matériel militaire à l'Angleterre
Attaque japonaise sur Pearl Harbor

1942 Débarquement des troupes américaines en Afrique du Nord
Guerre du Pacifique (îles Salomon, Guadalcanal). Raid sur Tokyo

1943 Bombardements sur l'Allemagne
Débarquement en Italie
Accords de Téhéran entre Staline et Roosevelt

1944 Débarquement en France. Prise de Guam. Réélection de Roosevelt

Littérature

Ernest Hemingway, *The Sun also Rises*	1926
William Faulkner, *The Sound and the Fury*	1929
Ernest Hemingway, *A Farewell to Arms*	1929
Katherine Anne Porer, *Flowering Judas*	1930
Eugene O'Neill, *Mourning Becomes Electra*	1931
William Faulkner, *Light in August*	1932
Francis Scott Fitzgerald, *Tender is the Night*	1934
William Carlos Williams, *Collected Poems*	1934
James T. Farrell, *Studs Lonigan*	1934
Thomas Wolfe, *Of Time and The River*	1935
John Dos Passos, *USA*	1936
Carl Sandburg, *The People, Yes*	1936
John Steinbeck, *Of Mice and Men*	1937
E. E. Cummings, *Collected Poems*	1938
Thornton Wilder, *Our Town*	1938
Robert Frost, *Collected Poems*	1939
John Steinbeck, *The Grapes of Wrath*	1939
Ernest Hemingway, *For Whom the Bell Tolls*	1940
Richard Wright, *Native Son*	1940

Histoire

1945 Conférence de Yalta
Harry Truman devient Président à la mort de Roosevelt. Il proposera un « Fair Deal »
Bataille d'Iwo Jima
Victoire des Alliés sur l'Allemagne nazie
Bombe atomique sur Hiroshima, puis Nagasaki

1946 Première assemblée de l'ONU

1947 Plan Marshall. Doctrine Truman. Début de la Guerre froide. Début du maccarthysme
Loi Taft-Hartley sur les syndicats

1948 Election de Truman à la Présidence

1949 Signature du Pacte de l'Atlantique Nord (OTAN)

1950 Guerre de Corée
Le général McArthur prêt à envahir la Chine populaire, en conflit avec Truman

1951 Condamnation à mort des époux Rosenberg déclarés coupables d'espionnage au profit de l'Union soviétique

1952 Dwight Eisenhower élu Président. Richard Nixon est vice-Président

1953 Earl Warren devient Chief Justice de la Cour suprême

1954 McCarthy est désavoué
Fondation de l'OTASE et pacte de défense pour l'Asie du Sud-Est
Affaire Brown-Topeka et arrêt de la Cour suprême sur la déségrégation des écoles

1956 Réélection d'Eisenhower

1958 Création de la NASA

1959 Hawaii est admis comme Etat de l'Union

1960 John Kennedy élu Président

1961 Programme de la Nouvelle Frontière
Aide au Viet-nam du Sud

Littérature

Tennessee Williams, *The Glass Menagerie*	1945
Richard Wright, *Black Boy*	1945
Robert Penn Warren, *All the King's Men*	1946
Tennessee Williams, *A Street Car Named Desire*	1947
Arthur Miller, *Death of a Salesman*	1949
John Hawkes, *The Cannibal*	1949
J. D. Salinger, *The Catcher in the Rye*	1951
William Styron, *Lie Down in Darkness*	1951
Ralph Ellison, *Invisible Man*	1952
Ernest Hemingway, *The Old Man and the Sea*	1952
James Baldwin, *Go Tell it on the Mountain*	1953
Arthur Miller, *The Crucible*	1953
Theodore Roethke, *The Waking*	1953
Wallace Stevens, *Collected Poems*	1954
Flannery O' Connor, *A Good Man is Hard to Find*	1954
John Barth, *The Floating Opera*	1956
Allen Ginsberg, « Howl »	1956
Jack Kerouac, *On the Road*	1957
Bernard Malamud, *The Assistant*	1957
Edward Albee, *The Zoo Story*	1958
Vladimir Nabokov, *Lolita*	1958
Robert Lowell, *Life Studies*	1959
William Burroughs, *The Naked Lunch*	1959
John Updike, *Rabbit, Run*	1960
John Barth, *The Sot-Weed Factor*	1960
Joseph Heller, *Catch-22*	1960
Walker Percy, *The Moviegoer*	1961

Histoire

1962 Blocus de Cuba

1963 Grande marche sur Washington et discours de Martin Luther King (I have a dream)
Lyndon Johnson devient Président après l'assassinat de Kennedy

1964 Election triomphale de Johnson à la Présidence contre Barry Goldwater
Programme de la « Grande Société »
Civil Rights Act
Résolution du golfe du Tonkin

1965 Premiers bombardements du Viet-nam du Nord
Marche pour les droits civiques en Alabama conduite par Martin Luther King
Emeutes raciales à Watts, Los Angeles
Manifestations contre la guerre du Viet-nam

1966 Emeutes raciales à Chicago, Atlanta. Montée du « pouvoir noir »

1967 Présence de 500 000 militaires américains au Viet-nam
Manifestations contre la guerre à Berkeley et New York

1968 Assassinat de Martin Luther King
Assassinat de Robert Kennedy à Los Angeles
Emeutes à la Convention des Démocrates à Chicago
Lyndon Johnson renonce à un nouveau mandat et engage des négociations pour la paix au Viet-nam
Election de Richard Nixon à la Présidence. Spiro Agnew est vice-Président

1969 Manifestations à Harvard sur la guerre du Viet-nam
Mission Apollo sur la Lune

1970 Grève des ouvriers de l'automobile
Recrudescence de la criminalité urbaine

1971 Politique de redressement économique. Nixon revient sur les accords de Bretton-Woods et laisse désormais flotter le dollar

1972 Début de l'affaire du Watergate révélée par le *Washington Post*
L'Equal Right Amendment soumis au Congrès (Droits des femmes). Non encore ratifié

Littérature

Edward Albee, *Who's Afraid of Virginia Woolf?*	1962
Ken Kesey, *One Flew over The Cuckoo's Nest*	1962
Katherine Anne Porter, *Ship of Fools*	1962
Kurt Vonnegut, *Cat's Cradle*	1963
Mary McCarthy, *The Group*	1963
John Berriman, *Dream Songs*	1963
Saul Bellow, *Herzog*	1964
Robert Lowell, *For the Union Dead*	1964
Richard Brautigan, *A Confederate Soldier from Big Sur*	1964
Thomas Berger, *Little Big Man*	1964
Sylvia Plath, *Ariel*	1965
Norman Mailer, *An American Dream*	1965
Theodore Roethke, *Collected Poems*	1966
John Gardner, *The Resurrection*	1966
Truman Capote, *In Cold Blood*	1966
William Styron, *The Confessions of Nat Turner*	1967
Richard Brautigan, *Trout Fishing in America*	1967
Tom Wolfe, *The Electric Kool-Acid Test*	1968
John Barth, *Lost in the Funhouse*	1968
William Gass, *In the Heart of the Heart of the Country*	1968
Philip Roth, *Portnoy's Complaint*	1969
Donald Bartheleme, *City Life*	1970
James Dickey, *Deliverance*	1970
Eudora Welty, *Losing Battles*	1970
John Hawkes, *The Blood Oranges*	1971
Eudora Welty, *The Optimist's Daughter*	1971

Histoire

1973	Démission de Spiro Agnew, remplacé comme vice-Président par Gerald Ford War Powers Act. Limitation des pouvoirs présidentiels en cas de conflit armé Accord de cessez-le-feu au Viet-nam à la Conférence de Paris
1974	Démission de Nixon à la suite du Watergate. Ford devient Président
1976	Fêtes du Bicentenaire de l'indépendance des Etats-Unis Jimmy Carter élu Président
1978	Contestation de l' « affirmative action ». Arrêt Bakke à la Cour suprême
1979	Affaires des otages de Téhéran Chômage et inflation Incident à la centrale nucléaire de Three Mile Island, Pennsylvanie
1980	Election de Ronald Reagan
1981	Mise en œuvre de la « reaganomie » Attentat contre le Président à Washington
1982	Les Marines sont envoyés au Liban
1983	Attentat contre les Marines à Beyrouth Ralentissement spectaculaire du taux d'inflation Taux de pauvreté à 15 %
1984	En hausse constante, le dollar est à son taux record Les Jeux Olympiques consacrent le modèle américain Réélection de Reagan
1986	Tension avec la Libye Taux de pauvreté le plus élevé depuis 1969 Assouplissement des lois sur l'immigration Intensification de la lutte contre la drogue
1987	Des scandales secouent le milieu des télé-évangélistes Rencontre de Reagan avec Gorbatchev à Washington Crise financière à Wall Street Taux de chômage le plus faible (6,2 %) depuis 1978
1988	George Bush est élu Président

Littérature

Thomas Pynchon, *Gravity's Rainbow*	1973
Erica Jong, *Fear of Flying*	1973
John Irving, *The World According to Garp*	1978
Joyce Carol Oates, *Unholy Loves*	1979
John Updike, *Rabbit is Rich*	1981
John Irving, *The Hotel New Hampshire*	1981
Toni Morrison, *Tar Baby*	1981
Alice Walker, *The Color Purple*	1982
Ann Beattie, *The Burning House*	1982
Mary Robison, *An Amateur's Guide to the Night*	1983
Marge Piercy, *Fly Away Home*	1984
Louise Erdrich, *Love Medicine*	1984
Joyce Carol Oates, *Wild Night*	1985
Tom Wolfe, *The Bonfire of the Vanities*	1987

Eléments de filmographie

Les indications sommaires que nous donnons ici portent exclusivement sur les auteurs qui figurent dans l'anthologie. Nous avons parfois jugé utile d'étendre les références à des œuvres non incluses dans l'ouvrage, dans la mesure où elles ouvrent un champ d'interprétation tant de la fiction littéraire que de son adaptation cinématographique ou télévisuelle. A ce propos, on lira avec profit Jean-Loup Bourget, *Le mélodrame hollywoodien* (Stock, 1985), afin de mieux saisir la spécificité de la fiction à l'écran. Il y eut plusieurs versions cinématographiques des romans de James Fenimore Cooper sur la saga de Leatherstocking. En 1909, l'un des premiers films de D. W. Griffith, pour Biograph, fut inspiré des aventures de Natty Bumppo. Les prises de vue se firent à Cuddebackville dans l'Etat de New York. Le film allemand *Lederstumpf* (Luna-Film, 1911) eut un tel succès qu'il passa aux Etats-Unis en 1921 avec pour titre *The Deerslayer*. En 1922 fut produite l'une des meilleures versions en Amérique de *The Last of the Mohicans*, réalisée par Maurice Tourneur et Clarence Brown. La première version du parlant date de 1932 avec Harry Carey et Edwina Booth. La plus connue des versions du roman est *The Last of the Mohicans* de 1936, réalisée par George B. Seitz avec Randolph Scott dans le rôle de Hawkeye (Associated Producers). En 1947, Columbia appela sa version *The Last of the Red Men* (réalisation de George Sherman). Il existe aussi une version de *The Deerslayer* (Twentieth Century Fox, réalisation de Kurt Neufeld) avec Lex Barker et Rita Moreno. Une série télévisée sur Leatherstocking fut produite en 1962 par

International Television Corporation, une autre en 1977 (MTV, réalisation James Conway) sur *The Last of the Mohicans*.

Les nouvelles d'Edgar Allan Poe ont été maintes fois portées à l'écran. On ne retiendra ici que *Tales of Terror* (Warner Bros, 1963) réalisé par Roger Corman et qui inclut « The Black Cat ».

Nombreuses sont les adaptations cinématographiques de *The Scarlet Letter*. En muet, on citera la version Metro Goldwyn Mayer de 1926 réalisée par Victor Sjostrom avec Lillian Gish. Une version pour la télévision de Wim Wenders a été réalisée en 1973.

Moby Dick fut adapté deux fois. La première en 1930, réalisation de Lloyd Bacon avec John Barrymore, la seconde en 1956, produite par Warner Bros fut réalisée par John Huston avec Gregory Peck dans le rôle d'Achab, et Orson Welles.

Life on the Mississippi fut adapté en 1980 par la chaîne de télévision WNET à New York et réalisé par Peter Hunt avec David Knell et Robert Lansing. Hormis les versions pour la télévision, il existe plusieurs adaptations de *Huckleberry Finn*, dont celle de 1939 (Metro Goldwyn Mayer), réalisée par Richard Thorpe avec Mickey Rooney dans le rôle de Huck. Deux autres versions méritent d'être mentionnées. Celle de 1960 (Metro Goldwyn Mayer, réalisateur Michael Curtiz) et celle de 1974 (United Artists), réalisée par J. Lee Thompson.

« The Blue Hotel » a été réalisé en 1977 par le réseau de la télévision publique dans la série « American Short Story Series » dirigée par Jan Kadar. « Soldier's Home » (1977) est sorti dans la même série. *The Red Badge of Courage*, adapté par Metro Goldwyn Mayer en 1951, a été réalisé par John Huston avec Audy Murphy dans le rôle de Henry Fleming.

Adapté de *The Awakening* de Kate Chopin, un film intitulé *The End of August* a été produit par Enterprise en 1981 ; réalisation de Bob Graham avec Sally Sharp et David Marshall.

Inspiré de *Sister Carrie* de Dreiser, le film *Carrie* produit par Paramount fut réalisé par William Wyler en 1952 avec Laurence Olivier dans le rôle de Hurstwood et Jennifer Jones dans celui de Carrie. Il existe une première version de *An American Tragedy* de Paramount, 1931, réalisée par Josef von Sternberg. La version la plus connue est celle de 1951 (Paramount), intitulée *A Place in the Sun*. Réalisation de George Stevens avec Montgomery Clift et Elizabeth Taylor.

Il existe deux versions de *Babbitt*. La première date de 1924

(Warner Bros). Elle fut réalisée par Harry Beaumont avec Willard Louis, la seconde en 1934 (First National) dirigée par William Keighley avec Guy Kibee et Aline McMahon.

Il existe deux versions de *A Farewell to Arms*. La première fut réalisée par Frank Borzage en 1932 (Paramount) avec Gary Cooper dans le rôle de Frederic Henry. La seconde date de 1957 (Twentieth Century Fox). Réalisation de Charles Vidor avec Rock Hudson et Jennifer Jones dans le rôle de Catherine Barkley. Borzage dut lutter pour imposer la fin du roman dans le film. Une autre version du dénouement prévoyait une *happy end*.

The Great Gatsby a fait l'objet de deux adaptations. La première en 1949 (Paramount, réalisation Elliott Nugent) avec Alan Ladd dans le rôle de Gatsby. La seconde date de 1974 (Paramount), réalisée par Jack Clayton avec Robert Redford et Mia Farrow. La qualité visuelle de ce film, notamment l'emploi du blanc, et la priorité donnée à l'intrigue semblent avoir pour la critique affaibli l'impact des personnages.

Auteur par excellence pour le cinéma comme l'est Emile Zola en France, John Steinbeck a inspiré de nombreux films. *The Grapes of Wrath* (Twentieth Century Fox, 1940) fut réalisé par John Ford avec Henry Fonda (Tom Joad) et John Carradine (Jim Casy). La version filmée s'achève sur une vision plus idyllique que ne le suggère le roman. On notera aussi *Of Mice and Men* (United Artists, 1939, réalisation de Lewis Milestone) avec Burgess Meredith. Il existe une autre version avec Robert Blake et Randy Quaid (1981).

Il y a plusieurs films tirés des œuvres de William Faulkner. On citera *The Sound and the Fury* (Twentieth Century Fox, 1959), réalisé par Martin Ritt avec Yul Brynner et Joanne Woodward, *Sanctuary* (Twentieth Century Fox, 1960) avec Lee Remick et Yves Montand, *The Reivers* (Warner Bros, 1969), réalisé par Mark Rydell avec Steve McQueen.

La pièce de Tennessee Williams, *The Glass Menagerie*, eut sa version filmée en 1950 de Warner Bros, réalisée par Irving Rapper avec Arthur Kennedy, Gertrude Lawrence, Jane Wyman et Kirk Douglas. En 1973, c'est Anthony Harvey qui dirigea la nouvelle version à laquelle participèrent Katherine Hepburn, Sam Waterston, Joanna Miles et Michael Moriarty. Enfin en 1987, Paul Newman réalisa une nouvelle version avec Joanne Woodward et Karen Allen. Une quinzaine de pièces de Tennessee

Williams ont eu une adaptation cinématographique, dont *Cat on a Hot Tin Roof, A Streetcar Named Desire.*

All My Sons de Arthur Miller fut adapté en 1948 (United Artists). Le réalisateur était Irving Reis, et les acteurs Edward G. Robinson, Burt Lancaster et Howard Duff. On citera également *Les Sorcières de Salem* (1957), film français inspiré de *The Crucible* réalisé par Raymond Rouleau avec Yves Montand et Simone Signoret.

Parmi les œuvres de Norman Mailer portées à l'écran, on réservera une mention spéciale à *The Naked and the Dead* (Warner Bros, 1958) réalisé par Raoul Walsh avec Aldo Ray, Raymond Massey et Cliff Robertson.

Basée sur *The Natural* de Bernard Malamud, on citera l'adaptation de Barry Levinson avec Robert Redford et Robert Duvall en 1984. *The Fixer* (Metro Goldwyn Mayer, 1969) a été réalisé par John Frankenheimer avec Dirk Bogarde et Alan Bates.

End of the Road, inspiré de John Barth, fut produit par Continental Films en 1969, réalisé par Aram Avakian avec Stacy Keach et Dorothy Tristan.

Rabbit Run de John Updike a été porté à l'écran par Warner Bros en 1969. Le réalisateur était Jack Smight et les interprètes James Caan et Arthur Hill.

Kurt Vonnegut a inspiré le film *Slaughterhouse-Five* réalisé par George Roy en 1972 (United Artists), avec Michael Sacks, Sharon Gans et Ron Liebman.

Titré initialement *Head Over Heels* avec une fin différente, *Chilly Scenes of Winter* est adapté d'un roman d'Ann Beattie (1982, réalisé par Joan Micklin Silver, avec John Heard, Mary Beth Hurt et Gloria Grahame).

Index

Imprimé en France
Imprimerie des Presses Universitaires de France
73, avenue Ronsard, 41100 Vendôme
Février 1991 — N° 36 356